Database Management Systems

Database Management Systems

Designing and Building Business Applications

Third Edition

Gerald V. Post
University of the Pacific

Tata McGraw-Hill Publishing Company Limited
NEW DELHI

McGraw-Hill Offices

New Delhi New York St Louis San Francisco Auckland Bogotá Caracas
Kuala Lumpur Lisbon London Madrid Mexico City Milan Montreal
San Juan Santiago Singapore Sydney Tokyo Toronto

Tata McGraw-Hill

DATABASE MANAGEMENT SYSTEMS:
DESIGNING AND BUILDING BUSINESS APPLICATIONS

Tata McGraw-Hill Edition 2005

Ninth reprint
RZXYCDDXRBZAB

Reprinted in India by arrangement with The McGraw-Hill Companies, Inc., New York

Sales territories: India, Pakistan, Nepal, Bangladesh, Sri Lanka and Bhutan

Library of Congress Cataloging-in-Publication Data

Post, Gerald V.
Database management systems : designing and building business applications / Gerald V. Post. —3rd ed.
p. cm.
Includes index.
ISBN 0-07-291919-1 (alk. paper)
1. Database management. 2. Database design. 3. Business—Databases. Management information systems. I Title.
QA76.9.D3P675 2005
005.74—dc22 2003066454

ISBN-13: 978-0-07-063526-5
ISBN-10: 0-07-063526-9

Published by Tata McGraw-Hill Publishing Company Limited,
7 West Patel Nagar, New Delhi 110 008, and printed at
Pashupati Printers Pvt. Ltd., Delhi 110 095

The McGraw·Hill Companies

To my wife Sarah and to Jessie and Simon who would rather chase my mountain bike than watch me write. The Pet Store case is named in memory of Sarah's mother.

Preface

A Tale of Two Websites

The Orinoco Music Company is proud of their website. The graphics are cool, the audio clips are hot, and initial excitement in the press has brought record numbers of potential customers to the site. Orders are coming in through the Web order form. After a few weeks, some problems arise. Clerks are making mistakes in copying the orders from the Web form into the company's existing mail order system. Customers are canceling orders because many of the shipments are backordered—they complain that if they had known the item was not in stock, they would never have ordered it. After a couple of months, the press begins to downgrade the site, noting that the graphics are old and they cannot get audio clips for the new bands. Because of the expense of constantly changing the site, Orinoco Music is thinking about removing the site and returning to a basic company-information site.

Customers have been flocking to the new website for Salt Peanuts Music Company. In the month since the site was activated, orders have almost doubled—in terms of the number of customers and in the value of each order. Customers can instantly see if an item is in stock. With a couple of clicks, they get background information on any artist and can play short clips from any song. Registered customers can download songs to their computers for a fee and play them as often as they like. Customers can also contact sales representatives with instant messaging. The reps have instant access to all of the customer data. But everyone's favorite feature is that the system tracks individual purchases and suggests similar groups. These selections are based partly on expert opinions, but are primarily driven by grouping sales. Customers can see what products are bought by groups of similar customers. Everyone is happy with the system. Company managers like it because it increases sales and provides detailed data on trends. Customers like it because they have instant access to the information they want. Recording artists like it because it gives everyone access to the music and increases sales.

The difference between the two websites is that the Salt Peanuts site is built on a database management system that integrates the company's data. It enables the company to create a more complete, interactive site.

Introduction

Databases are one of the most important and useful tools available to management and information technology professionals. Databases provide the foundation for collecting, organizing, and sharing data across an organization. Virtually every area of management uses a database management system (DBMS). For example, marketing professionals use databases to analyze sales data, human resource managers to evaluate employees, operations managers to track and improve quality, accountants to integrate data across the firm, and financial analysts to analyze a company's performance.

The database management approach provides several significant advantages over traditional programming techniques. Primary advantages include shorter development times, easier modification, better data integrity and security, and improved data sharing and integration. However, a DBMS is one of the most complex technology tools available. Databases have to be carefully designed to gain these advantages. A large-scale commercial DBMS provides thousands of options and costs hundreds of thousands of dollars. It can take several months to learn all of the features of a particular DBMS.

Although databases are often created and maintained by information technology professionals, increasingly management professionals in other disciplines are designing and creating their own database applications. This text is targeted to the primary business database course at the junior level. Students from any major should be able to understand the material, but it will be easier if they have taken an introductory programming course.

Goals and Philosophy

The goal of this text is straightforward: At the end of the text, students should be able to evaluate a business situation and build a database application.

The heart of this text consists of two crucial topics that every student must learn before building databases: database design (normalization) and SQL (queries). These two topics are standardized across all major database systems. Normalization shows how to carefully design databases to gain the strengths of the DBMS approach. SQL is a standard query language that is used for virtually every step of application development. These two topics must be covered carefully and thoroughly, particularly because they are both difficult topics for students.

Although some students might learn how to build an application through a general discussion or lecture, most require examples and hands-on practice supported by comments from a knowledgeable instructor. This text supports the learning process through clear exposition, many examples, exercises, and sample databases. The accompanying workbooks provide even more detail on building applications within a specific database system.

Building applications using a relational database requires three specific skills: database design, knowledge of SQL, and programming. Each of these areas is complex, and each is crucial to building successful applications.

Database design is the foundation for building applications. A well-designed database can simplify building, maintaining, and expanding an application. An important strength of relational database design is its flexibility. A properly designed database can be expanded to meet changing business conditions. On the other hand, if the design is weak, building an application will be substantially harder and more time-consuming. It is often better to throw away a poorly designed database and start over, instead of trying to fix or expand it.

SQL is a powerful query language. One of its greatest strengths is that it is available in many different products. Once you learn the foundations of SQL, you will be able to retrieve data from almost every major database system. Many queries in SQL are relatively simple, so the foundations can be learned rapidly. Yet SQL can also be used to answer complex questions.

Programming skills form the third level of knowledge needed to build solid business applications. Some applications and some database systems require detailed programming skills. However, in many cases, programming is used sparingly. It can be used as a glue to combine various components or add new features that make the application easier to use.

Most applications experience trade-offs among database design, SQL, and programming. The weaker the design, the less you rely on SQL and the more programming you will need to build the application. Because coding is more likely to create errors and is harder to change, application developers should rely on proper database design and the power of SQL.

Learning Assessment

Learning assessment is important to students as well as faculty and employers. Students need to determine what aspects they are strong in and which ones need additional work. Students need to understand that if they can successfully learn this material, they will have acquired several skills that will get them jobs and help them contribute to businesses by being able to quickly build and maintain business applications.

Learning assessment in this course is straightforward: At the end of the course, students should be able to analyze a business situation and develop a database application. The complexity of the application and tools used will depend on the specific class and the background of the students. Assigning a term-length project is often a good approach to assessing this overall skill. The final project can be evaluated in terms of (1) correctly meeting the business needs, (2) an efficient database structure, and (3) usability.

It is also useful to assess individual skills independently—particularly if groups are used to create the final project. In this case, assessment consists of individual exams for (1) database design and normalization, (2) SQL and creating queries from business questions, and (3) selected topics including database programming, security, data mining, and distributed systems.

Organization

The organization of the text follows the basic steps of application development: design, queries, applications, administration, and advanced topics. Some instructors might prefer to teach queries before database design, so the initial chapters are written with that flexibility.

The introduction explains the importance of databases and relates database applications to topics the students have likely seen in other classes.

The section on database design has two chapters: Chapter 2 on general design techniques (systems techniques, diagramming, and control) and Chapter 3, which details data normalization. The objective is to cover design early in the term so that students can get started on their end-of-term projects.

Queries are covered in two chapters. Chapter 4 introduces queries and focuses on the fundamentals of converting business questions to SQL queries. Chapter 5 discusses more complex queries, including subqueries and outer joins.

Part 3 describes the development of database applications, beginning with the essentials of forms, reports, and application development in Chapter 6. Chapter 7 examines the common problems created in a multiuser environment. It explains the common techniques used to handle data integrity and transactions. Chapter 8 explains why analytical processing requires a different database configuration than transaction processing. It covers the main tools for analysis and data mining in a nonstatistical context.

Part 4 examines various topics in database administration. Chapter 9 examines management issues emphasizing planning, implementation, performance, and security. It explains the major tasks and controls needed by an administrator. Chapter 10 investigates the growing importance of providing distributed access to databases. It examines the impact of various network configurations. It also discusses methods to connect databases to websites to provide access through browsers.

Additionally, four chapters have appendixes that discuss programming concepts that are more technical. The appendix to Chapter 2 describes the online database design system that is available to instructors and students. It provides immediate feedback on database designs, making it easier for students to understand the problems and explore different designs. The appendix to Chapter 3 presents the formal definitions of normalization. They are provided for instructors and students who want to see the more formal set-theory definitions. The appendix to Chapter 4 is a convenient list of the primary SQL statements. The appendix to Chapter 5 provides an introduction to programming. It is designed as a summary or simple reminder notes.

Pedagogy

The educational goal of the text is straightforward and emphasized in every chapter: By the end of the text, students should be able to build business applications using a DBMS. The text uses examples to apply the concepts described in the text. Students should be encouraged to apply the knowledge from each chapter by solving the exercises and working on their final projects.

Each chapter contains several sections to assist in understanding the material and in applying it to the design and creation of business applications:

- **What You Will Learn in This Chapter.** A brief discussion highlights the importance and use of the chapter material.
- **Chapter Summary.** A brief review of the chapter topics.
- **A Developer's View.** Each chapter opens and closes with a scenario example of how the material in the chapter applies to building applications.
- **Key Terms.** A list of terms introduced in the chapter. A full glossary is provided at the end of the text.
- **Additional Reading.** References for more detailed investigation of the topics.
- **Website References.** Some sites provide detailed information on the topic. Some are newsgroups where developers share questions and tips.
- **Review Questions.** Designed as a study guide for the exams.
- **Exercises.** Problems that apply the concepts presented in the chapter. Most require the use of a DBMS.
- **Projects.** Several longer projects are presented in an appendix at the end of the text. They are suitable for an end-of-term project.
- **Workbook.** New to the third edition, the workbook explains the detailed tasks for building a database with a specific tool. Each workbook

chapter illustrates tasks that match the discussion in the textbook. The workbook also provides exercises to build six other databases for different companies.

- **Sample Databases.** Two sample databases are provided to illustrate the concepts. Sally's Pet Store illustrates a database in the early design stages, whereas Rolling Thunder Bicycles presents a more finished application, complete with realistic data. Exercises for both databases are provided in the chapters.

Features of the Text

1. Focus on modern business application development.
   - Database design explained in terms of business modeling.
   - Application hands-on emphasis with many examples and exercises.
   - Emphasis on modern graphical user interface applications.
   - Chapters on database programming and application development.
   - Appendixes on programming and development details.
2. Hot topics.
   - Description and use of the unified modeling language (UML) for modeling and system diagrams. This new standard will soon be required for all designers.
   - In-depth discussion of security topics in a database environment.
   - Development of databases for the Internet and intranets.
   - Emphasis on SQL 92, with an introduction to SQL 99 and the XML features of SQL 200x.
   - Integrated applications and objects in databases.
3. Applied business exercises and cases.
   - Many database design problems.
   - Exercises covering all aspects of application development.
   - Sample cases suitable for end-of-term projects.
4. A complete sample database application (Rolling Thunder Bicycles).
   - Fully functional business database.
   - Sample data and data generator routines.
   - Program code to illustrate common database operations.
5. A second database (Sally's Pet Store) for comparison and additional assignments.
6. Lecture notes as PowerPoint slide show.
7. Workbooks built for specific database technologies that illustrate the hands-on steps needed to build an actual application. Initially, printed workbooks will be shipped for Microsoft Access and Oracle. Check with the publisher and the instructor for support for other systems and tools.
8. Additional information and chapters. To reduce the size of the book, some earlier chapters—notably the analysis of physical data storage (B-trees) has been moved to electronic chapters on the accompanying student CD.

End-of-Term Projects

Several projects are described in the appendix at the end of the text. These cases are suitable for end-of-term projects. Students should be able to build a complete application in one term. The grading focus should be on the final project. However, the instructor should evaluate at least two intermediate stages: (1) a list of the normalized tables collected shortly after Chapter 3 is completed and (2) a design preview consisting of at least two major forms and two reports collected shortly after Chapter 6. The six additional cases in the workbook can also be used as an end-of-term project.

Some instructors may choose to assign the projects as group assignments. However, it is often wiser to avoid this approach and require individual work. The project is a key learning tool. If some members of the group avoid working on the project, they will lose an important learning opportunity.

Database Design and the Unified Modeling Language

For several years, entity-relationship diagrams were the predominant modeling technique for database design. However, this approach causes problems for instructors (and students) because there are several different diagramming techniques. This edition continues to help solve these problems by incorporating the Unified Modeling Language (UML) method, instead of traditional entity-relationship (ER) diagramming, as the modeling technique for database design. This change will be most apparent in the replacement of the ER diagram notation and terminology with the parallel concepts in UML class diagrams.

UML class diagrams, although very similar to ER diagrams, are superior in several ways. First, they are standardized, so students (and instructors) need learn only one set of notations. Second, they are "cleaner" in the sense that they are easier to read without the bubbles and cryptic notations of traditional ER diagrams. Third, they provide an introduction to object-oriented design, so students will be better prepared for future development issues. Fourth, with the rapid adoption of UML as a standard design methodology, students will be better prepared to move into future jobs. Many of the systems design organizations have adopted UML as a standard method for designing systems. UML has the support of major authors in systems design (e.g., Booch, Rumbaugh, and Jacobsen) as well as being supported by the major software development firms including IBM, Microsoft, and Oracle. Note that Microsoft Access and SQL Server both use a diagramming tool that is similar to UML. In addition, students should have little difficulty transferring their knowledge of the UML method if they need to work with older ER methods.

The basic similarities between ER and class diagrams are (1) entities (classes) are drawn as boxes, (2) binary relationships (associations) are drawn as connecting lines, and (3) *n*-ary associations (relationships) are drawn as diamonds. Hence, the overall structures are similar. The main differences between UML and ER diagrams occur in the details. In UML the multiplicity of an association is shown as simple numerical notation instead of as a cryptic icon. An example is shown in the following two figures.

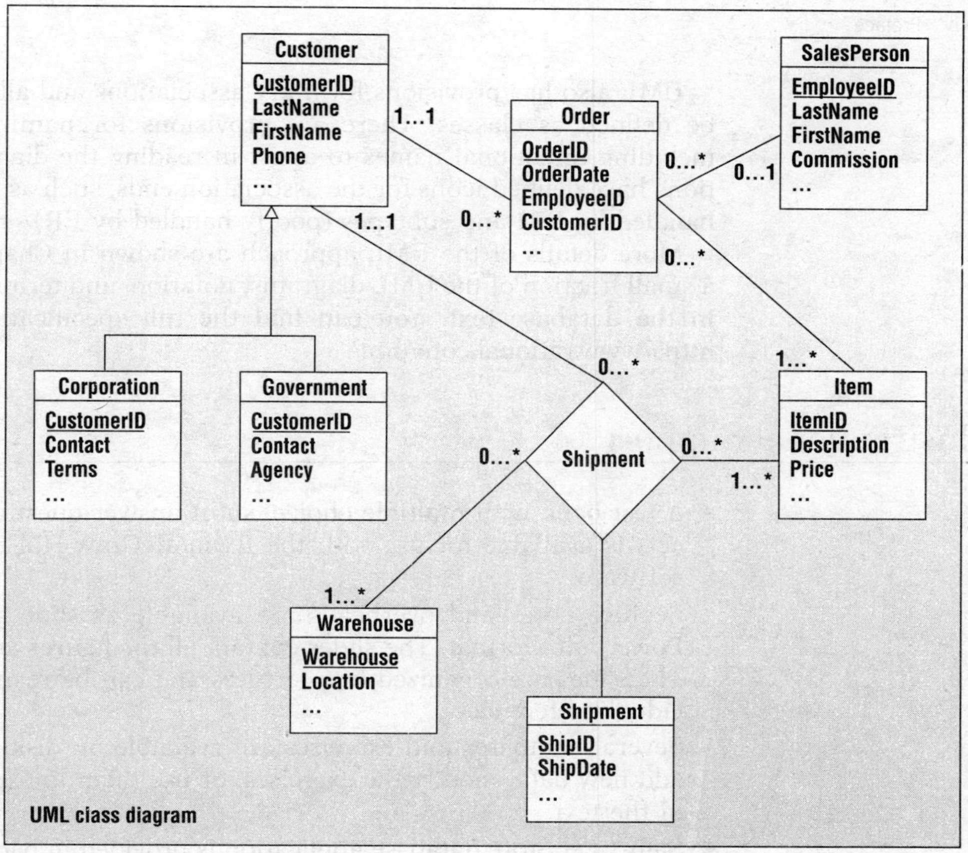

UML class diagram

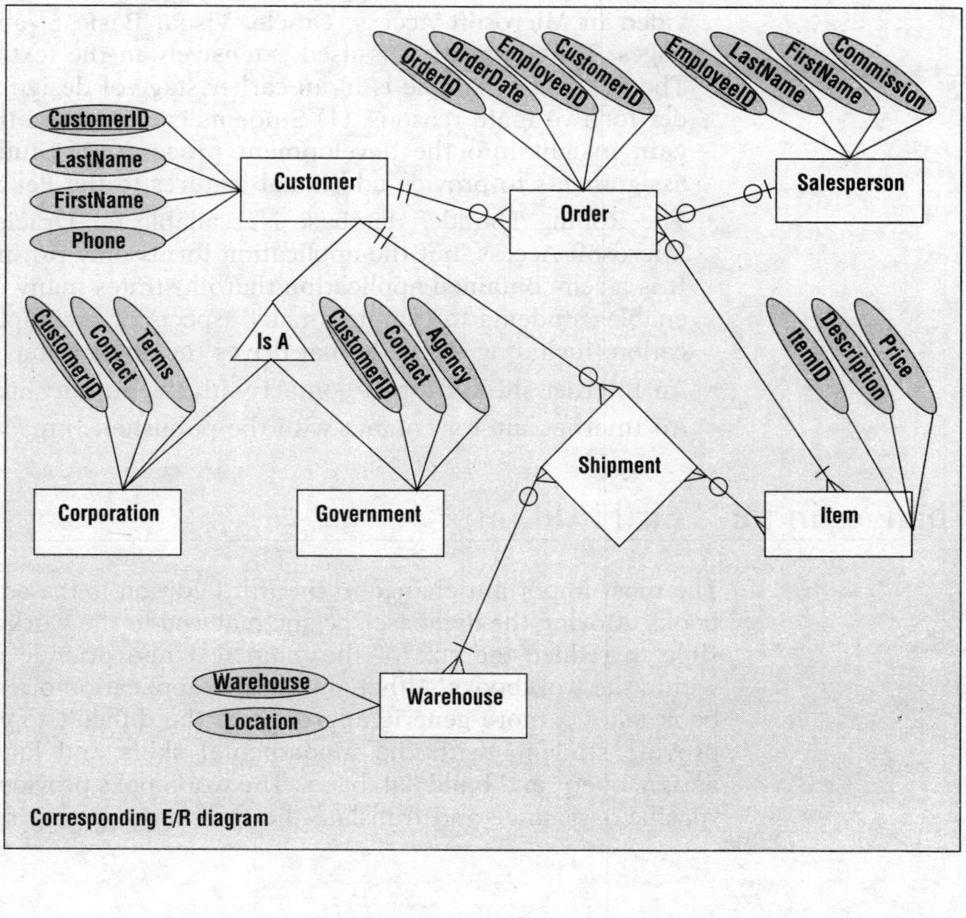

Corresponding E/R diagram

UML also has provisions for *n*-ary associations and allows associations to be defined as classes. There are provisions for naming all associations, including directional names to assist in reading the diagram. Several situations have defined icons for the association ends, such as composition (rarely handled by ER) and subtypes (poorly handled by ER).

More details of the UML approach are shown in Chapters 2 and 3. Only a small fraction of the UML diagrams, notation, and terminology will be used in the database text. You can find the full specification on the Web at http://www.rational.com/uml/.

Instructional Support

- A test bank with multiple choice, short answer questions, and short projects is available for use with the Irwin/McGraw-Hill electronic test bank software.
- Lecture notes and overheads are available as slide shows in Microsoft PowerPoint format. The slides contain all the figures and additional notes. The slides are organized into lectures and can be rearranged to suit individual preferences.
- Several databases and exercises are available on disk. The instructor can add new data, modify the exercises, or use them to expand the discussion in the text.
- Sally's Pet Store database application is provided in back-end database format for Microsoft Access, SQL Server, and Oracle. The front end is provided in Microsoft Access, Oracle, Visual Basic 6; and ASP Web server pages. The application is used extensively in the text to illustrate topics. The Pet Store example is in an earlier stage of design than Rolling Thunder for two main reasons. (1) Students can compare the applications and gain insight into the development process. (2) Students can be given assignments to provide additional features to the Pet Store application.
- The Rolling Thunder database is available for Oracle, SQL Server, and Microsoft Access, but the application forms only run in Microsoft Access. It is a self-contained application that illustrates many of the concepts and enables students to examine many aspects of a complete database application, including the code that drives the application.
- An Internet site for direct contact with the author: http://JerryPost.com.
- An Internet site for contact with the publisher: http://www.mhhe.com.

Changes in the Third Edition

The most important change in the third edition is the addition of the workbooks. Moving the database-specific material to the workbooks makes it possible to reduce the size of the main text and provide more detailed help within the workbooks. Although it is still application oriented, the main textbook takes a more generic approach to the difficult topics. The focus is to provide students with the fundamental skills and knowledge needed to design, query, and build databases. The workbooks provide detailed, database-specific assistance and translate the tasks into solving specific problems in building applications. The workbooks can be used in a lab setting, or as separate assignments that students can follow to help design and build their projects.

The third edition also contains an expanded discussion of data warehouses and data mining. The concepts have been expanded into a new chapter (Chapter 8). Chapter 7 on integrity and transactions contains expanded coverage of the importance of database triggers, transactions, and key generation issues. The concepts of building an application have been consolidated and simplified into Chapter 6. The detailed steps have been moved to the workbooks.

Again, note that most of the exercises have been replaced. The old exercises are available on the CD-ROM and the author's website. This edition contains five new end-of-term cases in the appendix, Database Projects. All of the old ones have been moved to the CD-ROM and website. In addition to providing new projects, the goal was to create slightly shorter cases that students can finish within one term.

Design Feedback Tool

Another important new element of the textbook is the availability of the online database design system. This online expert system is a major advance in teaching database design and data normalization. Students use a Java-enabled Web browser to draw the design diagrams and save them on the central sever. With a click of the mouse, the server evaluates the diagram and provides immediate feedback on the design. The feedback takes the form of pointers and questions to direct students to reconsider the table design. Instructors can set up classes and assignments in a few minutes and have the ability to customize the problems, solutions, and grading. Instructors can even create new problems, but the system already contains dozens of exercises, including all of the problems from the three editions of the textbook. Instructors need to sign up to use the system in class. Check the website at http://time-post.com/dbdesign.

Acknowledgments

Creating a new approach to teaching database management required the efforts and support of many people. The database class can be a difficult course to teach, but one of the most enjoyable. It requires considerable dedication by instructors to develop methods to teach the material. The dedication of the reviewers of both the first and second editions who shared their time and expertise to improve this book is greatly appreciated.

I specifically want to thank John Gerdes for his work on the test bank, along with the following talented professionals who contributed their time and talent to reviews that guided the improvements found in this edition.

Dr. Bhagyavati
Columbus State University

Sudip Bhattacharjee
The University of Connecticut

Andy Borchers
Kettering University

Subhasish Dasgupta
The George Washington University

Dr. Sherif Elfayoumy
The University of North Florida

John Gerdes, Jr.
The University of California

Allen Gray
Loyola Marymount University

Jim Kattke
Augsburg College

T. M. Rajkumar
Miami University

Dr. Sudha Ram
The University of Arizona

Dr. Karlene Sanborn
Friends University

Ashraf Shirani
San Jose State University

Leon Zhao
The University of Arizona

Great thanks are also due to the instructors who considered and encouraged the decision to organize the third edition as a core text and two workbooks. They are

Barbara Beccue
Illinois State University

Jim Chen
St. Cloud State University

Mike Collins
High Point University

Donald Dawley
Miami University—Oxford

Carlos Ferran
Rochester Institute Technology

Philip Friedlander
St. Petersburg College—Clearwater

Monica Garfield
University of South Florida—Tampa

Marilyn Griffin
Virginia Polytechnic Institute

Jeff Guan
University of Louisville—Louisville

John Molluzzo
Pace University

Anne Nelson
High Point University

Larisa Preiser
California State Polytechnic University—Pomona

Steve Rau
Marquette University

Werner Schenk
University of Rochester

Richard Segall
Arkansas State University—State University

Tarun Sen
Virginia Polytech Institute

Conrad Shayo
California State University—San Bernardino

Kazem Taghva
University of Nevada—Las Vegas

S. Varden
Pace University

James Yao
Montclair State University

Brian Zelli
University at Buffalo—The State University of New York

It is always a pleasure to work with the staff at McGraw-Hill/Irwin. Paul Ducham's guidance and willingness to try new ideas were crucial to producing this text. The support of Charlie Fisher and Greta Kleinert and the unparalleled attention to detail by the design and production staff help create better books. The entire staff made my job much easier and more enjoyable.

Jerry Post

Brief Contents

Contents

Chapter 1

Introduction

Chapter Outline

What You Will Learn in This Chapter

- What is a database? 2
- What is a database management system? 2
- What are the major components of a database management system? 4
- What are the advantages of using a database management system? 10
- What are the main types of database management systems? 13

A Developer's View

Miranda: My uncle just called me and said his company was desperate. It needs someone to build an application for the sales team. The company wants a laptop system for each salesperson to enter orders. The system needs to track the order status over time and generate notices and weekly reports. My uncle said that because I know a lot about computers, I should call and get the job. His company is willing to pay $6,000, and I can work part-time.

Ariel: Wow! Sounds like a great job. What's the problem?

Miranda: Well, I know how to use basic computer tools, and I can program a little, but I'm not sure I can build a complete application. It could take a long time.

Ariel: Why not use a database management system? It should be easier than writing code from scratch.

Miranda: Do you really think so? What can a database system do? How does it work?

Introduction

Do you want to build computerized business applications? Do you want to create business applications that operate in multiple locations? Do you want to conduct business on the Internet? Do you want to enable customers to place orders using the Web? If you are going to build a modern business application, you need a database management system.

A modern database system is one of the most powerful tools you can use to build business applications. It provides many features that represent significant advantages over traditional programming methods. Yet database systems are complex. To gain the advantages, data must be carefully organized. To retrieve data and build applications, you need to learn to use a powerful query language. Once you understand the concepts of database design, queries, and application building, you will be able to create complex applications in a fraction of the time it would take with traditional programming techniques.

A **database** is a collection of data stored in a standardized format, designed to be shared by multiple users. A **database management system (DBMS)** is software that defines a database, stores the data, supports a query language, produces reports, and creates data entry screens.

Some of the most challenging problems in building applications arise in storing and retrieving data. Problems include conserving space, retrieving data rapidly, sharing data with multiple users at the same time, and providing backup and recovery of the data. Initially programmers had to solve these problems for every application they created. Today, the DBMS already provides some of the best solutions to these problems. Making the database the foundation of an application means that you get all of the powerful features and security without much additional work.

Databases and Application Development

In the last few years, database systems have become the foundation of almost all application development projects. From large enterprise relationship systems, to e-business websites, to stand-alone business applications, database

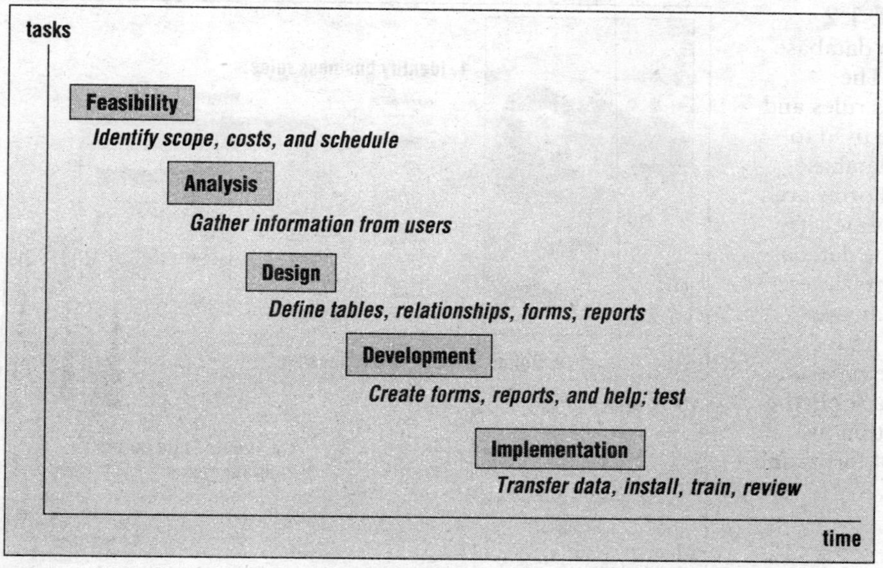

FIGURE 1.1
Systems development. Particularly for large projects, it is useful to divide application development into separate steps. They can be used to track the progress of the development team and highlight the steps remaining. For some projects, it is possible to overlap or even iterate the tasks, but steps should not be skipped.

systems store and retrieve data efficiently, provide security, and make it easier to build the applications. Today, when you build or modify an application, you will first create the database. To understand the capabilities of a DBMS and how you will use them to create applications, it is best to examine the process used to develop applications.

Organizations typically follow the basic steps outlined in Figure 1.1 when creating technology applications. Larger projects may require several people in each phase, while smaller projects might be created entirely by one or two developers. Organizations can rearrange the tasks that fall within each step, but all of the tasks must be completed for a project to be successful. The feasibility step defines the project and provides estimates of the costs. During the analysis phase, systems analysts collect data definitions, forms, and reports from users. These are used to design the database and all of the new forms, reports, and user interactions. During the development step, the forms, reports, and application features such as help files are created. Implementation generally consists of the transfer of data, installation, training, and review.

For database-driven applications, the design stage is critical. Database systems and the associated development tools are incredibly powerful, but databases must be carefully designed to take advantage of this power. Figure 1.2 shows that the business rules and processes are converted into database table and relationship definitions. Forms are defined that transfer data into the database, and reports use queries to retrieve and display data needed by users. These forms and reports along with features such as menus and help screens constitute applications. Users generally see only the application and not the underlying database or tables.

Designing the database tables and relationships is a key step in creating a database application. The process and rules for defining tables are detailed in Chapters 2 and 3. Using the database requires the ability to retrieve and manipulate the data. These tasks are handled by the query system, which is described in Chapters 4 and 5. With these foundations, it is relatively easy to use the tools to create forms and reports and build them into applications as discussed in Chapter 6.

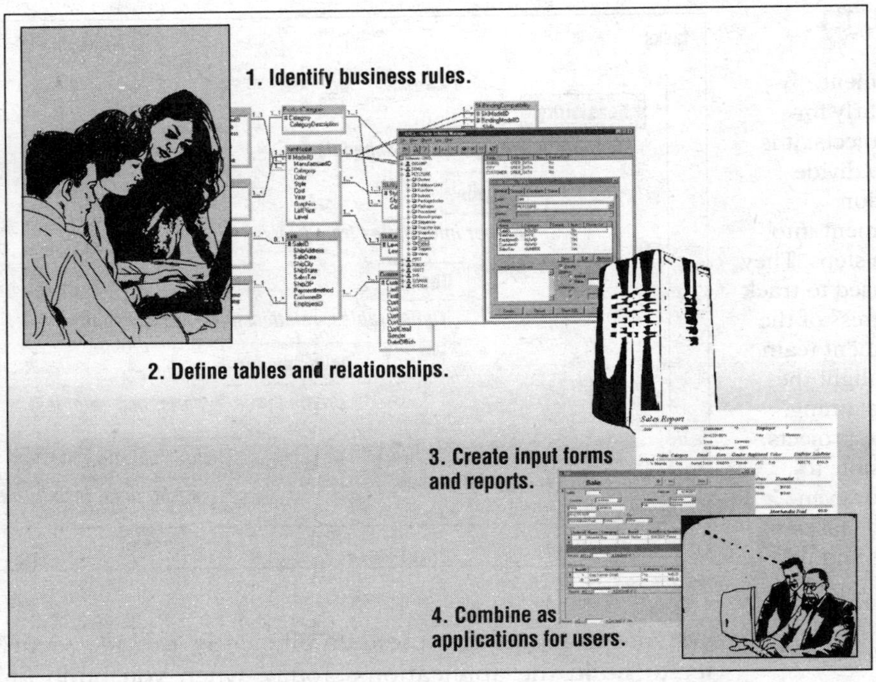

FIGURE 1.2
Steps in database design. The business rules and data are used to define database tables. Forms are used to enter new data. The database system retrieves data to answer queries and produce reports. Users see only the application in terms of forms and reports.

Components of a Database Management System

To understand the value of a DBMS, it helps to see the components that are commonly provided. This basic feature list is also useful when you have to evaluate the various products to determine which DBMS your company should use. Each DBMS has unique strengths and weaknesses. You can evaluate the various products according to how well they perform in each of these categories. A DBMS is evaluated based on the database engine, data dictionary, query processor, report writer, forms generator, application generator, communication and integration, and security.

Database Engine

The **database engine** is the heart of the DBMS. It is responsible for storing, retrieving, and updating the data. This component is the one that most affects the performance (speed) and the ability to handle large problems (scalability). The other components rely on the engine to store not only the application data but also the internal system data that defines how the application will operate. Figure 1.3 illustrates the primary relationship between the database engine and the data tables.

With some systems the database engine is a stand-alone component that can be purchased and used as an independent software module. For example, the Microsoft "jet engine" forms the foundation of Access. Similarly, the database engine for Oracle and Microsoft SQL Server can be purchased separately.

The database engine is also responsible for enforcing business rules regarding the data. For example, most businesses would not allow negative prices to be used in the database. Once the designer creates that rule, the database engine will warn the users and prevent them from entering a negative value.

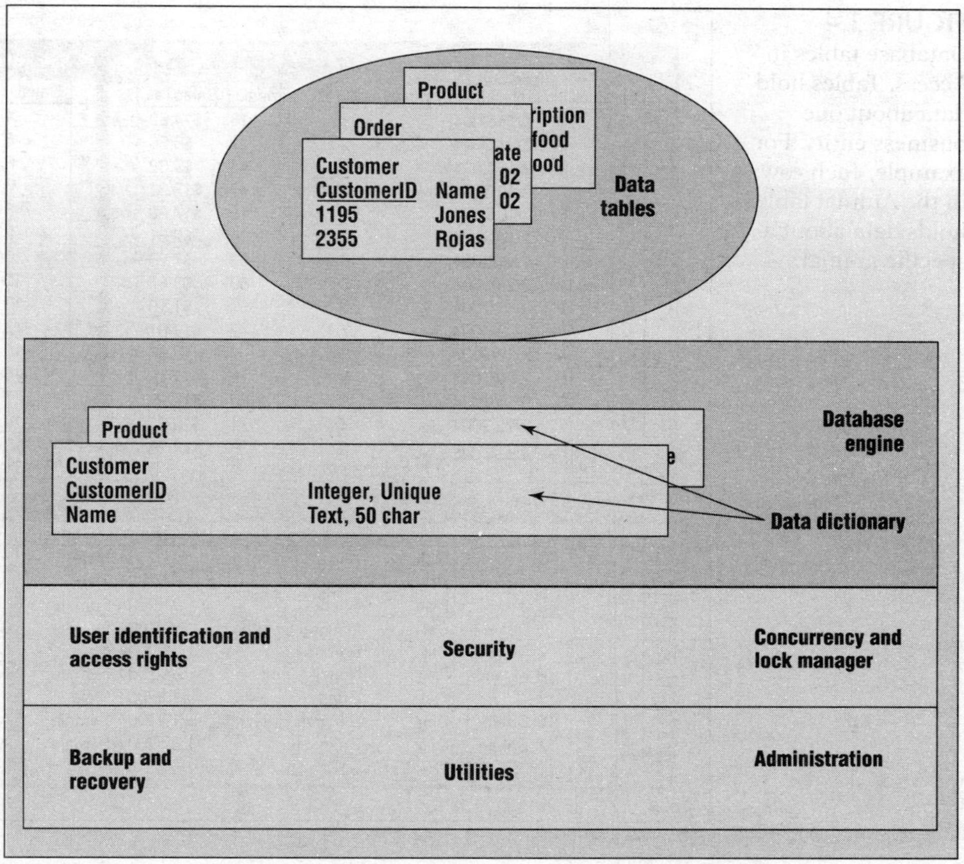

FIGURE 1.3
Database engine. The engine is responsible for defining, storing, and retrieving the data. The security subsystem of the engine identifies users and controls access to data.

As shown in Figure 1.4, the database engine stores data in carefully designed tables. Tables are given names that reflect the data they hold. Columns represent simple attributes that describe the object, such as an employee's name, phone, and address. Each row represents one object in the table.

Database performance is an important issue. The speed of your application depends on the hardware, the DBMS software, the design of your database, and on how you choose to store your data. Chapter 9 discusses some popular methods, such as indexing, that improve the performance of a database application.

Data Dictionary

The **data dictionary** holds the definitions of all of the data tables. It describes the type of data that is being stored, allows the DBMS to keep track of the data, and helps developers and users find the data they need. Most modern database systems hold the data dictionary as a set of system tables. For example, Microsoft Access keeps a list of all the tables in a hidden system table called MsysObjects. Oracle includes several system tables that provide information from the data dictionary. For instance, sys.dba_tables holds data about the tables in the database.

These tables are used by the system, and you will rarely need to use them directly. The DBMS should provide other tools that help you examine the structure of the database. For example, Oracle, SQL Server, Access, and DB2 provide an administration tool that lists the tables and contains a visually oriented tool to help you enter column names and select data types and other properties.

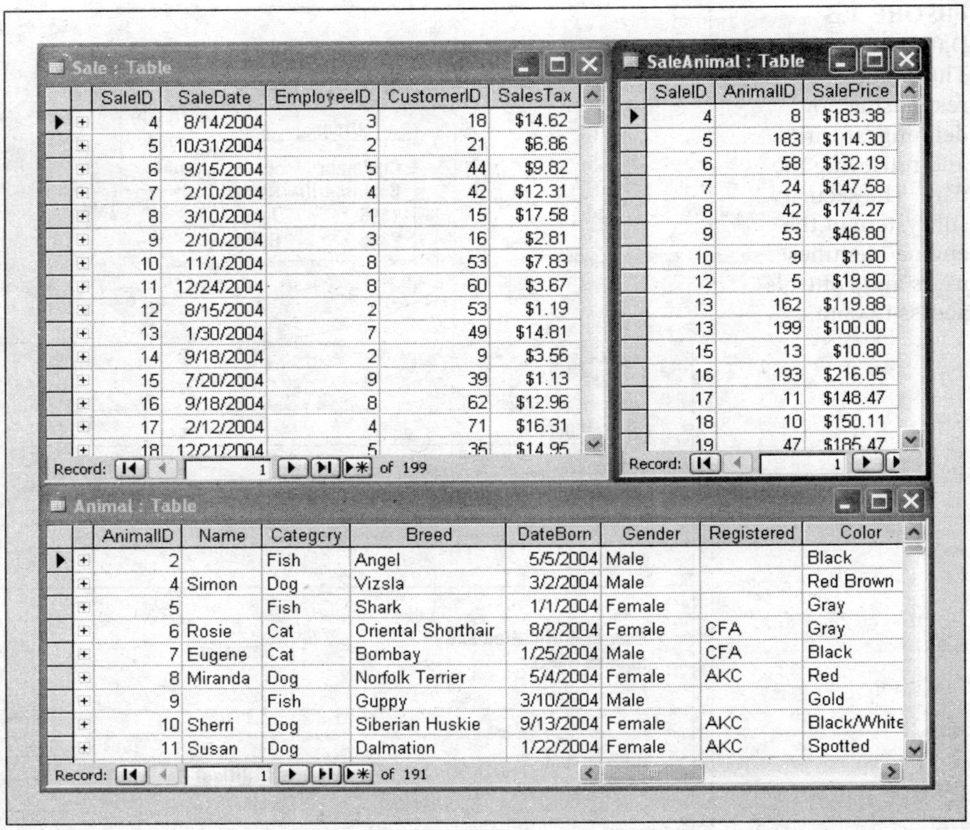

FIGURE 1.4
Database tables in Access. Tables hold data about one business entity. For example, each row in the Animal table holds data about a specific animal.

Query Processor

The query processor is a fundamental component of the DBMS. It enables developers and users to store and retrieve data. In some cases the query processor is the only connection you will have with the database. That is, all database operations can be run through the query language. Chapters 4 and 5 describe the features and power of query languages—particularly standard SQL.

Queries are derived from business questions. The query language is necessary because natural languages like English are too vague to trust with a query. To minimize communication problems and to make sure that the DBMS understands your question, you should use a query language that is more precise than English. As shown in Figure 1.5, the DBMS refers to the data dictionary to create a query. When the query runs, the DBMS query processor works with the database engine to find the appropriate data. The results are then formatted and displayed on the screen.

Report Writer

Most business users want to see summaries of the data in some type of report. Many of the reports follow common formats. A modern **report writer** enables you to set up the report on the screen to specify how items will be displayed or calculated. Most of these tasks are performed by dragging data onto the screen. Professional-level writers enable you to produce complex reports in a short time without writing any program code. Chapter 6 describes several of the common business reports and how they can be created with a database report writer.

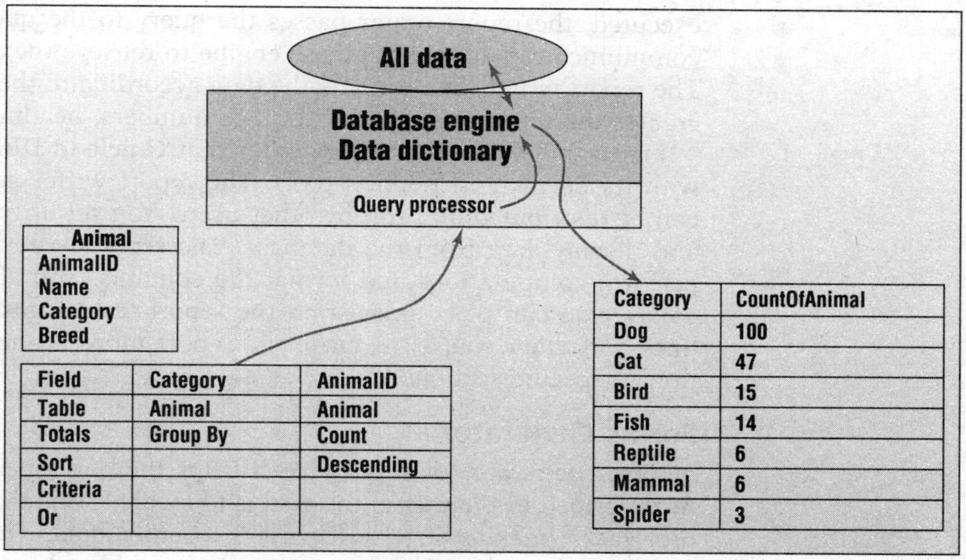

FIGURE 1.5
Database query processor. The data dictionary determines which tables and columns should be used. When the query is run, the query processor communicates with the database engine to retrieve the requested data.

The report writer can be integrated into the DBMS, or it can be a stand-alone application that the developer uses to generate code to create the needed report. As shown in Figure 1.6, the developer creates a basic report design. This design is generally based on a query. When the report is

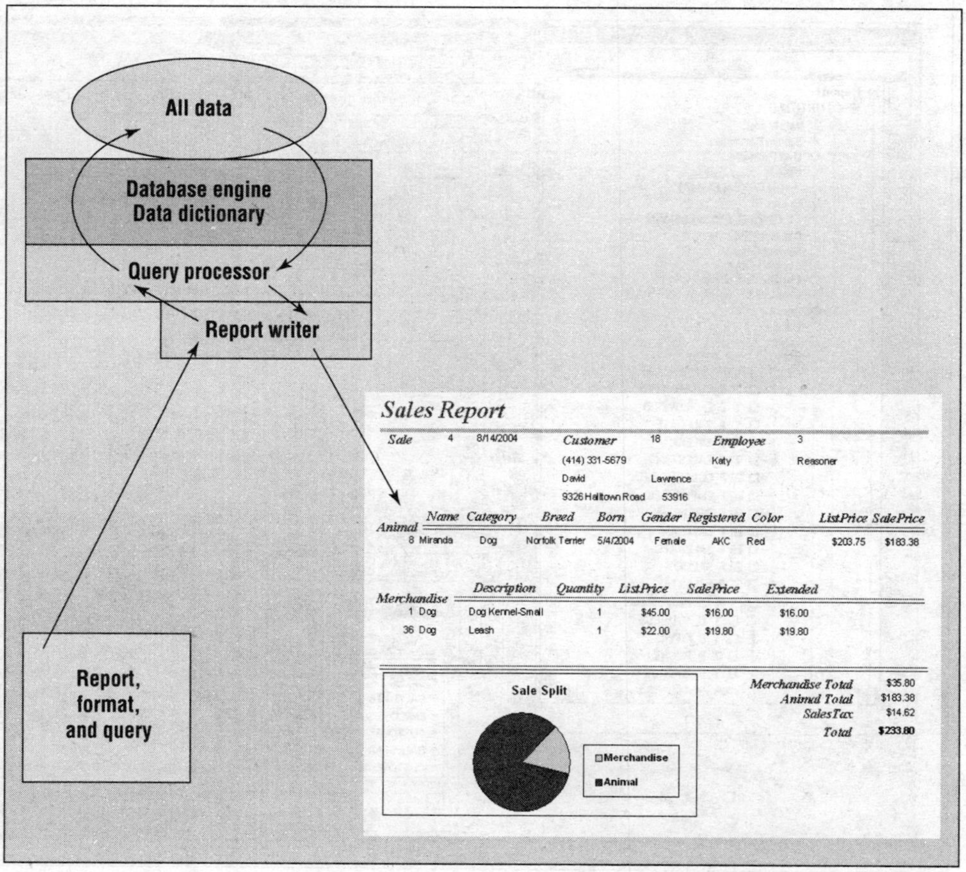

FIGURE 1.6
Database report writer. The design template sets the content and layout of the report. The report writer uses the query processor to obtain the desired data. Then it formats and prints the report.

executed, the report writer passes the query to the query processor, which communicates with the database engine to retrieve the desired rows of data. The report writer then formats the data according to the report template and creates the report complete with page numbers, headings, and footers.

Figure 1.7 shows the report writer that Oracle (a DBMS vendor) provides with its Forms and Reports tools. The report writer generates reports that can be distributed and run by other users. You set up sections on the report and display data from the database. The report writer includes features to perform computations and format the columns. You also have control over colors, you can place images on the report (e.g., logos), and you can draw lines and other shapes to make the report more attractive or to call attention to specific sections.

Forms Generator

A **forms generator** or input screen helps the developer create input forms. As described in Chapter 6, the goal is to create forms that represent common user tasks, making it easy for users to enter data. The forms can include graphs and images. The forms generator enables developers to build forms

FIGURE 1.7

Oracle Reports report writer. The Data Model is used to create a query and select the data to be displayed. Then Reports creates the basic report layout. You can modify the layout and add features to improve the design or highlight certain sections.

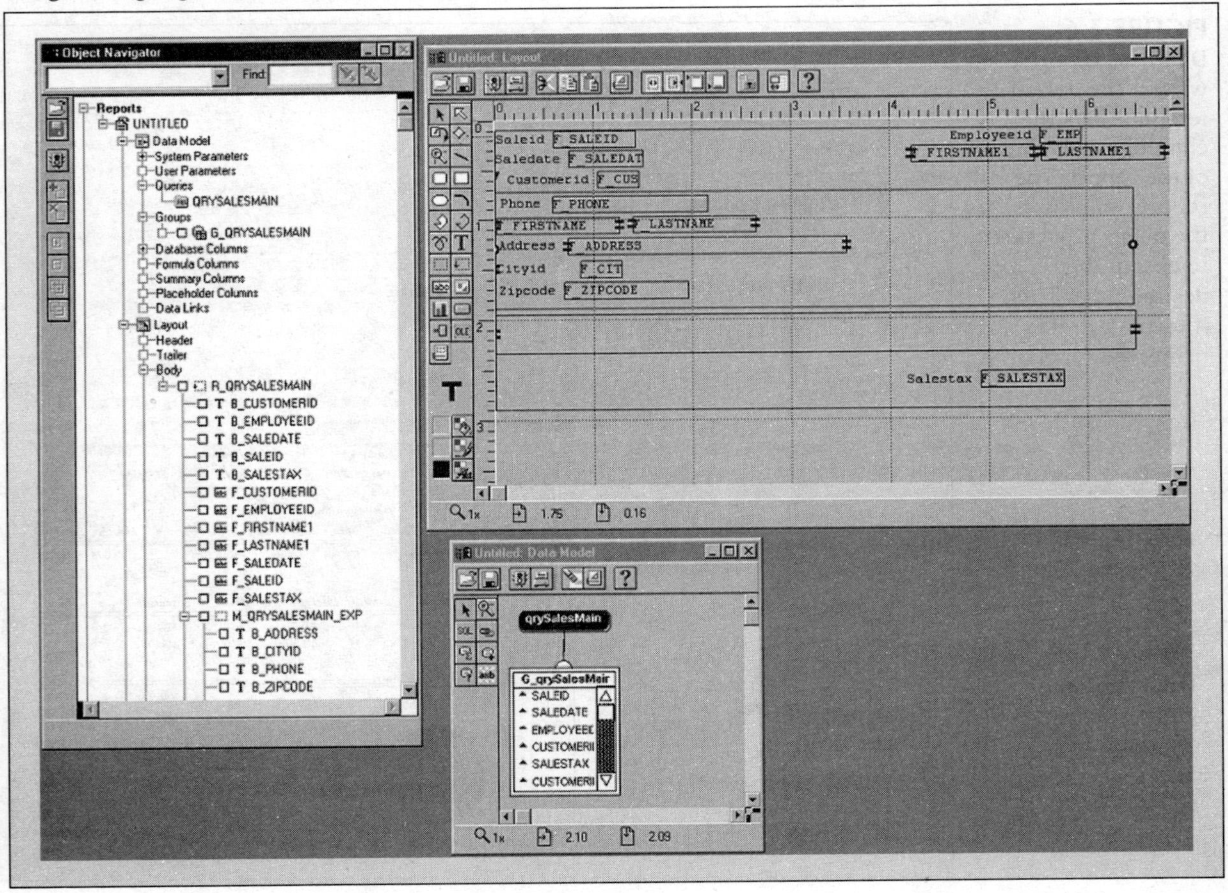

FIGURE 1.8
Database form. A form is used to collect data. It is designed to match the tasks of the user, making it easy to enter data and look up information. The query processor is used to obtain related data and fill in look-up data in combo boxes.

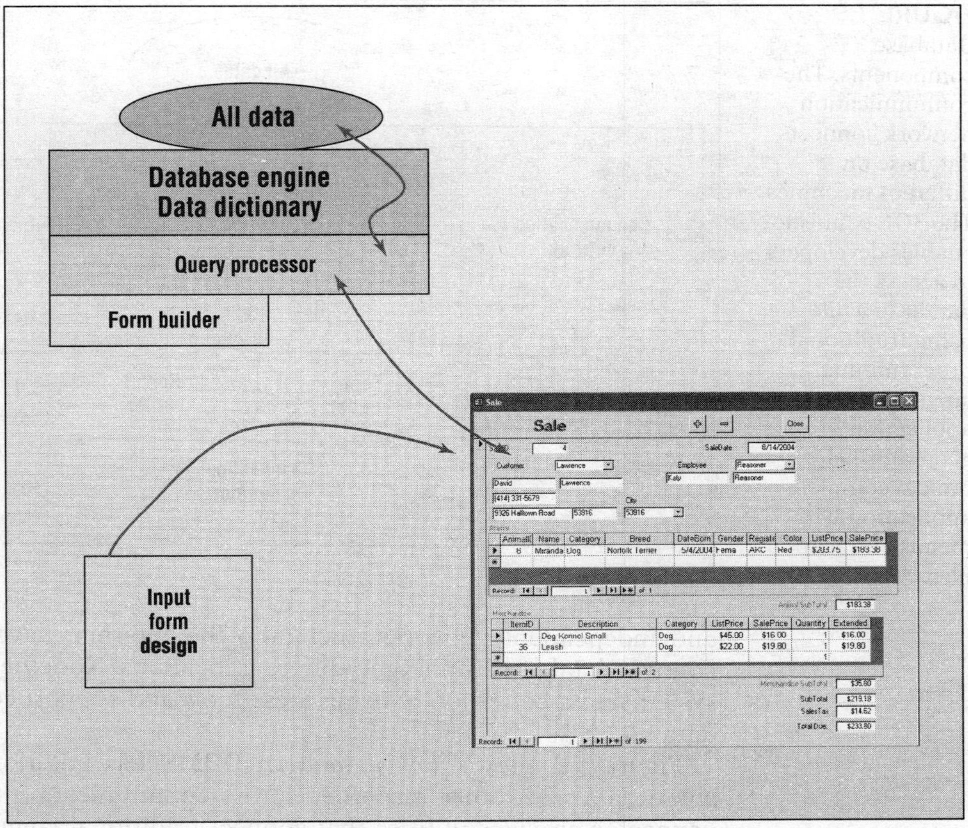

by dragging and dropping items on the screen. Figure 1.8 shows that forms make heavy use of the query processor to display data on the form.

Many database systems also provide support for traditional, third-generation languages (3GL) to access the database. The issues in writing programs and accessing data through these programs are directly related to the topics discussed in Chapter 7.

Application Generator

An application is a collection of forms and reports designed for a specific user task. It is the final package that you are trying to create. The Pet Store database that accompanies this text shows the start of an application. The Rolling Thunder database is a more complete application. Applications can be small and consist of a few input forms and reports, or they can be large, complex systems that integrate data from several databases with hundreds of forms and reports.

A good DBMS contains an **application generator,** which consists of tools that assist the developer in creating a complete application package. As discussed in Chapter 6, popular development tools include menu and toolbar generators and an integrated context-sensitive help system.

Communication and Integration

Some database systems provide special communication and integration utilities designed to store and use data in several databases running on different machines, even if they are in different locations. Modern operating systems

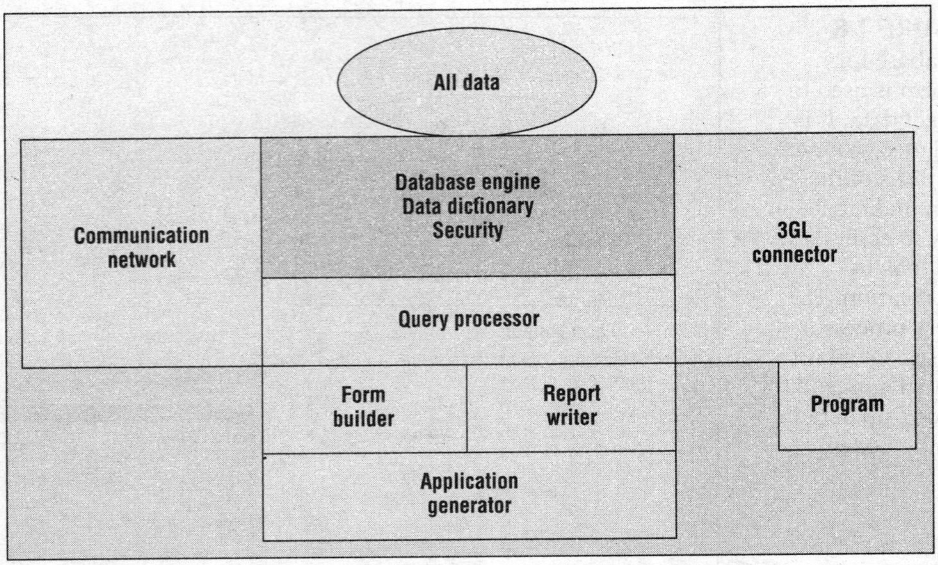

FIGURE 1.9 Database components. The communication network connects database on different machines. The 3GL connector enables developers to access the database while using traditional programming languages. The application generator helps build a complete application with menus and help files.

and independent networks, including the Internet, have made it easier to connect databases running in different locations. Nonetheless, some database systems do a better job of using these tools and support connections to share data globally.

Figure 1.9 shows how a modern DBMS has additional components to share data with other machines across communication networks. The 3GL connector provides utilities that connect traditional languages (Visual Basic, COBOL, C++, etc.) with the database engine. Developers can use the power and flexibility of these languages and still use the query processor to retrieve and store data in the database.

Security and Other Utilities

Because a primary goal of a database is to share data with multiple users, the DBMS must also be responsible for establishing and maintaining security access controls. Chapter 10 describes how individuals or groups of users can be granted specific privileges and how their actions can be restricted to specific areas of the database.

Security is a complex issue with databases running on personal computers, because most personal computer operating systems have few controls. The DBMS has to take responsibility for more aspects of security. In particular, it must identify the user and then provide or limit access to various parts of the database.

Various administrative utilities are provided by the DBMS and discussed in Chapter 10. Common features include backup and recovery, user management, data storage evaluation, and performance-monitoring tools.

Advantages of the Database Management System Approach

Many business applications need the same features (efficient storage and retrieval of data, sharing data with multiple users, security, and so on). Rather than re-create these features within every application program, it

FIGURE 1.10
Advantages of a DBMS. The DBMS provides a solution to basic data storage and retrieval problems. By using a DBMS to handle data storage problems, programmers can concentrate on building applications—saving time and money in developing new systems and simplifying maintenance of existing applications.

- Minimal data redundancy
- Data consistency
- Integration of data
- Sharing of data
- Enforcement of standards
- Ease of application development
- Uniform security, privacy, and integrity
- Data independence

makes more sense to purchase a database management system that includes these basic facilities. Then developers can focus on creating applications to solve business problems. The primary benefits provided by a DBMS are shown in Figure 1.10.

First, the DBMS stores data efficiently. As described in Chapters 2 and 3, if you set up your database according to a few basic rules, the data will be stored with minimal wasted space. Additionally, the data can be retrieved rapidly to answer any query. Although these two goals seem obvious, they can be challenging to handle if you have to write programs from scratch every time.

The DBMS also has systems to maintain data consistency with minimal effort. Most systems enable you to create basic business rules when you define the data. For example, price should always be greater than zero. These rules are enforced for every form, user, or program that accesses the data. With traditional programs, you would have to force everyone to follow the same rules. Additionally, these rules would be stored in hundreds or thousands of separate programs—making them hard to find and hard to modify if the business changes.

The DBMS, particularly the query language, makes it easy to integrate data. For example, one application might collect data on customer sales. Another application might collect data on customer returns. If programmers created separate programs and independent files to store this data, combining the data would be difficult. In contrast, with a DBMS any data in the database can be easily retrieved, combined, and compared using the query system.

Focus on Data

With the old programming-file method, developers focused on the process and the program. Developers started projects by asking these kinds of questions: How should the program be organized? and What computations need to be made? The database approach instead focuses on the data. Developers now begin projects by asking, What data will be collected? This change is more than just a technicality. It alters the entire development process.

Think about the development process for a minute. Which component changes the most: programs (forms and reports) or the data? Yes, companies collect new data all the time, but the structure of the data does not change often. And when it does change, the reason is usually that you are adding new elements—such as cellular phone numbers. On the other hand, users constantly need modifications to forms and reports.

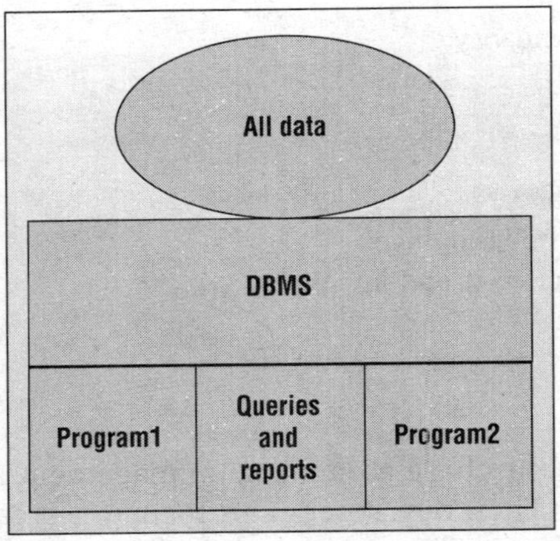

FIGURE 1.11
DBMS focus on data. First, define the data. Then all queries, reports, and programs access the data through the DBMS. The DBMS always handles common problems such as concurrency and security.

As shown in Figure 1.11, the database approach concentrates on the data. The DBMS is responsible for defining, storing, and retrieving the data. All requests for data must go through the database engine. Hence the DBMS is responsible for efficient data storage and retrieval, concurrency, data security, and so on. Once the data structure is carefully defined, additional tools like the report writer, forms generator, and query language make it faster and easier to develop business applications.

Data Independence

The other important feature of focusing on the data is the separation of the data definition from the program—known as **data independence.** Data independence enables you to change the data definition without altering the program. Similarly, data can be moved to new hardware or a completely different machine. Once the DBMS knows how to access the data, you do not have to alter the forms, reports, or programs that use that data. You can alter individual programs without having to change the data definitions.

There are exceptions to this idealistic portrayal. Obviously, if you delete entire chunks of the database structure, some of your applications are not going to work properly. Similarly, if you make radical changes to the data definitions—such as changing phone number data storage from a numeric to a text data type—you will probably have to alter your reports and forms. However, a properly designed database rarely needs these radical changes.

Consider the problem of adding cell phone numbers to an Employee table. Figure 1.12 shows part of the data definition for employees. Regardless of

FIGURE 1.12
Adding cellular phone numbers to the Employee table. Adding a new element to a table does not affect the existing queries, reports, forms, or programs.

Field Name	Data Type	Description
EmployeeID	Number	Autonumber . . .
TaxpayerID	Text	Federal ID
LastName	Text	
FirstName	Text	
. . .		
Phone	Text	
. . .		
CellPhone	Text	Cellular . . .

how many forms, reports, or programs exist, the procedure is the same. Simply go to the table definition and insert the entry for CellPhone. The existing queries, forms, reports, and programs will function exactly as they did before. Of course, they will ignore the new phone number entry. If you want to see the new values on a report, you will have to insert it. With a modern report writer, this change can be as simple as dragging the CellPhone item to the appropriate location on the form or report.

The focus on data and careful design enable database systems to avoid the problems experienced with traditional programming-file methods. The consolidation of common database functions within one application enables experts to create powerful database management systems and frees application programmers to focus on building applications that solve business problems.

Data Independence and Client/Server Systems

Increasingly powerful personal computers developed over the past 10 years have opened up new methods of designing and building business applications. The most important of these is the client/server model. Database management systems have played important roles in creating client/server systems. In a simple client/server approach, the data is stored in a DBMS on a centralized computer. The decentralized personal computers run a front-end application that retrieves and displays data from the server.

The power of data independence is that the client-side applications are essentially independent from the database. Developers can create new applications without altering the database. Similarly, they can expand the database or even move it to multiple servers, and the applications remain the same. Users continue to work with their familiar personal computer applications. Developers retain control over the data. The DBMS can monitor and enforce security and integrity conditions to protect the data, yet still give access to authorized users. Chapter 10 discusses the use of distributed database systems in more detail, including building client/server systems on the World Wide Web.

Leading Commercial Databases

Some of the leading database systems include DB2, Oracle, CA-Ingres, SQL Server, and Informix. Tools from IBM, Oracle, and CA-Ingres are available for a variety of platforms, from large to midrange to personal computers. The Informix database system is also available for various hardware platforms but is primarily designed to run on computers using the UNIX operating system. Many database packages are available for personal computers, but most of the vendors recommend that their use be limited to small applications. Microsoft Access is a common example of a small-system database, but Microsoft also provides a low-cost version of SQL Server called MSDE that provides the same capabilities of SQL Server but is limited to five users. Oracle provides Personal Oracle for stand-alone use.

Choosing a database system can be a major challenge. Many larger organizations standardize on a major vendor, negotiate reduced license costs, and make it available throughout the organization for all projects. However, if you need to choose a DBMS for a specific project, you need to carefully investigate the vendor options.

The premiere database systems are useful for large projects, offer extensive options and control over thousands of detailed features. However, these options make it difficult for beginners to understand the major concepts. It is generally best if you begin your studies with a simpler database system such as Microsoft Access. In structure, Access is similar to the large databases: it is easy to change your designs at any time, it has wizards to help build forms and reports, and the SQL queries follow most of the SQL-92 standard. It is also relatively inexpensive and widely available. However, even Microsoft recommends that you use Access only for relatively small, self-contained applications. For better performance, security, and data protection, you will eventually need to use a more powerful database system.

Brief History of Database Management Systems

Developers quickly realized that many business applications needed a common set of features for sharing data, and they began developing database management systems. Developers gradually refined their goals and improved their programming techniques. Many of the earlier database approaches still survive, partly because it is difficult to throw away applications that work. It is worth understanding some of the basic differences between these older methods. The following discussion simplifies the concepts and skips the details. The purpose is to highlight the differences between these various database systems—not to teach you how to design or use them.

The earliest database management systems were based on a hierarchical method of storing data. The early systems were an extension of the COBOL file structure. To provide flexible access, these systems were extended with network databases. However, the relational database approach originated by E. F. Codd eventually became the dominant method of storing and retrieving data. Recently, the object-oriented approach has been defined. In some ways it is an extension of the relational model. In other ways it is different. However, it is so new that systems based on the concept are still evolving.

Hierarchical Databases

The **hierarchical database** approach begins by claiming that business data often exhibits a hierarchical relationship. For example, a small office without computers might store data in filing cabinets. The cabinets would be organized by customer. Each customer section would contain folders for individual orders, and the orders would list each item being purchased. To store or retrieve data, the database system must start at the top—with a customer in this example. As shown in Figure 1.13, when the database stores the customer data, it stores the rest of the hierarchical data with it.

The hierarchical database approach is relatively fast—as long as you only want to access the data from the top. The most serious problem related to data storage is the difficulty of searching for items in the bottom or middle of the hierarchy. For example, to find all of the customers who ordered a specific item, the database would have to inspect each customer, every order, and each item.

Network Databases

The **network database** has nothing to do with physical networks (e.g., local area networks). Instead, the network model is named from the network of

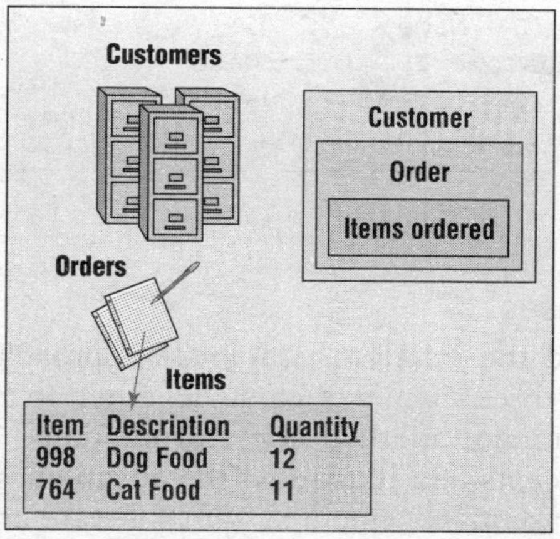

FIGURE 1.13
Hierarchical database. To retrieve data, the DBMS starts at the top (customer). When it retrieves a customer, it retrieves all nested data (order, then items ordered).

connections between the data elements. The primary goal of the network model was to solve the hierarchical problem of searching for data from different perspectives.

Figure 1.14 illustrates the Customer, Order, and Item data components in a network model. First, notice that the items are now physically separated. Second, note that they are connected by arrows. Finally, notice the entry points, which are indicated with arrows. The entry points are predefined items that can be searched. In all cases the purpose of the arrows is to show that once you enter the database, the DBMS can follow the arrows to find and display matching data. As long as there is an arrow, the database can make an efficient connection.

Although this approach seems to solve the search problem, the cost is high. All arrows must be physically implemented as indexes or embedded pointers. Essentially, an index duplicates every key data item in the associated data set and associates the item with a pointer to the storage location of the rest of the data. The problem with the network approach is that the indexes must be built before the user can ask a question. Consequently, the developer must anticipate every possible question that users might ask about the data. Worse, building and maintaining the indexes can require huge amounts of processor time and storage space.

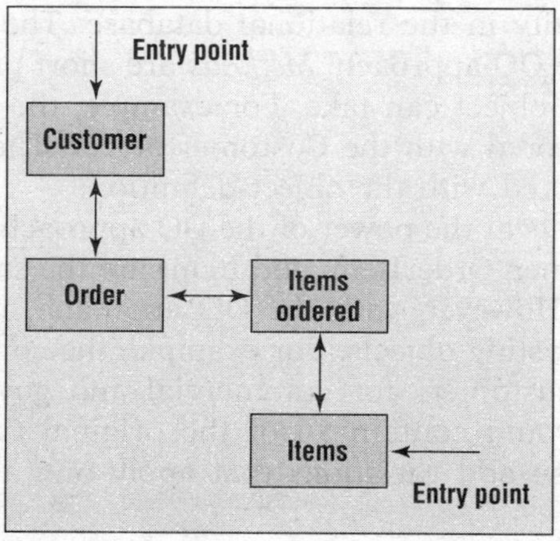

FIGURE 1.14
Network database. All data sets must be connected with indexes as indicated by the arrows. Likewise, all entry points (starting point for a query) must be defined and created before the question can be answered.

FIGURE 1.15
Relational database. Data is stored in separate sets of data. The tables are not physically connected; instead, data is linked between columns. For example, when retrieving an order, the database can match and retrieve the corresponding customer data based on CustomerID.

```
Customer(CustomerID, Name, . . .
Order(OrderID, CustomerID, OrderDate, . . .
ItemsOrdered(OrderID, ItemID, Quantity, . . .
Items(ItemID, Description, Price, . . .
```

Relational Databases

E. F. Codd originated the **relational database** approach in the 1970s, and within several years three elements came together to make the relational database the predominant method for storing data. First, theoreticians defined the basic concepts and illustrated the advantages. Second, programmers who built database management system software created efficient components. Third, hardware performance improved to handle the increased demands of the system.

Figure 1.15 illustrates how the four basic tables in the example are represented in a relational database. The key is that the tables (called "relations" by Codd) are sets of data. Each table stores attributes in columns that describe specific entities. These data tables are not physically connected to each other. The connections exist through the matching data stored in each table. For example, the Order table contains a column for CustomerID. If you find an order that has a CustomerID of 15, the database can automatically find the matching CustomerID and retrieve the related customer data.

The strength of the relational approach is that the designer does not need to know which questions might be asked of the data. If the data is carefully defined (see Chapters 2 and 3), the database can answer virtually any question efficiently (see Chapters 4 and 5). This flexibility and efficiency is the primary reason for the dominance of the relational model. Most of this book focuses on building applications for relational databases.

Object-Oriented Databases

An **object-oriented (OO) database** is a new and evolving method of organizing data. The OO approach began as a new method to create programs. The goal is to define objects that can be reused in many programs—thus saving time and reducing errors. As illustrated in Figure 1.16, an object has three major components: a name, a set of properties or attributes, and a set of methods or functions. The properties describe the object, just as attributes describe an entity in the relational database. The "methods" are the true innovation of the OO approach. *Methods* are short programs that define the actions that each object can take. For example, the code to add a new customer would be stored with the Customer object. The innovation is that these methods are stored with the object definition.

Figure 1.16 also hints at the power of the OO approach. Note that the base objects (Order, Customer, OrderItem, and Item) are the same as those for the relational approach. However, with the OO approach, new objects can be defined in terms of existing objects. For example, the company might create separate classes of customers for commercial and government accounts. These new objects would contain all of the original Customer properties and methods, and also add variations that apply only to the new types of customers.

FIGURE 1.16
Object-oriented database. Objects have properties—just as relational entities have attributes—that hold data to describe the object. Objects have methods that are functions the objects can perform. Objects can be derived from other objects.

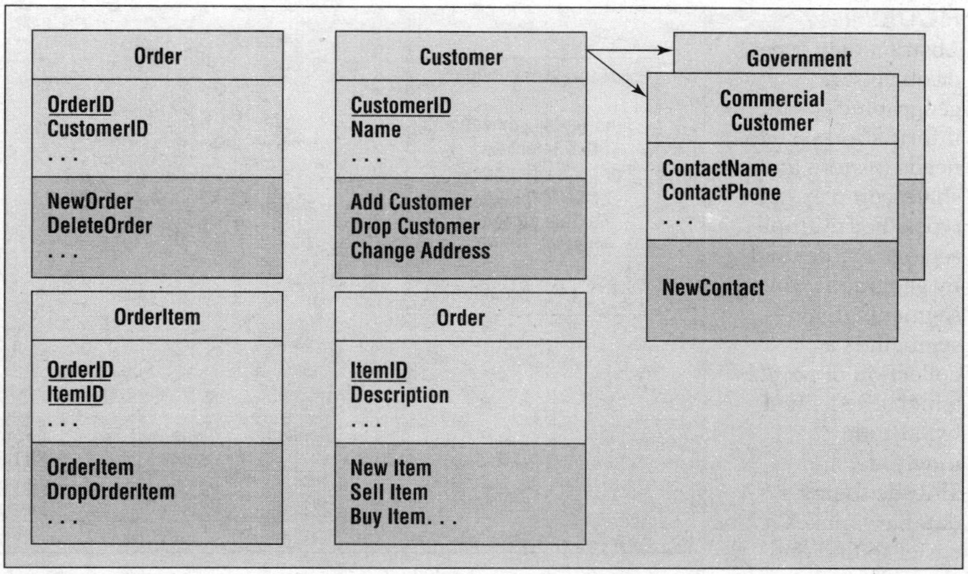

The OO approach is fundamentally altering the way programmers create applications. As an application developer, you will be using DBMS software that was created with an OO approach. Hence, you will use the objects, properties, and methods that have already been defined.

There are two basic approaches to handling true object-oriented data: (1) extend the relational model so that it can handle typical OO features or (2) create a new object-oriented DBMS. Today, most commercially successful database systems follow the first approach by adding object features to the relational model.

The approach that adds OO features to the relational model is best exemplified by the American National Standards Institute (ANSI). Object-oriented features were a major component to the SQL 99 version. The proposed SQL 200x standard clarified some of the OO issues as well. In 1997 the SQL3 development group merged with the Object Database Management Group (ODMG). Three features are suggested to add OO capabilities: (1) abstract data types, (2) subtables, and (3) persistent stored modules. Database management system vendors have implemented some of the features, a few of the more advanced ones.

Object Properties

The first issue involves defining and storing properties. In particular, OO programmers need the ability to create new composite properties that are built from other data types. SQL supports **abstract data types** to enable developers to create new types of data derived from existing types. This technique supports inheritance of properties. The type of data stored in a column can be a composite of several existing abstract types. Consider the example shown in Figure 1.17, which shows part of a database for a geographic information system (GIS). The GIS defines an abstract data type for location in terms of latitude, longitude, and altitude. Similarly, a line segment (e.g., national boundary) would be a collection of these location points. By storing the data in tables, the application can search and retrieve information

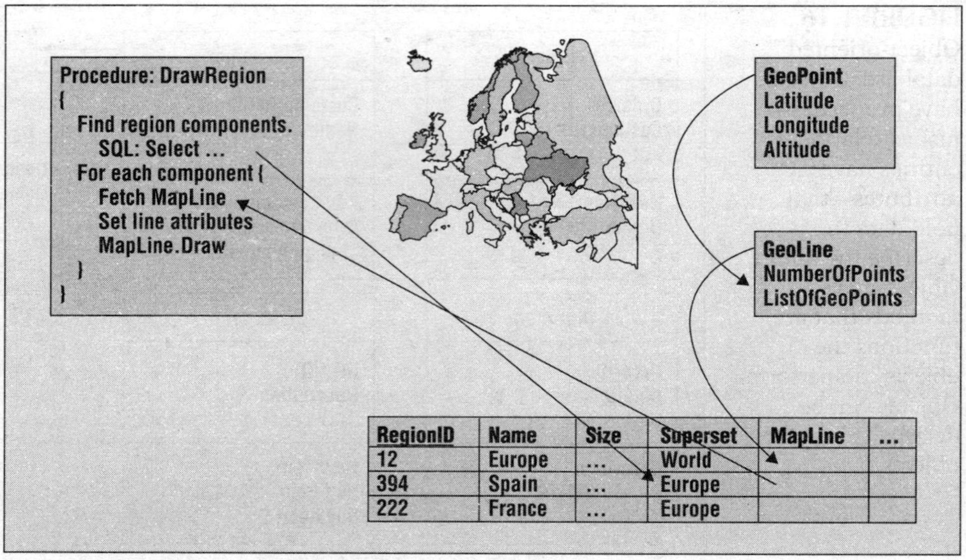

FIGURE 1.17
Abstract data types or objects. A geographic information system needs to store and share complex data types. For example, regions are defined by geographic line segments. Each segment is a collection of points, which are defined by latitude, longitude, and altitude. Using a database makes it easier to find and share data.

based on user requirements. The database also makes it easier to share and to update the data. In the GIS example, the database handles the selection criteria (Region = Europe). The database can also match and retrieve demographic data stored in other tables. The advantage to this approach is that the DBMS handles the data storage and retrieval, freeing the developer to concentrate on the application details.

The abstract data type enables developers to create and store any data needed by the application. The abstract data type can also provide greater control over the application development. First, by storing the data in a DBMS, it simplifies and standardizes the way that all developers access the data. Second, the elements within the data type can be encapsulated. By defining the elements as private, application developers (and users) can only access the internal elements through the predefined routines. For example, developers could be prevented from directly modifying the latitude and longitude coordinates of any location by defining the elements as private.

SQL provides a second method to handle inheritance by defining subtables. A **subtable** inherits all the columns from a base table and provides inheritance similar to that of the abstract data types; however, all the data is stored in separate columns. The technique is similar to the method shown in Figure 1.16, which stores subclasses in separate tables. The difference is that the OO subtables will not need to include the primary key in the subtables. As indicated in Figure 1.18, inheritance is specified with an UNDER statement. You begin by defining the highest level tables (e.g., Customer) in the hierarchy. Then, when you create a new table (e.g., CommercialCustomer), you can specify that it is a subtable by adding the UNDER statement. If you use the unified modeling language (UML) triangle-pointer notation for inheritance, it will be easy to create the tables in SQL. Just define the properties of the table and add an UNDER statement if there is a "pointer" to another table.

Do not worry about the details of the CREATE TABLE command. Instead, it is important to understand the difference between abstract data types and subtables. An abstract data type is used to set the type of data that will be stored in one column. With a complex data type, many pieces

FIGURE 1.18
SQL subtables. A subtable inherits the columns from the selected supertable. Queries to the Commercial-Customer table will also retrieve data for the CustomerID, Address, and Phone columns inherited from the Customer table.

```
CREATE SET TABLE Customer
(
   CustomerID       INTEGER,
   Address          VARCHAR,
   Phone            CHAR(15)
)

CREATE SET TABLE CommercialCustomer
(
   Contact          VARCHAR,
   VolumeDiscount   NUMERIC(5,2)
)
   UNDER Customer;
```

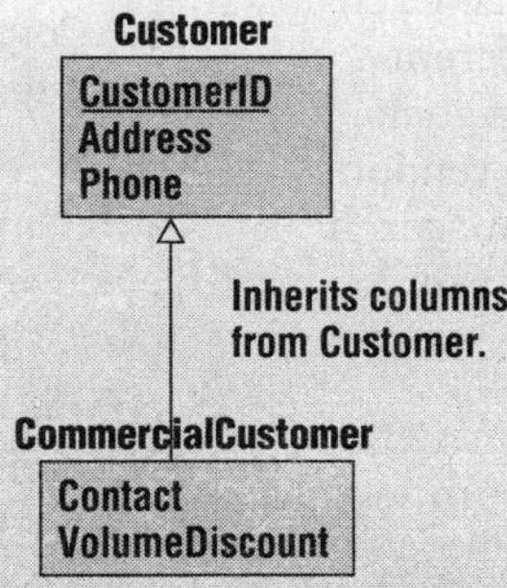

of data (latitude, longitude, etc.) will be stored within a single column. With a subtable the higher level items remain in separate columns. For example, a subtable for CommercialCustomer could be derived from a base Customer table. All the attributes defined by the Customer table would be available to the CommercialCustomer as separate columns.

Object Methods

Each abstract data type can also have methods or functions. In SQL, the routines are called **persistent stored modules**. They can be written as SQL statements. The SQL language is also being extended with programming commands—much like Oracle's PL/SQL extensions. Routines are used for several purposes. They can be used as code to support triggers, which have been added to SQL. Persistent routines can also be used as methods for the abstract data types. Designers can define functions that apply to individual data types. For example, a GIS location data type could use a subtraction operator that computes the distance between two points.

To utilize the power of the database, each abstract data type should define two special functions: (1) to test for equality of two elements and (2) to compare elements for sorting. These functions enable the DBMS to perform searches and to sort the data. The functions may not apply to some data types (e.g., sound clips), but they should be defined whenever possible.

Object-Oriented Languages and Sharing Persistent Objects

The development of true OODBMS models was initiated largely in response to OO programmers who routinely create their own objects within memory. They needed a way to store and share those objects. Although the goals may appear similar to the modified-relational approach, the resulting database systems are unique.

Most OO development has evolved from programming languages. Several languages were specifically designed to utilize OO features. Common examples include C++, Smalltalk, and Java. Data variables within these languages are defined as objects. Each class has defined properties and methods. Currently, developers building applications in these languages must either create their own storage mechanisms or translate the internal data to a relational database.

Complex objects can be difficult to store within relational databases. Most languages have some facility for storing and retrieving data to files, but not

FIGURE 1.19
OODBMS vendors and products. Each tool has different features and goals. Contact the vendors for details or search the Web for user comments.

GemStone Systems, Inc.
Hewlett Packard, Inc. (OpenODB)
IBEX Corporation, SA.
Illustra (Informix, Inc.)
Matisse Software, Inc.
O2 Technology, Inc.
Objectivity, Inc.
Object Design, Inc.
ONTOS, Inc.
POET Software Corporation.
UniSQL
Unisys Corporation (OSMOS)
Versant Object Technology

to databases. For example, C++ libraries have a serialize function that transfers objects directly to a disk file. There are two basic problems with this approach: (1) it is difficult to search files or match data from different objects, and (2) the developer is responsible for creating all sharing, concurrency, and security operations. However, this approach causes several problems because data is now intrinsically tied to the programs and is no longer independent.

Essentially, OO programmers want the ability to create **persistent objects**, that is, objects that can be saved and retrieved at any time. Ideally, the database would standardize the definitions, control sharing of the data, and provide routines to search and combine data. The basic difficulty is that no standard theory explains how to accomplish all these tasks. Nonetheless, as shown in Figure 1.19, several OODBMS exist, and users have reportedly created many successful applications with these tools.

The key to an OODBMS is that to the programmer it simply looks like extended storage. An object and its association links are treated the same whether the object is stored in RAM or shared through the DBMS. Clearly, these systems make development easier for OO programmers. The catch is that you have to be an OO programmer to use the system at all. In other words, if your initial focus is on OO programming, then a true OODBMS may be useful. If you started with a traditional relational database, you will probably be better off with a relational DBMS that has added OO features.

In theory, the 1997 agreements between ANSI and ODMG were designed to bring the SQL and OODBMS models closer to a combined standard. In practice, it could take a few years and considerable experimentation in the marketplace. For now, if you are serious about storing and sharing objects, you will have to make a choice based on your primary focus: OO programming or the relational database.

Application Development

If you carefully examine Figures 1.14, 1.15, and 1.16, you will notice that they all have essentially the same data sets. This similarity is not an accident. Database design methods described in Chapters 2 and 3 should be followed regardless of the method used to implement the database. In other words, any database project begins by identifying the data that will be needed and analyzing that data to store it as efficiently as possible.

The second step in building applications is to identify forms and reports that the users will need. These forms and reports are based on queries, so you must create any queries or views that will be needed to produce the reports and forms as described in Chapters 4 and 5. Then you use the report writer and forms generator to create each report and form as described in Chapter 6. The next step is to combine the forms and reports into an application that handles all of the operations needed by the user. The goal is to create an application that matches the jobs of the users and helps them to do their work.

Chapter 7 describes how to deal with common problems in a multiuser environment to protect the integrity of the data and support transactions. Chapter 8 shows one more design method of storing data: the data warehouse. To deal with large databases, transaction processing systems use indexes and other features to optimize storage tasks. Today, managers want to retrieve and analyze the data. Data warehouses provide special designs and tools to support **online analytical processing (OLAP)**.

When the application is designed and while it is being used, several database administration tasks have to be performed. Setting security parameters and controlling access to the data is one of the more important tasks. Chapter 9 discusses various administration and security issues.

As an organization grows, computer systems and applications become more complex. An important feature in modern organizations is the need for users to access and use data from many different computers throughout the organization. At some point you will need to increase the scope of your application so that it can be used by more people in different locations. Distributed databases discussed in Chapter 10 are a powerful way to create applications that remove the restrictions of location. The Internet is rapidly becoming a powerful tool for building and implementing database applications that can be used by anyone around the world. The same technologies can be used for applications that are accessed only by in-house personnel. Systems that use Internet technology but limit access to insiders are called **intranets**.

Sally's Pet Store

A young lady with a love for animals is starting a new type of pet store. Sally wants to match pets with owners who will take good care of the animals. One of her key objectives is to closely monitor breeders to make sure that they take good care of all of their animals and that baby animals receive proper care and attention so they will become friendly pets. A second objective is to develop long-term relationships with customers. She wants to help them choose the best type of animal for each situation and to make sure the customers have all of the support and information they need to care for the animals properly.

Sally realizes that meeting these two objectives requires her to collect and monitor a large amount of data. After taking an information systems course in an MBA program, she realizes that she needs a database to help her collect data and monitor the operations of the store.

At the moment Sally has only one store, but she dreams of expanding into additional cities. She wants to hire and train workers to be "animal friends," not salespeople. These friends will help customers choose the proper animal. They will answer questions about health, nutrition, and pet behavior. They will even be taught that some potential customers should be convinced not to buy an animal.

Because the workers will spend most of their time with the customers and animals, they will need technology to help them with their tasks. The new system will also have to be easy to use, since little time will be available for computer training.

Even based on a few short discussions with Sally, it is clear that the system she wants will take time to build and test. Fortunately, Sally admits that she does not need the complete system immediately. She has decided that she first needs a basic system to handle the store operations: sales, orders, customer tracking, and basic animal data. However, she emphasizes that she wants the system to be flexible enough to handle additional features and applications.

Details of Sally's Pet Store will be examined in other chapters. For now, you might want to visit a local pet store or talk to friends to get a basic understanding of the problems they face and how a database might help them.

Rolling Thunder Bicycles

The Rolling Thunder Bicycle Company builds custom bicycles. Its database application is much more complete than the Pet Store application, and it provides an example of how the pieces of a database system fit together. This application also contains many detailed forms that illustrate the key concepts of creating a user interface. Additionally, most of the forms contain programming code that handle common business tasks. You can study this code to help you build your own applications. The Rolling Thunder application has a comprehensive help system that describes the company and the individual forms. The database contains realistic data for hundreds of customers and bicycles.

One of the most important tasks at the Rolling Thunder Bicycle Company is to take orders for new bicycles. Several features have been included to help nonexperts select a good bicycle. As the bicycles are built, the employees record the construction on the Assembly form. When the bicycle is shipped, the customers are billed. Customer payments are recorded in the financial forms. As components are installed on bicycles, the inventory quantity is automatically decreased. Merchandise is ordered from suppliers, and payments are made when the shipments arrive.

The tasks performed at Rolling Thunder Bicycles are similar to those in any business. By studying the application and the techniques, you will be able to create solid applications for any business.

The Feasibility Study

Ideas for information systems can come from many sources: users, upper management, information system analysts, competitors, or firms in other industries. Ideas that receive initial support from several people might be proposed as new projects. If the project is small enough and easy to create, it might be built in a few days. Larger projects require more careful study. If the project is going to involve critical areas within the organization, require expensive hardware, or require substantial development time, then a more formal **feasibility study** is undertaken.

FIGURE 1.20
Common costs and benefits from introducing a database management system. Note that benefits can be hard to measure, especially for tactical and strategic decisions. But it is still important to list potential benefits. Even if you cannot assign a specific value, managers need to see the complete list.

Costs	Benefits
Up-front/one-time	Cost savings
Software	Software maintenance
Hardware	Fewer errors
Communications	Less data maintenance
Data conversion	Less user training
Studies and design training	Increased value
Ongoing costs	Better access to data
Personnel	Better decisions
Software upgrades	Better communication
Supplies	More timely reports
Support	Faster reaction to change
Software and hardware maintenance	New products and services
	Strategic advantages
	Lock out competitors

Feasibility studies are covered in detail within systems analysis texts. However, because of their unique nature, it is helpful to examine the typical costs and benefits that arise with the database approach.

The goal of a feasibility study is to determine whether a proposed project is worth pursuing. The study examines two fundamental categories: costs and potential benefits. As noted in Figure 1.20, costs are often divided into two categories: up-front or one-time costs and ongoing costs once the project is operational. Benefits can often be found in one of three categories: reduced operating costs, increased value, or strategic advantages that lock out competitors.

Costs

Almost all projects will entail similar up-front costs. The organization will often have to purchase additional hardware, software, and communication equipment (e.g., expand a local area network). The cost of developing the system is listed here, including the cost for all additional studies. Other one-time costs include converting data to the new system and initial training of users. Database management systems are expensive software items. For example, for larger projects, the cost for software such as Oracle can easily run to several million dollars. You will also have to purchase "maintenance" upgrades of the software at least on an annual basis.

Hardware and software costs can be estimated with the help of vendors. As long as you know the approximate size of the final system (e.g., number of users), vendors can provide reasonably accurate estimates of the costs. Data conversion costs can be estimated from the amount of data involved. The biggest challenge often lies in estimating the costs of developing the new system. If an organization has experience with similar projects, historical data can be used to estimate the time and costs based on the size of the project. Otherwise, the costs can be estimated based on the projected number of people and hours involved.

Once the project is completed and the system installed, costs will arise from several areas. For example, the new system might require additional personnel and supplies. Software and hardware will have to be modified and replaced—entailing maintenance costs. Additional training and support might be required to deal with employee turnover and system modifications. Again, most of these costs are straightforward to estimate, as long as you know the size of the project.

Unfortunately, information system (IS) designers have not been very successful at estimating the costs. For example, in January 1995 *PC Week* reported that 31 percent of new IS projects are canceled before they are completed. Additionally, 53 percent of those that are completed are 189 percent over budget. The greatest difficulty is in estimating the time it takes to design and develop new software. Every developer is different with large variations in programmer productivity. In large projects, where the staff members are constantly changing, accurately predicting the amount of time needed to design and develop a new system is often impossible. Nonetheless, managers need to provide some estimate of the costs.

Benefits

In many cases benefits are even more difficult to estimate. Some benefits are tangible and can be measured with a degree of accuracy. For instance, transaction processing systems are slightly easier to evaluate than a DSS, since benefits generally arise from their ability to decrease operations costs. A system might enable workers to process more items, thus allowing the firm to expand without increasing labor costs. A database approach might reduce IS labor costs by making it easier for workers to create and modify reports. Finally, a new information system might reduce errors in the data, leading to improved decisions.

Many benefits are intangible and cannot be assigned specific monetary values. For instance, benefits can arise because managers have better access to data. Communication improves, better decisions are made, and managers can react faster to a changing environment. Similarly, the new system might enable the company to produce new products and services or to increase the sales of ancillary products to existing customers. Similarly, firms might implement systems that provide a competitive advantage. For example, an automated order system between a firm and its customers often encourages the customers to place more orders with the firm. Hence the firm gains an advantage over its competitors.

When information systems are built to automate operations-level tasks and the benefits are tangible, evaluating the economic benefits of the system is relatively straightforward. The effects of improving access to data are easy to observe and measure in decreased costs and increased revenue. However, when information systems are implemented to improve tactical and strategic decisions, identifying and evaluating benefits is more difficult. For example, how much is it worth to a marketing manager to have the previous week's sales data available on Monday instead of waiting until Wednesday?

In a database project benefits can arise from improving operations—which leads to cost savings. Additional benefits occur because it is now easier and faster to create new reports for users, so less programmer time will be needed to modify the system. Users can also gain better access to data through creating their own queries—instead of waiting for a programmer to write a new program.

Database projects can provide many benefits, but the organization will receive those benefits only if the project is completed correctly, on time, and within the specified budget. To accomplish this task, you will have to design the system carefully. More than that, your team will have to communicate with users, share work with each other, and track the progress of the development. You need to follow a design methodology.

Summary

One of the most important features of business applications is the ability to share data with many users at the same time. Without a DBMS sharing data causes several problems. For example, if data definitions are stored within each separate program, making changes to the data file becomes very difficult. Changes in one program and its data files can cause other programs to crash. Every application would need special code to provide data security, concurrency, and integrity features. By focusing on the data first, the database approach separates the data from the programs. This independence makes it possible to expand the database without crashing the programs.

A DBMS has many components. Required features include the database engine to store and retrieve the data and the data dictionary to help the DBMS and the user locate data. Other common features include a query language, which is used to retrieve data from the DBMS to answer business questions. Application development tools include a report writer, a forms generator, and an application generator to create features like menus and help files. Advanced database systems provide utilities to control secure access to the data, cooperate with other software packages, and communicate with other database systems.

Database systems have evolved through several stages. Early hierarchical databases were fast for specific purposes but provided limited access to the data. Network databases enabled users to build complex queries but only if the links were built with indexes in advance. The relational database is currently the leading approach to building business applications. Once the data is defined carefully, it can be stored and retrieved efficiently to answer any business question. The OO approach is a new technique for creating software. Object-oriented systems enable you to create your own new abstract data types. They also support subtables, making it easier to extend a class of objects without redefining everything from scratch.

Regardless of the type of database implemented, application development follows similar steps. First, identify the user requirements, determine the data that needs to be collected, and define the structure of the database. Then, develop the forms and reports that will be used, and build the queries to support them. Next, combine the various elements into a polished application that ties everything together to meet the user needs. If necessary, distribute the database across the organization or through an Internet or intranet. Additional features can be provided by integrating the database with powerful analytical and presentation tools, such as spreadsheets, statistical packages, and word processors.

A Developer's View

For Miranda to start on her database project, she must first know the strengths of the tools she will use. At the starting point of a database project, you should collect information about the specific tools that you will use. Get the latest reference manuals. Install the latest software patches. Set up work directories and project space. For a class project, you should log on, get access to the DBMS, make sure you can create tables, and learn the basics of the help system.

Key Terms

abstract data type, *17*
application generator, *9*
data dictionary, *5*
data independence, *12*
database, *2*
database engine, *4*
database management system (DBMS), *2*
feasibility study, *22*
forms generator, *8*
hierarchical database, *14*
intranet, *21*
network database, *14*
object-oriented (OO) database, *16*
online analytical processing (OLAP), *21*
persistent objects, *20*
persistent stored modules, *19*
relational database, *16*
report writer, *6*
subtable, *18*

Review Questions

1. What are the advantages of the DBMS approach to application development?
2. What are the basic components of a DBMS?
3. Why is the relational database approach better than earlier methods?
4. How is the object-oriented approach different from the relational approach?
5. How are abstract data types and subtables a cross between the relational and object approaches?
6. What are the main steps in application development with a database system?
7. What is the purpose of a feasibility study?

Exercises

Employee(<u>EmployeeID</u>, LastName, FirstName, Address, DateHired)

EmployeeID	LastName	FirstName	Address	DateHired
332	Ant	Adam	354 Elm	5/5/1964
442	Bono	Sonny	765 Pine	8/8/1972
553	Cass	Mama	886 Oak	2/2/1985
673	Donovan	Michael	421 Willow	3/3/1971
773	Moon	Keith	554 Cherry	4/4/1972
847	Morrison	Jim	676 Sandalwood	5/5/1968

Client(<u>ClientID</u>, LastName, FirstName, Balance, EmployeeID)

ClientID	LastName	FirstName	Balance	EmployeeID
1101	Jones	Joe	113.42	442
2203	Smith	Mary	993.55	673
2256	Brown	Laura	225.44	332
4456	Dieter	Jackie	664.90	442
5543	Wodkoski	John	984.00	847
6673	Sanchez	Paula	194.87	773
7353	Chen	Charles	487.34	332
7775	Hagen	Fritz	595.55	673
8890	Hauer	Marianne	627.39	773
9662	Nguyen	Suzie	433.88	553
9983	Martin	Mark	983.31	847

Report

Ant, Adam	5/5/1964	
	Brown, Laura	225.24
	Chen, Charles	487.34
		712.58
Bono, Sonny	8/8/1972	
	Dieter, Jackie	664.90
	Jones, Joe	114.32
		779.22

1. Create a new database with the two tables shown in the figure. Feel free to add more data. Be sure to set a primary key for the underlined columns. Next, create a query that includes every column in the two tables. Create a report based on this query similar to the one shown in the figure. Hint: Use the wizard to create the report.
2. Read the documentation to your DBMS and write a brief outline that explains how to:
   a. Create a table.
   b. Create a simple query.
   c. Create a report.
3. Interview a friend or a relative about his or her job and sketch two forms that could be used in a database application for that job.
4. Find a recent reference that compares at least two DBMS software packages. List the major strengths of each package. Describe the basic features (query, report writer, etc.) for each package.
5. Describe how a university club or student organization could use a database to improve its service operations.
6. Using Internet resources, select a DBMS vendor, identify the components needed, and estimate the cost of purchasing a complete system for use on a medium-size project. The database will include at least 100 primary tables and approximately 800 megabytes of data storage. The system will be used by at least 20 users at the same time—most of whom use personal computers attached to a central server.
7. A company is considering a new system for tracking employee evaluations. On talking with users, you learn the potential benefits include less time spent to determine raises; a reduction of one full clerical position; elimination of printing 3,000 pages of reports four times a year; and better merit decisions, which should reduce the $250,000 per year EEO lawsuits. Costs include the initial development costs ($35,000); new hardware ($12,000); new software ($10,000); and annual maintenance costs estimated to be $4,000. There will also be some annual training costs of about $6,000. Prepare a feasibility study for this project. Examine the alternatives under different interest rates (2, 5, 8, and 10 percent) and different expected lifetimes of the project (1, 3, 5, and 10 years). Are there additional benefits and costs that should be considered?
8. A company wants you to create a small application to help management track sales orders. The orders will arrive by phone or e-mail from a website, and a clerk will enter the data into your application. Currently, the company receives many orders by phone, and it requires two clerks on duty much of the time to prevent busy signals. If 50 percent of the orders shift to the online system (which is already developed), the company can eliminate one of the phone clerks (at minimum wage). The company already has a computer but would need to buy the DBMS. How much would the company be willing to pay for the application? Assuming the products are straightforward and the data transfer is easy, how long should it take you to develop the system?

Sally's Pet Store

9. Install the Pet Store database or find it on your local area network if it has already been installed. Print out (or write down) the list of the tables used in the database. Use the Help command to find the version number of Microsoft Access that you are using.
10. Visit a local pet store and make a list of 10 merchandise items and five animals for sale. Enter this data into the appropriate Pet Store database tables.
11. Create a mailing label report that lists the customers who live in California (CA). First create a query that includes the Customer and City tables. Then use the Report Wizard to create a label report based on that query.

12. Outline the basic tasks that take place in running a pet store. Identify some of the basic data items that will be needed.

Rolling Thunder Bicycles

13. Install the Rolling Thunder database or find it on your local area network if it has already been installed. Using the BicycleOrder form, create an entry for a new bicycle.
14. Use the Rolling Thunder Help system to briefly describe the firm and its major processes. Identify the primary business entities in the company.
15. As bicycles are built, how is the data entered into the database? What problems would you anticipate at this stage?
16. Refer to the relationship/class diagram to explain what a Component is and how it is connected to a Bicycle. Give an example from the data.

Website References

Site	Description
http://www.microsoft.com/office/access	Microsoft Access
http://www.microsoft.com/sql/	Microsoft SQL Server
http://www.oracle.com	Oracle
http://otn.oracle.com	Oracle technology network with software downloads
http://www.cai.com/products/ingres.htm	Ingres
http://www.sybase.com	Sybase
http://www.software.ibm.com/data/db2/	IBM DB2
http://www.mysql.com	Free but limited DBMS
http://www.postgresql.org	A better free DBMS
http://www.acm.org	Association for Computing Machinery
http://groups.google.com/groups?group=comp.databases	Newsgroups for database questions
http://dbforums.com	
http://dbaclick.com	
http://www.devx.com/dbzone/Door/7022	

Additional Reading

Anderson, V. *Access 2002: The Complete Reference.* Berkeley: Osborne McGraw-Hill, 2002. [One of many reference books on Access. Spend some time at your local (or electronic) bookstore and choose your favorite.]

Loney, K., and G. Koch. *Oracle 9i: The Complete Reference.* Berkeley: Osborne McGraw-Hill, 2002. [One in series of reference books on Oracle.]

Shapiro, J. *SQL Server 2000: The Complete Reference.* New York: McGraw-Hill, 2001. [One of many reference books for SQL Server.]

Willis, T. *Beginning SQL Server 2000 for Visual Basic Developers*. Indianapolis: Wrox Press, 2000. [One of many introductions to SQL Server 2000.]

Zikopoulos, P. C., and R. B. Melnyk. *DB2: The Complete Reference,* New York: McGraw-Hill, 2001. [One of few reference books on DB2 and written by IBM employees.]

Part 1

Systems Design

To create a useful application, you must first understand the business and determine how to help the users. In a database context, the most important issue is to identify the data that must be stored. This process requires two basic steps. In Chapter 2 you will design a logical (or conceptual) data model that examines business entities and their relationships. This logical data model is displayed on a class diagram and specifies the various business rules of the company.

The second design step is to create an implementation model of how the data will be stored in the database management system. This step usually consists of creating a list of nicely behaved tables that will make up the relational database. Chapter 3 describes how to create this list of tables and explains why it is important to define them carefully.

Chapter 2

Database Design

Chapter Outline

What You Will Learn in This Chapter

A Developer's View

Miranda: Well, Ariel, you were right as usual. A database seems like the right tool for this job.

Ariel: So you decided to take the job for your uncle's company?

Miranda: Yes, it's good money, and the company seems willing to let me learn as I go. But, it's only paying me a small amount until I finish the project.

Ariel: Great. So when do you start?

Miranda: That's the next problem. I'm not really sure where to begin.

Ariel: That could be a problem. Do you know what the application is supposed to do?

Miranda: Well, I talked to the manager and some workers, but there are a lot of points I'm not clear about. This project is bigger than I thought. I'm having trouble keeping track of all the details. There are so many reports and terms I don't know. And one salesperson started talking about all these rules about the data—things like customer numbers are five digits for corporate customers but four digits and two letters for government accounts.

Ariel: Maybe you need a system to take notes and diagram everything they tell you.

Introduction

The goal of any information system is to add value for the users. To achieve this goal requires answering two important questions: Who are the users? and How can an information system help them? Both of these questions can be difficult to answer and usually require research and interviews.

Before spending large amounts of money on a project, most organizations perform a feasibility study to provide initial answers to these two questions. Organizations are particularly interested in evaluating benefits in three key areas: (1) reduction of costs, (2) increase in sales or revenue, and (3) competitive advantage or long-term benefits.

Completing a project on time and within the budget is a challenge. Small projects that involve a few users and one or two developers are generally straightforward. However, you still must carefully design the databases so they are flexible enough to handle future needs. Likewise, you have to keep notes so that future developers can easily understand the system, its goals, and your decisions. Large projects bring additional complications. With many users and several developers, you need to split the project into smaller problems, communicate ideas between users and designers, and track the team's progress.

As explained in systems analysis and design courses, several formal methodologies have been created for designing systems and managing projects. Details can be found in any systems development textbook. Recently, several attempts have been made to speed the development process, known as **rapid application development (RAD)**. Steve McConnell's book, *Rapid Development: Taming Wild Software Schedules,* presents an excellent analysis of the importance of design, how development time can be reduced, and when it cannot be reduced. Development of database applications can take place within any of these methodologies.

An important step in all of these methodologies is to build models of the system. A *model* is a simplified abstraction of a real-world system. In many cases the model consists of a drawing that provides a visual picture of the system.

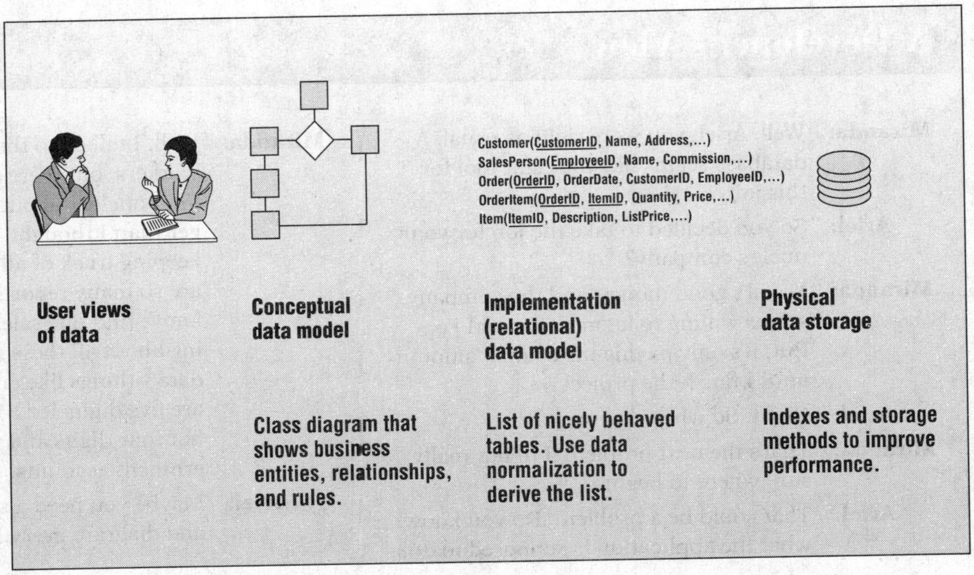

FIGURE 2.1
Design models. The conceptual model records and describes the user views of the system. The implementation model describes the way the data will be stored. The final physical database may utilize storage techniques like indexing to improve performance.

Just as contractors need blueprints to construct a building, information system developers need designs to help them create useful systems. As shown in Figure 2.1, conceptual models are based on user views of the system. Implementation models are based on the conceptual models and describe how the data will be stored. The implementation model is used by the DBMS to store the data.

Three common types of models are used to design systems: process models, class or object models, and event models. Process models are displayed with a **collaboration diagram** or a data flow diagram (DFD). They are typically explained in detail in systems analysis courses and are used to redesign the flow of information within an organization. Class diagrams or the older entity-relationship diagrams are used to show the primary entities or objects in the system. Event models such as a sequence or statechart diagram are newer and illustrate the timing of various events and show how messages are passed between various objects. Each of these models is used to illustrate a different aspect of the system being designed. A good designer should be able to create and use all three types of models. However, the class diagrams are the most important tools used in designing and building database applications.

Database applications can be part of a larger project, which require formal project management techniques to control costs and monitor progress. Alternatively, database projects can be shorter, independent projects developed by a small team working closely with users to rapidly build a new system. The project management controls and system design methodologies will be different in these two approaches. However, certain fundamental database design techniques will be the same. This book focuses on the database design elements and leaves the system and project management issues for systems development textbooks.

Getting Started

Today's DBMS tools are flashy and alluring. It is always tempting to jump right in and start building the forms and reports that users are always anxious to see. However, before you can build forms and reports, you must

FIGURE 2.2
Initial steps in database design. A database design represents the business rules of the organization. You must carefully interview the users to make sure you correctly identify all of the business rules. The process is usually iterative, as you design classes you have to return to the users to obtain more details.

1. Identify the exact goals of the system.
2. Talk with the users to identify the basic forms and reports.
3. Identify the data items to be stored.
4. Design the classes (tables) and relationships.
5. Identify any business constraints.
6. Verify the design matches the business rules.

design the database correctly. If you make a mistake in the database design it will be hard to create the forms and reports, and it will take considerable time to change everything later.

Before you try to build anything, determine exactly what data will be needed by talking with the users. Occasionally, the users know exactly what they want. Most times, users have only a rough idea of what they want and a vague perception of what the computer is capable of producing. Communicating with users is a critical step in any development project. The most important aspect is to identify (1) exactly what data to collect, (2) how the various pieces of data are related, and (3) how long each item needs to be stored in the database. Figure 2.2 outlines the initial steps in the design process.

Once you have identified the data elements, you need to organize them properly. As described in detail in this chapter and the next, the rules for arranging data into tables are straightforward. However, one problem that developers always face is that the database structure ultimately depends on the business rules. The real challenge lies in identifying the business rules. For instance, consider standard orders from customers: Do orders come from only one customer, or can two or more customers jointly place an order? The answer to this question (and similar ones) dramatically affects the design of the database. Hence, the entire point of database design is to identify and formalize the business rules.

To build business applications, you must understand the business details. The task is difficult, but not impossible and almost always interesting. Although every business is different, many common problems exist in the business world. Several of these problems are presented throughout this book. The patterns you develop in these exercises can be applied and extended to many common business problems.

Designing Databases

Information systems are complex, constantly changing, and expensive to create and maintain. But a well-designed system can generate enormous benefits to an organization. Building a useful system requires that you understand and communicate with the user. It often requires organizing and controlling a team of developers. System designs are models that are used to facilitate this communication and teamwork. Designs are a simplification or picture of the underlying business operations. The design models also record the fundamental features, assumptions, and restrictions present in any business.

Identifying User Requirements

One challenging aspect of designing a system is to determine the requirements. You must thoroughly understand the business needs before you can create a useful system. A key step is to interview users and observe the operations of the firm. Although this step sounds easy, it can be difficult—especially when users disagree with each other. Even in the best circumstances, communication can be difficult. Excellent communication skills and experience are important to becoming a good designer.

One of the most important tasks in designing a database application is to correctly identify the data that needs to be stored. As long as you collect the data and organize it carefully, the DBMS makes it easy to create and modify reports. As you talk with users, you will collect user documents, such as reports and forms. These documents provide information about the basic data and operations of the firm. You need to gather three basic pieces of information for the initial design: (1) the data that needs to be collected, (2) the data type (domain), and (3) the amount of data involved.

Business Objects

Database design focuses on identifying the data that needs to be stored. Later, queries can be created to search the data, input forms to enter new data, and reports to retrieve and display the data to match the user needs. For now, the most important step is to organize the data correctly so that the database system can efficiently handle it.

All businesses deal with entities or objects, such as customers, products, employees, and sales. From a systems perspective, an **entity** is some item in the real world that you wish to track. That entity is described by its **attributes** or **properties.** For example, a customer entity has a name, address, and phone number. In modeling terms, an entity listed with its properties is called a **class.** In a programming environment, a class can also have **methods** or functions that it can perform, and these can be listed with the class. For example, the customer class might have a method to add a new customer. Database designs seldom need to describe methods, so they are generally not listed.

Database designers need some way to keep notes and show the list of classes to users and other designers. Several graphical techniques have been developed, but the more modern approach is to use a class diagram. A **class diagram** displays each class as a box containing the list of properties for the class. Class diagrams also show how the classes are related to each other by connecting them with lines. Figure 2.3 shows how a single class is displayed.

FIGURE 2.3
Class. A class has a name, properties, and methods. The properties describe the class and represent data to be collected. The methods are actions the class can perform and are seldom used in a database design.

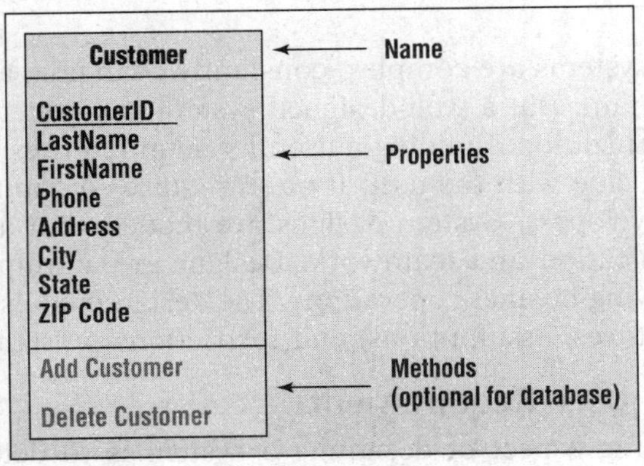

Tables and Relationships

The primary objective in database design is to identify the data that will be needed by the users. This data has to be stored carefully so the database can efficiently store and retrieve the data. Relational databases achieve these efficiencies by storing data in tables. These tables represent the business classes, where the properties become columns in the table, and each row represents data for one of the objects. So, as you talk with users and begin identifying the data to be collected, you need to organize it into classes. Although this process is not difficult, you need to be careful. The data tables have to meet certain requirements.

Classes, which eventually become tables, are related to each other. For example, the Sales class contains an attribute to identify the Customer participating in the sale; so the Customer class is connected to the Sales class. In a class diagram, this relationship is shown by a line connecting the two classes. These relationships have a numerical value as well that contains additional business information. In the Customer/Sales example, most companies have a policy that only one customer is listed on a sale, but a customer can participate in many different sales. So, there is a one-to-many relationship between Customer and Sales. These relationships are critical to proper design of the database.

Definitions

To learn how to create databases that are useful and efficient, you need to understand some basic definitions. The main ones are shown in Figure 2.4. E. F. Codd created formal mathematical definitions of these terms when he defined relational databases, and these formal definitions are presented in the Appendix to Chapter 3. However, for designing and building business applications, the definitions presented here are easier to understand.

A **relational database** is a collection of carefully defined tables. A **table** is a collection of columns (attributes or properties) that describe an entity. Individual objects are stored as rows (tuples) within the table. For example, EmployeeID 12512 represents one instance of an employee and is stored as one row in the Employee table. An attribute (property) is a characteristic or descriptor of an entity. Two important aspects to a relational database are that (1) all data must be stored in tables and (2) all tables

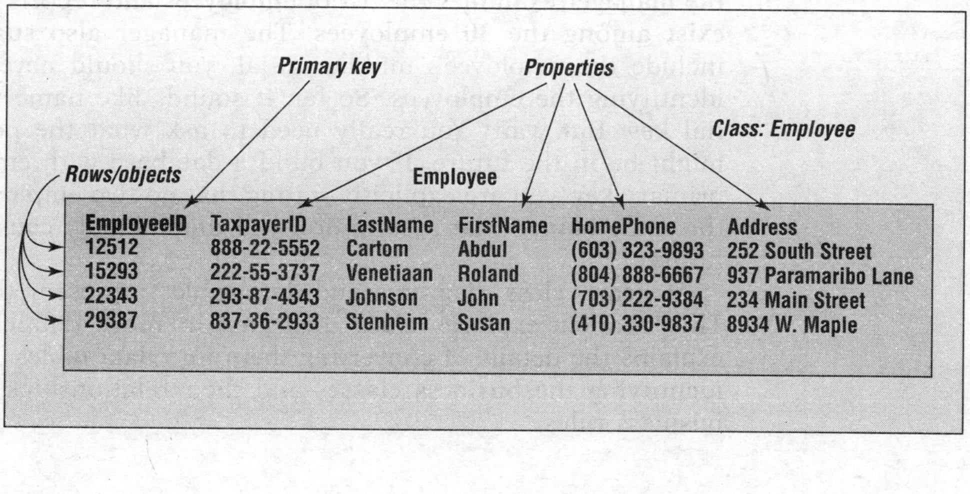

FIGURE 2.4
Basic database definitions. Codd has more formal terms and mathematical definitions, but these are easier to understand. One row in the data table represents a single object, a specific employee in this situation. Each column (attribute) contains one piece of data about that employee.

must be carefully defined to provide flexibility and minimize problems. **Data normalization** is the process of defining tables properly to provide flexibility, minimize redundancy, and ensure data integrity. The goal of database design and data normalization is to produce a list of nicely behaved tables. Each table describes a single type of object in the organization.

Primary Key

Every table must have a primary key. The **primary key** is a column or set of columns that identifies a particular row. For example, in the Customer table you might use a customer's name to find a particular entry. But that column does not make a good key. What if eight customers are named John Smith? In most cases separate keys will be created to ensure they are unique. For example, a customer identification number is often created to ensure that all customers are correctly separated. The relationship between the primary key and the rest of the data is one-to-one. That is, each entry for a key points to exactly one customer row. To highlight the primary key, the names of the columns that make up the key will be underlined.

In some cases there will be several choices to use as a primary key. In the customer example you could choose name or phone number, or create a unique CustomerID. If you have a choice, the primary key should be the smallest set of columns needed to form a unique identifier.

Some U.S. organizations might be tempted to use personal Social Security numbers (SSN) as the primary key. Even if you have a need to collect the SSN, you will be better off using a separate number as a key. One reason is that a primary key must always be unique, and with the SSN you run a risk that someone might present a forged document. Also, primary keys are used and displayed in many places within a database. If you use the SSN, too many employees will have access to your customers' private information. Because SSNs are used for many financial, governmental, and health records, you should protect customer privacy by limiting employee access to these numbers.

The most important issue with a primary key is that it can never point to more than one row or object in the database. For example, assume you are building a database for the human resource management department. The manager tells you that the company uses names of employees to identify them. You ask whether or not two employees have the same name so the manager examines the list of employees and reports that no duplicates exist among the 30 employees. The manager also suggests that if you include the employee's middle initial, you should never have a problem identifying the employees. So far, it sounds like name might be a potential key. But wait! You really need to ask what the possible key values might be in the future. If you build a database with employee name as a primary key, you are explicitly stating that no two employees will ever have the same name. That assumption will undoubtedly cause problems in the future.

At heart, class diagrams and data tables represent the same concepts. This chapter explores class diagrams in more detail, while Chapter 3 explains the details of converting them into data tables. For now, focus on identifying the business classes and their relationships as defined by the business rules.

Class Diagrams

The DBMS approach focuses on the data. In many organizations data remains relatively stable. For example, companies collect the same basic data on customers today that they collected 20 or 30 years ago. Basic items such as name, address, and phone number are always needed. Although you might choose to collect additional data today (cell phone number and Internet address, for example), you still utilize the same base data. On the other hand, the way companies accept and process sales orders has changed over time, so forms and reports are constantly being modified. The database approach takes advantage of this difference by focusing on defining the data correctly. Then the DBMS makes it easy to change reports and forms. The first step in any design is to identify the things or entities that you wish to observe and track.

Classes and Entities

It is best to define a few terms before illustrating the models. The basic definitions are given in Figure 2.5. Note that these definitions are informal. Each entry has a more formal definition in terms of Codd's relational model and precise semantic definitions in the **Unified Modeling Language (UML)**. However, you can develop a database without learning the mathematical foundations.

To design a database you must understand the difference between classes, properties, and associations. Your solution depends on how the business deals with the entities and what data needs to be collected. For example, consider an employee. The employee is clearly a separate entity because you always need to keep detailed data about the employee (date hired, name, address, and so on). But what about the employee's spouse? Is the spouse an attribute of the Employee entity, or should he or she be treated as a separate entity? If the organization only cares about the spouse's name, it can be stored as an attribute of the Employee entity. On the other hand, if the organization wants to keep additional information about the spouse (e.g., birthday and occupation), it might be better to create a separate Spouse

FIGURE 2.5
Basic definitions. These terms describe the main concepts needed to create a class diagram. The first step is to identify the business entities and their properties. Methods are less important than properties in a database context, but you should identify important functions or calculations.

Term	Definition	Pet Store Examples
Entity	Something in the real world that you wish to describe or track.	Customer, Merchandise, Sales
Class	Description of an entity that includes its attributes (properties) and behavior (methods).	Customer, Merchandise, Sale
Object	One instance of a class with specific data.	Joe Jones, Premium Cat Food, Sale #32
Property	A characteristic or descriptor of a class or entity.	LastName, Description, SaleDate
Method	A function that is performed by the class.	AddCustomer, UpdateInventory, ComputeTotal
Association	A relationship between two or more classes.	Each sale can have only one customer

entity with its own attributes. Your first step in designing a database is to identify the entities and their defining attributes. The second step is to specify the relationships among these entities.

Associations and Relationships

An important step in designing databases is identifying associations or relationships among entities. Details about these relationships represent the business rules. It is critical that you identify these business relationships correctly. Entities are usually related to other entities. Similarly, attributes within an entity can be related to other attributes. **Associations** or **relationships** represent business rules. For example, it is clear that a customer can place many orders. But the relationship is not as clear from the other direction. How many customers can be involved with one particular order? Many businesses would say that each order could come from only one customer. Hence there would be a one-to-many relationship between customers and orders. On the other hand, some organizations might have multiple customers on one order, which creates a many-to-many relationship.

Associations can be named: UML refers to the **association role.** Each end of a binary association can be labeled. It is often useful to include a direction arrow to indicate how the label should be read. Figure 2.6 shows how to indicate that one customer places many sales orders.

Unified Modeling Language uses numbers and asterisks to indicate the **multiplicity** in an association. As shown in Figure 2.6, the asterisk (*) represents many. So each supplier can receive many purchase orders. Some older entity-relationship design methods used multiple arrowheads or the letters *M* and *N* to represent the "many" sides of a relationship.

Correctly identifying relationships is important for you to properly design a database application. Remember that the relationships are determined by the business rules, so it is important to speak with the users to identify these relationships carefully. When you collect forms and reports from users, go through them and identify the initial entities—such as customer, order, and product. Then talk with the users to determine how the business handles the relationships between these entities.

Be sure you understand the importance of establishing the relationship or association between two classes. For example, the business rule in the Customer/Sales association means that no one should be able to enter a

FIGURE 2.6
Associations. Three types of relationships (one-to-one, one-to-many, and many-to-many) occur among entities. They can be drawn in different ways, but they represent business or organizational rules. Avoid vague definitions where almost any relationship could be classified as many-to-many. They make the database design more complex.

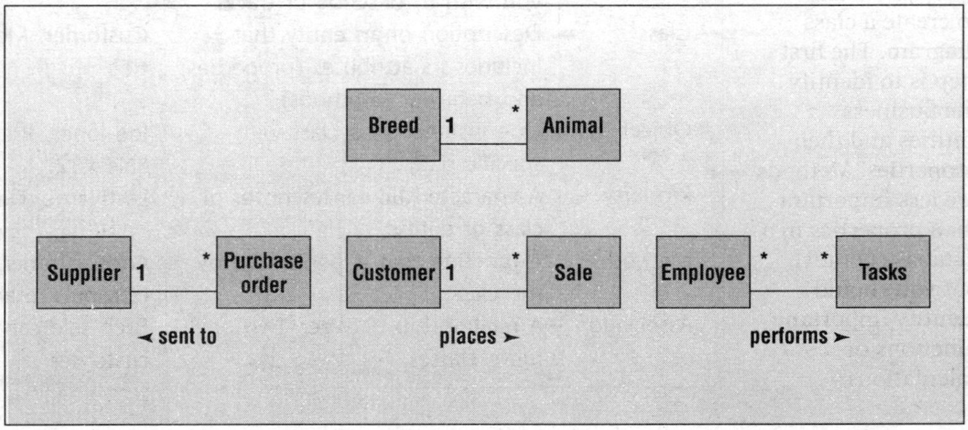

customer value into a sale, unless that specific customer data already exists in the customer table.

Class Diagram Details

A class diagram is a visual model of the classes and associations in an organization. These diagrams have many options, but the basic features that must be included are the class names (entities) in boxes and the associations (relationships) connecting them. Typically, you will want to include more information about the classes and associations. For example, you will eventually include the properties of the classes within the box.

Associations also have several options. One of the most important database design issues is the multiplicity of the relationship, which has two aspects: (1) the maximum number of objects that can be related, and (2) the minimum number of objects, if any, that must be included. As indicated in Figure 2.6, multiplicity is shown as a number for the minimum value, ellipses (. . .), and the maximum value. An asterisk (*) represents an unknown quantity of many. In the example in Figure 2.6, exactly one customer (1 . . . 1) can be involved with zero to many (0 . . .*) sales.

Many times a relationship requires both of the entities to exist. For example, what happens if you have a sale form that lists a customer, but there is no data on file for that customer? There is a referential relationship between the order and the customer entities. Business rules require that customer data must already exist before that customer can make a purchase. This relationship can be denoted by specifying the minimum value of the relationship (0 if it is optional, 1 if it is required).

Be sure to read relationships in both directions. For example, in Figure 2.7, the second part of the customer/sales association states that a customer can place from zero to many sales orders. That is, a customer is not required to place an order.

Moving down the diagram, note the many-to-many relationship between sale and item (asterisks on the right side for both classes). A sale must contain at least one item (empty sales orders are not useful in business), but the firm might have an item that has not been sold yet.

Association Details: N-ary Associations

Many-to-many associations between classes cause problems in the database design. They are acceptable in an initial diagram such as Figure 2.8, but they

FIGURE 2.7
Class diagram or entity-relationship diagram. Each customer can place zero or many orders. Each sale must come from at least one and no more than one customer. The zero (0) represents an optional item, so a customer might not have placed any orders yet.

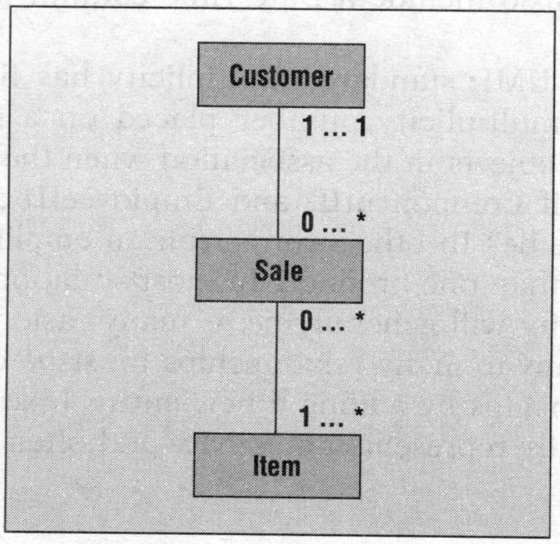

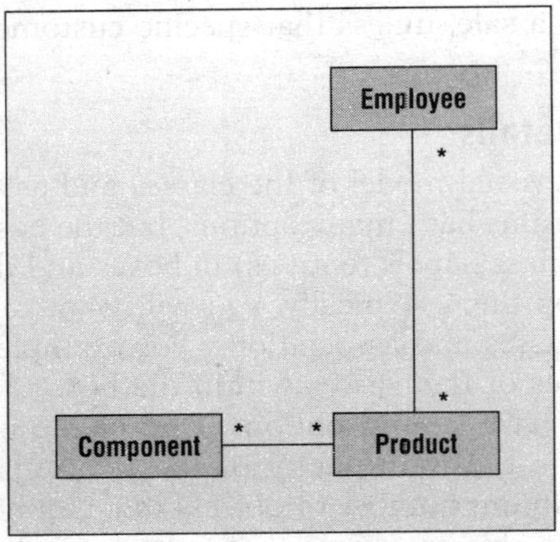

FIGURE 2.8
Many-to-many relationships cause problems for databases. In this example, many employees can install many components on many products, but we do not know which components the employee actually installed.

will eventually have to be split into one-to-many relationships. This process, and the reasons for it, are explained in detail in Chapter 3.

In a related situation, as shown in Figure 2.8, entities are not always obvious. Consider a basic manufacturing situation in which employees assemble components into final products. At first glance, it is tempting to say that there are three entities: employees, components, and products. This design specifies that the database should keep track of which employees worked on each product and which components go into each product. Notice that two many-to-many relationships exist.

To understand the problem caused by the many-to-many relationships, consider what happens if the company wants to know which employees assembled each component into a product. To handle this situation, Figure 2.9 shows that the three main entities (Employee, Product, and Component) are actually related to each other through an Assembly association. When more than two classes are related, the relationship is called an **n-ary association** and is drawn as a diamond. This association (actually any association) can be described by its own class data. In this example an entry in the assembly list would contain an EmployeeID, a ComponentID, and a ProductID. In total, many employees can work on many products, and many components can be installed in many products. Each individual event is captured by the Assembly association class. The Assembly association solves the many-to-many problem, because a given row in the Assembly class holds data for one employee, one component, and one product. In real life you would also include a Date/Time column to record when each event occurred.

According to the UML standard, multiplicity has little meaning in the n-ary context. The multiplicity number placed on a class represents the potential number of objects in the association when the other n-1 values are fixed. For example, if ComponentID and EmployeeID are fixed, how many products could there be? In other words, can an employee install the same component in more than one product? In most situations the answer will be yes, so the multiplicity will generally be a "many" asterisk.

Eventually, all many-to-many relationships must be converted to a set of one-to-many relationships by adding a new entity. Like the Assembly entity, this new entity usually represents an activity and often includes a date/time stamp.

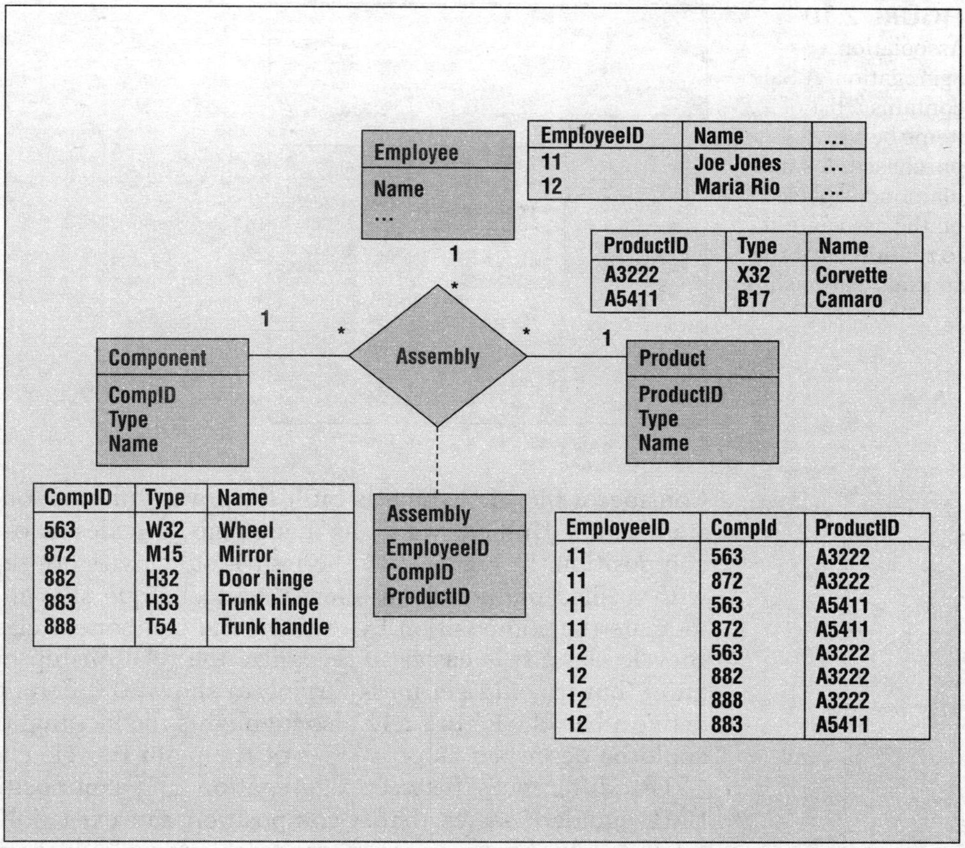

FIGURE 2.9
Many-to-many associations are converted to a set of one-to-many relationships with an n-ary association, which includes a new class. In this example each row in the Assembly class holds data for one employee, one component, and one product. Notice that the Assembly class (box) is connected to the Assembly association (diamond) by a dashed line.

As a designer you will use class diagrams for different purposes. Sometimes you need to see the detail; other times you only care about the big picture. For large projects, it sometimes helps to create an overview diagram that displays the primary relationships between the main classes. On this diagram it is acceptable to use many-to-many relationships to hide some detail entities.

Association Details: Aggregation

Some special types of associations arise often enough that UML has defined special techniques for handling them. One category is known as an **aggregation** or a collection. For example, a Sale consists of a collection of Items being purchased. As shown in Figure 2.10, aggregation is indicated by a small diamond on the association line next to the class that is the aggregate. In the example the diamond is next to the Sale class. Associations with a many side can be ordered or unordered. In this example the sequence in which the Items are stored does not matter. If order did matter, you would simply put the notation {ordered} underneath the association. Be sure to include the braces around the word.

Association Details: Composition

The simple aggregation indicator is not used much in business settings. However, **composition** is a stronger aggregate association that does arise more often. In a composition, the individual items become the new object.

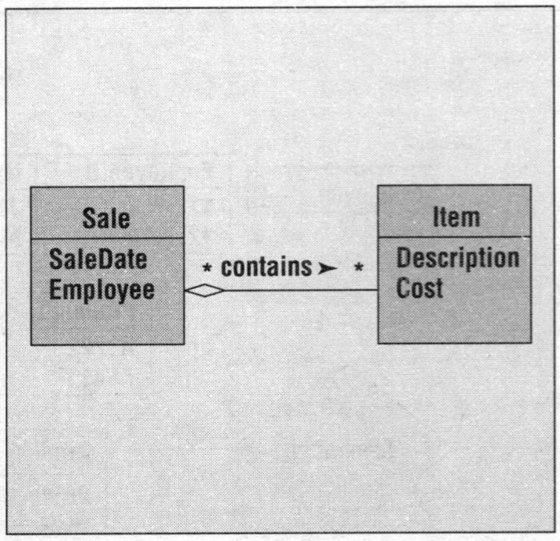

FIGURE 2.10
Association aggregation. A Sale contains a list of items being purchased. A small diamond is placed on the association to remind us of this special relationship.

Consider a bicycle, which is built from a set of components (wheels, crank, stem, etc.). Unified Modeling Language provides two methods to display composition. In Figure 2.11 the individual classes are separated and marked with a filled diamond. An alternative technique shown in Figure 2.12 is to indicate the composition by drawing the component classes inside the main Bicycle class. It is easier to recognize the relationship in the embedded diagram, but it could get messy trying to show 20 different objects required to define a bicycle. Figure 2.12 also highlights the fact that the component items could be described as properties of the main Bicycle class.

The differences between aggregation and composition are subtle. The UML standard states that a composition can exist only for a one-to-many relationship. Any many-to-many association would have to use the simple aggregation indicator. Composition relationships are generally easier to recognize than aggregation relationships, and they are particularly common in manufacturing environments. Just remember that a composition exists only when the individual items become the new class. After the bicycle is built, you no longer refer to the individual components.

Association Details: Generalization

Another common association that arises in business settings is **generalization**. This situation generates a class hierarchy. The most general description

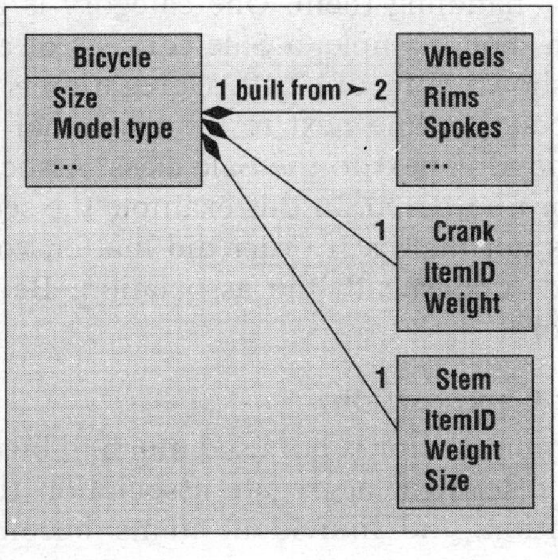

FIGURE 2.11
Association composition. A bicycle is built from several individual components. These components no longer exist separately; they become the bicycle.

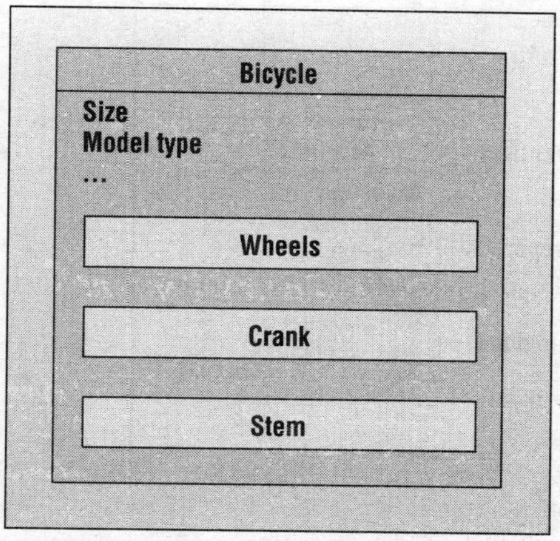

FIGURE 2.12
Association composition. It is easier to see the composition by embedding the component items within the main class.

is given at the top, and more specific classes are derived from it. Figure 2.13 presents a sample from Sally's Pet Store. Each animal has certain generic properties (e.g., DateBorn, Name, Gender, ListPrice), contained in the generic Animal class. But specific types of animals require slightly different information. For example, for a mammal (perhaps a cat), buyers want to know the size of the litter and whether or not the animal has claws. On the other hand, fish do not have claws, and customers want different information, such as whether they are fresh- or saltwater fish and the condition of their scales. Similar animal-specific data can be collected for each species. There can be multiple levels of generalization. In the pet store example, the Mammal category could be further split into Cat, Dog, and Other.

A small, unfilled triangle is used to indicate a generalization relationship. You can connect all of the subclasses into one triangle as in Figure 2.13, or you can draw each line separately. For the situation in this example, the collected approach is the best choice because the association represents a disjoint (mutually exclusive) set. An animal can fall into only one of the subclasses.

An important characteristic of generalization is that lower-level classes inherit the properties and methods of the classes above them. Classes often begin with fairly general descriptions. More detailed classes are **derived** from these base classes. Each lower-level class inherits the properties and

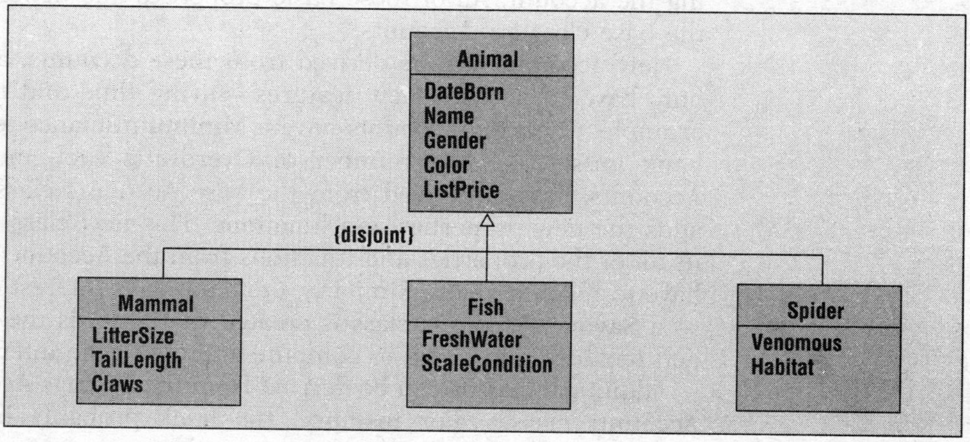

FIGURE 2.13
Association generalization. The generic Animal class holds data that applies to all animals. The derived subclasses contain data that is specific to each species.

FIGURE 2.14
Class inheritance. Object classes begin with a base class (e.g., Accounts). Other classes are derived from the base class. They inherit the properties and methods, and add new features. In a bank, all accounts need to track basic customer data. Only checking accounts need to track overdraft fees.

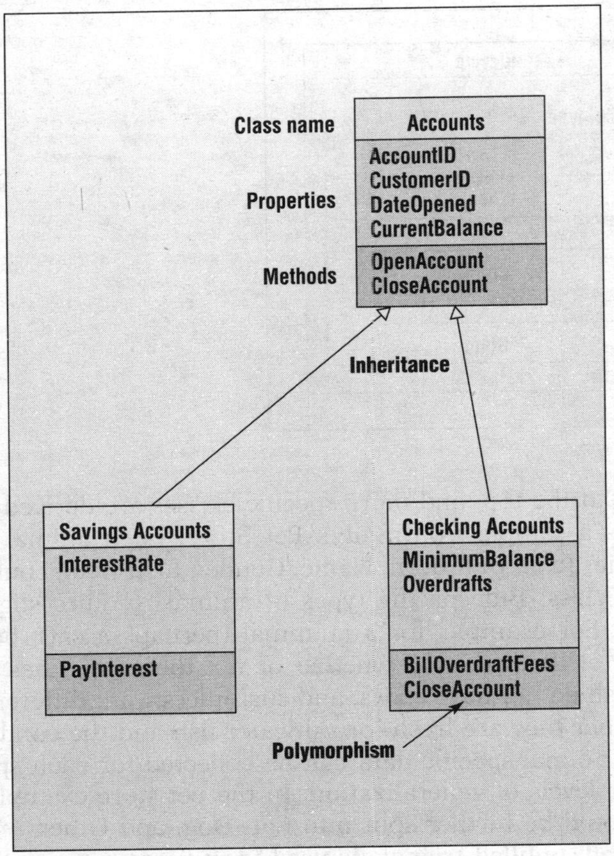

functions from the higher classes. **Inheritance** means that objects in the derived classes have all of the properties from the higher classes, as well as those defined in their own class. Similarly, functions defined in the related classes are available to the new class.

Consider the example of a bank accounting system displayed in Figure 2.14. A designer would start with the basic description of a customer account. The bank is always going to need basic information about its accounts, such as AccountID, CustomerID, DateOpened, and CurrentBalance. Similarly, there will be common functions including opening and closing the account. All of these basic properties and actions will be defined in the base class for Accounts.

New accounts can be derived from these accounts, and designers would only have to add the new features—saving time and reducing errors. For example, Checking Accounts have a MinimumBalance to avoid fees, and the bank must track the number of Overdrafts each month. The Checking Accounts class is derived from the base Accounts class, and the developer adds the new properties and functions. This new class automatically inherits all of the properties and functions from the Accounts class, so you do not have to redefine them. Similarly, the bank pays interest on savings accounts, so a Savings Accounts class is created that records the current InterestRate and includes a function to compute and credit the interest due each month.

Additional classes can be derived from the Savings Accounts and Checking Accounts classes. For instance, the bank probably has special checking accounts for seniors and for students. These new accounts might offer lower fees, different minimum balance requirements, or different interest rates. To accommodate these changes, the design diagram is simply expanded by adding new classes below these initial definitions. These diagrams display the **class hierarchy**, which shows how classes are derived from each other, and highlights which properties and functions are inherited. The UML uses open diamond arrowheads to indicate that the higher-level class is the more general class. In the example, the Savings Accounts and Checking Accounts classes are derived from the generic Accounts class, so the association lines point to it.

Each class in Figure 2.14 can also perform individual functions. Defining properties and methods within a class is known as **encapsulation**. It has the advantage of placing all relevant definitions in one location. Encapsulation also provides some security and control features because properties and functions can be protected from other areas of the application.

Another interesting feature of encapsulation can be found by noting that the Accounts class has a function to close accounts. Look carefully, and you will see that the Checking Accounts class also has a function to close accounts (CloseAccount). When a derived class defines the same function as a parent class, it is known as **polymorphism**. When the system activates the function, it automatically identifies the object's class and executes the matching function. Designers can also specify that the derived function (CloseAccount in the Checking Accounts class) can call the related function in the base class. In the banking example, the Checking Account's CloseAccount function would cancel outstanding checks, compute current charges, and update the main balance. Then it would call the Accounts CloseAccount function, which would automatically archive the data and remove the object from the current records.

Polymorphism is a useful tool for application builders. It means that you can call one function regardless of the type of data. In the bank example you would simply call the CloseAccount function. Each different account could perform different actions in response to that call, but the application does not care. The complexity of the application has been moved to the design stage (where all of the classes are defined). The application builder does not have to worry about the details.

Note that in complex situations, a subclass can inherit properties and methods from more than one parent class. In Figure 2.15, a car is motorized,

FIGURE 2.15
Multiple parent classes. Classes can inherit properties from several parent classes. The key is to draw the structure so that users can understand it and make sure that it matches the business rules.

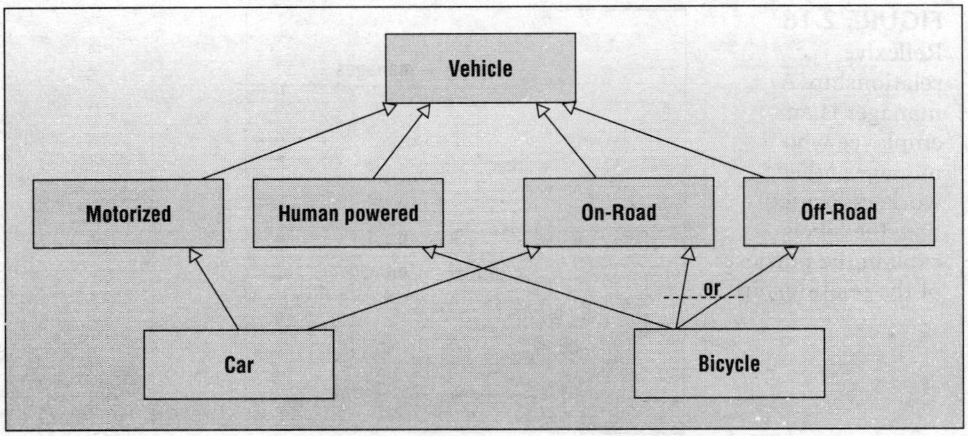

and it is designed for on-road use, so it inherits properties from both classes (and from the generic Vehicle class). The bicycle situation is slightly more complex because it could inherit features from the On-Road class or from the Off-Road class, depending on the type of bicycle. If you need to record data about hybrid bicycles, the Bicycle class might have to inherit data from both the On-Road and Off-Road classes.

Association Details: Reflexive Association

A reflexive relationship is another situation that arises in business that requires special handling. A **reflexive association** is a relationship from one class back to itself. The most common business situation is shown in Figure 2.16. Some employees are managers, and they manage other employees. Hence there is an association from Employee (the manager) back to Employee (the workers). Notice how UML enables you to label both ends of the relationship (manager and worker). Also, the "◀manages" label indicates how the association should be read. The labels and the text clarify the purpose of the association. Some associations may not need to be labeled, but reflexive relationships should always be carefully explained.

Association Details: Summary

These last few sections represent more than minor changes to your class diagram. They represent common business situations. You need to recognize these situations because they will affect the way you design and build database applications. To create a class diagram, first identify the main classes, including their properties. Then note the associations among the classes, paying particular attention to the proper multiplicity. Be on the lookout for many-to-many relationships. When you see them, look for n-ary associations or new classes that will provide one-to-many relationships. Look for cases of composition or aggregation. Is one class made up of several smaller objects? If so, consider embedding the subclasses within the main class. Watch for examples of generalization. Are there classes that have similar purposes? If so, try to define a generic class and derive the detailed classes using inheritance. Watch for disjoint (or mutually exclusive) classes. Be sure to indicate them on the diagram. Finally, look for reflexive associations where objects in one class are related to other objects in the same class. You should always see this relationship in the

FIGURE 2.16
Reflexive relationship. A manager is an employee who manages other workers. Notice how the labels explain the purpose of the relationship.

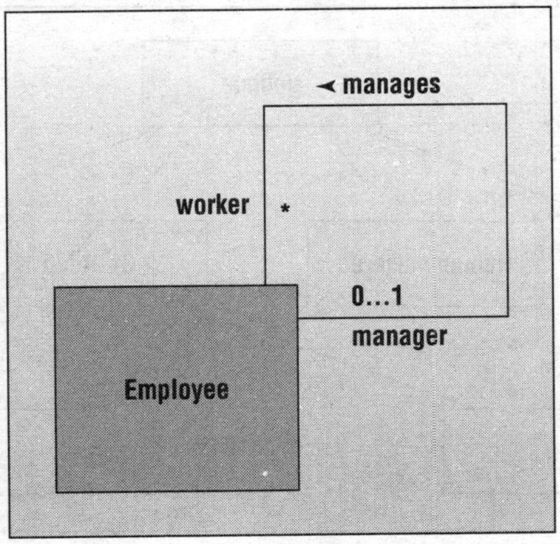

Employee class, but it can show up in other classes as well. For instance, a company can produce products that are built from other products.

At this point, you do not have to be concerned with drawing a perfect class diagram. Just make sure that you have correctly identified all the business rules. Chapter 3 explains how to analyze the classes and associations and how to create an improved set of classes.

Sally's Pet Store Class Diagram

Remember that Sally, the owner of the pet store, wants to create the application in sections. The first section will track the basic transaction data of the store. Hence you need to identify the primary entities involved in operating a pet store.

The first step in designing the Pet Store database application is to talk with the owner (Sally), examine other stores, and identify the primary components that will be needed. After talking with Sally, it becomes clear that the pet store has some features that make it different from other retail stores. The most important difference is that the store must track two separate types of sales: animals are handled differently from products. For example, the store tracks more detailed information on each animal. Also, products can be sold in multiple units (e.g., six cans of dog food), but animals must be tracked individually. Figure 2.17 shows an initial class diagram for Sally's Pet Store that is based on these primary entities. The diagram highlights the two separate tracks for animals and merchandise.

Because of Sally's philosophy of providing good homes for the pets, she wants to collect detailed information about each customer. Sally also monitors suppliers more carefully than most store owners. She is even thinking about hiring people to inspect various breeders. The inspectors would provide reports on a variety of features, such as cleanliness, number of animals boarded, number of trainers, type of food served at each meal, and quality of veterinary care.

FIGURE 2.17
Initial class diagram for the PetStore. Animal purchases and sales are tracked separately from merchandise because the store needs to monitor different data for the two entities.

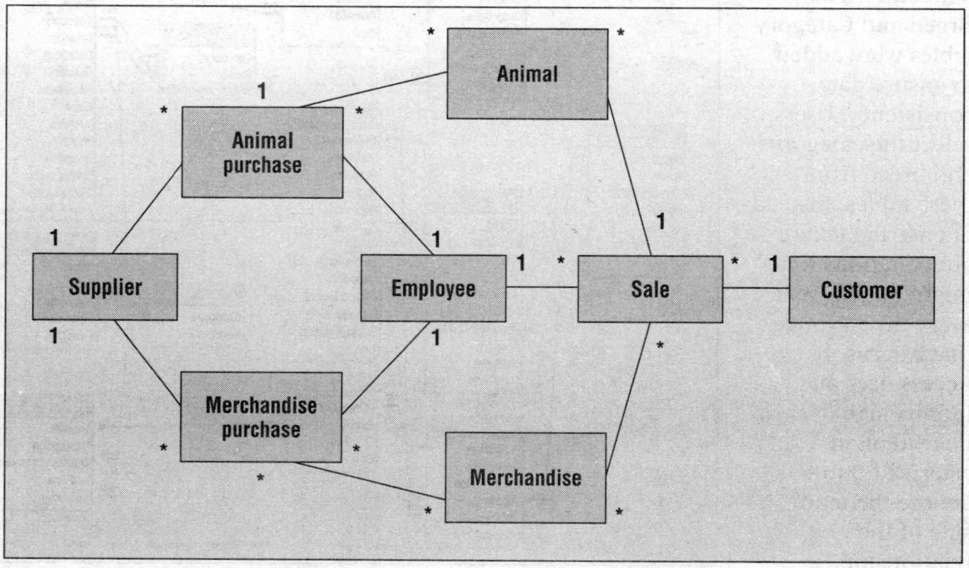

While talking with Sally, a good designer will write down some of the basic items that will be involved in the database. This list consists of entities for which we need to collect data. For example, for the Pet Store database you will clearly need to collect data on customers, suppliers, animals, and products. Likewise, you will need to record each purchase and each sale. Right from the beginning, you will want to identify various attributes or characteristics of these entities. For instance, customers have names, addresses, and phone numbers. For each animal, you will want to know the type of animal (cat, dog, etc.), the breed, the date of birth, and so on.

The detailed class diagram will include the attributes for each of the entities. Notice that the initial diagram in Figure 2.17 includes several many-to-many relationships. All of these require the addition of an intermediate class. Consider the MerchandiseOrder class. Several items can be ordered at one time, so you will create a new entity (OrderItem) that contains a list of items placed on each MerchandiseOrder. The AnimalOrder and Sale entities will gain similar classes.

Figure 2.18 shows the more detailed class diagram for the pet store with these new intermediate classes. It also contains new classes for City, Breed, and Category. Postal codes and cities raise issues in almost every business database. There is a relationship between cities and postal codes, but it is not one-to-one. One simple solution is to store the city, state, and postal code for every single customer and supplier. However, for local customers, it is highly repetitive to enter the name of the city and state for every sale. A solution is to store city and postal code data in a separate class. Commonly used values can be entered initially. An employee can select the desired city from the existing list without having to reenter the data.

The Breed and Category classes are used to ensure consistency in the data. One of the annoying problems of text data is that people rarely enter data consistently. For example, some clerks might abbreviate the dalmatian dog breed

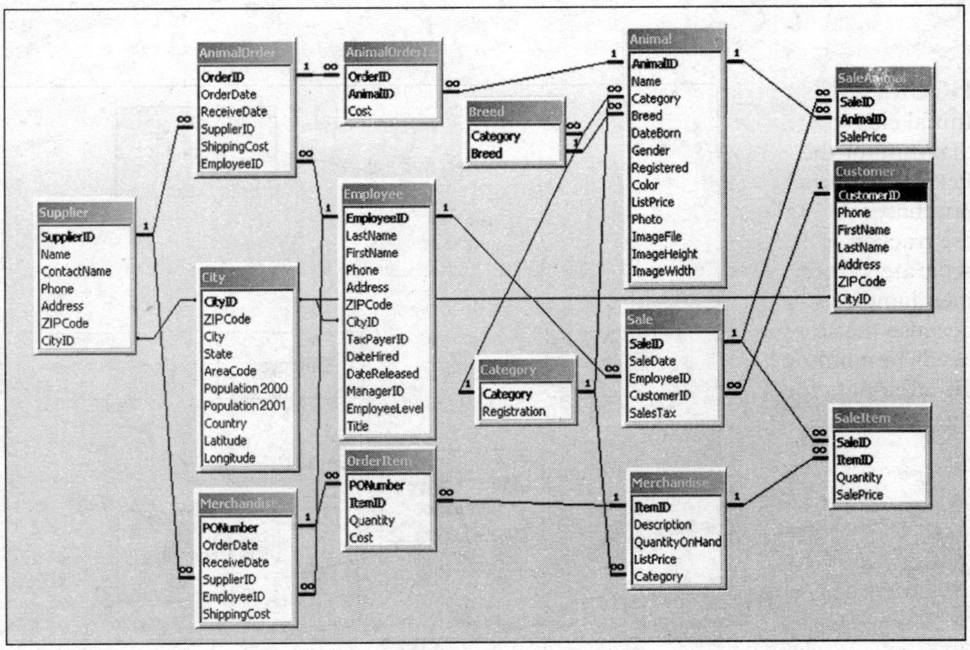

FIGURE 2.18
Detailed class diagram for the pet store. Notice the tables added to solve many-to-many problems: OrderItem, AnimalOrderItem, SaleItem, and SaleAnimal. The City table was added to reduce data entry. The Breed and Category tables were added to ensure data consistency. Users select the category and breed from these tables, instead of entering text or abbreviations that might be different every time. Notice that Microsoft Access uses an infinity sign (∞) instead of an asterisk (*) to denote the many side of the relationship.

as *Dal*, others might use *Dalma,* and a few might enter the entire name. To solve this problem, we want to store all of the category and breed names one time in separate classes. Then employees simply choose the category and breed from the list in these classes. Hence data is entered exactly the same way every time.

Both the overview and the detail class diagrams for the Pet Store can be used to communicate with users. Through the entities and relationships, the diagram displays the business rules of the firm. For instance, the separate treatment of animals and merchandise is important to the owner. Similarly, capturing only one customer per each sale is an important business rule. This rule should be confirmed by Sally. If a family purchases an animal, does she want to keep track of each member of the family? If so, you would need to add a Family class that lists the family members for each customer. The main point is that you can use the diagrams to display the new system, verify assumptions, and get new ideas.

Data Types (Domains)

As you list the properties within each class, you should think about the type of data they will hold. Each attribute holds a specific **data type** or data domain. For example, what is an EmployeeID? Is it numeric? At what value does it start? How should it be incremented? Does it contain letters or other alphanumeric characters? You must identify the domain of each attribute or column. Figure 2.19 identifies several common domains. The most common is text, which holds any characters.

FIGURE 2.19
Data types (domains). Common data types and their variations in three database systems. The text types in SQL Server and Oracle beginning with an "N" hold Unicode character sets, particularly useful for non-Latin-based languages.

	Access	SQL Server	Oracle
Text			
fixed		char,	CHAR
variable	Text	varchar	VARCHAR2
Unicode		nchar, nvarchar	NVARCHAR2
memo	Memo	text	LONG
Number			
Byte (8 bits)	Byte	tinyint	INTEGER
Integer (16 bits)	Integer	smallint	INTEGER
Long (32 bits)	Long	int	INTEGER
(64 bits)	NA	bigint	NUMBER(127,0)
Fixed precision	NA	decimal(p,s)	NUMBER(p,s)
Float	Float	real	NUMBER, FLOAT
Double	Double	float	NUMBER
Currency	Currency	money	NUMBER(38,4)
Yes/No	Yes/No	bit	INTEGER
Date/Time	Date/Time	datetime smalldatetime	DATE
Interval	NA	interval year . . .	INTERVAL YEAR . . .
Image	OLE Object	image	LONG RAW, BLOB
AutoNumber	AutoNumber	Identity rowguidcol	SEQUENCES ROWID

Note that any of the domains can also hold missing data. Users do not always know the value of some item, so it may not be entered. Missing data is defined as a **null** value.

Text

Text columns are often limited to no more than 255 characters. Some database management systems ask you to distinguish between fixed-length and variable-length text. Fixed-length strings always take up the amount of space you allocate and are most useful to improve speed in handling short strings like identification numbers or two-letter state abbreviations. Variable-length strings are stored so they take only as much space as needed for each row of data.

Memo or note columns are also used to hold variable-length text data. The difference from variable-length text is that the database can allocate more space for memos. The exact limit depends on the DBMS and the computer used, but memos typically range up to 32K or 64K bytes in one database column. Memo columns are often used for long comments or even short reports. However, some systems limit the operations that you can perform with memo columns, such as not allowing you to sort the column data.

Numbers

Numeric data is also common, and computers recognize several variations of numeric data. The most important decision you have to make about numeric data columns is choosing between integer and floating-point numbers. Integers cannot hold fractions (values to the right of a decimal point). Integers are often used for counting and include values such as 1; 2; 100; and 5,000. Floating-point numbers can include fractional values and include numbers like 3.14159 and 2.718.

The first question raised with integers and floating-point numbers is, Why should you care? Why not store all numbers as floating-point values? The answer lies in the way that computers store the two types of numbers. In particular, most machines store integers in 2 (or 4) bytes of storage for every value; but they store each floating-point number in 4 (or 8) bytes. Although a difference of 2 bytes might seem trivial, it can make a huge difference when multiplied by several million rows of data. Additionally, arithmetic performed on integers is substantially faster than computations with floating-point data. Something as simple as adding two numbers together can be 10 to 100 times faster with integers than with floating-point numbers. Although machines have become faster and storage costs keep declining, performance is still an important issue when you deal with huge databases and a large customer base. If you can store a number as an integer, do it—you will get a measurable gain in performance.

Most systems also support long integers and double-precision floating-point values. In both cases the storage space is doubled compared to single-precision data. The main issue for designers involves the size of the numbers and precision that users need. For example, if you expect to have 100,000 customers, you cannot use an integer to identify and track customers (a key value). Note that only 65,536 values can be stored as 16-bit integers. To count or measure larger values, you need to use a long integer, which can range between +/− 2,000,000,000. Similarly, floating-point numbers can support about six significant digits. Although the magnitude (exponent) can be

FIGURE 2.20

Data sizes. Make sure that you choose a data type that can hold the largest value you will encounter. Choosing a size too large can waste space and cause slow calculations, but if in doubt, choose a larger size.

	Size		
Data Types	**Access**	**SQL Server**	**Oracle**
Text (characters)			
fixed		8K, 4K	2K
variable	255	8K, 4K	4K
memo	64K	2M, 1M	2G
Numeric			
Byte (8 bits)	255	255	38 digits
Integer (16 bits)	+/− 32767	+/− 32767	38 digits
Long (32 bits)	+/− 2 B	+/− 2 B	38 digits
(64 bits)	NA	18 digits	p: 38 digits
Fixed precision	NA	+/− 1 E 38	p: −84 to 127; s: 1 to 38
Float	+/− 1 E 38	+/− 1 E 38	38 digits
Double	+/− 1 E 308	+/− 1 E 308	38 digits
Currency	+/− 900.0000 trillion	+/− 900.0000 trillion	38 digits
Yes/No	0/1	0/1	
Date/Time	1/1/100 – 12/31/9999 (1 sec)	1/1/1753 – 12/31/9999 (3 ms) 1/1/1900 – 6/6/2079 (1 min)	1/1/−4712, 1/31/9999 (sec)
Image	OLE Object	2 GB	2 GB, 4 GB
AutoNumber	Long (2 B)	2 B or 18 digits with bigint	Column: 38 digit maximum

larger, no more than six or seven digits are maintained. If users need greater precision, use double-precision values, which maintain 14 significant digits. Figure 2.20 lists the maximum sizes of the common data types.

Many business databases encounter a different problem. Monetary values often require a large number of digits, and users cannot tolerate round-off errors. Even if you use long integers, you would be restricted to values under 2,000,000,000 (20,000,000 if you need two decimal point values). Double-precision floating-point numbers would enable you to store numbers in the billions even with two decimal values. However, floating-point numbers are often stored with round-off errors, which might upset the accountants whose computations must be accurate to the penny. To compensate for these problems, database systems offer a currency data type, which is stored and computed as integer values (with an imputed decimal point). The arithmetic is fast, large values in the trillions can be stored, and round-off error is minimized. Some systems offer a generic fixed-precision data type. For example, you could specify that you need 4 decimal digits of precision, and the database will store the data and perform computations with exactly 4 decimal digits.

Dates and Times

All databases need a special data type for dates and times. Most systems combine the two into one domain; some provide two separate definitions.

Many beginners try to store dates as string or numeric values. Avoid this temptation. Date types have important properties. Dates (and times) are actually stored as single numbers. Dates are typically stored as integers that count the number of days from some base date. This base date may vary between systems, but it is only used internally. The value of storing dates by a count is that the system can automatically perform date arithmetic. You can easily ask for the number of days between two dates, or you can ask the system to find the date that is 30 days from today. Even if that day is in a different month or a different year, the proper date is automatically computed. Although most systems need 8 bytes to store date/time columns, doing so removes the need to worry about any year conversion problems.

A second important reason to use internal date and time representations is that the database system can convert the internal format to and from any common format. For example, in European nations, dates are generally displayed in day/month/year format, not the month/day/year format commonly used in the United States. With a common internal representation, users can choose their preferred method of entering or viewing dates. The DBMS automatically converts to the internal format, so internal dates are always consistent.

Databases also need the ability to store time intervals. Common examples include a column to hold years, months, days, minutes, or even seconds. For instance, you might want to store the length of time it takes an employee to perform a task. Without a specific interval data type, you could store it as a number. However, you would have to document the meaning of the number—it might be hours, minutes, or seconds. With a specified interval type, there is less chance for confusion.

Binary Objects

A relatively new domain is a separate category for objects or **binary large objects (BLOB)**. It enables you to store any type of object created by the computer. A useful example is to use a BLOB to hold images and files from other software packages. For example, each row in the database could hold a different spreadsheet, picture, or graph. An engineering database might hold drawings and specifications for various components. The advantage is that all of the data is stored together, making it easier for users to find the information they need and simplifying backups. Similarly, a database could hold several different revisions of a spreadsheet to show how it changed over time or to record changes by many different users.

Computed Values

Some business attributes can be computed. For instance, the total value of a sale can be calculated as the sum of the individual sale prices plus the sales tax. Or an employee's age can be computed as the difference between today's date and the DateOfBirth. At the design stage, you should indicate which data attributes could be computed. The UML notation is to precede the name with a slash (/) and then describe the computation in a note. For example, the computation for a person's age is shown in Figure 2.21. The note is displayed as a box with folded corner. It is connected to the appropriate property with a dashed line.

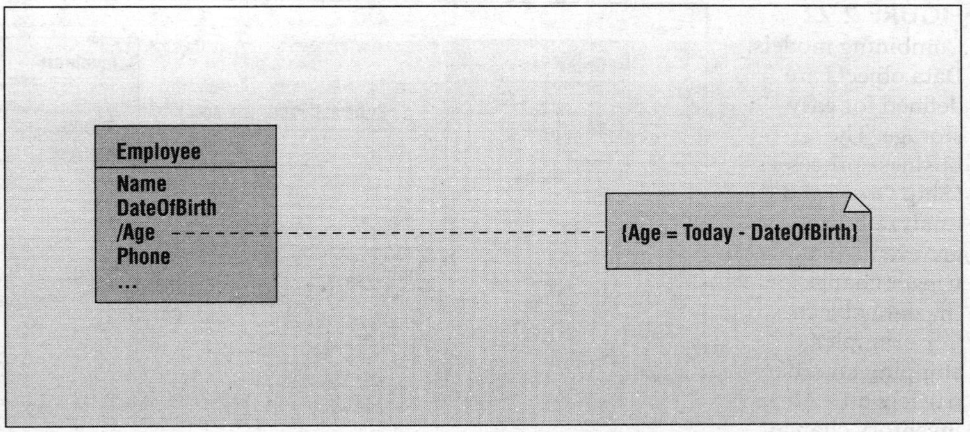

FIGURE 2.21
Derived values. The Age attribute does not have to be stored, since it can be computed from the date of birth. Hence, it should be noted on the class diagram. Computed attribute names are preceded with a slash.

User-Defined Types (Domains/Objects)

A relatively recent object-relational feature is supported by a few of the larger database systems. You can build your own domain as a combination of existing types. This domain essentially becomes a new object type. The example of a geocode is one of the easiest to understand. You can define a geographic location in terms of its latitude and longitude. You also might include altitude if the data is available. In a simple relational DBMS, this data is stored in separate columns. Anytime you want to use the data, you have to look up and pass all values to your code. With a user-defined data type, you can create a new data type called location that includes the desired components. Your column definition then has only the single data type (location), but actually holds two or three pieces of data. These elements are treated by the DBMS as a single entry. Note that when you create a new domain, you also have to create functions to compare values so that you can sort and search using the new data type.

Events

Events are another important component of modern database systems that you need to understand. Three basic types of events occur in a database environment:

1. Business events that trigger some function, such as a sale triggering a reduction in inventory.
2. Data changes that signal some alert, such as an inventory that drops below a preset level, which triggers a new purchase order.
3. User interface events that trigger some action, such as a user clicking on an icon to send a purchase order to a supplier.

Events are actions that are dependent on time. UML provides several diagrams to illustrate events. The collaboration diagram is probably the most useful for recording business processes and events. Complex user interface events can be displayed in sequence diagrams or statechart diagrams. These latter diagrams are beyond the scope of this book. You can consult an OO design text for more details on how to draw them.

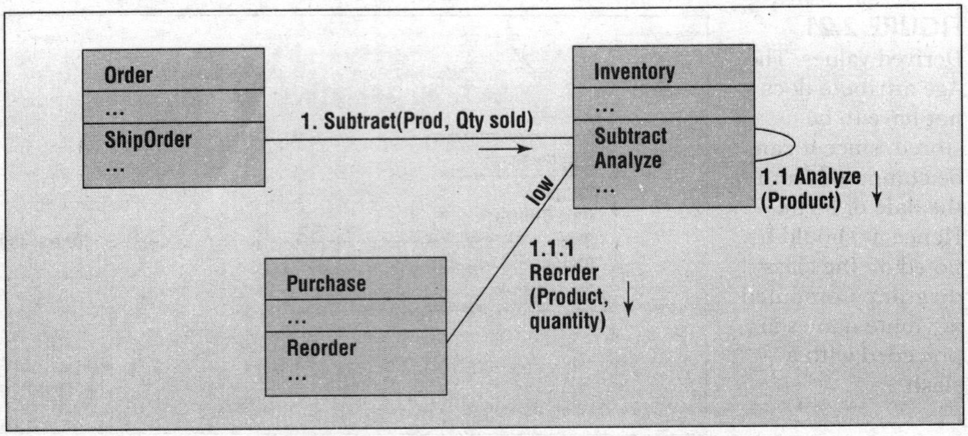

FIGURE 2.22
Combining models. Data objects are defined for easy storage. The business processes (Ship Order and Analyze Inventory) are events that trigger changes in the data objects. For example, shipping an order triggers an inventory change, which in turn triggers an analysis of the current level, which can trigger a new inventory order.

Business events can be related so that one event can trigger a second one, and so on. For complex chains of events, you should probably draw a process diagram to show the desired sequence of the events. Figure 2.22 is a small collaboration diagram. It shows how three classes interact by exchanging messages and calling functions from the various classes. Note that because the order is important, the three major trigger activities are numbered sequentially. First, the Order class is called to ship an order, which triggers a message to the Inventory class to subtract the appropriate quantity. When an inventory quantity changes, an automatic trigger calls a routine to analyze the current inventory levels. If the appropriate criteria are met, a purchase order is generated and the product is reordered.

The example represents a linear chain of events, which is relatively easy to understand and to test. More complex chains can be built that loop back on themselves and involve more complex alternatives. The UML sequence diagram can be used to show more detail on how individual messages are handled in the proper order. The UML statechart diagrams highlight how a class/object status varies over time. Events are important in building a system and can involve complicated interactions. For now you should be able to draw simple collaboration diagrams that indicate the primary message events.

In simpler situations you can keep a list of important events. You can write events as triggers, which describe the event cause and the corresponding action to be taken. For example, a business event based on inventory data could be written as shown in Figure 2.23. Large database systems such as Oracle and SQL Server support triggers directly. You define the event and attach the code that will be executed when the condition arises.

These triggers can be written in any basic format (e.g., pseudocode) at the design stage, and later converted to database triggers or program code. Unified Modeling Language also provides an Object Constraint Language (OCL) that you can use to write triggers and other code fragments. It is generic and will be useful if you are using a tool that can convert the OCL code into the database you are using.

FIGURE 2.23
Sample trigger. List the condition and the action.

```
ON (QuantityOnHand < 100)
THEN Notify Purchasing Manager
```

Large Projects

If you build a small database system for yourself or for a single user, you will probably not take the time to draw diagrams of the entire system. However, you really should provide some documentation so the next designer who has to modify your work will know what you did. On the other hand, if you are working on large projects involving many developers and users, everyone must follow a common design methodology. What is a large project and what is a small project? There are no fixed rules, but you start to encounter problems such as those listed in Figure 2.24 when several developers and many users are involved in the project.

Methodologies for large projects begin with diagrams such as the class and collaboration diagrams described in this chapter. Then each company or team adds details. For example, standards are chosen to specify naming conventions, type of documentation required, and review procedures.

The challenge of large projects is to split the project into smaller pieces that can be handled by individual developers. Yet the pieces must fit together at the end. Project managers also need to plan the project in terms of timing and expenses. As the project develops, managers can evaluate team members in terms of the schedule.

Several types of tools can help you design database systems, and they are particularly useful for large projects. To assist in planning and scheduling, managers can use project-planning tools (e.g., Microsoft Project) that help create Gantt and PERT charts to break projects into smaller pieces and highlight the relationships among the components. Computer-assisted software engineering (CASE) tools (like Rational Rose) can help teams draw diagrams, enforce standards, and store all project documentation. Additionally, groupware tools (like Lotus Notes/Domino) help team members share their work on documents, designs, and programs. These tools annotate changes, record who made the changes and their comments, and track versions.

As summarized in Figure 2.25, CASE tools perform several useful functions for developers. In addition to assisting with graphical design, one of the most important functions of CASE tools is to maintain the data repository for the project. Every element defined by a developer is stored in the data repository, where it is shared with other developers. In other words, the

FIGURE 2.24
Development issues on large projects. Large projects require more communication, adherence to standards, and project monitoring.

Design is harder on large projects
- Communication with multiple users
- Communication between IT workers
- Need to divide project into pieces for teams
- Finding data/components
- Staff turnover—retraining

Need to monitor design process
- Scheduling
- Evaluation

Build systems that can be modified later
- Documentation
- Communication/underlying assumptions and model

FIGURE 2.25
CASE tool features. CASE tools help create and maintain diagrams. They also support teamwork and document control. Some can generate code from the designs. Others can examine applications and create the matching code through reverse engineering.

Computer-Aided Software Engineering
- Diagrams (linked)
- Data dictionary
- Teamwork
- Prototyping
  - Forms
  - Reports
  - Sample data
- Code generation
- Reverse engineering

data repository is a specialized database that holds all of the information related to the project's design. Some CASE tools can generate databases and applications based on the information you enter into the CASE project. In addition, reverse-engineering tools can read files from existing applications and generate the matching design elements. These CASE tools are available from many companies, including Rational Software, IBM, Oracle, and Sterling Software. CASE tools can speed the design and development process by improving communication among developers and through generating code. They offer the potential to reduce maintenance time by providing complete documentation of the system.

Good CASE tools have existed for several years, and yet many firms do not use them, and some that have tried them have failed to realize their potential advantages. Two drawbacks to CASE tools are their complexity and their cost. The cost issue can be mitigated if the tools can reduce the number of developers needed on a given project. But their complexity presents a larger hurdle. It can take a developer several months to learn to use a CASE tool effectively. Fortunately, some CASE vendors provide discounts to universities to help train students in using their tools. If you have access to a CASE tool, use it for as many assignments as possible.

Rolling Thunder Bicycles

The Rolling Thunder Bicycle case illustrates some of the common associations that arise in business settings. Because the application was designed for classroom use, many of the business assumptions were deliberately simplified. The top-level view is shown in Figure 2.26. Loosely based on the activities of the firm, the elements are grouped into six packages: Sales, Bicycles, Assembly, Employees, Purchasing, and Location. The packages will not be equal: Some contain far more detail than the others. In particular, the Location and Employee packages currently contain only one or two classes. They are treated as separate packages because they both interact with several classes in multiple packages. Because they deal with independent, self-contained issues, it makes sense to separate them.

Each package contains a set of classes and associations. The Sales package is described in more detail in Figure 2.27. To minimize complexity, the associations with other packages are not displayed in this figure. For example, the Customer and RetailStore classes have an association with the Location::City class. These relationships will be shown in the Location package. Consequently, the Sales package is straightforward. Customers place orders

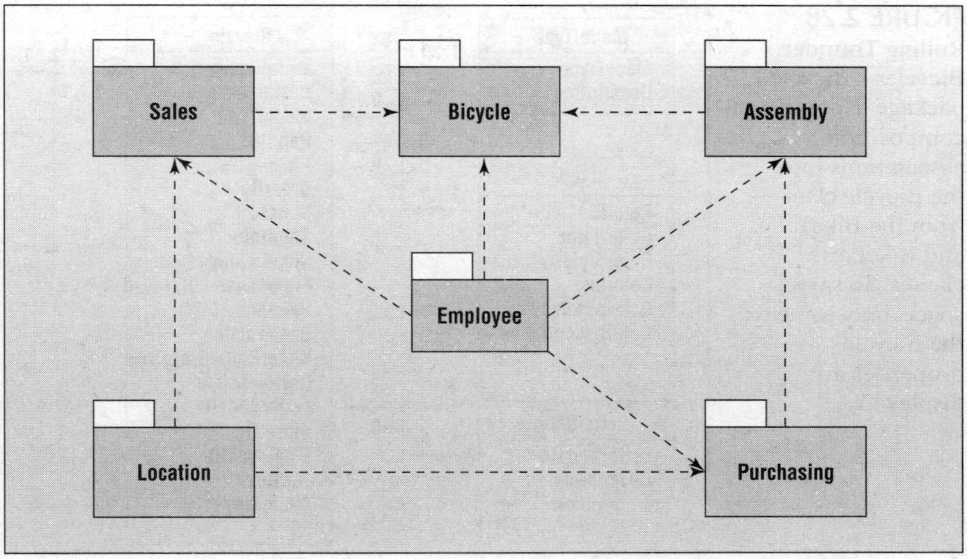

FIGURE 2.26
Rolling Thunder Bicycles—top-level view. The packages are loosely based on the activities of the firm. The goal is for each package to describe a self-contained collection of objects that interacts with the other packages.

for Bicycles. They might use a RetailStore to help them place the order, but they are not required to do so. Hence the association from the RetailStore has a (0 . . . 1) multiplicity.

The Bicycle package contains many of the details that make this company unique. To save space, only a few of the properties of the Bicycle class are shown in Figure 2.28. Notice that a bicycle is composed of a set of tubes and a set of components. Customers can choose the type of material used to create the bicycle (aluminum, steel, carbon fiber, etc.). They can also select the components (wheels, crank, pedals, etc.) that make up the bicycle. Both of these classes have a composition association with the Bicycle class. The Bicycle class is one of the most important classes for this firm. In conjunction with the BicycleTubeUsed and BikeParts classes, it completely defines each bicycle. It also contains information about which

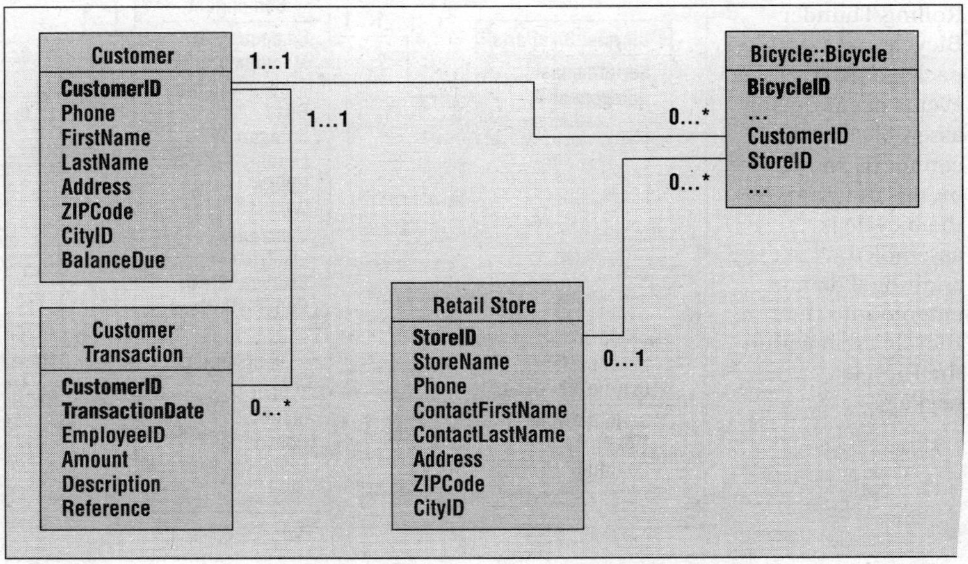

FIGURE 2.27
Rolling Thunder Bicycles—Sales package. Some associations with other packages are not shown here. (See the other packages.)

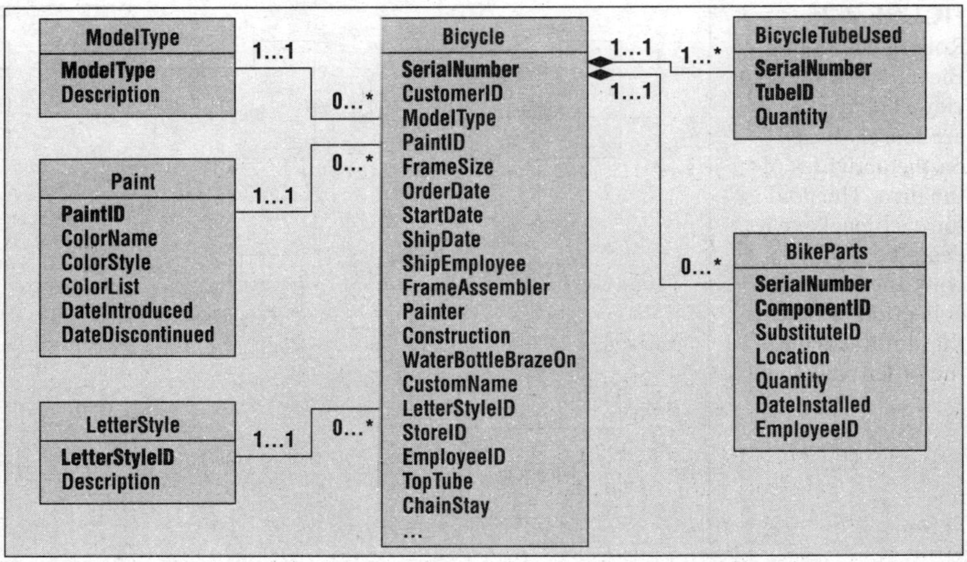

FIGURE 2.28 Rolling Thunder Bicycles—Bicycle package. Note the composition associations into the Bicycle class from the BikeTubes and BikeParts classes. To save space, only some of the Bicycle properties are displayed.

employees worked on the bicycle. This latter decision was a design simplification choice. Another alternative would be to move the ShipEmployee, FrameAssembler, and other employee properties to a new class within the Assembly package.

As shown in Figure 2.29, the Assembly package contains more information about the various components and tube materials that make up a bicycle. In practice, the Assembly package also contains several important events. As the bicycle is assembled, data is entered that specifies who did the work and when it was finished. This data is currently stored in the Bicycle class within the Bicycle package. A collaboration diagram or a sequence diagram would have to be created to show the details of the various events within the Assembly package. For now, the classes and associations are more important, so these other diagrams are not shown here.

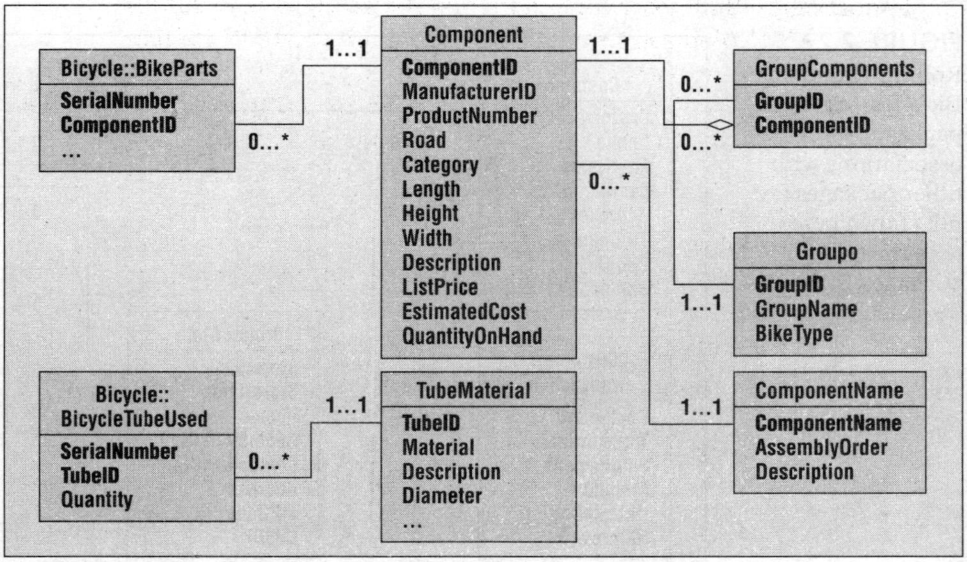

FIGURE 2.29 Rolling Thunder Bicycles—Assembly package. Several events occur during assembly, but they cannot be shown on this diagram. As the bicycle is assembled, additional data is entered into the Bicycle table within the Bicycle package.

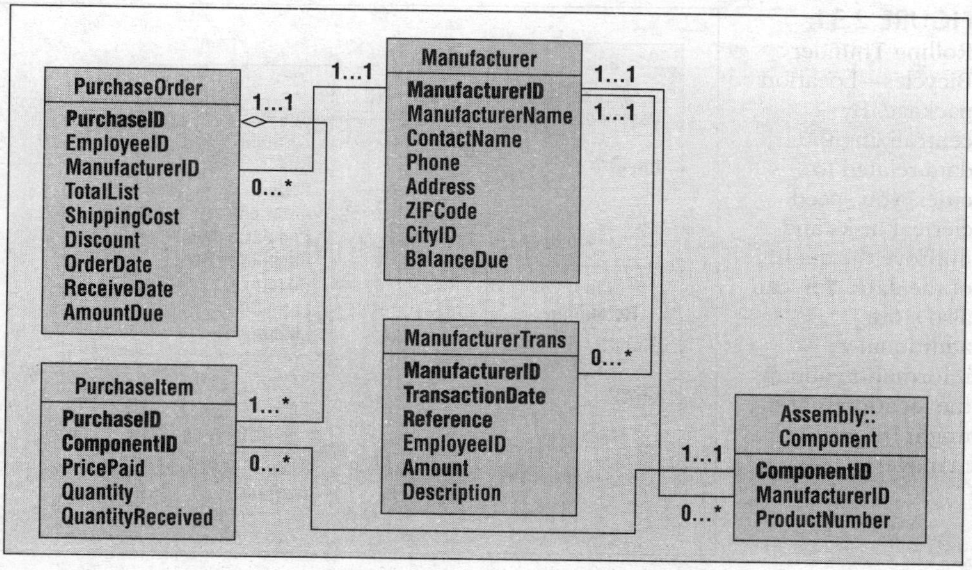

FIGURE 2.30 Rolling Thunder Bicycles—Purchasing package. Note the use of the Transaction class to store all related financial data for the manufacturers in one location.

All component parts are purchased from other manufacturers (suppliers). The Purchase package in Figure 2.30 is a fairly traditional representation of this activity. Note that each purchase requires the use of two classes: PurchaseOrder and PurchaseItem. The PurchaseOrder is the main class that contains data about the order itself, including the date, the manufacturer, and the employee who placed the order. The PurchaseItem class contains the detail list of items that are being ordered. This class is specifically included to avoid a many-to-many association between the PurchaseOrder and Component classes.

Notice from the business rules that a ManufacturerID must be included on the PurchaseOrder. It is dangerous to issue a purchase order without knowing the identity of the manufacturer. Chapter 10 explains how security controls can be imposed to provide even more safety for this crucial aspect of the business.

An additional class (ManufacturerTransactions) is used as a transaction log to record each purchase. It is also used to record payments to the manufacturers. On the purchase side, it represents a slight duplication of data (AmountDue is in both the PurchaseOrder and Transaction classes). However, it is a relatively common approach to building an accounting system. Traditional accounting methods rely on having all related transaction data in one location. In any case the class is needed to record payments to the manufacturers, so the amount of duplicated data is relatively minor.

The Location package in Figure 2.31 was created to centralize the data related to addresses and cities. Several classes have address properties. In older systems it was often easier to simply duplicate the data and store the city, state, and ZIP code in every class that referred to locations. Today, however, it is relatively easy to obtain useful information about cities and store it in a centralized table. This approach improves data entry, both in speed and data integrity. Clerks can simply choose a location from a list. Data is always entered consistently. For example, you do not have to worry about abbreviations for cities. If telephone area codes or ZIP codes are changed, you need to change them in only one table. You can also store additional

FIGURE 2.31
Rolling Thunder Bicycles—Location package. By centralizing the data related to cities, you speed clerical tasks and improve the quality of the data. You can also store additional information about the location that might be useful to managers.

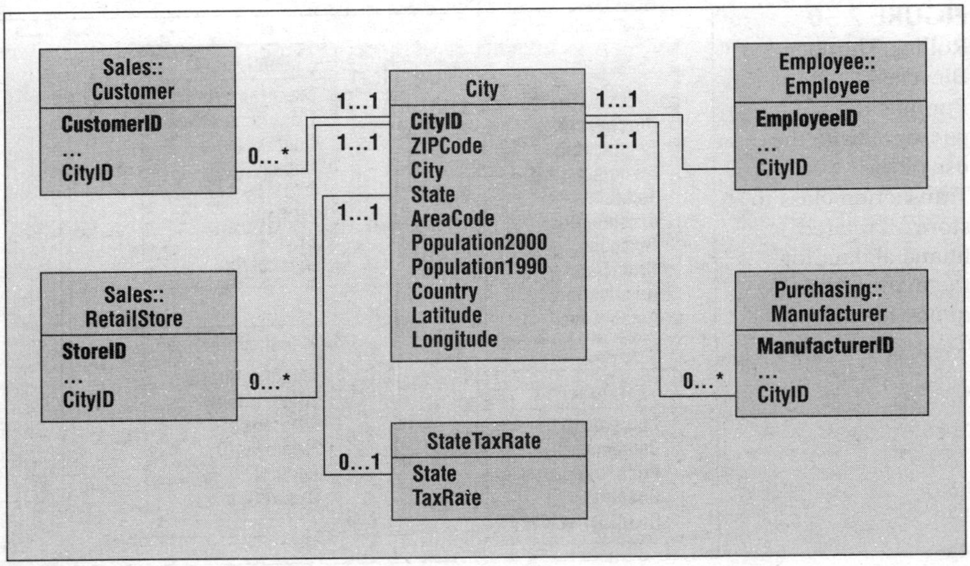

information that will be useful to managers. For example, the population and geographical locations can be used to analyze sales data and direct marketing campaigns.

The Employee package is treated separately because it interacts with so many of the other packages. The Employee properties shown in Figure 2.32 are straightforward. Notice the reflexive association that denotes the management relationship. For the moment there is only one class within the Employee package. In actual practice this is where you would place the typical human resources data and associations. For instance, you would want to track employee evaluations, assignments, and promotions over time. Additional classes would generally be related to benefits such as vacation time, personal days, and insurance choices.

FIGURE 2.32
Rolling Thunder Bicycles—Employee package. Note the reflexive association to indicate managers.

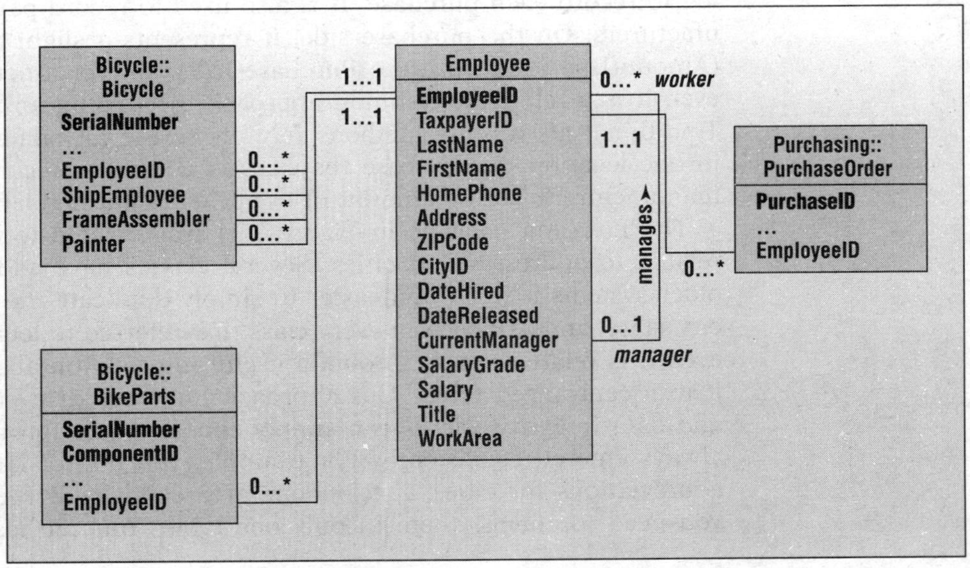

FIGURE 2.33
Rolling Thunder detailed class diagram. Microsoft Access varies slightly from UML. For example, Access uses an infinity sign (∞) instead of an asterisk (*) to indicate a many relationship. The class diagram is a nice reference tool for understanding the organization, but for many organizations this diagram will be too large to display at this level of detail.

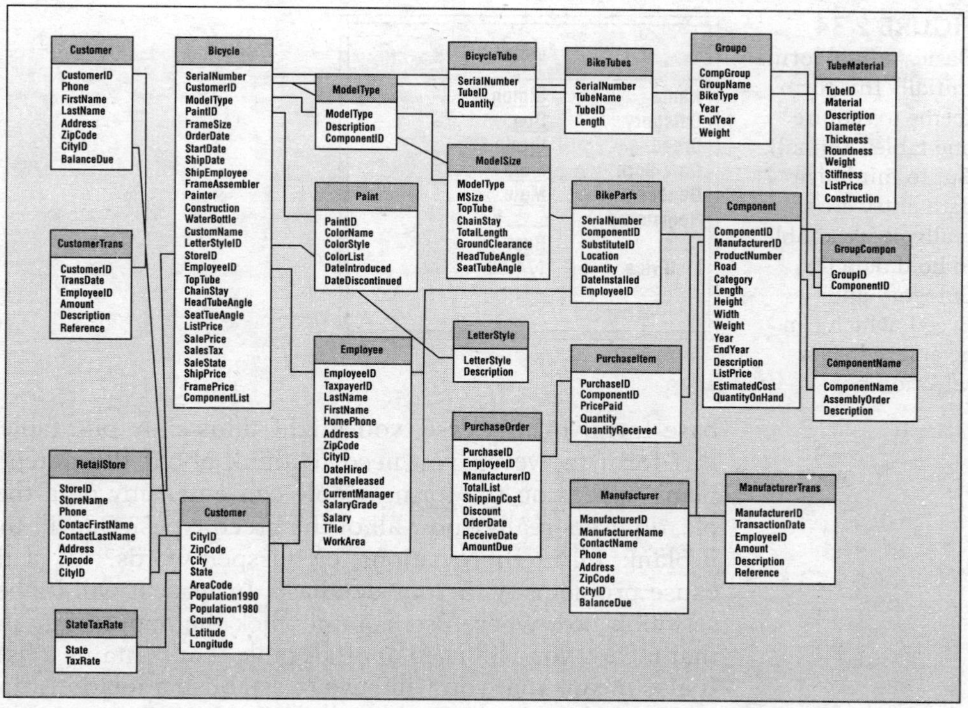

A detailed, combined class diagram for Rolling Thunder Bicycles is shown in Figure 2.33. Some associations are not included—partly to save space. A more important reason is that all of the drawn associations are enforced by Microsoft Access. For example, once you define the association from Employee to Bicycle, Access will only allow you to enter an EmployeeID into the Bicycle class that already exists within the Employee class. This enforcement makes sense for the person taking the order. Indeed, financial associations should be defined this strongly. On the other hand, the company may hire temporary workers for painting and frame assembly. In these cases the managers may not want to record the exact person who painted a frame, so the association from Employee to Painter in the Bicycle table is relaxed.

Application Design

The concept of classes and attributes seems simple at first, but can quickly become complicated. Practice and experience make the process easier. For now, learn to focus on the most important objects in a given project. It is often easiest to start with one section of the problem, define the basic elements, add detail, then expand into other sections. As you are designing the project, remember that each class becomes a table in the database, where each attribute is a column, and each row represents one specific object.

You should also begin thinking about application design in terms of the forms or screens that users will see. Consider the simple form in Figure 2.34. On paper, this form would simply have blanks for each of the items to be entered. Eventually, you could build the same form with blanks as a data-

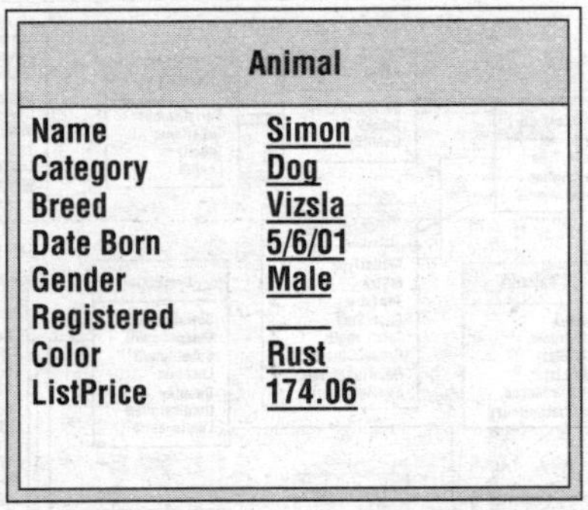

FIGURE 2.34
Basic Animal form. Initially this form seems to require one table (Animal). But to minimize data-entry errors, it really needs a table to hold data for Category and Breed, which can be entered via a selection box.

base form. In this case, you might think only one table is associated with this form; however, you need to think about the potential problems. With blank spaces on the form, people can enter any data they want. For example, do users really know all of the breed types? Or will they sometimes leave it blank, fill in abbreviations, or misspell words? All of these choices would cause problems with your database. Instead, it will be better to give them a selection box, where users simply pick the appropriate item from a list. But that means you will need another table that contains a list of possible breeds. It also means that you will have to establish a relationship between the Breed table and the Animal table. In turn, this relationship affects the way the application will be used. For example, someone must enter all of the predefined names into the Breed table before the Animal table can even be used.

At this point in the development, you should have talked with the users and collected any forms and reports they want. You should be able to sketch an initial class diagram that shows the main business objects and how they relate to each other, including the multiplicity of the association. You should also have a good idea about what attributes will be primary keys, or keys that you will need to create for some tables. You also need to specify the data domains of each property.

Summary

Managing projects to build useful applications and control costs is an important task. The primary steps in project management are the feasibility study, systems analysis, systems design, and implementation. Although these steps can be compressed, they cannot be skipped.

The primary objective is to design an application that provides the benefits needed by the users. System models are created to illustrate the system. These models are used to communicate with users, communicate with other developers, and help us remember the details of the system. Because defining data is a crucial step in developing a database application, the class diagram is a popular model.

The class diagram is created by identifying the primary entities in the system. Entities are defined by classes, which are identified by name and defined by the properties of each entity. Classes can also have functions that they perform.

Associations among classes are important elements of the business design because they identify the business rules. Associations are displayed as connecting lines on the class diagram. You should document the associations by providing names where appropriate, and by identifying the multiplicity of the relationship. You should be careful to identify special associations, such as aggregation, composition, generalization, and reflexive relationships.

Designers also need to identify the primary events or triggers that the application will need. There are three types of events: business events, data change events, and user events. Events can be described in terms of triggers that contain a condition and an action. Complex event chains can be shown on sequence or statechart diagrams.

Designs generally go through several stages of revision, with each stage becoming more detailed and more accurate. A useful approach is to start with the big picture and make sure that your design identifies the primary components that will be needed in the system. Packages can be defined to group elements together to hide details. Detail items are then added in supporting diagrams for each package in the main system diagram.

Models and designs are particularly useful on large projects. The models provide a communication mechanism for the designers, programmers, and users. CASE tools are helpful in creating, modifying, and sharing the design models. In addition to the diagrams, the CASE repository will maintain all of the definitions, descriptions, and comments needed to build the final application.

A Developer's View

Like any developer, Miranda needs a method to write down the system goals and details. The feasibility study documents the goals and provides a rough estimate of the costs and benefits. The class diagram identifies the main entities and shows how they are related. The class diagram, along with notes in the data dictionary, records the business rules. For your class project, you should study the case. Then create a feasibility study and an initial class diagram.

Key Terms

aggregation, *44*
association, *38*
association role, *38*
attribute, *34*
binary large object (BLOB), *52*
class, *34*
class diagram, *34*
class hierarchy, *45*
collaboration diagram, *32*
composition, *41*
data normalization, *36*
data type, *49*
derived classes, *43*
encapsulation, *45*
entity, *34*
generalization, *42*
inheritance, *44*
method, *34*
multiplicity, *38*
n-ary association, *40*
null, *50*
polymorphism, *45*
primary key, *36*
property, *34*
rapid application development (RAD), *31*
reflexive association, *46*
relational database, *35*
relationship, *38*
table, *35*
Unified Modeling Language (UML), *37*

Review Questions

1. How are business rules represented in class diagrams?
2. What is the purpose of a class diagram (or entity-relationship diagram)?
3. What is a reflexive association and how is it shown on a class diagram?
4. What is a primary key?
5. What is multiplicity and how is it shown on a class diagram?
6. What are the primary data types used in business applications?
7. How is inheritance shown in an entity-relationship diagram?
8. How do events and triggers relate to objects or entities?
9. What problems are complicated with large projects?
10. How can computer-aided software engineering tools help on large projects?

Exercises

1. A small company that rents canoes needs a database to track basic information about the rental and the canoes. Eventually, the firm wants to identify customers who cause problems by damaging the canoes, but for now, the managers just want to track the costs. The managers have outlined the data as a form. Create the class diagram for this case.

Rental ID	Canoe Rental	Rent Date

Customer	
Last Name, First Name	Credit Card Number
Email Phone	Expiration Date
Address	Name on Card
City, State PostalCode	Deposit Amount
Country	

Number	Description: Length, Material	Returned Date	Fee	Damage Charge	Total
					Total

2. A small company that specializes in pet grooming needs a database to record the work done by its employees. Currently, the company uses a paper sheet similar to the form shown here. For each time slot, the employee records information about the customer, the pet, and the tasks performed. All tasks have a base fee, but the employee can alter the amount depending on the difficulty and the animal. The employees are also encouraged to record comments regarding the pet and the specific task. Create the class diagram for this case.

Employee	Daily Grooming Record
Last Name	
First Name	Date
DateHired	
Specialty	

Start Time
Owner Name, Phone, Address
Pet Name, Category, Gender

Task	Time	Fee	Comments

3. A dentist who runs a small office employing himself, three hygienists, and a receptionist wants a database to schedule appointments. He has a commercial billing system to handle payments and insurance, but appointments are currently written on a paper form similar to the sample shown here. The form currently tracks only the patient name and the primary procedure to be performed (cleaning, X ray, filling, and so on). He wants to add a little more detail and list all of the procedures planned, the estimated fee for each procedure, and the estimated insurance coverage. The base fees should be stored with the procedures, but the insurance amounts are highly variable and will be entered by the receptionist who can get estimates from the billing system. The system also has to track the patient's phone number and e-mail address and record how he or she wants to be notified. Eventually, it could send e-mail messages to patients as reminders. Create the class diagram for this case.

Date Time	Dentist	Hygienist: Mary	Hygienist: Susan	Hygienist: David
10:00	Patient Name Procedure Fee	Patient Name Procedure		
10:30			Patient Name Procedure	
11:00				

4. An aging shoe manufacturing company has decided to abandon the highly competitive market for low-cost mass-market shoes. Instead, it wants to have customers order custom shoes that will be made on demand. Customers will trace or scan their feet and molds will be built specifically for each customer. The foot information will be digitized and stored in the database so it can be retrieved and used whenever the customer orders shoes. The firm will produce a variety of standard styles of shoes. Customers will select a style, choose a color and size, and in many cases choose a material. The orders are sent to company factories that customize the shoe to each person. Customers can also specify minor adjustments to most shoes—such as asking for slightly wider shoes for certain tasks. The basic information is entered on the sample form, but the company needs everything in a database. Create the normalized tables for this case.

OrderID Order Date
Estimated Ship Date Actual Ship Date Shipping Cost

Customer
Last Name, First Name, Phone, Email
Address, City, State, PostalCode
Country

LeftFootID, RightFoodID, Comments

Shipping Address
City, State, PostalCode
Country

StyleID	Description	Color	Material	Size	Adjustments	Price

5. Experience exercise: Talk to a manager of a local store and create a class diagram for the store's system.
6. Identify the typical relationships between the following entities. Write down any assumptions or comments that affect your decision. Be sure to include minimum and maximum values.
   a. Bookstore, Book
   b. Van, Driver
   c. Computer, IP address
   d. Patient, Prescription glasses
   e. House, Kitchen
   f. Cruise ship, Pool
   g. Cruise ship, Docking berth
   h. Bank, Federal Reserve district
   i. Company, Director

j. Television show, Time slot
k. Company, NAICS 6-digit code
l. Checking account number, Customer
m. Automobile, VIN
n. Fishing license, Fisherperson
o. Driver's license, Driver
p. Plane ticket, Passenger
q. Prescription, Patient
r. Latitude longitude point, Road

7. For each of the entities in the following list (left side), identify whether each of the items on the right should be an attribute of that entity or a separate entity.

a.	Shoes	Size, Sale date, Color, Price, Salesperson, Style, Manufacturer
b.	Automobile	Model, Owner, Manufacturer, Salesperson, Engine, Driver
c.	Factory	Machine, City, Employee, Manager, Owner, Size
d.	Prison	Guard, Prisoner, Warden, Location, State/Federal, Capacity
e.	Party	Location, Occasion, Guest, Menu, Start time, Caterer, Band

8. Your college radio station has a problem. To broadcast songs—particularly those streamed over the Internet, the station has to keep a detailed log of what songs were played. The studios also want to know how many listeners received the song. For Internet streams, this number is shown by the streaming software. Although the studios want detailed information on each song, the station's DJs find it easier to pick the songs by the artist and the CD. The station wants an easy-to-use database that lets the DJ quickly pick the song each time it is played, enter the number of listeners, and any comments—particularly if the song does not play all the way through for some reason. Based on your knowledge of music and the sample log page, create the class diagram for this case.

Date Time	Song	Employee Artist CD	Studio	Comments	#Listeners

9. A local company is creating a new in-car toll system. Customers will purchase an emitter, which is a small transmitter placed in the car. They will register a credit card number with the company. Whenever the customer drives past the toll collection point, the emitter sends an ID signal that is picked up at the booth. The time and fee are recorded, the customer is sent a statement at the end of the month, and the credit card is automatically billed for the total monthly amount. The slightly complicated part is that each location charges different fees based on the day of the week and the time of day. For instance, rush hour charges are generally higher than at other times. The report below provides a partial picture of the fee structure and the data collected at a single location. Of course, there are multiple locations, and the customer data has to be consolidated to provide a total bill. To help reduce theft, emitters are identified with specific vehicles, but customers can transfer them when they sell a car. Create the class diagram for this case.

Location Description Traffic Log Date			Fee Structure			
Time	EmitterID	Fee	DayOfWeek	Start Time	End Time	Fee
			MTWTF	6:00	8:00	$3
			MTWT	15:00	18:00	$3
			F	15:00	18:00	$5
			SS	00:00	24:00	$2

Sally's Pet Store

10. Do some initial research on retail sales and pet stores. Identify the primary benefits you expect to gain from a transaction processing system for Sally's Pet Store. Estimate the time and costs required to design and build the database application.
11. Extend the class diagram for Sally's Pet Store by including the details needed to track the genealogy of all of the animals.
12. Extend the class diagram for Sally's Pet Store by including the details needed to track the health and veterinary records for the animals.
13. Extend the pet store class diagram to include scheduling of appointments for pet grooming.

Rolling Thunder Bicycles

14. Redesign the Rolling Thunder class diagram using an object-oriented approach. Identify all of the classes, properties, and methods.
15. Rolling Thunder Bicycles is thinking about opening a chain of bicycle stores. Explain how the database would have to be altered to accommodate this change. Add the proposed components to the class diagram.

16. If Rolling Thunder Bicycles wants to add a website to sell bicycles over the Internet, what additional data needs to be collected? Extend the class diagram to handle this additional data.

Website References

Site	Description
http://www.rational.com/uml/	The primary site for UML documentation and examples
http://www.iconixsw.com	UML documentation and comments
http://otn.oracle.com/docs/products/oracle9i/doc_library/release2/server.920/a96540/sql_elements2a.htm#54201	Oracle data type description
http://msdn.microsoft.com/library/default.asp?url=/library/en-us/odbc/htm/odappdpr_2.asp	SQL Server data type description
http://time-post.com/dbdesign	Database design system

Additional Reading

Codd, E. F. "A Relational Model of Data for Large Shared Data Banks." *Communications of the ACM* 13 no. 6 (1970), pp. 377–87. [The paper that initially described the relational model.]

Constantine, L. "Under Pressure." *Software Development,* October 1995, pp. 111–12. [The importance of design.]

———. "Re: Architecture." *Software Development*, January 1996, pp. 87–88. [Update on a design competition.]

McConnell, S. *Rapid Development: Taming Wild Software Schedules.* Redmond: Microsoft Press, 1996. [An excellent introduction to building systems, with lots of details and examples.]

Penker, M., and H. Eriksson. *Business Modeling with UML: Business Patterns at Work.* New York: John Wiley & Sons, 2000. [Detailed application of UML to business applications.]

Silverston, L. *The Data Model Resource Book, Vols. 1 and 2,* New York: John Wiley & Sons, 2001. [A collection of sample models for a variety of businesses.]

Database Design System

Many students find database design to be challenging to learn. The basic concept seems straightforward: define a table that represents one basic entity with columns that describe the properties to hold the necessary data. For example, a Customer table will have columns for CustomerID, LastName, FirstName, and so on. But it is often difficult to decide exactly which columns belong in a table. It is also difficult to identify the key columns, which are used to establish relationships among tables. The design is complicated by the fact that the tables reflect the underlying business rules, so students must also understand the business operations and constraints in order to create a design that provides the functionality needed by the business.

In addition to reading Chapters 2 and 3 closely, one of the most important steps in learning database design is to work as many problems as possible. The catch is that students also need feedback to identify problems and improve the design. An online expert system is available to instructors and students to provide this immediate feedback. This online system is available at: http://time-post.com/dbdesign. This appendix uses the DB Design system to highlight a graphical approach to designing a database. However, even if you do not use the DB Design system, this appendix provides a useful summary of how to approach database design.

Sample Problem: Customer Orders

It is easiest to understand database design and the DB Design system by following an example. Customer orders are a common situation in business databases, so consider the simple order form displayed in Figure 2.1A. The layout of the form generally provides information about the business rules and practices. For example, there is space for only one customer on the order, so it seems reasonable that no more than one customer can participate in an order. Conversely, the repeating section shows multiple rows to allow several items to be ordered at one time. These one-to-many relationships are important factors in the database design.

Getting Started: Identifying Columns

One of the first steps in creating the database design is to identify all of the properties or items for which you need to collect data. In the example, you will need to store customer first name, last name, address, and so on. You will also need to store

FIGURE 2.1A
Typical order form. Each order can be placed by one customer but can contain multiple items ordered as shown by the repeating section.

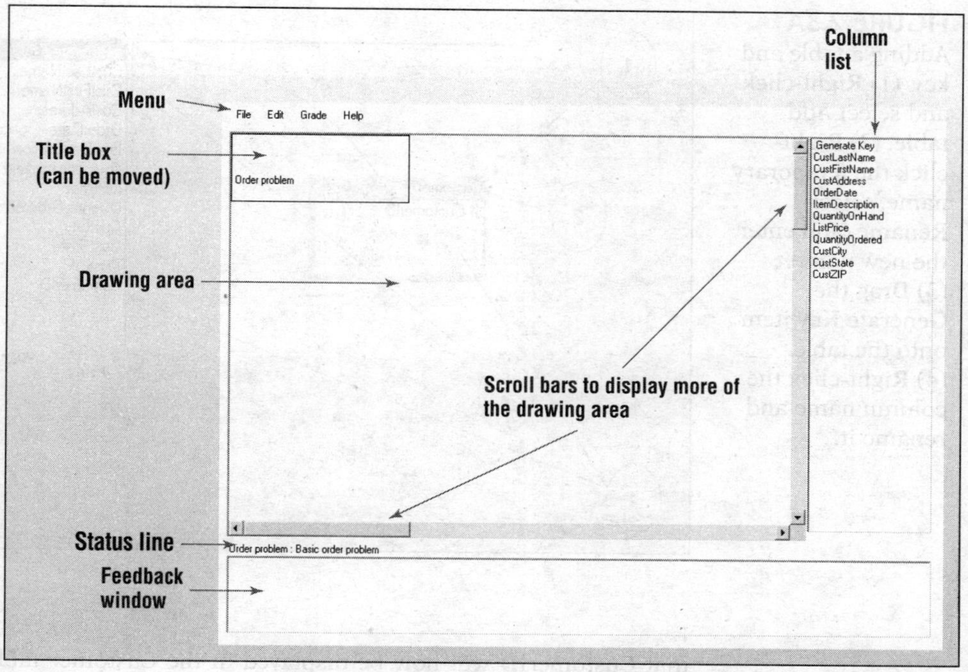

FIGURE 2.2A
DB Design screen. Once you log in, use the File menu option to Open the Order Problem. The Help menu has an option to View the Problem. The right-hand window contains a list of the available columns that will be placed into tables. Selecting the Grade menu option generates comments in the feedback window.

an order number, order date, item description, and more. Basically, you identify each item on the form and give it a unique name. Note that some items can be easily computed and will not need to be stored. For instance, value is list price times quantity, and the order total is the sum of the value items.

As shown in Figure 2.2A, after you have opened a problem, the DB Design system provides you with a list of items from the form. This list is presented in the right-hand column. The list of columns is the foundation for the database design. Your job is to create tables and then select the columns that belong in each table. You can rename the columns by right-clicking the column name and selecting the Rename option. You should make sure that the names are unique. The system does not care, but you will have trouble identifying columns in the main list if some have the same name. To get a better grasp of the columns available, you can sort the list by right-clicking the list and selecting the Sort option.

Creating a Table and Adding Columns

The main objective is to create tables and specify which columns belong in each table. It is fairly clear that this problem will need a table to hold customer data, so begin by right-clicking the main drawing window and selecting the option to add a table. Then, right-click on the top gray border of the table and select the rename option. Enter "Customer" to provide the new name.

Each table must have a primary key—one or more columns that uniquely identify each row in the table. Looking at the order form and in the column list, you will not see a column that can be used as a primary key. You might consider using the customer phone number, but that presents problems when customers change their numbers. Instead, it is best to generate a new column called CustomerID. The values for this number might be assigned by the marketing department or created automatically by the database system. To create a new key, drag the Generate Key item from the column list and drop it on the Customer table. Then, right-click the column name and select the rename option and enter CustomerID as the new name. Notice

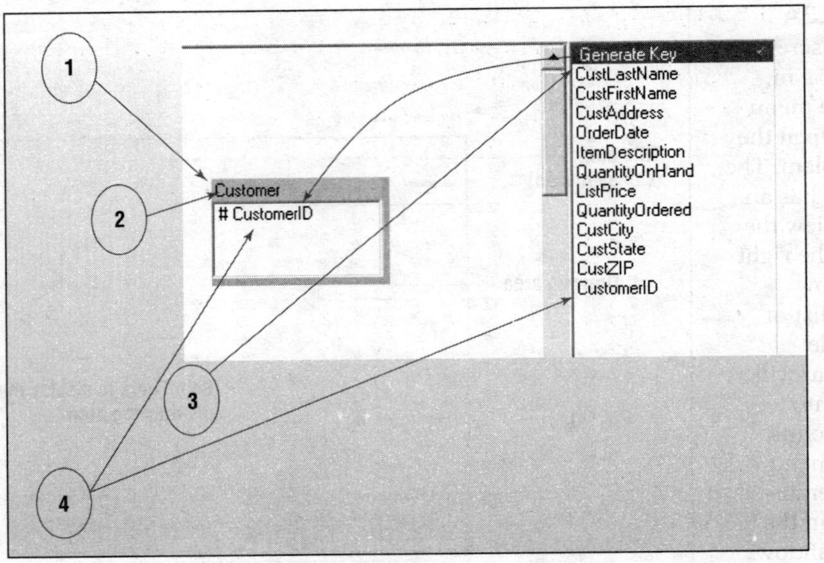

FIGURE 2.3A Adding a table and key. (1) Right-click and select Add table. (2) Right-click the temporary name, select Rename, and enter the new name. (3) Drag the Generate Key item onto the table. (4) Right-click the column name and rename it.

that CustomerID will now be displayed in the Customer table and as a new column in the column list. Also, notice in Figure 2.3A that the CustomerID is marked with a flag (#) to indicate that it is part of the primary key in the Customer table. You can set and unset columns as primary keys by right-clicking the column. When you double-click a table's column name, the table will be automatically resized to display all of its columns.

Now that the table and primary key are established, you can add other columns to the table. But which columns? The Customer table should contain columns that identify attributes specifically about a customer. So, find each column that is strictly identified by the new primary key CustomerID and drag it onto the Customer table.

It is also fairly clear that the database design will need an Orders table. Add a new table, name it "Orders," and generate a key for OrderID. Once again, you need to identify the columns that belong in the Order table. Looking at the Order form, you should add the OrderDate column. Notice that the order form also contains customer information. But it would seem to be a waste of effort to require clerks to enter a customer's name and address for every order. Instead, you need to add only the CustomerID in the Order table. Remember that CustomerID will not be a primary key in the Order table, because for each order, there can be only one customer. If it were keyed, you would be indicating that more than one customer could take part in an order. Your tables should be similar to Figure 2.4A. Be sure to save your work as you go. If you wait too long, the Internet connection will time-out and you may lose your changes.

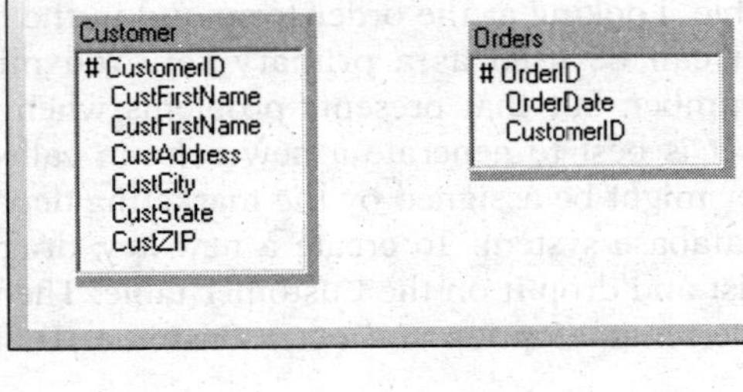

FIGURE 2.4A Two tables. Each table represents a single entity, and all columns are data collected for that entity. The Orders table contains the CustomerID, which provides a method to obtain the matching data in the Customer table.

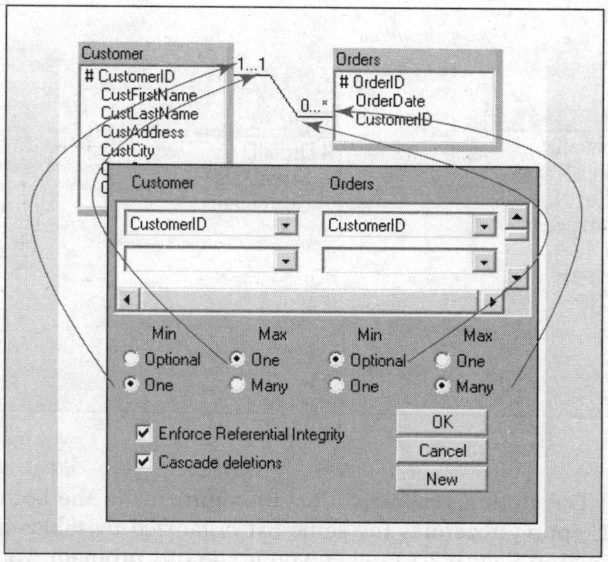

FIGURE 2.5A
Relationships. Drag the CustomerID column from the Customer table and drop it onto the CustomerID column in the Orders table. Then set the minimum and maximum values for each side of the relationship. An order must have exactly one customer, and a customer can place from zero to many orders.

Relationships: Connecting Tables

The database system eventually needs to know that the CustomerID in the Orders table constitutes a relationship with the CustomerID in the Customer table. You need to draw a line in the diagram to link the tables to show this relationship. The easiest way to create this link is to drag the CustomerID from the Customer table and drop it onto the CustomerID column in the Orders table. The second step is to indicate the minimum and maximum values for each side of the relationship. Figure 2.5A shows how the selections in the relationship design are displayed on the diagram. In this case, an order can be placed by exactly one customer, so the minimum customer value is one and the maximum value is also one. On the other side of the relationship, each customer can place from zero to many orders. Some might argue that if a customer has not placed any orders, then he or she is only a potential customer, but the difference is not critical to the database.

Grading: Detecting and Solving Problems

You will repeat these same steps to create the database design: add a table, set the primary key, add the data columns, and link the tables. The DB Design system makes the process relatively easy, and you can drag tables around to display them conveniently. You can save your work and come back at a later time to retrieve it and continue working on the problem. However, you still do not know if your design is good or bad.

Consider adding another table to the sample order problem. Add a table for Items and generate a new key column called ItemID. Add the columns for ItemDescription, ListPrice, and QuantityOnHand. The problem you face now is that you need to link this new table with the Orders table. But, so far, they do not have any related columns. So, as an experiment, try placing the OrderID column into the Items table. Now build a relationship from Items to Orders by linking the OrderID columns, as shown in Figure 2.6A.

At any time, you can submit the current design to see if there are problems. In fact, it is a good idea to check your work several times as you create the tables, so you can spot problems early. Use the Grade option on the menu to Grade and Mark the

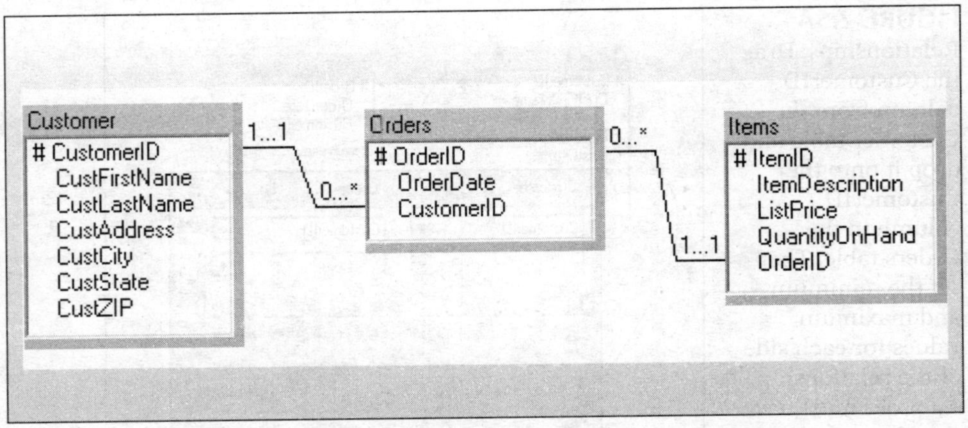

FIGURE 2.6A Creating errors. To demonstrate a potential problem, add the OrderID column to the Items table and then link it to the Orders table.

diagram. This option generates a list of comments in the bottom window. The Grade to HTML option generates the same list organized by tables in a separate window.

As shown in Figure 2.7A, when you grade this problem, you get a reasonably good score (88.3). However, there are several important comments. When you double-click on a comment the system highlights the error. In this case, most of the comments indicate that there is a problem with the Items table. In particular, the OrderID column is presenting a problem. This problem is partially highlighted by the relationship. Can an order have more than one item on it? If you reexamine Figure 2.1A, you will see that yes, an order has rows to hold multiple items. You could try to fix the relationship by making it a many-to-many relationship, but relational databases do not work with many-to-many relationships directly between two tables. If you look more carefully at the Items table, you will see the problem. It currently has only ItemID as a key. Because OrderID is not keyed, an item can appear on only one order, which means that each item could never be sold more than once.

You might try making OrderID a key as well as ItemID. To see the problem, try both fixes. Figure 2.8A shows the result of these changes. First, notice that the score

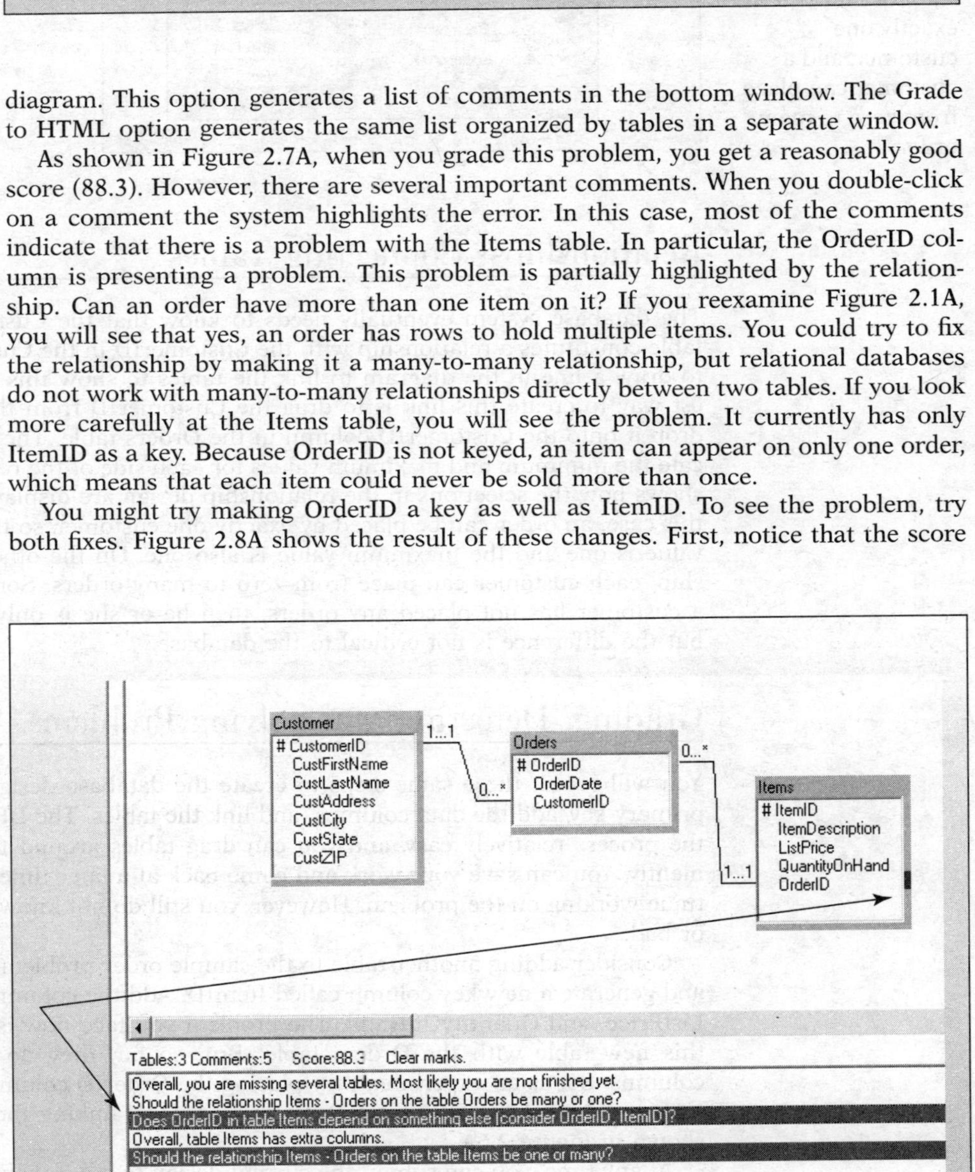

FIGURE 2.7A Grading the exercise. Double-click a comment to highlight the table and column causing problems. Use the comments to recognize which table and which column are causing the problems. In this case, think about why the OrderID might not belong in the Items table.

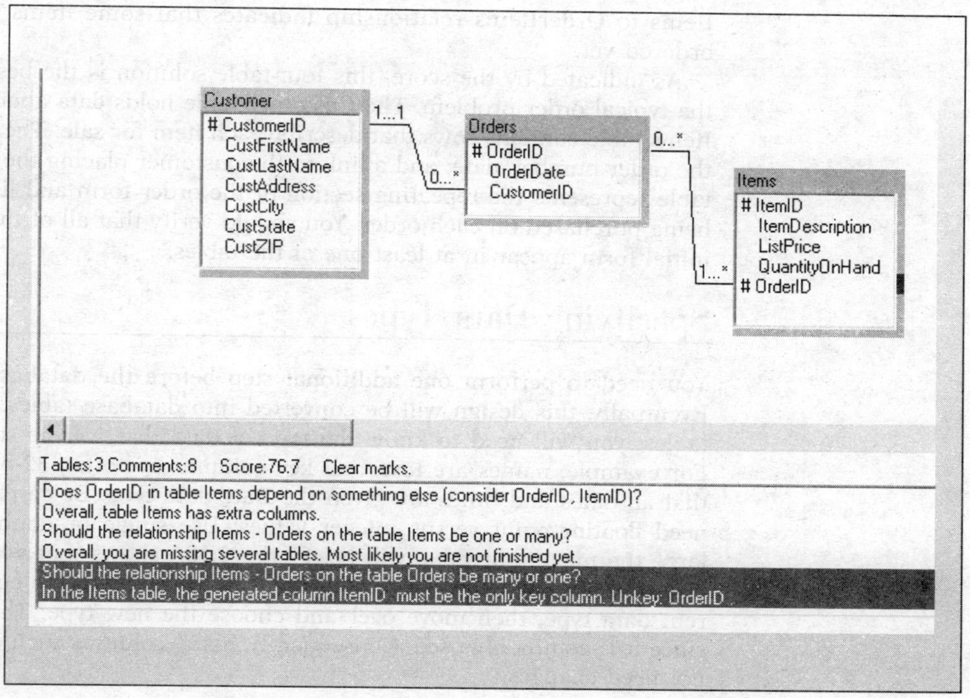

FIGURE 2.8A Trying to fix the problems. Notice that the score decreased, so the "fix" actually made the situation worse. The problems with the OrderID and the relationship have not been solved.

decreased! The DB Design system is still pointing out problems with the relationship between Orders and Items, and it is showing a problem with making OrderID a key. In particular, note that ItemID was created as a generated key, so it is always guaranteed to be unique. If that is true, then you would never need a second key column in the same table.

The solution is to realize that a relational database cannot support a direct many-to-many relationship between two tables. Instead, you must insert a new table between the first two. In this case, call it an OrderItem table. Then be sure to add the key columns from both of the linked tables (OrderID and ItemID). As shown in Figure 2.9A, add both relationships as one-to-many links. Notice that the

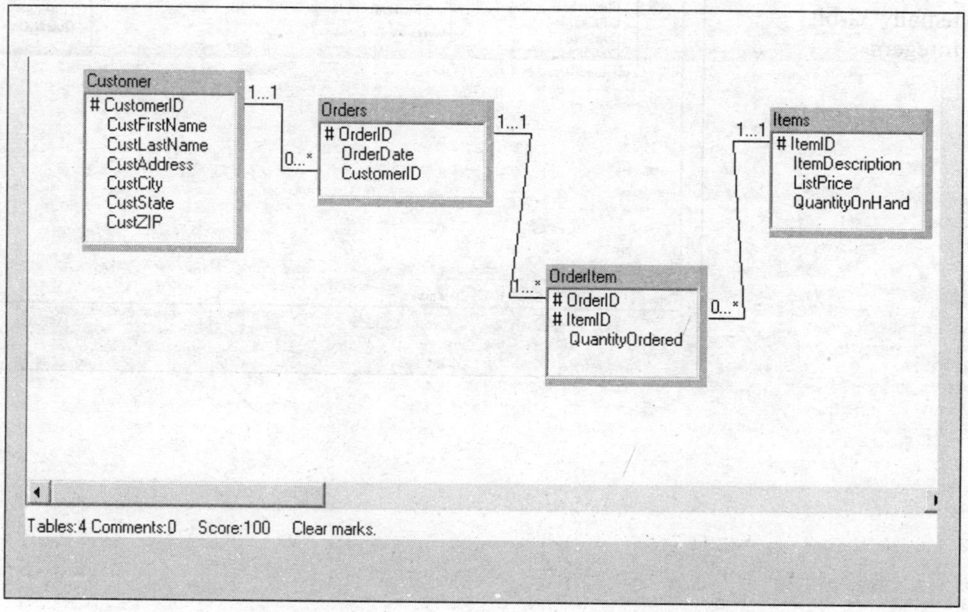

FIGURE 2.9A A solution. Add the intermediate table OrderItem and include keys from both tables (OrderID and ItemID). Use one-to-many relationships to link it to both tables.

Items to OrderItems relationship indicates that some items might not have been ordered yet.

As indicated by the score, this four-table solution is the best database design for the typical order problem. The Customer table holds data about each customer. The Items table contains rows that describe each item for sale. The Orders table provides the order number, date, and a link to the customer placing the order. The OrderItem table represents the repeating section of the order form and lists the multiple items being purchased on each order. You should verify that all of the data items from the initial form appear in at least one of the tables.

Specifying Data Types

You need to perform one additional step before the database design is complete. Eventually, this design will be converted into database tables. When you create the tables, you will need to know the type of data that will be stored in each column. For example, names are text, and key columns are often 32-bit integers. Make sure that all dates and times are given the Date data type. Be careful to check when you need floating-point versus integer values: Use single or double depending on how large the maximum value will be. Figure 2.10A shows that you set the data type by right-clicking the column name in the table, then move the cursor to select the current data type, then move over and choose the new type. The default value is text since it is commonly used. Consequently, many columns such as customer name will not need changes.

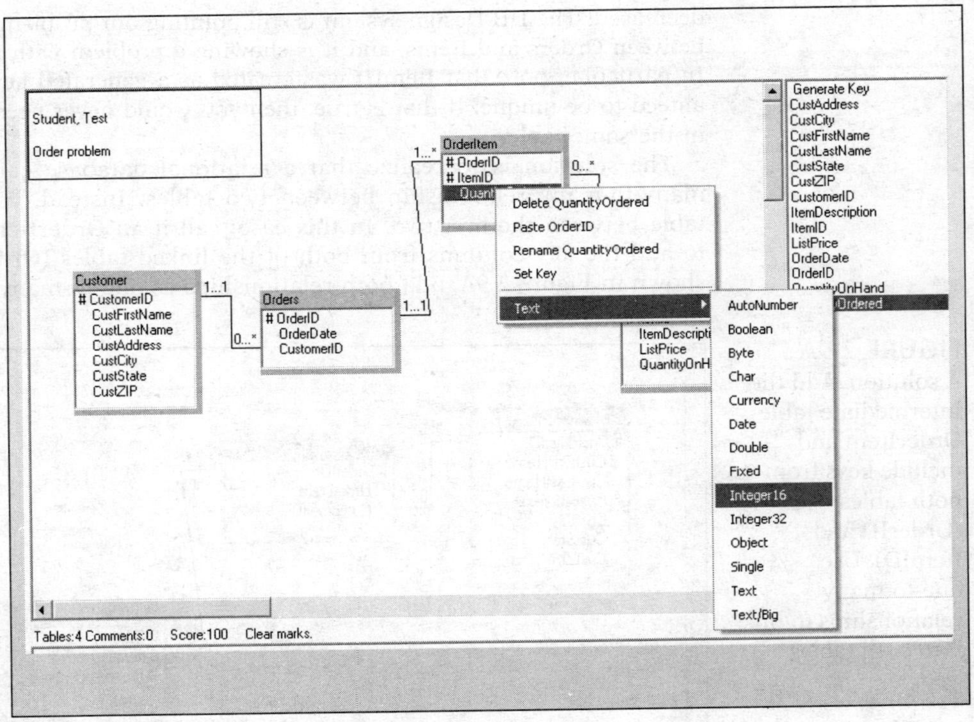

FIGURE 2.10A
Data types. Right-click a column name and set its data type. The default is Text, so you do not have to change common columns like the customer name. Key columns are usually 32-bit integers.

Chapter 3

Data Normalization

Chapter Outline

What You Will Learn in This Chapter

A Developer's View

Miranda: That was actually fun. I learned a lot about the company's procedures and rules. I think I have everything recorded properly on the class diagram, along with some notes in the data dictionary.

Ariel: Great! We should go to the concert tonight and celebrate.

Miranda: I could use a night off. Maybe giving my brain cells a rest will help me figure out what to do next.

Ariel: What do you mean? How much longer do you think the project will take?

Miranda: That's the problem. I put all this time in, and I don't really have a start on the application at all.

Ariel: Well, isn't the data the most important aspect to building a database application? I heard that database systems are touchy. You have to define the data correctly the first time; otherwise, you will have to start over.

Miranda: Maybe you're right. I'll take the night off; then I'll study these rules to see how I can turn the class diagram into a set of database tables.

Introduction

A database is a powerful tool. It provides many advantages over traditional programming and hierarchical files. However, you get these advantages only if you design the database correctly. Recall that a database is a collection of tables. The goal of this chapter is to show you how to design the tables for your database.

The essence of data normalization is to split your data into several tables that will be connected to each other based on the data within them. Mechanically, this process is not very difficult. There are perhaps four rules that you need to learn. On the other hand, the tables have to be created specifically for the business or application that you are dealing with. Therefore, you must first understand the business, and your tables must match the rules of the business. So the challenge in designing a database is to first understand how the business operates and what its rules are. Some of these rules were hinted at in Chapter 2 with the focus on relationships. Business relationships (one-to-one and one-to-many) form the foundation of data normalization. These relationships are crucial to determining how to set up your database. These rules vary from firm to firm and sometimes even depend on which person you talk to in the organization. So when you create your database, you have to build a picture of how the company works. You talk to many people to understand the relationships among the data. The goal of data normalization is to identify the business rules so that you can design good database tables.

By designing database tables carefully, you (1) save space, (2) minimize duplication, (3) protect the data to ensure its consistency, and (4) provide faster transactions by sending less data. One method for defining database tables is to use the graphical approach presented in Chapter 2 and build a class diagram. A related method is to collect the basic paperwork, starting with every form and every report you might use. Then take apart each collection of data and break it down into respective tables. Most people find that a combination of both approaches helps them find the answer. However, the discussion will begin by describing the two methods separately.

Tables, Classes, and Keys

Chapter 2 focuses on identifying the business classes and associations. Now, these classes need to be more carefully defined so they can be converted into database tables. Of course, as you modify the tables, you will also update the class diagram. The relationships among the classes are critical to determining the final form of the tables. These relationships are also expressed in terms of the primary keys of the tables. A primary key consists of a collection of columns that uniquely identify each row. Since the key must be guaranteed to always be unique, it is common to create a new key column that holds generated keys. But, in many cases, you will use multiple columns to make up the primary key. These situations are important enough to require a detailed explanation.

Composite Keys

In many cases, as you design a database, you will have tables that will use more than one column as part of the primary key. These are called **composite keys.** You need composite keys when the table contains a one-to-many or many-to-many relationship with another table.

As an example of composite keys, look at the OrderItems table in Figure 3.1. These two tables are common in business and they form a **master-detail** or parent-child relationship. The Orders table is straightforward. It has one column as a primary key, where you created the OrderID. This table contains the basic information about an order, including the date and the customer. The OrderItems table has two columns as keys: OrderID and Item. The purpose of the OrderItems table is to show which products the customers chose to buy. In terms of keys the important point is that each order can contain many different items. In the example OrderID 8367 has three items. Because each order can have many different items, Item must be part of the key. Reading the table description from left to right you can say that each OrderID may have many Items. The "many" says that Item must be keyed. What about the other direction in the OrderItems table? Do you really need to key OrderID? The answer is yes because the firm can sell the same item to many different people (or to the same customer at different times). For example, Item 229 appears on OrderIDs 8367 and

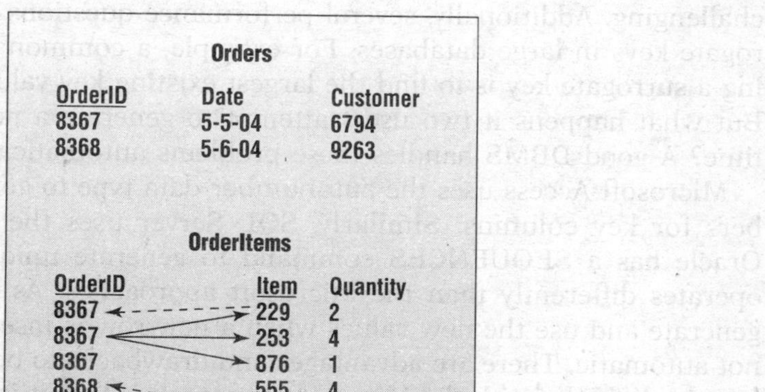

FIGURE 3.1
Composite keys. OrderItems uses a composite key (OrderID + Item) because there is a many-to-many relationship. Each order can contain many items (shown by the solid arrows). Each item can show up on many different orders (dotted arrows).

8368. Because each item can appear on many different orders, the OrderID must be part of the primary key. For comparison, reconsider the Orders table in Figure 3.1. Each OrderID can have only one Customer, so Customer is not keyed.

To be sure you understand how keys and relationships interact, look again at the OrderItems table. Looking at the ItemID column, ask yourself, For each OrderID, can there be one or many ItemIDs? If the answer is many, then ItemID must be keyed (underlined). Now, look at OrderID and ask yourself, Can an ItemID appear on one or many orders? Again, the answer is many, so OrderID must also be keyed.

Look at the CustomerID column in the Order table and ask, For each order, can there be one or many customers? The common business rule says there is only one customer per order, so CustomerID is not part of the primary key. On the other hand, because CustomerID is a primary key within the Customer table, it is known as a **foreign key** in the Order table. Think of it as a foreign dignitary visiting a different country (table). It is required in the Order table because it serves as a link to the rest of the customer data in the Customer table.

To properly normalize the data and store the data as efficiently as possible, you must identify keys properly. Your choice of the key depends on the business relationships, the terminology in the organization, and the one-to-many and many-to-many relationships within the company.

Surrogate Keys

It can be difficult to ensure that any real-world data will always generate a unique key. Consequently, you will often ask the database system to generate its own key values. These surrogate keys are used only within the database and are often hidden so users do not even know they exist. For example, the database system could assign a unique key to each customer, but clerks would look up customers by conventional data such as name and address. Surrogate keys are especially useful when there is some uncertainty with the business key. Think about the problems that you would face if a company changed the format of its product numbers every 2 years. If you rely on business keys, you must trust that they will always be consistent and never be duplicated.

The use of surrogate keys can be tricky when the database becomes large. With many simultaneous users, creating unique numbers becomes more challenging. Additionally, several performance questions arise involving surrogate keys in large databases. For example, a common method of generating a surrogate key is to find the largest existing key value and increment it. But what happens if two users attempt to generate a new key at the same time? A good DBMS handles these problems automatically.

Microsoft Access uses the **autonumber** data type to generate unique numbers for key columns. Similarly, SQL Server uses the Identity data type. Oracle has a SEQUENCES command to generate unique numbers, but it operates differently than the Microsoft approaches. As a programmer, you generate and use the new values when a new row is inserted—the process is not automatic. There are advantages and drawbacks to both approaches. The biggest difficulty with the Microsoft approach is that it is sometimes difficult to obtain the new value that was generated when a row is inserted. The drawback to the Oracle approach is that you must ensure that all users and

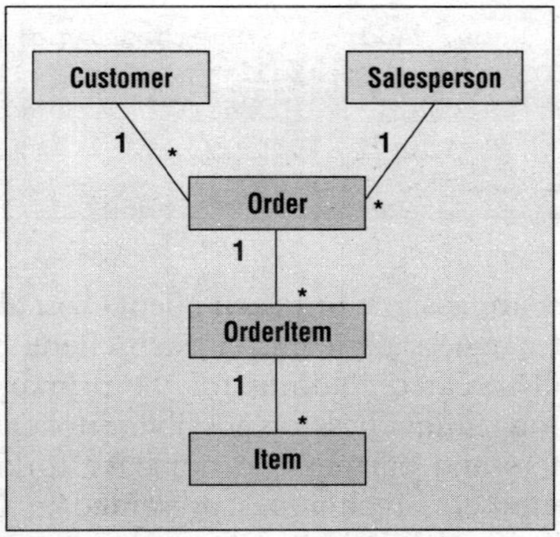

FIGURE 3.2
A small class diagram for a basic order system. The numbers indicate relationships. For instance, each customer can place many orders, but a given order can come from only one customer.

developers use the proper number generation commands throughout the application. Additionally, both approaches can cause problems when transferring data—particularly to other database systems.

Notation

A detailed class diagram can describe each table and include all properties within each class and marked key columns. The advantage to using class diagrams is that they highlight the associations among the classes. Additionally, some people understand the system better with a visual representation. Figure 3.2 shows a simple example class diagram, but it leaves out the properties.

The drawback to class diagrams is that they can become very large. By the time you get to 30 classes, it is hard to fit all the information on one page. Also, many of the association lines will cross, making the diagram harder to read. CASE tools help resolve some of these problems by enabling you to examine a smaller section of the diagram.

However, you can also use a shorter notation, as shown in Figure 3.3. The notation consists of a straight listing of the tables. Each column is listed with the table name. The primary keys are underlined and generally listed first. This notation is easy to write by hand or to type, and it can display many tables in a compact space. However, it is hard to show the relationships between the tables. You can draw arrows between the tables, but your page can become messy.

Designers frequently create both the class diagram and the list of tables. The list identifies all of the columns and the keys. The class diagram shows the relationships between the tables. The class diagram can also contain additional details, such as existence constraints and minimum requirements.

Consider the example in Figure 3.4 of a small client-billing system. Basic data includes clients and partners. You probably have a relationship that

FIGURE 3.3
Table notation. Column details are easier to see in a simple listing of the tables. This list is also useful when the tables are entered into the database.

```
Customer(CustomerID, Name, Address, City, Phone)
Salesperson(EmployeeID, Name, Commission, DateHired)
Order(OrderID, OrderDate, CustomerID, EmployeeID)
OrderItem(OrderID, ItemID, Quantity)
Item(ItemID, Description, ListPrice)
```

FIGURE 3.4
Client-billing example. Note the business rule that each client can be assigned many partners results in both PartnerID and ClientID being keys in the PartnerAssignment table.

```
Client(ClientID, Name, Address, BusinessType)
Partner(PartnerID, Name, Speciality, Office, Phone)
PartnerAssignment(PartnerID, ClientID, DateAcquired)
Billing(ClientID, PartnerID, Date/Time, Item,
Description, Hours, AmountBilled)
```

shows which partners are assigned to each client. You also want to track the amount of work that partners perform for each client. The Client and Partner tables use specially created columns for the primary key. Hence you do not have to worry about uniqueness or possible duplication of names. Keep in mind that customers and partners do not have to know anything about their identification numbers. Techniques presented in Chapter 8 will show how to look up client data while hiding key values.

Notice that in the PartnerAssignment table, both PartnerID and ClientID are keyed. Just by writing the table in this form, you have identified an assumption about the way the firm operates. First, each partner performs work for many clients—a fairly common practice. Additionally, each client could be assigned many partners. This second assumption might not hold in some firms. Smaller firms might simply assign a primary partner to each client. If a different partner performs work for the client, the partner could still be listed in the billing table. The choice of keys in the PartnerAssignment table depends on the way that the business operates.

Figure 3.5 illustrates what happens in a firm with a rule that each client is assigned to exactly one primary partner. In this case PartnerID is no longer a key in the PartnerAssignment table. Notice also that the Client and PartnerAssignment tables have exactly the same keys (ClientID). If these keys are correct, the columns should be combined into one table (Client). There is no reason to have two tables with exactly the same key. Hence the data tables for the second firm will be different from those of the first firm—simply because of a difference in business procedures.

The Billing table in Figure 3.6 has three columns in the primary key: ClientID, PartnerID, and Date/Time. The keys indicate that for each client many partners can perform work. Conversely, each partner can work for many different clients. Similarly, each client can have work performed by each partner at many different times. Consider the implications if you did not key

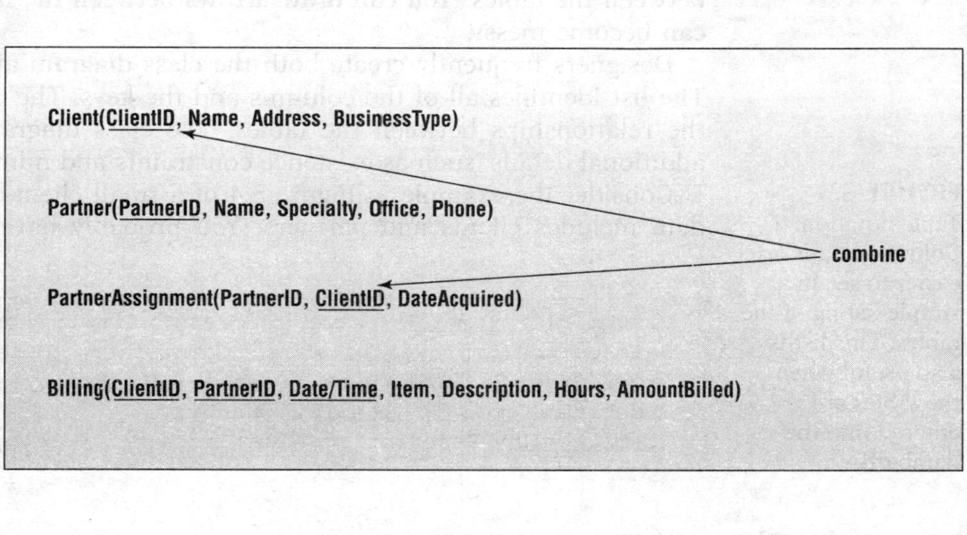

FIGURE 3.5
Simplified client billing. If each client is assigned exactly one primary partner, then the PartnerID cannot be keyed in the PartnerAssignment table. However, now the client table and the PartnerAssignment table have the same key (ClientID). Hence, the columns should be combined into one (Client) table.

FIGURE 3.6
Sample data for the Billing table. Note that Partner 963 can perform the same task for Client 115 several times because Date/Time is part of the primary key.

Billing

ClientID	PartnerID	Date/Time	Item	Description	Hours	AmountBilled
115	963	8-4-04 10:03	967	Stress analysis	2	$500
295	967	8-5-04 11:15	754	New Design	3	$750
115	963	8-8-04 09:30	967	Stress analysis	2.5	$650

Date/Time. Then each client could be billed by many partners, but only one time for each partner. Although the clients might be happy with that constraint, it is not realistic from the perspective of the firm using the database. The problem with not keying Date/Time is that rows 1 and 3 would no longer be unique. To test your primary keys, enter sample data and cover up the other columns. Looking at the first two columns in the table, you see duplicate entries for rows 1 and 3. To solve the problem, you have to ask, How can a partner perform work for a client more than once? The answer is that the work must be performed at different times. Hence the Date/Time column is added and becomes part of the primary key.

Already you can see how the business rules affect the database design. The choice of the primary key depends heavily on the business relationships, and can be different for each organization. Be careful to double-check all of your keys. If you make a mistake in the keys, it will be difficult to get the rest of the database correct. In the case of simple entities (customer, employee, etc.) you will generally create a unique key. For more complex entities, you need to watch for one-to-many and many-to-many relationships. You test composite keys by looking at the first underline (ClientID) and then ask, for all other underlined columns (in this case, PartnerID), Are there many of these partners? If so, the column should be keyed. If there is only one entry, then the column should not be a key. Be sure to check the reverse relationship as well (PartnerID to ClientID).

Sample Database for a Video Store

The best way to illustrate data normalization is to examine a sample problem. Remember that the results you get (the tables you create) depend heavily on the specific example and the assumptions you make. The following example uses a case that is familiar to most students: the main task at a video store.

One of the most important functions of a video store is to check out the videos for rental. A sample checkout screen is displayed in Figure 3.7.

The main components of the sample form are the customer and the videos being rented. When the form is built in the database, it will automatically keep track of the total amount due. It should also automatically assign a RentalID that is unique. Note that the form also has buttons and controls to help the user enter data with a minimum of effort. Forms and controls are discussed in Chapter 5. For now, as you talk with the manager, you should sketch the desired features of the form. Values that can be computed (e.g., subtotals) should be marked, and the appropriate equations provided if needed. For the most part you do not want to store computed values in the data tables.

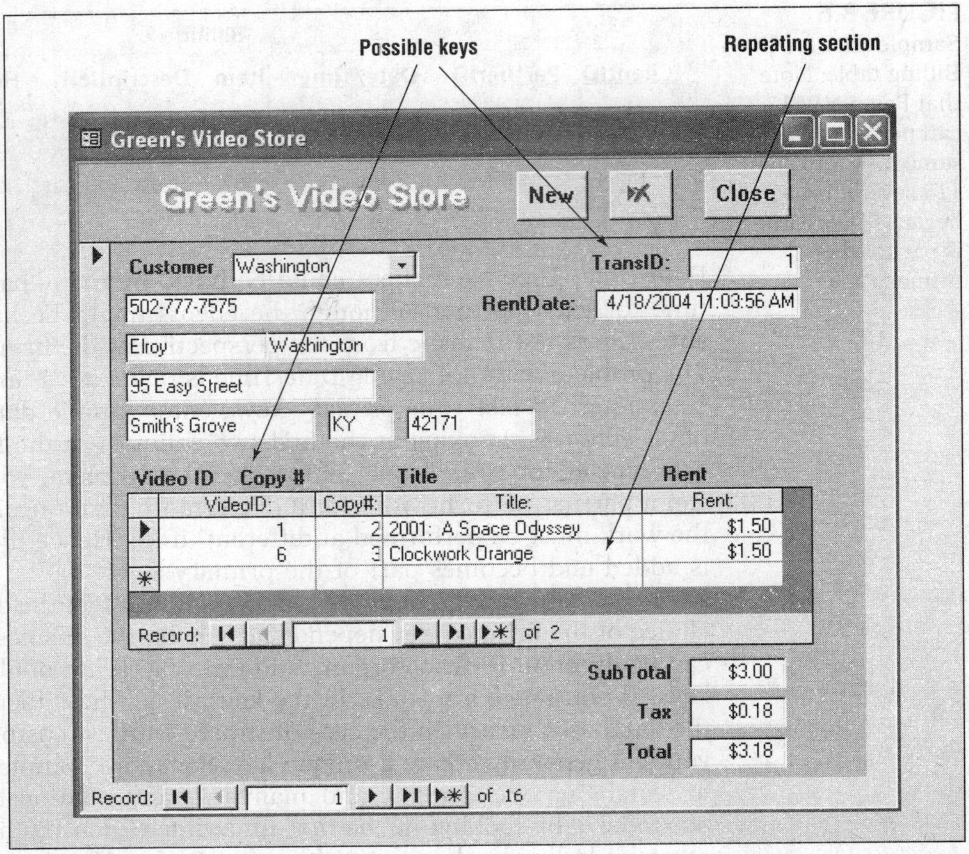

FIGURE 3.7
Sample video rental screen. First look for possible keys, keeping in mind that repeating sections (one-to-many relationships) will eventually need concatenated keys.

Initial Objects

Begin by identifying the main objects that you will need. The obvious ones are customers and videos. In real life you would also have employees, VCRs to rent, and possibly other sale items, but you can ignore those for now. However, managers also need to keep track of who rented specific videos. For example, if a video is not returned on time, managers need to know who to call. Hence you need two additional objects. The first is a transaction that records the date and the customer. The second is a list of the videos rented by that customer at that time.

Examine the initial objects in Figure 3.8. You need a primary key for customers (and videos). Clearly, Name will not work, but you might consider using the Phone number. This approach would probably work, but it might cause some minor difficulties down the road. For example, if a customer gets a new phone number, you would have to change the corresponding phone number in every table that referred to it. As a primary key, it could appear in several different tables. A bigger problem would arise if a customer (Adams) moves, freeing up the phone number, which the phone company reassigns to another person (Brown) several months later. If Brown opens an account at your store, your database might mistakenly identify customer Brown as the customer Adams. The safest approach is to have the database create a new number for every customer.

The Video object (which could include video games) also needs a key. In practice you might be able to use the product identifiers created by the

FIGURE 3.8
Initial objects for the video store. Note that the transaction has two parts, RentalTransaction and VideosRented, because many videos can be rented at one time.

Initial Objects	Key	Sample Properties	Comment
Customer	Assign CustomerID	Name Address Phone	
Video	Assign MovieID	Title RentalPrice Rating Description	
RentalTransaction	Assign TransactionID	CustomerID Date	Event/Relationship
VideosRented	TransactionID + MovieID	VideoCopy#	Event/Repeating list

publisher. For now, it is easiest to assign a separate number. Common properties would include Title, Rating, Description, and RentalPrice. More attributes can be added later if necessary.

Every transaction must be recorded. A *transaction* is an event that identifies which customer rented a video and when the rental occurred. This object refers to the base rental form and is also assigned a unique key value. Remember this approach. Almost all of the problems you encounter will end up with a table to hold data for the base form or report.

An important issue in many situations is the presence of a repeating section, which can cause problems for storing data (see "Problems with Repeating Sections"). Hence, the section is split from the main transaction and stored in its own table. Keys here include the TransactionID from the Transaction table and the VideoID. Note that the key is composite because a many-to-many relationship exists. A customer can rent many videos at one time, and a video can be rented (at different times) by more than one customer.

The VideoCopy# in the VideosRented table indicates which copy of the movie is being rented. (There can be multiple copies of each movie.) When the movie is returned, the copy number tells the manager who returned the video. Notice that you have a choice about making VideoCopy# a key. If VideoCopy# is not a key—the way it is drawn—the corresponding business assumption is that a given customer can rent many movies but only one copy of that movie. By designing the database this way, you are saying that a customer will never rent two copies of the same movie at the same time. Whether that is a reasonable assumption depends on the business. The catch is that if you build the database this way, a customer can never rent more than one copy of a given movie at a time. If a customer wanted to rent two copies, you would have to write two separate transactions.

Initial Form Evaluation

Without practice, it can be difficult to identify all four of the tables in Figure 3.9. Most people should be able to identify the Customer and Video tables. Some will recognize the need for a RentalTransaction table. However, the purpose of the VideosRented table is not as clear. Fortunately, there is a method to derive the individual tables by starting with the entire form and breaking it into pieces. This method is the data normalization

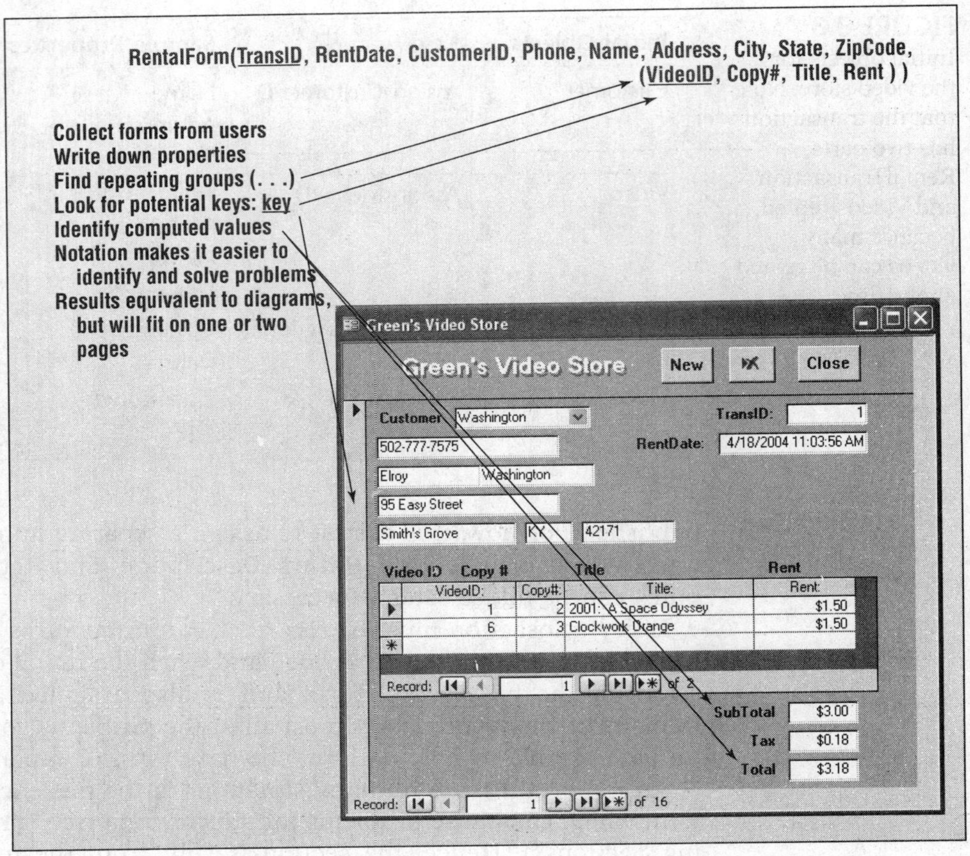

FIGURE 3.9
Initial form evaluation. Once you have collected basic user forms, you can convert them into a more compact notation. The notation makes the normalization steps easier by highlighting potential issues.

approach, and it is a mechanical process that follows from the business assumptions.

Figure 3.9 shows the first step in the evaluation. As you learn normalization, you should be careful to write out this first step. As you gain experience, you might choose to skip this step. The procedure is to look through the form or report and write down everything that you want to store. The objective is to write it in a structured format.

Give the form a name and then list the items as column names. You can generally start at the top left of the form and write a column name for each data element. Try to list items together that fall into natural groupings—such as all customer data. The RentalForm begins with the TransID, which looks like it would make a good key. The RentDate and CustomerID are listed next, followed by the basic customer data. The next step is slightly more complicated because you have to signify that the section with the videos contains repeating data. That is, it has multiple lines of data or the potential for several similar entries. Repeating data represents a one-to-many relationship that must be handled carefully. An easy way to signify the repeating section is to put it inside another set of parentheses. Some people also list it on a new line.

Observe that computed attributes (subtotal, tax, and total) were not included, since they can be recalculated when they are needed. However, in some cases you might want to store computed data. Just be careful to list the columns with the overall form—not inside the repeating data section.

Also, you should mark these items, or make a notation in the data dictionary so that you remember they are computed values.

While you are working on the first step, be sure to write down every item that you want to store in the database. In addition, make sure to identify every repeating section. Here you have to be careful. Sometimes repeating sections are obvious: They might be in a separate section, highlighted by a different color, or contain sample data so you can see the repetition. Other times, repeating sections are less obvious. For example, on large forms repeating sections might appear on separate pages. Other times, some entries might not seem to be repeating. Consider a phone number. In a business environment, some customers will have only one phone number, but others might have several phone numbers: office, work, cellular, pager, and so on. If you need to store multiple phone numbers, they become a repeating entry and should be marked. For instance, the phone numbers could be stored as (<u>PhoneType</u>, Number). You should also try to mark potential keys at this point, both to indicate repeating sections and to highlight columns that you know will contain unique data.

Problems with Repeating Sections

The reason you have to be so careful in identifying repeated sections or one-to-many relationships is that they can cause problems in the database. The situation in Figure 3.10 shows what happens when you try to store the data from the form exactly the way it is written now. The first problem with this

RentalForm(<u>TransID</u>, RentDate, CustomerID, Phone, Name, Address, City, State, ZIPCode, (<u>VideoID</u>, Copy#, Title, Rent))

Storing data in this raw form would not work very well. For example, repeating sections will cause problems.

Note the duplication of data.

Repeating section

Also, what if a customer has not yet checked out a movie—where do we store that customer's data?

Causes duplication

TransID	RentDate	CustomerID	LastName	Phone	Address	VideoID	Copy#	Title	Rent
1	4/18/04	3	Washington	502-777-7575	95 Easy Street	1	2	2001: A Space Odyssey	$1.50
1	4/18/04	3	Washington	502-777-7575	95 Easy Street	6	3	Clockwork Orange	$1.50
2	4/30/04	7	Lasater	615-888-4474	67 S. Ray Drive	8	1	Hopscotch	$1.50
2	4/30/04	7	Lasater	615-888-4474	67 S. Ray Drive	2	1	Apocalypse Now	$2.00
2	4/30/04	7	Lasater	615-888-4474	67 S. Ray Drive	6	1	Clockwork Orange	$1.50
3	4/18/04	8	Jones	615-452-1162	867 Lakeside Drive	9	1	Luggage Of The Gods	$2.50
3	4/18/04	8	Jones	615-452-1162	867 Lakeside Drive	15	1	Fabulous Baker Boys	$2.00
3	4/18/04	8	Jones	615-452-1162	867 Lakeside Drive	4	1	Boy And His Dog	$2.50
4	4/18/04	3	Washington	502-777-7575	95 Easy Street	3	1	Blues Brothers	$2.00
4	4/18/04	3	Washington	502-777-7575	95 Easy Street	8	1	Hopscotch	$1.50
4	4/18/04	3	Washington	502-777-7575	95 Easy Street	13	1	Surf Nazis Must Die	$2.50
4	4/18/04	3	Washington	502-777-7575	95 Easy Street	17	1	Witches of Eastwick	$2.00

FIGURE 3.10
Problems with repeating data. Storing repeating data with the main form results in duplicating the base data for every entry in the repeated section. In this case customer data must be entered for every video that is rented—even those rented at the same time.

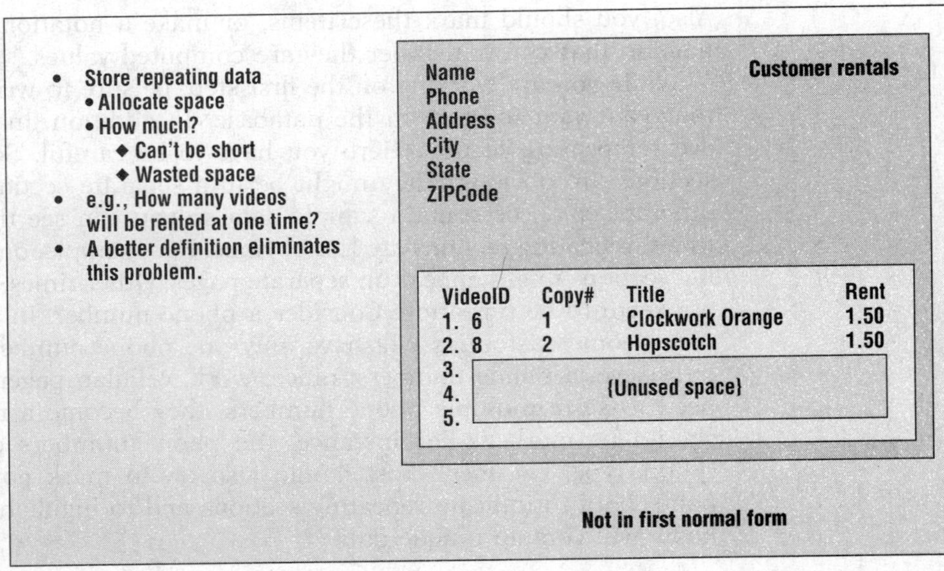

FIGURE 3.11 Allocation problems with repeating data. Storing repeating data in a hierarchical format generally forces designers to allocate a fixed amount of space for each repeating entry. There is no good way to determine how much space will be needed, so the database tends to have considerable unused space.

raw format is that it contains duplicate data. For example, every time a customer rents a video, the clerk would have to reenter the address, phone, and so on, because the repeating data is in the same table as the base data. Therefore, every video that is rented requires a copy of all the base data. Computers may be fast and have lots of memory, but it is pointless to list the customer more than once.

A related problem occurs when someone wants to become a member at the video store. Because they have not rented any videos yet, you cannot store the personal information in the database. Conversely, what if you delete old data, such as all of last year's rentals? As you delete rentals, you also delete customer data. Suddenly, you notice that you deleted half of the customer base. Technically, these problems are known as an **insertion anomaly** and a **deletion anomaly**; that is, when the data is not stored in a proper format, you encounter difficulties as you try to add or delete data. These problems arise because you tried to store all the data in one table.

Another problem with using repeating sections illustrated in Figure 3.11 resembles the problem that COBOL programmers used to encounter. In older, hierarchical files the database designer had to allocate a certain amount of space for each repeating section. In the video store case the programmer would have to allocate space for a fixed number of videos rented on each form. The challenge was to estimate the maximum number of spaces that would be needed. The problem is that if one or two customers might rent many videos (say 10 or more), the program would always allocate 10 spaces for each rental. Yet this space would go unused and be wasted for most transactions. On the other hand, failure to set aside enough spaces might cause problems and upset the best customers. Think about the issue with phone numbers again. If you do not treat them as repeating, how many columns do you need to allocate for various phone numbers, and how can you be sure you have enough? By moving the repeating data to a separate table, each entry takes one row, and you do not have to guess how many rows might be necessary. The database simply allocates a new row as it is needed.

First Normal Form

The answer to the problem with repeating sections is to put them into a separate table. When a table has no repeating groups, it is said to be in **first normal form (1NF)**. That is, for each cell in a table (one row and one column), there can be only one value. This value should be *atomic* in the sense that it cannot be decomposed into smaller pieces.

Repeating Groups

As shown in some of the prior examples, some **repeating groups** are obvious. Others are more subtle and deciding whether to split them into a separate table is more difficult. The first normalization rule is clear: If a group of items repeats, it should be split into a new table. The problem is that items that repeat in one case might not be an issue in another situation. Consider the phone number example. In many cases, you can easily include one or two columns for a phone number within a customer table (treated as nonrepeating). In a different situation, with a huge number of customers and the potential to store a widely varying set of phone numbers, the best solution is to split the phone numbers into a new table.

Return to the video store example, as shown in Figure 3.12, and notice the repeating section that is highlighted by the parentheses. To split this form, first separate everything that is not in the repeating group. These columns might need other changes later, but the section contains no repeating groups. Second, put all the columns from the repeating video rentals section into a new table. However, be careful. When you pull out a repeating section, you must bring down the key from the original table. The RentalForm table has TransID as a primary key. This key, along with the VideoID key, must become part of the new table RentalLine. You need the TransID key so that the data from the two tables can be recombined later. Note that the new table (RentalLine) will always have a composite key—signifying the many-to-many relationship between rentals and videos.

Splitting off the repeating groups solves several basic problems. First, it reduces the duplication: You no longer have to enter customer data for every video that is rented. In addition, you do not have to worry about allocating

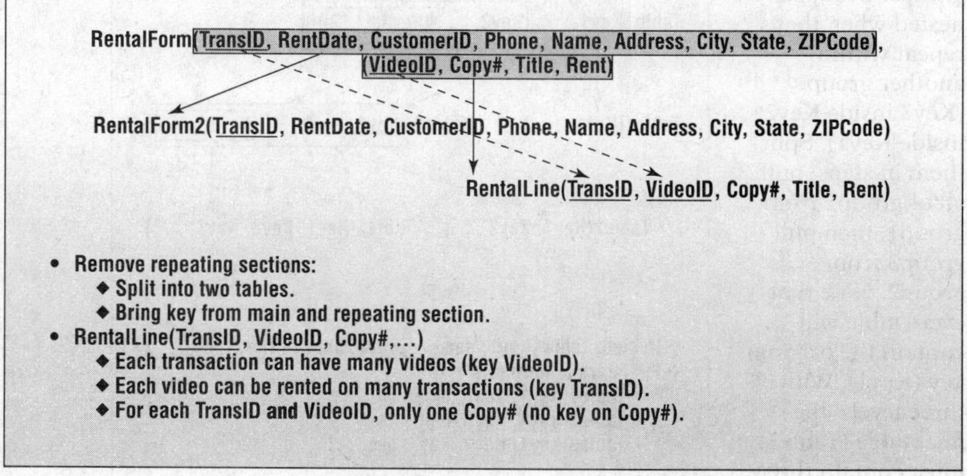

FIGURE 3.12
First normal form. All repeating groups must be split into new tables. Be sure that the new table includes a copy of the key from the original table. The table holding the repeating group must have a concatenated key so that the data can be recombined in queries.

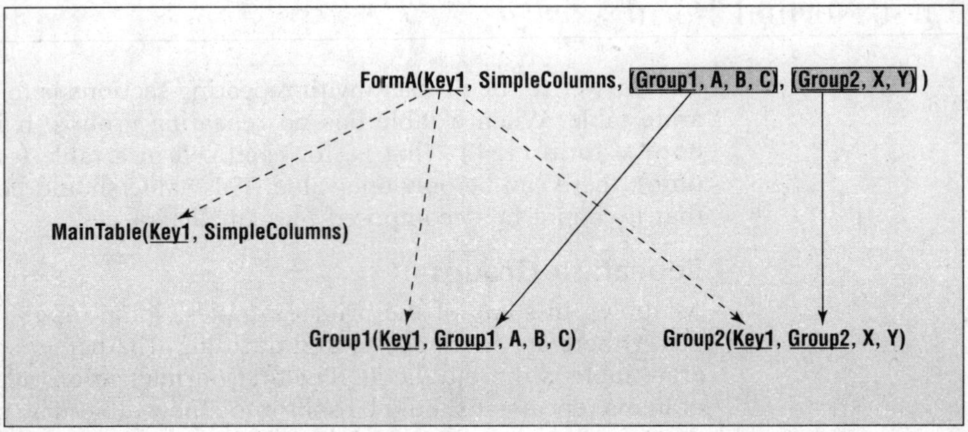

FIGURE 3.13
Independent groups. In this example, two groups are repeating independently of each other. They are split separately into new tables. Remember to include the original key (Key1) in every new table.

storage space: Each video rented will be allocated to a new row. By storing rental data for all customers in one table, you avoid the problem of allocating space for each customer.

Many forms will have several different groups that repeat. As shown in Figure 3.13, if they repeat independently of each other, the split is straightforward; each group becomes a new table. Just be careful to include the original key in every new table so the tables can be linked together later. Using the base notation, groups are independent if the parentheses do not overlap. For example, a more complex video store case would have the repeating group for the videos rented, and it might have a separate section that lists the family members related to a particular customer. The list of family members would be stored independently from the list of videos rented.

Nested Repeating Groups

More complicated situations arise when several different repeating groups occur within a table—particularly when one repeating group is nested inside another group. The greatest difficulty lies in identifying the nested nature of the groups. As illustrated in Figure 3.14, after you identify the relationships,

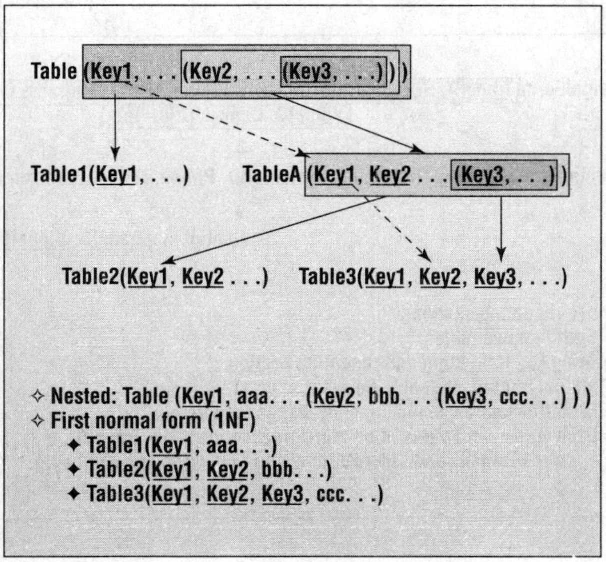

FIGURE 3.14
Nested repeating groups. Groups are nested when they repeat within another group (Key3 inside Key2 inside Key1). Split them in steps: pull all of group2 from group1, then pull group3 from group2. Note that every table will contain the original key (Key1). With three levels, the final table (Table3) must contain three columns in the key.

splitting the tables is straightforward. Just go one step at a time, pulling the outermost groups first. Always remember to bring along the prior key each time you split the tables. So when you pull the second group (Key2 . . . (Key3 . . .)) from the first group (Key1 . . .), the new TableA must include Key1 and Key2. When you pull Table3 from TableA, you must bring along all the prior keys (Key1 and Key2) and then add the third key (Key3).

A more sophisticated video database would encounter nested repeating groups. For example, the store might rent to business clients where several departments might rent videos at the same time. In this situation the rental form would have a repeating section for the departments (or family members). A second, nested repeating section for each department lists the videos rented by that department. For example, Department(<u>DepartmentID</u>, . . . (<u>VideoID</u>, . . .)).

Second Normal Form

It was straightforward to reach first normal form: Just identify the repeating groups and put them into their own table that is linked to the main table through the initial key. The next step is a little more complicated because you have to look at relationships between the key value and the other (nonkey) columns in the table. Correct specification of the keys is crucial. At this point it would be wise to double-check all the keys to make sure they are unique and that they correctly identify many-to-many relationships.

Problems with First Normal Form

You can guess by the names of the tables in Figure 3.12 that first normal form might still have problems storing data efficiently. Consider the situation in Figure 3.15 that illustrates the current Video Rental table. Every time someone rents video 6, the database stores the title *Clockwork Orange*. The problem is that the movie title depends on only part of the key (VideoID). If you know the VideoID, you always know the corresponding title. The movie title does not change with every transaction. There is an additional problem,

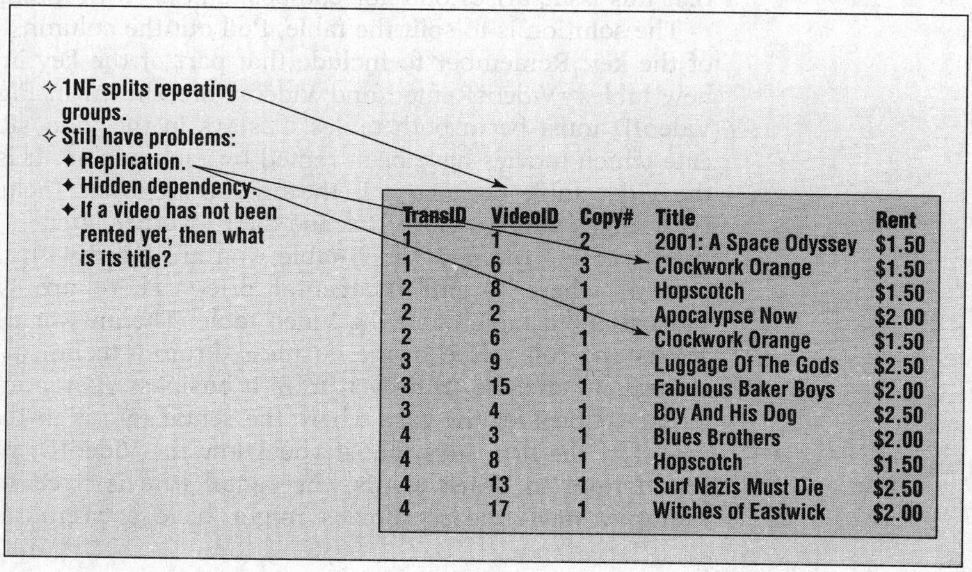

<u>TransID</u>	<u>VideoID</u>	Copy#	Title	Rent
1	1	2	2001: A Space Odyssey	$1.50
1	6	3	Clockwork Orange	$1.50
2	8	1	Hopscotch	$1.50
2	2	1	Apocalypse Now	$2.00
2	6	1	Clockwork Orange	$1.50
3	9	1	Luggage Of The Gods	$2.50
3	15	1	Fabulous Baker Boys	$2.00
3	4	1	Boy And His Dog	$2.50
4	3	1	Blues Brothers	$2.00
4	8	1	Hopscotch	$1.50
4	13	1	Surf Nazis Must Die	$2.50
4	17	1	Witches of Eastwick	$2.00

FIGURE 3.15
Problems with first normal form. There are no repeating groups, but the Video Rental table still contains duplicated data. Every time a video is rented, we have to reenter its title. Also, if a video has not yet been rented, what is its title? The problem is that the title depends only on the VideoID, not on the TransID).

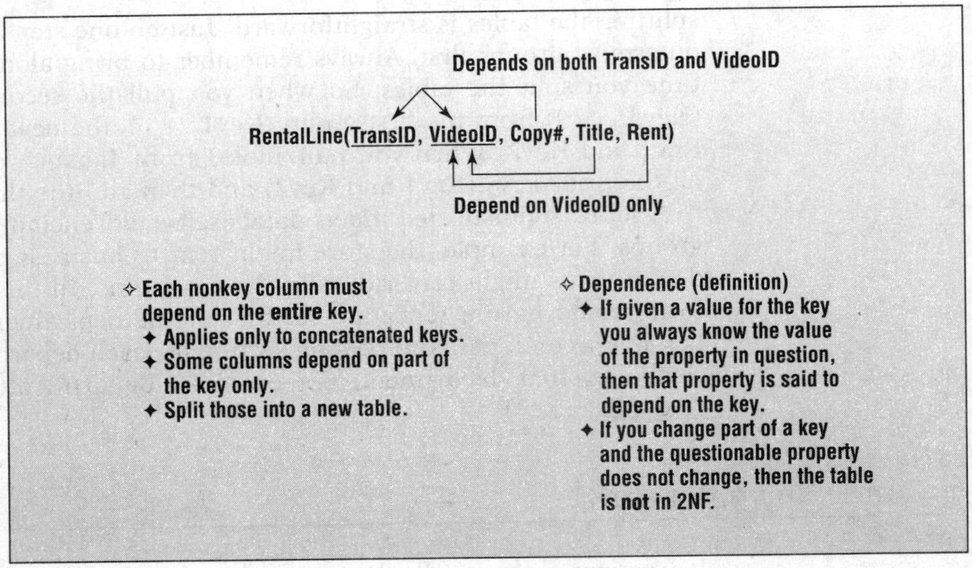

FIGURE 3.16
Second normal form definition. Each nonkey column must depend on the entire key. It is only an issue with concatenated keys. The solution is to split off the parts that only depend on part of the key.

then, besides the waste of space: If a video has not yet been rented, what is its title? Because movies are only entered into the database with a transaction, this data will not be stored in the database. Similarly, if all the rows for video 8 are deleted, you will lose all the associated information about that movie.

Second Normal Form Definition

The problem with the preceding example is that once you know the VideoID, you always know the movie title. A one-to-one relationship exists between the VideoID and the Title (perhaps many-to-one). As shown in Figure 3.16, the important point is that the transaction does not matter. If someone rents video 6 in June, the title is *Clockwork Orange*. If someone rents video 6 in December, the title is still *Clockwork Orange*. Hence, the title depends on only part of the key (the VideoID and not the TransID). A table is in **second normal form (2NF)** if every nonkey column depends on the entire key (not just part of it). Note that this issue arises only for composite keys (with multiple columns).

The solution is to split the table. Pull out the columns that depend on part of the key. Remember to include that part of the key in the new table. The new tables (VideosRented and Videos) are shown in Figure 3.17. Note that VideoID must be in both tables. It stays in the VideosRented table to indicate which movies have been rented by each person. It is the primary key in the Video table because it is the unique identifier. Including the column in both tables enables us to link the data together later.

In creating the new Video table, you are faced with the interesting question of where to put the rental price. There are two choices: in the VideosRented table or in the Video table. The answer depends on the operations and rules used in the business. From a technical standpoint you can choose either table. However, from a business standpoint there is a big difference. Consider the case where the rental rate is in the Videos table. This model of the firm says that if you know the VideoID, you always know the rental rate. In other words, the rental rate is fixed for each movie. For example, new release movies might have a premium rental rate. Now

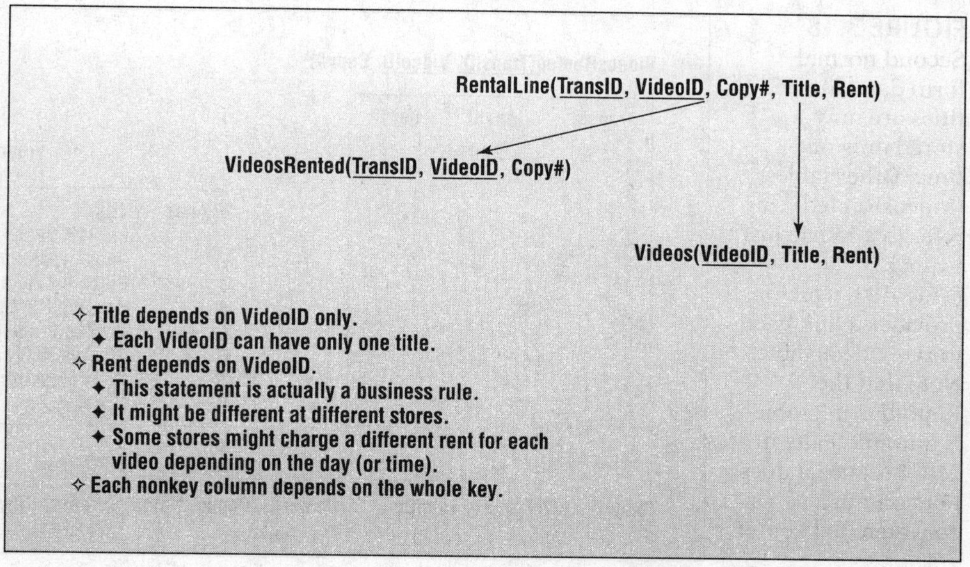

FIGURE 3.17
Creating second normal form. Split the original table so that the items that depend on only part of the key are moved to a separate table. Note that both tables must contain the VideoID key.

consider the interpretation when the rental rate is stored in the VideosRented table. Here you are explicitly saying that the rental rate depends on both the VideoID and on the specific transaction. In other words, for one customer the rental rate for *Clockwork Orange* might be $2.00, whereas another customer might pay only $1.50. The price difference might arise because you give discounts if someone rents several movies or because the store charges different prices on different days. Most business database designers quickly encounter the problem of where to store prices. One solution is to store prices in both tables. That is, the price in the Videos (product) table would be the list price. The price in the VideosRented table would be the actual rental price paid that incorporates various discounts. The key point is that the final list of tables depends not just on these mechanical rules but is also determined by the operations of the business. The assumptions you make about how a particular business operates determine the tables you get. For now, you will stick with the simpler assumption that assigns a fixed rate to each video.

Figure 3.18 gives sample data for the new tables. Notice that 2NF resolves the problem of repeating the movie title each time it is rented. The base movie data is stored one time in the Videos table. It is referenced in the VideosRented table by the VideoID. Looking through the VideosRented table, you can easily get the corresponding title by finding the matching ID in the Videos table. Chapter 4 explains how the database query system handles this link automatically.

Dependence

The discussion of 2NF (and 3NF) uses the term *depends.* That is, the attribute Y depends on X if and only if each value of X determines exactly one value of Y. In the video case, if you know the VideoID (6), there is only one corresponding movie title (*Clockwork Orange*). Similarly, if you are given a CustomerID (3), there is only one LastName (Washington).

The issue arose in 2NF by noting that if the TransID was changed, the movie title remained the same. Hence, the movie title did not depend on the

FIGURE 3.18
Second normal form data. Movie titles are now stored only one time. Other tables (VideosRented) can refer to a movie just by its key (VideoID), which provides a link back to the Videos table. Note that the RentalForm2 table is automatically in 2NF because it does not contain a concatenated key.

VideosRented(TransID, VideoID, Copy#)

TransID	VideoID	Copy#
1	1	2
1	6	3
2	2	1
2	6	1
2	8	1
3	4	1
3	9	1
3	15	1
4	3	1
4	8	1
4	13	1
4	17	1

Videos(VideoID, Title, Rent)

VideoID	Title	Rent
1	2001: A Space Odyssey	$1.50
2	Apocalypse Now	$2.00
3	Blues Brothers	$2.00
4	Boy And His Dog	$2.50
5	Brother From Another Planet	$2.00
6	Clockwork Orange	$1.50
7	Gods Must Be Crazy	$2.00
8	Hopscotch	$1.50

(Unchanged)

RentalForm2(TransID, RentDate, CustomerID, Phone, Name, Address, City, State, ZIPCode)

TransID. This dependence (or lack of it) presents the greatest difficulty to most students. Once you know the relationships in the data, normalization is mechanical. The problem lies in determining those relationships in real life. **Dependence** is an issue of business assumptions and operations. When you write down the final list of normalized tables (3NF or beyond), you have explicitly stated those business relationships.

In practice, you can generally ask clients to clarify relationships between attributes. However, avoid using terms such as *one-to-one* and *dependence*. Instead, ask questions like these: Can more than one entry occur for each item?, or Can different customers be charged different prices? However, as a database designer, you will find that you rarely have time to ask clients all the questions you want to ask. Try to identify common relationships yourself and save the difficult questions for the clients. Many business problems have similar rules and assumptions. Experience saves you time, because you will not have to ask users to spell out every rule.

Third Normal Form

The logic, analysis, and elements of designing for **third normal form (3NF)** are similar to those used in deriving 2NF. In particular, you still concentrate on the issue of dependence. With experience, most designers combine the derivation of 2NF and 3NF into a single step. Technically, a table in 3NF must also be in 2NF.

Problems with Second Normal Form

At this point, you need to examine the RentalForm2 table that was ignored in the earlier analysis. It is displayed in Figure 3.19. In particular, notice that TransID is the key. The problem can be seen in the sample data. Every time a customer rents a video, the database stores his or her name, address, and phone number again. This unnecessary duplication is a waste of space and probably a waste of the clerk's data entry time. Consider what happens when

FIGURE 3.19
Problems with second normal form. The hidden dependency in the customer data leads to duplicating the customer address each time a customer rents videos from the store. Similarly, if old transaction rows are deleted, the firm might lose all of the data for some customers.

RentalForm2(<u>TransID</u>, RentDate, CustomerID, Phone, Name, Address, City, State, ZIPCode)

TransID	RentDate	CustID	Phone	LastName	FirstName	Address	City	State	ZIPCode
1	4/18/04	3	502-777-7575	Washington	Elroy	95 Easy Street	Smith's Grove	KY	42171
2	4/30/04	7	615-888-4474	Lasater	Les	67 S. Ray Drive	Portland	TN	37148
3	4/18/04	8	615-452-1162	Jones	Charlie	867 Lakeside Drive	Castalian Springs	TN	37031
4	4/18/04	3	502-777-7575	Washington	Elroy	95 Easy Street	Smith's Grove	KY	42171

- Even in 2NF problems remain:
  - Replication.
  - Hidden dependency.
  - If a customer has not rented a video yet, where do we store the customer's personal data?
- Solution: split table.

a customer moves. You would have to find the address and change it for every transaction the customer had with us.

If the customer has not yet rented any movies, you do not have a place to store the customer data. Similarly, if you delete old transactions from the database, you risk losing customer data. Once again, you have to deal with a hidden dependency.

Third Normal Form Definition

The problems in the previous section are fairly clear. The customer name, address, phone, and so on depend on the CustomerID. The catch is that CustomerID is not part of the key for the table. In other words, some nonkey columns do not depend on the key. So why are they in this table? The question also provides the solution. If columns do not depend on the primary key, they should be placed in a separate table.

To be in 3NF a table must already be in 2NF, and every nonkey column must depend on nothing but the key. In the video example in Figure 3.20, the problem is that basic customer data columns depend on the CustomerID, which is not part of the key.

At first glance, two solutions seem possible: (1) make CustomerID part of the key or (2) split the table. If the table is already in 2NF, option (2) is the only choice that will work. The problem with the first option is that making CustomerID part of the key is equivalent to stating that each transaction can involve many customers. This assumption is not likely to be true. However, even if it is, your table would no longer be in 2NF, since the customer data would then depend on only part of the key (CustomerID and not TransID). Hence the correct solution is to split the table into two parts: the columns that depend on the whole key and the columns that depend on something else (CustomerID).

The solution in the video store example is to pull out the columns that are determined by the CustomerID. Remember to include the CustomerID column in both tables so they can be relinked later. The resulting tables are displayed in Figure 3.21. Notice that CustomerID is not a key in the Rentals

FIGURE 3.20
Third normal form definition. This table is not in 3NF, since some of the columns depend on CustomerID, which is not part of the key.

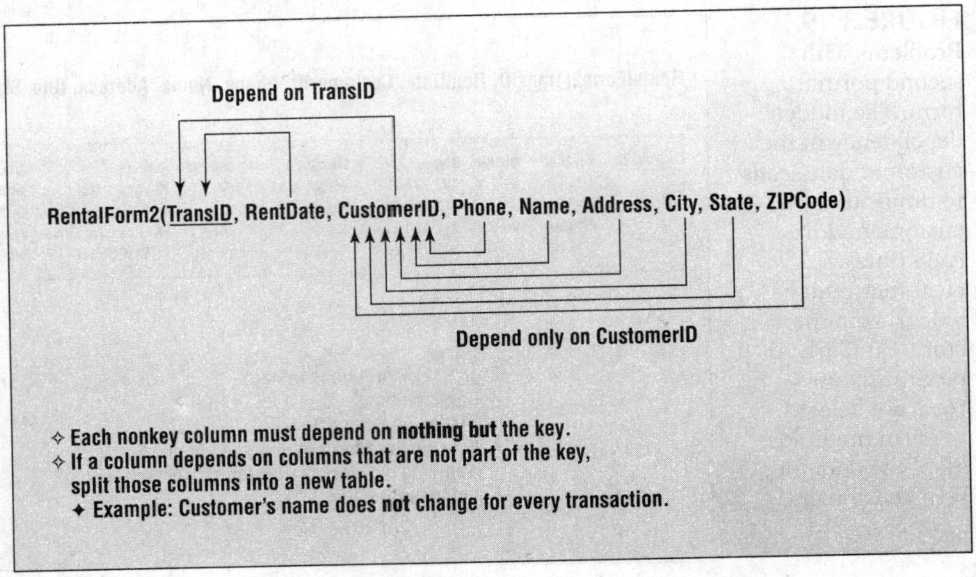

FIGURE 3.21
Third normal form. Putting customer data into a separate table eliminates the hidden dependency and resolves the problems with duplicate data. Note that CustomerID remains in both tables, but it is still not a key in the Rentals table.

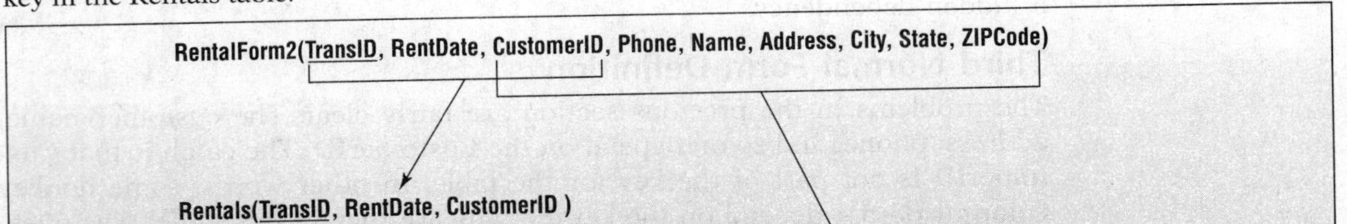

TransID	RentDate	CustomerID
1	4/18/04	3
2	4/30/04	7
3	4/18/04	8
4	4/18/04	3

CustomerID	Phone	LastName	FirstName	Address	City	State	ZIPCode
1	502-666-7777	Johnson	Martha	125 Main Street	Alvaton	KY	42122
2	502-888-6464	Smith	Jack	873 Elm Street	Bowling Green	KY	42101
3	502-777-7575	Washington	Elroy	95 Easy Street	Smith's Grove	KY	42171
4	502-333-9494	Adams	Samuel	746 Brown Drive	Alvaton	KY	42122
5	502-474-4746	Rabitz	Victor	645 White Avenue	Bowling Green	KY	42102
6	615-373-4746	Steinmetz	Susan	15 Speedway Drive	Portland	TN	37148
7	615-888-4474	Lasater	Les	67 S. Ray Drive	Portland	TN	37148
8	615-452-1162	Jones	Charlie	867 Lakeside Drive	Castalian Springs	TN	37031
9	502-222-4351	Chavez	Juan	673 Industry Blvd.	Caneyville	KY	42721
10	502-444-2512	Rojo	Maria	88 Main Street	Cave City	KY	42127

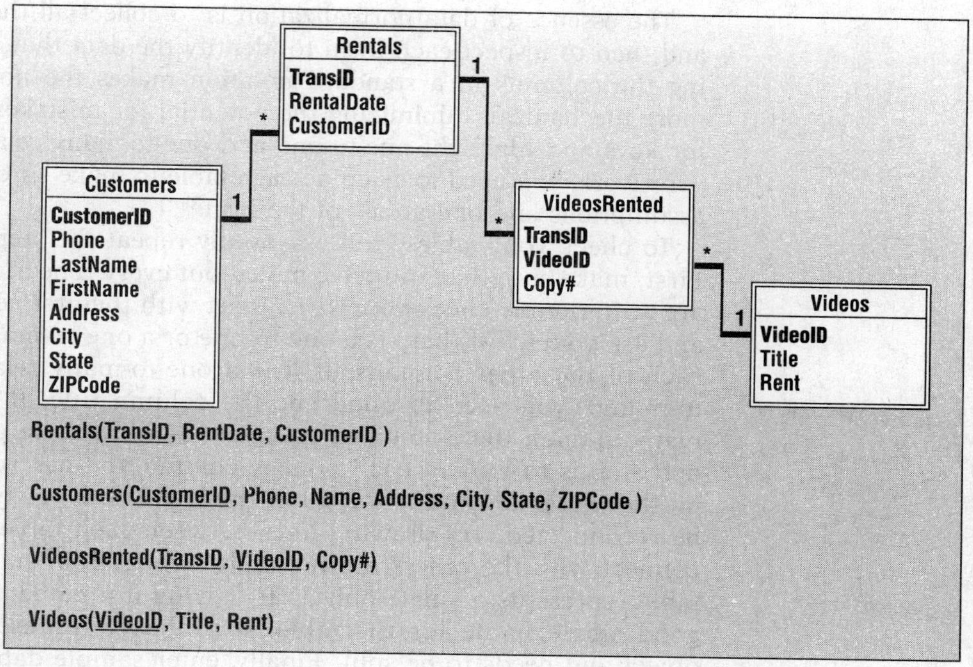

FIGURE 3.22
Third normal form tables. There are no repeating groups within a table, and each nonkey column depends on the whole key and nothing but the key.

table. Tables can be linked by columns even if they are not part of a key. Figure 3.21 also illustrates how splitting the tables resolves the problems from the hidden dependency.

The final collection of tables is presented in Figure 3.22. This list is in 3NF: There are no repeating groups within a table (1NF), and each nonkey column depends on the whole key (2NF) and nothing but the key (3NF). The tables are displayed in notational form and in a class diagram format. The class diagram was created within the Microsoft Access database management system and shows how the tables are linked together through the columns they have in common.

The astute reader should raise a question about the address data. That is, City, State, and ZipCode have some type of dependent relationship. Perhaps the Customer table is not really in 3NF? In theory, it is true, ZIP codes were created as a means to identify locations. The catch is that at a five-digit level, the relationship is relatively weak. A ZIP code identifies an individual post office. Each city can have many ZIP codes, and a ZIP code can be used for more than one city. At the moment, it is true that a ZIP code always identifies one state. However, can you be certain that this relationship will always hold—even in an international setting? Hence it is generally acceptable to include all three items in the same table. On the other hand, as pointed out in the pet store discussion in Chapter 2, there are some advantages to creating a separate City table. The most important advantage is that you can reduce data entry time and errors by selecting a city from a predefined list.

Checking Your Work

At this critical point, you must double-check your work. In large projects it is beneficial to have several team members participate in the review to make sure the assumptions used in defining the data tables match the business operations.

The essence of data normalization is to collect all the forms and reports and then to inspect each form to identify the data that will be stored. Writing the columns in a standard notation makes the normalization process more mechanical, minimizing the potential for mistakes. In particular, look for keys and highlight one-to-one and one-to-many relationships. To check your work, you need to examine each table to make sure it demonstrates the assumptions and operations of the firm.

To check your tables, you essentially repeat the steps in normalization. First, make sure that you have pulled out every repeating group. While you are at it, double-check your keys. Start with the first key column in a table and ask yourself if there is a one-to-one or a one-to-many relationship with each of the other columns. If it is a one-to-many relationship (or many-to-many), you need to underline the column title. If it is one-to-one (or many-to-one), the column in question should not be underlined. The second step is to look at each nonkey column and ask yourself if it depends on the whole key and nothing but the key. Third, verify that the tables can be reconnected. Try drawing lines between each table. Tables that do not connect with the others are probably wrong. Fourth, ask yourself if each table represents a single object. Try giving it a name. If you cannot find a good single name for the table, it probably represents more than one object and needs to be split. Finally, enter sample data for each table and make sure that you are not entering duplicate rows. Some underlying problems may become obvious when you begin to enter data. It is best to enter test data during the design stage, instead of waiting until the final implementation.

Beyond Third Normal Form

In designing relational database theory, E. F. Codd first proposed the three normalization rules. On examining real-world situations, he and other writers realized that additional problems could occur in some situations. In particular, Codd's initial formal definition of 3NF was probably too narrow. Hence he and Boyce defined a new version, which is called **Boyce-Codd normal form (BCNF)**.

Other writers eventually identified additional problems that could arise and created further "normal forms." Fortunately, these situations do not arise often in practice. If you are careful in designing your database—particularly in creating keys—you should not have too many problems with these issues. However, occasionally problems arise, so a good database designer will check for the problems described in the following sections. In particular, in large projects with many designers, one member of the team should check the final list of tables.

Boyce-Codd Normal Form

You have already seen how problems can arise when hidden dependencies occur within a table. A secondary relationship between columns within a table can cause problems with duplication and lost data. Consider the example in Figure 3.23, which contains data about employees. From the business rules, it is clear that the table is in 3NF. The keys are correct, and from rule (*c*) the nonkey column (Manager) depends on the entire key. That is, each

FIGURE 3.23
Boyce-Codd normal form. There is a hidden dependency (*d*) between manager and specialty. If we delete rows from the original table, we risk losing data about our managers. The solution is to add a table to make the dependency explicit. For flexibility, it might be wise to leave the original table—just in case the assumptions change.

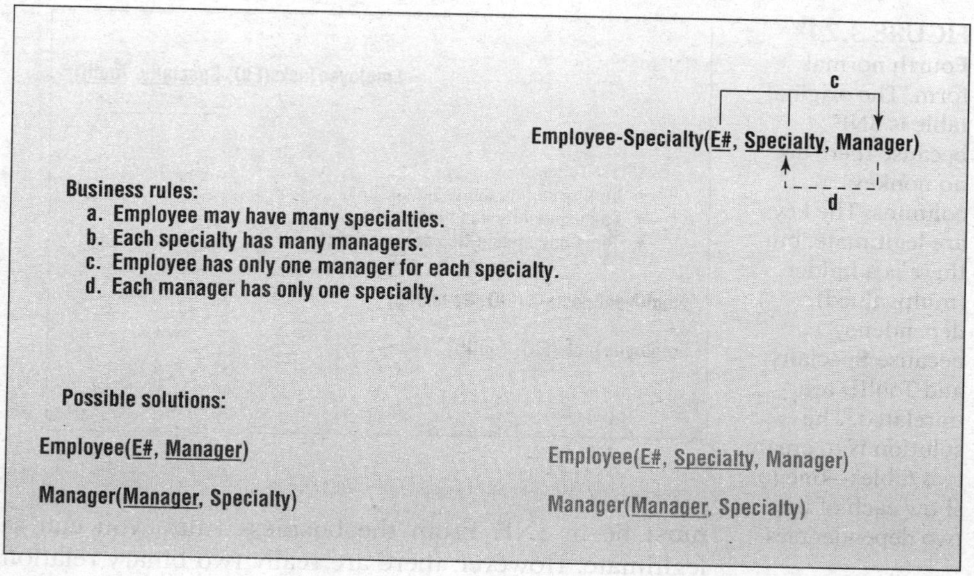

employee can have a different manager for each specialty. The problem arises because of business rule (*d*): Each manager has only one specialty. The manager determines the specialty, but since Manager can never be a key for the entire table, you have a **hidden dependency** (Manager → Specialty) in the table. What if you delete old data rows and delete all references to one manager? Then you lose the data that revealed that manager's specialty. The BCNF prevents this problem by stating that any dependency must be explicitly shown in the keys.

The solution is to add a table to make the dependency explicit. Because each specialty can have many managers, the best solution is to add the table Manager(<u>Manager</u>, Specialty). Note that technically, you can now remove the Specialty column from the original table (and key Manager). Because a manager can have only one specialty, as soon as you know the manager, you can use a link to obtain the specialty. However, the database is more flexible if you retain the three columns in the original table, even though it results in some duplication of data. The reason is that it takes some unusual assumptions to cause this particular problem. If these assumptions change, you would have to change the tables. In the example it is not very realistic to believe the firm will always have managers with only one specialty. It is better to leave the original table and add the new Manager table. Then if the assumptions change, you simply need to make Specialty a key in the Manager table. The main point is that you have explicitly recorded the hidden relationship—so you no longer need to worry about losing important relationships when you delete rows.

Fourth Normal Form

Fourth normal form (4NF) problems arise when there are two binary relationships, but the modeler attempts to show them as one combined relationship. An example should clarify the situation.

In Figure 3.24, employees can have many specialties, and they perform many tasks for each specialty. Because all three columns are keyed, the table

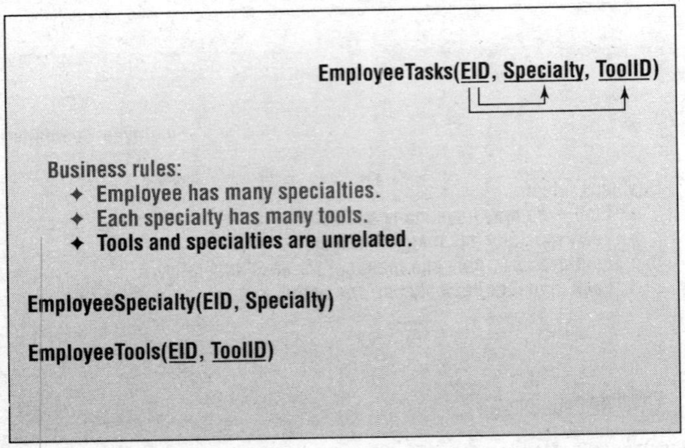

FIGURE 3.24
Fourth normal form. The original table is 3NF because there are no nonkey columns. The keys are legitimate, but there is a hidden (multivalued) dependency because Specialty and ToolID are unrelated. The solution is to create two tables—one to show each of the two dependencies.

must be in 3NF. From the business rules, you can see that the keys are legitimate. However, there are really two binary relationships instead of one ternary relationship: Employee → Specialty and Employee → Tool.

Since the third business rule specifies that Specialty and ToolID are not directly dependent on each other, you need to break up the original table into two tables to remove the hidden dependency. The problem you would face with the original is that there could be considerable duplication of data if for every employee you have to list each tool for every specialty. It is more efficient to list specialties and tools separately.

Fourth normal form problems are relatively rare in practice. However, they can occur and they can cause problems, so you should be able to spot them. The main trick is to watch for hidden dependencies, and make sure they are made explicit.

Domain-Key Normal Form

In 1981 Fagin described a different approach to normalized tables when he proposed the **domain-key normal form (DKNF)**. This describes the ultimate goal in designing a database. If a table is in DKNF, Fagin proved that it must also be in 4NF, 3NF, and all of the other normal forms. The catch is that there is no defined method to get a table into DKNF. In fact, it is possible that some tables can never be converted to DKNF.

Despite these difficulties, DKNF is important for application developers because it is a goal to work toward when designing applications. Think of it as driving to the mall when you do not have exact directions. You can still get there as long as you know how to start (1NF, 2NF, and 3NF are well-defined) and can recognize the mall when you arrive (DKNF).

The goal of DKNF is to have each table represent one topic and for all the business rules to be expressed in terms of domain constraints and key relationships. That is, all business rules are explicitly described by the table rules. Domain constraints are straightforward—they represent limitations placed on the data held in a column. For example, prices cannot be negative.

All other business rules must be expressed in terms of relationships with keys. In particular, there can be no hidden relationships. Consider the example in Figure 3.25, which shows a table for students and advisors. It could be

FIGURE 3.25
DKNF example. The tables are not in DKNF. Because a student can have more than one major, SID would not be a unique primary key. Also, Advisor is related to Major, which is a hidden relationship.

```
Student(SID, Name, Major, Advisor)
Advisor(FID, Name, Office, Discipline)

Business rules: A student can have many advisors,
but only one for each major.
  Faculty can be advisors for only their discipline.
```

in DKNF—you do not know until you examine the business rules. A typical university rule might be that a student can have multiple advisors, but only one for each major. Additionally, faculty members can be advisors only for students majoring in the instructor's discipline. With these two rules the two tables are clearly not in DKNF. First, the primary key SID would not be unique. Second, there must be an explicit rule concerning the major and discipline. Figure 3.26 shows three new tables that are in DKNF. Notice that all of the business rules are now explicitly stated in terms of the primary key and foreign key relationships.

To define a set of tables in DKNF, you can start by working through the 3NF rules. Then be sure that you have a complete list of the business rules. Next make certain that the business rules are all expressed in terms of domain constraints and key relationships. Check the primary keys to be sure they are unique—and that you have captured all of the many-to-many relationships. Be sure there are no hidden rules or dependencies. Set foreign key relationships to enforce existence rules and to match data in other tables.

Domain-key normal form returns to the beginning of Chapter 2. The goal in designing the database is to build a model of the organization, and DKNF clarifies this goal by stating that the best database design is one that explicitly states all business rules as database rules.

In theory, there can be no normal forms beyond DKNF. That is a nice theory, but since there is no well-defined way to put a set of tables in DKNF, it is not always helpful. Several authors have identified other potential problems and derived additional versions of normal forms, such as fifth normal form. For the most part these definitions are not very useful in practice; they will not be described here. You can consult C. J. Date's textbooks for details and examples of more theoretical concepts.

FIGURE 3.26
DKNF solution. Splitting the tables makes the primary keys unique. The previously hidden relationship between Major and Discipline is made explicit through a foreign key constraint.

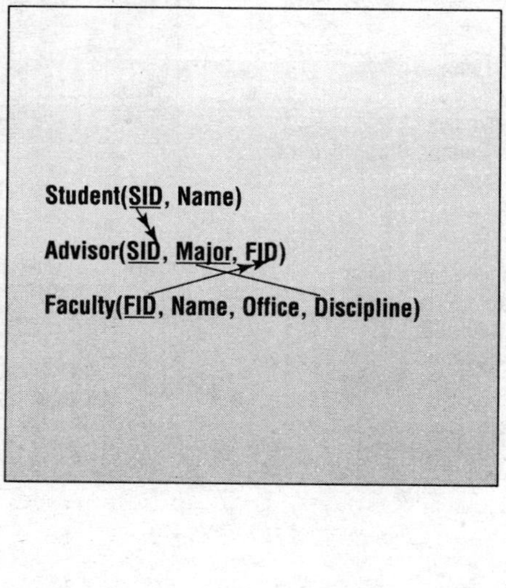

Data Rules and Integrity

As you talk to users and managers to design reports and tables, you also need to think about what business rules need to be enforced. One of the goals of a database designer is to ensure that the data remains accurate. In many cases there are straightforward business rules. For example, you typically want to make sure that price is greater than zero. Similarly, you may have a constraint that salaries should not exceed some number like $100,000 or that the date hired has to be greater than the date the company was founded. These **data integrity** constraints are easy to assign in most databases. Typically, you can go to the table definitions and add the simple constraints along with a message. The advantage of storing these constraints with the tables is that the DBMS enforces the conditions for every operation on the table, regardless of the source or method of data entry. No programming is necessary, and the constraint is stored in one location. If you need to change the condition, it is readily accessible (to authorized users).

A second type of constraint is to choose data from a set of predefined options. For example, gender may be listed as male, female, or unavailable. Providing a list helps clerks enter data, and it forces them to enter only the choices provided. For example, you do not have to worry whether someone might enter *f*, *F*, or *fem*. The data is more consistent.

A third type of data integrity is a bit more complicated but crucial in a relational database. The tables are nicely organized with properties that ensure efficient storage of the data. Yet you need to be able to reconnect the data in the tables to get the reports and forms the users need. Consider the video store example in Figure 3.27 when a clerk enters a customer number in the Rentals table. What happens if the clerk enters a customer number that does not exist in the Customer table? If the videotapes were not returned, you would have no way of finding the customer. Hence you need a constraint to ensure that when a customer number is entered into the Rentals table, that number must already exist in the Customer table. The

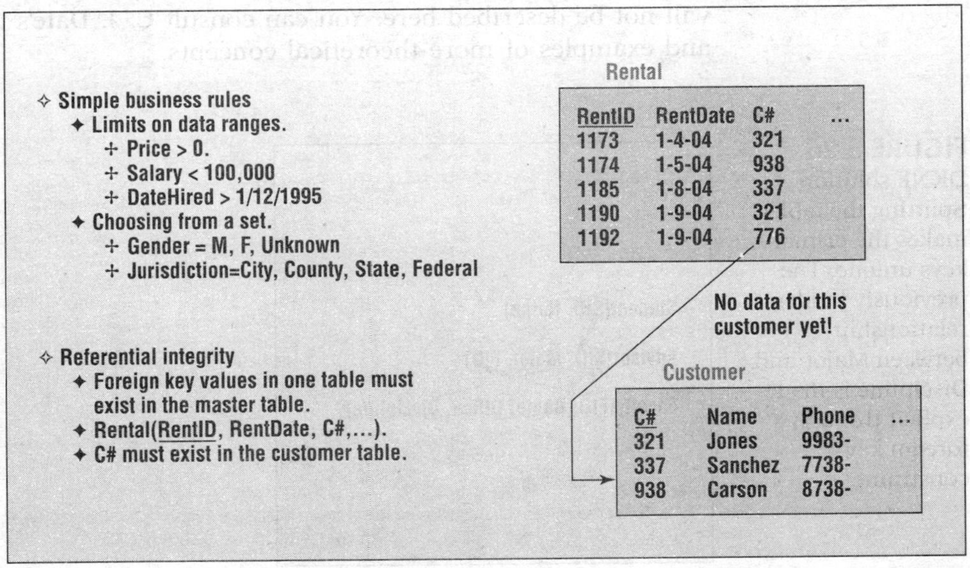

FIGURE 3.27 Data integrity. Integrity can be maintained by simple rules. Relational databases rely on referential integrity constraints to ensure that customer data exists before the customer number can be entered in the Rental table.

FIGURE 3.28
SQL referential integrity definition. In the Order table, declaring a column as a foreign key tells the DBMS to check each value in this table to find a matching value in the referenced (e.g., Customer) table.

```
CREATE TABLE Order
( OID     NUMBER(5) NOT NULL,
  Odate   DATE,
  CID     NUMBER(5),
          CONSTRAINT pk_Customer
            PRIMARY KEY (OID),
          CONSTRAINT fk_Customer
            FOREIGN KEY (CID)
            REFERENCES Customer (CID)
            ON DELETE CASCADE
)
```

CustomerID in the Rentals table is a foreign key in that table, and the constraint you need is known as referential integrity. **Referential integrity** exists when a value for a foreign key can be entered only if the corresponding value already exists in the originating table.

Essentially, once you define the relationship between tables, you can tell the DBMS to enforce referential integrity. The method for defining referential integrity depends on the specific DBMS. In Access, these relationships are built and displayed using a version of a class diagram where the connecting line indicates the referential integrity constraint. Most relational databases also support **cascading delete**, which uses the same concepts. If a user deletes a row in the Customer table, you also need to delete the related entries in the Rentals table. Then you need to delete the corresponding rows in the VideosRented table. If you build the relationships and specify cascade on delete, the database will automatically delete the related rows when a user deletes an entry in the Customer table. These actions maintain the consistency of the database by ensuring that links between the tables always refer to legitimate rows.

Oracle and SQL Server support referential integrity by declaring a foreign key when you create the VideosRented table. Figure 3.28 shows the command that can be used to create an Order table with three columns. The company wants to make sure that all orders are sent to legitimate customers, so the customer number (CID) in the Order table must exist in the Customer table. The foreign key constraint enforces this relationship. The constraint also specifies that the relationship should handle cascading deletes. Oracle and SQL Server use the standard SQL language to create tables.

When you start to enter data into a DBMS, you will quickly see the role played by referential integrity. Consider two tables: Order(<u>OrderID</u>, Odate, CustomerID) and Customer(<u>CustomerID</u>, Name, Address, etc.). You have a referential integrity constraint that links the CustomerID column in the Order table to the CustomerID column in the Customer table. Now say you enter sample data in the two tables, but you begin with the Order table. The DBMS will not accept any data because the corresponding CustomerID must already exist in the Customer table. That is, the referential integrity rules force you to enter data in a certain order. Clearly, these rules would present problems to users, so you cannot expect users to enter data directly into tables. Chapters 6, 7, and 8 explain how forms and applications will automatically ensure that the user enters data in the proper sequence.

FIGURE 3.29
Database design for a soccer league. The design and normalized tables depend on the business rules.

Location Date Played					Referee Name Phone Number, Address				
Team 1 Name Sponsor	Score				Team 2 Name Sponsor		Score		
Player Name	Phone	Age	Points	Penalties	Player Name	Phone	Age	Points	Penalties

The Effects of Business Rules

It is important to understand how different business rules affect the database design and the normalization process. As a database designer, you must identify the basic rules and build the database to match them. However, be careful because business rules can change. If you think a current business rule is too restrictive, you should design the database with a more flexible structure.

Consider the example shown in Figure 3.29. The local parks and recreation department runs a soccer league and collects basic statistics at the end of every match. You need to design the data tables for this problem.

To illustrate the effect of different rules, consider the two main rules and the resulting tables displayed in Figure 3.30. The first rule states that there can be only one referee per match. Hence the RefID can be placed in the Match table. Note that it is not part of the primary key. The second rule states that a player can play on only one team; therefore, the appropriate TeamID can be placed in the Player table.

Now consider what happens if these two rules are relaxed as shown in Figure 3.31. The department manager believes that some day there might

FIGURE 3.30
Restrictive rules. With only one referee per match, the referee key is added to the Match table. Similarly, the TeamID column is placed in the Player table.

There is one referee per match.
A player can play on only one team.

Match(MatchID, DatePlayed, Location, RefID)
Score(MatchID, TeamID, Score)
Referee(RefID, Phone, Address)
Team(TeamID, Name, Sponsor)
Player(PlayerID, Name, Phone, DoB, TeamID)
PlayerStats(MatchID, PlayerID, Points, Penalties)

FIGURE 3.31
Relaxing the rules to allow many-to-many relationships. You might try to make the RefID and TeamID columns part of the primary key, but the resulting tables are not in 3NF. Location does not depend on RefID, and Player Name does not depend on TeamID.

There can be several referees per match. A player can play on only several teams (substitute), but only on one team per match.

Match(MatchID, DatePlayed, Location, RefID)
Score(MatchID, TeamID, Score)
Referee(RefID, Phone, Address)
Team(TeamID, Name, Sponsor)
Player(PlayerID, Name, Phone, DoB, TeamID)
PlayerStats(MatchID, PlayerID, Points, Penalties)

be several referees per match. Also, the issue of substitute players presents a problem. A substitute might play on several different teams in a season—but only for one team during a match. To handle these new rules, the key values must change. You might be tempted to make the simple changes indicated in Figure 3.31; that is, make RefID part of the key in the Match table and make TeamID part of the primary key in the Player table. Now each Match can have many Referees, and each Player can play on many teams. The problem with this approach is that the Match and Player tables are no longer in 3NF. For example, DatePlayed does not depend on RefID. Likewise, Name in the Player table does not depend on the TeamID. For example, Paul Ruiz does not change his name every time he plays on a different team.

The solution is displayed in Figure 3.32. A new table is added to handle the many-to-many relationship between referees and matches. Similarly, the player's TeamID is moved to the PlayerStats table, but it is not part of the primary key. In this solution, each match has many players, and players can participate in many matches. Yet, for each match, each player plays for only one team. This new database design is different from the initial design. More importantly, it is less restrictive. As a designer, you must look ahead and build the database so that it can handle the future needs of the department.

Which of these database designs is correct? The answer depends on the needs of the department. In practice, it would be wiser to choose the more flexible design that can assign several referees to a match and allows players to substitute for different teams throughout the season. However, in practice you should make one minor change to this database design. If no matches have been played, how do you know which players are on each team? As it stands, the database cannot answer this question. The solution is to add a BaseTeamID to the Player table. At the start of the season, each team will submit a roster that lists the initial team members. Players can be listed on only one initial team roster. If someone substitutes or changes teams, the data can be recorded in the PlayerStats table.

FIGURE 3.32
Relaxing the rules and normalizing the tables. The RefereeMatch table enables the department to have more than one referee per match. Moving the TeamID to the PlayerStats table indicates that someone can play for more than one team—but for only one team during a given match.

Match(MatchID, DatePlayed, Location)
RefereeMatch(MatchID, RefID)
Score(MatchID, TeamID, Score)
Referee(RefID, Phone, Address)
Team(TeamID, Name, Sponsor)
Player(PlayerID, Name, Phone, DoB)
PlayerStats(MatchID, PlayerID, TeamID, Points, Penalties)

Converting a Class Diagram to Normalized Tables

Each normalized table represents a business entity or class. Hence a class diagram can be converted into a list of normalized tables. Likewise, a list of normalized tables can be drawn as a class diagram. Technically, the entities in a class diagram do not have to be in 3NF (or higher). Some designers use a class diagram as an overview, or big picture, of the business, and they leave out some of the normalized details. In this situation you will have to convert the classes into a list of normalized tables. As noted in Chapter 2, some features commonly arise on a class diagram, so you should learn how to handle these basic conversions.

Figure 3.33 illustrates a typical class diagram for a purchase order with four basic types of relationships: (1) a one-to-many relationship between supplier and the purchase order, (2) a many-to-many relationship between the purchase order and the items, (3) a subtype relationship that contains different attributes, and (4) a recursive relationship within the Employee entity to indicate that some employees are managers of others.

One-to-Many Relationships

The most important rule in converting class diagrams to normalized tables is that relationships are handled by placing a common column in each of the related tables. This column is usually a key column in one of the tables. This process is easy to see with one-to-many relationships.

The purchase order example has two one-to-many relationships. (1) Many different purchase orders can be sent to each supplier, but only one supplier appears on a purchase order. (2) Each purchase order is created by only one employee, but an employee can create many purchase orders. To create the normalized tables, first create a primary key for each entity (Supplier, Employee, and PurchaseOrder). As shown in Figure 3.34, the normalized tables can be linked by placing the Supplier key (SID) and Employee key (EID) into the PurchaseOrder table. Note carefully that all class diagram associations are expressed as relationships between keys.

Note also that SID and EID are not key columns in the PurchaseOrder table. You can verify which columns should be keyed. Start with the POID column. For each PurchaseOrder (POID), how many suppliers are there? The

FIGURE 3.33
Converting a class diagram to normalized tables. Note the four types of relationships: (1) one-to-many, (2) many-to-many, (3) subtype, and (4) recursive.

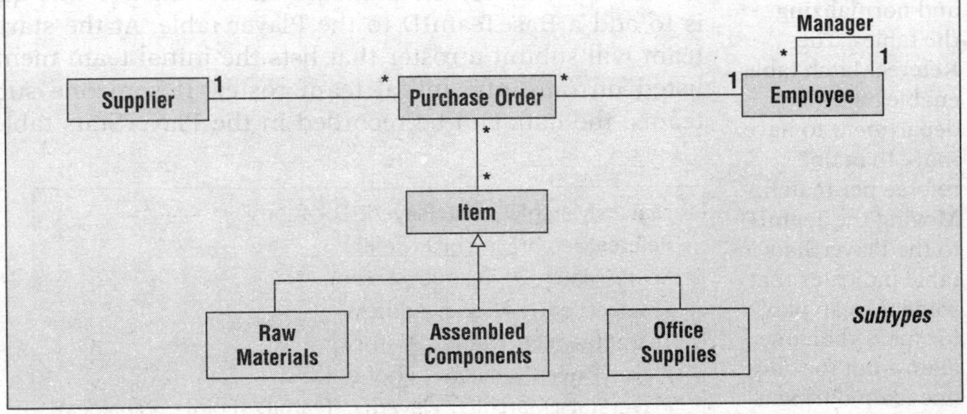

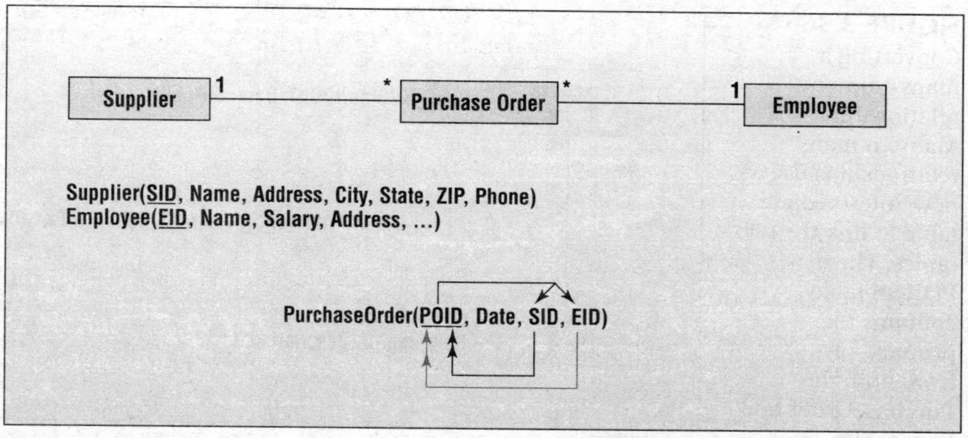

FIGURE 3.34 Converting one-to-many relationships. Add the primary key from the one-side into the many-side table. In the example SID and EID are added to the PurchaseOrder table. Note that they are not primary keys in the PurchaseOrder table.

business rule says only one supplier for a purchase order; therefore, SID should not be keyed, so do not underline SID. Now start with SID and work in the other direction. For each supplier, how many purchase orders are there? The business rule says many purchase orders can be sent to a given supplier, so the PID column needs to be a key. The same process indicates that EID should not be a key; it belongs in the PurchaseOrder table, since each Employee can place many orders. Figure 3.35 uses sample data to show how the tables are linked through the key columns.

Supplier

SID	Name	Address	City	State	ZIP	Phone
5676	Jones	123 Elm	Ames	IA	50010	515-777-8988
6731	Markle	938 Oak	Boston	MA	02109	617-222-9999
7831	Paniche	873 Hickory	Jackson	MS	39205	601-333-9932
8872	Swensen	773 Poplar	Wichita	KS	67209	316-999-3312

PurchaseOrder

POID	Date	SID	EID
22234	9-9-2004	5676	221
22235	9-10-2004	5676	554
22236	9-10-2004	7831	221
22237	9-11-2004	8872	335

Employee

EID	Name	Salary	Address
221	Smith	67,000	223 W. 2300
335	Sanchez	82,000	37 W. 7200
554	Johnson	35,000	440 E. 5200

FIGURE 3.35 Sample data for one-to-many relationships. The Supplier and PurchaseOrder tables are linked through the SID column. Similarly, the Employee table is linked through the data in the EID column. Both the SID and EID columns are foreign keys in the PurchaseOrder table, but they are not primary keys in that table.

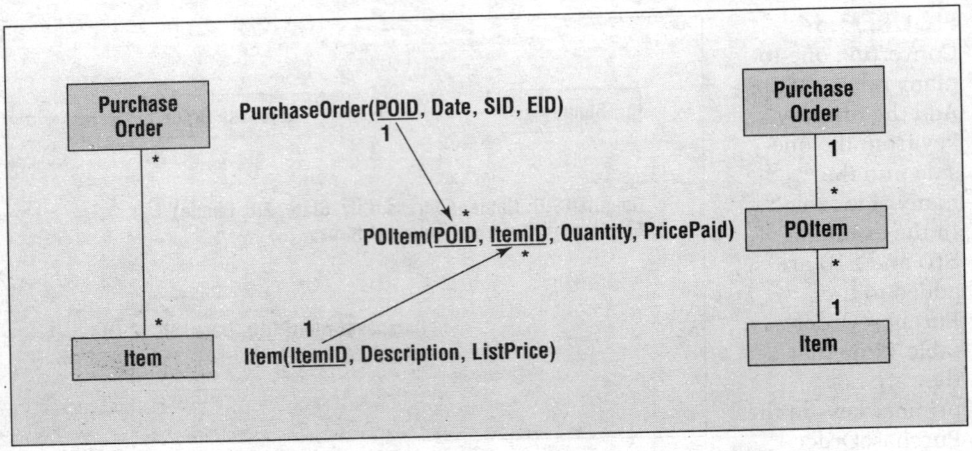

FIGURE 3.36
Converting a many-to-many relationship. Many-to-many relationships use a new, intermediate table to link the two tables. The new POItem table contains the primary keys from both the PurchaseOrder and Item tables.

Many-to-Many Relationships

Overview class diagrams often contain many-to-many relationships. However, in a relational database many-to-many relationships must be split into two one-to-many relationships to get to BCNF. Figure 3.36 illustrates the process with the PurchaseOrder and Item tables.

Each of the two initial entities becomes a table (PurchaseOrder and Item). The next step is to create a new table (POItem) that contains the primary keys from both of the other tables (POID and ItemID). This table represents the many-to-many relationship. Each purchase order (POID) can contain many items, so ItemID must be a key. Similarly, each item can be ordered on many purchase orders, so POID must be a key.

You must have a table that contains both POID and ItemID as keys. Can you create this relationship without creating a third table? In most cases the answer is no. Consider what happens if you try to put the ItemID column into the PurchaseOrder table and make it part of the primary key. The resulting entity would not be a 3NF table, because Date, SID, and EID do not depend on the ItemID. A similar problem arises if you try to place the POID key into the Item table. Hence the intermediate table is required. Figure 3.37 uses sample data to show how the three tables are linked through the keys.

N-ary Associations

As noted in Chapter 2, n-ary associations are denoted with a diamond. This diamond association also becomes a class. In a sense, an n-ary association is simply a set of several binary associations. As shown in Figure 3.38, the new association class holds the primary key from each of the other classes. As long as the binary associations are one-to-many, each column in the Assembly class will be part of the primary key. If for some reason a binary association is one-to-one, then the corresponding column would not be keyed.

Generalization or Subtypes

Some business entities are created as subtypes. Figure 3.39 illustrates this relationship with the Item entity. An item is a generic description of something that is purchased. Every item has a description and a list price. However, the company deals with three types of items: raw materials, assembled components, and office supplies. Each of these subtypes has some additional properties that you wish to track. For example, the company tracks the

PurchaseOrder

POID	Date	SID	EID
22234	9-9-2004	5676	221
22235	9-10-2004	5676	554
22236	9-10-2004	7831	221
22237	9-11-2004	8872	335

POItem

POID	ItemID	Quantity	PricePaid
22234	444098	3	2.00
22234	444185	1	25.00
22235	444185	4	24.00
22236	555828	10	150.00
22236	555982	1	5,800.00

Item

ItemID	Description	ListPrice
444098	Staples	2.00
444185	Paper	28.00
555828	Wire	158.00
555982	Sheet steel	5,928.00
888371	Brake assembly	152.00

FIGURE 3.37
Sample data for the many-to-many relationship. Note that the intermediate POItem table links the other two tables. Verify that the three tables are in 3NF, where each nonkey column depends on the whole key and nothing but the key.

weight of raw materials, the dimension of assembled components, and quantity discounts for office supplies.

In converting this design to a relational database, there are two basic approaches. (1) If subtypes are similar, you could ignore the subclasses and compress all the subclasses into the main class that would contain every property for all of the subclasses. In this case each item entry would have several null values. (2) In most cases a better approach is to create separate tables for each subclass. Each table will contain the primary key from the main Item class.

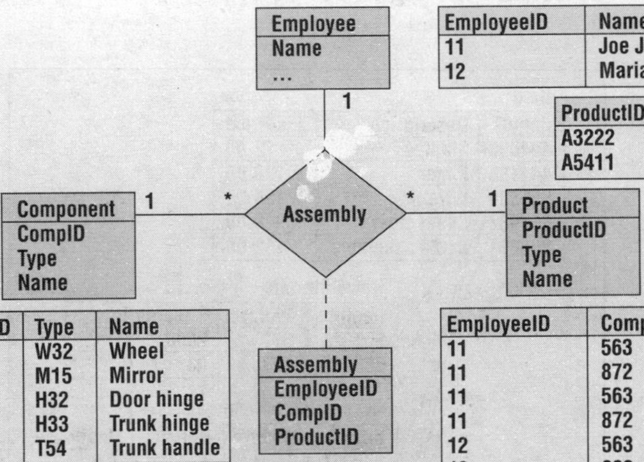

EmployeeID	Name	...
11	Joe Jones	...
12	Maria Rio	...

ProductID	Type	Name
A3222	X32	Corvette
A5411	B17	Camaro

CompID	Type	Name
563	W32	Wheel
872	M15	Mirror
882	H32	Door hinge
883	H33	Trunk hinge
888	T54	Trunk handle

EmployeeID	CompID	ProductID
11	563	A3222
11	872	A3222
11	563	A5411
11	872	A5411
12	563	A3222
12	882	A3222
12	888	A3222
12	883	A5411

FIGURE 3.38
N-ary association. The Assembly association is also a class. It can be modeled as a set of binary (one-to-many) associations. The primary key from each of the main classes is included in the new Assembly class.

FIGURE 3.39
Converting subtypes. Every item purchased has basic attributes, which are recorded in the Item table. Each item can be placed in one of three categories, which have different attributes. To convert these relationships to 3NF, create new tables for each subtype. Use the same key in the new tables and in the generic table. Add attributes specific to each of the subtypes.

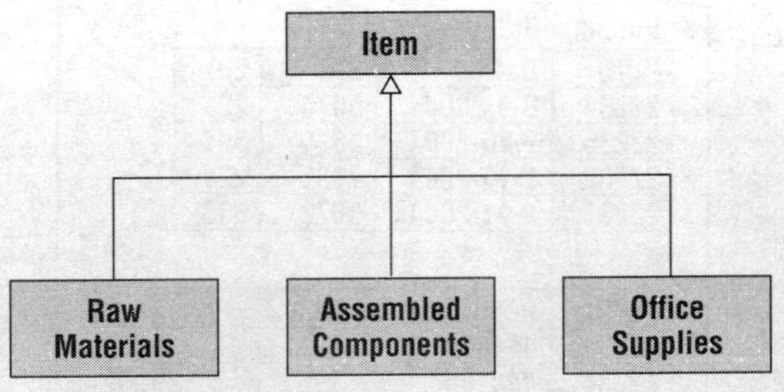

Item(ItemID, Description, ListPrice)

RawMaterials(ItemID, Weight, StrengthRating)

AssembledComponents(ItemID, Width, Height, Depth)

OfficeSupplies(ItemID, BulkQuantity, Discount)

As shown in Figure 3.40, each item has an entry in the Item table. There is another entry in one of the three subtype tables, depending on the specific item. For example, item 444098 is described in the Item table and has additional data in the OfficeSupplies table.

If the subclass relationships are not mutually exclusive, then each main item can have a matching row in more than one of the subclass tables.

Composition

In some ways composition is a combination of an n-ary association and subtypes. Consider the bicycle example in Figure 3.41, in which a bicycle is built from various components. The first decision to make is how to handle the many components. It is a question of subtypes. In this situation the business keeps almost identical data for each component (ID number, description, weight, cost, list price, and so on). Hence a good solution is to

FIGURE 3.40
Sample data for the subtype relationships. Notice how each Item has an entry in the Item table and a row in one of the three subtype tables.

Item

ItemID	Description	ListPrice
444098	Staples	2.00
444185	Paper	28.00
555828	Wire	158.00
555982	Sheet steel	5928.00
888371	Brake assembly	152.00

RawMaterials

ItemID	Weight	StrengthRating
555828	57	2000
555982	2578	8321

AssembledComponents

ItemID	Width	Height	Depth
888371	1	3	1.5

OfficeSupplies

ItemID	BulkQuantity	Discount
444098	20	10%
444185	10	15%

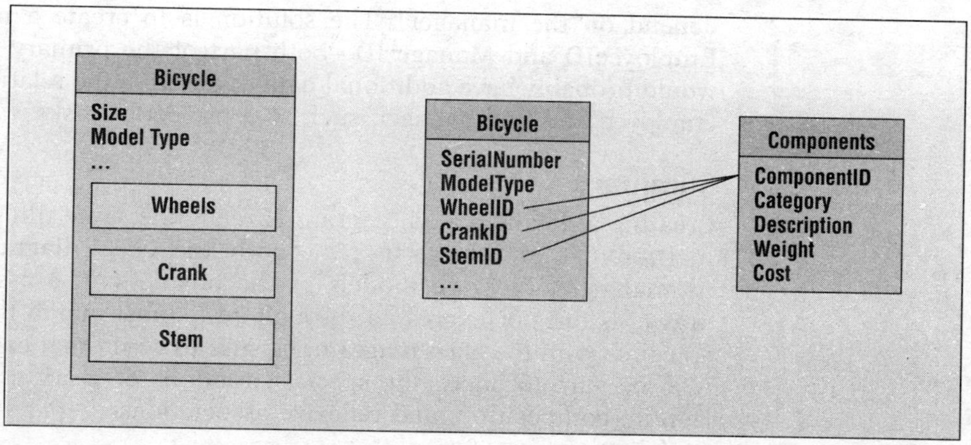

FIGURE 3.41 Normalizing a composition association. First decide how to handle the subclasses. In this case they are combined into one Components table. Second, handle the composition by storing the appropriate Component key values into the main Bicycle table.

compress each subtype into a generic Component class. However, it would also make sense to handle wheels separately because they are a more complex component.

You can solve the main composition problem by creating properties in the main Bicycle table for each of the component items (WheelID, CrankID, StemID, and so on). These columns are foreign keys in the Bicycle table (but not primary keys). When a bicycle is built, the ID values for the installed components are stored in the appropriate column in the Bicycle table. You can find more details by examining the actual Rolling Thunder database.

Reflexive Associations

Occasionally, an entity may be linked to itself. A common example is shown in Figure 3.42, where employees have managers. Because managers are also employees, the entity is linked to itself. This relationship is easy to see when you create the corresponding table. Simply add a Manager column to the Employee table. The data in this column consists of an EID. For example, the first employee (Smith, EID 221) reports to manager 335 (Sanchez). Is the Manager column part of the primary key? No, because the business rule states that each employee can have only one manager.

How would you handle a situation in which an employee can have more than one manager? Key the Manager column? No, because then the Employee table would not be in BCNF (an employee's address would not

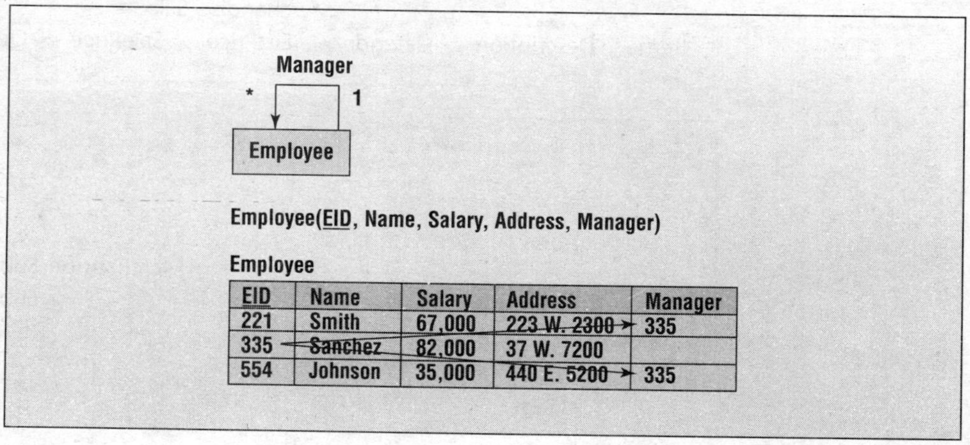

FIGURE 3.42 Converting recursive relationships. An employee can have only one manager, so add a Manager column to the Employee table which contains the EID to point to the manager. In the example, Smith reports to Manager 335 (Sanchez).

depend on the manager). The solution is to create a new table that lists EmployeeID and ManagerID—both part of the primary key. The new table would probably have additional data to describe the relationship between the employee and the manager, such as a project or task.

Summary

Creating a detailed class diagram is really the same thing as creating a normalized list of tables. In fact, both the class diagram and the list of normalized tables are models of the business. The associations, whether drawn as lines or expressed through keys, must match the business rules. If you start with the class diagram, be sure to verify that each class is in BCNF. Also be sure to check the special situations of n-ary associations, generalization, composition, and reflexive associations.

Sally's Pet Store Example

To design Sally's Pet Store database, you talk to the owner and investigate the way that other stores operate. In the process you collect ideas for various forms, and you begin to understand the business rules. To expedite the development and hold down costs, you and Sally agree to begin with a simplified model and add features later. The sales form sketched in Figure 3.43 contains the primary data that will be needed when sales are made.

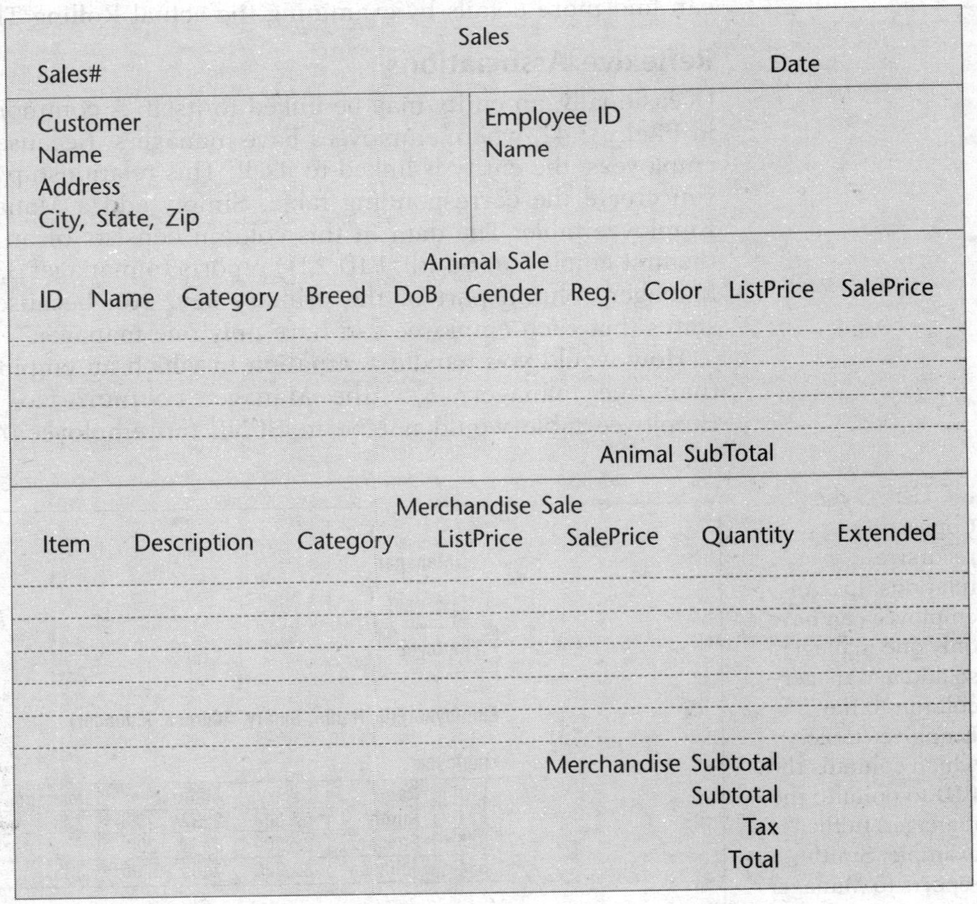

FIGURE 3.43
Pet Store sample sales form. Separate sections for selling animals and merchandise reflect a business rule to treat them differently.

FIGURE 3.44

Pet Store sample purchase order for animals. More information will be collected later—particularly data on each animal's health and lineage.

Purchase Order for Animals

Order# | Date Ordered | Date Received

Supplier	Employee ID
Name	Name
Contact	Home Phone
Phone	Date Hired
Address	
City, State **ZIPcode**	

Animal Descriptions

Name	Category	Breed	Gender	Registration	Price

Subtotal
Shipping Cost
Total

Sally wants you to create separate purchase orders for animals and products. She has repeatedly emphasized the importance of collecting detailed animal data from the breeders and eventually wants to collect the genealogical data for the animals whenever possible. With registered animals like cats and dogs, this data is readily available. However, she said it is hard to get good records for fish. Sally would also like to get medical records for the animals she buys. Common data would include their shots, any illnesses, and any medications or treatments they have received. For now, she is relying on the breeders to keep this information. However, once the sales and basic financial applications have been created, she wants to add these features to the database.

For the moment the most important job is to collect the transaction data. Figure 3.44 shows the minimal financial data that must be collected when purchasing animals from suppliers. Note the importance of collecting information on the animals, suppliers/breeders, customers, and employees. Because of the anticipated changes, it is important to design the database for flexibility. The design should make it easy to add new attributes for all of the major entities. It should also be easy to add new tables (such as health records) without making major alterations to the initial structure.

Purchasing merchandise from suppliers represents a similar process. However, there are some slight differences. In particular, you need to collect different data on the individual items.

A sample form is shown in Figure 3.45. Again, remember that Sally wants to start with a small database. Later you will have to collect additional data. For example, what happens if an order arrives and some items are missing? The current form can only record the arrival of the entire shipment. Similarly, each supplier probably uses a unique set of Item numbers. For example, a case of cat food from one supplier might be ordered with ItemID 3325, but the same case from a different supplier would be ordered with ItemID

FIGURE 3.45
Pet Store sample purchase order for merchandise. Note the similarities and differences between the two types of orders. Keep in mind that additional data will have to be collected later.

Purchase Order for Merchandise

Order# Data Ordered
Date Received

Supplier	Employee ID
Name	Name
Contact	Home Phone
Phone	
Address	
City, State **ZIPcode**	

Items Ordered

ItemID	Description	Category	Price	Quantity	Ext.	QOH

Subtotal
Shipping Cost
Total

A9973. Eventually, Sally will probably want to track the numbers used by her major suppliers. That way, when invoices arrive bearing their numbers, matching the products to what she ordered will be easier.

The next step in designing the Pet Store database is to take each form and create a list of normalized tables that will be used to hold data for that form. Figure 3.46 shows the tables that were generated from the Sales form. Before examining the results in detail, you should attempt to normalize the data yourself. Then see whether you derived the same answer. You should also derive the normalized tables for the other two forms. Remember to double-check your work. First make sure the primary keys are correct, then check to see that each nonkey column depends on the whole key and nothing but the key.

There is an interesting assumption in both the SaleAnimal and AnimalOrderItem (Figure 3.46) tables. The SaleAnimal table uses both SaleID and AnimalID as the primary key. This approach means that each sale can consist of several animals. It also means that each animal can be sold many times. Is this latter situation possible? Can the same animal be sold more than once? If not, then SaleID should not be part of the primary key—and it can simply be inserted into the Animal table. Likewise, can the same

FIGURE 3.46
Pet Store normalized tables for the basic sales form. You should do the normalization first and see if your results match these tables.

```
Sale(SaleID, Date, CustomerID, EmployeeID)
SaleAnimal(SaleID, AnimalID, SalePrice)
SaleMerchandise(SaleID, ItemID, SalePrice, Quantity)
Customer(CustomerID, Name, Address, City, State, Zip)
Employee(EmployeeID, Name)
Animal(AnimalID, Name, Category, Breed, DateOfBirth, Gender,
Registration, Color, ListPrice)
Merchandise(ItemID, Description, Category, ListPrice)
```

animal be purchased more than once? If not, the OrderID can be placed into the Animal table, but not as part of the key. The rest of the data in the SaleAnimal and AnimalOrderItem tables can also be placed in the Animal table. Although this approach appears realistic, it is less flexible. Designing the database this way means that the Pet Store can *never* sell the same animal twice. Then how would you handle return of an animal?

View Integration

Up to this point, database design and normalization have been discussed using individual reports and forms, which is the basic step in designing a database. However, most projects involve many reports and forms. Some projects involve teams of designers, where each person collects forms and reports from different users and departments. Each designer creates the normalized list of tables for the individual forms, and you eventually get several collections of tables related to the same topic. At this point you need to integrate all these tables into one complete, consistent set of table definitions.

When you are finished with this stage, you will be able to enter the table definitions into the DBMS. Although you might end up with a large list of interrelated tables, this step is generally easier than the initial derivation of the 3NF tables. At this point you collect the tables, make sure everything is named consistently, and consolidate data from similar tables. The basic steps involved in consolidating the tables are as follows:

- Collect the multiple views (documents, forms, etc.).
- Create normalized tables for each document.
- Combine the views into one complete model.

Sally's Pet Store Example

Figure 3.47 illustrates the view integration process for the Pet Store case. The tables generated from the three input forms are listed first. The integration occurs by looking at each table to see which ones contain similar data. A good starting point is to look at the primary keys. If two tables have exactly the same primary keys, the tables should usually be combined. However, be careful. Sometimes the keys are wrong, and sometimes the keys might have slightly different names.

Notice that the Employee table shows up three times in the example. By carefully checking the data in each listing, you can form one new table that contains all of the columns. Hence the Phone and DateHired columns are moved to one table, and the two others are deleted. A similar process can be used for the Supplier, Animal, and Merchandise tables. The goal is to create a complete list of normalized tables that will hold the data for all the forms and reports. Be sure to double-check your work and to verify that the final list of tables is in 3NF or BCNF. Also, make sure that the tables can be joined through related columns of data.

The finalized tables can also be displayed on a detailed class diagram. The class diagram for the Pet Store is shown in Figure 3.48. One strength of the diagram is the ability to show how the classes (tables) are connected through relationships. Double-check the normalization to make sure that the basic forms can be re-created. For example, the sales form will start

Sale(SaleID, Date, CustomerID, EmployeeID)
SaleAnimal(SaleID, AnimalID, SalePrice)
SaleItem(SaleID, ItemID, SalePrice, Quantity)
Customer(CustomerID, Name, Address, City, State, Zip)
Employee(EmployeeID, Name, Phone, DateHired)
Animal(AnimalID, Name, Category, Breed, DateOfBirth,
Gender, Registration, Color, ListPrice, Cost)
Merchandise(ItemID, Description, Category, ListPrice,
QuantityOnHand)

AnimalOrder(OrderID, OrderDate, ReceiveDate, SupplierID,
EmpID, ShipCost)
AnimalOrderItem(OrderID, AnimalID, Cost)
Supplier(SupplierID, Name, Contact, Phone, Address, City,
State, Zip)
~~Employee(EmployeeID, Name, Phone DateHired)~~
~~Animal(AnimalID, Name, Category, Breed, Gender,~~
~~Registration, Cost)~~

MerchandiseOrder(PONumber, OrderDate, ReceiveDate, SID,
EmpID, ShipCost)
MerchandiseOrderItem(PONumber, ItemID, Quantity, Cost)
~~Supplier(SupplierID, Name, Contact, Phone, Address, City,~~
~~State, Zip)~~
~~Employee(EmployeeID, Name, Phone)~~
~~Merchandise(ItemID, Description, Category, QuantityOnHand)~~

FIGURE 3.47 Pet Store view integration. Data columns from similar tables can be combined into one table. For example, we need only one Employee table. Look for tables that have the same keys. The goal is to have one set of normalized tables that can hold the data for all the forms and reports.

with the Customer, Employee, and Sale tables. Sales of animals requires the SaleAnimal and Animal tables. Sales of products requires the SaleItem and Merchandise tables. All of these tables can be connected by relationships on their attributes.

Most of the relationships are one-to-many relationships, but pay attention to the direction. Access denotes the many side with an infinity (∞) sign. Of course, you first have to identify the proper relationships from the business rules. For instance, there can be many sales to each customer, but a given sale can list only one customer.

This final list shown in the class diagram in Figure 3.48 has three new tables: City, Breed, and Category. These validation tables have been added to simplify data entry and to ensure consistency of data. Without these tables employees would have to repeatedly enter text data for city name, breed, and category. There are two problems with asking people to type in these values: (1) it takes time, and (2) people might enter different data each time. By placing standardized values in these tables, employees can select the proper value from a list. Because the standard value is always copied to the new table, the data will always be entered exactly the same way each time it is used.

Asking the DBMS to enforce the specified relationships raises an interesting issue. The relationships require that data be entered in a specific sequence. The foreign key relationship specifies that a value for the customer must exist in the Customer table before it can be placed in the Sale table. From a business standpoint the rule makes sense; you must first meet

FIGURE 3.48

Pet Store class diagram. The tables become entities in the diagram. The relationships verify that the tables are interconnected through the data. Some new data has been added for the employees. Also, cities have been defined in a single table to simplify data entry. Likewise, the new Breed and Category tables ensure consistency of data.

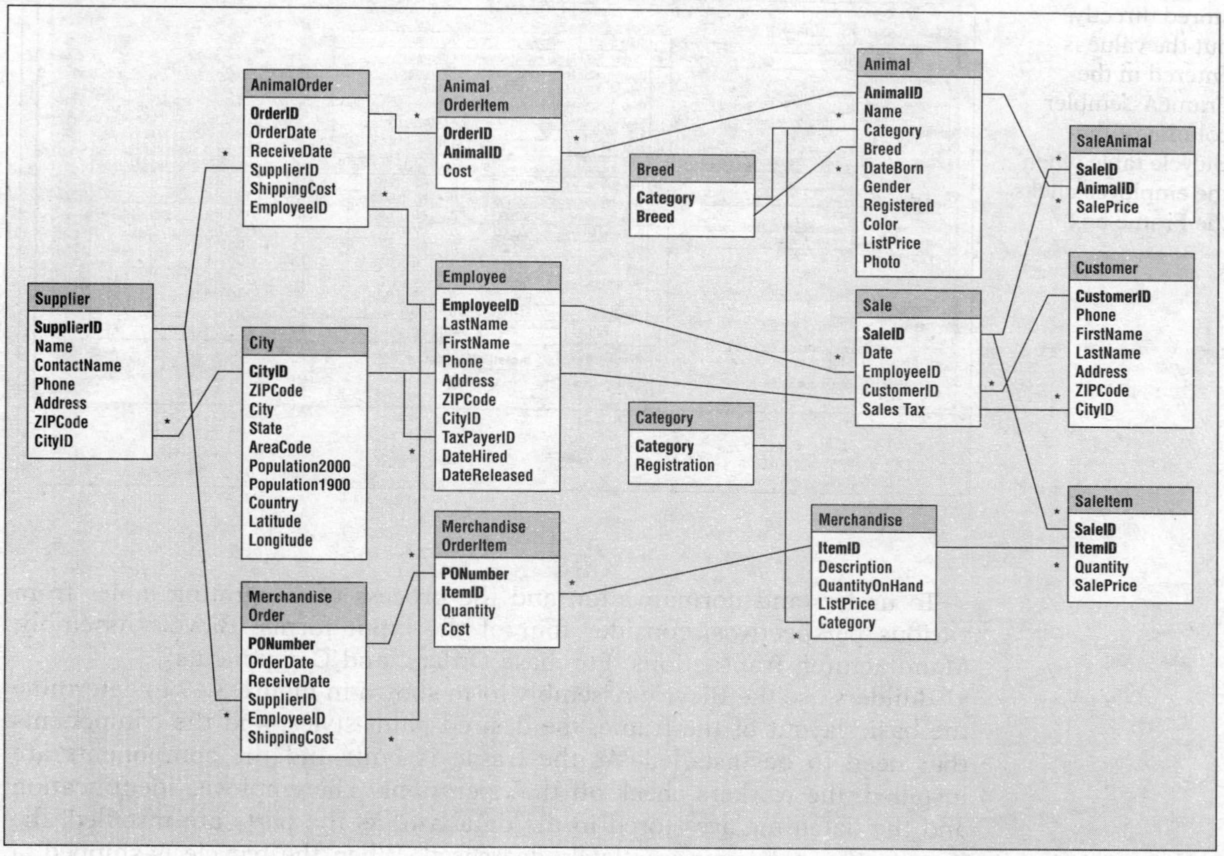

customers before you can sell them something. However, this rule may cause problems for clerks who are entering sales data. You need some mechanism to help them enter new Customer data before attempting to enter the Sales data. Chapters 6 and 7 explain one way to resolve this issue.

Rolling Thunder Sample Integration Problem

The only way to learn database design and understand normalization is to work through more problems. To practice the concepts of data normalization and to illustrate the methods involved in combining sets of tables, consider a new problem involving a database for a small manufacturer: Rolling Thunder Bicycles. The company builds custom bicycles. Frames are built and painted in-house. Components are purchased from manufacturers and assembled on the bicycles according to the customer orders. Components (cranks, pedals, derailleurs, etc.) are typically organized into groups so that the customer orders an entire package of components without having to specify every single item. Additional details about bicycles and the company operations are available in the Rolling Thunder database.

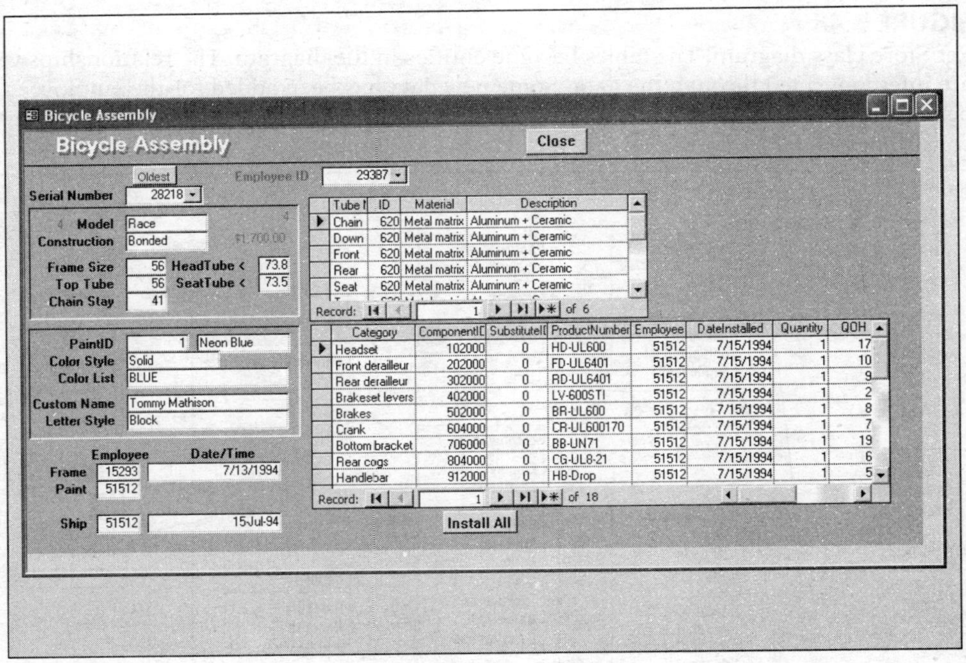

FIGURE 3.49
Bicycle Assembly form. The main EmployeeID control is not stored directly, but the value is entered in the FrameAssembler column of the Bicycle table when the employee clicks the Frame box.

To understand normalization and the process of integrating tables from various perspectives, consider four of the input forms: Bicycle Assembly, Manufacturer Transactions, Purchase Orders, and Components.

Builders use the Bicycle Assembly form shown in Figure 3.49 to determine the basic layout of the frame, the desired paint styles, and the components that need to be installed. As the frame is built and the components are installed, the workers check off the operations. The employee identification and the date/time are stored in the database. As the parts are installed, the inventory count is automatically decreased. When the bicycle is shipped, a trigger executes code that records the price owed by the customer so a bill can be printed and sent.

Collecting the data columns from the form results in the notation displayed in Figure 3.50. Notice that two repeating groups (tubes and components) occur, but they repeat independently of each other. They are not nested.

Components and other supplies are purchased from manufacturers. Orders are placed as supplies run low and are recorded on a Purchase Order form. Shown in Figure 3.51, the Purchase Order contains standard data on the manufacturer, along with a list of components (or other supplies) that are ordered.

The notation and the 4NF tables are derived in Figure 3.52. For practice you should work through the normalization on your own. Note that the computed columns do not need to be stored. However, be careful to store the shipping cost and discount, since those might be negotiated specifically on each order.

Payments to manufacturers are collected with a basic transaction form shown in Figure 3.53. Note that the initial balance and balance due are computed by code behind the form to display the effects of adding new

FIGURE 3.50
Notation for the BicycleAssembly form. There are two repeating groups, but they are independent. The 4NF tables from this form are displayed, but you should try to derive the tables yourself.

```
BicycleAssembly(
SerialNumber, Model, Construction, FrameSize, TopTube,
ChainStay, HeadTube, SeatTube, PaintID, PaintColor,
ColorStyle, ColorList, CustomName, LetterStyle, EmpFrame,
EmpPaint, BuildDate, ShipDate,
  (Tube, TubeType, TubeMaterial, TubeDescription),
  (CompCategory, ComponentID, SubstID, ProdNumber,
  EmpInstall, DateInstall, Quantity, QOH) )

Bicycle(SerialNumber, Model, Construction, FrameSize,
TopTube, ChainStay, HeadTube, SeatTube, PaintID,
ColorStyle, CustomName, LetterStyle, EmpFrame, EmpPaint,
BuildDate, ShipDate)
Paint(PaintID, ColorList)
BikeTubes(SerialNumber, TubeID, Quantity)
TubeMaterial(TubeID, Type, Material, Description)
BikeParts(SerialNumber, ComponentID, SubstID, Quantity,
DateInstalled, EmpInstalled)
Component(ComponentID, ProdNumber, Category, QOH)
```

transactions. Row entries for purchases are automatically generated by the Purchase Order form, so this form is generally used for payments or for corrections.

The 4NF tables resulting from the manufacturer transactions are shown in Figure 3.54. Again, work through the normalization yourself. Practice and experience are the best ways to learn normalization. Do not be misled: It is always tempting to read the "answers" in the book and say that normalization is easy. Normalization becomes much more complex when you face a blank page. Investigating and determining business rules is challenging when you begin.

The Component form in Figure 3.55 is used to add new components to the list and modify the descriptions of the components. It can also be used to

FIGURE 3.51
Tables from the Purchase Order form. Note that the computed columns (extension is price * quantity) are not stored in the tables.

```
PurchaseOrder(PurchaseID, PODate, EmployeeID, FirstName,
LastName, ManufacturerID, MfgName, Address, Phone, CityID,
CurrentBalance, ShipReceiveDate, (ComponentID, Category,
ManufacturerID, ProductNumber, Description, PricePaid,
Quantity, ReceiveQuantity, ExtendedValue, QOH,
ExtendedReceived), ShippingCost, Discount)

PurchaseOrder(PurchaseID, PODate, EmployeeID, ManufacturerID,
ShipReceiveDate, ShippingCost, Discount) Employee(EmployeeID,
FirstName, LastName)
Manufacturer(ManufacturerID, Name, Address, Phone, Address,
CityID, CurrentBalance)
City(CityID, Name, ZipCode)
PurchaseItem(PurchaseID, ComponentID, Quantity, PricePaid,
ReceivedQuantity)
Component(ComponentID, Category, ManufacturerID,
ProductNumber, Description, QOH)
```

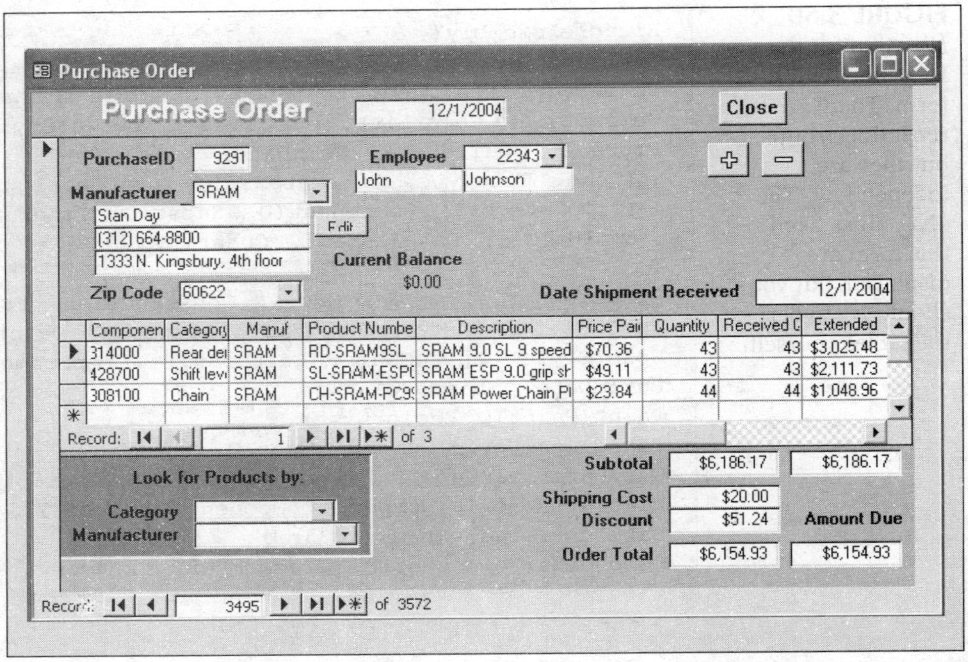

FIGURE 3.52
Purchase Order form. Only the items ordered is a repeating group. The Look for Products section is a convenience for users and does not store data. The Date Shipment Received box is initially blank and is filled in when the product arrives at the loading dock.

make changes to the manufacturer data. Notice the use of two identification numbers: one is assigned by Rolling Thunder, and the other is assigned by the manufacturer. Assigning our own number ensures consistency of the data format and guarantees a unique identifier. The manufacturer's product number is used to help place orders, since the manufacturer would have no use for our internal data.

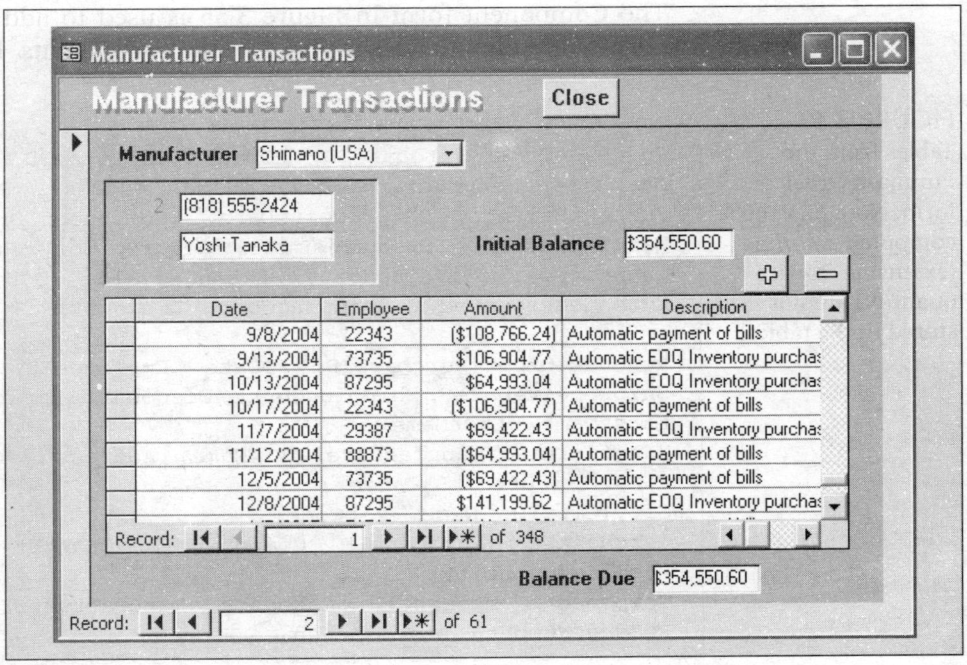

FIGURE 3.53
Manufacturer Transaction form. The balance due is stored in the database, but only one time. The Initial Balance and Balance Due boxes are computed by the form to display the effect of transactions added by the user.

FIGURE 3.54
Tables for Manufacturer Transaction form. This normalization is straightforward. Note that the TransactionDate column also holds the time, so it is possible to have more than one transaction with a given manufacturer on the same day.

```
ManufacturerTransactions(ManufacturerID, Name, Phone,
Contact, BalanceDue, (TransDate, Employee, Amount,
Description))

Manufacturer(ManufacturerID, Name, Phone, Contact,
BalanceDue)
ManufacturerTransaction(ManufacturerID, TransactionDate,
EmployeeID, Amount, Description)
```

The 4NF tables derived from the Component form are shown in Figure 3.56. For the most part they are straightforward. One interesting difference in Rolling Thunder is the treatment of addresses and cities. Many business tables for customers, employees, suppliers, and so on, contain columns for city, state, and ZIP code. Technically, there is a hidden dependency in this basic data because the three are related. Hence a database can save space and data entry time by maintaining a separate City table. Of course, a City table for the entire United States, much less the world, could become large. A more challenging problem is that there is not a one-to-one relationship between cities and ZIP codes. Some cities have many ZIP codes, and some ZIP codes cover multiple cities. Rolling Thunder resolves these two issues by keeping a City table based on a unique CityID. If space is at a premium, the table can be reduced to contain only cities used in the database. As customers arrive from new cities, the basic city data is added. The ZIP code problem is handled by storing a base ZIP code for each city. The specific ZIP code related to each address is stored with the appropriate table (e.g., Manufacturer). This specific ZIP code could also be a nine-digit code that more closely identifies the location of the

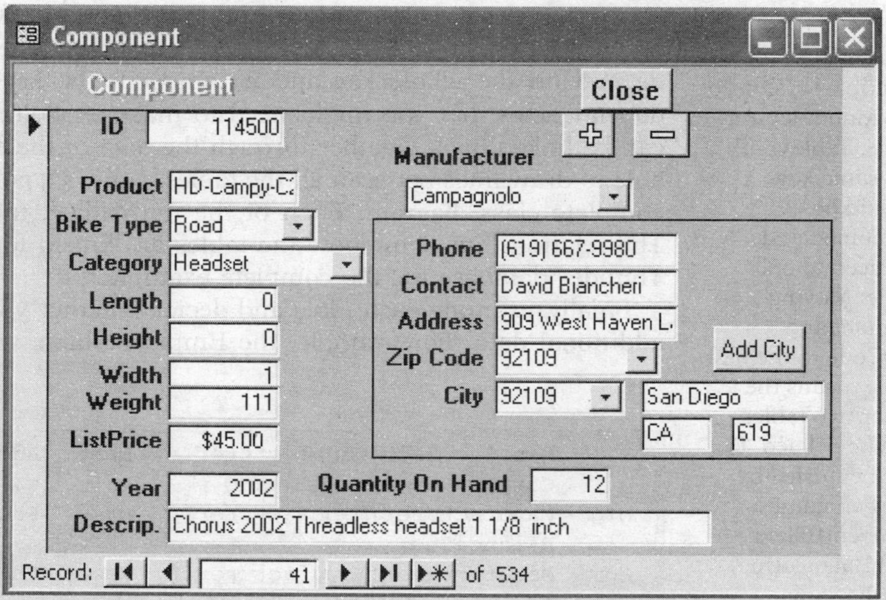

FIGURE 3.55
Component form. Note that components have an internal ID number that is assigned by Rolling Thunder employees. Products usually also have a Product number that is assigned by the manufacturer. It is difficult to rely on this number, since it might be duplicated across suppliers and the formats vary widely.

FIGURE 3.56
Tables derived from the Component form. The ZipCode in the Manufacturer table is specific to that company (probably a nine-digit code). The ZipCode in the City table is a base (five-digit) code that can be used for a reference point, but there are often many codes per city.

```
ComponentForm(ComponentID, Product, BikeType, Category,
Length, Height, Width, Weight, ListPrice, Description, QOH,
ManufacturerID, Name, Phone, Contact, Address, ZipCode,
CityID, City, State, AreaCode)

Component(ComponentID, ProductNumber, BikeType, Category,
Length, Height, Width, Weight, ListPrice, Description, QOH,
ManufacturerID)
Manufacturer(ManufacturerID, Name, Phone, Contact, Address,
ZipCode, CityID)
City(CityID, City, State, ZipCode, AreaCode)
```

customer or manufacturer. Although it is possible to create a table of complete nine-digit codes, the size is enormous, and the data tends to change. Companies that rely heavily on nine-digit mailings usually purchase verification software that contains authenticated databases to check their addresses and codes.

Look at the tables from Figures 3.50, 3.51, 3.54, and 3.56 again. Notice that similar tables are listed in each figure. In particular, look for the Manufacturer tables. Notice that the overlapping tables often contain different data from each form. In practice, particularly when there is a team of designers, similar columns might have different names, so be careful. The objective of this step is to combine the similar tables. The best way to start is to look for common keys. Tables that have the same key columns should be combined. For example, the Manufacturer variations are reproduced in Figure 3.57. The version from the PO table can be extended by adding the Contact and ZipCode columns from the other variations.

After combining duplicate tables, you should have a single list of tables that contain all of the data from the forms. This list is shown in Figure 3.58. It is also a good idea at this point to double-check your work. In particular, verify that the keys are unique and that composite keys represent many-to-many relationships. Then verify the 3NF rules: Does each nonkey column depend on the whole key and nothing but the key? Also look for hidden dependencies that you might need to make explicit. Be sure that the tables can be linked back together through the data in the columns. You should be able to draw lines between all the tables. Now is a good time to draw a more complete class diagram. Each of the normalized tables becomes an entity. The relationships show how the tables are linked together. (See the Rolling Thunder database for the complete example.)

Finally, examine each table and decide whether you might want to collect additional data. For example, the Employee table would undoubtedly need

FIGURE 3.57
Multiple versions of the Manufacturer table. Tables with the same key should be combined and reduced to one table. Moving Contact and ZipCode to the first table means the other two tables can be deleted. Do not be misled by the two names (CurrentBalance and BalanceDue) for the same column.

```
PO   Manufacturer(ManufacturerID, Name, Address, Phone,
     CityID, CurrentBalance)
Mfg  Manufacturer(ManufacturerID, Name, Phone, Contact,
     BalanceDue)
Comp Manufacturer(ManufacturerID, Name, Phone, Contact,
     Address, ZipCode, CityID)
```

FIGURE 3.58
Integrated tables. Duplicate tables have been combined, and normalization (4NF) has been verified. Also draw a class diagram to be sure the tables link together. Note the addition of the Reference column as an audit trail to hold the corresponding PurchaseID. Observe that some tables (e.g., Employee) will need additional data.

```
Bicycle(SerialNumber, Model, Construction, FrameSize,
TopTube, ChainStay, HeadTube, SeatTube, PaintID, ColorStyle,
CustomName, LetterStyle, EmpFrame, EmpPaint, BuildDate,
ShipDate)
Paint(PaintID, ColorList)
BikeTubes(SerialNumber, TubeID, Quantity)
TubeMaterial(TubeID, Type, Material, Description)
BikeParts(SerialNumber, ComponentID, SubstID, Quantity,
DateInstalled, EmpInstalled)
Component(ComponentID, ProductNumber, BikeType, Category,
Length, Height, Width, Weight, ListPrice, Description, QOH,
ManufacturerID)
PurchaseOrder(PurchaseID, PODate, EmployeeID, ManufacturerID,
ShipReceiveDate, ShippingCost, Discount)
PurchaseItem(PurchaseID, ComponentID, Quantity, PricePaid,
ReceivedQuantity)
Employee(EmployeeID, FirstName, LastName)
Manufacturer(ManufacturerID, Name, Contact, Address, Phone,
CityID, ZipCode, CurrentBalance)
ManufacturerTransaction(ManufacturerID, TransactionDate,
EmployeeID, Amount, Description, Reference)
City(CityID, City, State, ZipCode, AreaCode)
```

more data, such as Address and DateHired. Similarly, you saw that the ManufacturerTransaction table could use a Reference column that will contain the PurchaseID when a transaction is automatically generated by the Purchase Order form. This column functions as an audit trail and makes it easier to trace accounting transactions back to the source. Some people might use date/time for the same purpose, but a round-off to seconds could cause problems.

Data Dictionary

In the process of collecting data and creating normalized tables, be sure to keep a data dictionary to record the data domains and various assumptions you make. A **data dictionary** or **data repository** consists of **metadata**, which is data that describes the data stored in the database. It typically lists all of the tables, columns, data domains, and assumptions. It is possible to store this data in a notebook, but it is easier to organize if it is stored on a computer. Some designers create a separate database to track the underlying project data. Specialized computer tools known as computer-aided software engineering (CASE) tools help with software design. One of their strengths is the ability to create, store, and search a comprehensive data dictionary.

DBMS Table Definition

When the logical tables are defined and you know the domains for all of the columns, you can enter the tables into a DBMS. Most systems have a graphical interface that makes it easier to enter the table definitions. In some cases, however, you might have to use the SQL data definition commands described in Chapter 4. In both cases, the process is similar. Define the table name, enter the column names, select the data type for the column, and then identify the keys. Sometimes keys are defined by creating a separate index. Some systems enable you to create a description for each column and table. This description might contain instructions to users or it might be an extension of your data dictionary to help designers make changes in the future.

At this time, you should determine which keys you want to generate with an autonumber function. Similarly, identify any computed columns and specify the calculations needed for them. Some databases enable you to store these calculations within the database definition; others require that you write them into queries.

You can also set **default values** for each column to speed up data entry. In the video store example, you might set a default value for the base rental rate. Default values can be particularly useful for dates. Most systems enable you to set a default value for dates that automatically enters the current date. At this point you should also set validation rules to enforce data integrity. As soon as the tables are defined, you can set relationships. In Microsoft Access, go to the relationships screen, add all of the tables, then draw lines to show the connections (much like the class diagram). Be sure to check the boxes that specify "Enforce referential integrity," "Cascade on delete," and "Cascade on update." With SQL Server and Oracle, you specify referential integrity as constraints when you define the tables.

Figure 3.59 shows the form that Microsoft Access uses to define tables. Primary keys are set by selecting the appropriate rows and clicking an icon. Data type details such as character length and numeric subtype are set in

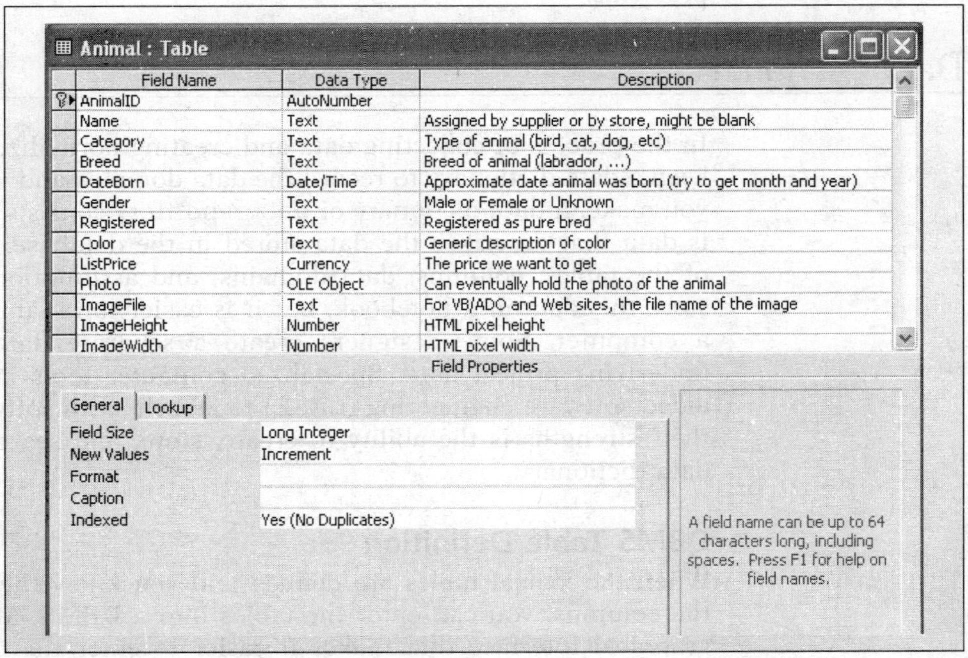
Animal : Table

Field Name	Data Type	Description
AnimalID	AutoNumber	
Name	Text	Assigned by supplier or by store, might be blank
Category	Text	Type of animal (bird, cat, dog, etc)
Breed	Text	Breed of animal (labrador, ...)
DateBorn	Date/Time	Approximate date animal was born (try to get month and year)
Gender	Text	Male or Female or Unknown
Registered	Text	Registered as pure bred
Color	Text	Generic description of color
ListPrice	Currency	The price we want to get
Photo	OLE Object	Can eventually hold the photo of the animal
ImageFile	Text	For VB/ADO and Web sites, the file name of the image
ImageHeight	Number	HTML pixel height
ImageWidth	Number	HTML pixel width

FIGURE 3.59
Table definition in Microsoft Access. Note the primary key indicator. Also note that text size limits and numeric subtypes are defined in the list at the bottom of the form.

FIGURE 3.60

Oracle Schema Manager for creating tables. Primary keys and foreign keys are set in the Constraints tab. For primary key columns, be sure to also check that the values cannot be null.

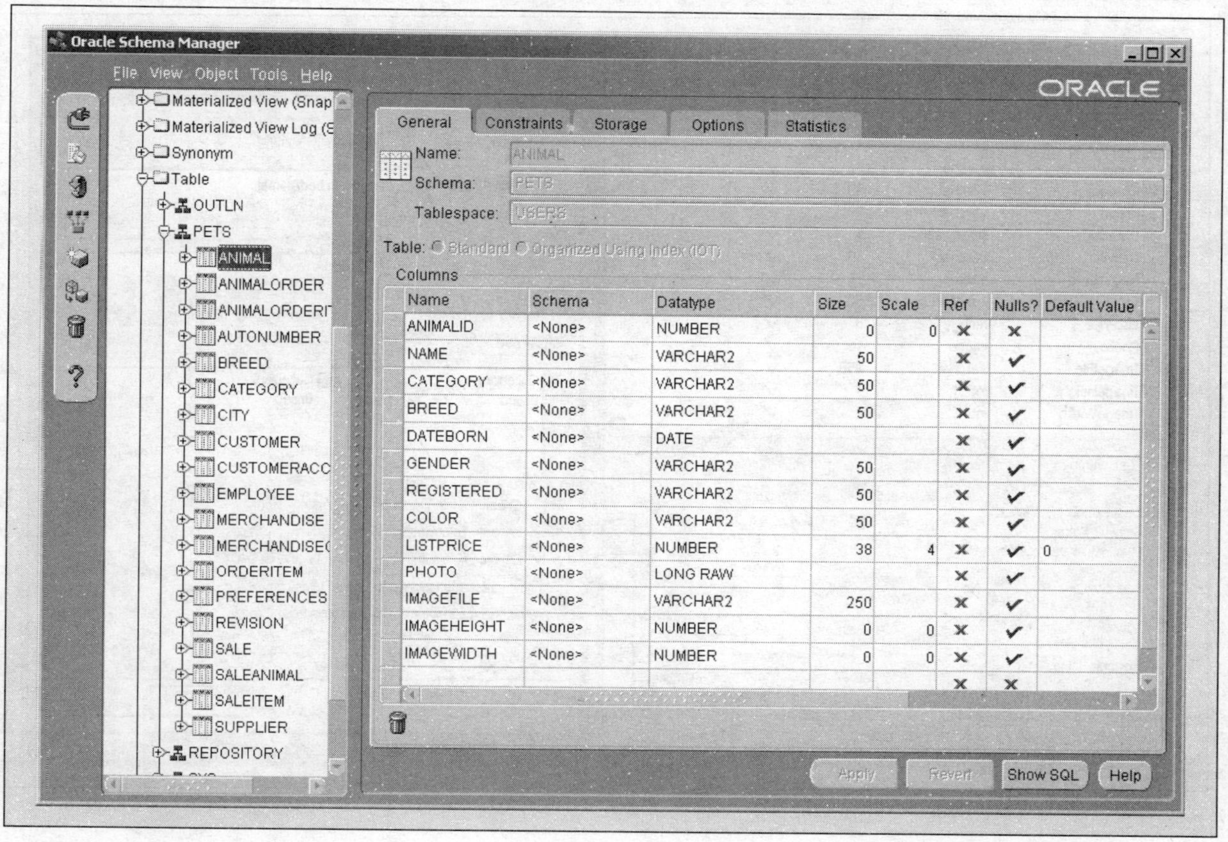

the list at the bottom of the form. Changes to the table can be made at any time, but if data already exists in the table, you might lose some information if you select a smaller data type.

Figure 3.60 shows the form that can be used within Oracle to create tables—it is the Schema Manager. Primary and foreign keys can be set using the Constraints tab. Keep in mind that once you create a table in Oracle (and SQL Server), it can be difficult to change later. It is always possible to add new columns, but you might not be permitted to change the data type of an existing column or to delete columns.

If you are using Oracle version 8 or above, perform one additional step once the tables have been created by telling it to analyze the tables. For example, use the SQL Plus tool to issue commands for each table similar to: Analyze table Animal compute statistics. These commands tell Oracle to generate statistics for each table (notice the Statistics tab in the Schema Manager). Oracle uses these statistics to dramatically improve performance of queries.

Figure 3.61 shows the forms that SQL Server uses to create and edit tables. The basic layout is similar to that used in Microsoft Access. But the relationships and constraints are specified on the properties form. The main

FIGURE 3.61
Microsoft SQL Server form for creating tables. Note the similarity to the Microsoft Access design form, but relationships and constraints are specified on the properties form.

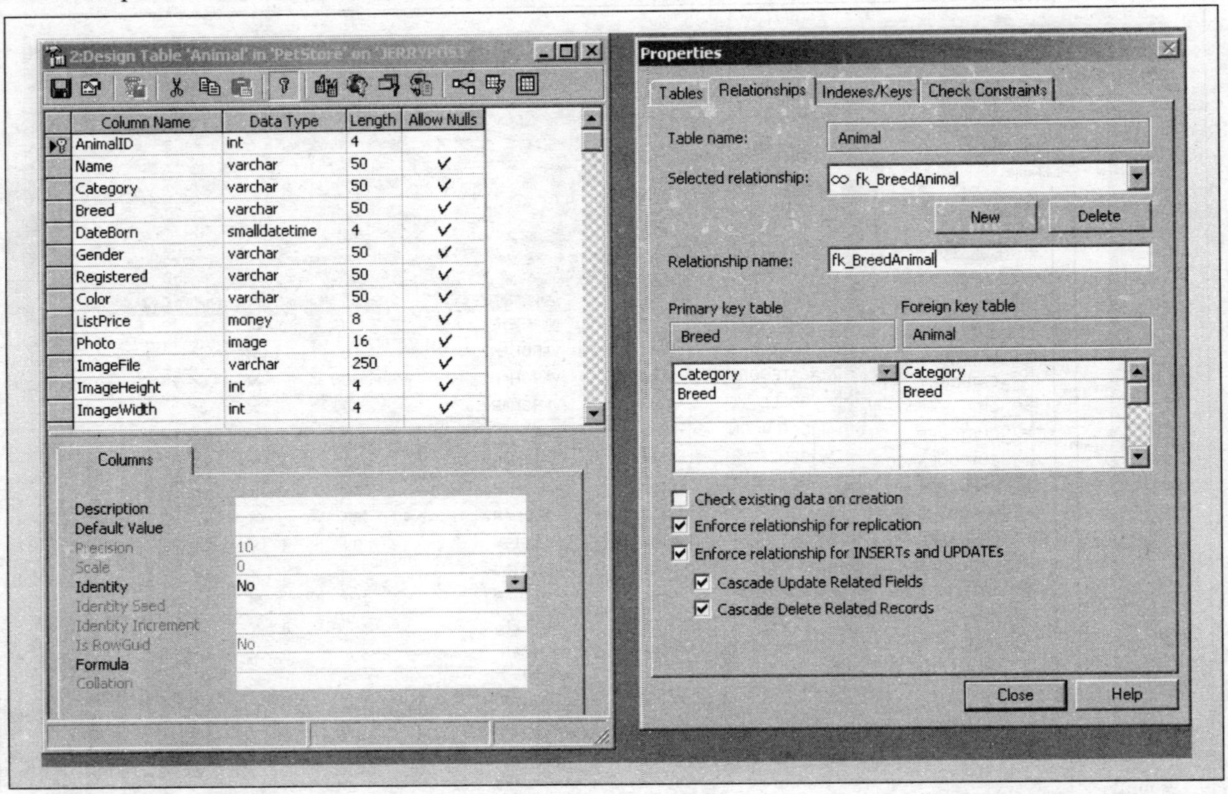

design form is activated from the Enterprise Manager, which lists the databases and all of the tables within the database.

It is easy to see the similarities of the database design tools for the various products. Yet more important differences between the systems lie in the data types used within each system. Although some of the data type names appear similar, be particularly careful with Oracle databases. Oracle's underlying data types are different—particularly in dealing with numbers. For both Oracle and SQL Server, the graphical forms seem easy to use; however, experienced developers almost always rely on direct SQL statements stored in a text file to create tables. Figure 3.62 gives an example for the Animal table. You simply create a list of all of the table creation statements and store them in a text file. This file is read by the database SQL processor to create the tables. The list has several advantages over the graphical approach: (1) It is easier to change the text file. (2) It is easier to re-create the tables on a different database or different computer. (3) Changing a table definition usually requires creating a new table, copying in the existing data, deleting the old table, and renaming the new one. With the text file, you can quickly define the new table and run the statement to create the table. (4) It is easier to specify the primary key and foreign key relationships in the text file. Most of the graphical approaches are cumbersome and hard to read. Also, some versions of Oracle had stricter

FIGURE 3.62
Oracle SQL Statements to create the Animal table. The statements for SQL Server are similar—just change the data types.

```
CREATE TABLE Animal
(
  AnimalID        INTEGER,
  Name            VARCHAR2(50),
  Category        VARCHAR2(50),
  Breed           VARCHAR2(50),
  DateBorn        DATE,
  Gender          VARCHAR2(50)
    CHECK (Gender='Male' Or Gender='Female'
      Or Gender='Unknown' Or Gender Is Null)
  Registered      VARCHAR2(50),
  Color           VARCHAR2(50),
  ListPrice NUMBER(38,4)
    DEFAULT 0,
  Photo           LONG RAW,
  ImageFile       VARCHAR2(250),
  ImageHeight     INTEGER,
  ImageWidth      INTEGER,
    CONSTRAINT pk_Animal PRIMARY KEY (AnimalID)
    CONSTRAINT fk_BreedAnimal FOREIGN KEY (Category, Breed)
    REFERENCES Breed(Category, Breed)
    ON DELETE CASCADE
  CONSTRAINT fk_CategoryAnimal FOREIGN KEY (Category)
    REFERENCES Category(Category)
    ON DELETE CASCADE
);
```

limits using the graphical interface that could be avoided by creating the SQL statements directly. (5) Because of the foreign key constraints, the order in which the tables are created is critical. You cannot refer to a table in the foreign key constraint unless that table already has been created. For example, the Category and Breed tables must be created before the Animal table. Keeping the table definitions in a text file means you only have to set up the sequence one time. If you are uncertain about the SQL syntax for creating a table, you can examine existing structure files, or you can use the Schema Manager to enter the basic information, then click the Show SQL button to cut and paste the underlying SQL code.

You need to be aware of one additional crucial feature when you create Oracle tables. Once you have created the table, you will need to tell Oracle to analyze the table and collect statistics about it. First, create the tables using SQL. Second, load any existing data into the tables. Third, use the SQL Plus utility to run the analyze command for each table. For example: Analyze table Animal compute statistics.

Data Volume and Usage

One more step is required when designing a database: estimating the size of the resulting database. The process is straightforward, but you have to ask a lot of questions of the users. When you design a database, it is important to estimate the overall size and usage of the database. These values enable you to estimate the hardware requirements and cost of the system. The first

FIGURE 3.63
Estimating data volume. First estimate the size of each row, and then estimate the number of rows in the table. If there is a concatenated key, you will usually multiply an average value times the number of rows in a prior table, as in the calculation for OrderItem.

Customer(C#, Name, Address, City, State, ZIP)
Row: 4 + 15 + 25 + 20 + 2 + 10 = 76

Order(O#, C#, Odate)
Row: 4 + 4 + 8 = 16

OrderItem(O#, P#, Quantity, SalePrice)
Row: 4 + 4 + 4 + 8 = 20

$$\textit{Orders in 3 yrs} = 1{,}000\ \textit{Customers} * \frac{10\ \textit{Orders}}{\textit{Customer}} * 3\ \textit{yrs} = 30{,}000$$

$$\textit{OrderItem} = 30{,}000\ \textit{Orders} * \frac{5\ \textit{Lines}}{\textit{Order}} = 150{,}000$$

- Business rules
  - 3-year retention.
  - 1,000 customers.
  - Average 10 orders per customer per year.
  - Average five items per order.

Customer	76 * 1,000	76,000
Order	16 * 30,000	480,000
OrderItem	20 * 150,000	3,000,000
Total		3,556,000

step is to estimate the size of the tables. Generally, you should investigate three situations: How big is the database now? How big will the database be in 2 or 3 years? and How big will the database be in 10 years?

Begin with the list of normalized tables. The process consists of estimating the average number of bytes in each row of the table and then estimating the number of rows in the table. Multiply the two numbers to get an estimate of the size of the table, and then add the table sizes to estimate the total database size. This number represents the minimum size of the database. Many databases will be three to five times larger than this base estimate. Some systems have more complex rules and estimation procedures. For example, Oracle provides a utility to help you estimate the storage required for the database. You still begin with the data types for each column and the approximate number of rows. The utility then uses internal rules about Oracle's procedures to help estimate the total storage space needed.

An example of estimating **data volume** is presented in Figure 3.63. Consider the Customer table. The database system sets aside a certain amount of storage space for each column of data. The amount used depends on the particular system, so consult the documentation for exact values. In the abbreviated Customer table, the identification number takes 4 bytes as a long integer, and you estimate that Names take an average of 15 characters. Other averages are displayed in the table. Better estimates could be obtained from statistical analysis of sample data. In any case the estimated size of one row of Customer data is 76 bytes. Evaluating the business provides an estimate of approximately 1,000 customers; hence, the Customer table would be approximately 76K bytes.

Estimating the size of the Order table follows a similar process, yielding an estimate of 16 bytes per row. Managers might know how many orders are placed in a given year. However, it might be easier to obtain the average number of orders placed by a given customer in 1 year. If that number is 10, then you could expect 10,000 orders in a given year. Similarly, to get the number of rows in the OrderItem table, you need to know the average number of products ordered on one order form. If that number is 5, then you can expect to see 150,000 rows in the OrderItem table in 1 year.

The next step is to estimate the length of time data will be stored. Some companies plan to keep their data online for many years, whereas others follow a strict retention and removal policy. For legal purposes data must be maintained for a certain number of years, depending on its nature. Keep in mind that agencies such as the IRS also require that retrieval software (e.g., the DBMS) be available to reproduce the data.

In addition to the basic data storage, your database will also reserve space for indexes, log files, forms, programs, and backup data. Experience with a particular database system will provide a more specific estimate, but the final total will probably be three to five times the size of the base estimate.

The final number will give you some idea of the hardware needed to support the database. Although performance and prices continue to change, only small databases can be run effectively on personal computers. Larger databases can be moved to a file server on a local area network (LAN). The LAN provides access to the data by multiple users, but performance depends heavily on the size of the database, the characteristics of the DBMS, and the speed of the network. As the database size increases (hundreds or thousands of megabytes), it becomes necessary to move to a dedicated computer to handle the data. Very large databases (terabytes) need multiple computers and specialized disk drives to minimize capacity and performance bottlenecks. The data estimates do not have to be perfect, but they provide basic information that you can give to the planning committee to help allocate funds for development, hardware, software, and personnel.

While you are talking with the users about each table, you should ask them to identify some basic security information. You will eventually need to assign security access rights to each table. Chapter 10 presents the details, but for now you should find out which people use the table, and which people should be denied some privileges. For example, clerks who order merchandise should not be allowed to acknowledge receipt of that merchandise. Otherwise, an unethical clerk could order merchandise, record it as being received, and then steal it. Four basic operations can be granted to data: read it, change it, delete it, or add new data. You should keep a list of who may or may not access each table.

Summary

Database design relies on normalization, or the process of splitting data into tables. Ultimately, each table refers to a single entity or concept. Each table must have a primary key that uniquely identifies each row of data. To create the tables, you begin with a collection of data—generally derived from a user form or report. You reach 1NF by finding the repeating groups of data and putting them in a separate table. Next, you go through each of the intermediate tables and identify primary keys. You reach 2NF by checking each nonkey column and asking whether it depends on the whole key. If not, put the column into a new table along with the portion of the key that it does depend on. To reach 3NF, you check to see whether the nonkey column depends on anything that is not in the key. If so, pull out the column and the dependent column and put them into a new table. BCNF and 4NF apply to similar problems within the primary key. In particular, you want to look for hidden dependencies within the keys. If you find one, create an additional table that makes that dependency explicit.

Each form, report, or description that you collect from a user must be analyzed and a set of 4NF tables defined. For large projects several analysts may be given different forms, resulting in several lists of normalized tables. These tables must then be integrated into one standardized set of normalized data tables. Along the way you must specify the domain, or type of data, for each column. This final list of tables, with any comments, will be entered into the DMBS to start the database construction.

You should also collect estimates of data volume in terms of number of rows for each table. These numbers will enable you to estimate the average and maximum size of the database so that you can choose the proper hardware and software. You should also collect information on security conditions: Who owns the data? Who can have read access? Who can have write access? All of these conditions can be entered into the DBMS when you create the tables.

At this point, after you review your work, you can enter sample data to test your tables. When you are certain that the design is complete and accurate, you can begin building the application by constructing queries and creating forms and reports.

A Developer's View

Miranda learned that the class diagram is converted into a set of normalized tables. These tables are the foundation of the database application. Database design is crucial to developing your application. Engrave the basic normalization rule onto the back of your eyelids: Each nonkey column depends on the whole key and nothing but the key. Since the design depends on the business rules, make certain that you understand the rules. Listen carefully to the users. When in doubt, opt for flexibility. For your class projects, you should now be able to create the list of normalized tables. You should also be able to estimate the size of the database.

Key Terms

autonumber, *80*
Boyce-Codd normal form (BCNF), *98*
cascading delete, *103*
composite key, *79*
data dictionary/repository, *123*
data integrity, *102*
data volume, *128*
default values, *124*
deletion anomaly, *88*
dependence, *94*
domain-key normal form (DKNF), *100*
first normal form (1NF), *89*
foreign key, *80*
fourth normal form (4NF), *99*
hidden dependency, *99*
insertion anomaly, *88*
master-detail, *79*
metadata, *123*
referential integrity, *103*
repeating groups, *89*
second normal form (2NF), *92*
third normal form (3NF), *94*

Review Questions

1. What is a primary key and why is it needed?
2. What is a composite key?
3. What are the main rules for normalization?
4. What problems do you encounter if data is not stored in normalized tables?
5. Explain the phrase *a column is dependent on another column.*
6. How are BCNF and 4NF different from 3NF?
7. What are the primary types of data that can be stored in a table?
8. Give examples of rules you would store as integrity constraints?
9. What elements do you look for when integrating views?
10. How do you estimate the potential size of a database?
11. Why is referential integrity important?
12. What complications are caused by setting referential integrity rules?

Exercises

1. A local retail firm is building a website and wants you to create a database to track information requests. The company wants to collect basic customer data and then record when potential customers return to track their comments by topic. The topic is a predefined list of items (which managers can change) that potential customers will choose via a selection box. Define the normalized tables needed for this project. Create the class diagram and list of normalized tables for this case.

Name
Phone
E-mail
Address
City, State ZIP
Country

Date/Time	IP Address	Comment	Topic

2. You have been hired to develop a small database for a company that wants to offer products for sale on the Internet. Create the class diagram and list of normalized tables for this case.

Date/Time	**Order Form**	
Customer	Credit Card	Internet
Name / Shipping Address	Card #	E-mail
Phone / City, State ZIP	Expiration Date	IP Address
	Bank	Referred From

Items

Item #	Name	Description	Quantity	List Price	Sale Price	Quantity Shipped	Back Order	Extended

Item Total	
Shipping	
Tax	
Total Due	

3. A local company needs help with its human resources department. The managers want to offer cafeteria-style benefits, where employees can choose which benefit packages they want. The firm kicks in a fixed amount of total money, and employees pay the difference if the cost of the items selected goes over the limit. The Human Resources department also wants to keep a listing of the jobs each employee has held. Currently, this information is collected on a form similar to the one shown here. Create the class diagram and list of normalized tables for this case.

Employee
Last Name, First Name
Office, Phone
Date Hired

Benefit	Date	Monthly Cost

Job/Title	Location	Start Date	End Date	Salary	Supervisor

4. A friend of yours has started a garage band. The band has already written several songs and has jobs (gigs) at several local nightclubs. To improve the performances and the band, she wants a database to track which songs were played and how well they were received. The band members also want to track who played on each song and indicate if there were problems (or highlights) so they know what to work on. The database has to be easy to use, and she has sketched out a sample form. Create the class diagram and list of normalized tables for this case.

Gig

Date	Location
Start Time	End Time
# People	Money
Comments	

Song	
Length	Actual
Author	
Style	Key
Comments	

Person	Instrument	Comment

Song	
Length	Actual
Author	
Style	Key
Comments	

Person	Instrument	Comment

5. A small firm that performs lawn care needs to track customer jobs and employees. Currently, the owner keeps daily records on a pad of paper. Similar to the form shown here, it lists the jobs by time. Employees can do several tasks for each customer, including lawn mowing, edging, and tree trimming. Create the class diagram and list of normalized tables for this case.

Lawn Care Date	
Time	Customer, Address Total Task Employee Time Charge

6. A local country club has a beautiful new clubhouse that the club rents out to individuals and companies for small parties and receptions. The clubhouse has four rooms of different sizes that can be rented separately, but the managers generally do not like to host more than two large events at one time. Clients must make reservations in advance, and can choose the room based on the number of expected guests. Clients can elect to have meals served or use a buffet. The meal costs depend on the items served. As shown in the sample form, for additional fees, clients can elect to have valet parking service and flowers provided by the club. Bar service is treated similar to a meal option. Create the class diagram and list of normalized tables for this case.

Reservation Form Date Employee Room/Hall Maximum Capacity	
Cancel Date Total Due Deposit	Event Date, Time, Length Event Title ☐ Valet Parking (cost:) ☐ Flowers (cost:)
Lunch (sit down) # Guests # Servers Menu Item Description Cost Quantity Subtotal	
Dinner (sit down) # Guests # Servers Menu Item Description Cost Quantity Subtotal Buffet … Bar …	

7. A small woodworking shop specializes in building grandfather clocks. The shop orders the wood, clockworks, and miscellaneous components from various suppliers. The wood panels are planed from rough wood, glued, shaped, and assembled. The ornate carvings for the top are purchased from a single supplier where they are hand carved. Some clocks are sold as custom orders where the client chooses such options as the height and the clockwork. For regular production, the owner usually fills out a sheet similar to the one shown just to keep track. The clocks are in high demand, and the owner makes a deliberate effort to hold down production so prices stay high. Based on the purchase order and the sales forms, create the class diagram and list of normalized tables needed for this case. Note that the item total on the Sale form does not equal the total price, because the total price includes some overhead charges, but not the delivery charge. Although not displayed on the form, the owner also wants to track the date each clock was started and finished.

Sale					Employee
Order Date					
Estimated Delivery Date					Customer
Actual Delivery Date					Phone
					Address
Total Price	Payment Method				City, State ZIP
Delivery Method	Delivery Charge				
Item/Feature	Color	Quantity	Price	Subtotal	
				Item Total	

Purchase Order				
Supplier				Order Date
Contact	Phone			Employee
Estimated Ship Date				
Date Received				
Item	Quantity	Cost	Quantity Received	Clock (custom orders)
Total Charges		Date Due		
Date Paid	Amount Paid			

8. A local pizza shop wants a database to track customer orders and deliveries. The basic order form is shown here, along with a simple form the driver fills out when the pizza is delivered. Drivers are encouraged to write down comments about the delivery or the order that might be useful to drivers who deliver the next time. Tips have to be recorded because they are reported to the IRS. Create the class diagram and list of normalized tables for this case.

Pizza Order

Customer
Phone
Address

Order Date/Time
Employee

For each pizza:
Crust Type
Size
Base Price
Specialty Pizza

Custom Toppings

Item	Cost	Comments (e.g., half/half)

Topping Cost
Tax
Discount/Coupon
Total

Delivery Time
Employee
Directions
Payment Method — Credit Card # — Expiration
Driver Tip
Comments (e.g., dog)

9. A company that creates animated videos wants you to build a database to track the progress in producing the video. Based on the accompanying forms, the main focus is on tracking the individual characters and on the scenes. A principal artist draws a character and the basic data is stored so other artists can retrieve it and place samples in their scenes. The company also asks workers to track the amount of time spent on producing the various scenes. Create the class diagram and list of normalized tables for this case.

Character				
Name Description Relative Size				Artist in Charge
Character Views: digitized and stored				
Front	Left	Right	Rear	Top

Scene		
Sequence/Position Lead Writer Synopsis		
Character View Role Action Description		

Work Status				
Date		Employee		
Time	Scene	Character	Changes/Work	Amount of Time

10. A company that makes designer jeans is in trouble. The managers need help matching production to orders and ensuring that products are delivered to customers on time. The problem is made more difficult because each of the several styles of jeans can have many sizes, and customers have very specific orders. The orders can be quite large and are often filled by production from several factories, so several deliveries are needed to fill an order. The order, delivery, and production forms show the main items needed. Each factory has several shifts. A production line consists of about five employees who work on different aspects of the jeans. Create the class diagram and list of normalized tables for this case.

Order

Order ID — Order Date
Customer PO — Exp. Delivery Date
Customer Contact — Phone

Style	Name	Size	Description	List Price	Sale Price	Value

Order Total

Delivery

Order ID — Delivery Date
Factory: Location — Manager — Phone
Shipping Costs

Style	Color	Size	Quantity

Factory Production

Address — Maximum Capacity
City, State ZIP
Country — Date

Shift	Line	Style	Gender	Quantity	Defective	Hours	# People

Sally's Pet Store

11. Define the tables needed to extend the Pet Store database to handle genealogy records for the animals.
12. Define the tables needed to extend the Pet Store database to handle health and veterinary records for the animals.

13. Sally wants to add payroll and monthly employee evaluation information to the database. Define the tables needed.
14. Sally wants to add pet grooming services. Define the tables necessary to schedule appointments, assuming two workers will be dedicated to this area.

Rolling Thunder Bicycles

15. Using the class diagram, identify five business rules that are described by the table definitions and table relationships (similar to the RentPrice rules described by the video store).
16. The company wishes to add more data for human resources, such as tax withholding, benefits selected, and benefit payments by the employees and by the company. Research common methods of handling this type of data and define the required tables.

Website References

Site	Description
http://www.intelligententerprise.com/info_centers/database/	*Database* magazine.
http://www.for.gov.bc.ca/isb/datadmin/	Canadian Ministry of Forests data administration site, with useful information on data administration and design. Start with the development standards.
http://support.microsoft.com/support/kb/articles/q209/5/34.asp	Introduction to normalization.
http://www.phpbuilder.com/columns/barry20000731.php3	Normalization examples.

Additional Reading

Date, C. J. *An Introduction to Database Systems*, 8th ed. Reading: Addison-Wesley, 2003. [A classic higher-level textbook that covers many details of normalization and databases.]

Diederich, J., and J. Milton. "New Methods and Fast Algorithms for Database Normalization." *ACM Transactions on Database Systems* 13, no. 3 (September 1988), pp. 339–65. [One of many attempts to automate the normalization process.]

Fagin, R. "Multivalued Dependencies and a New Normal Form for Relational Databases." *ACM Transactions on Database Systems* 2, no. 3 (September 1977), pp. 262–78. [A classic paper in the development of normal forms.]

———. "A Normal Form for Relational Databases That Is Based on Domains and Keys." *ACM Transactions on Database Systems* 6, no. 3 (September 1981), pp. 387–415. [The paper that initially described domain-key normal form.]

Kent, W. "A Simple Guide to Five Normal Forms in Relational Database Theory." *Communications of the ACM* 26, no. 2 (February 1983), 120–25. [A nice presentation of normalization with examples.]

Rivero, L., J. Doorn, and V. Ferraggine. "Elicitation and Conversion of Hidden Objects and Restrictions in a Database Schema." *Proceedings of the 2002 ACM Symposium on Applied Computing*, 2002, 463–69. [Good discussion of referential integrity issues and problems with weak designs heavily dependent on surrogate ID columns.]

Wu, M. S. "The Practical Need for Fourth Normal Form." *Proceedings of the Twenty-third SIGCSE Technical Symposium on Computer Science Education*, 1992, 19–23. [A small study showing that fourth normal form violations are common in business applications.]

Appendix

Formal Definitions of Normalization

One of the strengths of the relational database model is that it was developed from the mathematical foundations of set theory. Although it is not necessary to know the formal definitions, sometimes they make it easier to understand the process. For a more detailed description of the normal forms and the complications, you should read C. J. Date's advanced textbook. Keep in mind that the formal definitions use specific terms. Figure 3.1A lists the major terms and their common interpretation. Although the formal terms are more accurate, few people have a common understanding of the terms, so in most conversations, it is preferable to use the informal terms.

Initial Definitions

A *relation* is a set of attributes with data that changes over time. Each *attribute* has a corresponding domain and refers to some real-world characteristic. The formal definitions refer to subsets of attributes, which are collections of the columns. The data value returned within tuples for a specified subset of attributes X is denoted t[X].

The essence of normalization is to recognize that a set of attributes has some real-world relationships. The goal is to accurately portray these relationship constraints. These semantic constraints are known as *functional dependencies (FD)*.

Definition: Functional Dependency and Determinant

Where X and Y are subsets of attributes, a functional dependency is denoted as X → Y and holds when any rows of data that have identical values for the X attributes always have identical values for the Y attributes. That is, for tuples t1 and t2 of R, if t1[X] = t2[X], then t1[Y] = t2[Y]. In an FD, X is also known as a *determinant*, because given the dependency, once you are given the values for the X attributes, it determines the resulting values for the Y attributes.

Primary keys are important in relational databases because they are used to identify rows of data. Sometimes multiple attribute sets could be used to form different keys, so they are sometimes referred to as *candidate keys*.

FIGURE 3.1A
Terminology. The formal terms are more accurate and defined mathematically, but difficult for developers and users to understand.

Formal	Definition	Informal
Relation	A set of attributes with data that changes over time. Often denoted R.	Table
Attribute	Characteristic with a real-world domain. Subsets of attributes are multiple columns, often denoted X or Y.	Column
Tuple	The data values returned for specific attribute sets are often denoted as t[X].	Row of data
Schema	Collection of tables and constraints/ relationships	
Functional dependency	X → Y	Business rule dependency

Definition: Keys

A *key* is a set of attributes K such that, where U is the set of all attributes in the relation,

1. There is a functional dependency $K \rightarrow U$
2. If K′ is a subset of K, then there is no FD $K' \rightarrow U$

That is, a set of key attributes K functionally determines all other attributes in the relation, and it is the smallest set of attributes that will do so (there is no smaller subset of K that determines the other attributes).

Normal Form Definitions

The definition of first normal form is closely tied to the definition of an atomic attribute, so both need to be defined at the same time.

Definition: First Normal Form (1NF)

A relation is in *first normal form* if and only if all of its attributes are atomic.

Definition: Atomic Attributes

Atomic attributes are single valued, which means they cannot be composite, multivalued, or nested relations.

Essentially, a 1NF relation is a table with simple cells under each attribute column. You cannot play tricks and try to squeeze extra data, other relationships, or multiple columns into one column. Figure 3.2A provides an example of a table that is not in first normal form because it has two attributes that are not atomic.

Second normal form is defined in terms of primary keys and functional dependency.

Definition: Second Normal Form (2NF)

A relation is in *second normal form* if it is in first normal form and each nonkey attribute is fully functionally dependent on the primary key. That is, $K \rightarrow Ai$ for each nonkey attribute Ai. Consequently, there is no subset K′ such that $K' \rightarrow Ai$ for any attribute.

This definition corresponds closely to the simpler version presented in the chapter that each nonkey column depends on the entire key, not just a portion of the key. Figure 3.3A shows an example of a relation that is not in second normal form.

The formal definition of third normal form is a little harder to comprehend because it relies on a new concept: transitive dependency.

Definition: Transitive Dependency

Given functional dependencies $X \rightarrow Y$ and $Y \rightarrow Z$, the *transitive dependency* $X \rightarrow Z$ must also hold.

The concept of transitivity should be familiar from basic algebra. The fact that it holds true arises from the set-theory foundations. To understand the definition, remember that functional dependency represents business semantic relationships. Consider the relationship between OrderID, CustomerID, and customer Name

FIGURE 3.2A
Nonatomic attributes. This table is not in first normal form because the Name attribute is a composite of two elementary attributes, and the phone attribute is being used to handle multiple values.

Customer(CID, Name: First + Last, Phones, Address)

CID	Name: First + Last	Phones	Address
111	Joe Jones	111-2223 111-3393 112-4582	123 Main

FIGURE 3.3A
Not full dependency. The product description depends on just the ProductID and not the full key {OrderID, ProductID}, so this relation is not in second normal form.

OrderProduct(<u>OrderID</u>, <u>ProductID</u>, Quantity, Description)

<u>OrderID</u>	<u>ProductID</u>	Quantity	Description
32	15	1	Blue hose
32	16	2	Pliers
33	15	1	Blue hose

attributes. The business rule that there is only one customer per order translates to a functional dependency OrderID → CustomerID. Once you know the OrderID value you always know the CustomerID value. Likewise, the key relationship between CustomerID and other attributes such as Name means there is a functional dependency CustomerID → Name. Applying transitivity, once you know the OrderID value, you can obtain the CustomerID value, and in turn learn the value of the customer Name.

Definition: Third Normal Form (3NF)

A relation is in *third normal form* if and only if it is in second normal form and no nonkey attributes are transitively dependent on the primary key. That is, given second normal form: K → Ai for each attribute Ai, there is no subset of attributes X such that K → X → Ai.

In simpler terms, each nonkey attribute depends on the entire key, and not on some intermediate attribute. Figure 3.4A shows a common business example of a relation that is not in third normal form, because customer attributes depend transitively on the CustomerID.

As discussed in Chapter 3, Boyce-Codd normal form is a little harder to follow. It represents the same basic issue: removing a hidden dependency as seen by the formal definition.

Definition: Boyce-Codd Normal Form (BCNF)

A relation is in Boyce-Codd normal form if and only if it is in third normal form and every determinant is a candidate key. That is, K → Ai for every attribute, and there is no subset X (key or nonkey) such that X → Ai where X is different from K.

As shown in the example in Figure 3.5A, consider the situation where employees can have many specialties, there are many employees for each specialty, and an employee can have many managers, but each manager is manager for only one specialty. This functional dependency (ManagerID → Specialty) is not a key within the relation EmpspecMgr(<u>EID</u>, <u>Specialty</u>, ManagerID), so the relation is not in BCNF. It has to be decomposed to create new relations ManagerSpecialty(<u>ManagerID</u>, Specialty), and EmployeeManager(<u>EmployeeID</u>, <u>ManagerID</u>) that explicitly have each functional dependency as keys.

FIGURE 3.4A
Transitive dependency. The customer Name and Phone attributes transitively depend on the CustomerID, so this relation is not in third normal form.

Order(<u>OrderID</u>, OrderDate, CustomerID, Name, Phone)

<u>OrderID</u>	OrderDate	CustomerID	Name	Phone
32	5/5/2004	1	Jones	222-3333
33	5/5/2004	2	Hong	444-8888
34	5/6/2004	1	Jones	222-3333

FIGURE 3.5A
Boyce-Codd normal form. Notice that there is a functional dependency from ManagerID to Specialty. Because this FD is not a candidate key in the relation, it is hidden, and this relation is not in BCNF.

Example: Employees can have many specialties, and many employees can be within a specialty. Employees can have many managers, but a manager can have only one specialty: Mgr → Specialty

EmpSpecMgr(EID, Specialty, ManagerID)

EID	Speciality	ManagerID
32	Drill	1
33	Weld	2
34	Drill	1

FD ManagerID → Specialty is not currently a key.

Fourth normal form is slightly tricky but fortunately does not occur very often in practice. Yet, it can cause problems if it does arise, so you should understand its definition. The definition is closely tied to the definition of a multi-valued dependency.

Definition: Multi-Valued Dependency (MVD)

A *multi-valued dependency (MVD)* exists when there are at least three attributes in a relation (A, B, and C; which could be sets of attributes), and one attribute A determines the other two (B and C), but the other two are independent of each other. That is, A → B and A → C, but B and C are not functionally dependent on each other.

For example, employees can have many specialties and be assigned many tools, but tools and specialties are not directly related to each other.

Definition: Fourth Normal Form (4NF)

A relation is in *fourth normal form* if and only if it is in Boyce-Codd normal form and there are no multi-valued dependencies. That is, all attributes of the relation are functionally dependent on A. If A →→ B, then A → Ai for all attributes Ai.

In the multi-valued dependency example for employee specialties and tools, the relation EmpSpecTools(EID, Specialty, ToolID) is not in fourth normal form, because of the two functional dependencies: EID → Specialty and EID → ToolID. Solving the problem results in two simpler relations: EmployeeSpecialty(EID, Specialty) and EmployeeTools(EID, ToolID).

Part 2

Queries

An important step in building applications is creating queries to retrieve exactly the data that you want. Queries are used to answer business questions and serve as the foundation for forms and reports.

Chapter 4 shows you how to use two basic query systems: SQL and QBE. SQL has the advantage of being a standard that is supported by many database management systems. Once you learn it, you will be able to work with many different systems.

Chapter 5 shows some of the powerful aspects of SQL queries. In particular, it examines the use of subqueries to answer difficult business questions. It also shows that SQL is a complete database language that can be used to define new databases and tables. SQL is also a powerful tool to manipulate data.

Chapter 4

Data Queries

Chapter Outline

What You Will Learn in This Chapter

- How do you get answers to business questions from a database? 145
- Why do you need to learn a special query language to use a database system? 145
- What are the four questions that you need to answer to create a query? 146
- How can you perform computations with a query? 159
- How can you compare results by groups? 163
- Why and how do you join tables in a query? 166

A Developer's View

Miranda: Wow that was hard work! I sure hope normalization gets easier the next time.

Ariel: At least now you have a good database. What's next? Are you ready to start building the application?

Miranda: Not quite yet. I told my uncle that I had some sample data. He already started asking me business questions; for example. Which products were back-ordered most often? and Which employees sold the most items last month? I think I need to know how to answer some of those questions before I try to build an application.

Ariel: Can't you just look through the data and find the answer?

Miranda: Maybe, but that would take forever. Instead, I'll use a query system that will do most of the work for me. I just have to figure out how to phrase the business questions as a correct query.

Introduction

Why do you need a query language? Why not just ask your question in a natural language like English? Natural language processors have improved, and several companies have attempted to connect them to databases. Similarly, speech recognition is improving. Eventually, computers may be able to answer ad hoc questions using a natural language. However, even if an excellent natural language processor existed, it would still be better to use a specialized query language. The main reason for the problem is communication. If you ask a question of a database, a computer, or even another person, you can get an answer. The catch is, did the computer give you the answer to the question you asked? In other words, you have to know that the machine (or other person) interpreted the question in exactly the way you wanted. The problem with any natural language is that it can be ambiguous. If there is any doubt in the interpretation, you run the risk of receiving an answer that might appear reasonable, but is not the answer to the question you meant to ask.

A query system is more structured than a natural language so there is less room for misinterpretation. Query systems are also becoming more standardized, so that developers and users can learn one language and use it on a variety of different systems. **SQL** is the standard database query language. The standard is established through the ISO (International Organization of Standards) and it is updated every few years. Most database management systems implement at least some of the SQL-99 standard, but a few still use the SQL-92 version. The ISO working group is developing a new standard, but it will probably be a few years before it becomes implemented. Although these standards are accepted by most vendors, there is still room for variations in the SQL syntax, so queries written for one database system will not always work on another system.

Most database systems also provide a **query by example (QBE)** method to help beginners create SQL queries. These visually oriented tools generally let users select items from lists, and handle the syntax details to make it easier to create ad hoc queries. Although the QBE designs are easy to use and save time by minimizing typing, you must still learn to use the SQL commands.

Many times, you will have to enter SQL into programming code, or copy and edit SQL statements.

As you work on queries, you should also think about the overall database design. Chapter 3 shows how normalization is used to split data into tables that can be stored efficiently. Queries are the other side of that problem: They are used to put the tables back together to answer ad hoc questions and produce reports.

Three Tasks of a Query Language

To create databases and build applications, you need to perform three basic sets of tasks: (1) define the database, (2) change the data, and (3) retrieve data. Some systems use formal terms to describe these categories. Commands grouped as **data definition language (DDL)** are used to define the data tables and other features of the database. The common DDL commands include ALTER, CREATE, and DROP. Commands used to modify the data are classified as **data manipulation language (DML).** Common DML commands are DELETE, INSERT, and UPDATE. Some systems include data retrieval within the DML group, but the SELECT command is complex enough to require its own discussion. The appendix to this chapter lists the syntax of the various SQL commands. This chapter focuses on the SELECT command. The DML and DDL commands will be covered in more detail in Chapter 5.

The SELECT command is used to retrieve data; it is the most complex SQL command, with several different options. The main objective of the SELECT command is to retrieve specified columns of data for rows that meet some criteria.

Database management systems are driven by query systems. Virtually all tasks can be performed by issuing a DDL, DML, or query command. Modern systems simplify some of the database administration tasks (such as creating a table) by providing a graphical interface. The interface actually builds the appropriate CREATE TABLE command.

Four Questions to Retrieve Data

Every attempt to retrieve data from a relational DBMS requires answering the four basic questions listed in Figure 4.1. The difference among query systems is how you fill in those answers. You need to remember these four questions, but do not worry about the specific order. When you first learn to create queries, you should write down these four questions each time you construct a query. With easy problems, you can almost automatically fill in

FIGURE 4.1
Four questions to create a query. Every query is built by asking these four questions.

- What output do you want to see?
- What do you already know (or what constraints are given)?
- What tables are involved?
- How are the tables joined?

answers to these questions. With more complex problems, you might fill in partial answers and switch between questions until you completely understand the query.

Notice that in some easy situations you will not have to answer all four questions. Many easy questions involve only one table, so you will not have to worry about joining tables (question 3). As another example, you might want the total sales for the entire company, as opposed to the total sales for a particular employee, so there may not be any constraints (question 2).

What Output Do You Want to See?

You generally answer this question by selecting columns of data from the various tables stored in the database. Of course, you need to know the names of all of the columns to answer this question. Generally, the hardest part in answering this question is to wade through the list of tables and identify the columns you really want to see. The problem is more difficult when the database has hundreds of tables and thousands of columns. Queries are easier to build if you have a copy of the class diagram that lists the tables, their columns, and the relationships that join the tables.

The query system can generate aggregations, such as totals and averages. Similarly, the computer can perform basic arithmetic operations (add, subtract, multiply, and divide) on numeric data.

What Do You Already Know?

In most situations you want to restrict your search based on various criteria. For instance, you might be interested in sales on a particular date or sales from only one department. The search conditions must be converted into a standard Boolean notation (phrases connected with AND or OR). The most important part of this step is to write down all the conditions to help you understand the purpose of the query.

What Tables Are Involved?

With only a few tables, this question is easy. With hundreds of tables, it could take a while to determine exactly which ones you need. A good data dictionary with synonyms and comments will make it easier for you (and users) to determine exactly which tables you need for the query. It is also critical that tables be given names that accurately reflect their content and purpose.

One hint in choosing tables is to start with the tables containing the columns listed in the first two questions (output and criteria). Next decide whether other tables might be needed to serve as intermediaries to connect these tables.

How Are the Tables Joined?

This question relates to the issues in data normalization and is the heart of a relational database. Tables are connected by data in similar columns. For instance, an Order table has a CustomerID column. Corresponding data is stored in the Customer table, which also has a CustomerID column. In many cases matching columns in the tables will have the same name (e.g., CustomerID) and this question is easy to answer. However, the columns are not required to have the same name, so you sometimes have to think a little more carefully. For example, an Order table might have a column for

SalesPerson, which is designed to match the EmployeeID key in an Employee table.

Sally's Pet Store

The initial Pet Store database has been built, and some basic historical data has been transferred from Sally's old files. When you show your work to Sally, she becomes very excited. She immediately starts asking questions about her business and wants to see how the database can answer them.

The examples in this chapter are derived from the Pet Store database. The tables and relationships for this case are shown in Figure 4.2. After reading each section, you should work through the queries on your own. You should also solve the exercises at the end of the chapter. Queries always look easy when the answers are printed in the book. To learn to write queries, you must sit down and struggle through the process of answering the four basic questions.

Chapter 3 notes that data normalization results in a business model of the organization. The list of tables gives a picture of how the firm operates. Notice that the Pet Store treats merchandise a little differently than it treats

FIGURE 4.2

Tables for the Pet Store database. Notice that animals and merchandise are similar, but they are treated separately.

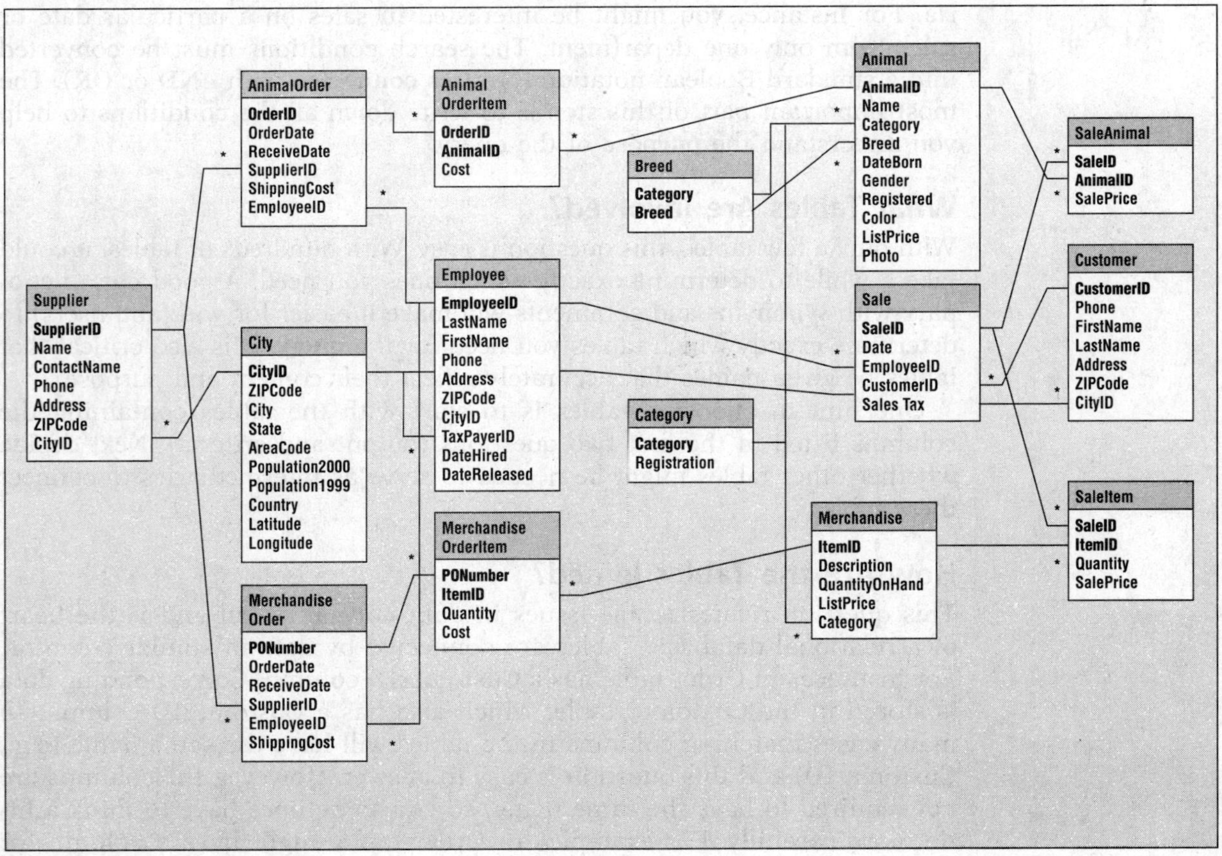

animals. For example, each animal is listed separately on a sale, but customers can purchase multiple copies of merchandise items (e.g., bags of cat food). The reason for the split is that you need to keep additional information about the animals that does not apply to general merchandise.

When you begin to work with an existing database, the first thing you need to do is familiarize yourself with the tables and columns. You should also look through some of the main tables to become familiar with the type and amount of data stored in each table. Make sure you understand the terminology and examine the underlying assumptions. For example, in the Pet Store case, an animal might be registered with a breeding agency, but it can be registered with only one agency. If it is not registered, the Registered column is NULL (or missing) for that animal. This first step is easier when you work for a specific company, since you should already be familiar with the firm's operations and the terms that it uses for various objects.

Vendor Differences

The SQL standards present a classic example of software development tradeoffs. New releases of the standards provide useful features, but vendors face the need to maintain compatibility with a large installed base of applications and users. Consequently, there are substantial differences in the database products. These differences are even more pronounced when you look at the graphical interfaces. To remain up to date, the presentation in this chapter (and the next one) will follow the most recent SQL standards. The current versions of most systems now support many of the SQL standards. For example, Oracle 9i supports the more modern JOIN syntax for multiple tables.

Query Basics

It is best to begin with relatively easy queries. This chapter first presents queries that involve a single table to show the basics of creating a query. Then it covers details on constraints, followed by a discussion on computations and aggregations. Groups and subtotals are then explained. Finally, the chapter discusses how to select data from several tables at the same time.

Figure 4.3 presents several business questions that might arise at the Pet Store. Most of the questions are relatively easy to answer. In fact, if there are not too many rows in the Animal table, you could probably find the answers by hand-searching the table. Actually, you might want to work some of the initial questions by hand to help you understand what the query system is doing.

The foundation of queries is that you want to see only some of the columns from a table and that you want to restrict the output to a set of rows that match some criteria. For example, in the first query (animals with yellow color), you might want to see the AnimalID, Category, Breed, and their Color. Instead of listing every animal in the table, you want to restrict the list to just those with a yellow color.

Single Tables

The first query to consider is, List all animals with yellow in their color. Note that an animal could have many colors. The designer of this database has chosen to store all the colors in one column of the database. So an animal's

FIGURE 4.3
Sample questions for the Pet Store. Most of these are easier since they involve only one table. They represent typical questions that a manager or customer might ask.

- List all animals with yellow in their color.
- List all dogs with yellow in their color born after 6/1/04.
- List all merchandise for cats with a list price greater than $10.
- List all dogs who are male and registered or who were born before 6/1/04 and have white in their color.
- What is the average sale price of all animals?
- What is the total cost paid for all animals?
- List the top 10 customers and the total amount they spent.
- How many cats are in the animal list?
- Count the number of animals in each category.
- List the CustomerID of everyone who bought something between 4/1/04 and 5/31/04.
- List the first name and phone of every customer who bought something between 4/1/04 and 5/31/04.
- List the last name and phone of anyone who bought a registered white cat between 6/1/04 and 12/31/04.
- Which employee has sold the most items?

colors could be described as "yellow, white, brown." Presumably, the primary color is listed first, but there is no mechanism to force the data to be entered that way.

First consider answering this question with a QBE system, as shown in Figure 4.4. The QBE system asks you to choose the tables involved. This situation involves only one table: Animal. Note that all the output columns

FIGURE 4.4
Sample query shown in QBE and SQL. Since there is only one table, only three questions need to be answered: What tables? What do you want to see? What conditions?

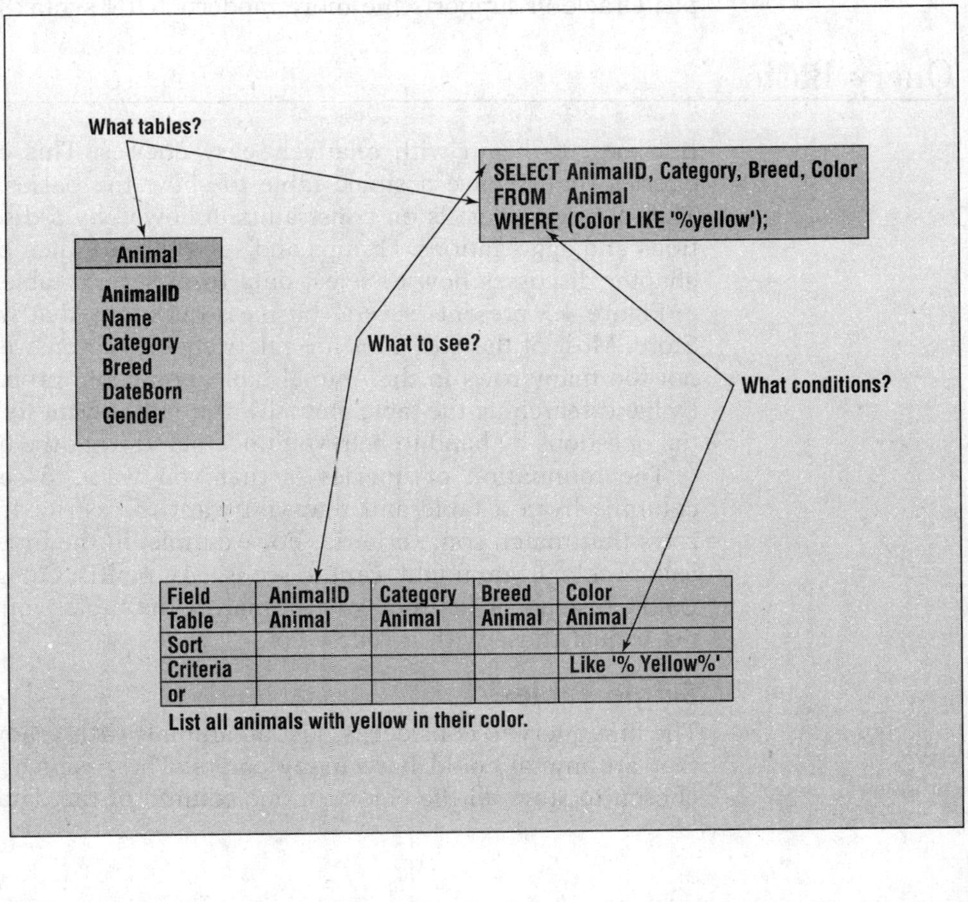

come from the Animal table. Similarly, the Color column in the criteria is also in the Animal table. With the table displayed, you can now choose which columns you want to see in the output. The business question is a little vague, so select AnimalID, Category, Breed, and the Color.

The next step is to enter the criteria that you already know. In this example, you are looking for animals with yellow in their color. On the QBE screen enter the condition "yellow" under the Color column. However, there is one catch: The Color column generally contains more than one word. For some animals, yellow might show up as the second or third color in the list. To match the animal regardless of where the word *yellow* is located, you need to use the LIKE pattern-matching function. By entering the condition LIKE '%yellow%', you are asking the query system to match the word *yellow* anywhere in the list (with any number of characters before or after the word). It is a good idea to run the query now. Check the Color column to make sure the word *yellow* appears somewhere in the list.

Introduction to SQL

SQL is a powerful query language. However, unlike QBE, you generally have to type in the entire statement. Some systems like Microsoft Access enable you to switch back and forth between QBE and SQL, which saves some typing. Perhaps the greatest strength of SQL is that it is a standard that most vendors of DBMS software support. Hence once you learn the base language, you will be able to create queries on all of the major systems in use today. Some people pronounce SQL as "sequel," arguing that it descended from a vendor's early DBMS called quel. Also, "Sequel" is easier to say than "ess-cue-el."

The most commonly used command in SQL is the SELECT statement, which is used to retrieve data from tables. A simple version of the command is shown in Figure 4.5, which contains the four basic parts: **SELECT**, **FROM**, **JOIN**, and **WHERE**. These parts match the basic questions needed by every query. In the example in Figure 4.4, notice the similarity between the QBE and SQL approaches.

Sorting the Output

Database systems treat tables as collections of data. For efficiency the DBMS is free to store the table data in any manner or any order that it chooses. Yet in most cases you will want to display the results of a query in a particular order. The SQL **ORDER BY** clause is an easy and fast means to display the output in any order you choose. As shown in Figure 4.6, simply list the columns you want to sort. The default is ascending (A to Z or low to high with numbers). Add the phrase **DESC** (for descending) after a column to sort from high to low. In QBE you select the sort order on the QBE grid.

In some cases you will want to sort columns that do not contain unique data. For example, the rows in Figure 4.6 are sorted by Category. In these situations you would want to add a second sort column. In the example, rows for each

FIGURE 4.5
The basic SQL SELECT command matches the four questions you need to create a query. The uppercase letters are used in this text to highlight the SQL keywords. They can also be typed in lowercase.

```
SELECT    columns       What do you want to see?
FROM      tables        What tables are involved?
JOIN      conditions    How are the tables joined?
WHERE     criteria      What are the constraints?
```

FIGURE 4.6
The ORDER BY clause sorts the output rows. The default is to sort in ascending order; adding the keyword *DESC* after a column name results in a descending sort. When columns like Category contain duplicate data, use a second column.

Animal
AnimalID
Name
Category
Breed
DateBorn
Gender

```
SELECT Name, Category, Breed
FROM Animal
ORDER BY Category, Breed
```

Field	Name	Category	Breed
Table	Animal	Animal	Animal
Sort		Ascending	Ascending
Criteria			
Or			

Name	Category	Breed
Cathy	Bird	African Grey
	Bird	Canary
Debbie	Bird	Cockatiel
	Bird	Cockatiel
Terry	Bird	Lovebird
	Bird	Other
Charles	Bird	Parakeet
Curtis	Bird	Parakeet
Ruby	Bird	Parakeet
Sandy	Bird	Parrot
Hoyt	Bird	Parrot
	Bird	Parrot

category (e.g., Bird) are sorted on the Breed column. The column listed first is sorted first. In the example, all birds are listed first, and birds are then sorted by Breed. To change this sort sequence in QBE, you have to move the entire column on the QBE grid so that Category is to the left of Breed.

Distinct

The SELECT statement has an option that is useful in some queries. The **DISTINCT** keyword tells the DBMS to display only rows that are unique. For example, the query in Figure 4.7 (*SELECT Category FROM Animal*) would return a long list of animal types (Bird, Cat, Dog, etc.). In fact, it would return the category for every animal in the table—obviously, there are many cats and dogs. To prevent the duplicates from being displayed, use the SELECT DISTINCT phrase.

Note that the DISTINCT keyword applies to the entire row. If there are any differences in a row, it will be displayed. For example, the query *SELECT*

FIGURE 4.7
The DISTINCT keyword eliminates duplicate rows of the output. Without it the animal category is listed for every animal in the database.

```
SELECT Category
FROM Animal;
```

Category
Fish
Dog
Fish
Cat
Cat
Dog
Fish
Dog
Dog
Dog
Fish
Cat
Dog
...

```
SELECT DISTINCT Category
FROM Animal;
```

Category
Bird
Cat
Dog
Fish
Mammal
Reptile
Spider

DISTINCT Category, Breed FROM Animal will return more than the seven rows shown in Figure 4.7 because each category can have many breeds. That is, each category/breed combination will be listed only once, such as Dog/Retriever. Microsoft Access supports the DISTINCT keyword, but you have to enter it in the SQL statement.

Criteria

In most questions identifying the output columns and the tables is straightforward. If there are hundreds of tables, it might take a while to decide exactly which tables and columns you want, but it is just an issue of perseverance. On the other hand, identifying constraints and specifying them correctly can be more challenging. More importantly if you make a mistake on a constraint, you will still get an "answer." The problem is that it will not be the answer to the question you asked—and it is often difficult to see that you made a mistake.

The primary concept of constraints is based on **Boolean algebra,** which you learned in mathematics. In practice, the term simply means that various conditions are connected with AND and OR clauses. Sometimes you will also use a **NOT** statement, which negates or reverses the truth of the statement that follows it. For example, NOT (Category = 'Dog') means you are interested in all animals except dogs.

Consider the example in Figure 4.8. The first step is to note that three conditions define the business question: dog, yellow, and date of birth. The second step is to recognize that all three of these conditions need to be true at the same time, so they are connected by AND. As the database system examines each row, it evaluates all three clauses. If any one clause is false, the row is skipped.

Notice that the SQL statement is straightforward—just write the criteria. The QBE is a little trickier. With QBE, every condition listed on the same criteria row is connected with an AND clause. Conditions on different criteria rows are joined with an OR clause. You have to be careful creating (and reading) QBE statements, particularly when there are many different criteria rows.

FIGURE 4.8
Boolean algebra. An example of three conditions connected by AND. Notice the # signs surrounding the date. They are a convention used by Microsoft Access to help it recognize a date. They are particularly useful if you want to enter a text date (e.g., June 1, 2004).

Animal
AnimalID
Name
Category
Breed
DateBorn
Gender

```
SELECT  AnimalID, Category,DateBorn
FROM    Animal
WHERE   ((Category = 'Dog')
        AND (Color Like '%Yellow%')
        AND (DateBorn > '01-Jun-2004'));
```

Field	AnimalID	Category	DateBorn	Color
Table	Animal	Animal	Animal	Animal
Sort				
Criteria	'Dog'		>'01-Jun-2004'	Like '%Yellow%'
Or				

List all dogs with yellow in their color born after 6/1/04.

a	b	a AND b	a OR b
T	T	T	T
T	F	F	T
F	T	F	T
F	F	F	F

FIGURE 4.9
A truth table shows the difference between AND and OR. Both clauses must be true when connected by AND. Only one clause needs to be true when clauses are connected by OR.

Boolean Algebra

One of the most important aspects of a query is the choice of rows that you want to see. Most tables contain a huge number of rows, and you want to see only the few that meet a business condition. Some conditions are straightforward. For example, you might want to examine only dogs. Other criteria are complex and involve several conditions. For instance, a customer might want a list of all yellow dogs born after June 1, 2004, or registered black labs. Conditions are evaluated according to Boolean algebra, which is a standard set of rules for evaluating conditions. You are probably already familiar with the rules from basic algebra courses; however, it pays to be careful.

The DBMS uses Boolean algebra to evaluate conditions that consist of multiple clauses. The clauses are connected by these operators: AND, OR, NOT. Each individual clause is evaluated as true or false, and then the operators are applied to evaluate the truth value of the overall criterion. Figure 4.9 shows how the primary operators (AND, OR) work. The DBMS examines each row of data and evaluates the Boolean condition. The row is displayed only if the condition is true.

A condition consisting of two clauses connected by AND can be true only if both of the clauses (a and b) are true. A statement that consists of two clauses connected by OR is true as long as at least one of the two conditions is true. Consider the examples shown in Figure 4.10. The first condition is false because it asks for both clauses to be true, and the first one is false. The second example is true because it requires only that one of the two clauses be true. Consider an example from the Pet Store. If a customer asks to see a list of yellow dogs, he or she wants a list of animals where the category is Dog AND the color is yellow.

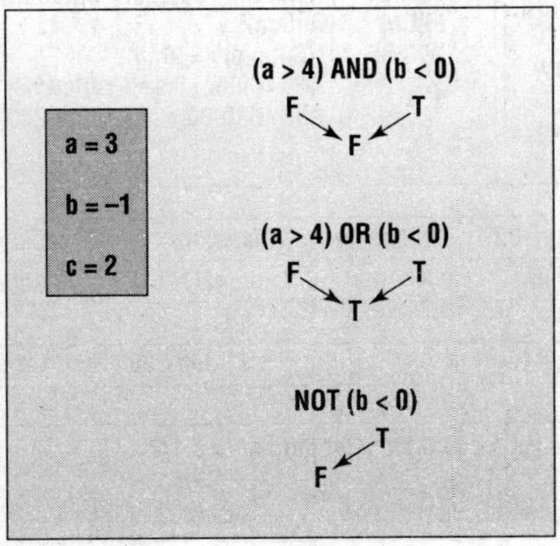

FIGURE 4.10
Boolean algebra examples. Evaluate each clause separately. Then evaluate the connector. The NOT operator reverses the truth value.

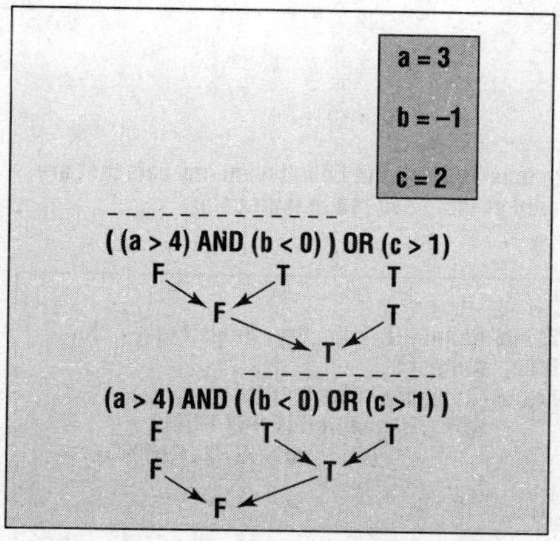

FIGURE 4.11
Boolean algebra mixing AND and OR operators. The result changes depending on which operator is applied first. You must set the order of evaluation with parentheses. Innermost clauses are evaluated first.

As shown in Figure 4.11, conditions that are more complex can be created by adding additional clauses. A complication arises when the overall condition contains both AND connectors and OR connectors. In this situation the resulting truth value depends on the order in which the clauses are evaluated. You should always use parentheses to specify the desired order. Innermost parentheses are evaluated first. In the example at the top of Figure 4.11, the AND operation is performed before the OR operation, giving a result of true. In the bottom example, the OR connector is evaluated first, leading to an evaluation of false.

If you do not use parentheses, the operators are evaluated from left to right. This result may not be what you intended. Yet the DBMS will still provide a response. To be safe, you should build complex conditions one clause at a time. Check the resulting selection each time to be sure you get what you wanted. To find the data matching the conditions in Figure 4.11, you would first enter the $(a > 4)$ clause and display all of the values. Then you would add the $(b < 0)$ clause and display the results. Finally, you would add the parentheses and then the $(c > 1)$ clause.

No matter how careful you are with Boolean algebra there is always room for error. The problem is that natural languages such as English are ambiguous. For example, consider the request by a customer who wants to see a list of "All dogs that are yellow or white and born after June 1." There are two interpretations of this statement:

1. (dogs AND yellow) OR (white AND born after June 1).
2. (dogs) AND (yellow OR white) AND (born after June 1).

These two requests are significantly different. The first interpretation returns all yellow dogs, even if they are older. The second interpretation requests only young dogs, and they must be yellow or white. Most people do not use parentheses when they speak—although pauses help indicate the desired interpretation. A good designer (or salesperson) will ask the customer for clarification.

DeMorgan's Law

Designing queries is an exercise in logic. A useful technique for simplifying complex queries was created by a logician named Augustus DeMorgan. Consider the Pet Store example displayed in Figure 4.12. A customer might

FIGURE 4.12
Sample problem with negation. Customer knows what he or she does not want. SQL can use NOT, but you should use DeMorgan's law to negate the Registered and Color statements.

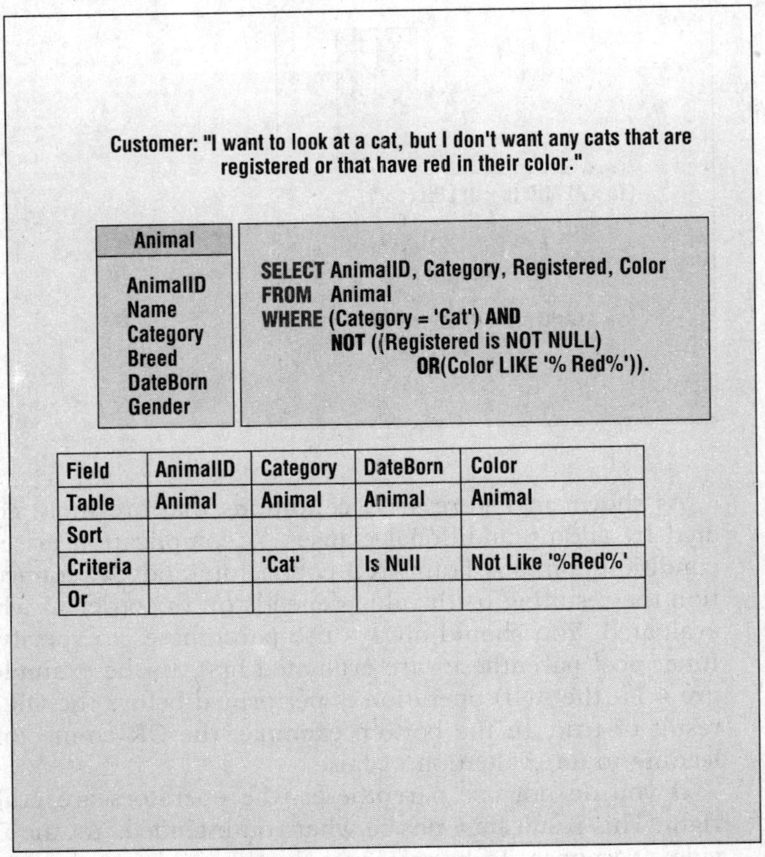

come in and say, "I want to look at a cat, but I don't want any cats that are registered or that have red in their color." Even in SQL, the condition for this query is a little confusing: (Category = "cat") AND NOT ((Registered is NOT NULL) OR (Color LIKE '%red%')). The negation (NOT) operator makes it harder to understand the condition. It is even more difficult to create the QBE version of the statement.

The solution lies with **DeMorgan's law**, which explains how to negate conditions when two clauses are connected with an AND or an OR. DeMorgan's law states that to negate a condition with an AND or an OR connector, you negate each of the two clauses and switch the connector. An AND becomes an OR, and vice versa. Figure 4.13 shows how to handle the negative condition for the Pet Store customer. Each condition is negated (NOT NULL becomes NULL, and red becomes NOT red). Then the connector is changed from OR to AND. Figure 4.13 shows that the final truth value stays the same when the statement is evaluated both ways.

The advantage of the new version of the condition is that it is a little easier to understand and much easier to use in QBE. In QBE you enter the individual clauses for Registration and Color. Placing them on the same line connects them with AND. In natural language the new version is expressed as follows: A cat that is not registered and is not red.

In practice DeMorgan's law is useful to simplify complex statements. However, you should always test your work by using sample data to evaluate the truth tables.

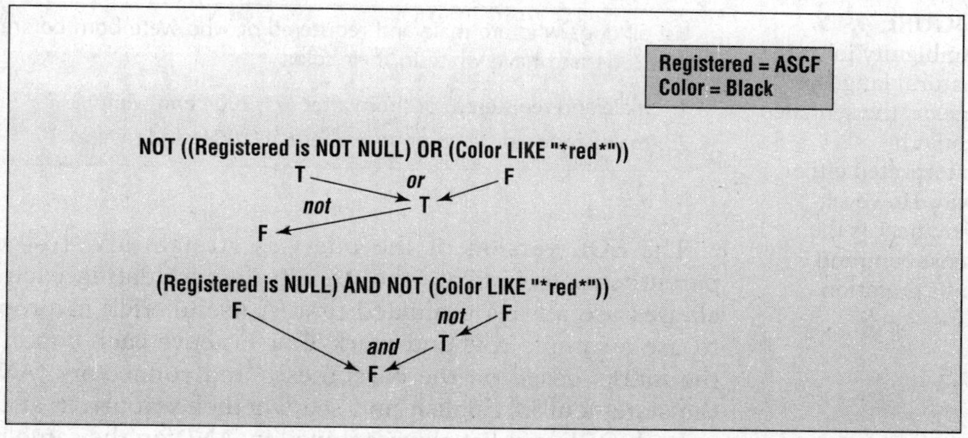

FIGURE 4.13
DeMorgan's law. Compound statements are negated by reversing each item and swapping the connector (AND for OR). Use truth tables to evaluate the examples.

Criteria can become more complex when you mix clauses with AND and OR in the same query. Consider the question in Figure 4.14 to list all dogs who are male and registered or who were born before 6/1/04 and have white in their color.

First, note that there is some ambiguity in the English statement about how to group the two clauses. Figure 4.15 shows the two possibilities. The use of the second *who* helps to clarify the split, but the only way to be absolutely certain is to use either parentheses or more words.

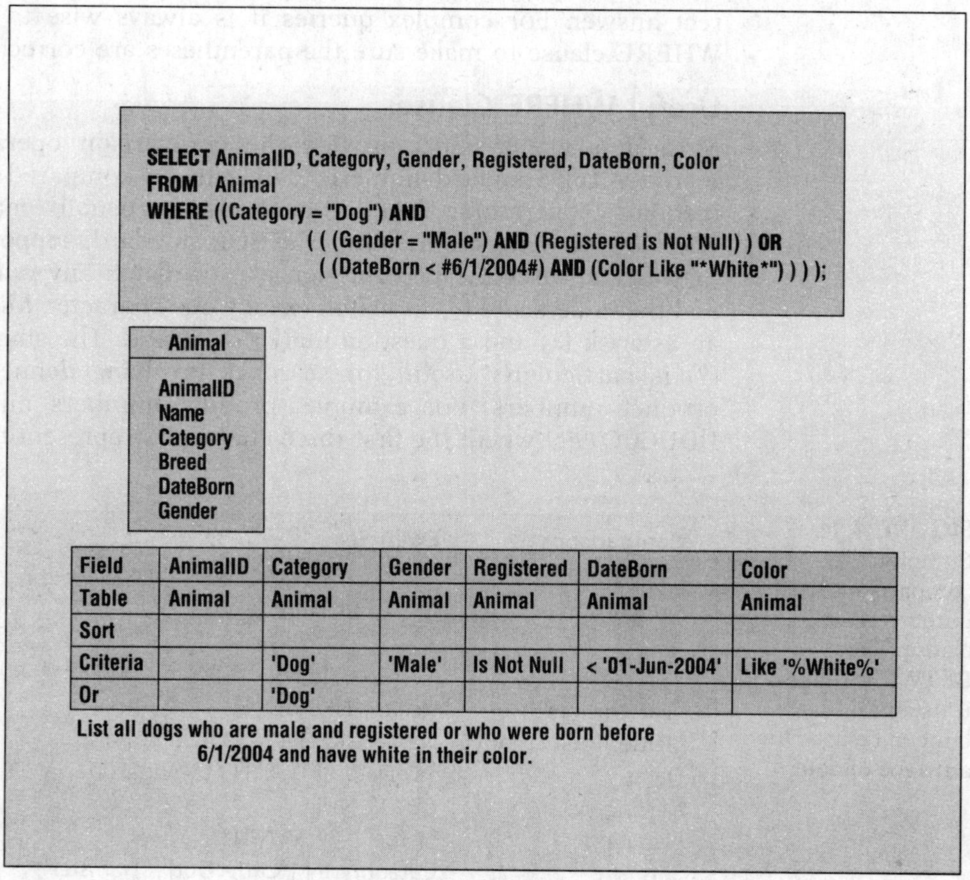

FIGURE 4.14
Boolean criteria—mixing AND and OR. Notice the use of parentheses in SQL to ensure the clauses are interpreted in the right order. Also note that QBE required duplicating the condition for "Dog" in both rows.

FIGURE 4.15
Ambiguity in natural languages means the sentence could be interpreted either way. However, version 1 is the most common interpretation.

List all dogs who are male and registered or who were born before 6/1/2004 and have white in their color.

1: (male and registered) or (born after 6/1/2004 and white)

2: (male) and (registered or born after 6/1/2004) and (white)

The SQL version of the query is straightforward—just be sure to use parentheses to indicate the priority for evaluating each phrase. Innermost clauses are always evaluated first. A useful trick in proofreading queries is to use a sample row and mark T or F above each condition. Next, combine the marks based on the parentheses and connectors (AND, OR). Then read the statement in English and see whether you arrive at the same result.

With QBE you list clauses joined by AND on the same row, which is equivalent to putting them inside one set of parentheses. Separate clauses connected by OR are placed on a new row. To interpret the query, look at each criteria row separately. If all of the conditions on one line are true, then the row is determined to be a match. A data row needs to match only one of the separate criteria lines (not all of them).

A second hint for building complex queries is to test just part of the criteria at one time—particularly with QBE. In this example, you would first write and test a query for male and registered. Then add the other conditions and check the results at each step. Although this process takes longer than just leaping to the final query, it helps to ensure that you get the correct answer. For complex queries it is always wise to examine the SQL WHERE clause to make sure the parentheses are correct.

Useful WHERE Clauses

Most database systems provide the comparison operators displayed in Figure 4.16. Standard numeric data can be compared with equality and inequality operators. Text comparisons are usually made with the **LIKE** operator for pattern matching. The SQL standard, supported by Oracle and SQL Server, uses the percent sign (%) to match any number of characters and the underscore (_) to match exactly one character. Microsoft Access uses an asterisk (*) and a question mark (?) instead. The single-character match (?) is particularly useful for searches involving defined text strings like product numbers. For example, product numbers might be defined as DDDCCC9999 where the first three characters represent the department, the

FIGURE 4.16
Common comparisons used in the WHERE clause. The BETWEEN clause is useful for dates but can be used for any type of data.

Comparisons	Examples
Operators	<, =, >, <>, BETWEEN, LIKE, IN
Numbers	AccountBalance > 200
Text	
Simple	Name > 'Jones'
Pattern match one	License LIKE 'A__82_'
Pattern match any	Name LIKE 'J%'
Dates	SaleDate BETWEEN '15-Aug-2004' AND '31-Aug-2004'
Missing data	City IS NULL
Negation	Name IS NOT NULL
Sets	Category IN ('Cat', 'Dog', 'Hamster')

next three the product category, and the last four digits are a unique number. Then to find all products that refer to the Dog category you could use the WHERE condition: ProductID LIKE "___dog____". Most systems also provide an option that controls whether text comparisons are sensitive to upper- and lowercase. Many people prefer to ignore case, since it is easier to type words without worrying about case.

The **BETWEEN** clause is not required, but it saves some typing and makes some conditions a little clearer. The clause (SaleDate BETWEEN '15-Aug-2004' AND '31-Aug-2004' is equivalent to (SaleDate >= '15-Aug-2004' AND SaleDate <= '31-Aug-2004'). The date syntax shown here can be used on most database systems. Some systems allow you to use shorter formats, but on others, you will have to specify a conversion format. These conversion functions are not standard. For example, Access can read almost any common date format if you surround the date by pound signs (#) instead of quotes. Oracle often requires the TO_DATE conversion function, such as SaleDate >=TO_DATE('8/15/04','mm/dd/yy'). Be sure that you test all date conversions carefully, especially when you first start working with a new DBMS.

Another useful condition is to test for missing data with the NULL comparison. Two common forms are IS NULL and IS NOT NULL. Be careful—the statement (City = NULL) will not work with most systems, because NULL is not really a value. You must use (City IS NULL) instead.

Computations

For the most part you would use a spreadsheet or write separate programs for serious computations. However, queries can be used for two types of computations: aggregations and simple arithmetic on a row-by-row basis. Sometimes the two types of calculations are combined. Consider the row-by-row computations first.

Basic Arithmetic Operators

SQL and QBE can both be used to perform basic computations on each row of data. This technique can be used to automate basic tasks and to reduce the amount of data storage. Consider a common order or sales form. As Figure 4.17 shows, the basic tables would include a list of items purchased: OrderItem(<u>OrderID</u>, <u>ItemID</u>, Price, Quantity). In most situations you would need to multiply Price by Quantity to get the total value for each item ordered. Because this computation is well defined (without any unusual conditions), there is no point in storing the result—it can be recomputed whenever it is needed. Simply build a query and add one more column. The new column uses elementary algebra and lists a name: Price * Quantity AS Extended. Remember that the computations are performed for each row in the query.

Some systems provide additional mathematical functions. For example, basic mathematical functions such as absolute value, logarithms, and trigonometric functions might be available. Although these functions provide extended capabilities, always remember that they can operate only on data stored in one row of a table or query.

Aggregation

Databases for business often require the computation of totals and subtotals. Hence, query systems provide functions for **aggregation** of data. The common functions listed in Figure 4.18 can operate across several rows of

FIGURE 4.17
Computations. Basic computations (+,−,*,/) can be performed on numeric data in a query. The new display column should be given a meaningful name.

OrderItem(<u>OrderID</u>, <u>ItemID</u>, Price, Quantity)

```
Select OrderID, ItemID, Price, Quantity,
Price*Quantity As Extended
From OrderItem;
```

OrderID	ItemID	Price	Quantity	Extended
151	9764	19.50	2	39.00
151	7653	8.35	3	25.05
151	8673	6.89	2	13.78

data and return one value. The most commonly used functions are Sum and Avg, which are similar to those available in spreadsheets.

With SQL, the functions are simply added as part of the SELECT statement. With QBE, the functions are generally listed on a separate Total line. With Microsoft Access, you first have to click the summation (Σ) button on the toolbar to add the Total line to the QBE grid. In both SQL and QBE, you should provide a meaningful name for the new column.

The Count function is useful in many situations, but make sure you understand the difference between Sum and Count. Sum totals the values in a numeric column. Count simply counts the number of rows. You can supply an argument to the Count function, but it rarely makes a difference—generally you just use Count(*). The difficulty with the Count function lies in knowing when to use it. You must first understand the English question. For example, the question How many employees does Sally have? would use the Count function: SELECT Count(*) From Employee. The question *How many units of Item 9764 have been sold?* requires the Sum function: SELECT

FIGURE 4.18
Aggregation functions. Sample query in QBE and SQL to answer: What is the average sale price for all animals? Note that with Microsoft Access you have to click the summation button on the toolbar (Σ) to display the Total line on the QBE grid.

```
SELECT Avg(SalePrice) AS AvgOfSalePrice
FROM SaleAnimal;
```

SaleAnimal
SaleID
AnimalID
SalePrice

Sum
Avg
Min
Max
Count
StDev or StdDev
Var

Field	SalePrice
Table	SaleAnimal
Total	Avg
Sort	
Criteria	
Or	

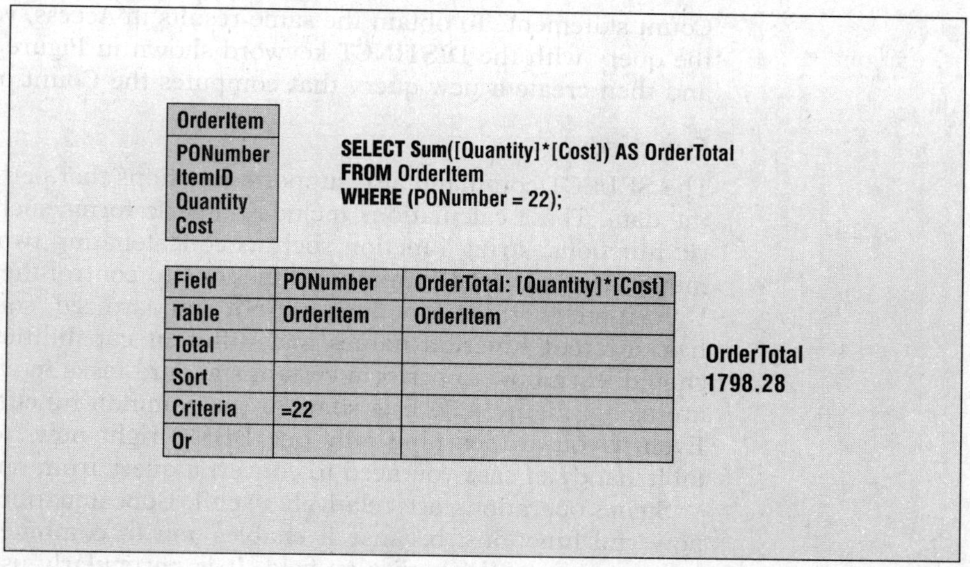

FIGURE 4.19
Computations. Row-by-row computations (Quantity * Cost) can be performed within an aggregation function (Sum), but only the final total will be displayed in the result.

Sum(Quantity) FROM OrderItem. The difference is that there can be only one employee per row in the Employee table, whereas a customer can buy multiple quantities of an item at one time. Also keep in mind that Sum can be used only on a column of numeric data (e.g., Quantity).

In many cases you will want to combine the **row-by-row calculations** with an aggregate function. The example in Figure 4.19 asks for the total value of a particular order. To get total value, the database must first calculate Quantity * Cost for each row and then get the total of that column. The example also shows that it is common to specify a condition (WHERE) to limit the rows used for the total. In this example, you want the total for just one order.

There is one important restriction to remember with aggregation. You cannot display detail lines (row by row) at the same time you display totals. In the order example you can see either the detail computations (Figure 4.17) or the total value (Figure 4.19). In most cases it is simple enough to run two queries. However, if you want to see the detail and the totals at the same time, you need to create a report as described in Chapter 6.

Note that you can compute several aggregate functions at the same time. For example, you can display the Sum, Average, and Count at the same time: SELECT Sum(Quantity), Avg(Quantity), Count(Quantity) From OrderItem. In fact, if you need all three values, you should compute them at one time. Consider what happens if you have a table with a million rows of data. If you write three separate queries, the DBMS has to make three passes through the data. By combining the computations in one query, you cut the total query time to one-third. With huge tables or complex systems, these minor changes in a query can make the difference between a successful application and one that takes days to run.

Sometimes when using the Count function, you will also want to include the DISTINCT operator. For example, *SELECT COUNT (DISTINCT Category) FROM Animal* will count the number of different categories and ignore duplicates. Although the command is part of the SQL standard, some systems (notably Access) do not support the use of the DISTINCT clause within the

Count statement. To obtain the same results in Access, you would first build the query with the DISTINCT keyword shown in Figure 4.7. Save the query and then create a new query that computes the Count on the saved query.

Functions

The SELECT command also supports functions that perform calculations on the data. These calculations include numeric forms such as the trigonometric functions, string function such as concatenating two strings, date arithmetic functions, and formatting functions to control the display of the data. Unfortunately, these functions are not standardized, so each DBMS vendor has different function names and different capabilities. Nonetheless, you should learn how to perform certain standard tasks in whichever DBMS you are using. Figure 4.20 lists some of the common functions you might need. Even if you are learning only one DBMS right now, you should keep this table handy in case you need to convert a query from one system to another.

String operations are relatively useful. Concatenation is one of the more powerful functions, because it enables you to combine data from multiple columns into a single display field. It is particularly useful when you want to combine a person's last and first names. Other common string functions convert the data to all lowercase or all uppercase characters. The length function counts the number of characters in the string column. A substring

FIGURE 4.20
Differences in SQL functions. This table shows some of the differences that are commonly encountered when working with these database systems. Queries are often used to perform basic computations, but the syntax for handling these computations depends on the specific DBMS.

Task	Access	SQL Server	Oracle
Strings			
Concatenation	FName & " " & LName	FName +' '+ LName	FName || ' ' || LName
Length	Len(LName)	Length(LName)	LENGTH(LName)
Uppercase	UCase(LName)	Upper(LName)	UPPER(LName)
Lowercase	LCase(LName)	Lower(LName)	LOWER(LName)
Partial string	MID(LName,2,3)	Substring(LName,2,3)	SUBSTR(LName,2,3)
Dates			
Today	Date( ), Time( ), Now( )	GetDate()	SYSDATE
Month	Month(myDate)	DateName(month, myDate)	TRUNC(myDate, 'mm')
Day	Day(myDate)	DatePart(day, myDate)	TRUNC (myDate, 'dd')
Year	Year(myDate)	DatePart(year, myDate)	TRUNC (myDate, 'yyyy')
Date arithmetic	DateAdd DateDiff	DateAdd DateDiff	ADD_MONTHS MONTHS_BETWEEN LAST_DAY
Formatting	Format(item, format)	Str(item, length, decimal) Cast, Convert	TO_CHAR(item, format) TO_DATE(item, format)
Numbers			
Math functions	Cos, Sin, Tan, Sqrt	Cos, Sin, Tan, Sqrt	COS, SIN, TAN, SQRT
Exponentiation	2 ^ 3	Power(2,3)	POWER(2,3)
Aggregation	Min, Max, Sum, Count,	Min, Max, Sum, Count,	MIN, MAX, SUM, COUNT,
Statistics	Avg StDev, Var	Avg, StDev, Var, LinReqSlope, Correlation	AVG, STDDEV, VARIANCE, REGR, CORR

function is used to return a selected portion of a string. For example, you might choose to display only the first 20 characters of a long title.

The powerful date functions are often used in business applications. Date columns can be subtracted to obtain the number of days between two dates. Additional functions exist to get the current date and time or to extract the month, day, or year parts of a date column. Date arithmetic functions can be used to add (or subtract) months, weeks, or years to a date. One issue you have to be careful with is entering date values into a query. Most systems are sensitive to the fact that world regions have different standards for entering and displaying dates. For example, whereas 5/1/2004 is the first day in May in the United States, it is the fifth day in January in Europe. To make sure that the DBMS understands exactly how you want a date interpreted, you might have to use a conversion function and specify the date format. Additional formatting functions can be used for other types of data, such as setting a fixed number of decimal points or displaying a currency sign.

A DBMS might have dozens of numeric functions, but you will rarely use more than a handful. Most systems have the common trigonometric functions (e.g., sine and cosine), as well as the ability to raise a number to a power. Most also provide some limited statistical calculations such as the average and standard deviation, and occasionally correlation or regression computations. You will have to consult the DBMS documentation for availability and details on additional functions. However, keep in mind that you can always write your own functions and use them in queries just as easily as the built-in functions.

Subtotals and GROUP BY

To look at totals for only a few categories, you can use the Sum function with a WHERE clause. For example, you might ask How many cats are in the animal list? The query is straightforward: SELECT Count (AnimalID) FROM Animal Where (Category = "Cat"). This technique will work, and you will get the correct answer. You could then go back and edit the query to get the count for dogs or any other category of animal. However, eventually you will get tired of changing the query. Also, what if you do not know all the categories?

Consider the more general query: Count the number of animals in each category. As shown in Figure 4.21, this type of query is best solved with the GROUP BY clause. This technique is available in both QBE and SQL. The SQL syntax is straightforward: just add the clause GROUP BY Category. The **GROUP BY** statement can be used only with one of the aggregate functions (Sum, Avg, Count, and so on). With the GROUP BY statement, the DBMS looks at all the data, finds the unique items in the group, and then performs the aggregate function for each item in the group.

By default, the output will generally be sorted by the group items. However, for business questions, it is common to sort (ORDER BY) based on the computation. The Pet Store example is sorted by the Count, listing the animals with the highest count first.

Be careful about adding multiple columns to the GROUP BY clause. The subtotals will be computed for each distinct item in the entire GROUP BY clause. So if you include additional columns (e.g., Category and Breed), you might end up with a more detailed breakdown than you wanted.

Microsoft added a useful feature that can be used in conjunction with the ORDER BY statement. Sometimes a query will return thousands of lines of

FIGURE 4.21
GROUP BY computes subtotals and counts for each type of animal. This approach is much more efficient than trying to create a WHERE clause for each type of animal. To convert business questions to SQL, watch for phrases such as *by* or *for each* which usually signify the use of the GROUP BY clause.

Animal
AnimalID
Name
Category
Breed
DateBorn
Gender

```
SELECT     Category, Count(AnimalID) AS CountOfAnimalID
FROM       Animal
GROUP BY   Category
ORDER BY   Count(AnimalID) DESC;
```

Field	Category	AnimalID
Table	Animal	Animal
Total	Group By	Count
Sort		Descending
Criteria		
Or		

Category	CountOfAnimalID
Dog	100
Cat	47
Bird	15
Fish	14
Reptile	6
Mammal	6
Spider	3

output. Although the rows are sorted, you might want to examine only the first few rows. For example, you might want to list your 10 best salespeople or the top 10 percent of your customers. When you have sorted the results, you can easily limit the output displayed by including the **TOP** statement; for example, SELECT TOP 10 SalesPerson, SUM(Sales) FROM Sales GROUP BY SalesPerson ORDER BY SUM(Sales) DESC. This query will compute total sales for each salesperson and display a list sorted in descending order. However, only the first 10 rows of the output will be displayed. Of course, you could choose any value instead of 10. You can also enter a percentage value (e.g., TOP 5 PERCENT), which will cut the list off after 5 percent of the rows have been displayed. These commands are useful when a manager wants to see the "best" of something and skip the rest of the rows. Note that Oracle does not support the TOP condition.

Conditions on Totals (HAVING)

The GROUP BY clause is powerful and provides useful information for making decisions. In cases involving many groups, you might want to restrict the output list, particularly when some of the groups are relatively minor. The Pet Store has categories for reptiles and spiders, but they are usually special-order items. In analyzing sales the managers might prefer to focus on the top-selling categories.

One way to reduce the amount of data displayed is to add the **HAVING** clause. The HAVING clause is a condition that applies to the GROUP BY output. In the example presented in Figure 4.22, the managers want to skip any animal category that has fewer than 10 animals. Notice that the SQL statement simply adds one line. The same condition can be added to the criteria grid in the QBE query. The HAVING clause is powerful and works much like a WHERE statement. Just be sure that the conditions you impose apply to the computations indicated by the GROUP BY clause. The HAVING clause is a possible substitute in Oracle which lacks the TOP statement. You can sort a set of subtotals and cut off the list to display only values above a certain limit.

FIGURE 4.22
Limiting the output with a HAVING clause. The GROUP BY clause with the Count function provides a count of the number of animals in each category. The HAVING clause restricts the output to only those categories having more than 10 animals.

Animal
AnimalID
Name
Category
Breed
DateBorn
Gender

```
SELECT     Category, Count(AnimalID) AS CountOfAnimalID
FROM       Animal
GROUP BY   Category
HAVING     Count(AnimalID ) > 10
ORDER BY   Count(AnimalID) DESC;
```

Field	Category	AnimalID
Table	Animal	Animal
Total	Group	Count
Sort		Descending
Criteria		>10
Or		

Category	CountOfAnimalID
Dog	100
Cat	47
Bird	15
Fish	14

WHERE versus HAVING

When you first learn QBE and SQL, WHERE and HAVING look very similar, and choosing the proper clause can be confusing. Yet it is crucial that you understand the difference. If you make a mistake, the DBMS will give you an answer, but it will not be the answer to the question you want.

The key is that the WHERE statement applies to every single row in the original table. The HAVING statement applies only to the subtotal output from a GROUP BY query. To add to the confusion, you can even combine WHERE and HAVING clauses in a single query—because you might want to look at only some rows of data and then limit the display on the subtotals.

Consider the question in Figure 4.23 that counts the animals born after June 1, 2004, in each Category, but lists only the Category if there are more

FIGURE 4.23
WHERE versus HAVING. Count the animals born after June 1, 2001, in each category, but list the category only if it has more than 10 of these animals. The WHERE clause first determines whether each row will be used in the computation. The GROUP BY clause produces the total count for each category. The HAVING clause restricts the output to only those categories with more than 10 animals.

Animal
AnimalID
Name
Category
Breed
DateBorn
Gender

```
SELECT     Category, Count(AnimalID) AS CountOfAnimalID
FROM       Animal
WHERE      DateBorn > #6/1/2004#
GROUP BY   Category
HAVING     Count(AnimalID) > 10
ORDER BY   Count(AnimalID) DESC;
```

Field	Category	AnimalID	DateBorn
Table	Animal	Animal	Animal
Total	Group By	Count	Where
Sort		Descending	
Criteria		>10	>'01-Jun-2004'
Or			

Category	CountOfAnimalID
Dog	30
Cat	18

than 10 of these animals. The structure of the query is similar to the example in Figure 4.22. The difference in the SQL statement is the addition of the WHERE clause (DateBorn >#6/1/2004#). This clause is applied to every row of the original data to decide whether it should be included in the computation. Compare the count for dogs in Figure 4.23 (30) with the count in Figure 4.22 (100). Only 30 dogs were born after June 1, 2004. The HAVING clause then limits the display to only those categories with more than 10 animals.

The query is processed by first examining each row to decide whether it meets the WHERE condition. If so, the Category is examined and the Count is increased for that category. After processing each row in the table, the totals are examined to see whether they meet the HAVING condition. Only the acceptable rows are displayed.

The same query in QBE is a bit more confusing. Both of the conditions are listed in the criteria grid. However, look closely at the Total row, and you will see a Where entry for the DateBorn column. This entry is required to differentiate between a HAVING and a WHERE condition. To be safe, you should always look at the SQL statement to make sure your query was interpreted correctly.

The Best and the Worst

Think about the business question, Which product is our best-seller? How would you build a SQL statement to answer that question? To begin, you have to decide if "best" is measured in quantity or revenue (price times quantity). For now, simply use quantity. A common temptation is to write a query similar to SELECT Max(Quantity) FROM SaleItem. This query will run. It will return the individual sale that had the highest sale quantity, but it will not sum the quantities. A step closer might be SELECT ItemID, Max(Sum(Quantity)) FROM SaleItem GROUP BY ItemID. But this query will not run because the database cannot compute the maximum until after it has computed the sum. So, the best answer is to use SELECT ItemID, Sum(Quantity) FROM SaleItem GROUP BY ItemID ORDER BY Sum(Quantity) DESC. This query will compute the total quantities purchased for each item and display the result in descending order—the best-sellers will be at the top of the list.

The one drawback to this approach is that it returns the complete list of items sold. Generally, most businesspeople will want to see more than just the top or bottom item, so it is not a serious drawback—unless the list is too long. In that case, you can use the TOP or HAVING command to reduce the length of the list.

Multiple Tables

All the examples so far have used a single table to keep the discussion centered on the specific topics. In practice, however, you often need to combine data from several tables. In fact, the strength of a DBMS is its ability to combine data from multiple tables.

Chapter 3 shows how business forms and reports are dissected into related tables. Although the normalization process makes data storage more efficient and avoids common problems, ultimately, to answer the business question, you need to recombine the data from the tables. For example, the Sale table contains just the CustomerID to identify the specific customer. Most people

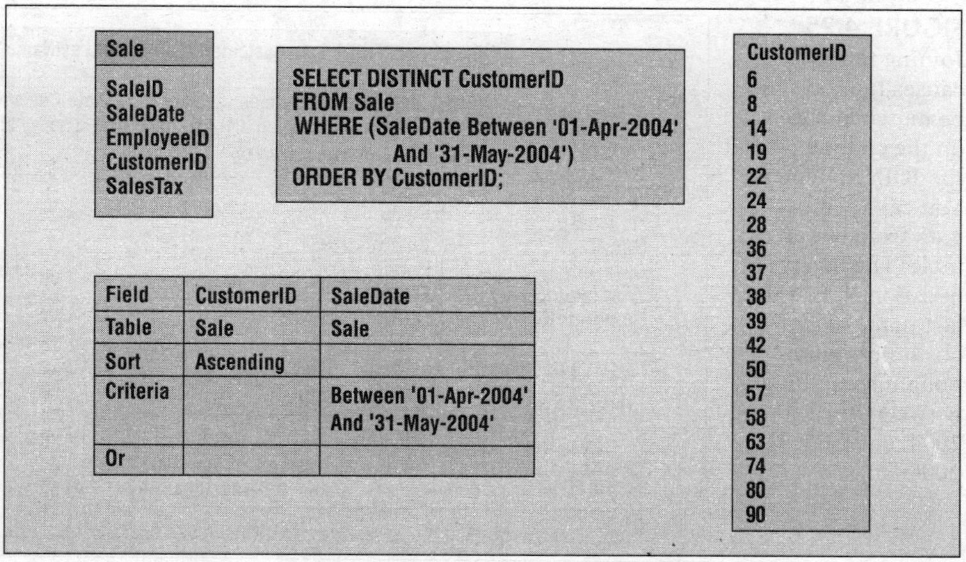

FIGURE 4.24
List the CustomerID of everyone who bought something between April 1, 2004, and May 31, 2004. Most people would prefer to see the name and address of the customer—those attributes are in the Customer table.

would prefer to see the customer name and other attributes. This additional data is stored in the Customer table—along with the CustomerID. The objective is to take the CustomerID from the Sale table and look up the matching data in the Customer table.

Joining Tables

With modern query languages, combining data from multiple tables is straightforward. You simply specify which tables are involved and how the tables are connected. QBE is particularly easy to use for this process.

To understand the process, first consider the business question posed in Figure 4.24: List the CustomerID of everyone who bought something between 4/1/2004 and 5/31/2004. Because some customers might have made purchases on several days, the DISTINCT clause can be used to delete the duplicate listings.

Most managers would prefer to see the customer name instead of CustomerID. However, the name is stored in the Customer table because it would be a waste of space to copy all of the attributes to every table that referred to the customer. If you had these tables only as printed reports, you would have to take the CustomerID from the sales report and find the matching row in the Customer table to get the customer name. Of course, it would be time-consuming to do the matching by hand. The query system can do it easily.

As illustrated in Figure 4.25, the QBE approach is somewhat easier than the SQL syntax. However, the concept is the same. First, identify the two tables involved (Sale and Customer). In QBE, you select the tables from a list, and they are displayed at the top of the form. In SQL, you enter the table names on the FROM line. Second, you tell the DBMS which columns are matched in each table. In this case, you match CustomerID in the Sale table to the CustomerID in the Customer table. Most of the time the column names will be the same, but they could be different.

In SQL, tables are connected with the JOIN statement. This statement was changed with the introduction of SQL 92—however, you will encounter many older queries that still use the older SQL 89 syntax. With SQL 89, the

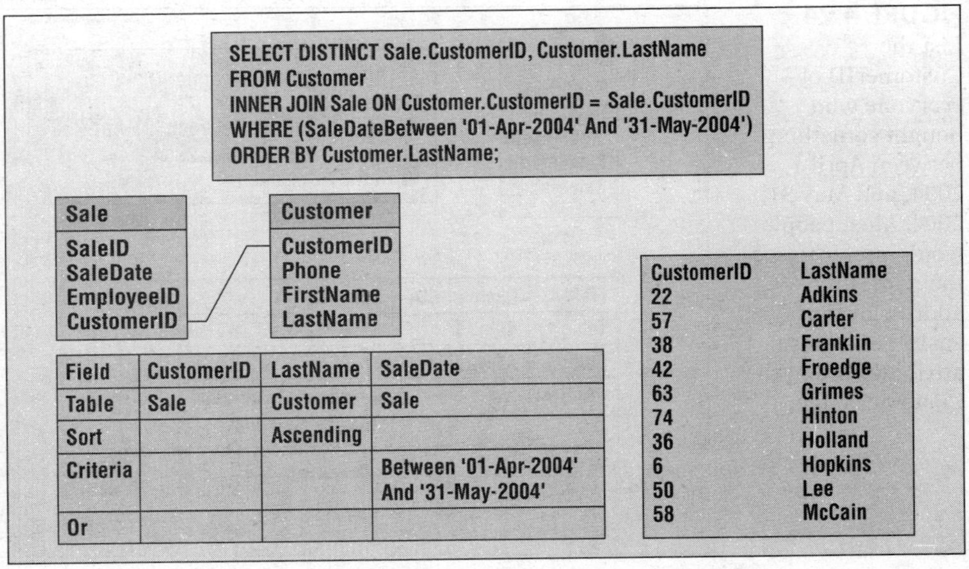

FIGURE 4.25
Joining tables causes the rows to be matched based on the columns in the JOIN statement. You can then use data from either table. The business question is, List the last name of customers who bought something between April 1, 2004, and May 31, 2004.

JOIN condition is part of the WHERE clause. Most vendors are converting to the SQL 92 syntax, so this text will rely on that format. As Chapter 5 shows, the SQL 92 syntax is much easier to understand when you need to change the join configuration.

The syntax for a JOIN is displayed in Figure 4.26. An informal syntax similar to SQL 89 is also shown. The DBMS will not accept statements using the informal syntax, but when the query uses many tables, it is easier to write down the informal syntax first and then add the details needed for the proper syntax. Note that with both QBE and SQL, you must specify the tables involved and which columns contain matching data.

Identifying Columns in Different Tables

Examine how the columns are specified in the SQL JOIN statement. Because the column CustomerID is used in both tables, it would not make sense to write CustomerID = CustomerID. The DBMS would not know what you meant. To keep track of which column you want, you must also specify the name of the table: Sale.CustomerID. Actually, you can use this syntax

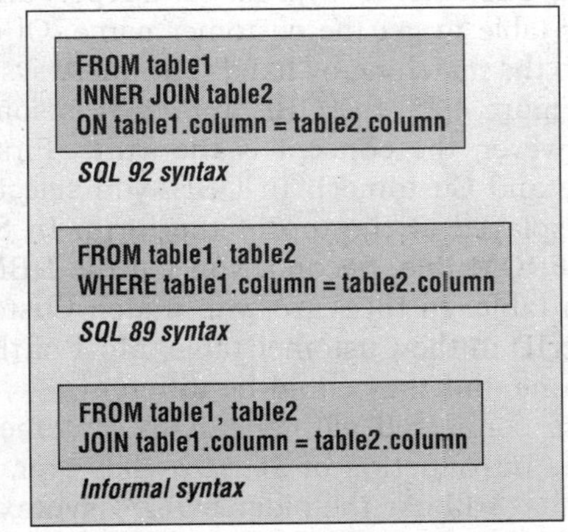

FIGURE 4.26
SQL 92 and SQL 89 syntax to join tables. The informal syntax cannot be used with a DBMS, but it is easier to read when you need to combine many tables.

anytime you refer to a column. You are required to use the full table.column name only when the same column name is used in more than one table. If you use QBE with Microsoft Access, you will see that it always includes the table name—to avoid confusion as tables are added.

Joining Many Tables

A query can use data from several different tables. The process is similar regardless of the number of tables. Each table you want to add must be joined to one other table through a data column. If you cannot find a common column, either the normalization is wrong or you need to find a third table that contains links to both tables.

Consider the example in Figure 4.27: List the name and phone number of anyone who bought a registered white cat between two given dates. An important step is to identify the tables needed. For large problems involving several tables, it is best to first list the columns you want to see as output and the ones involved in the constraints. In the example, the name and phone number you want to see are in the Customer table. The Registration status, Color, and Category (cat) are all in the Animal table. The SaleDate is in the Sale table. However, when you try to join these three tables, you quickly realize that the Animal table cannot be connected to the other two. Remember that customers might purchase more than one animal at a time, so this repeating list is stored in a separate table, SaleAnimal, which includes columns for SaleID and AnimalID. Hence the query uses four tables.

```
SELECT DISTINCTROW Customer.LastName, Customer.Phone
FROM Customer INNER JOIN (Sale INNER JOIN (Animal INNER JOIN SaleAnimal
ON Animal.AnimalID = SaleAnimal.AnimalID) ON Sale.SaleID = SaleAnimal.SaleID)
ON Customer.CustomerID = Sale.CustomerID
WHERE ((Animal.Category = 'Cat') AND (Animal.Registered Is Not Null)
AND (Color Like '%White%') AND (SaleDate Between '01-Jun-2004' And '31-Dec-2004'));
```

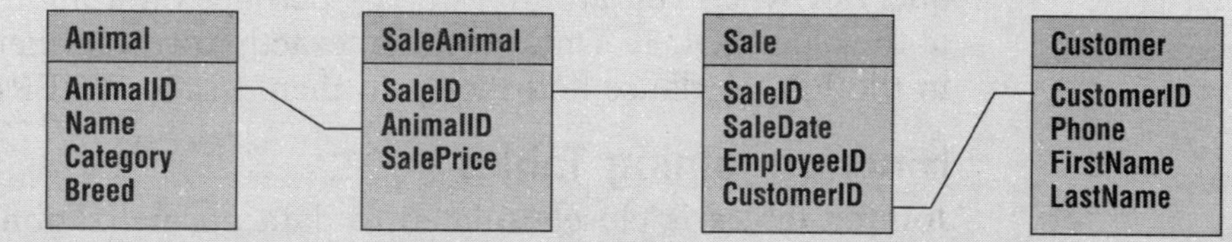

Field	LastName	Phone	Category	Registered	Color	SaleDate
Table	Customer	Customer	Animal	Animal	Animal	Sale
Sort	Ascending					
Criteria			'Cat'	Is Not Null	Like '%White%'	Between '01-Jun-2004' And '31-Dec-2004'
Or						

FIGURE 4.27
Joining multiple tables. QBE makes joining multiple tables relatively easy—just connect the tables with a line. With SQL, just start with two tables and expand outward; for example, start with (Animal INNER JOIN SaleAnimal ON Animal.AnimalID = SaleAnimal.AnimalID), and then add a third table (Sale) with its JOIN.

FIGURE 4.28
Joining multiple tables. With SQL 92 syntax, first join two tables within parentheses and then add a table and its JOIN condition. When you want to focus on the tables being joined, use the easier notation—just remember that it must be converted to SQL 92 syntax for the computer to understand it.

SQL 92 syntax to join three tables:

```
FROM Table1
  INNER JOIN (Table2 INNER JOIN Table3 ON Table2.ColA = Table3.ColA)
  ON Table1.ColB = Table2.ColB
```

Easier notation, but not correct syntax:

```
FROM   Table1, Table2, Table3
JOIN   Table1.ColB = Table2.ColB
       Table2.ColA = Table3.ColA
```

When the database contains a large number of tables, complex queries can be challenging to build. You need to be familiar with the tables to determine which tables contain the columns you want to see. For large databases, an entity-relationship diagram (ERD) or a class diagram can show how the tables are connected. If the database is built in Access, be sure that you pre-define relationships when you create the tables. Chapter 3 explains how Access sets referential integrity for foreign key relationships. Access uses the relationships to automatically add the JOINs to QBE when you choose a table. You can also use the ERD to help users build queries.

When you first see it, the SQL 92 syntax for joining more than two tables can look confusing. In practice, it is best not to memorize the syntax. When you are first learning SQL, understanding the concept of the JOIN is far more important than worrying about syntax. Figure 4.28 shows the syntax needed to join three tables. To read it or to create a similar statement, start with the innermost JOIN (in the parentheses). Then add a table with the corresponding ON condition. If you need additional tables, continue adding parentheses and ON statements, working out from the center. Just be sure that the new table can be joined to one of the tables inside the parentheses. Figure 4.28 also shows an easier syntax that is faster to write when you are first developing a query or when you are in a hurry—perhaps on a midterm exam. It is similar to the older SQL 89 syntax (but not exactly correct) where you list all the tables in the FROM clause and then join them in the WHERE statement.

Hints on Joining Tables

Joining tables is closely related to data normalization. Normalization splits data into tables that can be stored and searched more efficiently. Queries and SQL are the reverse operation: JOINs are used to recombine the data from the tables. If the normalization is incorrect, it might not be possible to join the tables. As you build queries, double-check your normalization to make sure it is correct. Students often have trouble with JOINs, so this section provides some hints to help you understand the potential problems.

Remember that any time you use multiple tables, you must join them together. Interestingly, many database query systems will accept a query even if the tables are not joined. They will even give you a result. Unfortunately, the result is usually meaningless. The joined tables also create a huge query. Without any constraints most query systems will produce a **Cross JOIN**, where every row in one table is paired with every row in the other table. In algebra, a Cross JOIN is known as a Cartesian product of two sets. If the tables have *m* and *n* rows each, the resulting query will have $m * n$ rows!

Where possible, you should double-check the answer to a complex query. Use sample data and individual test cases in which you can compute the answer by hand. You should also build a complex query in stages. Start with one or two tables and check the intermediate results to see if they make sense. Then add new tables and additional constraints. Add the summary calculations last (e.g., Sum, Avg). It's hard to look at one number (total) and decide whether it is correct. Instead, look at an intermediate listing and make sure it includes all of the rows you want; then add the computations.

Columns used in a JOIN are often key columns, but you can join tables on any column. Similarly, joined columns may have different names. For example, you might join an Employee.EmployeeID column to a Sale.SalesPerson column. The only technical constraint is that the columns must contain the same type of data (domain). In some cases, you can minimize this limitation by using a function to convert the data. For example, you might use Left(ZipCode,5) = ZipCode5 to reduce a nine-digit ZipCode string to five digits. Just make sure that it makes sense to match the data in the two columns. For instance, joining tables on Animal.AnimalID = Employee.EmployeeID would be meaningless. The DBMS would actually accept the JOIN (if both ID values are integers), but the JOIN does not make any sense because an Employee can never be an Animal (except in science-fiction movies).

Avoid multiple ties between tables. This problem often arises in Access when you have predefined relationships between tables. Access QBE automatically uses those relationships to join tables in a query. If you select the four tables shown in Figure 4.29 and leave all four JOINs, you will not get the answer you want. The four JOINs will return AnimalOrders only where the Employee placing the order has the same CityID as the Supplier! If you only need the City for the Supplier, the solution is to delete the JOIN between Employee and City. In general, if your query uses four tables, you should have three JOINs (one less than the number of tables).

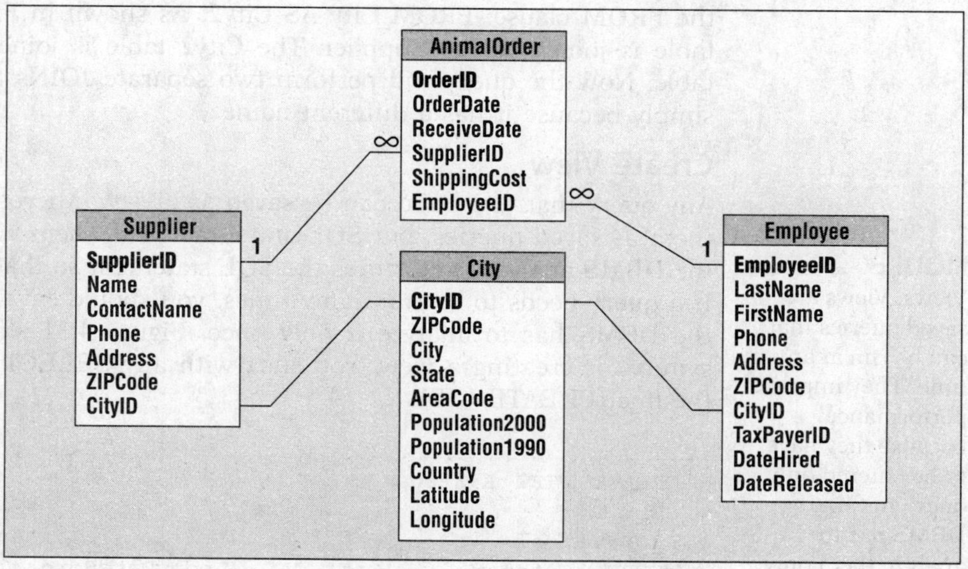

FIGURE 4.29
A query with these four tables with four JOINS would return only rows where the Employee had the same CityID as the Supplier. If you need only the supplier city, just delete the JOIN between Employee and CityID. If you want both cities, add a second copy of the City table as a fifth table.

FIGURE 4.30
Table alias. The City table is used twice. The second time, it is given the alias City2 and treated as a separate table. Hence, different cities can be retrieved for Supplier and for Employee.

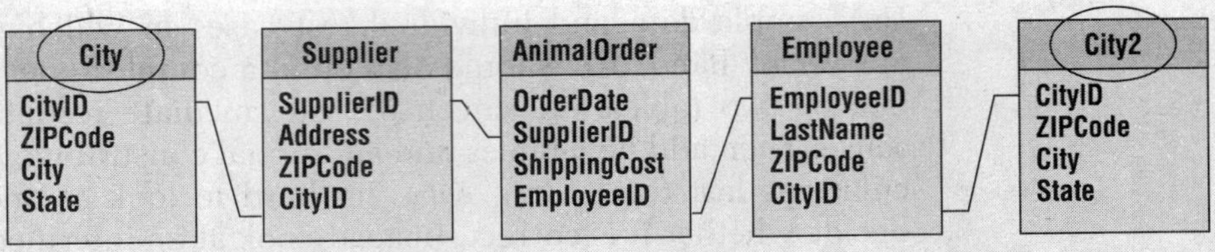


```
SELECT Supplier.SID, Supplier.CityID, City.City, Employee.EID,
Employee.Last Name, Employee.CityID, City2.City
FROM (City INNER JOIN Supplier ON City.CityID = Supplier.CityID) INNER JOIN
((City AS City2 INNER JOIN Employee ON City2.CityID = Employee.CityID)
INNER JOIN AnimalOrderON Employee.EmployeeID = AnimalOrder.EmployeeID)
ON Supplier.SupplierID = AnimalOrder.SupplierID;
```

SID	Supplier.CityID	City.City	EID	LastName	Employee.CityID	City2.City
4	7972	Middlesboro	5	James	7083	Orlando
2	10896	Springfield	1	Reeves	9201	Lincoln
4	7972	Middlesboro	3	Reasoner	8313	Springfield
9	10740	Columbia	8	Carpenter	10592	Philadelphia
5	10893	Smyrna	3	Reasoner	8313	Springfield

Table Alias

Consider the preceding example in more detail. What if you really want to display the City for the Supplier and the City for the Employee? Of course, you want to allow the cities to be different. The answer involves a little-known trick in SQL: just add the City table twice. The second "copy" will have a different name (e.g., City2). You give a table a new name (**alias**) within the FROM clause: FROM City AS City2. As shown in Figure 4.30, the City table is joined to the Supplier. The City2 table is joined to the Employee table. Now the query will perform two separate JOINs to the same table—simply because it has a different name.

Create View

Any query that you build can be saved as a **view**. Microsoft simply refers to them as saved queries, but SQL and Oracle call them *views*. In either case, the DBMS analyzes and stores the SQL statement so that it can be run later. If a query needs to be run many times, you should save it as a view so that the DBMS has to analyze it only once. Figure 4.31 shows the basic SQL syntax for creating a view. You start with any SELECT statement and add the line (CREATE VIEW . . .).

FIGURE 4.31
Views. Views are saved queries that can be run at any time. They improve performance because they have to be entered only once, and the DBMS has to analyze them only once.

```
CREATE VIEW Kittens AS
SELECT *
FROM Animal
WHERE (Category = 'Cat' AND (TodayDateBorn < 180);
```

FIGURE 4.32
Queries based on views. Views can be used within other queries.

```
SELECT Avg(ListPrice)
FROM Kittens
WHERE (Color LIKE '%Black%');
```

The most powerful feature of a view is that it can be used within another query. Views are useful for queries that you have to run many times. You can also create views to handle complex questions. Users can then create new, simpler queries based on the views. In the example in Figure 4.31, you would create a view (Kittens) that displays data for Cats born within the last 180 days. As shown in Figure 4.32, users could search the Kittens view based on other criteria such as color.

As long as you want to use a view only to display data, the technique is straightforward. However, if you want a view that will be used to change data, you must be careful. Depending on how you create the view, you might not be able to update some of the data columns in the view. The example shown in Figure 4.33 is an updatable view. The purpose is to add new data for ordering items. The user enters the OrderID and the ItemID. The corresponding description of that Item is automatically retrieved from the Item table.

Figure 4.34 illustrates the problem that can arise if you are hasty in choosing the columns in a view. Here the OrderLine view uses the ItemID value from the Item table (instead of from the OrderItem table). Now you will not be able to add new data to the OrderLine view. To understand why, consider what happens when you try to change the ItemID from 57 to 32. If it works at all, the new value is stored in the Item table, which simply changes the ItemID of cat food from 57 to 32.

To ensure that a view can be updated, the view should be designed to change data in only one table. The rest of the data is included simply for display—such as verifying that the user entered the correct ItemID. You should never include primary key columns from more than one table. Also, to remain updatable, a view cannot use the DISTINCT keyword or contain a GROUP BY or HAVING clause.

Views have many uses in a database. They are particularly useful in helping business managers work with the database. A database administrator (DBA) or IS worker can create views for the business managers, who see the section of the database expressed only in the views. Hence, you can hide the

FIGURE 4.33
Updatable view. The OrderLine view is designed to change data in only one table (OrderItem). The Description from the Item table is used for display to help the user verify that the ItemID was entered correctly.

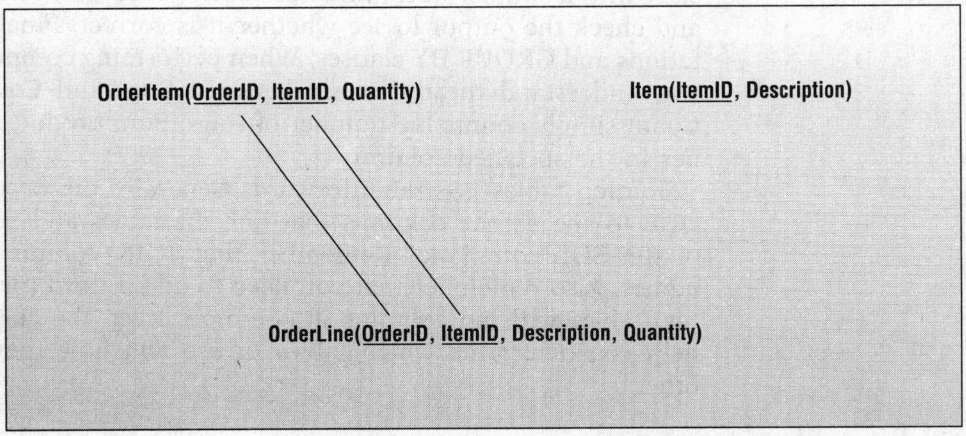

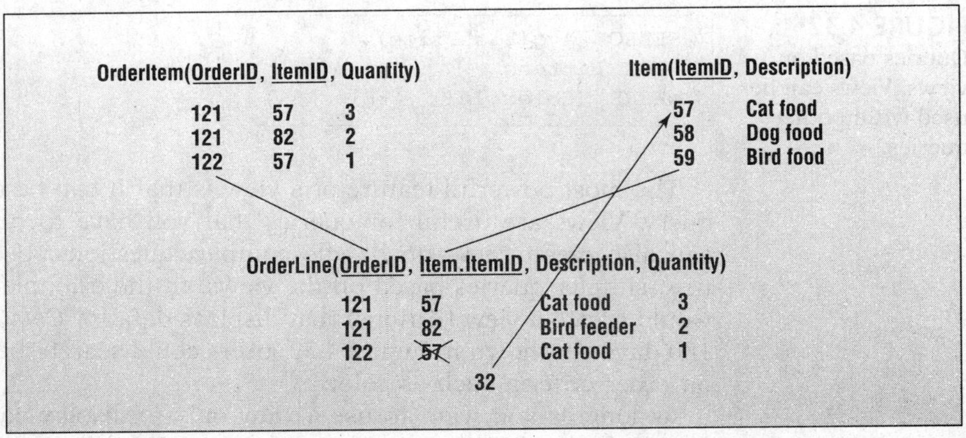

FIGURE 4.34
Nonupdatable view. Do not mix primary keys from different tables. If this view works at all, it will not do what you want. If you try to change the ItemID from 57 to 32, you will only change the ItemID of cat food. You will not be able to enter new data into the OrderItem table.

view's complexity and size. Most important, you can hide the JOINs needed to build the view, so managers can work with simple constraints. By keeping the view updatable, managers never need to use the underlying raw tables.

Note that some database systems place restrictions on commands allowed within a view. For example, older Oracle and newer SQL Server systems do not allow you to use the ORDER BY clause in a saved view. The reason for this restriction was to enable the system to provide better performance by optimizing the query. To sort a result, you had to add the ORDER BY statement to a new query that called the saved view. Finally, no matter how careful you are at constructing a view with a JOIN statement, the DBMS might still refuse to consider it updateable. When the DBMS accepts it, updatable views can save some time later when building forms. But, at other times you have to give up and go with simpler forms.

Summary

The key to creating a query is to answer four questions: (1) What output do you want to see? (2) What constraints do you know? (3) What tables are involved? (4) How are the tables joined? The essence of creating a query is to use these four questions to get the logic correct. The WHERE clause is a common source of errors. Be sure that you understand the objectives of the query. Be careful when combining OR and AND statements and use DeMorgan's law to simplify the conditions.

Always test your queries. The best method to build complex queries is to start with a simpler query and add tables. Then add conditions one at a time and check the output to see whether it is correct. Finally, enter the computations and GROUP BY clauses. When performing computations, be sure that you understand the difference between Sum and Count. Remember that Count simply counts the number of rows; Sum produces the total of the values in the specified column.

Joining tables is straightforward. Generally the best approach is to use QBE to specify the columns that link the tables and then check the syntax of the SQL command. Remember that JOIN columns can have different names. Also remember that you need to add a third (or fourth) table to link two tables with no columns in common. Keep the class diagram handy to help you determine which tables to use and how they are linked to each other.

A Developer's View

As Miranda noted, SQL and QBE are much easier than writing programs to retrieve data. However, you must still be careful. The most dangerous aspect of queries is that you may get a result that is not really an answer to the business question. To minimize this risk, build queries in pieces and check the results at each step. Be particularly careful to add aggregation and GROUP BY clauses last, so that you can see whether the WHERE clause was entered correctly. If you name your columns carefully, it is easier to see how tables should be joined. However, columns do not need the same names to be joined. For your class project, you should identify some common business questions and write queries for them.

Key Terms

aggregation, *159*
alias, *172*
BETWEEN, *159*
Boolean algebra, *153*
Cross JOIN, *170*
data definition language (DDL), *146*
data manipulation language (DML), *146*
DeMorgan's law, *156*
DESC, *151*
DISTINCT, *152*
FROM, *151*
GROUP BY, *163*
HAVING, *164*
JOIN, *151*
LIKE, *158*
NOT, *153*
NULL, *149*
ORDER BY, *151*
query by example (QBE), *145*
row-by-row calculations, *161*
SELECT, *151*
SQL, *145*
TOP, *164*
view, *172*
WHERE, *151*

Review Questions

1. What are the four questions used to create a query?
2. What is the basic structure of the SQL SELECT command?
3. What is the purpose of the DISTINCT operator?
4. Why is it important to use parentheses in complex (Boolean) WHERE clauses?
5. What is DeMorgan's law, and how does it simplify conditions?
6. What is the difference between the ORDER BY and GROUP BY commands?
7. How do the basic SQL arithmetic operators (+, −, etc.) differ from the aggregation (SUM, etc.) commands?
8. What basic aggregation functions are available in the SELECT command?
9. What is the difference between Count and Sum? Give an example of how each would be used.
10. What is the difference between the WHERE and HAVING clauses? Give an example of how each would be used.
11. What is the SQL syntax for joining two tables?

Exercises

Sally's Pet Store

Write the SQL statements that will answer questions 1 through 25 based on the tables in the Pet Store database.

1. List the cats born in May.
2. List the customers who shopped at the store the first seven days in June.
3. What was the most expensive item sold in July?
4. Which suppliers sent orders that took more than 10 days to arrive?
5. List the items that have fewer than 10 units in stock.
6. List the cats that are brown and cost less than $300, or any brown female animal priced less than $150.
7. What is the total value of animals sold in December?

8. How many cats were sold in October?
9. Which employees ordered merchandise from suppliers in Tennessee in April?
10. List the suppliers in Nebraska who sold birds to Sally's Pet Store.
11. Which employee placed the most expensive order in August?
12. Which state holds most of Sally's customers?
13. To what state did the Pet Store sell the most merchandise (by value) in July?
14. List the employees who report to Reasoner.
15. List the customers who have purchased cats from Gibson.
16. Did the store sell more cats or dogs in the first quarter?
17. Did the store sell more female or male animals in the fourth quarter?
18. List the registered dogs sold in January with white in their color.
19. Which supplier sold the Pet Store the most dog merchandise in the first quarter?
20. Which employees sold the most dog merchandise in July and August?
21. Which cats were preordered, meaning they were sold before they were ordered?
22. Which animals sold for less than their cost?
23. Which cats sold for at least 50 percent more than their cost?
24. For each merchandise supplier, what is the average shipping cost?
25. During the third quarter, which items have been ordered the most times in more than 5-unit quantities?

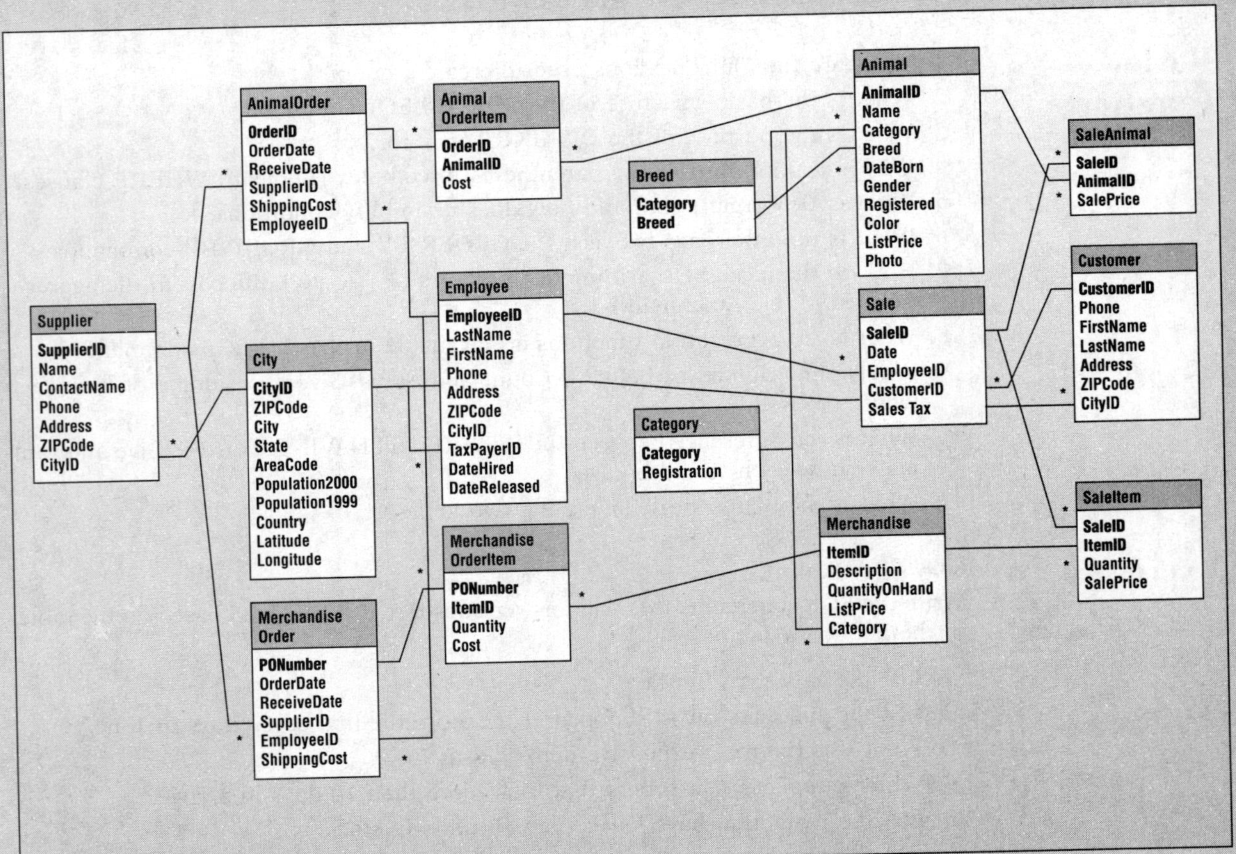

Rolling Thunder Bicycles

Write the SQL statements that will answer questions 26 through 50 based on the tables in the Rolling Thunder database. Build your queries in Access.

26. List the customers from California who bought red mountain bikes in September 2003.
27. List the employees who sold racing bikes shipped to Wisconsin without the help of a retail store in 2001.
28. List all of the (distinct) rear derailleurs installed on road bikes sold in Florida in 2002.
29. Who bought the largest (frame size) full-suspension mountain bike sold in Georgia in 2004?
30. Which manufacturer gave Rolling Thunder the largest discount on an order in 2003?
31. Which customer received the greatest percentage discount on a racing bike purchased since January 1, 2000?
32. Which employee has installed the most headsets in mountain bikes?
33. Which non-American company has received the most orders?
34. What is the most expensive road bike component Rolling Thunder stocks that has a quantity on hand greater than 200 units?
35. Which inventory item represents the most money sitting on the shelf based on estimated cost?

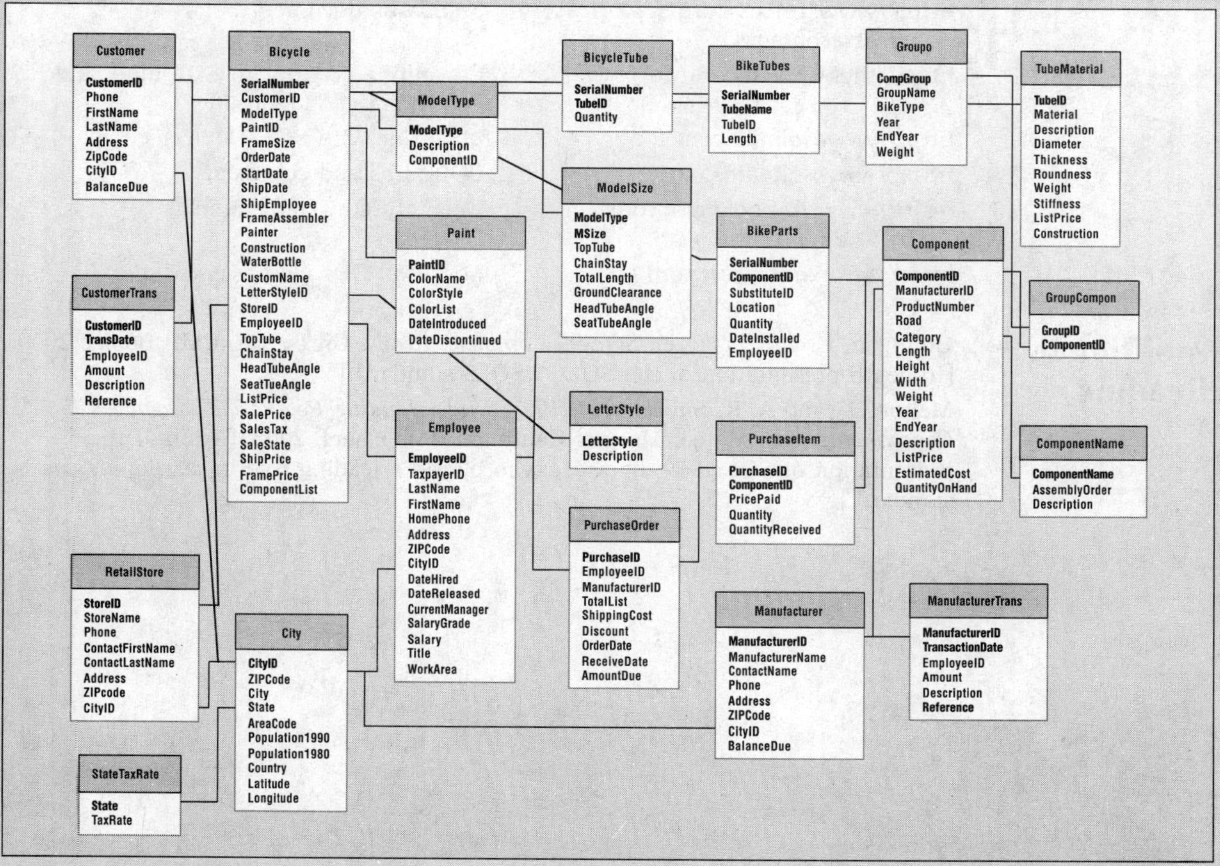

36. What is the greatest number of components installed in one day by one employee?
37. What was the most popular letter style on racing bikes in 2003?
38. Which customer spent the most money with the company, and how many bicycles did that person buy in 2002?
39. Have the sales of mountain bikes (full suspension or hard tail) increased or decreased from 2000 to 2004 (by count not by value)?
40. Which component did the company spend the most money on in 2003?
41. Which employee painted the most red racing bikes in May 2003?
42. Which California bike shop helped sell the most bikes (by value) in 2003?
43. What is the total weight of the components on bicycle 11356?
44. What is the total list price of all items in the 2002 Campy Record group?
45. In 2003, were more race bikes built from carbon or titanium (based on the down tube)?
46. What is the average price paid for the 2001 Shimano XTR rear derailleurs?
47. What is the average top tube length for a 54-cm (frame size) road bike built in 1999?
48. On average, which has the higher list price: road tires or mountain bike tires?
49. In May 2003, which employees sold road bikes that they also painted?
50. In 2002, was the Old English letter style more popular with some paint jobs?

Website References

Site	Description
http://www.opengroup.org	Standards group including SQL.
http://www.jtc1sc32.org/sc32/jtc1sc32.nsf/Attachments	Standards documents, start at 742.
http://thebestweb.com/db	Consulting group with SQL hints and lots of links to other sites.
http://www.sqlmag.com	Magazine with SQL emphasis.
http://www.sqlteam.com	SQL hints and comments.
http://www.vb-bookmark.com/SqlTutorial.html	General SQL reference links.
http://msdn.microsoft.com	Microsoft SQL Server notes.

Additional Reading

Gulutzan, P., and T. Pelzer. *SQL-99 Complete, Really.* Gilroy, CA: CMP Books, 2000. [In-depth presentation of the SQL-99/SQL3 standard.]

Melton, J., and A. R. Simon. *SQL 1999: Understanding Relational Language Components.* San Mateo: Morgan Kaufmann Publishers, 2002. [An in-depth presentation of SQL 1999, by those who played a leading role in developing the standard.]

SQL Syntax

Alter Table

```
ALTER TABLE table
     ADD COLUMN column datatype (size)
     DROP COLUMN column
```

Commit Work

```
COMMIT WORK
```

Create Index

```
CREATE [UNIQUE] INDEX index
ON table (column1, column2, ...)
WITH {PRIMARY|DISALLOW NULL|IGNORE NULL}
```

Create Table

```
CREATE TABLE table
(
    column1    datatype (size) [NOT NULL] [index1],
    column2    datatype (size) [NOT NULL] [index2],
    ...,
    CONSTRAINT pkname PRIMARY KEY (column, ...),
    CONSTRAINT fkname FOREIGN KEY (column)
          REFERENCES existing_table (key_column)
)
```

Create Trigger

```
CREATE TRIGGER triggername {BEFORE|AFTER}
    {DELETE|INSERT|UPDATE}
    ON table {FOR EACH ROW}
    {program code block}
```

Create View

```
CREATE VIEW viewname AS
SELECT ...
```

Delete

```
DELETE
FROM table
WHERE condition
```

Drop

```
DROP INDEX index ON table

DROP TABLE

DROP TRIGGER

DROP VIEW
```

Insert

```
INSERT INTO table (column1, column2, ...)
VALUES (value1, value2, ...)

INSERT INTO newtable (column1, column2, ...)
SELECT ...
```

Grant

```
GRANT privilege    privileges
ON object        ALL, ALTER, DELETE, INDEX,
TO user|PUBLIC   INSERT, SELECT, UPDATE
```

Revoke

```
REVOKE privilege      privileges
ON object           ALL, ALTER, DELETE, INDEX,
FROM user|PUBLIC INSERT, SELECT, UPDATE
```

Rollback

```
SAVEPOINT savepoint

ROLLBACK WORK
    TO savepoint
```

Select

```
SELECT DISTINCT table.column {AS alias}, ...
FROM table/view
INNER JOIN table/view ON T1.ColA = T2.ColB
WHERE (condition)
GROUP BY column
HAVING (group condition)
ORDER BY table.column
{UNION, INTERSECT, EXCEPT, ...}
```

Select Into

```
SELECT column1, column2, ...
INTO newtable
FROM tables
WHERE condition
```

Update

```
UPDATE table
SET column1 = value1, column2 = value2, ...
WHERE condition
```

Chapter 5

Advanced Queries and Subqueries

Chapter Outline

What You Will Learn in This Chapter

- What is a subquery? 184
- How do you find something that is not in a list? 187
- How do you join tables when some items exist in only one of the tables? 188
- When would you want to join a table to itself? 195
- Can SQL be used to change and delete data? 201

A Developer's View

Ariel: Hi, Miranda. You look happy.

Miranda: I am. This query system is great. I can see how it will help the managers. Once I get the application done, they can get answers to any questions they have. They won't have to call me for answers every day. Plus, I can really see how the query system relates to data normalization. With normalization I split the tables so the database could store them properly. Now the query system helps me rejoin them to answer my questions.

Ariel: Does that mean you're finally ready to create the application?

Miranda: Close, but I'm not quite ready. Yesterday my uncle asked me a question that I don't know how to answer.

Ariel: Really, I thought you could do anything with SQL. What was the question?

Miranda: Something about customers who did not order anything last month. I tried several times to get it to work, but the answers I get just aren't right.

Ariel: It doesn't sound like a hard question.

Miranda: I know. I can get a list of customers and orders that were placed any time except last month. But every time I join the Customer table to the Order table, all I get are the customers who did place orders. I don't know how to find something that's *not* there.

Introduction

Now that you understand the basics of the SQL SELECT statement as described in Chapter 4, it is time to study more complex questions. One of the most powerful features of the SQL SELECT command is known as a **subquery** or **nested query**. This feature enables you to ask complex questions that entail retrieving different types of data or data from different sources. SQL is also more than a query language. It can be used to create the entire database (data definition language). SQL also has powerful commands to alter the data (data manipulation language).

Two key points will help you learn how to use subqueries: (1) SQL was designed to work with sets of data—avoid thinking in terms of individual rows, and (2) you can split nested queries into their separate parts and deal with the parts individually.

The features of SQL covered in Chapter 4 are already quite powerful. Why do you need more features? Consider this common business question for Sally's Pet Store: Which animals have not been sold? Think about how you might answer that question using the SQL you know to this point. The first step might be to choose the tables: SaleAnimal and Animal appear to be likely choices. Second, select the columns as output: AnimalID and Name. Third, specify a condition. Fourth, join the tables. These last two steps cause the most problems in this example. How do you specify that an animal has not been sold? You cannot refer to any data in the SaleAnimal table. Because the animal has not been sold, the SaleAnimal table will not contain any entries for it.

Actually, the fourth step (joining the tables) causes you even more problems. Say you wrote a query like this: SELECT AnimalID, Name FROM Animal INNER JOIN SaleAnimal ON (Animal.AnimalID = SaleAnimal.AnimalID). As soon as you write that JOIN condition, you eliminate all the animals you

FIGURE 5.1
Harder questions. Even though there are few constraints on the problems, these questions are more complex. To answer many of them, we need to use subqueries or outer joins.

- How many cats are in stock on 10/01/04?
- Which cats sold for more than the average price?
- Which animals sold for more than the average price of animals in their category?
- Which animals have not been sold?
- Which customers (who bought something at least once) did not buy anything between 11/01/04 and 12/31/04?
- Which customers who bought dogs also bought products for cats (at any time)?

want to see. The JOIN clause restricts the output—just like a WHERE clause would. In this example, you told the DBMS to return only those animals that are listed in both the Animal and SaleAnimal tables. But only animals that have been sold are listed in the SaleAnimal table, so this query can never tell you anything about animals that have not been sold.

The following sections describe two solutions to this problem: Either fix the JOIN statement so that it is not as restrictive or use a subquery.

Sally's Pet Store

Figure 5.1 shows some more business questions that Sally needs to answer to manage her business. Again, think about how you might answer these questions using the basic SQL of Chapter 4. At first glance they do not seem too difficult. However, even the easiest question—to identify cats that sold for more than the average price—is harder than it first appears. All of these questions require an additional tool: the subquery.

Subqueries

Calculations or Simple Lookup

Perhaps the easiest way to see the value of a subquery is to consider the relatively simple question: Which cats sold for more than the average price of cats? If you already know the average sale price of cats (say, $170), the query is easy, as shown in the top half of Figure 5.2.

If you do not know the average SalePrice of cats, you could look it up with a basic query. You could write the result down on paper and then run the original query. However, with a subquery, you can go one step further: The result (average) from the query can be transferred directly to the original query. Simply replace the value ($170) with the complete SELECT AVG query as shown in the lower half of Figure 5.2. In fact, anytime you want to insert a value or comparison, you can use a subquery instead. You can even go to several levels, so a subquery can contain another subquery and so on. The DBMS generally evaluates the innermost query first and passes the results back to the higher level.

Two useful practices you should follow when building subqueries are to indent the subquery to make it stand out so humans can read it and to test the subquery before inserting it into the main query. Fortunately, most modern database systems make it easy to create a subquery and then cut and paste the SQL into the main query. Similarly, if you have problems getting a complex query to work, cut out the inner subqueries and test them separately.

FIGURE 5.2
Subqueries for calculation. If we do not know the average SalePrice of cats, we can use a query to look up the value. With a subquery we can put the result of that calculation directly into the original query (the subquery in parentheses replaces the 170 in the original query).

- **Which cats sold for more than the average sale price of cats?**
  - **Assume we know the average price is $170.**
  - **Usually we need to compute it first.**

```
SELECT SaleAnimal. AnimalID, Animal.Category, SaleAnimal.SalePrice
FROM Animal
INNER JOIN SaleAnimal ON Animal. AnimalID = SaleAnimal. AnimalID
WHERE ((Animal.Category="Cat") AND (SaleAnimal.SalePrice>170));
```

```
SELECT SaleAnimal. AnimalID, Animal.Category, SaleAnimal.SalePrice
FROM Animal
INNER JOIN SaleAnimal ON Animal. AnimalID = SaleAnimal. AnimalID
WHERE ((Animal.Category="Cat") AND (SaleAnimal.SalePrice>
   ( SELECT AVG(SalePrice)
     FROM Animal
     INNER JOIN SaleAnimal ON Animal. AnimalID = SaleAnimalID
     WHERE (Animal.Category="Cat") ) ) );
```

Subqueries and Sets of Data

Some special SQL operators (**IN, ALL, ANY, EXISTS**) are often used with subqueries. They are a little easier to understand if you begin with simple numbers instead of a subquery. Consider the relatively easy query illustrated in Figure 5.3: List all customers who purchased one of the following items: 1, 2, 30, 32, 33.

You might consider writing a basic SQL statement to answer this question. Just use lots of OR connectors in the WHERE statement. You might start: ItemID = 1 OR ItemID = 2 OR ItemID = 30. Although this approach would work for this simple example, it would entail some extra typing. A better approach is to treat the list as a set of data and use the IN operator: WHERE ItemID IN (1,2,30,32,33). This condition is true if ItemID matches any of the values in the set of numbers.

Although the IN operator saved some typing in this example, it actually has considerably more power. The power comes by noting that the list of numbers can be generated from a subquery. For example, the manager might want a list of customers who bought products for cats. Although you could look up all ItemID values for cat products, it is easier to let the DBMS do it. Simply change the WHERE clause to ItemID IN (SELECT ItemID FROM Merchandise WHERE Category = 'Cat').

Notice one crucial feature with the IN operator: The values in the list must be of the same data type (domain) as the variable being tested. The example in Figure 5.4 compares SaleItem.ItemID to SELECT ItemID. Like a JOIN statement, the IN operator compares similar types of data. For example, mixing ItemID with EmployeeID would lead to a nonsensical result. In fact, the IN operator can be used as a substitute for a JOIN statement—although a JOIN query is usually performed faster.

Subquery with ANY and ALL

The ANY and ALL operators combine comparison of numbers with subsets. In the preceding section, the IN operator compared a value to a list of items in a set; however, the comparison was based on equality. The test item had

FIGURE 5.3
Queries with sets (In). Could use OR statements, but the IN operator is easier. The WHERE condition is true if the ItemID matches any of the ID values in the accompanying list. List all customers who purchased one of the following items (1,2,30, 32,33).

```
SELECT Customer.LastName, Customer.FirstName, SaleItem.ItemID
FROM (Customer INNER JOIN Sale ON Customer.CustomerID = Sale.CustomerID)
 INNER JOIN SaleItemON Sale.SaleID = SaleItem.SaleID
WHERE (SaleItem.ItemID In (1,2,30,32,33))
ORDER BY Customer.LastName, Customer.FirstName;
```

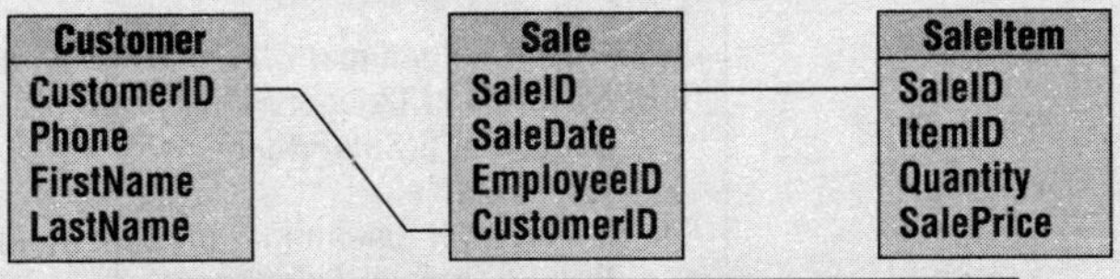

Field	LastName	FirstName	ItemID
Table	Customer	Customer	SaleItem
Sort	Ascending	Ascending	
Criteria			In (1,2,30,32,33)'
Or			

to exactly match an entry in the list. The ANY and ALL operators work with a less than (<) or greater than (>) operator and compare the test value to a list of values.

Figure 5.5 illustrates the use of the ANY query. It is hard to find a solid business example that needs the ANY operator. In the example, it would be just as easy to first find the minimum value in the list and then do the comparison. However, it is sometimes clearer to use the ANY operator. The word *SOME* can be used in place of the word *ANY*, but they work exactly the same way.

The ALL operator behaves similarly, but the test value must be greater than all of the values in the list. In other words, the test value must exceed the largest value in the list. Hence, the ALL operator is much more restrictive. The ALL operator can be a powerful tool—particularly when used with an equals (=) comparison. For instance, you might want to test whether one salesperson made all of the sales on a particular day, so the WHERE clause

FIGURE 5.4
Using IN with a subquery. List all customers who bought items for cats. The subquery generates a list of ItemIDs designated as cat products. The main query then matches if the ItemID being purchased is in that subquery list.

```
SELECT Customer.LastName, Customer.FirstName, SaleItem.ItemID
FROM (Customer
  INNER JOIN Sale ON Customer.CustomerID = Sale.CustomerID)
  INNER JOIN SaleItem ON Sale.SaleID = SaleItem.SaleID
WHERE (SaleItem.ItemID In
  (SELECT ItemID FROM Merchandise WHERE Category='Cat')
);
```

FIGURE 5.5
Subquery with ANY and ALL. The example computes 80 percent of the list price of each cat sold. Then it identifies any animal that sold for more than any of those amounts. In other words, it lists animals that sold for prices close to the list price of cats.

```
SELECT Animal.AnimalID, Name, SalePrice, ListPrice
FROM Animal
INNER JOIN SaleAnimal ON Animal.AnimalID =
SaleAnimal.AnimalID
WHERE ((SalePrice > Any

  (SELECT 0.80*ListPrice
  FROM Animal
  INNER JOIN SaleAnimal ON Animal.AnimalID =
  SaleAnimal.AnimalID
  WHERE Category = 'Cat'))

AND (Category='Cat');
```

would contain this statement: WHERE EmployeeID = ALL (SELECT EmployeeID FROM Sale WHERE SaleDate = Date()).

Subtraction: NOT IN

One question that commonly arises in business settings is illustrated in Figure 5.6 with the question: Which animals have not been sold? This question is deceptive. At first glance it looks like you could just join the Animal table to the SaleAnimal table. But then what? The standard JOIN statement will display only those animals that appear in both the Animal and the SaleAnimal tables. As soon as you enter the JOIN statement, you automatically restrict your list to only those animals that have been sold. One way to solve this problem is to change the behavior of the JOIN command, which is explored in the next section.

Another useful approach is to think about the problem in terms of sets of data. Think about how you would solve this problem if you had only

FIGURE 5.6
Subquery for NOT IN. Which animals have not been sold? Start with a list of all the animals and then subtract the list of those that were sold.

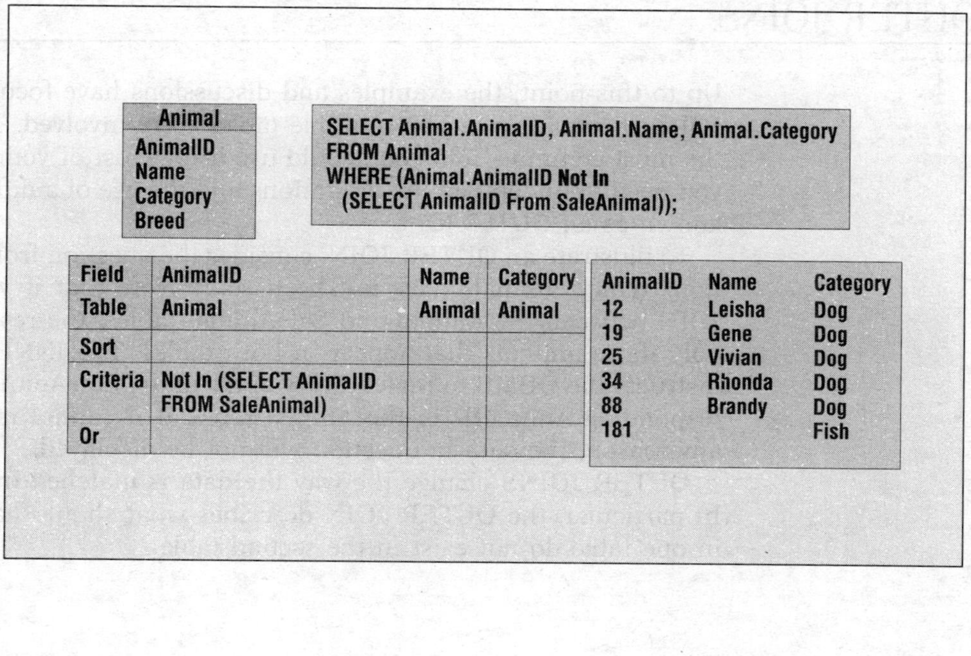

FIGURE 5.7
Sample data for subtraction subquery. The NOT IN statement removes animals that have been sold, leaving only those that were not sold.

Animal

ID	Name	Category	Breed
~~2~~		~~Fish~~	~~Angel~~
~~4~~	~~Gary~~	~~Dog~~	~~Dalmation~~
5		Fish	Shark
~~6~~	~~Rosie~~	~~Cat~~	~~Oriental Shorthair~~
~~7~~	~~Eugene~~	~~Cat~~	~~Bombay~~
~~8~~	~~Miranda~~	~~Dog~~	~~Norfolk Terrier~~
9		Fish	Guppy
~~10~~	~~Sherri~~	~~Dog~~	~~Siberian Huskie~~
~~11~~	~~Susan~~	~~Dog~~	~~Dalmation~~
12	Leisha	Dog	Rottweiler

SaleAnimal

ID	SaleID	SalePrice
2	35	$10.80
4	80	$156.66
6	27	$173.99
7	25	$251.59
8	4	$183.38
10	18	$150.11
11	17	$148.47

paper lists: one list of all the animals the store has purchased and one list of all the animals that have been sold. As illustrated in Figure 5.7, to answer the question you would go through the main Animal list and cross off all the animals that have been sold (which appear on the SaleAnimal list). The ones remaining on the Animal list are the animals that have not been sold.

SQL can accomplish the same task in a similar fashion using a subquery. The first step is to list all the animals—as shown in the main part of the query in Figure 5.6. But only list the animals that do not appear in the SaleAnimal table (the subquery).

The SQL NOT IN command is a useful tool. It is particularly useful for complex queries that involve several constraints. By moving the relevant constraints to the subquery, the main query becomes easier to understand.

OUTER JOINS

Up to this point, the examples and discussions have focused on the INNER JOIN (or **equi-join**) when multiple tables were involved. This type of join is the most common, and you should use it for most of your queries. However, you need to understand its limitations and the use of a different type of JOIN known as an **OUTER JOIN.**

To illustrate an OUTER JOIN, consider the question from the previous section: Which animals have not been sold? Note that if you use an INNER JOIN between the Animal and SaleAnimal tables, the result will be a list of only those animals that appear in both tables. The INNER JOIN command instructs the DBMS to match every entry in the SaleAnimal table with a corresponding AnimalID in the Animal table. If it cannot make the match for any reason, the data in question will not be displayed.

OUTER JOINS change the way the data is matched from the two tables. In particular, the OUTER JOIN describes what should happen when values in one table do not exist in the second table.

FIGURE 5.8
Left OUTER JOIN. Which animals have not been sold? The left JOIN includes all rows from the Animal (left) table and any matching rows from the SaleAnimal table. If an animal has not been sold, there will be no entry in the SaleAnimal table, so the corresponding entries will be NULL.

```
SELECT Animal.AnimalID, Animal.Name, Animal.Category
FROM Animal LEFT JOIN SaleAnimal
ON Animal.AnimalID = SaleAnimal.AnimalID
WHERE (SaleAnimal.SaleID Is Null);
```

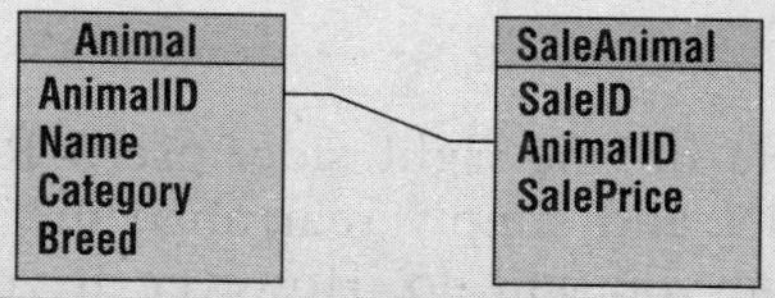

Field	AnimalID	SaleID	Name	Category
Table	Animal	SaleAnimal	Animal	Animal
Sort				
Criteria		Is Null		
Or				

In joining two tables, you have to consider two basic situations: (1) A value might exist in the left table with no matching value in the right table, or (2) a value might exist in the right table with no matching value in the left table. Of course, it really does not matter which table is on the left or right. However, you have to be careful about not mixing them up after you list the tables. In QBE, the tables are physically displayed in the order mentioned. With SQL, the left table is listed first.

The query in Figure 5.8 illustrates a typical left OUTER JOIN (or just **LEFT JOIN**). With a LEFT JOIN, all rows in the table on the left will be displayed in the results. If there is no matching value from the table on the right, NULL values will be inserted into the output. Note how the LEFT JOIN resolves the problem of identifying animals that have not been sold. Because the query will now list all animals, the rows where the SaleID is NULL represent animals that are not in the Sale table and have not been sold. Sample output from the query is displayed in Figure 5.9.

The **RIGHT JOIN** behaves similarly to the LEFT JOIN. The only difference is the order of the tables. If you want to use all the rows from the

FIGURE 5.9
Results from the left outer join. Note the missing (Null) values for animals that have not been sold.

ID	Name	Category	Breed	ID	SaleID	SalePrice
2		Fish	Angel	2	35	$10.80
4	Gary	Dog	Dalmation	4	80	$156.66
5		Fish	Shark	Null	Null	Null
6	Rosie	Cat	Oriental Shorthair	6	27	$173.99
7	Eugene	Cat	Bombay	7	25	$251.59
8	Miranda	Dog	Norfolk Terrier	8	4	$183.38
9		Fish	Guppy	Null	Null	Null
10	Sherri	Dog	Siberian Huskie	10	18	$150.11
11	Susan	Dog	Dalmation	11	17	$148.47
12	Leisha	Dog	Rottweiler	Null	Null	Null

FIGURE 5.10
Older syntax for LEFT JOIN. Which animals have not been sold? Note the asterisk-equals operator (*=), which is used for a LEFT JOIN. The reverse (=*) would be used for a RIGHT JOIN.

```
SELECT ALL
FROM Animal, SaleAnimal
WHERE Animal.AnimalID *= SaleAnimal.AnimalID
And SaleAnimal.SaleID Is Null
```

table on the right side, use a RIGHT JOIN. Why not just have a LEFT JOIN and simply rearrange the tables? Most of the time, that is exactly what you will do. However, if you have a query that joins several tables, it is sometimes easier to use a RIGHT JOIN instead of trying to rearrange the tables.

Another join is the full OUTER JOIN (**FULL JOIN**) that combines every row from the left table and every row from the right table. Where the rows do not match (from the ON condition), the join inserts NULL values into the appropriate columns.

Warning: Be careful with outer joins—particularly full joins. With two large tables that do not have much data in common, you end up with a very large result that is not very useful. Also be careful when using OUTER JOINS on more than two tables in one query. You get different results depending on the order in which you join the tables.

Finally, note that you have been relying on the SQL 92 syntax, which is fairly easy to read and understand. Some database systems do not yet support that syntax. A common older technique to specify OUTER JOINS is to use an asterisk in conjunction with an equals sign; for example, (*=) indicates a left OUTER JOIN, since the asterisk is to the left of the equals sign. The animal query for SQL Server is displayed in Figure 5.10. Although the syntax is different from SQL 92, the effect is the same. Be on the lookout for this syntax when you read queries developed for older systems—that little asterisk (*) can be hard to spot, but it radically alters the query results.

Older Oracle queries used yet another syntax to signify an outer join. The WHERE statement in Figure 5.10 would become Animal.AnimalID = (+) SaleAnimal.AnimalID. The plus sign in parentheses (+) indicates an OUTER JOIN, but be careful. The plus is to the right of the equals sign. In other words, if you want a left OUTER JOIN, you place the plus sign to the right of the equals sign. It is opposite from what you might expect and opposite from the asterisk notation.

Correlated Subqueries Are Dangerous

Recall the example in Figure 5.2 that asked, Which cats sold for more than the average price of cats? This example used a subquery to first find the average sale price of cats and then examined all sales of cats to display the ones that had higher prices. It is a reasonable business question to extend this idea to other categories of animals. Managers would like to identify all animals that were sold for a price greater than the average price of other animals within their respective categories (dogs greater than the average price of dogs, fish compared to fish, etc.).

FIGURE 5.11
Correlated subquery creation. List the animals that have sold for more than the average price of other animals in their category. The subquery needs to compute the average sale price for the category of animal shown in the main query. But both tables are called "Animal" so this query will not work yet.

```
SELECT AnimalID, Name, Category, SalePrice
FROM Animal INNER JOIN SaleAnimal ON
Animal.AnimalID = SaleAnimal.AnimalID
WHERE (SaleAnimal.SalePrice>
  (SELECT Avg(SaleAnimal.SalePrice)
  FROM Animal INNER JOIN SaleAnimal ON
  Animal.AnimalID = SaleAnimal.AnimalID
  WHERE (Animal.Category = Animal.Category)) )
ORDER BY SaleAnimal.SalePrice DESC;
```

Although this business question is perfectly reasonable, it can lead to serious problems as a query. To start with, it is not immediately obvious how to build this query. One approach might be to take the query in Figure 5.2 and substitute the category "Dog" for "Cat" in both the main and the subquery. This approach will work, but you will first have to find all of the categories and then edit the query for each category.

Instead of having you enter each category by hand, perhaps the subquery can get the category from the main query and then compute the average sale price for that category. Figure 5.11 shows a first attempt to create this query. The difficulty is that the main query refers to the Animal table and the subquery also uses the Animal table. Consequently, the WHERE constraint does not make sense. It needs to specify that one of the Animal tables is in the main query and the other is in the subquery. To do that, you need to rename (alias) the tables, as shown in Figure 5.12.

The query in Figure 5.12 will run. However, it is extremely inefficient. Even on a fast computer, queries of this type have been known to run for several days without finishing! This type of query is called a **correlated subquery**, because the subquery refers to data rows in the main query. The calculation in the subquery must be recomputed for each entry in the main table. The problem is illustrated in Figure 5.13. Essentially, the DBMS starts at the top row of the main Animal table. When it sees the category is Fish, it computes the average sale price of fish ($37.78). Then it moves to the next row and computes the average sale price for dogs. When the DBMS encounters the third row and sees Fish again, it must recompute the average for fish (still $37.78). Recomputing the average sale price for every single row in the main query is time-consuming. To compute an average, the DBMS must go through every row in the table that has the same category of

FIGURE 5.12
Correlated subquery that will run. Note the use of aliases to distinguish the two tables. However, never use this approach—it is incredibly inefficient!

```
SELECT A1.AnimalID, A1.Name, A1.Category,
SaleAnimal.SalePrice
FROM Animal As A1 INNER JOIN SaleAnimal ON
A1.AnimalID = SaleAnimal.AnimalID
WHERE (SaleAnimal.SalePrice>
  (SELECT Avg(SaleAnimal.SalePrice)
  FROM Animal As A2 INNER JOIN SaleAnimal ON
  A2.AnimalID = SaleAnimal.AnimalID
  WHERE (A2.Category = A1.Category)) )
ORDER BY SaleAnimal.SalePrice DESC;
```

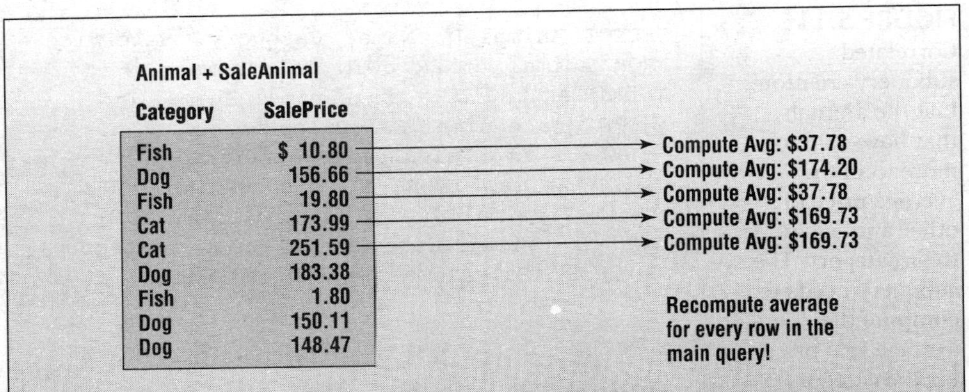

FIGURE 5.13 Problem with correlated subquery. The average is recomputed for every row in the main query. Every time the DBMS sees a fish, it computes the average to be $37.78. It is inefficient (and very slow) to force the machine to recalculate the average each time.

animal. Consider a relatively small query of 100,000 rows and five categories of animals. On average, there are 20,000 rows per category. To recompute the average each time, the DBMS will have to retrieve 100,000 * 20,000 or 2,000,000,000 rows!

Unfortunately, you cannot just tell the manager that it is impossible to answer this important business question. Is there an efficient way to answer this question? The answer illustrates the power of SQL and highlights the importance of thinking about the problem before you try to write a query. The problem with the correlated subquery lies in the fact that it has to continually recompute the average for each category. Think about how you might solve this problem by hand. You would first make a table that listed the average for each category and then simply look up the appropriate value when you needed it. As shown in Figure 5.14, the same approach can be used with SQL. Just create the query for the averages using GROUP BY and save it. Then join it to the Animal and SaleAnimal tables to do the comparison. Although this approach requires two complete passes through the query rows, or reading 200,000 rows in our small example, it is 10,000 times more efficient than the correlated subquery! If this new query takes a minute to run, the correlated subquery could take seven days to finish!

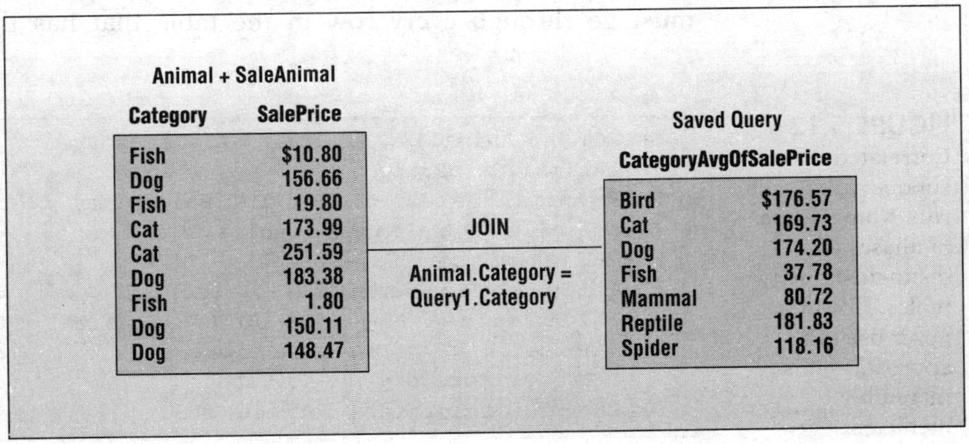

FIGURE 5.14 More efficient solution. Create and save a query to compute the averages using GROUP BY Category. Then join the query to the Animal and SaleAnimal tables to do the comparison.

More Features and Tricks with SQL SELECT

As you may have noticed, the SQL SELECT command is powerful and has plenty of options. There are even more features and tricks that you should know about. Business questions can be difficult to answer. It helps to study different examples to gain a wider perspective on the problems and solutions you will encounter.

UNION, INTERSECT, EXCEPT

Up to this point, the tables you have encountered have contained unique columns of data. The JOIN command links tables together so that a query can display and compare different columns of data from tables. Occasionally you will encounter a different type of problem where you need to combine rows of data from similar tables. The **UNION** operator is designed to accomplish this task.

As an example, assume you work for a company that has offices in Los Angeles and New York. Each office maintains its own database. Each office has an Employee file that contains standard data about its employees. The offices are linked by a network, so you have access to both tables (call them EmployeeEast and EmployeeWest). But the corporate managers often want to search the entire Employee file—for example, to determine total employee salaries of the marketing department. One solution might be to run their basic query twice (once on each table) and then combine the results by hand.

As shown in Figure 5.15, the easier solution is to use the UNION operator to create a new query that combines the data from the two tables. All searches and operations performed on this new query will treat the two tables as one large table. By combining the tables with a view, each office can make changes to the original data on its system. Whenever managers need to search across the entire company, they use the saved query, which automatically examines the data from current versions of both tables.

The most important concept to remember when creating a UNION is that the data from both tables must match (e.g., EID to EID, Name to Name). Another useful trick is to insert a constant value in the SELECT statement. In this example, the constant keeps track of which table held the original data. This value can also be used to balance out a SELECT statement if one

```
SELECT EID, Name, Phone, Salary, 'East' AS Office
FROM EmployeeEast
UNION
SELECT EID, Name, Phone, Salary, 'West' AS Office
FROM EmployeeWest
```

EID	Name	Phone	Salary	Office
352	Jones	3352	45,000	East
876	Inez	8736	47,000	East
372	Stoiko	7632	38,000	East
890	Smythe	9803	62,000	West
361	Kim	7736	73,000	West

FIGURE 5.15
The UNION operator combines rows of data from two SELECT statements. The columns in both SELECT lines must match. The query is usually saved and used when managers need to search across both tables. Note the use of a new, constant column (Office) to track the source of the data.

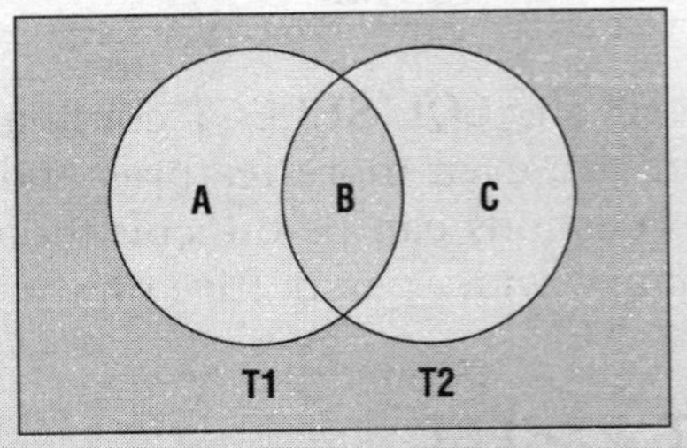

T1 UNION T2	A + B + C
T1 INTERSECT T2	B
T1 EXCEPT T2	A

FIGURE 5.16 Operators for combining rows from two tables. UNION selects all of the rows. INTERSECT retrieves only the rows that are in both tables. EXCEPT retrieves rows that exist in only one table.

of the queries will produce a column that is not available in the other query. To make sure both queries return the same number of columns, just insert a constant value in the query that does not contain the desired column. Make sure that it contains the same type of data that is stored in the other query (domains must match).

The UNION command combines matching rows of data from two tables. The basic version of the command automatically eliminates duplicate rows of data. If you want to keep all the rows—even the duplications—use the command UNION ALL. Two other options for combining rows are **EXCEPT** and **INTERSECT**. Figure 5.16 shows the difference between the three commands. They all apply to sets of rows, and the Venn diagram shows that the tables might have some data in common (area B). The UNION operator returns all the rows that appear in either one of the tables, but rows appearing in both tables are only listed once. The INTERSECT operator returns the rows that appear in both tables (area B). The EXCEPT operator returns only rows that appear in the first table (area A). Notice that the result of the EXCEPT operator depends on which table is listed first.

Multiple JOIN Columns

Sometimes you will need to join tables based on data in more than one column. In the Pet Store example, each animal belongs to some category (Cat, Dog, Fish, etc.). Each category of animal has different breeds. For example, a Cat might be a Manx, Maine Coon, or Persian; a Dog might be a Retriever, Labrador, or St. Bernard. A portion of the class diagram is reproduced in Figure 5.17. Notice the two lines connecting the Breed and Animal tables. This relationship ensures that only breeds listed in the Breed table can be entered for each type of Animal. A real store might want to include additional features in the Breed table (such as registration organization, breed description, or breed characteristics). The key point is that the tables must be connected by both the Category and the Breed.

In Microsoft Access QBE, the JOIN can be created by marking both columns and simultaneously dragging the two columns to the Animal table. The syntax for the SQL JOIN command is given in Figure 5.17. Simply expand the ON statement by listing both column connections. In this case, you want both sets of columns to be equal at the same time, so the statements are connected with an AND.

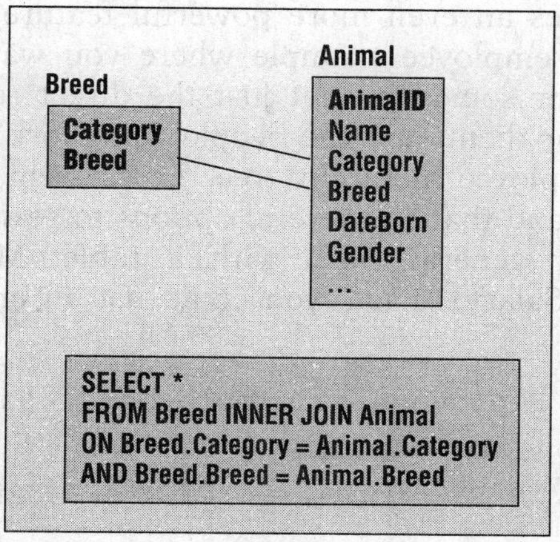

FIGURE 5.17 Multiple JOIN columns. The values in the tables are connected only when both the category and the breed match.

Reflexive Join

A **reflexive join** or **self-join** means simply that a table is joined to itself. One column in the table is used to match values in a second column in the same table. A common business example arises with an Employee table as illustrated in Figure 5.18. Employees typically have one manager. Hence the manager's ID can be stored in the row corresponding to each employee. The table would be Employee(<u>EID</u>, Name, Phone, . . . , Manager). The interesting feature is that a manager is also an employee, so the Manager column actually contains a value for EID. To get the corresponding name of the manager, you need to join the Employee table to itself.

The only trick with this operation is that you have to be careful with the ON condition. For instance, the following condition does not make sense: ON Employee.Manager = Employee.EID. The query would try to return employees who were their own managers, which is not likely to be what you wanted. Instead, you must use two instances of the Employee table and use an alias (say, E2) to rename the second copy. Then the correct ON condition becomes ON Employee.Manager = E2.EID. The key to self-joins is to make sure that the columns contain the same type of data and to create an alias for the second copy of the table.

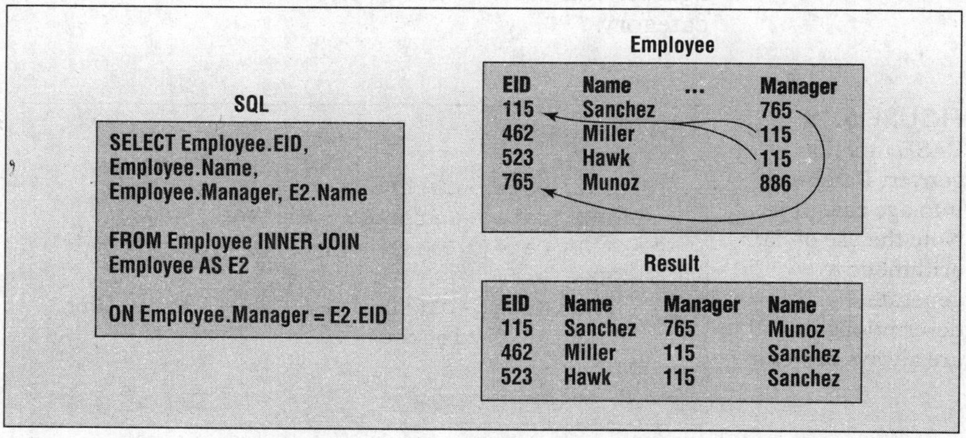

FIGURE 5.18 Reflexive JOIN to connect Employee table with itself. A manager is also an employee. Use a second copy of the Employee table (renamed to E2) to get the manager's name.

SQL 1999 provides an even more powerful feature related to reflexive joins. Consider the employee example where you want to list all of the people who work for someone—not just the direct reports, but also the people who work for them, and the people who work for that group, and so on down the employee hierarchy tree. The system provides the WITH RECURSIVE command that has several options to search a data tree. Consider the relatively general case, with a table: Manages(<u>ManagerID</u>, <u>EmployeeID</u>, Title, Salary). Then, you could list all employees, beginning with the CEO:

```
WITH RECURSIVE EmployeeList (EmployeeID, Title, Salary) AS
 (SELECT EmployeeID, Title, 0.00
 FROM Manages WHERE Title = "CEO" --starting level
 UNION ALL
 SELECT Manages.EmployeeID, Manages.Title, Manages.Salary
 FROM EmployeeList INNER JOIN Manages
 ON EmployeeList.EmployeeID = Manages.ManagerID)
SELECT EmployeeID, Count(Title), Sum(Salary)
FROM EmployeeList
GROUP BY EmployeeEID;
```

The only drawback at the moment is that DBMS vendors do not yet support the WITH RECURSIVE statement. Without this powerful statement, you need to write substantial code to accomplish the same task.

CASE Function

SQL 92 added the **CASE** function to simplify certain types of queries. However, many database systems have not yet implemented all the features of SQL 92. Hence, Microsoft Access 97 does not support it, whereas Microsoft SQL Server version 6.5 does provide this function.

Perhaps the managers want to classify the animals in Sally's Pet Store based on their age. Figure 5.19 shows the SQL statement that would create four categories based on different ages. Note the use of date arithmetic using today's date—Date()—and DateBorn. Whenever this query is executed, it will use the current day to assign each animal to the appropriate category. Of course, the next logical step is to run a GROUP BY query against this view to count the number of animals falling within each age category.

FIGURE 5.19
CASE function to convert DateBorn into age categories. Note the use of date arithmetic to generate descriptions that are always current.

```
Select AnimalID,
 CASE
  WHEN Date()-DateBorn <90 Then "Baby"
  WHEN Date()-DateBorn >= 90
   AND Date()-DateBorn <270 Then "Young"
  WHEN Date()-DateBorn >=270
   AND Date()-DateBorn <365 Then "Grown"
  ELSE "Experienced"
 END
FROM Animal;
```

Inequality Joins

A JOIN statement is actually just a condition. Most problems are straightforward and use a simple equality condition. For example, the following statement joins the Customer and Order tables: FROM Customer INNER JOIN Order ON (Customer.CustomerID = Order.CustomerID).

SQL supports complex conditions including **inequality joins**, where the comparison is made with inequality operators (less than, greater than) instead of an equals sign. The generic name for any inequality or equality join is a theta join.

There are a few situations where this type of join can be useful. For example, consider a common business problem. You have a table for AccountsReceivable(<u>TransactionID</u>, CustomerID, Amount, DateDue). Managers would like to categorize the customer accounts and determine how many transactions are past due by 30, 90, and 120 or more days. There are a couple of ways to build this query. For instance, you could write three separate queries. However, what happens if managers decide to change the business rules or add a new category? Then someone has to find your three queries and modify them. A more useful trick is to create a new table to hold the business rules or categories. For example, as shown in Figure 5.20, create the table LateCategory(<u>Category</u>, MinDays, MaxDays, Charge, etc.). This table defines the late categories based on the number of days past due. Now use inequality conditions to join the two tables. First, compute the number of days late using the current date (Date() − AR.DateDue). Finally, compare the number of days late to minimum and maximum values specified in the LateCategory table.

The ultimate value of this approach is that the business rules are now stored in a simple table (LateCategory). If managers want to change the conditions or add new criteria, they simply alter the data in the table. You can even build a form that makes it easy for managers to see the rules and quickly make the needed changes. With any other approach, a programmer would have to rewrite the code for the queries.

Questions with "Every" Need the EXISTS Clause

Some queries need the EXISTS condition. Consider the business question: Which employees have sold an animal in every category? The word *every* is the key here. Think about how you would answer that question if you did not have a computer. For each employee you would make a list of animal categories (Bird, Cat, Dog, etc.). Then you would go through the list of

FIGURE 5.20
Inequality join. Managers want to classify the AccountsReceivable (AR) data into three categories of overdue payments. First, store the business rules/categories in a new table. Then join the table to the AR data through inequality joins.

AR(TransactionID, CustomerID, Amount, DateDue)
LateCategory(<u>Category</u>, MinDays, MaxDays, Charge, . . .)

Month	30	90	3%
Quarter	90	120	5%
Overdue	120	9999	10%

```
SELECT *
FROM AR INNER JOIN LateCategory
ON ((Date() - AR.DateDue) >= Category.MinDays)
AND ((Date() - AR.DateDue) < Category.MaxDays)
```

FIGURE 5.21
List the animal categories that have not been sold by EmployeeID 5. Use a basic NOT IN query.

```
SELECT Category
FROM Category
  WHERE (Category <> "Other") And Category NOT IN
    (SELECT Animal.Category
    FROM Animal INNER JOIN (Sale INNER JOIN SaleAnimal
      ON Sale.SaleID = SaleAnimal.SaleID)
      ON Animal.AnimalID = SaleAnimal.AnimalID
    WHERE Sale.EmployeeID = 5)
```

AnimalSales and cross off each animal category sold by the employee. When finished, you would look at the employee list to see which people have every animal crossed off (or an empty list). You will do the same thing using queries.

First, you need a query that lists all the animal categories that have not been sold by an employee. Consider the list for EmployeeID 5, with the query shown in Figure 5.21. Notice that it uses the basic NOT IN query. You could also use an OUTER JOIN, but with three tables, it is easier to use NOT IN.

Remember, if this query returns any rows at all, then the selected employee has not sold every one of the animals. What you really want then is a list of employees for whom this query returns no rows of data. In other words, the rows from this query should NOT EXIST.

The next step is to examine the entire list of employees and see which ones do not retrieve any rows from the query in Figure 5.22. The final query is shown in Figure 5.24. Note that the specific EmployeeID 5 has been replaced with the EmployeeID matching the value in the outer loop. Notice that this action results in a correlated subquery. Unfortunately, you cannot avoid the correlated subquery in this type of problem. This query returns one employee (Reasoner) who has sold every type of animal.

The type of query in Figure 5.22 is commonly used to answer questions that include some reference to "every" item. In some cases, a simpler solution is to just count the number of categories for each employee. One catch to this approach is that the DBMS must support the Count(DISTINCT) format. In general, these complex questions are probably better answered with multiple queries, or with tools provided by a data warehouse approach as described in Chapter 8.

FIGURE 5.22
Example of NOT EXISTS clause. List the employees who have sold an animal from every category (except "Other").

```
SELECT Employee.EmployeeID, Employee.LastName
FROM Employee
WHERE Not Exists
(SELECT Category
  FROM Category
  WHERE (Category <> "Other") And Category NOT IN
    (SELECT Animal.Category
    FROM Animal INNER JOIN (Sale INNER JOIN SaleAnimal
      ON Sale.SaleID = SaleAnimal.SaleID)
      ON Animal.AnimalID = SaleAnimal.AnimalID
    WHERE Sale.EmployeeID = Employee.EmployeeID)
);
```

FIGURE 5.23
SQL SELECT options. Remember that WHERE statements can have subqueries.

```
SELECT DISTINCT Table.Column {AS Alias}, . . .
FROM Table/Query
INNER JOIN Table/Query ON T1.ColA = T2.ColB
WHERE (Condition)
GROUP BY Column
HAVING (Group Condition)
ORDER BY Table.Column
{UNION Second Select}
```

SQL SELECT Summary

The SQL SELECT command is powerful and has many options. To help you remember the various options, they are presented in Figure 5.23. Each DBMS has a similar listing for the SELECT command, and you should consult the relevant Help system for details to see if there are implementation differences. Remember that the WHERE clause can have subqueries.

Most database systems are picky about the sequence of the various components of the SELECT statement. For example, the WHERE statement should come before the GROUP BY statement. Sometimes these errors can be hard to spot, so if you receive an enigmatic error message, verify that the segments are in the proper order. Figure 5.24 presents a mnemonic that may help you remember the proper sequence. Also, you should always build a query in pieces, so you can test each piece. For example, if you use a GROUP BY statement, first check the results without it to be sure that the proper rows are being selected.

SQL Data Definition Commands

So far you have focused on only one aspect of a database: retrieving data. Clearly, you need to perform many more operations with a database. SQL was designed to handle all common operations. One set of commands is described in this section: data definition commands to create and modify the database and its tables. Note that the SQL commands can be cumbersome for these tasks. Hence, most modern database systems provide a visual or menu-driven system to assist with these tasks. The SQL commands are generally used when you need to automate some of these tasks and set up or make changes to a database from within a separate program.

The five most common data definition commands are listed in Figure 5.25. In building a new database, the first step is to **CREATE a SCHEMA**. A schema

FIGURE 5.24
Mnemonic to help remember the proper sequence of the SELECT operators.

```
Someone               SELECT
From                  FROM
Ireland               INNER JOIN
Will                  WHERE
Grow                  GROUP BY
Horseradish and       HAVING
Onions                ORDER BY
```

FIGURE 5.25
Primary SQL data definition commands. In most cases, you will avoid these commands and use a visual or menu-driven system to define and modify tables.

```
CREATE SCHEMA AUTHORIZATION DBName Password
CREATE TABLE TableName (Column Type, . . .)
ALTER TABLE Table {Add, Column, Constraint, Drop}
DROP {Table TableName | Index IndexName ON TableName}
CREATE INDEX IndexName ON TableName (Column ASC/DESC)
```

is a collection of tables. In some systems, the command is equivalent to creating a new database. In other systems, it simply defines a logical area where each user can store tables, which might or might not be in one physical database. The Authorization component describes the user and sets a password for security.

CREATE TABLE is one of the main SQL data definition commands. It is used to define a completely new table. The basic command lists the name of the table along with the names and data types for all of the columns. Figure 5.26 shows the format for the data definition commands. Additional options include the ability to assign default values with the DEFAULT command.

SQL 92 provides several standard data types, but system vendors do not yet implement all of them. SQL 92 also enables you to create your own data types with the **CREATE DOMAIN** command. For example, to ensure consistency you could create a domain called DomAddress that consists of CHAR (35). Then any table that used an address column would refer to the DomAddress.

With SQL 92, you identify the primary key and foreign key relationships with constraints. SQL **constraints** are rules that are enforced by the database system. Figure 5.27 illustrates the syntax for defining both a primary key and a foreign key for an Order table. First, notice that each constraint is given a name (e.g., pkorder). You can choose any name, but you should pick one that you will recognize later if problems arise. The primary key constraint simply lists the column or columns that make up the primary key. Note that each column in the primary key should also be marked as NOT NULL.

The foreign key constraint is easier to understand if you examine the relevant class diagram. Here you want to place orders only to customers who have data in the Customer table. That is, the CustomerID in the Order table must already exist in the Customer table. Hence, the constraint lists the column in the original Order table and then specifies a REFERENCE to the Customer table and the CustomerID.

The **ALTER TABLE** and **DROP TABLE** commands enable you to modify the structure of an existing table. Be careful with the DROP command, as it

FIGURE 5.26
The CREATE TABLE command defines a new table and all of the columns that it will contain. The NOT NULL command typically is used to identify the key column(s) for the table. The ALTER TABLE command enables you to add and delete entire columns from an existing table.

```
CREATE TABLE Customer
( CustomerID      INTEGER NOT NULL,
  LastName        VARCHAR(10),
  . . .
);

ALTER TABLE Customer
   DROP COLUMN ZIPCode;

ALTER TABLE Customer
   ADD COLUMN CellPhone VARCHAR(15);
```

```
CREATE TABLE Order
   (OrderID INTEGER NOT NULL,
    OrderDate DATE,
    CustomerID INTEGER

    CONSTRAINT pkorder PRIMARY KEY (OrderID),
    CONSTRAINT fkorder FOREIGN KEY (CustomerID)
       REFERENCES Customer (CustomerID));
```

FIGURE 5.27
Identifying primary and foreign keys in SQL. Keys are defined as constraints that are enforced by the DBMS. The primary key constraint lists the columns that make up the primary key. The foreign key lists the column (CustomerID) in the current table (Order) that is linked to a column (CustomerID) in a second table (Customer).

will remove the entire table from the database, including its data and structural definition. The ALTER TABLE command is less drastic. It can be used to ADD or DELETE columns from a table. Obviously, when you drop an entire column, all the data stored in that column will be deleted. Similarly, when you add a new column, it will contain NULL values for any existing rows.

You can use the CREATE INDEX and DROP INDEX commands to improve the performance of the database. Chapter 9 describes the strengths and weaknesses of using indexes. In general, these commands are issued once for a table, so it is usually easier to set them using a menu-driven interface.

Finally, as described in Chapter 4, the **CREATE VIEW** creates and saves a new query. The basic syntax is straightforward: CREATE VIEW myview AS SELECT. . . . The command simply gives a name and saves any SELECT statement. Again, these commands are almost always easier to create and execute from a menu-driven interface. However, because you may have to create SQL data definition statements by hand sometime, so it is good to know how to do so.

SQL Data Manipulation Commands

A third set of SQL commands demonstrates the true power of SQL. The SELECT command retrieves data, whereas data manipulation commands are used to change the data within the tables. The basic commands and their syntax are displayed in Figure 5.28. These commands are used to insert data, delete rows, and update (change) the values of specific cells. Remember two points when using these commands: (1) They operate on sets of data at one time—avoid thinking in terms of individual rows, and (2) they utilize the power of the SELECT and WHERE statements you already know.

INSERT and DELETE

As you can tell from Figure 5.28, the **INSERT** command has two variations. The first version (VALUES) is used to insert one row of data at a time. Except for some programming implementations, it is not very useful. Most database systems provide a visual or tabular data entry system that makes it easy to enter or edit single rows of data. As discussed in Chapter 6, you

FIGURE 5.28 Common SQL commands to add, delete, and change data within existing tables. The commands operate on entire sets of data, and they utilize the power of the SELECT and WHERE statements, including subqueries.

```
INSERT INTO target (column1, column2, . . .)
  VALUES (value1, value2, . . .)

INSERT INTO target (column1, column2, . . .)
  SELECT . . . FROM . . .

DELETE FROM table WHERE condition

UPDATE table
  SET Column1=Value1, Column2=Value2, . . .
  WHERE condition
```

will also build forms to make it easier for users to enter and edit single rows of data.

The second version of the INSERT command is particularly useful at copying data from one table into a second (target) table. Note that it accepts any SELECT statement, including one with subqueries, making it far more powerful than it looks. For example, in the Pet Store database, you might decide to move older Animal files to a different computer. To move records for all animals ordered before January 1, 2004, you would issue the INSERT command displayed in Figure 5.29. Notice that the subquery selects the animals based on the date they were ordered. The INSERT command then copies the associated rows in the Animal table into an existing OldAnimals table.

The query in Figure 5.29 just copies the specified rows to a new table. The next step is to delete them from the main Animals table to save space and improve performance. The **DELETE** command performs this function easily. As Figure 5.30 illustrates, you simply replace the first two rows of the query (INSERT and SELECT) with DELETE. Be careful not to alter the subquery. You can use the cut-and-paste feature to delete only rows that have already been copied to the backup table. Be sure you recognize the difference between the DROP and DELETE commands. The DROP command removes an entire table. The DELETE command deletes rows within a table.

UPDATE

The syntax of the **UPDATE** command is similar to the INSERT and DELETE commands. It, too, makes full use of the WHERE clause, including subqueries. The key to the UPDATE command is to remember that it acts on an

FIGURE 5.29 INSERT command to copy older data rows. Note the use of the subquery to identify the rows to be copied.

```
INSERT INTO OldAnimals
SELECT *
FROM Animal
WHERE AnimalID IN
  (SELECT AnimalOrderItem.AnimalID
  FROM AnimalOrder INNER JOIN AnimalOrderItem
  ON AnimalOrder.OrderID = AnimalOrderItem.OrderID
  WHERE (AnimalOrder.OrderDate= '01-Jan-2004') );
```

FIGURE 5.30
DELETE command to remove the older data. Use cut and paste to make sure the subquery is exactly the same as the previous query.

```
DELETE
FROM Animal
WHERE AnimalID IN
  (SELECT AnimalOrderItem.AnimalID
  FROM AnimalOrder INNER JOIN AnimalOrderItem
  ON AnimalOrder.OrderID = AnimalOrderItem.OrderID
  WHERE (AnimalOrder.OrderDate<'01-Jan-2004') );
```

entire collection of rows at one time. You use the WHERE clause to specify which set of rows need to be changed.

In the example in Figure 5.31, managers wish to increase the ListPrice of the cats and dogs. The price for cats should increase by 10 percent and the price for dogs by 20 percent. Because these are two different sets of animals, you will often use two separate UPDATE statements. However, this operation provides a good use for the CASE function. You can reduce the operation to one UPDATE statement by replacing the 1.10 and 1.20 values with a CASE statement that selects 1.10 for Cats and 1.20 for Dogs.

There are some additional features of the UPDATE statement. For example, you can change several columns at the same time. Just separate the calculations with a comma. You can also build calculations from any row within the table or query. For example, an animal's list price could take into consideration the animal's age with the command SET ListPrice = ListPrice * (1 − 0.001 * (Date() − DateBorn)). This command takes $\frac{1}{10}$ of 1 percent off the list price for each day since the animal was born.

Notice the use of the internal Date( ) function to provide today's date in the last example. Most database systems provide several internal functions that can be used within any calculation. These functions are not standardized, but you can generally get a list (and the syntax chart) from the system's Help commands. In Microsoft Access, you can get a complete list by searching Help for Functions, Reference. The Date, String, and Format functions are particularly useful.

When using the UPDATE command, remember that all the data in the calculation must exist on one row within the query. There is no way to refer to a previous or next row within the table.

Quality: Testing Queries

The greatest challenge with complex queries is that even if you make a mistake, you usually get results. The problem is that the results are not the answer to the question you wanted to ask. The only way to ensure the results

FIGURE 5.31
Sample UPDATE command. If the CASE function is not available, use two separate statements to increase the list price by 10 percent for cats and 20 percent for dogs.

```
UPDATE Animal
SET ListPrice = ListPrice * 1.10
WHERE Category = 'Cat';
```

```
UPDATE Animal
SET ListPrice = ListPrice * 1.20
WHERE Category = 'Dog';
```

FIGURE 5.32
Steps to building quality queries. Be sure there are recent backups of the database before you execute UPDATE or DELETE queries.

- Break questions into smaller pieces.
- Test each query.
  - Check the SQL.
  - Look at the data.
  - Check computations.
- Combine into subqueries.
  - Use the cut-and-paste feature to reduce errors.
  - Check for correlated subqueries.
- Test sample data.
  - Identify different cases.
  - Check final query and subqueries.
  - Verify calculations.
- Test SELECT queries before executing UPDATE queries.

are correct is to thoroughly understand SQL, to build your queries carefully, and to test your queries.

Figure 5.32 outlines the basic steps for dealing with complex queries. The first step is to break complex queries into smaller pieces, particularly when the query involves subqueries. You need to examine and test each subquery separately. You can do the same thing with complex Boolean conditions. Start with a simple condition, check the results, and then add new conditions. When the subqueries are correct, use cut-and-paste techniques to combine them into one main query. Be sure to avoid correlated subqueries. If necessary, save the initial queries as views, and use a completely new query to combine the results from the views. The third step is to create sample data to test the queries. Find or create data that represents the different possible cases.

Consider the example in Figure 5.33: List customers who bought dogs and also bought cat products. The query consists of four situations:

1. Customers bought dogs and cat products on the same sale.
2. Customers bought dogs and then cat products at a different time.
3. Customers bought dogs and never bought cat products.
4. Customers never bought dogs but did buy cat products.

FIGURE 5.33
Sample query: Which customers who bought dogs also bought cat products (at any time)? Build each query separately. Then paste them together in SQL and add the connecting link. Use sample data to test the results.

```
SELECT DISTINCT Animal.Category, Sale.CustomerID
FROM Sale INNER JOIN (Animal INNER JOIN SaleAnimal
  ON Animal.AnimalID = SaleAnimal.AnimalID)
  ON Sale.SaleID = SaleAnimal.SaleID
WHERE (((Animal.Category)='Dog'))

  AND Sale.CustomerID IN (

  SELECT DISTINCT Sale.CustomerID
  FROM Sale INNER JOIN (Merchandise INNER JOIN SaleItem
    ON Merchandise.ItemID = SaleItem.ItemID)
    ON Sale.SaleID = SaleItem.SaleID
  WHERE (((Merchandise.Category)='Cat'))
);
```

Because there are only four cases, you should create data and test each one. If there were thousands of possible cases, you might have to limit your testing to the major possibilities.

The final step in building queries involves data manipulation queries (such as UPDATE). You should first create a SELECT query that retrieves the rows you plan to change. Examine and test the rows to make sure they are the ones you want to alter. When you are satisfied that the query is correct, make sure you have a recent backup of the database—or at least a recent copy of the tables you want to change. Now you can convert the SELECT query to an UPDATE or DELETE statement and execute it.

Summary

Always remember that SQL operates on sets of data. The SELECT command returns a set of data that matches some criteria. The UPDATE command changes values of data, and the DELETE command deletes rows of data that are in a specified set. Sets can be defined in terms of a simple WHERE clause. They can also be defined by complex conditions involving subqueries and multiple tables. The key to understanding SQL is to think of the WHERE clause as defining a set of data.

Subqueries are powerful, but be careful to avoid correlated subqueries where the inner loop has to be repeated for each value in the outer query loop. In these cases, create a view first and store the intermediate results in a separate query. Also, test your subquery separately before placing it in the final query.

In everyday situations, data can exist in one table but not another. For example, you might need a list of customers who have not placed orders recently. The problem can also arise if the DBMS does not maintain referential integrity—and you need to find which orders have customers with no matching data in the customer table. Outer joins (or the NOT IN subquery) are useful in these situations.

Each database system has several internal functions that can be used in SQL statements. Unfortunately, these functions are not standardized, so each DBMS uses a different syntax. Nonetheless, some standard functions are commonly available and useful for business queries. Some important functions deal with dates and times. For example, the Month function will extract the month from a generic date column, enabling queries to compute totals by month.

The most important thing to remember when building queries is that if you make a mistake, most likely the query will still execute. Unfortunately, it will not give you the results you wanted. That means you have to build your queries carefully and always check your work. Begin with a smaller query and then add elements until you get the query you want. To build an UPDATE or DELETE query, always start with a SELECT statement and check the results. Then change it to UPDATE or DELETE.

A Developer's View

Miranda saw that some business questions are more complex than others. SQL subqueries and outer joins are often used to answer these questions. Practice the SQL subqueries until you thoroughly understand them. They will save you hundreds of hours of work. Think about how long it would take to write code to answer some of the questions in this chapter! For your class project, you should create several queries to test your skills, including subqueries and outer joins. You should build and test some SQL UPDATE queries to change sets of data. You should be able to use SQL to create and modify tables.

Key Terms

ALL, *185*
ALTER TABLE, *200*
ANY, *185*
CASE, *196*
constraint, *200*
correlated subquery, *191*
CREATE DOMAIN, *200*
CREATE SCHEMA, *199*
CREATE TABLE, *200*
CREATE VIEW, *201*
DELETE, *202*
DROP TABLE, *200*
equi-join, *188*
EXCEPT, *194*
EXISTS, *185*
FULL JOIN, *190*
IN, *185*
inequality join, *197*
INSERT, *201*
INTERSECT, *194*
LEFT JOIN, *189*
nested query, *183*
OUTER JOIN, *188*
reflexive join, *195*
RIGHT JOIN, *189*
schema, *199*
self-join, *195*
subquery, *183*
UNION, *193*
UPDATE, *203*

Review Questions

1. What is a subquery and in what situations is it useful?
2. What is a correlated subquery and why does it present problems?
3. How do you find items that are not in a list, such as customers who have not placed orders recently?
4. What are the three general categories of SQL commands?
5. How do you join tables when the JOIN column for one table contains data that is not in the related column of the second table?
6. How do you join tables when two or more columns need to be matched?
7. What are inequality joins and when are they useful?
8. What is the SQL UNION command and when is it useful?
9. What is a reflexive join? Give an example of when it might be used.
10. What is the purpose of the SQL CASE function?
11. What are the basic SQL data definition commands?
12. What are the basic SQL data manipulation commands?
13. How are UPDATE and DELETE commands similar to the SELECT statement?

Exercises

Sally's Pet Store

Write the SQL statements that will answer questions 1 through 25 based on the tables in the Pet Store database. Test your queries in the database. *Hint:* Many are easier if you split the question into multiple queries.

1. List the products with a list price greater than the average list price of all products.
2. On average, which sold in less time: male cats or female cats?
3. List the cats that took longer than average cats to sell.
4. Which merchandise items have an average sale price more than 50 percent higher than their average purchase cost?
5. List the employees and their total merchandise sales expressed as a percentage of total merchandise sales for all employees.
6. On average, which supplier charges the highest shipping cost as a percent of the merchandise order total?
7. Which customer has given us the most total money for animals and merchandise?
8. Which customers who bought more than $100 in merchandise in May also spent more than $50 on merchandise in October?

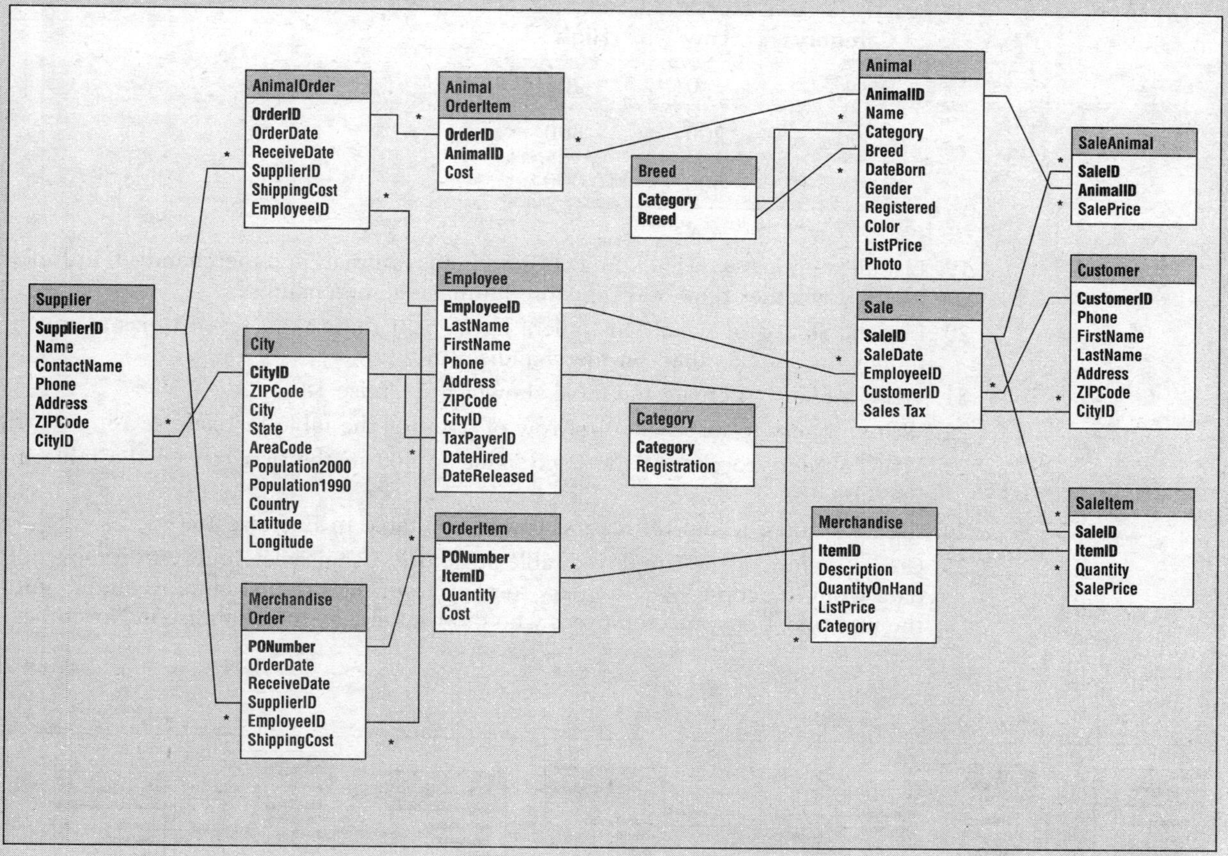

9. List the customers who bought dogs in the first quarter and also bought dog food in the fourth quarter.
10. What was the net change in quantity on hand for premium canned dog food between January 1 and July 1?
11. Which merchandise items with a list price of more than $50 were not sold in July?
12. Which merchandise items with more than 100 units on hand have not been ordered in 2004? Use an OUTER JOIN to answer the question.
13. Which merchandise items with more than 100 units on hand have not been ordered in 2004? Use a subquery to answer the question.
14. Which cat products with a quantity on hand greater than 500 have not been sold in the month of July?
15. Which dog breeds have never been sold at the Pet Store? Use an OUTER JOIN to answer the question.
16. Which dog breeds have never been sold at the Pet Store? Use a subquery to answer the question.
17. List the employees who report to Gibson.
18. Save a query to answer Exercise 7: the total amount of money spent by each customer. Create the table shown to categorize customers based on sales. Write a query that lists each customer from the first query and displays the proper label.

Category	Low	High
Weak	0	200
Good	200	800
Best	800	10,000

19. List all suppliers who sold the Pet Store items (animals and merchandise) in June. Identify whether they sold the store animals or merchandise.
20. List the states for which customers have spent more than seven times as much money on animals than on merchandise (in total).
21. Write a query to create the table shown in Exercise 18.
22. Write a query to insert the first row of data for the table in Exercise 18.
23. Write a query to change the High value to 400 in the first row of the table in Exercise 18.
24. Create a query to delete the first row of the table in Exercise 18.
25. Create a copy of the Employee table structure. Use a delete query to remove all data from the copy. Write a query to copy from the original employee table into the new one. Copy the employees who did not sell any merchandise in November.

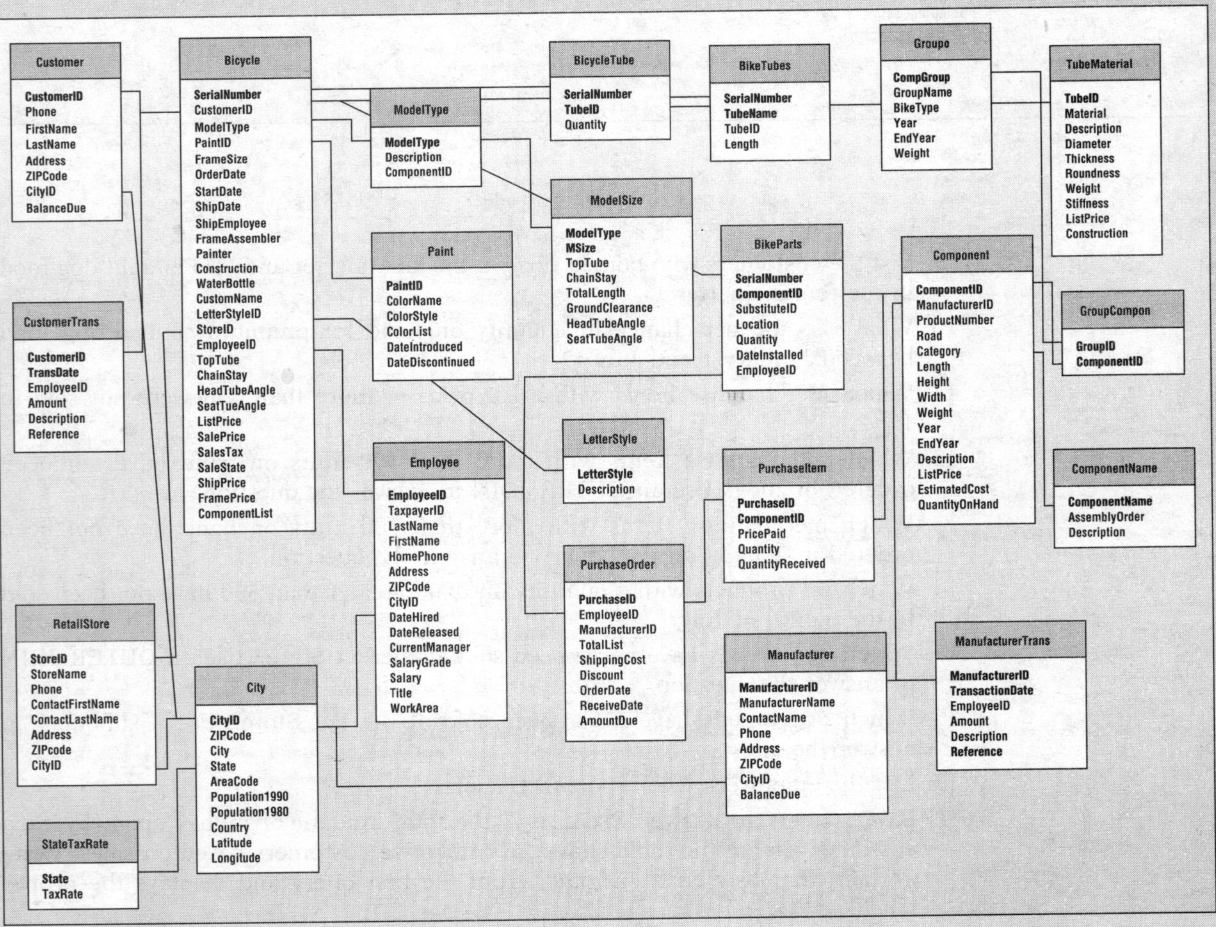

Rolling Thunder Bicycles

Write the SQL statements that will answer questions 26 through 50 based on the tables in the Rolling Thunder database. Build your queries in Access.

26. Which racing bikes in 2003 sold for more than the average price of racing bikes in 2002?
27. In 2002, which bicycles took more than twice as long as the average (for 2002) to produce?
28. List the sales for 2003 by bicycle type in terms of the percentage of total sales for that year.
29. The Campy R2 2002 rear derailleur was installed on what percentage of racing bikes in 2002?
30. List the customers who have purchased at least one road bike and one mountain bike (at any time). Use a subquery.
31. List the customers who have purchased at least one road bike and one mountain bike at any time. Use a JOIN with a saved query. Compare the performance to Exercise 30.
32. List the customers who have bought hard-tail mountain bikes, but have not yet purchased a full-suspension mountain bike. Use a subquery.
33. List the customers who have bought hard-tail mountain bikes, but have not yet purchased a full-suspension mountain bike. Use an OUTER JOIN and compare the performance to Exercise 32.
34. Which component that had no sales (installations) in 2004 has the highest inventory value (cost basis)?
35. Create a vendor contacts list of all manufacturers and retail stores in California. Include only the columns for VendorName and Phone. The retail stores should only include stores that participated in the sale of at least one bicycle in 2004.
36. List all of the employees who report to Venetiaan.
37. List the components where the company purchased at least 25 percent more units than it used through June 30, 2000.
38. List the component and year/month where the total value of the purchases for that month exceed the total value sold of that item for the same month.
39. In which years did the average build time for the year exceed the overall average build time for all years?
40. List the customers who spent at least $7,000 (not counting tax and shipping) from 1997 to 1999, but have not bought any bicycles in 2003 and 2004.
41. List all of the employees who worked on racing bikes ordered the first three days of July 2003. Work includes only assembling, painting, or installing parts. Label the task performed by each person.
42. Which employee had the highest percentage increase in sales from 2001 to 2002?
43. For each model type, what was the percentage change in annual sales value from 2002 to 2003 to 2004?
44. How many customers who purchased road or racing bikes since 2000 have also purchased some type of mountain bike since 2000?

45. Create a new table (CustomerSize) and enter the data shown in the table. Write a query that assigns the appropriate size label to each customer, then create a query to count the number of bicycles built in 2003 and 2004 that fall into each size category by model type.

Size	RoadLow	RoadHigh	MTBLow	MTBHigh
Small	45	52	14	15.5
Medium	52	57	15.5	17
Big	57	65	17	23

46. Write the CREATE TABLE query to create the table described in Exercise 45.
47. Write the query to insert the first row into the table shown in Exercise 45.
48. Write a query to change the RoadLow value for the small bike to 40 in the table for Exercise 47.
49. Write a query to delete the first row in the table for Exercise 46.
50. Write a query to delete the entire table created for Exercise 46.

Website References

Site	Description
http://www.acm.org/sigmod/	Association for Computing Machinery—Special Interest Group: Management of Data.
http://www.acm.org/dl	ACM digital library containing thousands of searchable full-text articles. See if your library has a subscription.

Additional Reading

Celko, J. *Joe Celko's SQL Puzzles & Answers.* San Mateo: Morgan Kaufmann, 1997. [Challenging SQL problems with solutions.]

Iseminger, D., ed. *Microsoft SQL Server 2000 Reference Library.* Redmond: Microsoft Press, 2000. [The hardcopy documentation that does not ship with SQL Server.]

Kreines, D., and K. Jacobs. *Oracle SQL: The Essential Reference.* Cambridge, MA: O'Reilly & Associates, 2000. [Reference book for Oracle's version of SQL.]

Appendix

Introduction to Programming

Many books will help you learn to write computer programs. The purpose of this appendix is to review the highlights of programming and to point out some of the features that are important to programming within a DBMS. If you are new to programming, you should consider reading several other books to explain the details and logic behind programming.

Variables and Data

One of the most important consequences of programming in a database environment is that there can be three categories of data: (1) data stored in a table, (2) data held in a control on a form or report, and (3) traditional data variables that are used to hold temporary results. Chapter 3 focuses on storing data within tables. Chapter 6 describes how to create forms and the role of data controls. Chapter 8 provides more details of how the three types of variables interact when building applications. For now, you must learn details about basic programming variables.

Any procedure can create variables to hold data. A program **variable** is like a small box: It can hold values that will be used or transferred later. Variables have unique names. More importantly, variables can hold a certain **data type.** Common types of variables are displayed in Figure 5.1A. They can generally be classified into three categories: integers (1, 2, −10, . . .); reals (1.55, 3.14, . . .); and strings ('123 Main Street', 'Jose Rojas', . . .).

Each type of variable takes up a defined amount of storage space. This space affects the size of the data that the variable can hold. The exact size depends on the particular DBMS and the operating system. For example, a simple integer typically takes 2 bytes of storage, which is 16 bits. Hence it can hold 2^{16} values or numbers between −32,768 and 32,767. Real numbers can have fractional values. There are usually two sizes: single and double precision. If you do not need many variables, it is often wise to choose the larger variables (long integers and double-precision reals). Although double-precision variables require more space and take longer to process, they provide room for expansion. If you choose too small of a variable, a user might crash your application or get invalid results. For example, it would be a mistake to use a 2-byte integer to count the number of customers—since a firm could generally anticipate having more than 65,000 customers. Along the same lines, you should use the Currency data type for monetary values. In

FIGURE 5.1A
Program variable types. Sizes are given for Microsoft Access. Note that currency variables help prevent round-off errors.

Integer
- 2 bytes
- −32768 32767

Long
- 4 bytes
- +/− 2,147,483,648

Single
- 4 bytes
- +/− 3.402823 E 38
- +/− 1.401298 E-45

Global, Const, Static

Double
- 8 bytes
- +/− 1.79769313486232 E-308
- +/− 4.94065645841247 E-324

Currency
- 8 bytes
- +/− 922,337,203,685,477.5808

String & String*n

Variant
- Any data type
- Null

addition to handling large numbers, it avoids round-off errors that are common to floating-point numbers.

Microsoft Access provides the Variant data type, which is useful when transferring data from a database table or from an input form. The Variant data type has two unique properties: (1) It can hold any type of data (including dates), and (2) it can identify missing data. If you think of a variable as a box that can hold values, you can see how it would be useful to know when the box is empty. Standard programming variables do not have a means to test for this condition. Access provides the IsNull function that will tell you whether a Variant data variable has not yet been assigned a value.

Variable Scope

The scope and lifetime of a variable are crucial elements of programming, particularly in an event-driven environment. Variable **scope** refers to where the variable is accessible, that is, which procedures or code can access the data in that variable. The **lifetime** identifies when the variable is created and when it is destroyed. The two properties are related and are generally automatic. However, you can override the standard procedures by changing the way you declare the variable.

All data variables should be explicitly declared; they should be identified before they are used. The most common method is to use a Dim statement, for example, Dim i1 As Integer. In the default case, the lifetime and scope of the variable depend on where the variable is created. Most commonly, the variable is created within the event procedure and is a **local variable.** When the procedure starts, the local variable is created. Any code within that procedure can use the variable. Code in other procedures cannot see the variable. When the procedure ends, the local variable and its data are destroyed.

Figure 5.2A shows two buttons on a form. Each button responds to a Click event, so two procedures are defined. Each procedure can have a variable called *i*1, but these two variables are completely separate. In fact, the variables are not created until the button is clicked. Think of the procedures as two different rooms. When you are in one room, you can see the data for that room only. When you leave the room, the data is destroyed.

However, what if you do not want the data to be destroyed when the code ends, or you want to access the variable from other procedures? You have two choices: (1) Change the lifetime of the variable by declaring it static, or (2) Change the scope of the variable by declaring it in a different location. You should avoid declaring a static variable unless it is absolutely necessary (which is rare). If the variable is

FIGURE 5.2A
Variable scope and lifetime. Each event has its own procedure with independent variables that are created and destroyed each time the button is clicked.

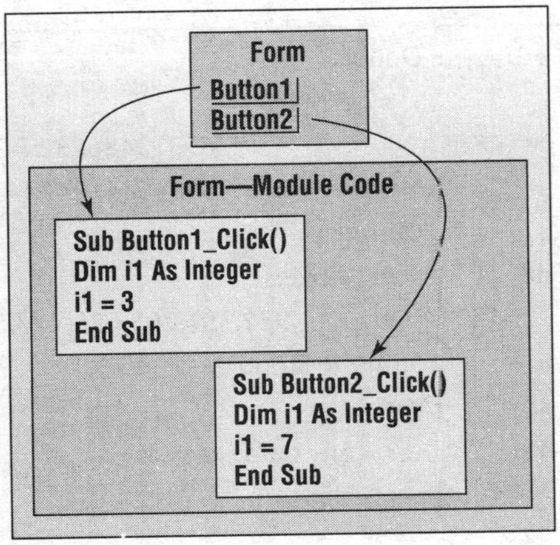

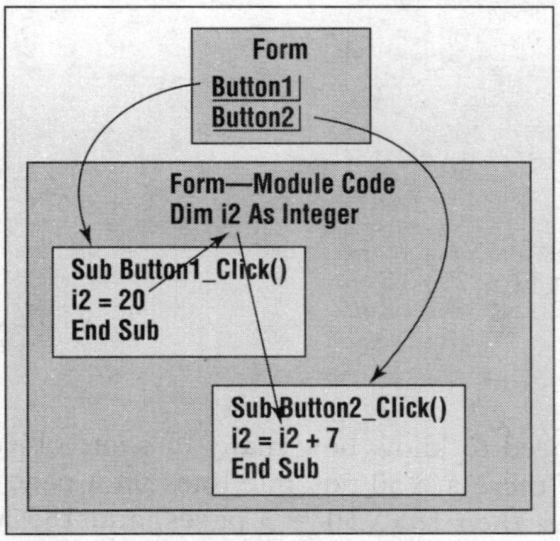

FIGURE 5.3A
Global variables. Variables that are defined in the form's General section are accessible by any function on that form (or module).

static, it keeps its value from the previous time the procedure was called. In the example, each time the button is clicked, the value for *i3* will remain from the prior click. You might use this trick if you need to count the number of times the button is clicked.

A more useful technique is to change where the variable is defined. Figure 5.3A shows that event procedures are defined within a form or a **module**, which is a collection of related procedures. The variable *i2* is defined for the entire form or module (within the General section in Access). The lifetime of the variable is established by the form, that is, the variable is created and destroyed as the form is opened and closed. The scope of the variable is that all procedures in the form can see and change the value. On the other hand, procedures in other forms or modules do not know that this variable exists.

Procedures or functions also have a scope. Any procedure that you define on a form can be used by other procedures on that form. If you need to access a variable or a procedure from many different forms or reports, you should define it on a separate module and then declare it as global (or public).

Be careful with global or public variables. A programmer who tries to revise your code might not know that the variable is used in other procedures and might accidentally destroy an important value. On forms the main purpose of a global variable is to transfer a value from one event to another one. For example, you might need to keep the original value of a text control—before it is changed by a user—and compare it to the new value. You need a global variable because two separate events examine the text control: (1) The user first enters the control, and (2) The user changes the data.

Computations

One of the main purposes of variables is to perform calculations. Keep in mind that these computations apply to individual variables—one piece of data at a time. If you need to manipulate data in an entire table, it is usually best to use the SQL commands described in Chapter 5. Nonetheless, there are times when you need more complex calculations.

Standard arithmetic operations (add, subtract, multiply, and divide) are shown in Figure 5.4A. These operators are common to most programming languages. Some nonstandard, but useful, operators include exponentiation (raise to a power, e.g., 2 ^ 3 = 2 * 2 * 2 = 8), and integer divide (e.g., 9 \ 2 = 4), which always returns an integer value. The mod function returns the modulus or remainder of an integer division (e.g., 15 mod 4 = 3, since 15 − 12 = 3). These last two functions

FIGURE 5.4A
Common arithmetic operators. Add (+), subtract (−), multiply (*), and divide (/). Exponentiation and integer arithmetic are often used for special tasks. For example, integer arithmetic is useful for dividing objects into groups.

- Arithmetic: + − * /
- Exponentiation ^
  2^3 = 2*2*2 = 8
- Integer divide \
  9 \ 2 = 4
- Modulus or remainder
  15 Mod 4 = 3, or 12 + 3 = 15

are useful when you need to know how many of some objects will fit into a fixed space. For example, if there are 50 possible lines on a page and you need to print a report with 185 lines, then 185 \ 50 = 3 pages, and 185 Mod 50 leaves 35 lines on a fourth page.

Most languages support string variables, which are used to hold basic text data, such as names, addresses, or short messages. A string is a collection (or array) of characters. Sometimes you will need to perform computations on string variables. How can you perform computations on text data? The most common technique is to **concatenate** (or add) two strings together. For example, if FirstName is "George" and LastName is "Jones", then FirstName & LastName is "GeorgeJones". Notice that if you want a space to appear between the names, you have to add one: FirstName & " " & LastName.

Figure 5.5A lists some of the common string functions. You can learn more about the functions and their syntax from the Help system within Access. Commonly used functions include the Left, Right, and Mid, which examine portions of the string. For example, you might want to see only the first five characters on the left side of a string.

Standard Internal Functions

As you may recall from courses in mathematics, several common functions are used in a variety of situations. As shown in Figure 5.6A, these functions include the standard trigonometric and logarithmic functions, which can be useful in mapping and procedures involving measurements. You also will need a function to compute the square root and absolute value of numbers. The Int (integer) function is useful for dropping the fractional portion of a number. Most languages also provide a random number generator, which will randomly create numbers between 0 and 1. If you need another range of numbers, you can get them with a simple conversion. For example,

FIGURE 5.5A
Common string functions to add strings, extract portions, examine characters, convert case, compare two strings, and format numerical data into a string variable.

& Concatenation
Left, Right, Mid
Trim, LTrim, RTrim
String
Chr, Asc
LCase, UCase
InStr
Len
StrComp
Format

"Frank" & "Rose" → "FrankRose"
Left("Jackson",5) → "Jacks"
Trim("   Maria   ") → "Maria"
Len("Ramanujan") → 9
String(5, "a") → "aaaaa"
InStr("8764 Main"," ") → 5

FIGURE 5.6A
Standard mathematical functions. Even in business applications, you often need basic mathematical functions.

Numeric
- Exp, Log
- Atn, Cos, Sin, Tan
- Sqr
- Abs
- Sgn
- Int, Fix
- Rnd, Randomize

$x = \log_e(e^x)$
Trigonometric functions ? $\phi = 30$ 92
$\sqrt{2} = 1.414$
Abs(−35) → 35
Sgn(−35) → −1
Int(17.893) → 17
Rnd() → 0.198474

to generate numbers between 40 and 90, use the following function: y = 40 + (90 − 40) * Rnd.

In a database environment, you will often need to evaluate and modify dates. It is also useful to have functions that provide the current date (Date) and time (Now). Two functions that are useful in business are the DateAdd and DateDiff functions. As illustrated in Figure 5.7A, the DateAdd function adds days to a given date to find some date in the future. The DateDiff function computes the difference between two dates. Usually, you will want to compute the number of days between various dates. However, the functions in VBA can compute number of months, weeks, and so on. You could even count the number of Fridays between two dates.

Recall that the Variant data type can contain any type of data, including dates, numbers, and strings. Sometimes you need to know exactly what type of data is stored in the Variant before you try to perform an operation. Several functions, such as IsDate, IsNumberic, and VarType, provide this information. These functions enable you to determine whether a variable is the proper type before using it in an inappropriate situation.

Another useful feature of the Variant data type is the ability to test for missing data. Traditional programming variables do not support this feature. Microsoft Access provides two functions for this purpose: IsNull and IsEmpty. The IsNull function can test data table values and examine data entry controls to see whether the user entered a value.

Input and Output

Handling input and output were crucial topics in traditional programming. These topics are still important, but the DBMS now performs most data-handling routines and the operating system handles most of the user interface. Common forms and reports (Chapter 6) are used for most input and output tasks.

FIGURE 5.7A
Date and time functions. Business problems often require computing the number of days between two dates or adding days to a date to determine when payments are due.

Date, Now, Time
DateAdd, DateDiff
- "y", "m", "q", . . .
- Firstweekday
- 1 = Sunday, . . .
- Can also be used to find number of Fridays, between two dates.

02/19/01 — today
03/21/01 — DateDue

DateDue = DateAdd("d", 30, Date())

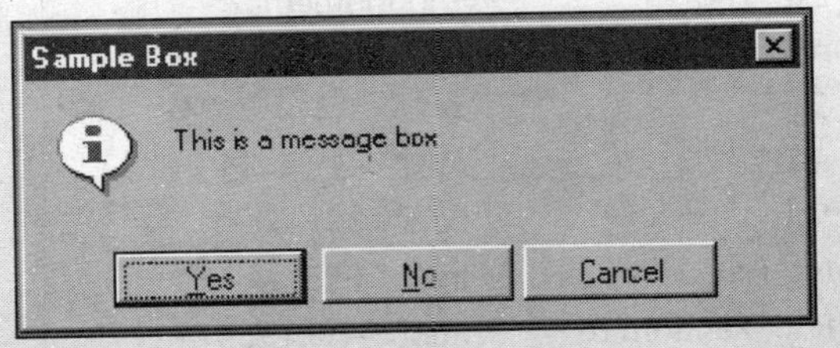


```
MsgBox ("This is a message box",
     vbYesNoCancel + vbInformation,
     "Sample Box")
```

FIGURE 5.8A
Sample message box. The message box interrupts the user and displays a few limited choices. It often handles errors or problems.

Remember that an important feature of a Windows interface is that users control the flow of data entry; that is, the designer provides a form, and users work at their own pace without interruption. Occasionally, you might choose to interrupt the user—either to provide information or to get a specific piece of data. One common reason is to display error messages. Two basic functions serve this purpose: MsgBox and InputBox. As shown in Figure 5.8A, a message box can contain buttons. The buttons are often used to indicate how the user wants to respond to some problem or error.

An InputBox is a special form that can be used to enter very small amounts of text or a single number. Neither the user nor the developer has much control over the form. In most cases, you would be better off creating your own blank form. Then you can have more than one text box, and you can specify and control the buttons. The InputBox is usually for temporary use when development time is extremely limited.

Conditions

The ability to test and respond to conditions is one of the most common reasons for writing your own procedures. The basic conditional statement (if . . . then . . . else) is relatively easy to understand. The structure is shown in Figure 5.9A. A condition is evaluated to be true or false. If it is true, then one set of statements is executed; otherwise, the second set is performed.

Conditions can be complex, particularly when the condition contains several AND and OR connectors. Some developers use a NOT statement to reverse the value of a condition. Be careful when writing conditions. Your goals are to make sure that the

```
If (Condition1) Then
  statements for true
Else
  statements for false
  If (Condition2) Then
    statements for true
  End If
End If
```

FIGURE 5.9A
Conditions. Basic conditions are straightforward. Indenting conditions highlights the relationships.

FIGURE 5.10A
Nested conditions to test for a user response. The code becomes harder to read as more conditions are added.

```
response = MsgBox (...)
If (response = vbYes) Then
  'statements for Yes
Else
  If (response = vbNo) Then
    'statements for No
  Else
    'statements for Cancel
  End If
End If
```

condition evaluates to the correct value and to make sure that other developers can understand the code.

You should always include parentheses to specify the order of evaluation and, for complex conditions, create sample data and test the conditions. Also, indent your code. Indenting is particularly important for **nested conditions,** in which the statements for one condition contain another conditional statement.

The Select Case statement is a special type of conditional statement. Many procedures will need to evaluate a set of related conditions. As a simple example, consider what happens if you use a message box with three buttons (Yes, No, and Cancel). You will have to test the user's choice for each option. Figure 5.10A shows how the code might look when you use nested conditions.

Figure 5.11A shows the same problem written with the Select Case statement. Note that this code is much easier to read. Now think about what will happen if you have 10 choices. The If . . . Then code gets much worse, but the Select Case code just adds new lines to the bottom of the list.

Loops

Iteration or loops are another common feature in procedures. Although you should use SQL statements (UPDATE, INSERT, etc.) as much as possible, sometimes you will need to loop through a table or query to examine each row individually.

Some of the basic loop formats are illustrated in Figure 5.12A. The For/Next loop is generally used only if you need a fixed number of iterations. The Do loop is more common. An important feature of loops is the ability to test the condition at the top or the bottom of the loop. Consider the example in which the condition says to execute the statements if ($x <= 10$). What happens when the starting value of x is 15? If you test the condition at the top of the loop, then the statements in the loop will never be executed. On the other hand, if you test the condition at the bottom, then

FIGURE 5.11A
The Select statement. The Select statement tests the response variable against several conditions. If the response matches a case in the list, the corresponding code is executed.

```
response = MsgBox(...)
Select Case response
  Case vbYes
    'statements for Yes
  Case vbNo
    'statements for No
  Case vbCancel
    'statements for Cancel
End Case
```

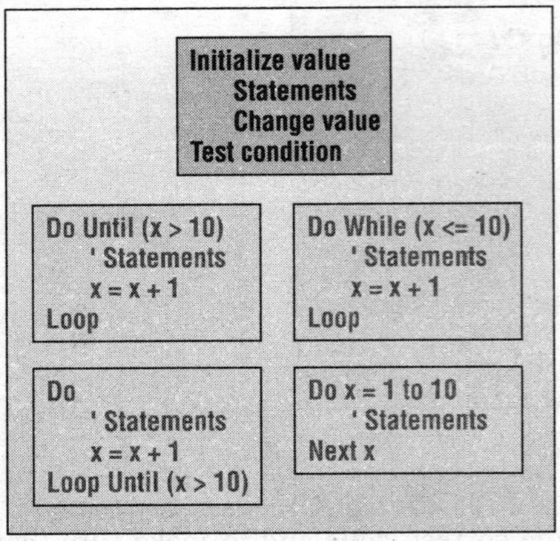

FIGURE 5.12A
Iteration. All versions of loops follow a common format: Initialize a counter value, perform statements, increment the counter, and test the exit condition. You can test the condition at the start or end of the loop.

the statements in the loop will be executed exactly one time—before the condition is tested.

Just as with conditions, it is good programming practice to indent the statements of the loop. Indents help others to read your code and to understand the logic. If there are no problems within a loop, your eye can easily find the end of the loop.

Be careful with loops: If you make a mistake, the computer may execute the statements of your loop forever. (On most personal computers, Ctrl+Break will usually stop a runaway loop.) A common mistake occurs when you forget to change the conditional variable (*x* in the examples). In tracking through a data query, you might forget to get the next row of data, in which case your code will perform the same operations forever on one row of data. A good programming practice is to always write loops in four steps: (1) Write the initial condition, (2) Write the ending statement, (3) Write a statement to update the conditional variable, and (4) Write the interior code. The first three statements give you the structure. By writing and testing them first, you know that you will be using the correct data.

Subroutines

An important concept in programming is the ability to break the program into smaller pieces as subroutines or functions. A **subroutine** is a portion of code that can be called from other routines. When the subroutine is finished, control returns to the program code that called it. The goal of using subroutines is to break the program into smaller pieces that are relatively easy to understand, test, and modify.

A subroutine is essentially a self-contained program that can be used by many other parts of the program. For example, you might create a subroutine that displays a status message on the screen. As illustrated in Figure 5.13A, you would write the basic routine once. Then anytime you need to display a status message, your program calls this routine. By passing the message to the subroutine, the actual message can change each time. The advantage of using the subroutine is that you have to write it only once. In addition, your status messages can be standardized because the subroutine specifies the location, style, and color. To change the format, you simply modify the few lines of code in the one subroutine. Without the subroutine, you would have to find and modify code in every location that displayed a status message.

A data variable that is passed to a function or a subroutine is known as a **parameter.** There are two basic ways to pass a parameter: by reference and by value. The default method used by Microsoft Access is pass-by-reference. In this case, the variable in the subroutine is essentially the same variable as in the original

FIGURE 5.13A
Subroutine. The StatusMessage subroutine can be called from any location. When the subroutine is finished, it returns to the calling program.

```
Main program
...
StatusMessage "Trying to connect."
...
StatusMessage "Verifying access."
...
End main program

Sub StatusMessage (Msg As String)
     ' Display Msg, location, color
End Sub
```

program. Any changes made to the data in the subroutine will automatically be returned to the calling program. For example, consider the two examples in Figure 5.14A. Changes to the variable *j*2 in the subroutine will automatically be passed back to the calling program. However, when only the value is passed, a copy is made in the subroutine. Changes made to the data in the subroutine will not be returned to the calling program. Unless you are absolutely certain that you want to alter the original value in the calling program, you should always pass variables by value. Subroutines that use pass-by-reference can cause errors that are difficult to find in programs. Some other programmer might not realize that your subroutine changed the value of a parameter.

Most languages also enable you to create new functions. There is a slight technical difference between functions and subroutines. Although subroutines and functions can receive or return data through pass-by-reference parameters, a function can return a result or a single value directly to the calling program. For instance, your main program might have a statement such as $v1 = \text{Min}(x, y)$. The function would choose the smaller of the two values and return it to the main program, where it is assigned to the variable *v*1.

FIGURE 5.14A
Two methods to pass data to a subroutine. Pass parameters by value as much as possible to avoid unwanted changes to data.

```
Main
j = 3
DoSum j
...   ' j is now equal to 8

Subroutine DoSum (j2 As Integer)
     j2 = 8
End Sub
```

By Reference
Changes to data in the subroutine are passed back.

```
Main
j = 3
DoSum j
...   ' j is still equal to 3

Subroutine DoSum (ByVal j2 As Integer)
     j2 = 8
End Sub
```

By Value
Creates a copy of the variable, so changes are not returned.

Summary

The only way to learn how to program is to write your own programs. Reading books, syntax documentation, and studying code written by others will help, but the only way to become a programmer is through experience.

As you write programs, remember that you (or someone else) might have to modify your code later. Choose descriptive variable names. Document your statements with comments that explain tricky sections and outline the purpose of each section of code. Write in small sections and subroutines. Test each section, and keep the test data and results in the documentation. Keep revision notes so that you know when each section was changed and why you changed it.

Part 3

Applications

Building business applications in a database environment begins with creating forms and reports. Most database management systems have tools to help you construct the basic forms and reports. However, Chapter 6 shows you that you have to design and modify forms and reports to make them useful and user-friendly. It also discusses the details needed to combine forms and reports into applications.

Chapter 7 focuses on the concepts of database integrity and transactions. It explores ways of maintaining data quality and preventing common problems that arise with multiple users in a large database.

Chapter 8 shows the conflicts between transaction-processing databases and systems designed for analysis. It introduces the issues of transferring data to data warehouses and explores some of the modern techniques for interactive data analysis in large databases.

Chapter 6

Forms, Reports, and Applications

Chapter Outline

What You Will Learn in This Chapter

- What is the purpose of input forms? Why not just enter data into tables? 223
- What are the main types of controls you can use on forms? 237
- What are the primary components of reports? 250
- What is the overall structure of a report? 252
- What additional features are needed to create an application? 255

A Developer's View

Ariel: Why the concerned look?

Miranda: Well, I finally figured out how to answer those hard questions. But I'm a little worried. Lots of times I got answers, but they were wrong. I have to be really careful with SQL.

Ariel: Oh, I'm sure you'll do fine. You're always careful about testing your work.

Miranda: I suppose it'll get easier.

Ariel: That's the spirit. Now, are you finally ready to start building the application?

Miranda: I sure am. I looked at some of the information about forms and reports. This is going to be easy.

Ariel: Really?

Miranda: Sure. And you know the best part? All the forms and reports are based on SQL. To get the initial forms and reports, all I have to do is build queries to get the data I want. There are even wizards that will help create the basic forms and reports.

Ariel: I always knew that someday people would call on spirits again.

Introduction

Forms and reports are an important part of the database application. Designers use them to create an integrated application, making it easier for users to perform their tasks. Decision makers and clerical workers use forms and reports on a daily basis. Years ago forms were used primarily as input devices, and reports were used to display results. However, as managers gained greater access to online databases, forms became increasingly important. Reports are still used for output that will be distributed or stored in paper form. However, forms can be distributed electronically and can display a variety of outputs. The Internet, and specifically the World Wide Web, is becoming an increasingly popular means of distributing data as electronic forms. The same design principles used for database forms also apply to the Web.

As summarized in Figure 6.1, forms are used to collect data, display results of queries, display analysis, and perform computations. They are also used as switchboards, or connectors, to other forms and reports. In sophisticated, Windows-based applications, a form can be used for direct manipulation of objects. A graphical interface enables users to drag-and-drop objects to indicate changes. With this type of form, users interact visually with a model of the firm.

FIGURE 6.1
Basic uses of database forms. It is important to understand the use of a form, since forms designed for data collection will be different from those designed to analyze data.

- Collect data
- Display query results
- Display analyses and computations
- Switchboard for other forms and reports
- Direct manipulation of objects
  - Graphics
  - Drag-and-drop

Reports are typically printed on paper, but they are increasingly being created for direct display on the screen. Reports are used to format the data and present results from complex analysis. Reports can be detailed and cover several pages; an example would be a detailed inventory report. Alternatively, reports can present summary data, incorporating graphs and totals. A common business example would be a weekly sales report comparing sales by division for the past few weeks. The report would generally be presented graphically and would occupy one page.

Applications are built as a collection of interrelated forms and reports. Because all user access to the database is through the forms and reports, they must be designed to match the tasks of the users. Additional features such as menus and help screens make it easier for workers to use the application.

Effective Design of Reports and Forms

The most important concept to remember when designing forms and reports is to understand that they are the primary contact with the users. Each form and report must be tailored to specific situations and business uses. For example, some forms will be used for **heads-down data entry**—where touch typists concentrate on entering data without looking at the screen. Other forms present exploratory analyses, and the decision maker will want to examine various scenarios. The features, layout, and capabilities of these two types of forms are radically different. If you choose the wrong design for the user, the form (or report) will be virtually useless.

The key to effective design is to determine the needs of the user. The catch is that users often do not know what they need (or want). In particular, they may not be aware of the capabilities and limitations of a modern DBMS. As a designer, you talk with the users to learn what they want to accomplish. Then you use your experience to provide features that make the form more useful. Just be careful to find the fine line between helping the user and trying to sell users an application they do not need.

Researchers in human factors have developed several guidelines to help you design forms. To begin, all forms and reports within an application (or even within an organization) should be as consistent as possible. Keystrokes, commands, and icons should be used for the same purposes throughout the application. Color, layout, and structure should be coordinated so users can understand the data and context on any form or report. Basing applications on a set of common tasks reduces the time it takes for users to learn new applications. The increasing importance of Web-based applications simplifies design to some extent, because you now have a limited set of tools that are understood by almost all users. Research into **human factors design** has also led to several hints and guidelines that designers should follow when building forms and reports.

Human Factors Design

Figure 6.2 summarizes some human factors design elements that system designers should incorporate in their applications. With current operating systems, the primary factor is that the users—not the programmer and not the application—should always have control. For example, do not expect

FIGURE 6.2
Basic human factors design elements. All designs should be evaluated in terms of these basic features.

Human Factors	Examples
User control	Match user tasks Respond to user control and events User customization
Consistency	Layout, design, and colors Actions
Clarity	Organization Purpose Terminology
Aesthetics	Art to enhance Graphics Sound
Feedback	Methods Visual Text Audio Uses Acceptance of input Changes to data Completion of tasks Events/Activation
Forgiveness	Anticipation and correction of errors Confirmation on delete and updates Backup and recovery

(or force) users to enter data in a particular sequence. Instead, set up the base forms and let users choose the data entry order that is easiest for them. In this approach, the user's choices trigger various events. Your application responds to these events or triggers by performing calculations, retrieving or storing data, and offering new choices.

Also, whenever possible, provide options for user customization. Many users want to change display features such as color, typeface, or size. Similarly, users have their own preferences in terms of sorting results and the data to be included.

Both the layout (design and color) and the required actions should be consistent across an application. In terms of user actions, be careful to ensure consistency in basic features, such as whether the user must press the Enter key at the end of an input, which function key invokes the Help system, how the arrow keys are used, and the role of each icon. These actions should be consistent across the entire application. This concept seems obvious, but it can be challenging to implement—particularly when many designers and programmers are creating the application. Two practices help ensure **consistency**: (1) At the start establish a design standard and basic templates for all designers to use, and (2) toward the end of the application development always go back and check for consistency.

Always strive for **clarity**. In many cases *clarity* means keeping the application simple and well organized. If the application has multiple forms and reports, organize them according to user tasks. It helps to have a clear purpose for an application and to make sure the design enhances that purpose. Use precise terminology, avoid jargon, and stick with terms that are used within the organization. If a company refers to its employees as "Associates," use that term, instead of "Employees."

Aesthetics also play an important role in the user interface. The goal is to use color and design (and sometimes sound) to enhance the forms and reports. Avoid the beginner's mistake of using different colors for every form or placing 10 different fonts on a page. Although design and art are highly subjective, bad designs are immediately obvious to others. If you have minimal experience in design aesthetics, consider taking a course or two in art or design. If nothing else, study work done by others to gain ideas, to train your artistic sensibility, and to stay abreast of current trends. Remember that graphics and art are important, and they provide an attractive and familiar environment for users.

Feedback is crucial to most human–computer interactions. People want to know that when they press a key, choose an option, or select an icon the computer recognized their action and is responding. Typical uses of feedback include accepting input, acknowledging changes of data, highlighting completion of a task, or signifying the start or completion of some event. Several options can be used to provide feedback. Visually, the cursor can be changed, text can be highlighted, a button can be "pushed in," or a box may change color. More direct forms of feedback, such as displaying messages on the screen, can be used in more complicated cases. Some systems use audio feedback, playing a musical theme or sound when the user selects a task or when the computer finishes an operation. If you decide to use audio feedback, be sure that you give users a choice—some people do not like "noisy" computers. On the other hand, do not be hasty to discard the use of audio feedback—it is particularly effective for people with low vision. Similarly, audio responses are useful when users need to focus their vision on an external task and cannot look at the computer screen.

Humans occasionally make mistakes or change their minds. As a designer, you need to understand these possibilities and provide for them within your application. In particular, your application should anticipate and provide for correction of errors. You should confirm deletions and major updates—giving users a chance to verify the changes, or even undo them. Finally, your overall application should include mechanisms for backup and recovery of data—both in case of natural disasters and in case of accidental deletions or loss of data.

Window Controls

Designing applications that run under Windows requires a solid understanding of the Windows interface—in part because you want to provide the standard controls and operations that Windows offers, but also because the Windows functionality enables you to easily provide additional, powerful features within your application.

A basic window is displayed in Figure 6.3. The components of the window consist of the frame, the title bar, a Control menu box, and various standard buttons. The frame can be resized by the user, or the programmer can set it to a fixed size. Be sure to provide a short, but descriptive, title for each

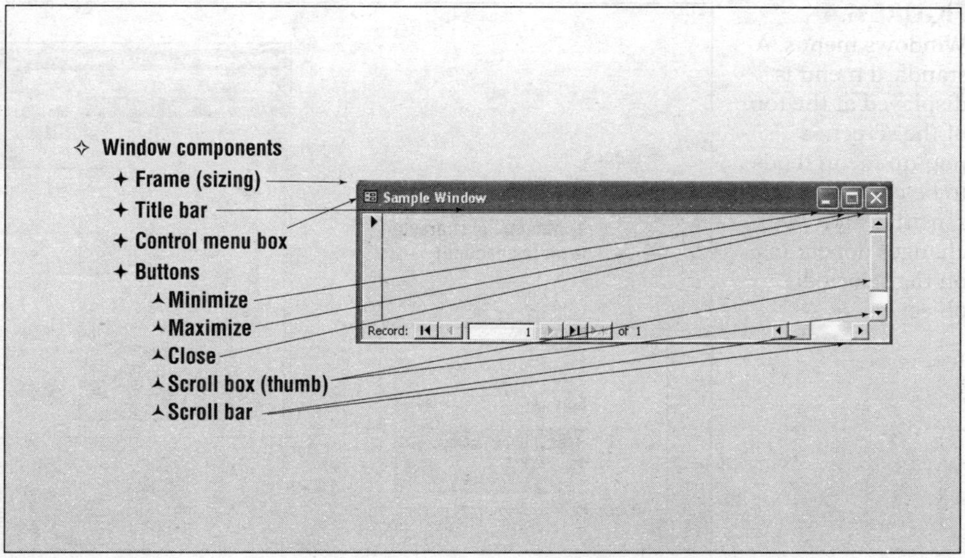

FIGURE 6.3
Windows interface. A window consists of several common components. The DBMS performs the main tasks required to maintain the window. However, you can often add features or commands to these operations.

form. The Control menu box provides standard commands to move, resize, and close the form. Common window buttons include Maximize (full screen) and Minimize (push to bottom of screen), and Close. **Scroll bars** enable the user to scroll the form horizontally and vertically. Your application or the DMBS typically handles these actions automatically. As you create a form, you have the ability to remove these standard controls, but avoid that temptation. More important, you can often override the standard actions and provide additional features. For instance, you might want to perform some cleanup operations when the user closes a form. Common cleanup operations include recomputing totals, storing changed data, triggering matching changes in other tables, or synchronizing the scrolling of one form as changes are made in a second form.

Menus are an important feature of any application. Most users (rightly) expect to have a menu that accesses the primary functions for each task. The most common menu is a drop-down menu displayed at the top of the screen, as shown in Figure 6.4. The menu contains a list of actions, often grouped by related commands, divided by a separator line. A pointer can activate the menu, or selections can be made from the keyboard using mnemonic letters. Mnemonic letters are generally underlined on the menu (e.g., the F in the File command). On a standard PC, the Alt key initiates these commands. Many applications also define shortcut keys—particularly for commands that are used frequently. These commands are generally initiated with a Ctrl key combination, such as the Ctrl+C command to copy a selection.

Occasionally developers use a pop-up or shortcut menu. An increasingly popular technique is to have the right mouse button trigger a pop-up menu to set properties of various objects on the screen. The biggest difference between a pop-up menu and a standard, fixed menu is that the pop-up menu is usually context sensitive. A **context-sensitive menu** is one that changes depending on the object selected by the user.

A useful feature within many forms and applications is a pop-up message box. As shown in Figure 6.5, a message box is a simple form, with few

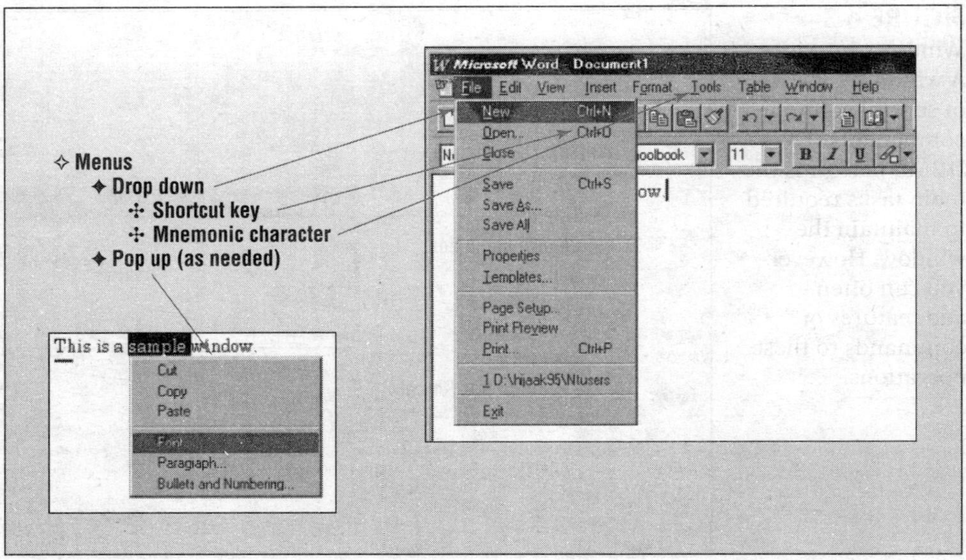

FIGURE 6.4 Windows menus. A standard menu is displayed at the top of the screen, a pop-up menu tends to be context sensitive and changes depending on the selected object.

controls. It is used to display short, one-line messages and obtain simple (usually yes/no) responses from the user. In general, it is best to avoid the use of message boxes—because they remove control from the user. In extreme cases, a **modal form** takes priority on the screen and forces the user to deal with it before continuing. This type of message box is commonly used to handle errors or to set up a printer—situations that require an interruption. You can make any form modal by setting its modal property to Yes. However, this advice is worth repeating: Avoid modal forms: They take away control from the user.

User Interface—Web Notes

In many ways, the Web environment is similar to the standard Windows environment. You have control over layout, color, and data entry. One of the useful features of Web pages and forms is that they can be standardized so they are displayed the same way on almost any type of client computer or browser. Users understand some basic interface features: Clicking a hyperlink

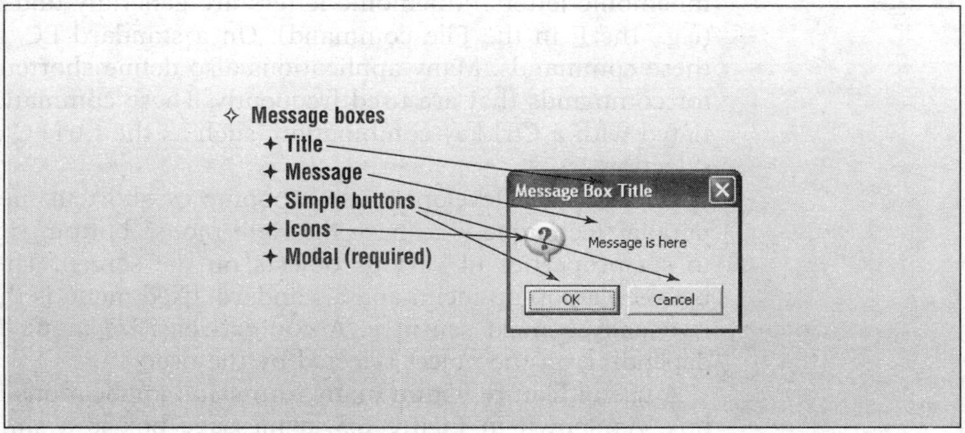

FIGURE 6.5 Message box. A message box is a simple form with a few buttons. This device should be used sparingly, since it interrupts the user's task. It is generally used to warn the user of problems or to offer immediate choices.

brings a new page, buttons are used to submit a form, drop-down lists are used to select an item, and so on.

When you develop applications for websites, be sure to incorporate style sheets. Style sheets can be powerful tools for designing consistent forms on the Web. They enable you to define a standard layout and color scheme that will be used by all of your pages. Altering a few parameters in the style sheet definition applies the changes to all of the pages, creating a new look for the website.

User Interface—Accessibility Issues

One of the greatest strengths of the Windows interface is its graphical orientation, which makes it easy for people to perform complex operations with a few moves of the mouse or selections on the screen. One of the drawbacks to this type of interface is that it is more difficult to make a system that is **accessible** to users facing some physical challenges. As a designer you can make your applications accessible to a wider base of users. To begin, your application should accept multiple sources of inputs. Do not rely on just a mouse or a pointer but also use the keyboard, and increasingly, the user's voice. Similarly, it is helpful if your application can provide multiple types of output. Increasingly, you should consider how to integrate sound and voice output. The user must also be able to set the color and size of the output.

Microsoft guidelines provide some suggestions for making your applications accessible to more users. Detailed ideas and current developments can be found on its website. Human factors experience with other applications has generated some specific suggestions. For example, do not use red–green color combinations. Approximately 10 percent of the U.S. male population experiences some difficulty distinguishing between red and green. Try to pick high-contrast colors that most people can distinguish (e.g., black and white, yellow, blue, and red). When in doubt, ask people to test your color combinations or let users select their own colors.

Second, avoid requiring rapid user responses. Do not put time limits on input. Although it might be fun in a game, many users have slower data entry skills. Some designers include pop-up messages to check on user progress after a delay in data entry. These messages are usually pointless and can be annoying. With modern screen-saver security systems, users can set their own delay controls and messages.

Third, avoid controls that flash rapidly on the screen. They tend to annoy most users. Worse, certain flash rates have been known to trigger epileptic seizures in some people. An interesting situation arose in Japan at the end of 1997 when a sequence of flashing graphics on an animated television show (*Pokemon*) sent about 700 children to the hospital.

Fourth, as much as possible, enable users to customize their screens. Let them choose typefaces, font sizes, and screen colors. That way, users can adjust the screen to compensate for any vision problems they may have. And if you use sound, let people control the volume, even pitch, if possible. In many cases, the Windows environment provides much of this functionality, so the key point is to avoid overriding that functionality. Also, you should test your applications on various computers. Some video systems may distort your choice of colors or will be incapable of displaying your forms at the desired resolution.

Form Layout

Individual forms or windows are your primary means of communicating with people who use your application. Forms are used to collect data, display results, and organize the overall system. From a database perspective, your application is built from several standard types of forms. As you begin working with these basic layouts, keep in mind that you can create complex forms that use features from several different form types. However, you should understand the layout and uses of each individual form type first.

You will be working with four basic types of forms: (1) **tabular forms,** which display data in rows and columns; (2) **single-row forms,** which show data for one row at a time and in which the designer can arrange the values in any format on the screen; (3) **subform forms,** which display data from two tables that have a one-to-many relationship; and (4) **switchboard forms,** or menus, which direct the user to other forms and reports in the application.

As indicated in Figure 6.6, forms have several things in common. They have properties, which you set to control the look and style of the form. Also, forms contain **controls,** which include labels and text boxes that are used to display basic text and data. Additionally, several events can occur with a form. For example, opening and closing a form are basic events for every form. You can control how the form operates by creating actions that are taken when each event occurs.

Although a form can have multiple controls (e.g., text boxes) on it, only one control at a time has the focus. The control that has the **focus** will receive keystrokes entered by the user. This control is often highlighted with an outline or a different color. The same concept applies when an application displays multiple forms on a screen. Only one form has the focus at a time. Within a form, users can usually use the Tab key to move to the next control in a sequence, which is known as the **tab order.** You must be sure to check the tab order on all forms so that it visually matches the layout of the form.

Tabular Forms

As shown in Figure 6.7, one of the simplest forms is the tabular form, which displays the columns and rows from a table or query. It can be used as a

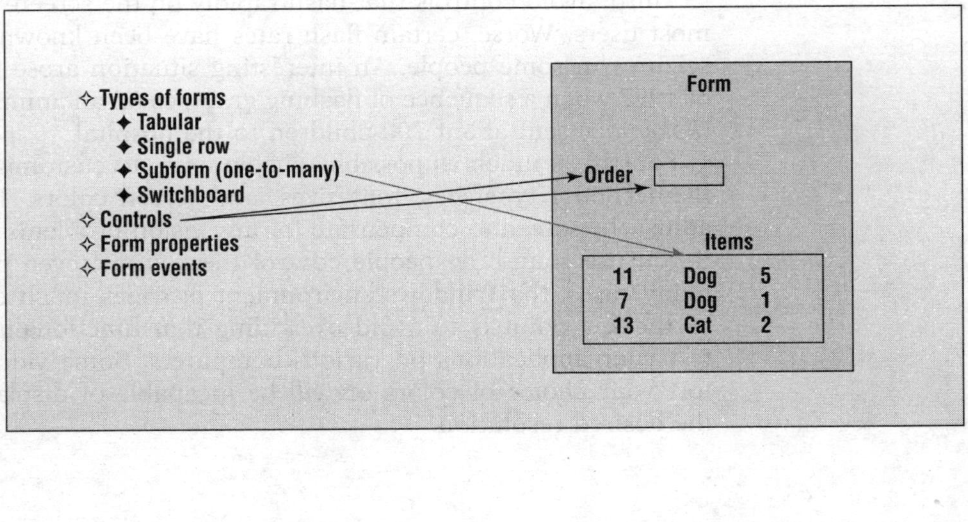

FIGURE 6.6
Form layout. Controls are placed on a form to display or collect data. A form's style is defined by its property settings. Form behavior is controlled by creating actions in response to form events.

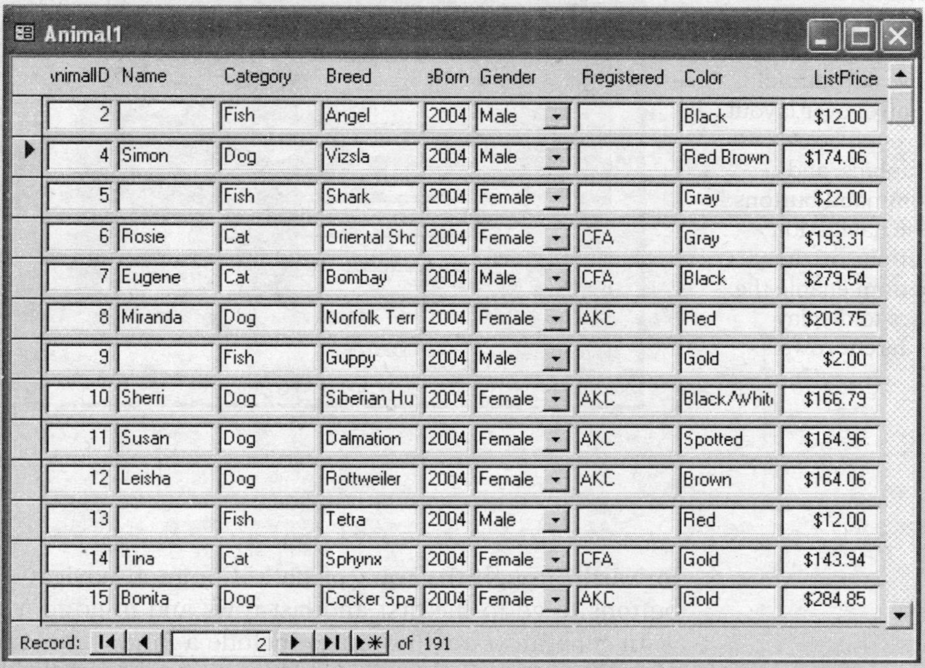

FIGURE 6.7
Sample tabular form. You define the controls for one row, and the DMBS displays data for all of the rows in the query. Scroll bars enable the user to see more rows (or columns of data).

subform and is rarely used as a stand-alone form. There are few differences between the tabular and datasheet forms. However, the tabular form provides a little more control over the display—such as three-dimensional controls and individual color settings. As a subform, the datasheet view takes up less space than the tabular form and looks like a spreadsheet.

The primary feature of the form is that it displays multiple rows of data for editing. Consequently, users can see and compare data across several items. It is useful for short lists of data. It can cause problems when the table to be edited is too large—both in terms of number of rows and too many columns. If the user has to scroll repeatedly to find a specific entry, a tabular form will not work very well.

Tabular forms are commonly used as subforms, where they collect and display a limited list of data that is related to the main form. For example, an order form often contains a subform tied to the OrderItem table to display the list of items being purchased on the currently displayed order.

Single-Row or Columnar Forms

A single-row form displays data for one row at a time. The goal is to display every column. Its greatest feature is that the designer can display the data at any location on the form. It is useful for designing a form that looks like a traditional paper form. The designer can also use color, graphics, and command buttons to make the form easier to use. As illustrated in Figure 6.8, this form design requires navigation controls that enable the user to scroll backward and

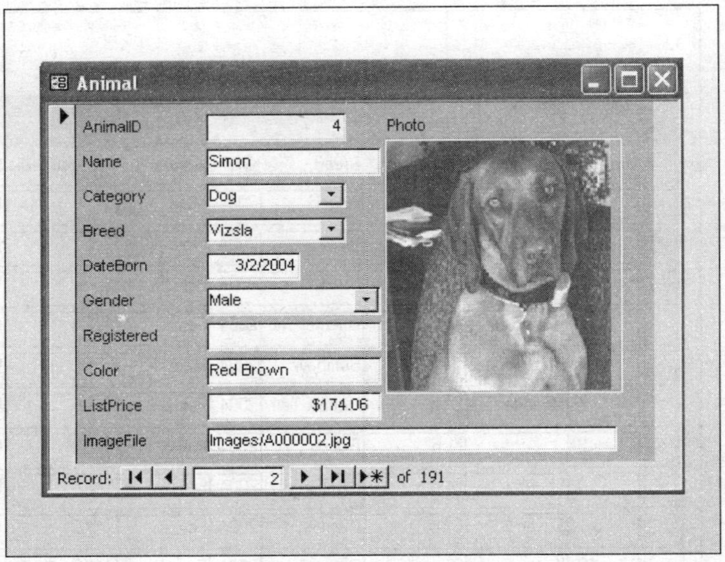

FIGURE 6.8
A simple single-row form. This form displays data for one row at a time. You have substantial control over layout through color, graphics, and command buttons. The navigation buttons on the bottom enable the user to display different rows.

forward through the rows of data. Common navigation controls also include buttons to go to the first and last rows and to go to a particular row of data.

In general, you will want to include a Find command that enables the user to locate a particular row of data—based on the values in some row. For example, a form displaying customer data should have a search option based on customer name. Similarly, the user will often want to sort the rows in different orders.

The single-row form is generally the most-used form layout. With careful design, you can use it to display substantial amounts of data. By including subforms, you can highlight relationships among various pieces of data and make it easy for users to enter data. You can also include charts to help users make decisions.

Subform Forms

A subform is usually a tabular form embedded on the main form. A subform generally shows a one-to-many relationship. In the example in Figure 6.9, a sale could include many animals, so you need a subform to display this repeating list. The main form must be a single-row form, and the subform should be a tabular view.

If you look at the underlying tables, you will see that SaleID links the main form (based on Sale) and subform (based on SaleAnimal) to each other. You will rarely display the linking column on the subform. In general, doing so would be pointless, since the linking column would always display the same value as the related column on the main form. Think about what that means for a minute. The Sale table has a SaleID that is generated by the DBMS when a new sale is created. The SaleAnimal table also has a SaleID column, and every animal sold must contain the same SaleID value from the main form. Yet it would be painful for the clerk to reenter the SaleID on the subform for each animal that is sold. By using the subform and specifying the SaleID as the link (Master and Child property), the DBMS automatically enters the main SaleID into the table for the subform.

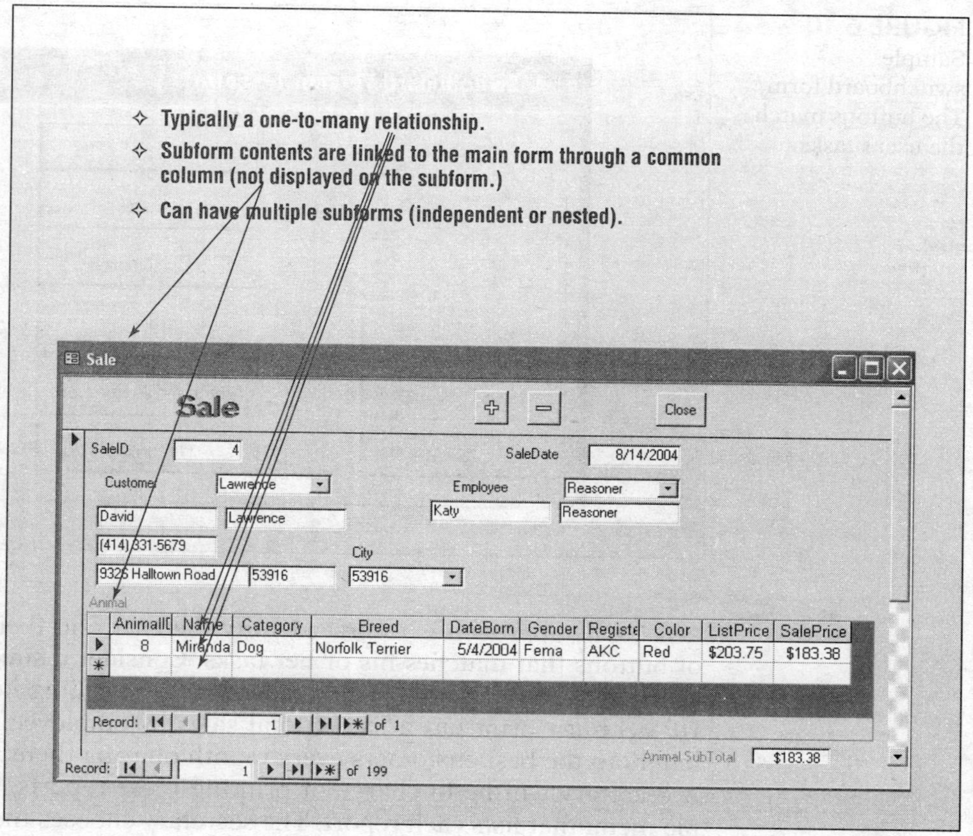

FIGURE 6.9
Subform example. The main form is based on the Sale table, which has a one-to-many relationship with the SaleAnimal table used on the subform. The datasheet view is used on the subform to display multiple rows at one time.

Most database systems enable you to create forms that have multiple subforms. The subforms can be either independent—as separate boxes on the main form—or nested—where each subform lies inside another. In most cases, you will want the parent forms to be single-row forms. However, some systems support tabular lists for both the main and the subforms. In most applications, users would find this approach disconcerting: They would first have to select a single row in the parent form and then deal with the matching list in the subform.

Switchboard Forms

Switchboard or menu forms provide the overall structure to an application. They are straightforward to create, although you may want the assistance of a graphics designer. The switchboard form often contains images, and the design reflects the style of the company.

You begin with a blank form and remove any scroll bars and navigation controls. Pictures can be inserted as background images or as individual controls that can be used as buttons to open another form. As shown in Figure 6.10, command buttons or links are the most important feature of the switchboard form. When the user selects a button, a corresponding form or report is opened. The main switchboard form will be used quite often, so you should pay careful attention to its design.

The key to a successful application begins with the switchboard form—not just its design but also its content. The forms should match the user's

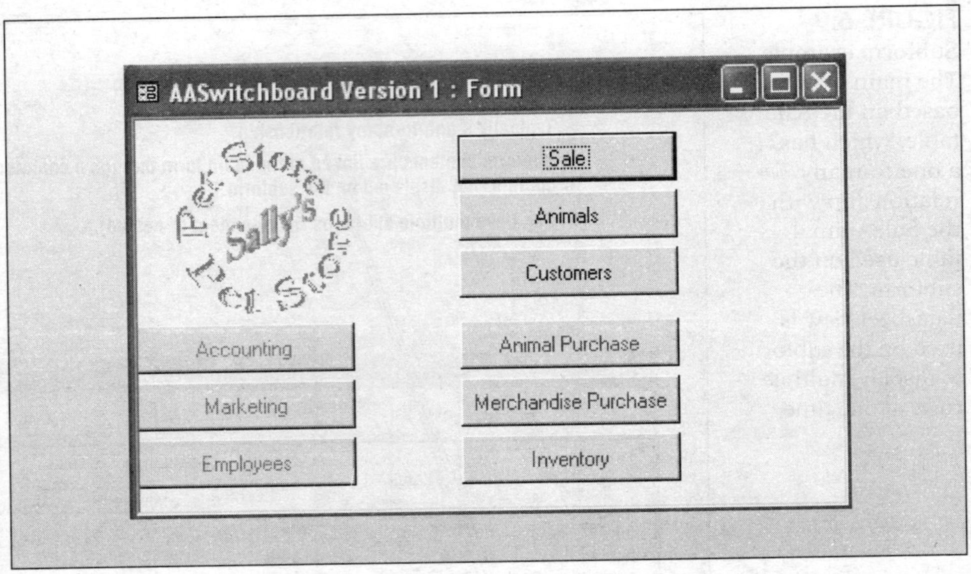

FIGURE 6.10 Sample switchboard form. The buttons match the user's tasks.

tasks. One approach is to first identify the user and then provide a selection of buttons that matches his or her tasks. Consider a simple example. A manager needs to print a daily sales report of best-selling items. Every week the DBMS must print out a list of total sales by employee. The firm also sends letters to the best customers every month offering them additional discounts. A secretary will be in charge of printing these reports, so you create a simple menu that lists each report. The secretary chooses the desired report from the list. Some reports might ask questions, such as which week to use. The secretary enters the answers, and the report is printed.

The first step in creating an application is to think about the people who will use it. How do they perform their jobs? How do the database inputs and reports fit into their job? The goal is to devise a menu system that reflects the way they work. Two examples of a first menu are shown in Figure 6.11. Which menu is easier for a clerk to understand? The one that best relates to the job. Once you understand the basic tasks, write down a set of related menus. Some menu options call up other menus, some print reports, and others activate the input screens you created.

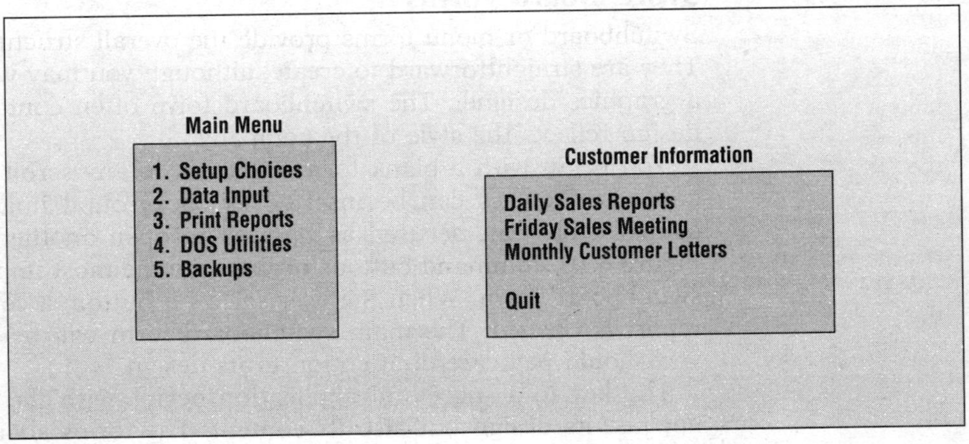

FIGURE 6.11 Designing menus for users. Which menu is easier for a secretary to understand? When designing applications, you should organize the application to match the processes users perform.

Creating Forms

The first step in creating a form is to be sure that you understand its purpose and how it will be used. Its usage dictates the specific data that needs to be displayed. Once you know the data needed, you can identify the database tables that hold that data. One important point to remember: A form should only attempt to update data to one table at a time. For example, a common sales form might display data about the Sale, the Customer, the SaleItems selected, and perhaps detailed data about the individual Products. Through the design process, this data needs to be stored in four related tables, so how can you create a form that updates only one table?

The answer to this question actually determines the characteristics of many database systems. The reason you can put only one table on a form is that multiple tables make it difficult for the form to understand exactly what the user is attempting to do. For instance, if the main Sales form contained all columns from the Sales table as well as the Customer table, what does it mean to add a new row? Should that row be added to the Sales table or the Customer table?

There are many times when you want to at least display data from multiple tables. Several approaches exist. You can use multiple, linked forms. You might be able to create sections within a form, where each section can hold data for a new, linked table. One of these sections could be a subform that contains repeating rows of data linked to the main form. Depending on the database system, you might be able to use an updateable query to display data from multiple tables.

Updateable Queries

The issue of multiple tables on a form is related to the problem of updateable queries. If a system can support queries that use multiple tables as updateable, then it is possible to put carefully selected columns from multiple tables on a single form. Figure 6.12 shows a common Sales Order main

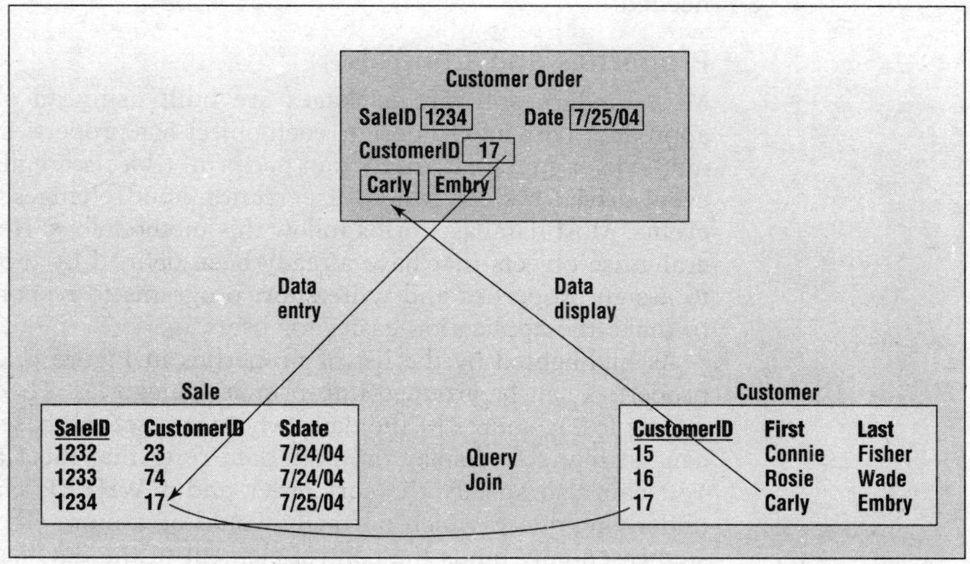

FIGURE 6.12
Basing the Order form on a query. The query contains all the columns from the Sale table and some columns from the Customer table. The query must never include the CustomerID column from the Customer table, which is the column used to join the two tables.

form. The Sale table holds the CustomerID as a foreign key. To record a sale, a salesperson simply needs to enter the ID number of the appropriate customer. But it is not easy to remember numbers, and it would be nice to display the matching customer data on the main form to verify the name and address.

Technically, a query could be built that includes all of the columns from the Sale Order table along with some of the descriptive columns from the Customer table. To remain updateable, the query must not include the primary key (CustomerID) from the Customer table. One potential drawback to this approach is that whenever a new CustomerID is entered into a sale, the form must make a trip to the database to look up the matching customer data. Consequently, some forms systems do not support this approach.

Linked Forms

Another approach to the problem is to use linked forms; these forms might be displayed separately, or they might be separate sections displayed on a single form. This latter approach is used for parent/child forms, where the child form contains data from a second table that has a one-to-many link to the parent form. Conceptually, displaying a related table on one form versus in a separate window is equivalent. The main difference lies in the amount of screen space needed. If you put several sections on one form, users will need large screens to see all of the data. By using multiple windows, the user will not be able to see all of the data at one time but can switch between the windows to see and edit the data.

Linked forms work by using a query to match the data displayed in the secondary form to a key value from the original form. For instance, from the main Sale Order form, the CustomerID can be used to display the matching customer data in a linked form. Similarly, a SaleItem subform can display the rows that match the SaleID from the main form. Each related portion of the data can be displayed in a separate form or region. Ideally, the forms system will have a method to automatically perform the linking and retrieve the matching data; otherwise, you will have to write customized code to modify the underlying query and refresh the data as needed.

Properties and Controls

Most modern software packages are built using an object-oriented (OO) approach. With an OO design, each object has properties that describe it and methods or functions that it can perform. Objects are also closely tied to an event-driven system, where user actions and changes can trigger various events. Most database forms follow this methodology. However, you will generally use objects that have already been defined by the DBMS. Your job is to assign properties and write short programs to respond to various events to make the application easier for users.

As highlighted by the list of properties in Figure 6.13, form and control properties can be grouped into primary categories. The first category (data) relates to the source of the data, where you set the base table or query. You can set filters to display only the data rows that meet a specific condition. You can also specify the sort order and a WHERE clause directly in the underlying query, which normally would be a more efficient approach. This step essentially binds the control element to the database.

FIGURE 6.13
Basic properties for forms. At a minimum, set the data source and basic format properties. Additional properties ensure consistency, protect data, and make the form easier to use.

Category	Properties
Data	Base table/query Filters Sort
Integrity	Edits Additions, deletions Locks
Format	Caption Scroll bars Record selectors Navigation buttons Size and centering Background/pictures Colors Tab order
Other	Pop-up menus Menu bar Help

A second set of properties refers to data integrity to help you control the type of editing and changes allowed on the form. For example, you might set the properties for individual users so that some users cannot add or delete data using a particular form. However, keep in mind that it is generally safer to set these conditions in SQL so that they apply throughout the database, and not just on one form. For example, sales clerks should probably be prevented from adding new suppliers.

A third level of properties controls the display of the form. Everything from the caption to scroll bars, form size, and background are set by display properties. Again, remember that consistency is a virtue. Before beginning a project, choose a design template and standards; then set all form and control properties to meet that standard.

Controls on Forms

Forms are built with controls. Controls consist of any object placed on a form. Common controls include simple text labels, text boxes for data entry, option buttons, pictures, and list boxes. More complex controls can be purchased from commercial software developers. Figure 6.14 shows the controls commonly available on most systems. Labels and text boxes are heavily used.

One property shared by all controls is the name. Every control must have a name. Be careful with this name; once you have set it, it is hard to change. The name is used by other controls and program code (much like a variable name) to retrieve and store data on the form. You need to pick a meaningful name when you first create the control. If you try to change it later, you will have to find every control or program that refers to that control—which can be a time-consuming and error-prone task. Some people name controls based on the type of control. For example, the name of a label control would start with lbl, such as lblAddress. This naming convention is helpful to other programmers who read your code later.

FIGURE 6.14
Sample controls. Notice the difference between a combo box and a list box. The combo box fills one line until the user clicks the arrow. Then it displays the list box so the user can choose an entry.

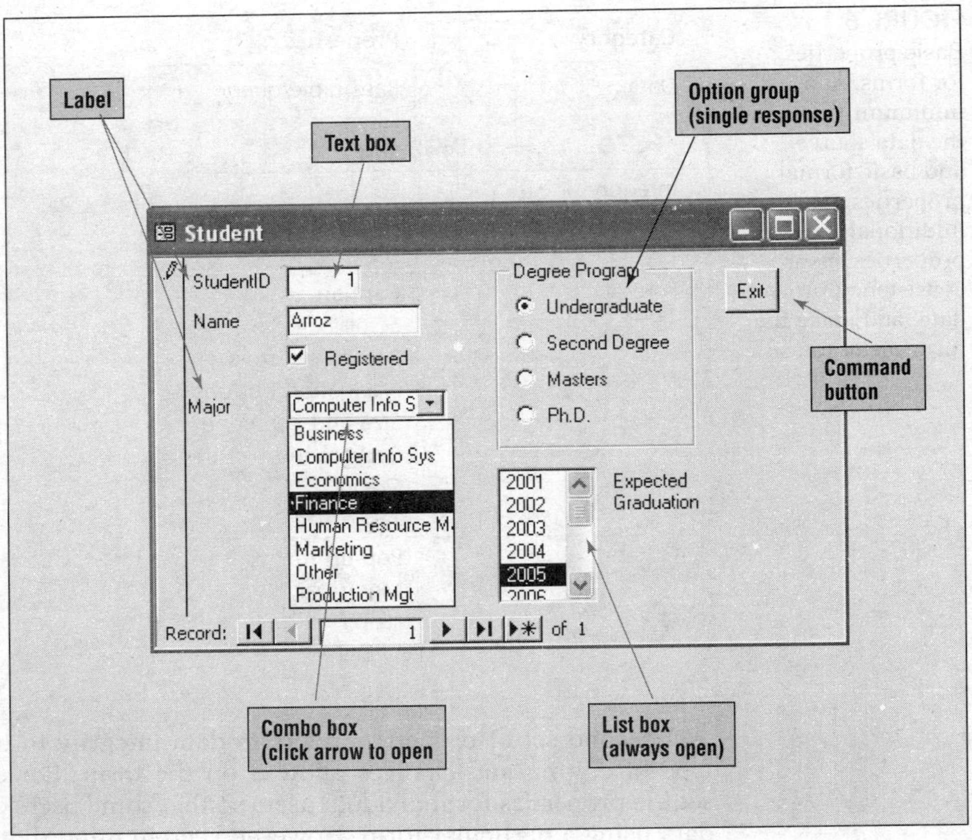

Label Controls and Text Boxes

The most basic controls are the label, the text box, and the command button. The label is plain text that cannot be changed directly by the user. The text box is used to display data from the database and to enter new values. A control that retrieves and stores data in a table is called a **bound control** because any data that is changed is automatically stored in the table. Data can be entered into an unbound control, but the values will not be stored in the database, and they will not change as the user scrolls through the table rows. Common properties of label and text box controls are color, typeface, and size. The difference between a bound and an unbound box is that a bound box has a control source (column in a table). With an unbound box, this property is empty.

Command Buttons

Command buttons typically have only one function: When the user clicks one, an event will be triggered (On_Click event), and some action will be performed. You have several choices for that action, including opening another form, printing a report, or running a custom program. Command buttons are the main component of switchboard forms, where they are used to open related forms.

Check Boxes and Option Buttons

These controls enable users to select from a choice of options. For example, clerks may indicate an animal's gender by picking one of three choices: male, female, and unknown. Notice that there are several ways to let users make a selection. Technically, there is no difference in the three methods. However, according to common user interface standards, they do have slightly different uses.

There are essentially two methods of making choices: mutually exclusive and multiple selections. Consider the example of an animal's gender. The three choices are mutually exclusive. An animal can be born as either male or female, or you may not know the true status. (Neutering is a separate consideration that does not affect the genetic determination of gender.) The **option button** group (round) was designed for mutually exclusive choices. Users know that when they see a group of option buttons, they can pick only one of the options. On the other hand, a customer might place an order for a dog with certain features: registered, brown or black in color, even temperament, and short hair. You should use a form with a group of **check boxes** (square) for this situation, because several of these items can be checked. The selection of one option does not affect any of the others.

Graphics Features

Occasionally you will want to add graphics features to your form. There are controls to add pictures, as well as simple lines and boxes. Lines and boxes are often used to create a three-dimensional effect for other controls by adding shading or highlighting.

To display an image from a table as shown in Figure 6.15, you must first define an Object or image column within that table. Then the bound object frame is used like a text box to position and display the image on the form.

To use an image or texture as a background, first use a graphics package to make sure the image is light enough to not interfere with the readability of the other boxes. Then set the Picture property of the form to the name of the image file. In most cases, you want to embed the image on the form so the picture is included directly with the database.

FIGURE 6.15
Image bound to a data column. Employee photo is scanned and stored in the database column.

Combo and List Boxes

The **list box** and **combo box** are useful controls in most database applications. The purpose of these two controls is to display a list of items from which the user can choose one value. There are two primary differences between the combo box and list box. The combo box displays only one of the available choices—until the user clicks on the down arrow. Second, a user can directly type in a value with the combo box. (The name for the combo box indicates that it is a combination of a list box and a text box.) Most designers rely on the combo box largely because it takes up less space than the list box.

A combo box has two basic uses. The first is to insert a value into a table. The second is to search for a particular row of data. If you decide to use both types of combo boxes in your application, you should use color or some other attribute to make the purpose clear to the user.

When you look through the normalized tables, you can see clearly why the combo box is so useful in a relational database. Many of the tables are joined together by internally generated ID numbers. For example, the Sale table uses the CustomerID to identify a customer. In Figure 6.12 a clerk would have to enter the value 17 to indicate which customer made the purchase. But how does the clerk know that value? You certainly cannot expect employees to memorize thousands of customer numbers. Similarly, you cannot ask customers to memorize their ID numbers. In some situations (e.g., a video rental store) you might ask customers to carry an ID card that contains the number. You might think about using some common ID number like a taxpayer ID or phone number. But it is hard to ensure that these numbers are unique and harder to convince customers to give them to you.

A better solution is to let the database use the internally generated ID and then have the clerk pick the customer from a list of names. Hence, most forms development systems provide combo boxes (sometimes called selection boxes). The combo box displays a list of all the entries in the Customer table (sorted by name or phone number). Entering the first few letters of a Customer's name forces the combo box to scroll to the matching entries. When the clerk selects the appropriate customer, the corresponding ID is entered into the Sale table.

Complex Controls

Additional control objects can be created using a variety of computer languages or purchased from commercial vendors.

A few additional controls are shown in Figure 6.16. The Tab and Calendar controls are particularly useful in business applications. There is also a Grid control that enables you to display data in a spreadsheet layout. These types of controls are not as easy to use as the standard bound controls. The developer has to write short programs to load data into the control and to respond to the control's events.

Charts

Database applications used for making decisions often contain charts or graphs. Charts are another type of control that can be placed on a form (or report). The first step in creating a useful chart is to discuss with the user exactly what type of data and what type of chart will be needed. Then you usually build a new SQL query that will collect the data to be displayed on

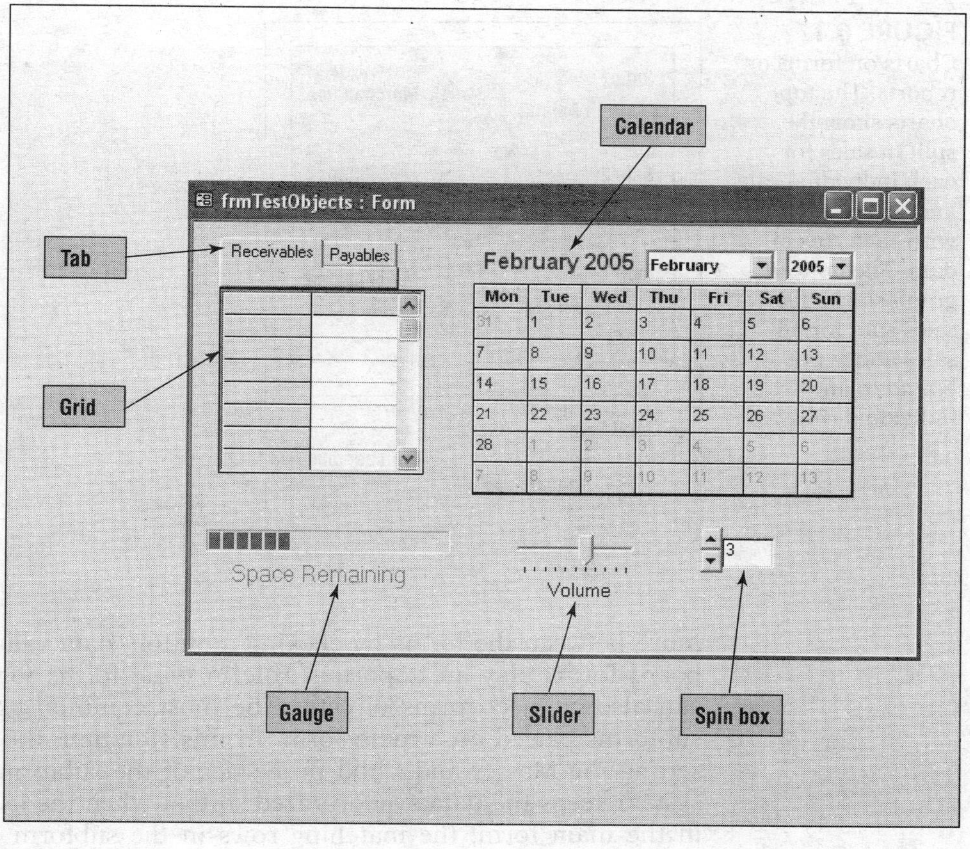

FIGURE 6.16
Additional controls. Thousands of controls are available to improve the user interface or perform specialized tasks. Common controls include tabs, grid, calendar, gauges, sliders, and the spin box. You can also create custom controls.

the chart. The chart control places the chart on the form and specifies the individual attributes (like type of chart, axis scale, and colors).

Two basic types of charts are used on database forms and reports: (1) graphs that show detail from the currently displayed row and (2) graphs that display summary data across all (or several) of the rows. The difference between the two approaches lies in the level of data displayed. Detail graphs change with each row of data displayed. Summary graphs are usually generated from totals or averages.

Figure 6.17 illustrates the two types of graphs as they might be used in the Pet Store database. Each chart shows the amount of money spent on animals versus the amount spent on merchandise. However, the top set of charts shows the split for each individual sale, so the graphs vary with each row in the Sale query. The bottom chart shows the overall total for the store—even if it is placed on a Sales form that shows each row of data, it will not change (except over time). To create the two types of charts, the main difference is in the query. The query for the detail charts contains a column (SaleID) that is linked to the row of data being displayed on the form (based on its SaledID). The summary graph computes the totals across all of the sales and is not linked to any particular sale.

Multiple Forms

As you can guess, an application will quickly spawn many different forms. Of course, the forms should be linked to each other so users can quickly

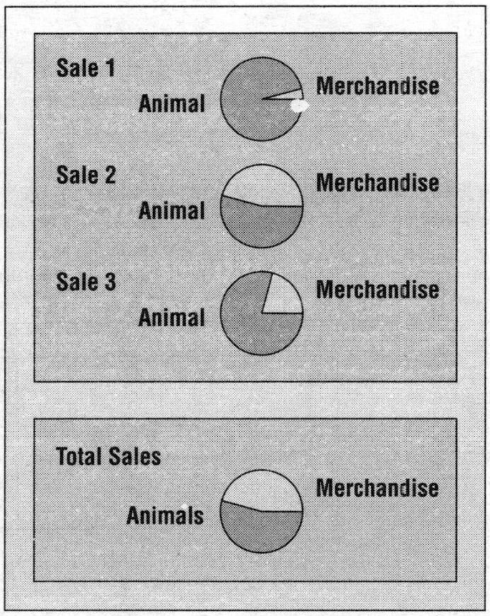

FIGURE 6.17
Charts on forms or reports. The top charts show the split in sales for each individual sale and will change with each row of data. The bottom graph shows the sales split for all sales and is not bound to an individual row.

move between the forms by clicking a button, data value, or image. Switchboard forms play an important role in tying forms together. However, you can also connect forms directly. The most common example is the use of subforms placed on a main form. In this situation, the forms are linked by setting the Master and Child properties of the subform. Then the database system keeps the data synchronized so that when the user selects a new row in the main form, the matching rows in the subform are located and displayed automatically.

When the forms contain related data, you sometimes want to open the new form and display only the row of data that is related. For example, if the Order form contains customer data, when the user clicks an Edit button (or double-clicks on the customer name), the application should open the Customer form. As shown in Figure 6.18, the Customer form should display

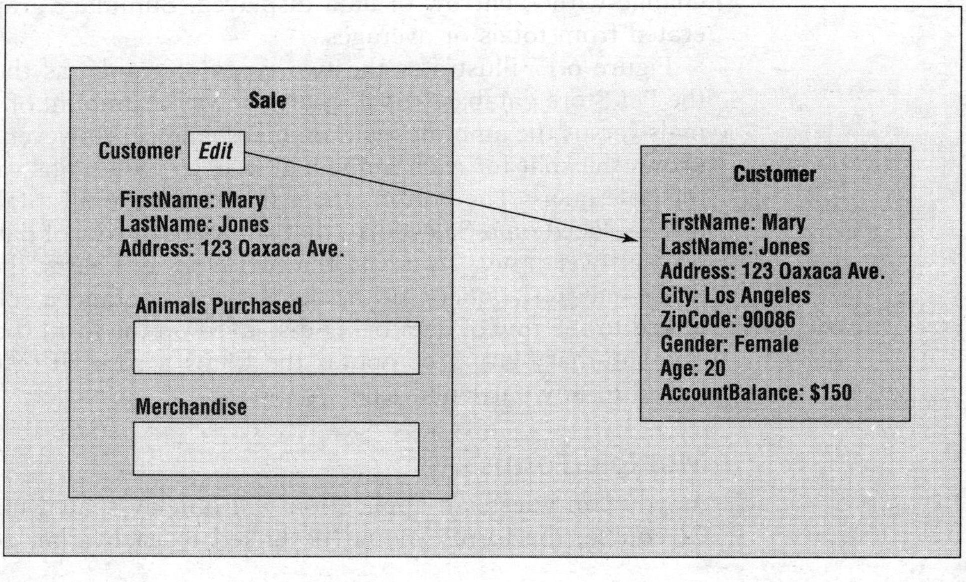

FIGURE 6.18
Connect forms with matching data. The Customer form is opened to display the data corresponding to the customer already entered in the Sale form.

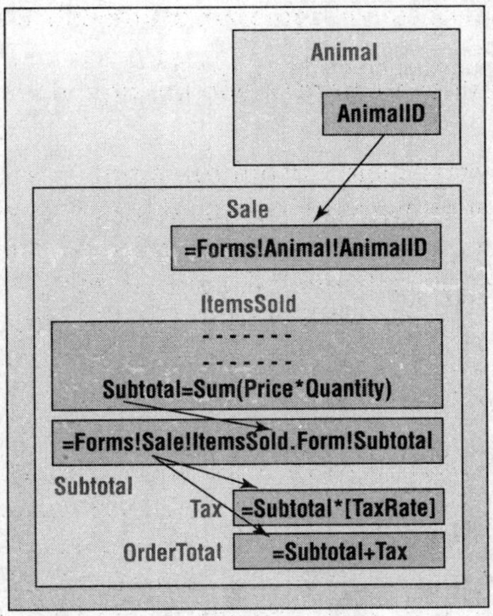

FIGURE 6.19
Copying data from a different form. The default AnimalID is copied into the Sale form from the Animal table. Likewise, the subtotal is first computed on the subform and then copied to the main form.

the data that corresponds to the customer on the Order form. The open form command uses a link criteria parameter to accomplish this task. The criteria limit the data displayed in the new form. In this example, the link criteria specifies that the CustomerID in the Customer form must match the CustomerID from the Sales form.

In most cases, the user would close the Customer form and return to the main Sale form. But what if users commonly keep both forms open at the same time? Then they would expect the data between the two forms to be synchronized so that when a new row is displayed on the Sale form, the matching data would be displayed on the Customer form. You might have to write a couple of lines of code to enable this synchronization to work. Essentially, whenever the Sale is changed, your code grabs the new CustomerID, passes it to the Customer form, requeries the database, and redisplays the form with the matching data.

A third, related situation is shown in Figure 6.19. Perhaps while looking at animal data, the customer decides to buy that animal. A Purchase button on the Animal form could quickly bring up the Sale form. It would be convenient if the button then copied the AnimalID into the appropriate space on the Sale form.

Again, you need to write a couple of lines of code to insert the AnimalID into the appropriate control on the Sale form. In some situations, you might want the Sales form to refer back to the ID value on the Animal table.

Business applications commonly need to compute subtotals from subforms. As shown in Figure 6.19, some systems treat subforms as entirely separate forms, so you must first do the subtotal calculation on the subform, and then copy its value back to the main form.

International Attributes

When designing forms and reports, you increasingly need to consider the use of the application in an international setting. An obvious complication is the need to translate the data to a different language. Some application development systems facilitate language translation by enabling developers to

FIGURE 6.20
International attributes. When creating forms and reports for international use, be careful to consider different formats for characters and data. Also, be sure to abide by all national laws—particularly in terms of data privacy.

- Language
- Character sets and punctuation marks
- Sorting
- Data formats
  - Date
  - Time
  - Metric versus English
  - Currency symbol and format
  - Separators (decimal, . . .)
  - Phone numbers
    - Separators
    - International code prefix
  - Postal codes
  - National ID numbers

store all written comments (e.g., screen names, labels, and error messages) in one location. You can do the same thing with a DBMS by creating a separate language table that holds the phrases that would need to be translated. Then build your form by looking up the appropriate phrase based on a code value. This separate table is then changed by the translators—without requiring any changes to your forms or code. The one drawback is that without a compiler, every form will take longer to load, since each phrase will have to be retrieved separately from the table.

As noted in Figure 6.20, another problem related to language is that most languages use special character sets. For example, Latin-based languages often include accents and other diacritical marks. Oriental languages are even more difficult, since they require thousands of different pictographs instead of a few characters. The computer must be capable of displaying the particular character set for each nation. Currently, the leading solution to this problem is based on a system known as **Unicode,** which is an international standard to store and display characters from virtually any language. Several operating systems support Unicode. For instance, Windows 95, Windows NT, NetWare, and some varieties of UNIX can handle the 2-byte character codes. Some modern applications and development tools support Unicode; if your application needs international support, be sure to choose tools that provide that support. The issue of language and characters also affects the sorting of data. Hence, databases typically enable you to set the sort order based on the character set being used.

Data formats for date, time, telephone numbers, postal codes, and currency all vary by region or nation. Most can be set within the Windows environment (control panel). However, be careful when converting data from one country to another. Dates and times will translate fine, since they are stored as a difference from a base date or time. But currencies will not convert correctly. Say you build a database application in the United States with a currency column and enter prices denoted in dollars (e.g., $18.20). What happens when you copy the database to a machine in London that has currency settings in pounds? The answer is that the currency sign will be changed, but not the data. In the example, the user would see £18.20, which is not the correct value (e.g., £11.44). You have two choices: (1) avoid the currency data type and leave the prices denominated in dollars or (2) write a query to convert all currency data to the new currency. It is possible in the first case to use the currency format and avoid conversion of the currency sign by defining your own currency type. The second method is probably the best for many applications and is easy to do with a query that multiplies the original value by a conversion factor. Of course, the conversion factor changes over time, so you have to be careful to track the conversion date.

A more difficult problem arises with respect to phone numbers and ZIP codes. When defining data and creating forms, be sure to allocate enough spaces to hold the country codes and longer phone numbers. Also note that postal codes in some countries contain letters as well as numbers. Programmers used to think that they could reduce data entry errors by restricting data entry of ZIP codes to five digits. In an international setting, you cannot make this assumption. One way to reduce data entry errors is to rely on combo boxes that pull data from a (huge) table of postal codes. A more reliable approach is to purchase software that automatically checks and updates postal codes in your database based on addresses.

Finally, be careful to abide by all national laws with respect to security and access to the data. For example, many European nations have strong privacy statutes—particularly with respect to customer data and national ID numbers. In some cases, it may be illegal to transfer data collected in Europe to the United States.

Direct Manipulation of Graphical Objects

In the last few years, the user interface to applications has been changing. The heavy use of graphics has led to an emphasis on **direct manipulation of objects**. Instead of typing in commands, the user can drag an item from one location on the screen to another to indicate a change. Most people have seen this approach used with basic operating system commands. For example, in the days of DOS you had to type a command such as COPY MYFILE.DOC A:MYFILE.DOC to copy a file. Today you click on the file icon and drag it to a disk drive icon.

Sally's Pet Store Example

A graphical approach can make your applications easier to use. However, it requires changing the way you think about applications, and a good dose of creativity. Consider the Pet Store example. The forms we designed earlier in this chapter were easy to create, and they will perform adequately. However, you could change the entire approach to the application.

Figure 6.21 shows a partial screen for the Pet Store example. Compare this form to the traditional data entry form shown in Figure 6.9. The traditional approach requires users to enter text into a box. With the graphical approach the user sees photos of the individual animals and drags them to the customer to indicate a sale. Double-clicking on an item provides more pictures or additional details. A similar approach would be used to special-order animals, using **drag-and-drop** techniques to define an animal (breed, color, etc.), and to place the order.

Note that you cannot entirely eliminate data entry. At some point, you need to collect basic data on customers (name, address, phone number, etc.). This data could be entered on a traditional form that is activated when the clerk double-clicks the customer icon or photo. That is, the form in Figure 6.21

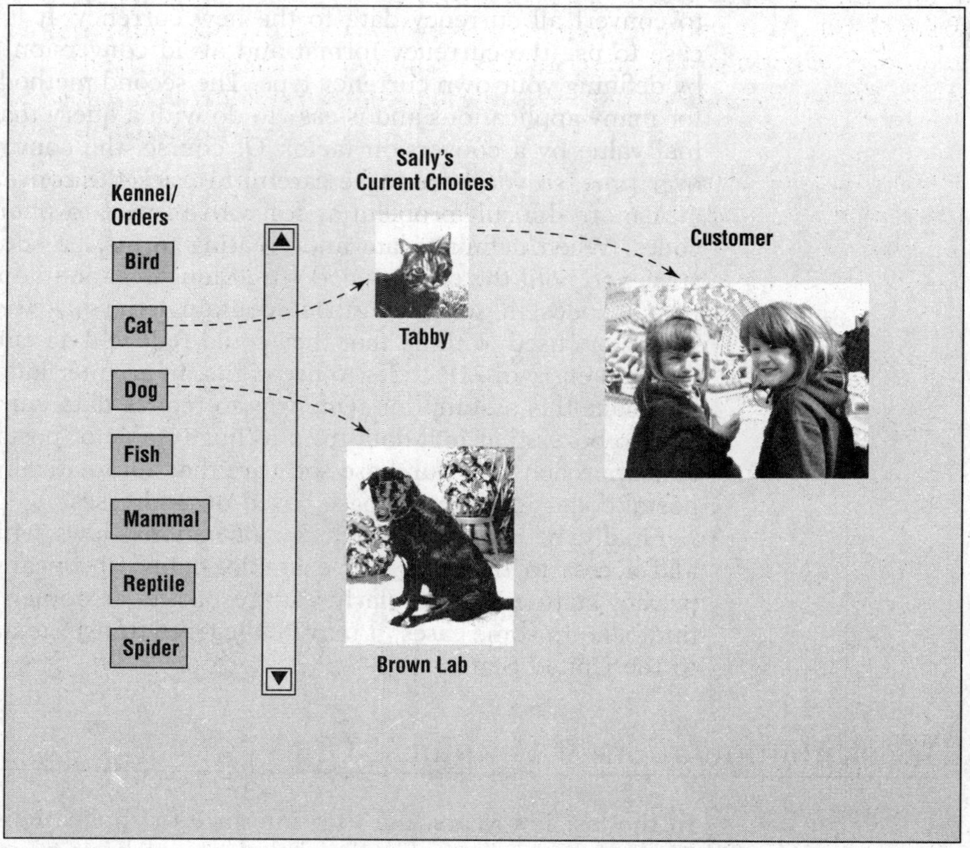

FIGURE 6.21 Direct manipulation of graphical objects at the Pet Store. Instead of entering an AnimalID into a box, you drag the picture of the animal to the customer to indicate a sale. Double-clicking on an item brings up more detail or related graphics screens.

replaces the traditional sales form but does not replace the basic customer form. Of course, once the customer data is on file, it can be dragged back to this main form whenever the customer returns.

The Internet

The emphasis on graphics and a direct manipulation of objects can be particularly valuable for forms used with the Internet. For starters, most of the users will have little experience with databases and only limited knowledge of your company. Creating a graphical model of the company and its processes achieves two important objectives: (1) It makes the site easier to use because it matches the physical purchase methods users already know, and (2) it limits the actions of the users to those that you have defined.

One of the goals of the graphical approach is to hide the use of the database. Yes, all basic product information, figures, and sales data are stored in the database. The database system provides search capabilities and stores user selections. It also provides reports and data analysis for managers. However, users never need to know about the database itself. Users simply see an image of a store and its products. They manipulate the objects to learn more or to place orders. One difficulty of the Internet is that you are limited by the capabilities of the user's browser. Browsers handle most simple data entry controls, but rarely have the ability to perform drag-and-drop operations. Nonetheless, searching for graphical approaches can help you find ways to make the forms more intuitive and easier to use.

Complications and Limitations of a Graphical Approach

There are several potential drawbacks to basing a form on the direct manipulation of graphical objects. The most important is that it can be an inefficient way to enter data. For example, you would not expect workers at a receiving dock to use a drag-and-drop form to record the receipt of several hundred boxes. A bar-code scanner would be considerably more efficient. Likewise, a quality control technician would prefer a simple keystroke (or voice) system so he or she could enter data without looking away from the task.

Even the Pet Store sales form is a debatable use of the drag-and-drop approach. Think about the operations at a typical large pet store. Consider what would happen when dozens of customers bring shopping carts full of merchandise to the checkout counter. If a clerk has to use a drag-and-drop screen, the checkout process would take forever. Again, bar-code scanners would speed up the process. On the other hand, perhaps the operations of the store could be improved by eliminating the checkout clerk. Think about how the store would function if shoppers used the store's drag-and-drop website to select products, which were then delivered, or bagged and stacked for drive-through pickup. The difference in the value of the approach depends on the operations of the business and on who will be using the application.

A second difficulty with the graphics approach is that each application requires a considerable amount of custom programming. The traditional approach is relatively straightforward. Common tools exist for entering data with forms made up of text boxes, combo boxes, and subforms. These tools can be used for virtually any database application. On the other hand, direct manipulation of objects requires that individual business objects be drawn on the screen and associated with data. Then each user action (double-click and drag-and-drop) has to be defined specifically for that application. In the future, tools may be created to assist in this programming. However, today, a graphical approach requires considerably more programming effort than other approaches.

Building graphical database applications across the Internet carries similar problems. There are two primary limitations: transmission speed and limitations of software tools. However, a huge amount of money and effort is being directed toward the Web. Many firms in several industries are working on solutions to both limitations.

Reports

When you understand forms, reports are straightforward. Increasingly, the main difference between forms and reports is that reports are designed to be printed, whereas forms are displayed on the screen. There are two additional differences: (1) forms can be used to collect data, and (2) reports are generally used to present summarized data. Consequently, reports cannot have controls that collect data. But, why, if you can print forms, would you need reports? The two main strengths of a report are that (1) it can easily handle multiple pages of output (with consistent page headers and page numbering) and (2) it can combine both detailed and summary data. Chapter 5 illustrates how SQL queries can produce relatively complex results with the GROUP BY clause. However, a single SQL query can be used to display either detail rows of data or the summaries—not both. A good DBMS report writer also provides additional control over the output, such as printing negative values in red.

• Report usage/user needs	• Security controls
• Report layout choices	Distribution list
Tabular	Unique numbering
Columns/subgroups	Concealed/nonprinted data
Charts/graphs	Secured printers
• Paper sizes	Transmissions limits
• Printer constraints	Print queue controls
• How often is it generated?	• Output concerns
• Events that trigger report	Typefaces
• Size of the report	Readability
• Number of copies	Size
• Availability of color	User disabilities
	OCR needs

FIGURE 6.22 Fundamentals of report design. Determine content and layout with users. Estimate size and printing times. Identify security controls. Check typefaces and sizing for user readability.

Report Design

As summarized in Figure 6.22, several issues are involved in designing reports. As in the development of forms, you and the users need to determine the content and layout. You must also identify the typical size of the report (number of pages and number of copies), along with noting how often it must be printed. Because of the physical steps involved, printing reports can be a time-consuming process. A report of a few dozen pages is no problem. However, when a report blooms into hundreds of pages with thousands of copies, you have to plan more carefully. First, you need a fast, heavy-duty printer. Then you need machines and people to assemble and distribute the report copies. You generally have to schedule time to use the printer for large reports.

Paper reports also present a different challenge to security. Paper reports require the use of more traditional security controls, such as written distribution lists, numbered copies, and control data. If security is an important issue in an organization, then these controls should be established when the report is designed.

Several physical and artistic aspects are involved in designing reports. The size of the page, the typeface used, and overall design of the page all must be determined. Newer DBMS report writers are relatively flexible, which is good and bad. The good part is that designers have greater control over the report. The bad part is that designers need to understand more about design—including the terminology.

Artistic design and a thorough treatment of design issues are beyond the scope of this book. If you are serious about design (for paper reports, forms, or Web pages), you should consider taking a course in graphic design. Nonetheless, it helps if you learn a few basic terms.

Terminology

Many of the basic terms come from typesetting and graphics design. The terms shown in Figure 6.23 will help you understand report writers and produce better reports. The first step is to choose the page layout, in terms of paper size; orientation (portrait versus landscape); and margins. The type of binding system will affect the margins, and you might have to leave an extra gutter margin to accommodate binding.

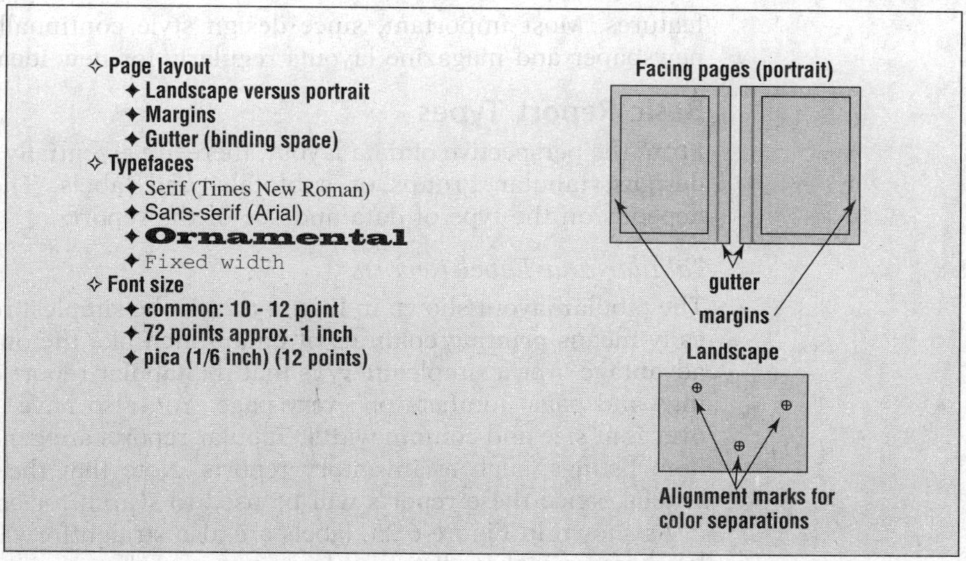

FIGURE 6.23
Basic publishing terminology. Understanding the basic design terms helps you design better reports and communicate with publishers and typesetters.

The next step is to choose the typeface and font size. In general, serif typefaces are easier to read, but sans serif faces have more white space, making them easier to read at larger and smaller sizes. Avoid ornamental typefaces except for covers and some headings. Columns of numbers are generally printed at a fixed width to keep columns aligned. Special fixed-width typefaces (e.g., Courier), in which all of the characters use exactly the same width, are especially appropriate if you need to align columns of nonnumeric data without the use of tab stops.

Font size is generally specified in terms of points. Most common printed material ranges from 10- to 12-point fonts. A useful rule of thumb is that a capitalized letter in a 72-point font is approximately 1 inch tall. Some report systems measure sizes and distance in picas. A pica is $\frac{1}{6}$ of an inch, or the same height as a 12-point font.

If your reports include graphs and images, the terminology becomes more complex. Be aware that the quality of bitmap images depends on the resolution of the original image and the resolution of the output device. Common laser printers have a 600-dots-per-inch (dpi) resolution. Typesetters typically achieve about 2,400-dpi resolution. An image that looks good on a 600-dpi laser may be too small or too jagged on a 2,400-dpi typesetter.

If your reports are in color, you quickly encounter additional problems. In particular, colors on your screen may not be the same as on the printer. Similarly, a sample report printed on a color ink jet might look completely different when submitted to a typesetter. The Pantone® color standard is designed to minimize these problems by providing numbers for many standard colors. The related issue you will encounter in color printing is the need to create color separations for all of your reports. For full-color submissions to print shops, each report page will need four separate color sheets. Denoted CMYK for each of the three primary colors—cyan (blue), magenta (red), and yellow—and the key color (black). In this case, each page will need high-resolution alignment marks so the colors can be reassembled properly.

One of the first elements of design that you must learn is to keep your reports simple and elegant. For instance, stick to one typeface and one or two font sizes on a page. Use plenty of white space to highlight columns and features. Most important, since design style continually changes, examine newspaper and magazine layouts regularly for new ideas and patterns.

Basic Report Types

From the perspective of data layout, there are essentially three types of report designs: tabular, groups or subtotals, and labels. The choice you make depends on the type of data and use of the report.

Tabular and Label Reports

The tabular layout shown in Figure 6.24 is the simplest report design. It basically means printing columns of data, much like the output of a query. The advantage over a simple query is that the tabular report can print page headings and page numbers on every page. You also have a little more control over font size and column width. Tabular reports are generally used for detail item listings, such as inventory reports. Note that the sort order becomes crucial, since these reports will be used to search for specific items.

As shown in Figure 6.25, labels are also straightforward. The essence of a label report is that all output for one row of data is printed in one "column" on the page. Then the next row is printed in the following column. The name *label report* comes from the use of preprinted or precut pages used for labels. These reports are sometimes named based on the number of physical columns. The example in Figure 6.25 has three labels across a page, so it is a three-up report. Before report writers, printing a label report was quite challenging, since the printer could only work from the top of the page. Hence, you had to write a program that printed the top line for three different rows of data, then return and print the second line, and so on. Today's printers are more flexible, and report writers make the job easy. Keep in mind that label reports can be useful for other tasks—whenever you want to group data for one row into separate locations on a page. For instance, by inserting blank rows and changing the label size, you might create a tic-tac-toe pattern of data. It could be an interesting effect for a cover page or advertising sheet, but avoid using such patterns for hundreds of pages of data.

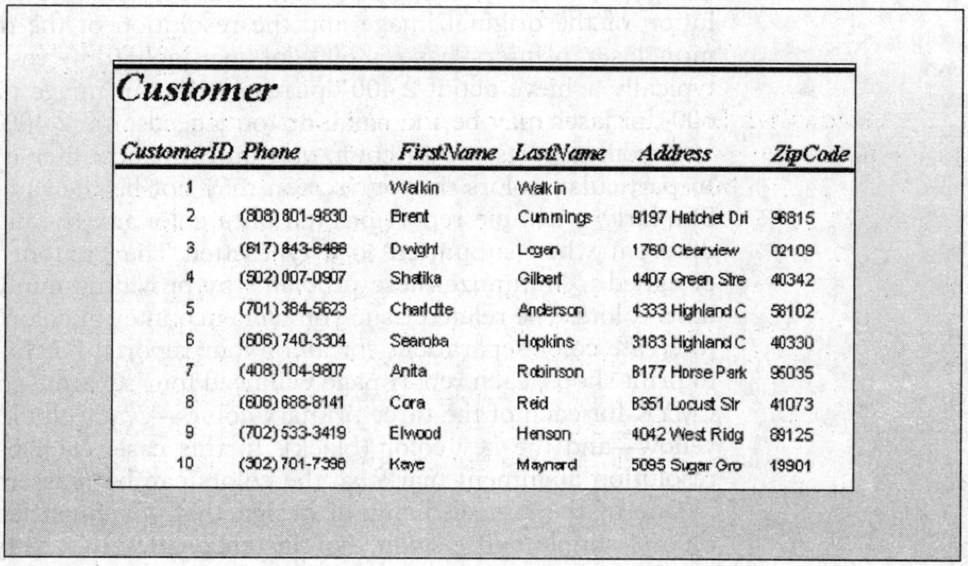

Customer

CustomerID	Phone	FirstName	LastName	Address	ZipCode
1		Walkin	Walkin		
2	(808) 801-9830	Brent	Cummings	9197 Hatchet Dri	96815
3	(617) 843-6488	Dwight	Logan	1760 Clearview	02109
4	(502) 007-0907	Shatika	Gilbert	4407 Green Stre	40342
5	(701) 384-5623	Charlotte	Anderson	4333 Highland C	58102
6	(606) 740-3304	Searoba	Hopkins	3183 Highland C	40330
7	(408) 104-9807	Anita	Robinson	8177 Horse Park	95035
8	(606) 688-8141	Cora	Reid	8351 Locust Str	41073
9	(702) 533-3419	Elwood	Henson	4042 West Ridg	89125
10	(302) 701-7398	Kaye	Maynard	5095 Sugar Gro	19901

FIGURE 6.24
Tabular report layout. Tabular reports have few options but are good for detailed data listings. They are used for itemized listings of data.

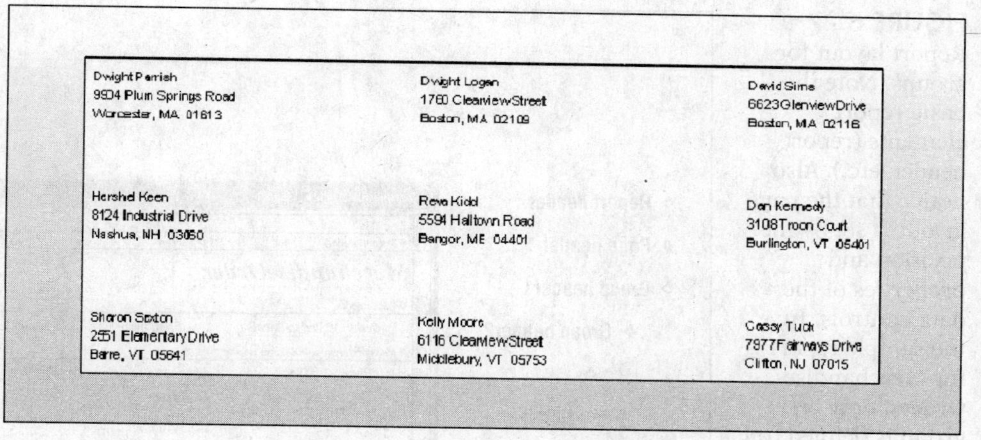

FIGURE 6.25
Label report layout. This three-up report is commonly used to print on label paper. It can be used for small sets of data that need to be printed across a page.

Groups or Subtotals

The most common type of report is based on groups and computes subtotals. It also provides the most flexibility over the layout of items on the report. Common examples include printing a receipt or a bill. Many times the report will print several rows of data, like the order form shown in Figure 6.26. Each order for the month is printed in one report, but the items are grouped together to show the individual order subtotals. Many people refer to these reports as control break reports.

The key to the subtotal report is to note that it includes both detail item listings (item ordered, quantity, cost, etc.), and group or total data (order date, customer, and order total). To create this report, you first build a query that contains the data that will be displayed. The example would probably include the Order, OrderItem, Merchandise, Customer, Employee, and Supplier tables. Be careful: If you want to see the detail, do not include a GROUP BY statement in the query. If you examine the data from this huge query, you will see a large number of rows and columns—many with repeating data.

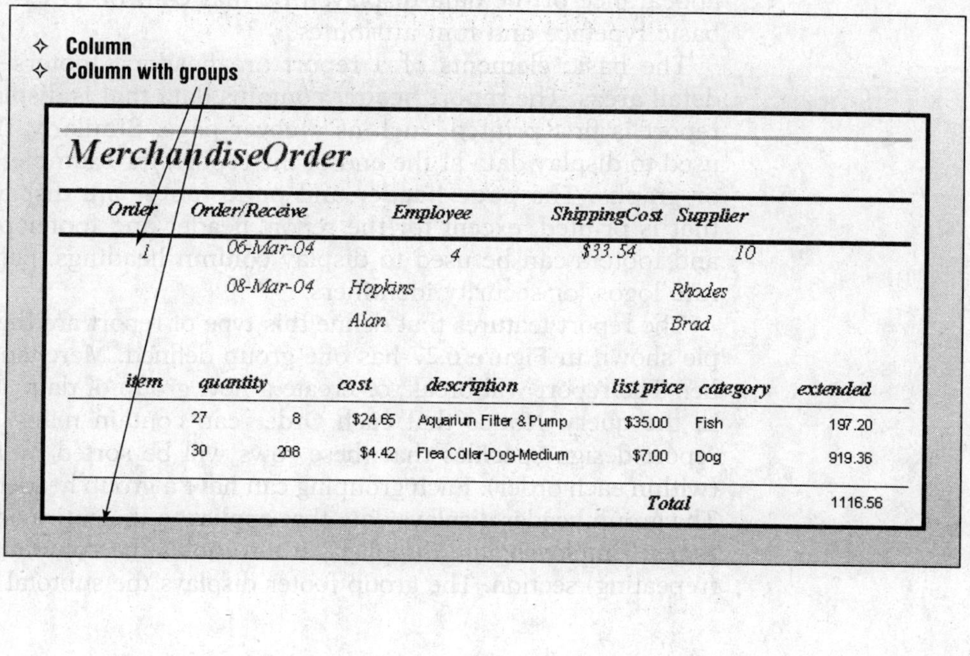

FIGURE 6.26
Group or subtotal report. Note that several orders are being printed. Each order has a detailed repeating section of items being ordered. The report can compute subtotals for each order and a total for the entire report.

FIGURE 6.27
Report layout for groups. Note the basic report elements (report header, etc.). Also notice that the page layout is set by the position and properties of the data controls. In the sample report for Merchandise Orders, only one group is defined (on the Order number).

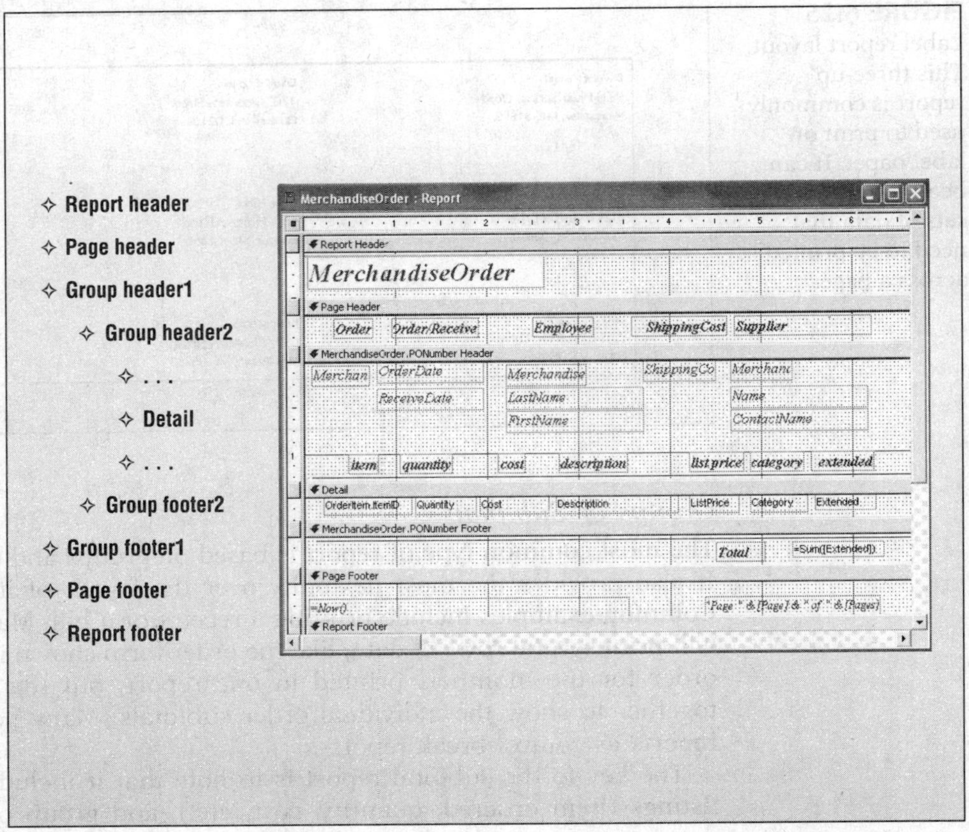

That is fine at this point, but not exactly what the user wants to see. The objective of the report is to clean up the display of the data.

To create a grouped report, examine the report design shown in Figure 6.27. This layout page shows the **group breaks** in the data and specifies the layout of each element on the page. Again, layout is set by the individual controls. The controls have properties that can be changed to alter the appearance of the data displayed by that control. For example, you can set basic typeface and font attributes.

The basic elements of a report are headers, footers, group breaks and detail areas. The **report header** contains data that is displayed only when the report is first printed, such as a cover page. Similarly, the **report footer** is used to display data at the end of the report, for example, summary statistics or graphs. The **page header** and **page footer** are displayed on every page that is printed, except for the report header and footer pages. Page headers and footers can be used to display column headings, page numbers, corporate logos, or security identifiers.

The report features that define this type of report are the groups. The example shown in Figure 6.27 has one group defined: MerchandiseOrder.PO Number. The report will break, or create a new group of data, for each PONumber in the query. Notice that each Order can contain many items ordered. The report design specifies that these rows will be sorted by the ItemID number (within each order). Each grouping can have a group header and a group footer. The group header displays data that applies to the entire order (e.g., Date, Customer, Employee, and Supplier). It also holds the column labels for the detail (repeating) section. The group footer displays the subtotal for each group.

FIGURE 6.28
Common uses for report layout elements. Most elements are available in pairs, but you are free to delete any components you do not need.

Report Section	Usage
Report header	Title pages that are printed one time for entire report.
Page header	Title lines or page notes that are printed at the top of every page.
Group header	Data for a group (e.g., Order) and headings for the detail section.
Detail	Innermost data.
Group footer	Subtotals for the group.
Page footer	Printed at the bottom of every page—page totals or page numbers and notes.
Report footer	Printed one time at the end of the report. Summary notes, overall totals, and graphs for entire data set.

The common uses of each report element are summarized in Figure 6.28. Note that all of the elements (except detail) can work in pairs—headers and footers. You are not required to use both. For instance, you might choose to display page numbers in a page header and delete the page footer to provide additional space on the page.

Note that groups represent one-to-many relationships. For example, each order can have many items in the detail section. If there are several one-to-many (or many-to-many) relationships in the data, you might want to use multiple levels of groups. As illustrated in Figure 6.29, each group is nested inside another group, with the detail at the innermost level.

To create this report, you must build a query that contains every item that will be displayed. Begin by focusing on the detail level and then join additional tables until you have all the columns you need. You can use computed columns for minor computations such as Price * Quantity. Be careful to avoid aggregate functions (e.g., Sum) and avoid the use of GROUP BY statements. The only time you might include these two features is if your "detail" row is actually a subtotal (or average) itself.

FIGURE 6.29
Nested groups. For example, each customer can place many orders, and each order has many detail lines. Two groups are used: (1) to show the total orders for each customer and (2) to show the total value of each order.

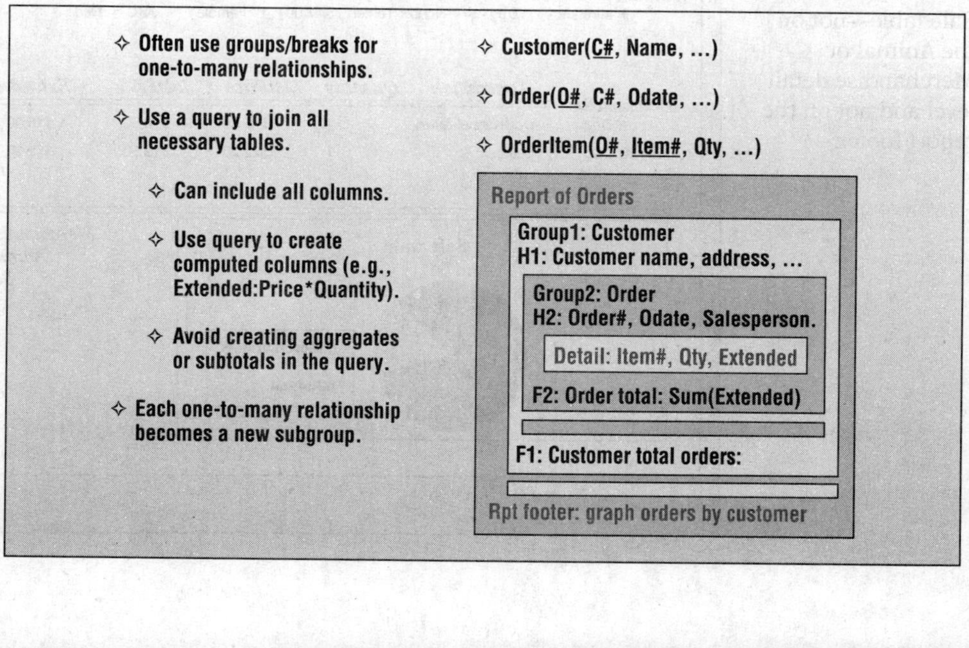

Group reports are generally used for computations—particularly subtotals. In general, computations on one row of data should be performed with the query. On the other hand, aggregations (Sum, Average, etc.) are handled by the report writer. Report writers have different methods of defining the scope of the operation, that is, what data should be included in the total.

Graphs

Graphs on reports are similar to graphs on forms. The first step is to decide with the user what type of graph will best illustrate the data. The second step is to determine where the graph should be positioned within the report elements. If you are graphing detail items, then the graph belongs in the detail section, where it will be redrawn for every row of data. If it is a summary graph, it belongs in a group footer, or perhaps in the report footer if it summarizes data across the entire report.

Once you have determined the type and location of the graph, you build a query to collect the data. This query can be different from the query used to produce the overall report. In particular, when the graph is in a group footer, you might need to use aggregation functions in the query for the graph. Be sure to include a column that links the graph to the data in the report—even if that column will not be displayed on the graph. Figure 6.30 shows one sale on the Sales report for the Pet Store. The totals for the graph are computed by a separate query.

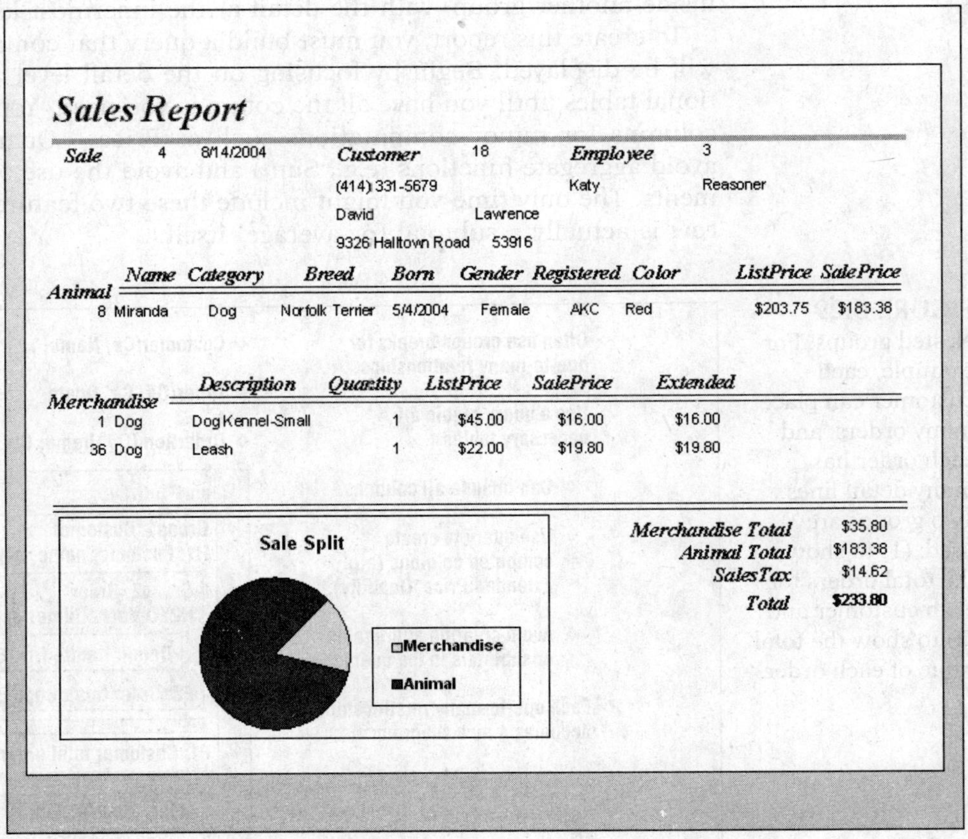

FIGURE 6.30
Sample graph on the sales report. It illustrates the portion of the sale spent on animals versus merchandise. Note that the graph appears on the same level as the Sale table—not on the Animal or Merchandise detail level and not on the report footer.

Application Features

Modern applications have several features that are designed to standardize the look and feel of applications and to make your applications relatively easy to use. Three features are particularly important: **menus, toolbars,** and the **Help system**.

The menu is a line of options displayed at the top of the application. The main menu is generally the same across the application. Hence, the menu centralizes choices that can be activated at any time. Menus are also useful for visually challenged workers and those who prefer to use the keyboard instead of a pointing device (mouse), because choices can be activated with the keyboard.

Toolbars consist of a set of icons or buttons that perform common tasks. Some applications enable users to customize the toolbar with specific buttons; usually users can also reposition toolbars. Current development tools take advantage of this feature and enable you to place menus into a custom toolbar.

The Help system is a crucial component of any application. In most applications, it replaces paper manuals. In theory, applications should be clear enough to use without a manual. Additional instructions and details are provided as text and pictures within the Help system.

Menus and Toolbars

A menu is simply a list of choices that perform some action when selected by the user. Most menus are hierarchical, that is, detailed choices are presented under a few keywords. The Windows interface standard specifies that menus should be displayed at the top of the application. However, users may want to move menus to a different location. Most applications use similar commands on their menus. For example, as illustrated in Figure 6.31, the main menu typically contains three common commands: File, Edit, and Help. The File command generally contains the New, Open, Save, and Close commands. As much as possible, your application should try to match these standards. By building applications with the same layout and the same words, users can understand your application with minimal training.

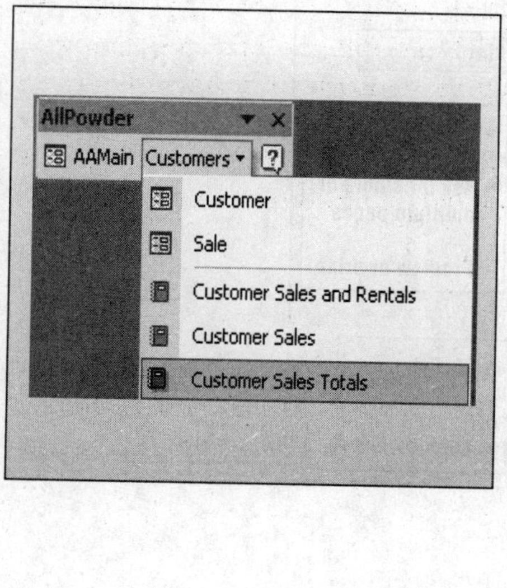

FIGURE 6.31
Sample menu. Note the hierarchical structure. The underlined letter represents the access key, which can be activated from the keyboard. You can also add shortcut keys (e.g., Ctrl+D), to activate a choice without going through the menu.

Purpose of the Menu

You might consider using the basic DBMS menu within your application. Then users will have full control over the database. In most cases, however, you will be better off building a custom menu for your application. A custom menu has several benefits. First, it can limit user actions. For example, if users do not need to delete data, the menu should not have the delete commands. You still have to set the appropriate security conditions to prevent them from using other methods to delete data. Removing a command from the menu helps to restrict user choices. A second advantage of a custom menu is that it simplifies the user interface. If entry-level users need only four or five commands, just display those options on the menu. Then they can find them faster. Third, you can add special functions to a custom menu. For example, you might add a special Help command to send e-mail to your support desk. Fourth, menu choices can be activated by keystrokes. Hence, touch typists and visually challenged workers can use your application without looking at the screen.

Toolbars

Custom menus are usually implemented on toolbars. A toolbar generally contains a collection of buttons and menu items. When the user clicks a toolbar button, a predefined operation is executed. A toolbar can contain traditional buttons, and it can contain textual menus. Most toolbars are **dockable**, which means that users can drag them to any place on the application window.

The purpose of a toolbar is to provide single-click access to complex actions or to commands that are used frequently. For example, many toolbars have an icon to immediately save the current work. As shown in Figure 6.32, you can put virtually any icon and any command on a toolbar. You can set different toolbars and menus for each form. You can even have multiple toolbars. For example, one toolbar might contain commands that apply to the entire application. Then special toolbars can be added as each form is opened.

Creating Menus and Toolbars

To support standardization and to simplify creating menus, most application development environments have a menu-generation feature. The exact steps

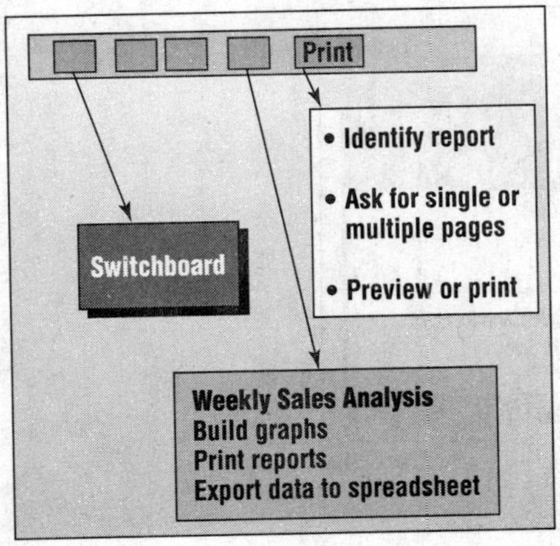

FIGURE 6.32
Sample toolbar. Toolbars can contain buttons and menus. Buttons generally display icons. When the pointer moves over them, a tooltip is displayed that briefly describes the button. When the button is clicked, an action is performed or a menu is displayed.

depend on the system you are using; however, three basic procedures are used to create a menu: (1) Choose the layout or structure, (2) Give each option a name and an access key, and (3) Define the action to be taken when each option is selected.

The basic steps to creating toolbars are similar: (1) Identify which tools you want to display for each form, (2) Choose or create an icon to represent a command, and (3) Define the action to be taken when the option is selected. A key feature in creating the toolbar is the choice of an icon. Never assume that users will recognize an icon or understand what it represents. Most systems enable you to define a **tooltip** for each option. When the user moves the pointer over the icon, the tooltip, or short comment, is displayed. Every toolbar button must have a tooltip.

Creating toolbars and menus is straightforward with recent application development systems. You can customize an existing toolbar by adding or deleting options. Similarly, you can create a new toolbar. Button icons and menus can be dragged to the toolbar.

The main step is to set the properties of each item. Menu names should be short and descriptive. You should also try to follow the standard names used in commercial software. To specify the access key, precede the key letter with an ampersand. For example, the &File text will appear as File, and the Alt plus F keys will activate that option. Shortcut keys (e.g., Ctrl+D) can be specified in the property settings of the detail menu item or the button command.

Most systems enable you to create multiple toolbars and then activate or deactivate toolbars for different users or in different areas within the application. You generally have to create a couple lines of code to activate or deactivate a specific toolbar.

Custom Help

Online Help systems have grown to replace paper manuals. The goal is to provide the background information and the specific instructions that a user might need to effectively use the application system. Help files can contain text-based descriptions, figures, and hypertext links to related topics. As much as possible, the help messages should be **context sensitive**. The users should be presented with information that is designed to help with the specific task they are working on at the time. Yet the Help system must also have an extensive search engine so that users can find information on any topic. Figure 6.33 illustrates a sample page from a Help system.

To maintain consistency, the Windows Help system displays the files, handles the links, table of contents, indexes, and searches almost automatically. As a developer, you can concentrate on creating the files that contain the basic information and the necessary links. Then the Help compiler converts your data into a special file that the Windows Help system can display and search. Once you learn the basic elements of creating a page, the hard part is writing the hundreds of pages needed for a complete Help system. Most directors of large development projects hire workers just to write the Help files.

Creating a Help File for Windows

The first and most important step in creating a Help file is to understand what information a user will need. Then you must write individual pages

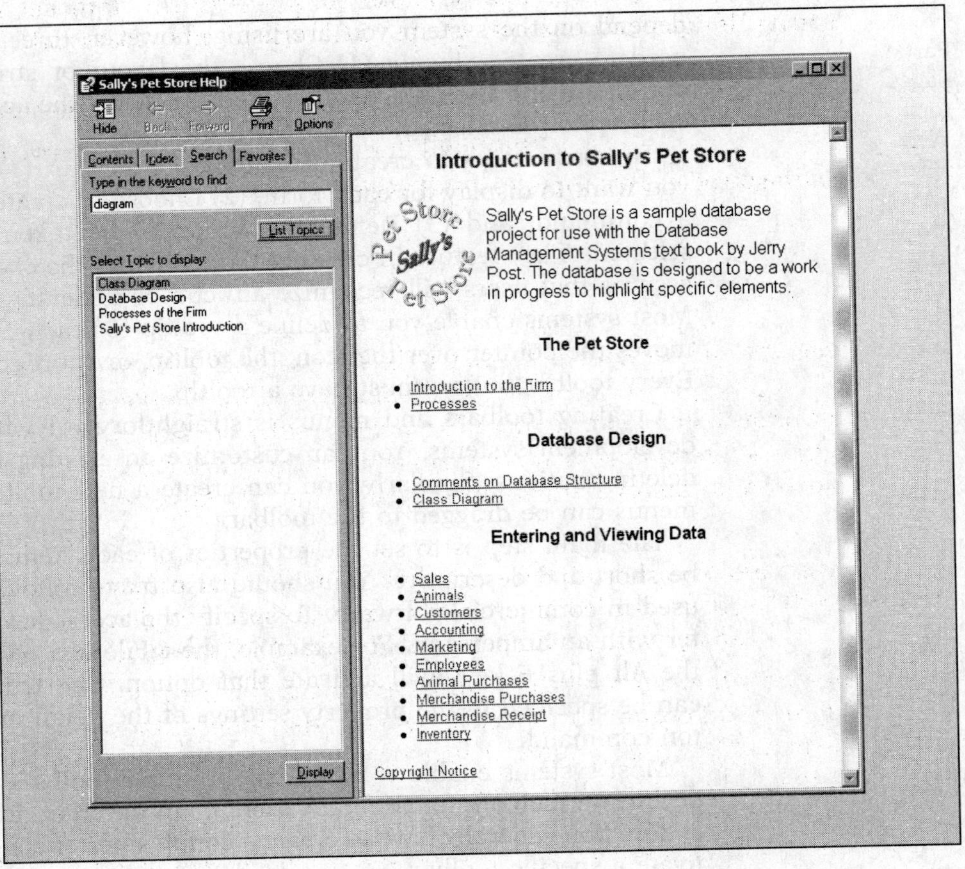

FIGURE 6.33
Sample help screen. The Windows help system handles all of the display and searches. You just have to write the HTML topic pages and specify keywords.

that explain the purpose of the system and how to use it. As with any communication project, you must first understand your audience. What types of people will use the application? What is their reading level? How much experience and training do they have with computers in general? Do they understand the business operations? The goal is to provide concise help information in a format that users can quickly understand.

Once you understand the needs of the users, you can write the individual Help pages. Five basic components are used to create a Help system: (1) text messages, (2) images, (3) hypertext links between topics, (4) keywords that describe each page, and (5) a topic name and a number for each page.

With the introduction of Windows 98, Microsoft changed the internal Help system. The old system still exists, but it is much easier to create Help files for the newer system using **hypertext markup language (HTML)**. Many good tools exist for creating Web pages. However, be careful with the tools: Some of them, such as Microsoft Word, create complex code that might not work well with the Help compiler. You want to use an HTML editor that produces basic HTML code without relying on XML or Javascript.

From a design perspective, it is crucial that you first design a style for your Help system and define that style using a cascading style sheet. A **style sheet** sets the typeface, font size, colors, and margins. The power of a style sheet is that you define all of the layout options in one place. Each page linked to the style sheet picks up those styles. So when you want to change the entire

```
<OBJECT type="application/x-oleobject"
classId="clsid:1e2a7bd0-dab9-11d0-b93a-00c04fc99f9e">
  <PARAM name="Keyword" value="Contents">
  <PARAM name="Keyword" value="Introduction">
  <PARAM name="Keyword" value="Sally's Pet Store">
  <PARAM name="Keyword" value="Management">
</OBJECT>
<HTML><HEAD>
<TITLE>Sally's Pet Store Introduction</TITLE>
<LINK rel="stylesheet" type="text/css"
href="PetHelpStyle.css">
</HEAD><BODY>
<H1>Introduction to Sally's Pet Store</H1>
<TABLE><TR>
<TD><IMG SRC='PetStoreLogo2.gif' border='0'></TD>
<TD>Sally's Pet Store is a sample database project for use
with the Database Management Systems textbook by Jerry
Post. The database is designed to be a work in progress
to highlight specific elements.</TD>
</TR></TABLE>
<H2>The Pet Store</H2>
<UL>
<LI><A HREF='FirmIntroduction.html'>Introduction to the
Firm</A></LI>
<LI><A HREF=`FirmProcesses.html'>Processes</A></LI>
</UL>
</BODY></HTML>
```

FIGURE 6.34
Partial sample Help page. Create each topic as a separate Web page using HTML. The anchor <A> tag links to other pages. The <IMG>tag loads images. Use style sheets to set fonts and design. Use a table or a style to control layout. Place keywords for the page in the <OBJECT>tag.

layout of your Help file, you make a few changes to the style sheet and every page uses that style.

Every topic is created as a separate HTML page. Users will be shown one page of material at a time. Try to keep topics short so they fit on one screen. Each Help page will contain links to other topics. Figure 6.34 shows part of a basic Help topic. Each page should have a title (marked with the <TITLE> tag). Pages generally have links to other topics (using the HTML standard <A HREF> tag). Images can be in one of two formats: joint photographic experts group (JPEG) and graphics interchange file (GIF). Most Help images will be line-art drawings and should be in the GIF format. Most graphics packages can create and store files in these formats. When you save the file, use only letters and numbers in the filename—do not include spaces. Because you will eventually have hundreds of pages, it is a good idea to keep a separate list of the pages along with a short description of the topic and when it was last modified.

Keywords are an important part of every Help page. They are used to create an index for the user. An index lists the keywords alphabetically, when a user double-clicks a word, the corresponding Help page is displayed. The HTML Help Workshop provides two ways to create the index: (1) manually listing each word and the corresponding topic, or (2) listing each keyword on the topic page. The second method is generally easier and less error prone, but it does scatter the words across all of the documents, making it harder to edit them as a group. The Help Workshop has a tool to place keywords on a topic page (Edit/Compiler Information/Keywords). But you have to load each page into the Workshop to use this method. Instead, it is often easier to copy everything in the <OBJECT> and </OBJECT> tags in Figure 6.34; then change the keywords within that list for each page. Each keyword is listed with a separate <PARAM> tag. If you want multiple levels, you can use a comma to list the hierarchy. For example, the three entries: (1) Sales; (2) Sales, Merchandise; and (3) Sales, Animal will create an index entry of Sales, followed by two indented lines for Animal and Merchandise.

Context-Sensitive Help

Users working on the Sales form in your application do not want to wade through several Help pages or try to think of search terms. Instead, when they press the Help key, they expect to see information on that particular form. At a minimum, you need to create different Help pages for each form in your application. But now you need some method in your database application to specify which Help page should be displayed for each form. As shown in Figure 6.35, each form has properties for Help File and Help Context ID. Oracle and Visual Basic forms have similar properties. You enter the name of the file (e.g., PetStore.chm) in the Help File property. The Help Context ID requires a number. This number is a long integer and can range from 1 to more than 2 billion.

It is crucial to note that applications require a topic number, but your Help file refers to pages by their filename—not by numbers. To get these two systems to match, you must assign a unique number to every topic page. With

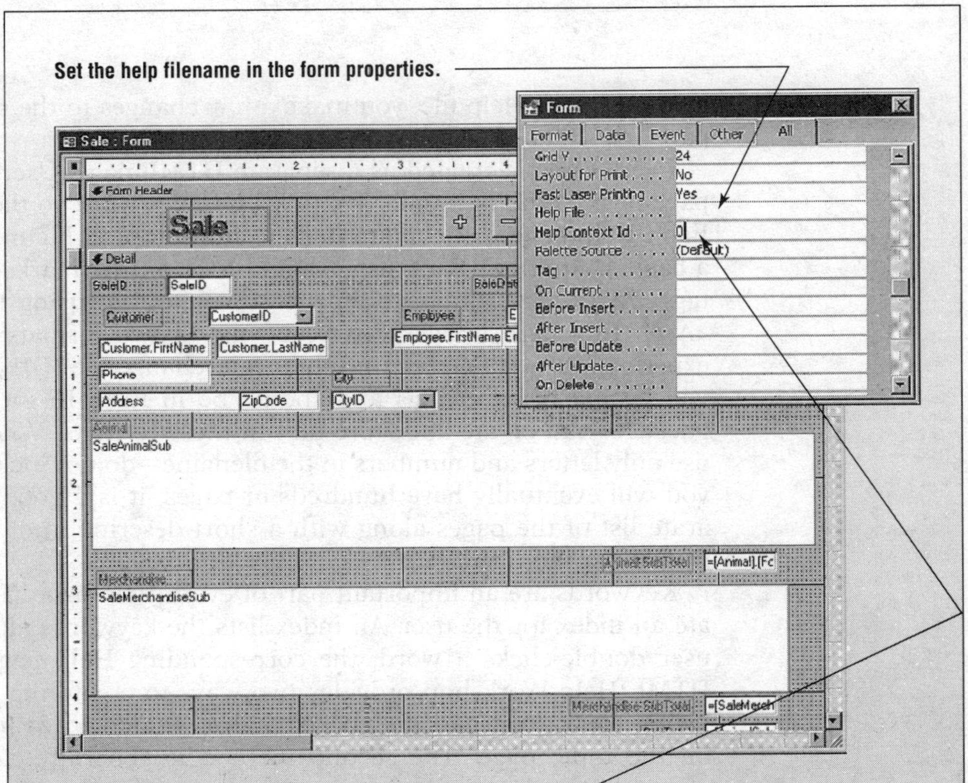

FIGURE 6.35
Setting context-sensitive help. In every form, enter the name of the Help file in the Help File property. Then enter the topic number for that form in the Help Context ID property. Every control or subform can also have a different Help topic—just enter the corresponding topic number.

FIGURE 6.36
Map file. Applications refer to topics by number, but the help system uses the filename. The map file (Topics.h) is a simple text file that assigns a number to each page.

```
#define PetStoreIntro              100
#define Accounting               10000
#define Animal                   20000
#define AnimalPurchase           30000
#define ClassDiagram             40000
#define Copyright                50000
#define Customer                 60000
#define DatabaseDesign           70000
#define Employee                 80000
#define FirmIntroduction         90000
#define FirmProcesses           100000
#define Inventory               110000
#define Marketing               120000
#define MerchandisePurchases    130000
#define MerchandiseReceipt      140000
#define Sale                    150000
```

HTML Help, you create a separate text file (usually called Topics.h) that maps this relationship. A sample file is shown in Figure 6.36. You can choose any number, but it is easier to remember them if you assign the numbers in groups. Also, with 2 billion numbers available, you can leave large gaps between the group numbers. For example, it is better to number by hundred thousands or millions instead of by ones (1, 2, 3, and so on). A useful technique is to assign numbers by business object (e.g., all Customer Help files might be numbered from 1,000,000 to 2,000,000). Once you have created the file, use the HtmlHelp API Information button (left side, fourth from the top) to tell the Help Workshop to include the file. Now, go through every form in your application and specify the filename and topic number for that form. Avoid changing the topic numbers in the Help file; they are hard to find in your application.

Summary

Forms must be designed to match the user's tasks and make your application easy to use. To meet this goal, you need to pay attention to design principles, operating system guidelines, and human limitations. Where possible, you should build the form to use direct manipulation of objects, such as dragging items from one location to another to signify shipment.

Forms are based on tables or queries. Each form has a single purpose and can store data in one table. More complex forms can be created by placing subforms onto the main form. Controls on the form are used to enter data into the tables, perform lookup functions, and manipulate data. Several standard controls are available for a Windows environment (e.g., text boxes, combo boxes, and option buttons). Additional controls can be purchased to handle more complex tasks, such as calendars for scheduling and three-dimensional imaging.

Reports are generally printed and differ from forms because reports are designed only to present data, not to collect it. There are several types of forms, but many business forms rely on subtotals or groupings to display different levels of data. For example, a sales report might be grouped by sales division or salesperson or both. You use a query to combine all data items needed for a report. There are two benefits to using a report writer: (1) It is a straightforward way to set data formats and alignment, and (2) The report can include detail listings as well as subtotals and totals.

A Developer's View

As Miranda noted, the database wizards can create basic forms for you. However, before you crank up the form wizard and generate hundreds of small forms, think about the tasks of the users and the overall design. Try to put the most important information on one central form with a few secondary forms to help. Strive for a clean, well-organized screen and use colors and graphics sparingly to enhance the appearance. You should also develop a design standard and layout for the application to ensure consistency. Just be sure to leave room for creativity. For your class project, you should begin creating the basic forms and reports.

Key Terms

accessibility, *229*
aesthetics, *226*
bound control, *238*
check box, *239*
clarity, *225*
combo box, *240*
command button, *238*
consistency, *225*
context-sensitive menu, *227*
controls, *230*
direct manipulation of objects, *245*
dockable, *256*
drag-and-drop, *245*
feedback, *226*
focus, *230*
group break, *252*
heads-down data entry, *224*
Help system, *255*
human factors design, *224*
hypertext markup language (HTML), *258*
list box, *240*
menu, *255*
modal form, *228*
option button, *239*
page footer, *252*
page header, *252*
report footer, *252*
report header, *252*
scroll bars, *227*
single-row form, *230*
style sheet, *258*
subform form, *230*
switchboard form, *230*
tab order, *230*
tabular form, *230*
toolbar, *255*
tooltip, *257*
Unicode, *244*

Review Questions

1. Which human factors are important to consider when designing forms?
2. How can you make your applications accessible to a wider group of workers?
3. What are the primary form types?
4. What are the main controls you can use on forms?
5. Explain the differences between a check box and an option button.
6. What is the purpose of subforms?
7. What are the main report types?
8. What are the primary sections of reports?
9. What features are needed to complete an application?
10. In general, what is the purpose of a menu and what items should be placed on it?
11. Why is context-sensitive help so important?
12. What steps are needed to create an HTML Help file?

Exercises

Create the tables and build the initial forms and reports for the databases described by the exercises in Chapters 2 and 3.

1. Canoe rental, Chapter 2, Exercise 1.
2. Pet grooming, Chapter 2, Exercise 2.
3. Dental appointments, Chapter 2, Exercise 3.
4. Custom shoes, Chapter 2, Exercise 4.
5. Radio station playlist, Chapter 2, Exercise 8.
6. Toll system, Chapter 2, Exercise 9.
7. Web comments, Chapter 3, Exercise 1.

8. Web sales, Chapter 3, Exercise 2.
9. HR benefits, Chapter 3, Exercise 3.
10. Garage band, Chapter 3, Exercise 4.
11. Lawn care, Chapter 3, Exercise 5.
12. Banquet facilities, Chapter 3, Exercise 6.
13. Clock builder, Chapter 3, Exercise 7.
14. Pizza delivery, Chapter 3, Exercise 8.
15. Animation studio, Chapter 3, Exercise 9.
16. Designer jeans, Chapter 3, Exercise 10.
17. For any existing database, create a main switchboard form. Build it as the final version, and include links for all necessary forms and reports—even if they are not built yet. Test the layout and structure with a potential user (or another student).
18. Generate a small Help file. Create at least three linked HTML pages, where one of the pages will be the startup page. Assign keywords to the pages and use H1, H2, and H3 tags to set up the table of contents. Define topic numbers. Use the HTML Help system to generate the compiled Help file. Test it. Add it to a database where each form points to a separate page. Test it.
19. Create a custom toolbar and menu to perform simple tasks, such as opening the main menu and showing the primary customer forms.
20. Review the documentation for the DBMS you are using and identify the features that it provides to support direct manipulation of objects such as drag-and-drop.

Sally's Pet Store

21. Create forms to handle the administration of the merchandise inventory, including forms for Breed, Category, and Merchandise tables.
22. Create a form to record orders of animals from suppliers.
23. Create forms to record orders and receipt of merchandise from suppliers.
24. Create a form to display a chart of merchandise sales by the main categories.
25. Identify all of the tasks that would need to be included in the database application, and redesign the main switchboard form.
26. Create a form that enables managers to select customers based on some common criteria (e.g., purchases of cat items, or purchases greater than some value), and then creates a mailing label report for the selected customers.
27. Create a report that lists employee sales by merchandise and animals and displays a chart comparing each employee total to the overall total.
28. Create a form that enables managers to select a time frame and then display a chart showing total merchandise purchases over that time period for each supplier.
29. Create a report that shows total sales of merchandise by category by week. Include a chart that compares the total sales by category.
30. Create a report that displays total sales by state.

Rolling Thunder Bicycles

31. Draw a diagram to show how the forms in Rolling Thunder are interconnected.
32. Build a version of the Bicycle form that is based on simple master/detail subforms. Compare the result to the existing form. What are the strengths and weaknesses?
33. Create a form to display a graph of bicycle sales (value and count) by model type for a specified time period. The time period should be entered as text boxes on the form, with a method to redraw the graph.
34. Create a form that enables the accountant to enter a day and generate a report that lists each supplier and the amount of money owed to the supplier as of that day.

35. Create a report that displays each state, the associated store within that state, and the total sales made with the help of that retail store. Include total sales by state.
36. Create a new toolbar/menu for the application. Include menus to select forms by Customer, Manufacturing, and Supplier. Include links to the appropriate forms and reports within those categories.
37. Create a report that displays sales of bicycles by model type by month. Include a chart that compares total sales by model type.
38. Create a report that displays sales of bicycles by employee by year. Include charts for each year that compare the sales across employees.
39. Create a report that charts the average length of time to build each bike model by month.
40. Create a form that enables managers to select a component and generate a chart that shows the purchases and sales of that component over time.

Website References

Site	Description
http://www.microsoft.com/enable	Accessibility guidelines.
http://www.unicode.org	Primary site for Unicode information.
http://www.acm.org/sigchi/	Association for Computing Machinery—Special Interest Group: Computer and Human Interaction.
http://www.acm.org/sigcaph/	Association for Computing Machinery—Special Interest Group: Computers and the Physically Handicapped.

Additional Reading

Cooper, A. *About Face: The Essentials of User Interface Design*. Foster City, CA: IDG Books, 1997. [A good discussion of various design issues.]

Ivory, M., and M. Hearst. "The State of the Art in Automating Usability." *Communications of the ACM* 33, no. 4 (December 2001), pp. 470–516. [General discussion on evaluating system usability.]

Koletzke, P. *Oracle Developer Advanced Forms and Reports*. Berkely: Osborne/McGraw-Hill, 2000.

Microsoft Corporation. *The Windows Interface: An Application Design Guide*. Redmond: Microsoft Press, 1992. [An important set of definitions and "standards" that designers should follow.]

O'Reilly, Inc., ed. *The Oracle PL/SQL CD Bookshelf: 7 Best Selling Books on CD ROM*. Cambridge, MA: O'Reilly & Associates, 2000. [A collection of several useful Oracle reference books on CD-ROM.]

Raskin, J. *The Humane Interface: New Directions for Designing Interactive Systems*. Reading, MA: Addison-Wesley, 2000. [The need for a new interface as explained by the creator of the Apple Macintosh project.]

Tsichritzis, D. "Form Management," *Communications of the ACM* 25, no. 7 (July 1982). [Basic concepts of database forms.]

Chapter 7

Database Integrity and Transactions

Chapter Outline

What You Will Learn in This Chapter

A Developer's View

Ariel: Well, is the application finished?

Miranda: No. The basic forms and reports are done. But I'm still running into some problems.

Ariel: I guess there is always more to do. What kinds of problems?

Miranda: Well, the numbers are sometimes wrong. It seems to happen when several people are working on the same data at the same time. And the application seems a little slow sometimes. And . . .

Ariel: Whoa. I get the picture. But these seem like common problems. Does the database system have any tools to help?

Miranda: I think so. I'm going to start by looking at some programming topics and data triggers. Then, I think indexes will help me with performance.

Introduction

Business applications often exhibit several common problems. For example, multiple users might try to change the same data at the same time, or multiple changes need to be made together, or you need to generate new ID numbers for a table. These situations must be handled correctly to ensure the integrity of the data. SQL commands are powerful tools, but in many of these situations, you need the ability to execute multiple statements or to choose which command should be run. Database systems have evolved procedural languages to handle these situations.

Although there are diverse methods to implement procedural languages, it is helpful when the language is embedded into the query system. With this approach, all of the code and conditions remain within the database definition and constraints are enforced automatically for all applications. These conditions are often written as data triggers—code that is executed when some data element is modified.

The issues of transactions, concurrent access, and key generation appear in almost every business application. This chapter explains the issues involved and provides the common solutions.

Performance is a tricky issue as databases expand into huge datasets. Complex queries across many large tables could take a long time to run. But, transaction-based applications need to process data quickly. Vendors have invested considerable money and time into improving performance. One common solution is to create indexes on the tables. You need to understand the basic index technologies to make informed choices to improve your application's performance.

Procedural Languages

A **procedural language** is a traditional programming language, where you specify the sequence of a set of commands. Common SQL commands are not procedural because you tell the DBMS only what you want done, not how to do it. Although SQL commands are powerful, there are times when

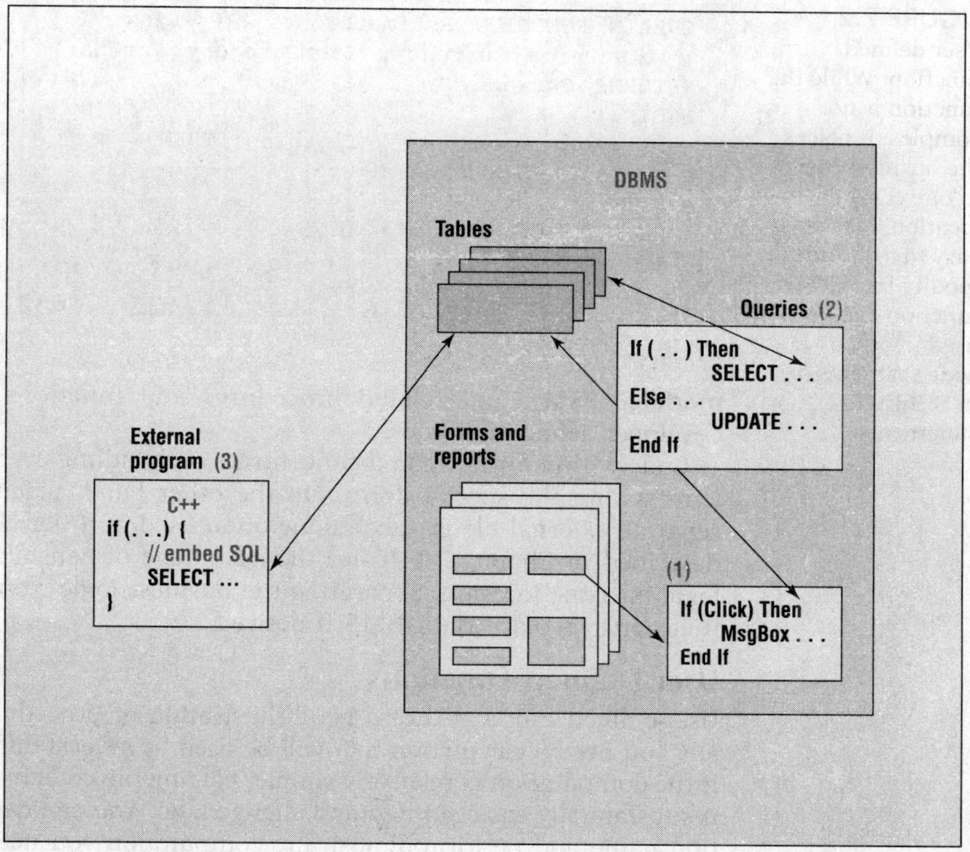

FIGURE 7.1
Location of procedural code. Code can usually be written in the query system, within a database form, or in an external program. When possible, code should be placed within the query system so that it cannot be bypassed.

you need the more precise control of a procedural language. For example, you might want to specify that a group of commands must be executed in a particular order and all must be completed for the transaction to succeed. Or, you might want to execute some commands only if certain external conditions are true. In more complex cases, you might need to step through each row in a table to perform some difficult computation.

Where Should Code Be Located?

Figure 7.1 shows that procedural code can often be placed in three locations: (1) within the query system, (2) within forms and reports, or (3) in external programs. In general, code that relates directly to the data should be placed within the query system. The reason is straightforward: by placing the code as close to the data as possible, it needs to be written only once, instead of copied into multiple forms. More importantly, the DBMS will ensure that the code is always executed and not bypassed. Think about a security situation where you want to write a note to a log table every time someone changes an employee salary. If you rely on programmers to implement this code in their forms, they might forget to do it or else do it incorrectly. Additionally, someone could create an entirely new form or even use a query to change the data directly, without executing the security code. Placing the code within the database provides a mechanism to ensure that it is run anytime the data is changed, regardless of how the modification is generated. In the SQL standard, procedural code stored within the database is called a **persistent stored**

FIGURE 7.2
User-defined function. While the function is not complex, it places the business logic in one central location, making it easy to find and modify later. This function can be used in other code segments or in SELECT statements.

```
CREATE FUNCTION EstimateCosts
  (ListPrice Currency, ItemCategory VarChar)
RETURNS Currency
BEGIN
  IF (ItemCategory = 'Clothing')THEN
    RETURN ListPrice * 0.5
  ELSE
    RETURN ListPrice * 0.75
  END IF
END
```

module (PSM), and related procedures and functions can be stored in developer-defined modules.

Code within forms should concentrate on handling events or custom problems within the specific form. On the other hand, placing the code into a separate external file is a technique often used in *n*-tier client/server systems described in Chapter 10. It has the advantage of consolidating the business logic into one location. Separating the business logic from the DBMS makes it easier to replace the DBMS if desired.

User-Defined Functions

User-defined functions are a good illustration of procedural code. Occasionally you need a calculation that will be used by several different queries. Even if the computation is relatively simple, placing the code in one location makes it substantially easier to find and change later. You can define your own function name and perform almost any computation you need using procedural code. You can pass in values from a table in the form of parameters. Figure 7.2 provides an example of a simple function to estimate item costs. In practice, this function would be better written using tables and queries, but it illustrates the basic concepts of a user-defined function. Functions are passed values and perform computations on these parameters. A value is returned to the calling routine. You can also create procedures, which are different from functions in that they do not return a value. However, in almost all cases, you will want to use functions—if only to return error codes.

Figure 7.3 shows a function that uses the input parameters to update the database. Notice that the parameters can be used in any SQL statement. You can also create local variables to modify the parameters and then use them

FIGURE 7.3
Function to update the database. The input parameters are used to specify values in the SQL statement. Additional computations can be performed and the parameters modified if needed.

```
CREATE FUNCTION IncreaseSalary
  (EmpID INTEGER, Amt CURRENCY)
RETURNS CURRENCY
BEGIN
  IF (Amt > 50000) THEN
    RETURN-1    --error flag
  END
  UPDATE Employee SET Salary = Salary + Amt
  WHERE EmployeeID = EmpID;
  RETURN Amt;
END
```

FIGURE 7.4
Looking up single data elements. The SELECT INTO statement can be used to return data from exactly one row in a table or query. The result is stored in a local variable (MaxAmount) that you can use in subsequent code or SQL statements.

```
CREATE FUNCTION IncreaseSalary
 (EmpID INTEGER, Amt CURRENCY)
RETURNS CURRENCY
DECLARE
  CURRENCY MaxAmount;
BEGIN
  SELECT MaxRaise INTO MaxAmount
  FROM CompanyLimits
  WHERE LimitName = 'Raise';

  IF (Amt > 50000) THEN
   RETURN-1   --error flag
  END
  UPDATE Employee SET Salary = Salary + Amt
  WHERE EmployeeID = EmpID;
  RETURN Amt;
END
```

in the SQL statement. Functions can be as complex as you need. The procedural language system contains the standard elements of any programming language: variables, conditions, loops, and subroutines.

Looking Up Data

Procedures and functions often need to be able to use data from tables or queries. Obtaining data from a single row is straightforward with the SELECT INTO statement. It behaves the same as a standard SELECT statement, but instead of displaying the values, if places them into local variables. However, you have to be careful to ensure that the SELECT statement returns only a single row of data. If you make a mistake in the WHERE condition and return multiple rows, it will generate an error.

Figure 7.4 shows how the SELECT INTO statement is used to retrieve a single value. The statement can be used to retrieve data from multiple columns, but only one row. Just add another COLUMN INTO VARIABLE on the SELECT line and separate it with a comma from the existing line. Notice the difference between Figures 7.3 and 7.4: The new approach looks up the maximum raise in a table. This approach is better than using a fixed value because you can create a form that enables an administrator to change this value quickly. If you leave fixed numbers in your program code, a programmer would have to wade through all of the modules to find the magic number. In addition, anytime someone has to change program code, there is a large risk that additional errors will be introduced. Whenever possible, you should place important values into a table and use the lookup process to get the current value when it is needed.

Data Triggers

Data **triggers** are procedures that are executed when some event arises within the database. The code is written in the query system and is saved as a procedure or function within the database. The common events are Update, Insert, and Delete, but some systems enable you to attach code to events related to

FIGURE 7.5
Data triggers. You can set procedures to execute whenever one of these actions occurs. Row events can be triggered before or after the specified event occurs.

users or the database instance. For example, you could create a procedure that is run whenever someone changes the Salary column in the Employee table. When the data is changed, your procedure is fired to record the person who made the change. With the log, auditors can go back and see who made changes. The salary example is a common use of data triggers, which is to add specific security or auditing features to the database. They can also be used to handle business events, such as monitoring when quantity on hand drops below some level and generating an e-mail message or an EDI order to a supplier.

Figure 7.5 lists the basic SQL commands that support triggers. The main data triggers on the rows and columns each have two attributes: BEFORE and AFTER. For example, you can specify a procedure for BEFORE UPDATE and a different procedure for AFTER UPDATE. The BEFORE UPDATE event is triggered when a user attempts to change data, but before the data is actually written to the database. The AFTER UPDATE trigger is fired once the data has been written. You choose the event based on what you want to do with your application. If you need to check data before it is written to the database, you need to use a BEFORE trigger. For instance, you might want to perform a complicated validation test before saving data. On the other hand, if you want to record when data was changed or need to alter a second piece of data, you can use an AFTER trigger.

Statement Versus Row Triggers

The SQL standard defines two levels of triggers: (1) triggers may be assigned to the overall table, or (2) they may be assigned to fire for each row of data being modified. Figure 7.6 shows the timing of the various triggers for an UPDATE command. Triggers created to the overall table are fired first (BEFORE UPDATE) or at the very end (AFTER UPDATE). Then individual row triggers are fired before or after each row being examined. For row-level triggers, you can also add conditions that examine the row data to decide if the trigger should be fired or ignored. For instance, you might add a row trigger in the Salary case that fires only for employees in a certain division. Note that this condition is completely separate from the original UPDATE WHERE statement. The trigger condition is used only to decide whether or not to fire the trigger.

Figure 7.7 shows a sample trigger that fires whenever a row is changed in the Employee table. Notice that it is a row-level trigger because of the FOR EACH ROW statement. The example also illustrates that triggers can examine and use the data stored in the target table before it is changed (OLD ROW) and after it has been changed (NEW ROW). In this situation, the original salary and new salary are both recorded to the log table. With this information, security managers and auditors can quickly query the log table to identify major changes to salary and then investigate further to ensure the

FIGURE 7.6
Update triggers can be assigned to the overall table and fire once for the entire command, or they can be assigned to fire for each row being updated.

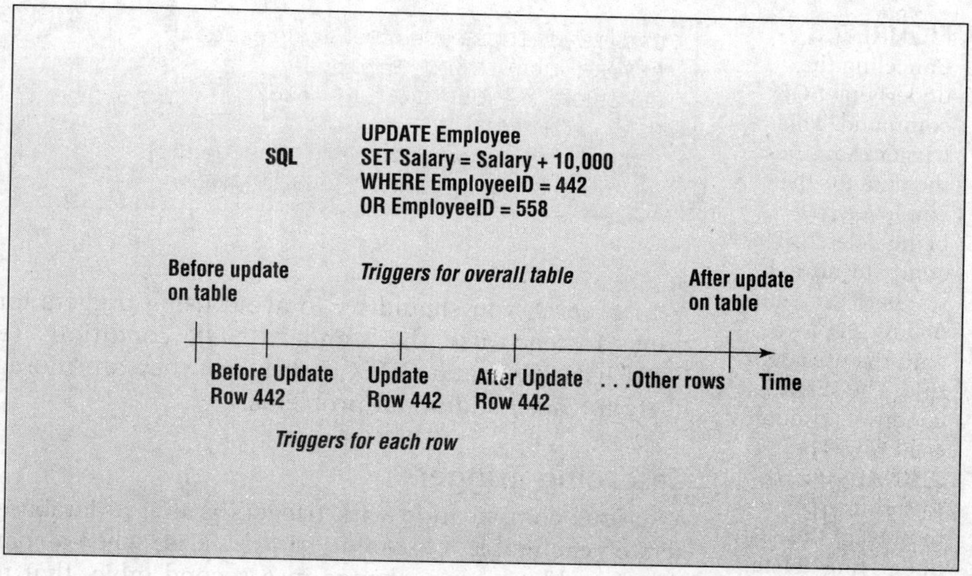

changes were legitimate. You do have to be careful with the OLD and NEW data. For example, the NEW data has not yet been created in a BEFORE UPDATE trigger, so it cannot be accessed.

Canceling Data Changes in Triggers

One of the uses of triggers is to examine changes in detail before they are written to the database. The BEFORE UPDATE and BEFORE INSERT triggers are often used to validate complex conditions. You also might want to provide more cautious checks before deleting data. In these cases, the structure of the trigger is straightforward. The only change is that you need a way to stop the original SQL statement from executing. The WHEN condition is used to examine the row that is scheduled to be deleted. As shown in Figure 7.8, the SIGNAL statement raises an error condition that prevents the row from actually being deleted. The actual signal condition (CANNOT_DELETE_PRESIDENT) can be almost anything, but it must be defined as a constant in the overall module. Note that most database system vendors have not yet adopted the SIGNAL keyword, so the actual syntax you need will depend on the system (and version) that you are using.

FIGURE 7.7
Trigger to log the users who change an employee salary. The trigger fires any time the salary is updated, regardless of the method used to alter the data. It is a useful security tracing technique for sensitive data because it cannot be circumvented, except by the owner of the trigger.

```
CREATE TRIGGER LogSalaryChanges
AFTER UPDATE OF Salary ON Employee
REFERENCING OLD ROW as oldrow
        NEW ROW AS newrow
FOR EACH ROW
  INSERT INTO SalaryChanges
  (EmpID, ChangeDate, User, OldValue, NewValue)
  VALUES
  (newrow.EmployeeID, CURRENT_TIMESTAMP,
  CURRENT_USER, oldrow.Salary,
newrow.Salary);
```

FIGURE 7.8
Canceling the underlying SQL command. This trigger examines the data for the employee row being deleted. The company always wants to keep data on any employee with the president title. The WHEN condition evaluates each row. The SIGNAL statement raises an error to prevent the underlying delete from executing.

```
CREATE TRIGGER TestDeletePresident
BEFORE DELETE ON Employee
REFERENCING OLD ROW AS oldrow
FOR EACH ROW
  WHEN (oldrow.Title = 'President')
      SIGNAL CANNOT_DELETE_PRES;
```

In general, you should try to avoid using triggers for simple check conditions. Instead, use the standard SQL conditions (e.g., PRIMARY KEY, FOREIGN KEY, and CHECK) because they are more efficient and are less likely to cause additional problems.

Cascading Triggers

A serious complication with triggers is that a database can have many triggers on each table. **Cascading triggers** arise when a change that fires a trigger on one table cause a change in a second table, that triggers a change in a third table, and so on. Figure 7.9 shows a common inventory situation. When an item is sold, a new row is added to the SaleItem table that contains the quantity sold. Because the item has been sold, the quantity on hand is updated in the Inventory table. A trigger on the Inventory table then checks to see if the QOH is below the reorder point. If it is, a new order is generated and sent electronically to a supplier, resulting in inserts on the Order and OrderItem tables.

There is nothing inherently wrong with cascading triggers. However, long chains of updates can slow down the system. They also make it difficult to debug the system and find problems. In the example, you might be looking at a problem in the OrderItem table, but it could have been caused by an error in the trigger code for the SaleItem table. The longer the chain, the more challenging it is to identify the source of problems.

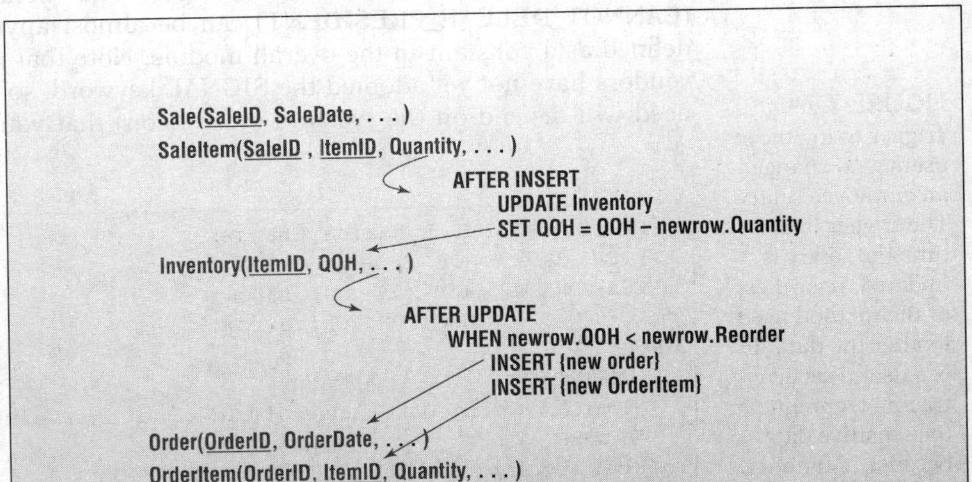

FIGURE 7.9
Cascading triggers. With triggers defined on multiple tables, a change in one table (SaleItem) can cascade into changes in other tables. Here, when an item is sold, quantity on hand is updated. If QOH is below the reorder point, a new order is generated and sent.

FIGURE 7.10
Trigger loop. Consider what happens when cascading triggers create a loop, where one trigger returns to alter a table that generated the original change. This loop would set up iterations that might converge or diverge. Even if the loop converges, it will eat up considerable resources.

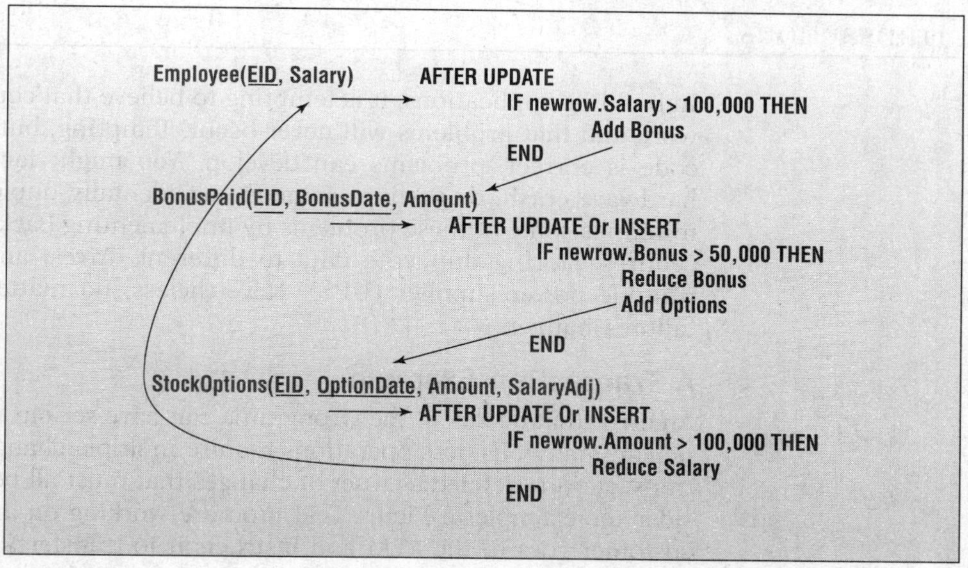

A more difficult problem can potentially arise with cascading triggers. What happens when the chain loops on itself? Figure 7.10 shows an example of the problem. A company has embedded several rules about the methods of paying employees. When the salary reaches a certain level, the employee is eligible for bonuses. When the employee has already received substantial bonuses, the bonus amount is limited and the employee is granted additional stock options. If the level of stock options is substantial, the original salary is reduced. But that takes the system back to the beginning, and the salary change could trigger another round of updates. Depending on the computations, this loop could diverge so that the numbers get larger and larger (or increasingly negative), and the computations never end. For this reason, the SQL standard is defined to forbid trigger loops. Systems that follow the standard are supposed to monitor the entire chain of updates, and if it encounters a loop, it should cancel changes and issue a warning. Even if the system is supposed to identify these loops, you should always check the system yourself to make sure that these problems will not arise. Obviously, the system is easier to check if there are only a limited number of triggers.

INSTEAD OF Triggers

Some database systems support the INSTEAD OF option as an even stronger type of trigger. A standard trigger runs your code in addition to performing the underlying function (DELETE, INSERT, or UPDATE). The INSTEAD OF option completely replaces the underlying command with your code. So, even if the change should be written to the database, you will have to write the additional SQL statements to take the appropriate action. It is a useful trick for making queries updateable. Note that a query that joins multiple tables generally is not updateable; data cannot be added to the query because the system does not always know which table gets the new row. To solve the problem, you can add an INSTEAD OF trigger to the query. Then changes that are needed can be written to the individual tables with separate SQL statements.

Transactions

In building applications, it is tempting to believe that components will always work and that problems will never occur. Tempting, but wrong. Even if your code is correct, problems can develop. You might face a power failure, a hardware crash, or perhaps someone accidentally unplugs a cable. You can minimize some of these problems by implementing backup and recovery procedures, storing duplicate data to different drives, and installing uninterruptible power supplies (UPS). Nevertheless, no matter how hard you try, failures happen.

A Transaction Example

An error that occurs at the wrong time can have serious consequences. In particular, many business operations require multiple changes to the database. A **transaction** is defined as a set of changes that must all be made together. Consider the example in Figure 7.11. You are working on a system for a bank. A customer goes to the ATM and instructs it to transfer $1,000 from savings to a checking account. This simple transaction requires two steps: (1) subtracting the money from the savings account balance and (2) adding the money to the checking account balance. The code to create this transaction will require two updates to the database. For example, there will be two SQL statements: one UPDATE command to decrease the balance in savings and a second UPDATE command to increase the balance in the checking account.

You have to consider what would happen if a machine crashed in between these two operations. The money has already been subtracted from the savings account, but it will not be added to the checking account. It is lost. You might consider performing the addition to checking first, but then the customer ends up with extra money, and the bank loses. The point is that both changes must be made successfully.

Starting and Ending Transactions

How do you know that both operations are part of the same transaction? It is a business rule—or the definition of a transfer of funds. The problem is, How does the computer know that both operations must be completed together? As the application developer, you must tell the computer system which operations

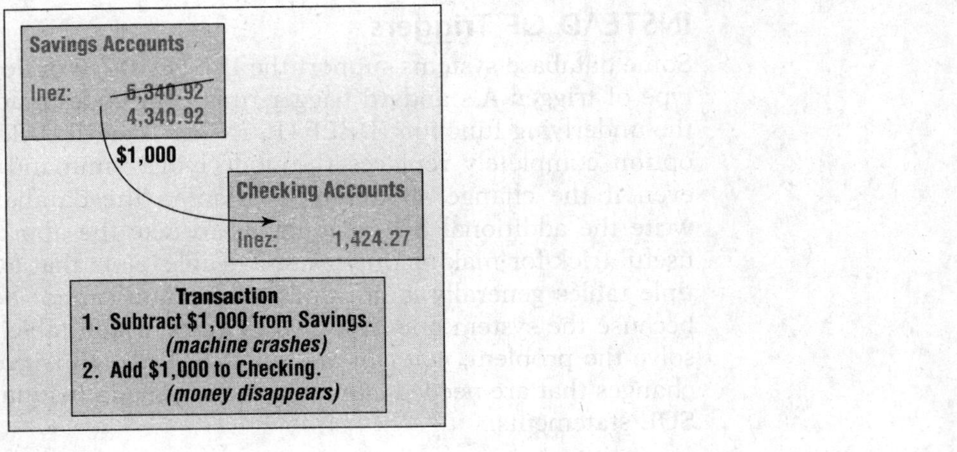

FIGURE 7.11
Transactions involve multiple changes to the database. All of the changes must be made, or the transaction will not be correct. To transfer money from a savings account to a checking account, for example, the system must subtract money from savings and add it to the checking balance. If the machine crashes after subtracting the money but before adding it to checking, the money will be lost.

FIGURE 7.12
Transaction to transfer money. If the system crashes before the end of the transactions (Commit), none of the changes are written to the database. On restart, the changes may all be rolled back, or the transaction restarted.

```
CREATE FUNCTION TransferMoney(Amount Currency,
    AccountFrom Number,AccountTo Number)
  RETURNS NUMBER
curBalance Currency;
BEGIN
  DECLARE HANDLER FOR SQLEXCEPTION
  BEGIN
    ROLLBACK;
    Return-2;             --flag for completion error
  END;
  START TRANSACTION;      --optional
  SELECT CurrentBalance INTO curBalance
  FROM Accounts WHERE (AccountID = AccountFrom);
  IF (curBalance < Amount) THEN
    RETURN-1;             --flag for insufficient funds
  END IF
  UPDATE Accounts
  SET CurrentBalance = CurrentBalance - Amount
  WHERE AccountID = AccountFrom;
  UPDATE Accounts
  SET CurrentBalance = CurrentBalance + Amount
  WHERE AccountID = AccountTo;
  COMMIT;
  RETURN 0;               --flag for success
End;
```

belong to a transaction. To do that you need to mark the start and the end of all transactions inside your code. When the computer sees the starting mark, it first writes all the changes to a log file. When it reaches the end mark, it makes the actual changes to the data tables. If something goes wrong before the changes are complete, when the DBMS restarts, it examines the log file and completes any transactions that were incomplete. From a developer's perspective, the nice part is that the DBMS handles the problem automatically. All you have to do is mark the start and the end of the transaction.

Transactions illustrate the need for procedural languages. As shown in Figure 7.12, the multiple UPDATE statements need to be stored in a module function or procedure. In this example, the two UPDATE statements must be completed together or fail together. The START TRANSACTION statement is optional (in the SQL 99 standard) but highlights the beginning of the transaction. If both updates complete successfully, the COMMIT statement executes, which tells the DBMS to save all of the changes. If an unexpected error arises, the ROLLBACK statement executes so none of the changes are saved. Most systems handle the transaction requirement by writing all changes to an intermediate log file. If something goes wrong with the transaction, the system can recover the log file and rollback or complete the transaction.

Notice that the START TRANSACTION line comes before the initial SELECT statement. This might seem unnecessary, since it appears that only the UPDATE commands need to be within the transaction. There is a syntax reason for placing this statement first: Any SELECT statement automatically initiates a new transaction. However, as will be explained in the section on concurrency, there is a good reason for starting the transaction before this SELECT statement.

FIGURE 7.13
SAVEPOINT. A SAVEPOINT enables you to rollback to an intermediate point in the procedure. You can set multiple SAVEPOINTS and choose how far back you want to rollback the changes.

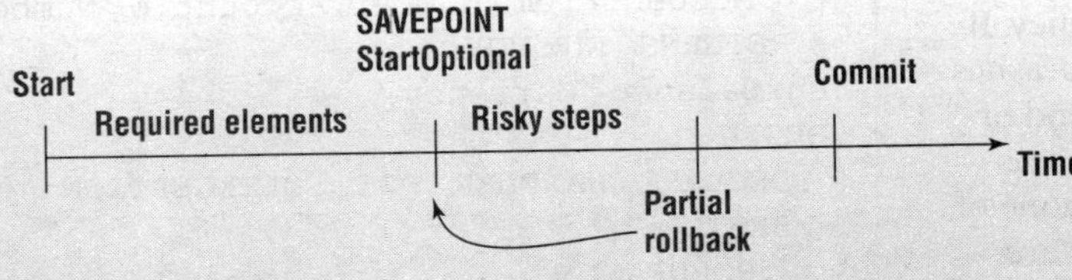


```
START TRANSACTION;
SELECT . . .
UPDATE . . .
SAVEPOINT StartOptional;
UPDATE . . .
UPDATE . . .
If error THEN
        ROLLBACK TO SAVEPOINT StartOptional;
END IF
COMMIT;
```

SAVEPOINT

Sometimes, you need intermediate points in a transaction. Some elements are more critical than others. You might have some optional changes that would be useful to save, but if they fail, you still need to ensure that the critical updates are committed. The SAVEPOINT technique divides transaction procedures into multiple pieces. You can rollback a transaction to the beginning, or to a specific SAVEPOINT. Figure 7.13 illustrates the process and shows the syntax to set a SAVEPOINT and rollback to it. As indicated, it can be used to mark a set of risky steps that you would like to include in the update but are not required to use. Consequently, if the updates fail for the risky section, you can discard those changes and still keep the required elements that were defined at the beginning of the transaction. Generally, you could accomplish the same thing by using multiple COMMIT statements, but sometimes the optional code might include a calculation that you want to include in the final result. Without the SAVEPOINT option, you might have to write the final value more than once.

Multiple Users and Concurrent Access

One of the most important features of a database is the ability to share data with many users or different processes. This concept is crucial in any modern business application: Many people need to use the application at the same time. However, it does create a potential problem with database integrity: What happens when two people try to change the same data at the same time? This situation is known as **concurrent access**. Consider the example of a mail-order system shown in Figure 7.14. The company records basic customer data and tracks charges and receipts from customers. Customers can have an outstanding balance, which is money they currently owe. In the example, Jones owes the company $800. When Jones makes a payment, a clerk receives the payment and checks for the current balance ($800). The clerk enters the amount paid ($200), and the computer subtracts to find the new balance due ($600). This

FIGURE 7.14
Concurrent access. If two processes try to change the same data at the same time, the result will be wrong. In this example the changes made when the payment is received are overwritten when a new order is placed at the same time.

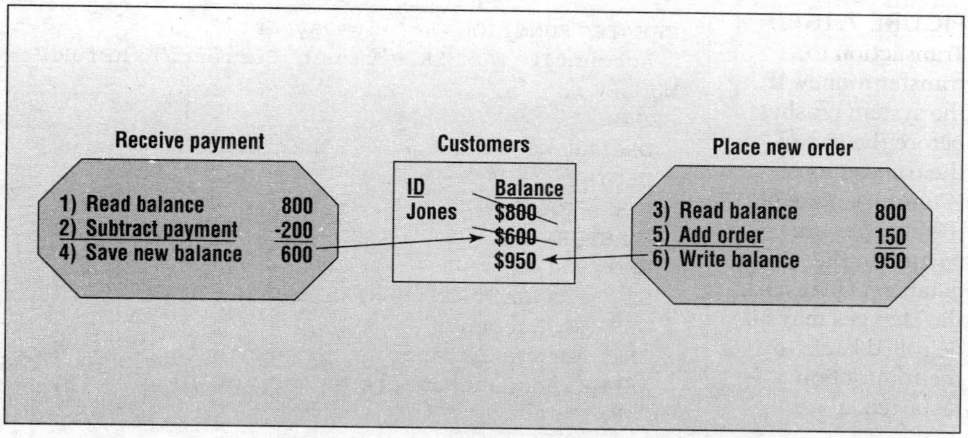

new value is written to the customer table, replacing the old value. So far, no problem. A similar process occurs if Jones makes a new purchase. As long as these two events take place at different times, there is no problem.

However, what happens if the two transactions do occur together? Consider the following intermingling: (1) The payments clerk receives the payment, and the computer retrieves the current amount owed by Jones ($800). (2) The clerk enters the $200 payment. Before the transaction can be completed, Jones is on the phone with a different clerk to place an order for $150 of new merchandise. (3) This clerk's computer also reads the current balance owed ($800) and adds the new purchases. Now, before this transaction can be completed, the first one finishes. (4) The payments clerk's computer determines that Jones now owes $600 and saves the balance due. (5) Finally, the order clerk's computer adds the new purchases to the balance due. (6) The order computer saves the new amount due ($950). Customer Jones is going to be justifiably upset when the next bill is sent. What happened to the $200 payment? The answer is that it was overwritten (and lost) when the new order change was mixed in with the receipt of the payment.

Pessimistic Locks: Serialization

One solution to the problem of concurrent access is to prevent it completely by forcing transactions to be completely isolated. As shown in Figure 7.15,

FIGURE 7.15
Serialization. The first process locks the data so that the second process cannot even read it. Concurrent changes are prevented by forcing each process to wait for the earlier ones to be completed.

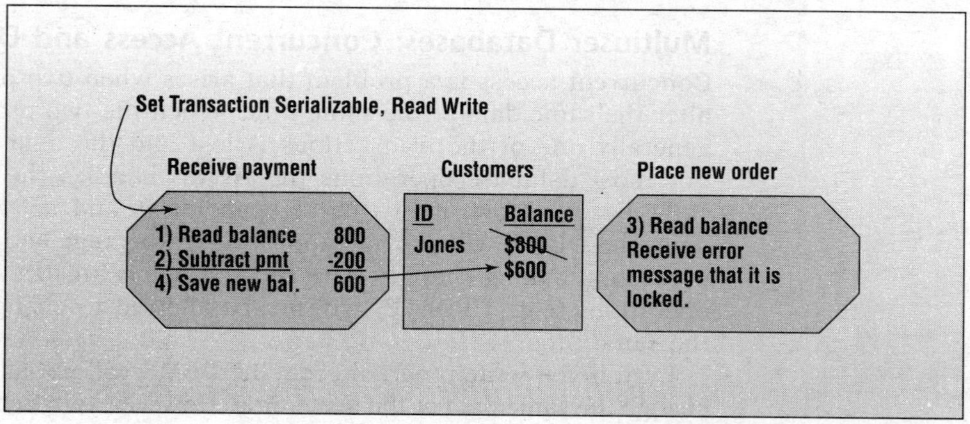

FIGURE 7.16
Transaction to transfer money. If the system crashes before the end of the transactions (Commit), none of the changes are written to the database. On restart, the changes may all be rolled back, or the transaction restarted.

```
CREATE FUNCTION ReceivePayment(
  AccountID NUMBER, Amount Currency) RETURNS
NUMBER
BEGIN
  DECLARE HANDLER FOR SQLEXCEPTION
  BEGIN
    ROLLBACK;
    RETURN-2;
  END
  SET TRANSACTION SERIALIZABLE, READ WRITE;
  UPDATE Accounts
  SET AccountBalance = AccountBalance - Amount
  WHERE AccountNumber = AccountID;
  COMMIT;
  RETURN 0;
END
```

the **serialization** process forces transactions to run separately so that a second process cannot even read the data being modified by the first process.

The method of invoking this type of lock mechanism depends heavily on the DBMS. SQL 99 defined a standard method of specifying the transaction lock, but it has not been widely implemented yet. Figure 7.16 shows the basic logic, but keep in mind that the syntax will be different for each DBMS. The main step is to specify the **isolation level** to SERIALIZABLE in the SET TRANSACTION statement. The DBMS then knows to lock each data element you will be using so that other transactions will be prevented from reading the data until the first changes have been committed. However, it is important that all of the transaction procedures contain error-handling code. Otherwise, when the second transaction (RecordPurchase is almost identical to this one) runs, it will crash and display a cryptic error message when it tries to update or read the data.

The concept of serialization is logical, and it emphasizes the importance of forcing each transaction to complete separately. However, it is based on the technique of a **pessimistic lock**—where each transaction assumes that concurrent interference will always occur. Every time the transaction runs, it places locks on all of the resources that will be needed. This technique can result in another serious problem described in the following section.

Multiuser Databases: Concurrent Access and Deadlock

Concurrent access is a problem that arises when two processes attempt to alter the same data at the same time. When the two processes intermingle, generally one of the transactions is lost and the data becomes incorrect. For most database operations the DBMS handles the problem automatically. For example, if two users open forms and try to modify the same data, the DBMS will provide appropriate warnings and prevent the second user from making changes until the first one is finished. Similarly, two SQL operations (e.g., UPDATE) will not be allowed to change the same data at the same time.

Even if you write program code, the DBMS will not allow two processes to change the same data at the same time. However, your code has to understand

FIGURE 7.17
Deadlock. Process 1 has locked Data A and is waiting for Data B. Process 2 has locked Data B and is waiting for Data A. To solve the problem, one of the processes has to back down and release its lock.

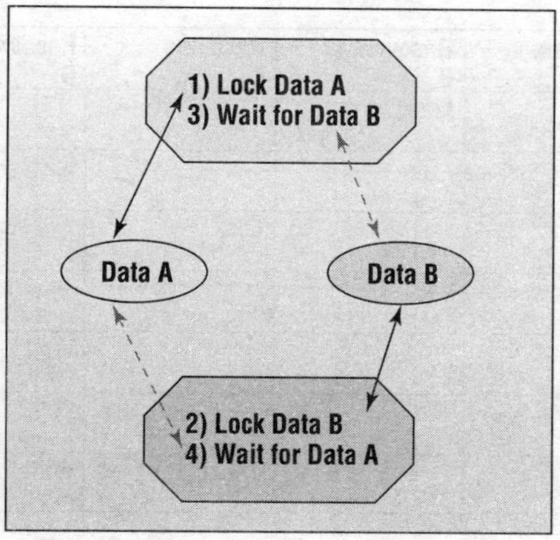

that sometimes a change to the data will not be allowed. This condition is often handled as an error.

The solution to the concurrency problem is to force changes to each piece of data to occur one at a time. If two processes attempt to make a change, the second one is stopped and must wait until the first process finishes. The catch is that this forced delay can cause a second problem: deadlock. **Deadlock** arises when two (or more) processes have placed locks on data and are waiting for the other's data. An example is presented in Figure 7.17. Process 1 has locked data item A. Process 2 has locked item B. Unfortunately, Process 1 is waiting for B to become free, and Process 2 is waiting for A to be released. Unless something changes, it could be a long wait.

Two common solutions exist for the deadlock problem. First, when a process receives a message that it must wait for a resource, the process should wait for a random length of time, try again, release all existing locks, and start over if it still cannot obtain the resource. This method works because of the random wait. Of the two deadlocked processes, one of them will try first, give up, and release all locks with a ROLLBACK statement. The release clears the way for the other process to complete its tasks. This solution is popular because it is relatively easy to program. However, it has the drawback of causing the computer to spend a lot of time waiting—particularly when there are many active processes, leading to many collisions.

A better solution is for the DBMS to establish a global lock manager as shown in Figure 7.18. A lock manager monitors every lock and request for a lock (wait). If the lock manager detects a potential deadlock, it will tell some of the processes to release their locks, allow the other processes to proceed, and then restart the other processes. It is a more efficient solution, because processes do not spend any time waiting. On the other hand, this solution can be implemented only within the DBMS itself. The lock manager must be able to monitor every process and its locks.

For typical database operations with forms and queries, the DBMS handles concurrent access and deadlock resolution automatically. When you write code to change data, the DBMS still tries to handle the situation automatically. However, the DBMS may rely on you to back out your transaction. Some systems may simply generate an error when the second process attempts to access the data, and it is your responsibility to catch the error and handle the problem.

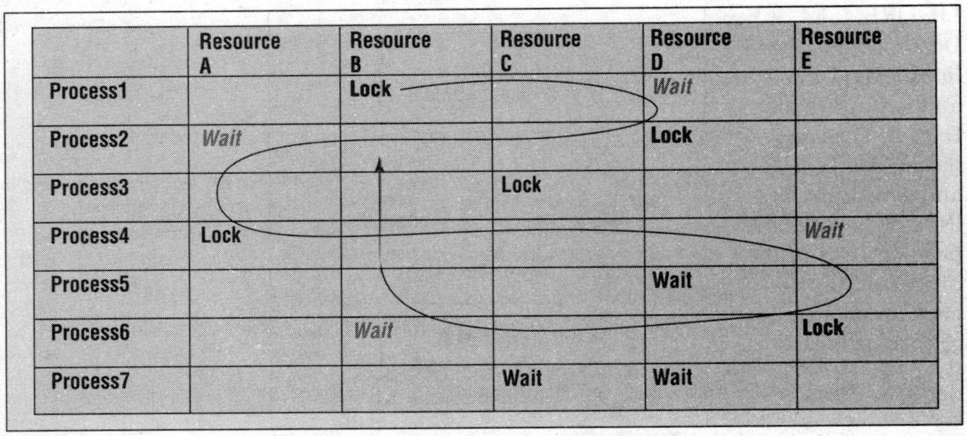

FIGURE 7.18
Lock manager. A global lock manager tracks all locked resources and associated processes. If it detects a cycle, then a deadlock exists, and the lock manager instructs processes to release locks until the problem is solved.

Optimistic Locks

Pessimistic locking and handling deadlocks was relatively standard in many systems for several years. Lately, a different approach seems to be gaining favor. As computer system performance increases, the DBMS can process transactions faster, resulting in a lower probability of concurrency problems. An **optimistic lock** begins with the assumption that collisions are rare and unlikely to arise. If they do arise, it is easier to handle the situation at that time. Pessimistic locks and deadlock resolution require considerable programming and computer resources to handle correctly. Particularly in distributed database environments, it is often easier and faster to use optimistic locking.

The key to understanding optimistic locks is to realize that they are not really locks; the DBMS lets your program read any piece of data needed. When your program attempts to change the data, the DBMS rereads the database and compares the currently stored value to the one it gave you earlier. If there is a difference between the two values, it signifies a concurrency problem because someone else changed the data before you were able to finish your task. The DBMS then raises an error and expects your program to deal with it. In summary, optimistic locking can improve performance, but it requires you to deal with potential collisions. Figure 7.19 outlines the basic process.

The preferred solution to collisions using optimistic locks is to rollback any changes you have already made, and restart your code to read the current value from the database, recompute your changes, and write the new value to the database. Consider the example of the orders in Figure 7.20. The function first reads the current value of the balance into memory. After completing some other tasks, it attempts the UPDATE command, with one twist. It specifies that the UPDATE command only applies to the row with the given Account Number and with the original Amount value. If the value was changed

FIGURE 7.19
Optimistic locking process. The steps assume that concurrency problems will not arise. If another transaction does change the data before this transaction finishes, the code receives an error message and must restart.

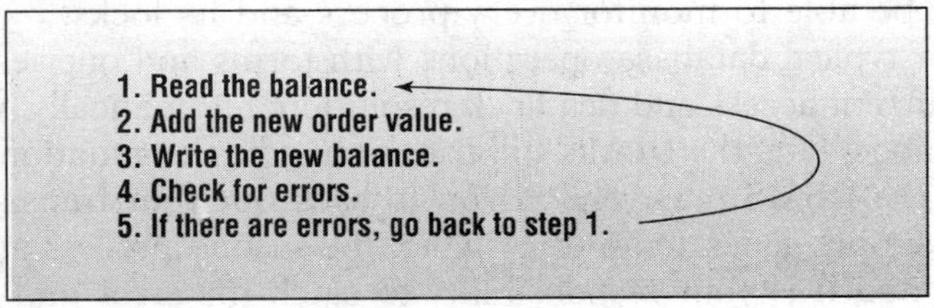

FIGURE 7.20
Optimistic concurrency with SQL. Keep the starting value within memory and then only do the update if that value is unchanged. If another transaction changed the data before this one completes, go back and get the new value and start over.

```
CREATE FUNCTION ReceivePayment (
 AccountID NUMBER, Amount Currency) RETURNS NUMBER
oldAmount Currency;
testEnd Boolean = FALSE;
BEGIN
 DO UNTIL testEnd = TRUE
 BEGIN
  SELECT Amount INTO oldAmount
  WHERE AccountNumber = AccountID;
  ...
  UPDATE Accounts
  SET AccountBalance = AccountBalance - Amount
  WHERE AccountNumber = AccountID
  AND Amount = oldAmount;
  COMMIT;
  IF SQLCODE = 0 And nrows > 0 THEN
   testEnd = TRUE;
   RETURN 0;
  END IF
  --keep a counter to avoid infinite loops
 END
END
```

by a second transaction, this UPDATE command will not alter any rows. The error test following the UPDATE command will recognize if the changes were successful or not. If successful, the routine is done and it exits. If the changes failed, you have complete control over what to do. In this case, it makes sense to go back and pick up the newly revised Amount and try again. To be safe, you should add a counter to the number of retries. If the number reaches too large of a number, this routine should simply give up and produce an error code indicating that it is not possible to update the data at this time.

One of the strengths of this approach is that it works even if multiple distributed databases are involved in the transactions. However, it does require that programmers write and validate the proper code for every single update. Consequently, it makes sense to create a code library that contains a generic version of the UPDATE command that can be called for almost any transaction.

The other powerful feature of this approach is that the program code can contain relatively sophisticated analysis to automatically handle common update problems. In this example, the pessimistic lock most likely prevented the transaction and required a clerk or customer to retry it later. On the other hand, the optimistic lock realized that it simply had to get the new balance and use it to compute the final amount. No intervention and almost no delay were involved.

ACID Transactions

The concept of integrity is fundamental to databases. One of the strengths of the database approach is that the DBMS has tools to handle the common problems. In terms of transactions, many of these concepts can be summarized in the acronym *ACID*. Figure 7.21 shows the meaning of the term.

FIGURE 7.21
ACID transactions. The acronym highlights four of the main integrity features required of transactions.

- **Atomicity: All changes succeed or fail together.**
- **Consistency: All data remain internally consistent (when committed) and can be validated by application checks.**
- **Isolation: The system gives each transaction the perception that it is running in isolation. There are no concurrent access issues.**
- **Durability: When a transaction is committed, all changes are permanently saved even if there is a hardware or system failure.**

Atomicity represents the central issue that all parts of a transaction must succeed or fail together. **Consistency** means that all data in the database must ultimately be consistent. Even though there might be temporary inconsistencies while a transaction is being processed, in the end, the database must be returned to a consistent state. This status should be able to be tested with application-defined code. For example, referential integrity must be maintained after a transaction is completed. **Isolation** means that concurrent access problems are prevented. Changes by one transaction do not result in errors in other transactions. Note that transactions are rarely completely isolated: they might encounter pessimistic or optimistic locking messages that need to be handled. **Durability** indicates that committed transactions are lasting. Once the transaction commits a change, it stays changed. This concept is critical in the face of hardware and software failures and is more difficult to maintain in a distributed database environment. Most systems ensure durability by writing changes to a log file. Then, even if a hardware failure interrupts an update, the changes will be finished when the system is restarted. Importantly, once the COMMIT statement is accepted, the DBMS cannot rollback the changes.

With SQL 99, the START TRANSACTION and SET TRANSACTION commands can be used to set the isolation level. In increasing isolation order, the four choices are READ UNCOMMITTED, READ COMMITTED, REPEATABLE READ, and SERIALIZABLE. These levels are supposed to be used to prevent different types of concurrency problems, but rarely is there a need for the intermediate levels, so many systems provide only the first and last.

The READ UNCOMMITTED level provides almost no isolation. It enables your routine to read data that another transaction has altered but not yet committed. This problem is sometimes called dirty read because the value you receive might be rolled back and the value ultimately may be inaccurate. If you select this level, SQL will not allow your transaction to update any data, because it might spread a false number throughout the database. The READ COMMITTED level is similar to optimistic concurrency. It will prevent your transaction from reading uncommitted data, but the data might still be changed or deleted by another transaction before the first transaction completes.

The REPEATABLE READ level prevents specific data you are using from being changed or deleted, but does not resolve the problem of phantom data. Consider a transaction that computes the sum of quantity on hand if the

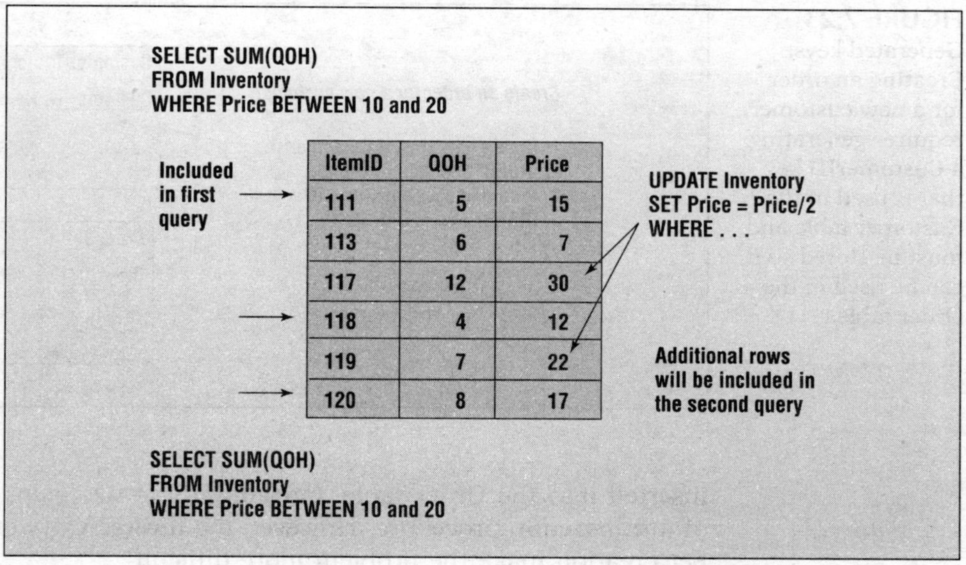

FIGURE 7.22
Phantom rows. The transaction on the left will initially select only three rows of data. When the second transaction runs, additional rows will match the criteria, so that the second time the query runs, it will return a different result.

price of an item falls within a specified range. Now, a second transaction reduces the prices of other items so that they now fall within the selected range. Reissuing the first command or creating a second command based on the same selection criteria will result in analyzing additional (phantom) rows of data. Figure 7.22 shows the process where the second transaction can cause new rows to meet the criteria, so that the first transaction now operates on a different set of rows.

The SERIALIZABLE isolation level prevents the phantom row problem by ensuring that all transactions behave as if they were run in sequence. However, keep in mind that this result is usually accomplished through the use of locks, so it requires database resources, and it does not guarantee that your transaction will be able to finish on the first try. You still need error handling to catch and resolve the problem when your transaction is blocked by another one.

Key Generation

As you know by now, the relational database relies heavily on primary keys, which must be unique. It can be difficult in business to guarantee that these keys are always created correctly. Hence, most relational databases have a mechanism to generate numeric keys that are unique. Although these methods work reasonably well for simple projects, you will eventually learn that generated key values present some challenges that must be handled with programming. Also, bear in mind that each DBMS uses a different mechanism to generate keys.

The main problem you encounter with generated keys is when you want to add a row to one table and then insert the matching key value into a second table. For example, when you add a new Customer, the system generates a CustomerID, which you need to insert into the Order table. Figure 7.23 shows the basic problem: the CustomerID key generated to create the new customer must be kept by the transaction procedure so that the key can be

FIGURE 7.23
Generated keys. Creating an order for a new customer requires generating a CustomerID key that is used in the Customer table and must be stored so it can be used in the Order table.

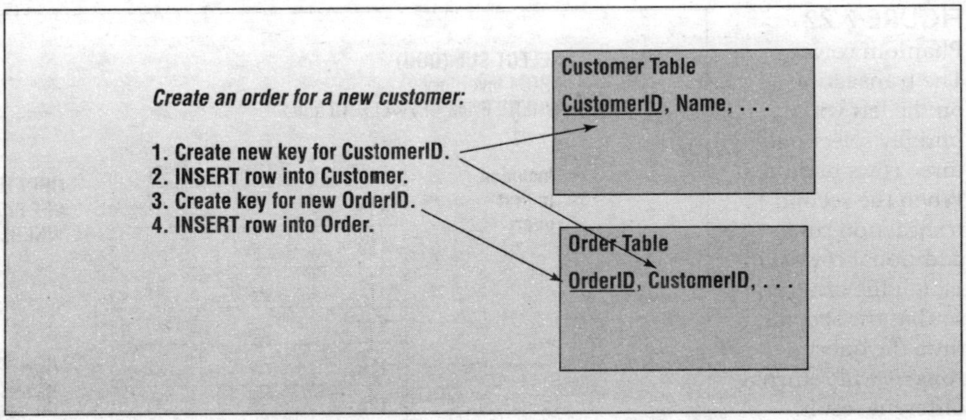

inserted into the Order table. Certainly these two steps must be made part of a transaction procedure. However, the diverse ways of handling the number creation make the problem more difficult.

Logically, generated keys could be created through two primary methods: (1) by an automatic method when a new row is added to a table, and (2) by a separate key generation routine. The advantage of the first method is that the process of adding a row to the initial (Customer) table is relatively simple. The drawback is that it is tricky to make sure you get the correct generated key to use in a second table. The second method solves the second problem, but makes it more difficult to create keys and requires programmers to ensure that the process is followed for every table and insertion operation.

As shown in Figure 7.24, if the DBMS automatically generates key values for each table, the code seems relatively simple. The complication is that problems arise when two transactions generate new key values on the same table at almost the same time. Step 2 can only pick up the most recently generated key value. If a second transaction generates a key value on the same table immediately after step 1, step 2 will receive the wrong value and the resulting sales order will be attributed to the wrong customer. To be safe, your code needs to verify after step 2 that the key value is correct. You need a SELECT INTO statement that retrieves the customer data for a newly created customer and compares the name, phone number, and other attributes. The alternative is to ignore the DBMS key value, and instead write a SELECT statement that always looks up the key value directly from the Customer table by specifying every customer attribute. The catch to this approach is that you must be certain that no two customers can ever have exactly the same two sets of attributes. Certainly it is possible that customers can have the same first and last names. But is it ever possible that they would have the same address and phone number? Be careful before you answer this question. What about a father and son with the same name living at the same address?

FIGURE 7.24
Auto-generated keys. The process seems relatively easy when the DBMS automatically generates keys. However, what happens at step 2 if two transactions generate a new key value on the same table at almost the same time?

1. INSERT row into Customer.
2. Get the key value that was generated.
3. Verify the key value is correct.
4. INSERT row into Order.

FIGURE 7.25
Key-generation routine. The steps are not difficult, but programmers must add them for every table and every routine that inserts data.

1. Generate a key for CustomerID.
2. INSERT row into Customer.
3. Generate a key for OrderID.
4. INSERT row into Order.

Because of the difficulties in obtaining an auto-generated key value, the second approach of calling a key generation routine has some benefits. Figure 7.25 shows the basic steps needed to create an order for a new customer. Notice that there is no uncertainty about the key value generated. The generation routine ensures that values are unique—even if two transactions request values at the same time. The drawback to this approach is that it is not automatic. This code must be added at every point where a key value is needed in the application.

Database Cursors

To this point, all of the procedures and functions have dealt with either DML statements or single-row SELECT statements. These statements either do not return values or they return only one row of data. This restriction simplifies the program logic and makes it easier to learn the foundations of SQL procedures. However, some applications will require more sophisticated queries: SELECT statements that return multiple rows of data.

Remember that SQL commands operate on sets of data—multiple rows at one time. What if you want more precise control? Perhaps you need to examine one row at a time to perform a complex calculation, compare some data from an external device, or display the row to the user and get a response. Or perhaps you need to compare one row of data to a second row. For example, you might want to subtract values across two rows. It is difficult to accomplish these tasks with standard SQL commands.

Cursor Basics

SQL does have a process that enables you to track through a set of data one row at a time. You create a **database cursor** that defines a SELECT statement and then points to one row at a time. A loop statement enables you to move the cursor to the next row and repeat your code to examine each row returned by the query.

Figure 7.26 shows the basic structure of a procedure to create a cursor and loop through the Customer table to calculate the total amount of money owed. Of course, this calculation can be done easier and faster with a simple SELECT statement. The goal here is to show the main structure of the code needed to implement a database cursor. The DECLARE CURSOR statement defines the SELECT statement that retrieves the rows to be examined. Although the example uses only one column, you can use any common SELECT statement including multiple columns, WHERE conditions, and ORDER BY lines. You must OPEN the cursor to use it, and eventually should CLOSE the cursor to free up database resources. When a cursor is first opened, it points to a location immediately before the first row of data. The FETCH statement retrieves one row of data and places the columns of data

FIGURE 7.26
SQL cursor structure. DECLARE, OPEN, FETCH, and CLOSE are the main statements in the SQL standard.

```
DECLARE cursor1 CURSOR FOR
  SELECT AccountBalance
  FROM Customer;
sumAccount, balance Currency;
SQLSTATE Char(5);
BEGIN
  sumAccount = 0;
  OPEN cursor1;
  WHILE (SQLSTATE = '00000')
  BEGIN
    FETCH cursor1 INTO balance;
    IF (SQLSTATE = '00000') THEN
      sumAccount = sumAccount + balance;
    END IF
  END
  CLOSE cursor1;
  --display the sumAccount or do a calculation
END
```

for that row into program variables. A loop is necessary to track through each row that matches the selection conditions.

Scrollable Cursors

By default, the FETCH command picks up the next row. If the FETCH command pushes the cursor past the end of the dataset, an error condition is created. You can use the WHENEVER statement to catch the specific error, or you can examine the SQLSTATE variable to see if an error was generated with the last SQL statement. A string value of five zeros indicates that the last command was successful.

Several options are available for the FETCH command to move the cursor to a different row. The common options are NEXT, PRIOR, FIRST, and LAST. These retrieve the indicated row. Figure 7.27 outlines the cursor procedure that begins at the last row and moves up to the first row. Note that you must declare the cursor as scrollable with the SCROLL keyword. Of course, it would be more efficient to simply sort the data in reverse order and then move forward; but the objective is to show that you can move in either direction. Additional FETCH scroll options include the ability to move to the first row (FETCH FIRST) and to jump to a specific row in the dataset. For example, FETCH ABSOLUTE 5 will retrieve the fifth row in the dataset. Since you rarely know the exact row number to retrieve, the relative scroll option is more useful. For instance, FETCH RELATIVE −3 skips back three rows from the current position.

FIGURE 7.27
FETCH options. A scrollable cursor can move in either direction. This code moves to the last row and then moves backward through the table. Other FETCH options include FIRST, ABSOLUTE, and RELATIVE.

```
DECLARE cursor2 SCROLL CURSOR FOR
SELECT ...
OPEN cursor2;
FETCH LAST FROM cursor2 INTO ...
Loop...
  FETCH PRIOR FROM cursor2 INTO ...
End loop
CLOSE cursor2;
```

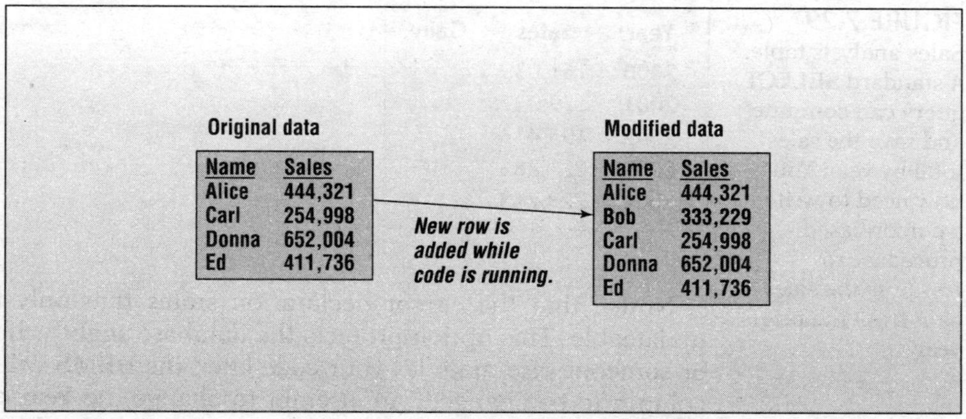

FIGURE 7.28
Transaction concurrency in cursor code. Your cursor code has tracked down through the data to Carl. It then tries to go back to the prior row with FETCH PRIOR. But, if another transaction has inserted a new row (Bob) in the meantime, your code will pick up that one instead of the original (Alice).

The ability to move backward in the list of rows highlights another transaction concurrency issue. What happens if you work your way down a set of rows and issue the FETCH PRIOR command? Most of the time, you would simply retrieve the row before the current one. But what happens if another transaction inserts a new row immediately before the FETCH PRIOR command is executed? Figure 7.28 shows the problem. Your code has tracked down to Carl, but a second process has inserted Bob into your list. The FETCH PRIOR command will return data for Bob instead of the data for Alice that you expected to see. The SQL standard solution to this problem is to make the dataset insensitive to other changes. You simply add a keyword to the cursor declaration (DECLARE cursor3 INSENSITIVE CURSOR FOR . . .). Effectively, the DBMS copies the results of the query into a temporary table that is not affected by other commands. Although this approach will work, it can be an expensive use of database resources. Instead, be sure to ask yourself why you need to move backward. In most cases, you will find that it is unnecessary. For example, if you want to calculate differences by subtracting the value on the current row from the value on the prior row, simply store the "prior" value in memory, then fetch the next row and perform the subtraction. There is no need to move backward and risk getting the wrong value.

You might notice that there is no procedure to find a row within the retrieved dataset and move the cursor to that row (such as a SEEK command). Although some systems provide this feature, it is rarely needed. Instead, you should create the WHERE condition to only retrieve exactly the rows you want.

Changing or Deleting Data with Cursors

A common situation that a cursor-based application encounters is the need to change or delete the data at the current row. For example, Figure 7.29 shows a table created to hold sales data for analysis. A standard SELECT command with a GROUP BY clause can compute the sales totals by year. You need to write a cursor-based procedure to compute the increase (or decrease) in sales for each year. The catch is that you need to store this computed value back into the table. To do that, you need to specify that the cursor is updateable, and then write an UPDATE statement that stores the calculation in the row currently pointed to by the cursor. Figure 7.30 shows the main code needed to perform the calculations.

FIGURE 7.29
Sales analysis table. A standard SELECT query can compute and save the sales total by year. You now need to write a cursor-based procedure to compute the sales gain from the prior year.

Year	Sales	Gain
2000	151,039	
2001	179,332	
2002	195,453	
2003	221,883	
2004	223,748	

Notice that the cursor declaration states that only the Gain column is updateable. This option protects the database slightly. If you make a mistake or someone else modifies your code later, the DBMS will only allow the Gain column to be changed. An attempt to change the Year or Sales column will generate an error. The other important element is the WHERE CURRENT OF cursor1 statement. This condition states that the row currently fetched, or pointed to by the cursor, is the one to be changed. The UPDATE statement will apply only to this row. An almost identical statement can be used to delete the current row (DELETE FROM SalesTable WHERE CURRENT OF cursor1).

Cursors with Parameters

Occasionally, you need a more dynamic query, where you want to pick the specific rows based on some variable within your procedure. For example, a user might enter a price, or your program compute a price based on some other query. Then you want to retrieve only the rows that are less than the specified price and perform some computation on those rows. You can enter local variables as parameters in the cursor query. Figure 7.31 shows the basic elements of the parameterized cursor. You enter the name of a variable within the cursor's SELECT statement. Within the procedure, you assign a value to this variable. The value might be computed from other variables, input by the user, or even retrieved from a different cursor or query. When

FIGURE 7.30
Cursor code for update. The FOR UPDATE option in the declaration enables the Gain column to be changed. The WHERE CURRENT OF statement specifies the row pointed to by the cursor.

```
DECLARE cursor1 CURSOR FOR
SELECT Year, Sales, Gain
FROM SalesTotal
ORDER BY Year
FOR UPDATE OF Gain;
priorSales, curYear, curSales, curGain
BEGIN
  priorSales = 0;
  OPEN cursor1;
  Loop:
    FETCH cursor1 INTO curYear, curSales, curGain
    UPDATE SalesTotal
    SET Gain = Sales - priorSales
    WHERE CURRENT OF cursor1;
    priorSales = curSales;
  Until end of rows
  CLOSE cursor1;
  COMMIT;
END
```

FIGURE 7.31
Parameterized cursor query. Your code sets the value of maxPrice through user input or calculation or another query. When this cursor is opened, the value is applied to the SELECT statement and only the matching rows are returned.

```
DECLARE cursor2 CURSOR FOR
SELECT ItemID, Description, Price
FROM Inventory
WHERE Price < :maxPrice;
maxPrice Currency;
BEGIN
  maxPrice = ... --from user or other query
  OPEN cursor2; --runs query with current value
  Loop:
    --Do something with the rows retrieved
  Until end of rows
  CLOSE cursor2;
END
```

the parameterized cursor is opened, the current value is substituted into the query, so that it returns only the rows that match the request. Parameterized queries in the cursor provide powerful tools to dynamically evaluate data automatically in response to other changes.

Merchandise Inventory at Sally's Pet Store

Handling inventory updates is often a tricky procedure in business database applications. In many situations, employees need to know the quantity on hand for a particular item. An employee may be looking at items to reorder, or a manager might want to know which items are overstocked and have not been selling fast enough. You have two basic choices in determining the quantity on hand in a database system. First, you could write a procedure that computes the current total on hand whenever it is needed. The routine would examine every purchase and sale of the item to reach the current inventory level. In a large application, this process might be slow. The second approach is to keep a running total of the quantity on hand in the inventory table. This value must then be updated whenever an item is purchased or sold. This second process provides the total very quickly but faces the drawback of some slightly complicated programming. Keep in mind that both methods also need an adjustment mechanism for "inventory shrink," to use the accountant's euphemistic term for inventory items that have disappeared.

Looking at the Merchandise table from Sally's Pet Store, shown in Figure 7.32, you will notice that it contains a column for QuantityOnHand, so the plan is to use the second inventory approach and keep an updated total for each item. Ultimately, you will need three sets of procedures: One to handle item purchases, one for item sales, and one to adjust for inventory shrinkage identified from physically counting the stock. The adjustment procedure is straightforward, but you have to work on the user interface to make it easy to use. The purchase and sale processes are similar to each other, so the discussion here will examine only the sale of an item.

When an item is sold, a new row is added to the SaleItem table keyed by the SaleID and ItemID. The row includes the quantity of the item being purchased, such as 10 cans of dog food. Whenever something changes in the SaleItem table, the total in the Merchandise table has to be adjusted.

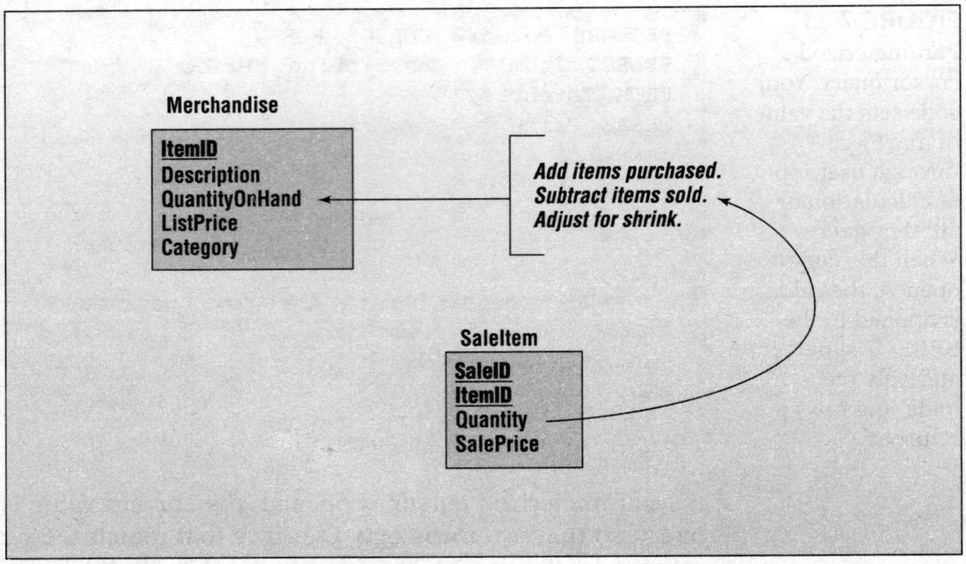

FIGURE 7.32 Processing inventory changes. When an item is sold, the quantity sold is entered into the SaleItem table. This value has to be subtracted from the QuantityOnHand in the Merchandise table.

Figure 7.33 shows the four basic changes that can arise in the SaleItem table. These events might not be immediately obvious, so consider the following business actions that drive them.

1. A new sale results in adding a row to the SaleItem table, so QuantityOnHand must be decreased by the quantity sold.
2. A clerical error or a customer changing his or her mind could result in the cancellation of a sale or of an item, so a row is removed from the SaleItem table. Any quantity that was already subtracted from the QuantityOnHand must be restored to the total.
3. An item could be returned, or the clerk might change the Quantity because of an error. The quantity adjustment must be applied to the QuantityOnHand total.

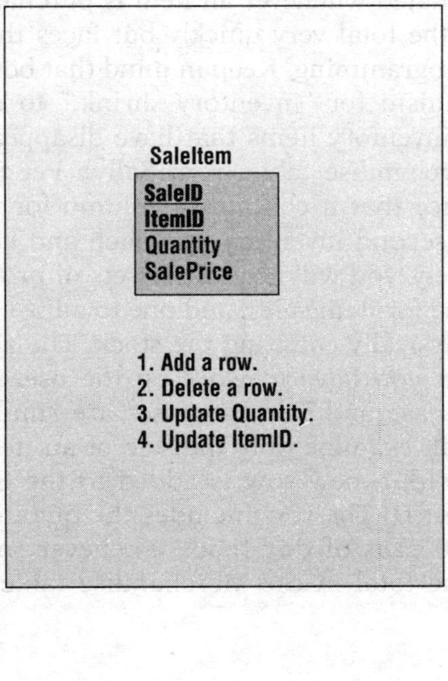

FIGURE 7.33 SaleItem events. Driven by business operations, four major events can arise in the SaleItem table. The QuantityOnHand must be altered in the Merchandise table for each of these events.

FIGURE 7.34
New Sale trigger. Inserting a new row triggers the event to subtract the newly entered quantity sold from the quantity on hand.

```
CREATE TRIGGER NewSaleItem
AFTER INSERT ON SaleItem
REFERENCING   NEW ROW AS newrow
FOR EACH ROW
  UPDATE Merchandise
  SET QuantityOnHand = QuantityOnHand – newrow.Quantity
  WHERE ItemID = newrow.ItemID;
```

4. An item might have been entered incorrectly, so the clerk changes the ItemID. The QuantityOnHand for the original ItemID has to be restored, and the QuantityOnHand for the new ItemID has to be reduced.

With database triggers, the entire process is not too difficult. If you are working with a DBMS without database triggers, the corresponding code has to be written into the forms; this process is not much more complex, but you need to validate each form to make sure it has the necessary code.

The first situation of adding a new row is straightforward. Figure 7.34 shows the logic needed for the databse trigger. Only one UPDATE statement is needed: Subtract the newly entered Quantity from the QuantityOnHand in the Merchandise table. If you are responsible for reviewing or fixing code in an existing application, you should find that this event is usually handled correctly. The problem is that many developers forget about the other events.

The second event of handling deleted rows is no more difficult than the code for inserting a row. Figure 7.35 shows the new trigger that is needed. Deleting a row from SaleItem indicates that the item was not really sold. Consequently, the trigger reverses the effect of the sale by adding the Quantity back to the QuantityOnHand.

The situation for changing data is more complex. You need to think about what it means when the Quantity value is changed. Say that the QuantityOnHand for the specified item begins at 50 units. Then, a SaleItem row was inserted with a Quantity of 10. The insert trigger fired and subtracted those 10 units, leaving the QuantityOnHand at 40 units. The clerk now changes the Quantity from 10 to 8. Since 2 fewer units were sold, the QuantityOnHand needs to be adjusted. As shown in Figure 7.36, the easiest way to understand the adjustment code is to think of it as adding the original 10 units back and then subtracting the new Quantity of 8 units. The net result will leave QuantityOnHand at 42 units.

The fourth change is one that is more difficult to portray. What happens if a clerk changes the ItemID value? The first complication you encounter is that database triggers might not have separate events for each column being

FIGURE 7.35
Delete Row trigger. This trigger reverses the original subtraction by adding the Quantity back in.

```
CREATE TRIGGER DeleteSaleItem
AFTER DELETE ON SaleItem
REFERENCING   OLD ROW AS oldrow
FOR EACH ROW
  UPDATE Merchandise
  SET QuantityOnHand = QuantityOnHand + oldrow.Quantity
  WHERE ItemID = oldrow.ItemID;
```

FIGURE 7.36
Update Quantity trigger. If Quantity is changed, you must add back the old value and then subtract the new value.

```
CREATE TRIGGER UpdateSaleItem
AFTER UPDATE ON SaleItem
REFERENCING    OLD ROW AS oldrow
               NEW ROW AS newrow
FOR EACH ROW
  UPDATE Merchandise
  SET QuantityOnHand = QuantityOnHand
    + oldrow.Quantity - newrow.Quantity
  WHERE ItemID = oldrow.ItemID;
```

changed. So you have to integrate the changes due to the ItemID into the previous code written to handle Quantity changes. Again, you need to think about the individual steps. Start with a QuantityOnHand of 50 for ItemID 1, then enter a sale of 10 items. The Insert trigger reduces QuantityOnHand to 40 units. Now the clerk changes the ItemID from 1 to 11. That means that no units of ItemID 1 were actually sold, so the 10 units have to be added back to its QuantityOnHand. Additionally, the 10 units have to be subtracted from the QuantityOnHand for ItemID 11. As shown in Figure 7.37, this trigger requires two separate UPDATE statements. Notice that the WHERE clause in the first statement uses the oldrow.ItemID and the second one uses the newrow.ItemID. Also, look more closely at the two SET statements. The first one adds the oldRow.Quantity; the second one subtracts the newRow.Quantity. Why is this difference important? First, it is possible that the clerk changed the Quantity along with the ItemID, and we need to make sure the old Quantity is used for the old ItemID. Second, and more importantly, this trigger also handles the simple change in Quantity, even if the ItemID is not changed. Assume the ItemID is set at 1 and is not changed. Start with a QuantityOnHand of 50 units, and an initial Quantity sold of 10, leaving a current QuantityOnHand of 40 units. Read through the code to see how it works if only the Quantity is changed from 10 to 8 units. First, the old Quantity (10) is added back to the QuantityOnHand. Second, the new Quantity (8) is subtracted, leaving 42 units on hand. This process is the same as that shown in Figure 7.36, but it is accomplished in two steps instead of one.

FIGURE 7.37
Final update trigger. If the ItemID is changed, you must restore the total for the original item and subtract the new quantity from the new ItemID.

```
CREATE TRIGGER UpdateSaleItem
AFTER UPDATE ON SaleItem
REFERENCING    OLD ROW AS oldrow
               NEW ROW AS newrow
FOR EACH ROW
BEGIN
  UPDATE Merchandise
  SET QuantityOnHand = QuantityOnHand + oldRow.Quantity
  WHERE ItemID = oldrow.ItemID;

  UPDATE Merchandise
  SET QuantityOnHand = QuantityOnHand - newRow.Quantity
  WHERE ItemID = newrow.ItemID;
  COMMIT;
END
```

Now you will have to write the same code for the purchase table (OrderItem). The logic is the same. However, there is a slight business complication in that you might want to wait to update the QuantityOnHand until the items actually arrive. If you do decide to wait, your primary initial trigger is not on the OrderItem INSERT event, but on the UPDATE event on the MerchandiseOrder table. Have the trigger look for an entry in the ReceiveDate column, and then do the QuantityOnHand updates.

Summary

Although SQL commands are powerful, you sometimes need a procedural language to gain detailed control over updates or to connect to other devices or applications. Depending on the DBMS, procedural code can exist within modules, within forms, or in external applications. Database triggers are an important application of procedural code. These procedures are triggered or executed in response to some database event, such as inserting, updating, or deleting data. Triggers can be used to enforce complex conditions or to execute business rules. For instance, a trigger might be attached to QuantityOnHand within an Inventory table to automatically notify a supplier when the value falls below a certain level. Cascading triggers arise when a change in one table fires a trigger that causes changes in additional tables, that might trigger even more events. Long cascades can be difficult to debug and use substantial server resources.

Transactions are critical applications in most business operations. They represent a collection of changes that must succeed or fail together. Setting start and ending points for transactions is an important step in application development to protect the integrity of the data. Concurrent access where multiple users attempt to modify the same data at the same time is another substantial threat to database integrity. Pessimistic locks have often been used to protect data through serialization so that only one transaction can see data at a time. However, multiple locks eat up resources and can lead to deadlock issues. Optimistic locks assume that collisions are unlikely, but code must be added to handle the situations when they do arise. The ACID acronym (atomicity, consistency, isolation, and durability) is a useful way to remember the main features desired of a DBMS to protect transaction integrity.

Generating keys is an important step in many relational databases, since it is difficult to trust humans to create unique identifiers. Two common methods are used to generate keys: (1) automatically create them when a row is added to a table, or (2) provide a separate function that generates keys on demand. Both methods create complications. The automatically generated keys are difficult to obtain and use in secondary tables. The generation functions require programmers to write code for every table and every insertion procedure.

Database cursors provide a method for your procedural code to retrieve multiple rows of data from a query and step through the rows one at a time. The cursor points to one current row that can be examined, modified, or deleted by your code. Scrollable cursors enable you to move forward or backward through the rows, but whenever possible, you should try to move in only one direction. With updateable cursors, your code can change or delete the data in the current row. With a parameterized query, your code can dynamically choose the rows to be retrieved in response to other conditions.

A Developer's View

Miranda learned that even a good DBMS often requires programming to handle some complex issues. In developing your application, you should examine all of the business processes and identify transaction elements. Also, be sure that your UPDATE and DELETE procedures can handle concurrency issues. Remember that a professional application anticipates and handles errors gracefully. Write data triggers or module code to automate basic processes and perform all needed calculations. Write additional cursor-based code if needed to perform advanced calculations.

Key Terms

atomicity, 282
cascading triggers, 272
concurrent access, 276
consistency, 282
database cursor, 285
deadlock, 278
durability, 282
isolation, 282
isolation level, 278
optimistic lock, 280
persistent stored module (PSM), 267
pessimistic lock, 278
procedural language, 266
serialization, 278
transaction, 274
trigger, 269

Review Questions

1. Why would you need a procedural language when SQL is available?
2. What is the purpose of data triggers?
3. Describe the sequence of the main data events.
4. What is the purpose of form events?
5. What are some of the main form events?
6. What is a transaction and why do they have to be defined by developers?
7. How do you start and finish a transaction?
8. How is pessimistic locking different from optimistic locks?
9. What code do you need to add to handle conflicts with optimistic locks?
10. What is an ACID transaction?
11. What are the most common methods used to generate keys?
12. How do you obtain the most recently generated key in the DBMS you are using?
13. What is a database cursor and why is it important?
14. What is the program logic to using a database cursor to alter data?

Exercises

1. Write a function to increase prices that accepts price as an input parameter. If the price is less than $10, the function adds 10 percent and returns the value. If the price is between $10 and $100, it adds 5 percent. Anything over $100 adds 2 percent. Test the function with a query.
2. Create a table that lists item category and the level of tax on that category. For example, food (0 percent), clothing (3 percent), entertainment (10 percent). Write a function with category and price as parameters. Compute and return the appropriate tax.
3. Create a data trigger that writes a row in a new table whenever employee salary is changed. Store the date changed, the employee, the old salary, and the new value.
4. Create a data trigger that will prevent anyone from increasing an employee salary by more than 50 percent.
5. Create a data trigger (or form code if triggers are not available) that adjusts inventory quantity on hand whenever an item is sold. You need a SaleItem and Item table.

6. Create the traditional bank account table (AccountID, CustomerID, TransactionDate, AccountType, Amount). Add a checking account and a savings account for the same person. Write the transaction code to safely transfer a specified amount from savings into checking.
7. Create a small table and build a form to edit data for that table. Write a procedure to change a value in the table. Set the form and write the code to correctly handle a pessimistic lock on the table.
8. Create a small table and build a form to edit data for that table. Write a procedure to change a value in the table. Set the form and write the code to correctly handle an optimistic lock on the table.
9. Create a small table that uses a generated key (for example, SalesOrder). Create a second table that includes that column as a foreign key (for example, OrderItem). Write code that enters a new row for the first table and uses the generated key to add a row to the second table.
10. Create a small table that lists sales by month and includes a column for PercentChange. Write a cursor-based procedure to loop through the table and compute the percent change from the prior month and store that value it the current row.

For the next five exercises, you will use a sample database that you create with the following tables:

```
Customer(CustomerID, LastName, FirstName, Phone, City,
AccountBalance)
Payment(PaymentID, CustomerID, DateReceived, Amount)
Item(ItemID, Description, ListPrice, QOH)
Sale(SaleID, CustomerID, SaleDate)
SaleItem(SaleID, ItemID, Quantity, SalePrice)
Shipping(City, Shipping)
```

11. Write a program that takes all of the sales and payments and computes the current AccountBalance for each customer and inserts the data into the Customer table.
12. Assume that all items start with 200 units on hand. Write a program that computes and stores the true quantity on hand for each time based on the total sales.
13. Write a program to calculate the difference in sales between Mondays and Tuesdays.
14. Write a program to update the Shipping table by the following percentages:

Madison	2%
New York	3%
San Francisco	4%
Chicago	2%
Other	5%

15. Create a form that enables the user to choose a City from the Shipping table, enter a percentage value to change the shipping charge, and click a button to have the Shipping value changed in the Shipping table.

Sally's Pet Store

16. Create a form that enables a manager to specify a quantity-on-hand percentage and a price reduction percentage. Write code that checks each merchandise item for sales (over the year). If the quantity on hand divided by the total sale of that item are less than the specified percentage, decrease its list price by the price percentage.
17. Create a form that has a text box for the user to enter an animal category and a percentage price increase. When the user clicks a button, update the list price of all the animals in the given category by the indicated percentage.

18. Using the appropriate query, write a program that will compute the change in sales revenue by month for each category of animal. For example; the user wants to know the percentage change in sales from January to February for cats. Write a program that will compute the changes and store the results in a new (temporary) table when the user clicks a button. Then display a graph of the results.
19. Write the code to increase quantity on hand when an item is purchased—specifically when the receive date is set. Be sure to handle it as a transaction, since quantity on hand can also be affected by sales.
20. The Pet Store is thinking about purchasing scanners to use at checkout. These scanners will pick up the ItemID of each merchandise item scanned. Assume that this data will trigger an event when an item is scanned. Write a function that can be called by this event. This function should create a new sale and store the data for the items sold. You can emulate the scanner trigger by creating a form with a control to select an ItemID and a button to fire the trigger.

Rolling Thunder Bicycles

21. Explain how the Rolling Thunder order form functions. In particular, why is code needed for the component choices? Outline the logic of the code used to handle the components. (Do not simply copy the code—describe each major section in a few sentences.)
22. Describe how the Rolling Thunder system estimates common dimensions (top tube length, chain stays, etc.) for bicycles that are not a standard size (e.g., 18.5-inch mountain bike).
23. A few states do not collect sales taxes on shipping charges, while a few require they be included. Modify the StateTaxRate table to handle this issue, and enter sample data. Write a function with parameters for the bicycle price, the shipping cost, and the state. This function will return the proper tax computation.
24. Write the proper code to increase the quantity on hand value for components when new purchases are received. Be sure to handle changes in values and to control for concurrent changes because the data can also be changed during a sale.
25. Create a query to compute sales by month for each model type. Create a temporary table to hold that data and to hold the percentage change. Write a program that executes the query, placing the data into the table. Then cursor-based code computes the percentage change in sales.
26. Write a transaction-based procedure to add a customer transaction for receipt of a new payment and update the BalanceDue in the Customer table.
27. Create a form that enables a manager to specify a value for quantity on hand, a year, and a percentage price change. Write a procedure that reduces the price of any component purchased before the selected year with a quantity on hand greater than the specified level.
28. Write a procedure to add an interest charge to customer accounts with a balance due. Make sure to handle concurrency/locking problems.
29. Write a program to automatically generate a new purchase order when quantity on hand falls below a specified level. Add the ReorderPoint column to the Component table and enter sample data.

Website References

Site	Description
http://www.acm.org/sigplan/	Association for Computing Machinery—Special Interest Group on Programming Languages (advanced).
http://support.microsoft.com/support/kb/articles/q115/9/86.asp	Avoiding common database programming mistakes.

Additional Reading

Baralis, E., and J. Widom. "An Algebraic Approach to Static Analysis of Active Database Rules." *ACM Transactions on Database Systems (TODS)* 25, no. 3 (September 2000), pp. 269–332. [Issues in database triggers and sequencing, but plenty of algebra.]

Ben-Gan, I., and T. Moreau. *Advanced Transact-SQL for SQL Server 2000,* Berkeley: Apress, 2000. [Discussion and examples of advanced topics for SQL Server.]

Feuerstein, S., B. Pribyl, and D. Russell. *Oracle Pl/SQL Programming,* 2nd ed. Cambridge, MA: O'Reilly & Associates, 1997. [Reference book on programming for Oracle.]

Gray, J., and A. Reuter. *Transaction Processing: Concepts and Techniques.* San Francisco: Morgan Kaufmann Publishers, 1993. [A classic reference on all aspects of transaction processing.]

ISO/IEC 14834. *Information Technology—Distributed Transaction Processing—The XA Specification,* 1996. [A discussion of the common method of handling transactions across multiple systems.]

Sanders, R., and J. Perna. *DB2 Universal Database SQL Developer's Guide.* Burr Ridge, IL: McGraw-Hill, 1999. [Using embedded SQL with IBM's DB2 database.]

Sceppa, D. *Microsoft ADO.NET (Core Reference).* Seattle: Microsoft Press, 2002. [Complete reference on using databases in the .NET framework.]

Sunderic, D., and T. Woodhead. *SQL Server 2000 Stored Procedure Programming.* Berkeley: Osborne McGraw-Hill, 2000. [One of many references providing an introduction to SQL Server programming.]

Chapter 8

Data Warehouses and Data Mining

Chapter Outline

What You Will Learn in This Chapter

A Developer's View

Miranda: Faster. Faster. Come on, run faster!

Ariel: What? Are you training for a marathon?

Miranda: No. It's just these queries they want me to write are taking forever to run. They worked OK when I tested them with small amounts of data. But now, I don't know.

Ariel: Maybe you just need a faster computer?

Miranda: No, I think I need a different system. These queries are retrieving data, but it is data from many different tables. And these managers want all of these strange subtotals.

Ariel: Wow! There are a lot of totals. How do you expect anyone to read those? I think I see four different levels of totals and that's on one page!

Miranda: Yes, and that's only part of what the managers want. I'm happy they are using the system, but I don't see how they can make any sense out of these reports. I think I might need a separate system to reorganize this data and create these reports for the managers. Then they want to do some type of statistical analysis as well!

Introduction

Relational database systems were designed to store large amounts of data efficiently. In particular, they are very good at quickly storing and retrieving basic transaction data. Look at the common Sale and SaleItem tables, and you will see data stored compactly. For example, the Pet Store SaleItem table has only four columns and they all contain simple numbers. An individual sale can be recorded or retrieved quickly. However, this structure causes problems for other types of queries. Queries that involve multiple tables use JOINs that can require the DBMS to match data values from millions of rows. Now ask the DBMS to analyze the data by computing subtotals on several different factors (such as employee, region, product category, and month). Computing breaks across many factors, multiple tables, and millions of rows of data can cause performance problems even on fast hardware. Vendors of database systems attempted to solve some of these problems by creating indexes on the tables. The indexes make it substantially faster for the DBMS to find individual rows of data within a table, and particularly to improve join performance. However, there is a trade-off: Adding indexes to a table speeds retrieval queries but slows down data updates and transactions because the indexes have to be continually rebuilt. This conflict has led to focusing the existing relational systems for **online transaction processing (OLTP)**, whereas new systems with different storage and retrieval systems are used for **online analytical processing (OLAP)**. Data from the OLTP is extracted and cleaned, and then it is placed in a data warehouse. The data warehouse is heavily indexed and optimized for data retrieval and analysis. Additional procedures and routines are available to analyze the data, support interactive exploration by managers, and statistically search it for meaningful correlations and information. Because the OLAP technologies are still evolving, there are few standards, and many tools are available.

Indexes

Although tables are often pictured as simple lists of rows and columns, a DBMS cannot simply store all data in sequential files. Sequential files take too long to search and require huge operations to insert new rows of data. Examine the short table of employees in Figure 8.1, and consider the steps involved to find the row where EmployeeID is 7. The DBMS would have to read each row sequentially and check the ID until it found the proper match. In this case, it would have to read 7 rows. On average, if there are *N* total rows, it takes about *N*/2 rows to find a match. If there are a million rows, a typical search would require reading 500,000 rows! Clearly, this method is not going to work for large datasets. The situation is even worse for inserting new rows of data—if you want to keep the list sorted. The system would have to read each row of data until it found the location for the new row, then continue reading every other row and copy it down by one row. Deletions are actually easy because the DBMS does not really remove the data. It simply marks a row as deleted. Later, the database can be reorganized or packed to remove these marked spaces.

Binary Search

Looking at the data, it is clear that the DBMS is not taking advantage of all of the information. In particular, if the data rows are sorted, there is a substantially faster search method. Figure 8.2 shows how to take advantage of the sorting. Think of the process as searching through a paper dictionary or a phone book. Instead of starting at the first page and checking each entry, you would open the book in the middle, then decide whether to search the first half or the second half of the book depending on what name you find in the middle. Finding the middle entry of Goetz, you know that Jones falls in the latter half of the data. With that one search, you instantly cut your search in half. Following the same process, you would divide the remaining entries in half and search only the appropriate section. In the example, only four attempts are needed to find the entry for Jones. This **binary search** process continues to divide the remaining data in half until the desired row is found. In general, with *N* total rows, a binary search will find the desired

FIGURE 8.1
Find an item in a sequential table. Even if you know the primary key value, the system has to start at the first row and continue until it finds the desired match. On average, with *N* total rows, it takes *N*/2 row retrievals to find a particular item.

ID	LastName	FirstName	DateHired
1	Reeves	Keith	1/29/2004
2	Gibson	Bill	3/31/2004
3	Reasoner	Katy	2/17/2004
4	Hopkins	Alan	2/8/2004
5	James	Leisha	1/6/2004
6	Eaton	Anissa	8/23/2004
7	Farris	Dustin	3/28/2004
8	Carpenter	Carlos	12/29/2004
9	O'Connor	Jessica	7/23/2004
10	Shields	Howard	7/13/2004

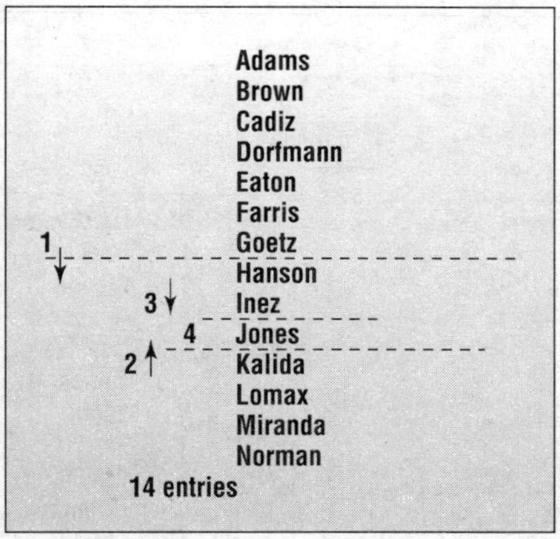

FIGURE 8.2
Binary search. To find the entry for Jones, divide the list in half. Jones falls below that value (Goetz), so divide the second part in half again. Jones falls above Kalida. Continue dividing the remaining sections in half until you find the matching row.

row in a maximum of $m = \log_2(N)$ attempts. Another way to understand this formula is to realize that because you cut the list in half each time, you are looking for m, where $2^m = N$. Now consider a table with a million rows of data. What is the maximum number of rows you have to read to find an entry? The value for m is 20, which is considerably better than the average of 500,000 for the sequential approach!

Pointers and Indexes

A binary search is a relatively good way to search data tables that are sorted, so it makes sense when you want to search by primary key, which is common for table joins. But what if the primary key is a numeric CustomerID and you want to search by LastName instead? How can the table be sorted in multiple ways? The answer lies with indexes and pointers.

Data is not actually stored in tables. It is usually broken into pieces and stored within a special file. When it is stored, each piece (perhaps an entire row) is placed at an open location and given an address. The address is a **pointer** that tells the operating system exactly where the piece of data is stored. It might be as simple as an offset number that specifies the number of bytes from the start of the file. Figure 8.3 shows that indexes can be created using the column to be searched (ID or LastName) along with the address pointer. The indexes are independent and have been sorted and so can be accessed quickly. As soon as the appropriate entry is found, the address pointer is passed to the operating system and the associated data is immediately retrieved. In practice, even the indexes are not stored sequentially. They are generally stored in pieces as B-trees. B-trees can be searched at least as quickly as can be done with a binary search, and they make it relatively easy to insert and delete key values. You can create indexes in SQL using the CREATE INDEX command.

Bitmap Index and Statistics

Some vendors provide highly compressed bitmap indexes for large tables. With a **bitmap index** each data key is encoded down to a small set of bits. The bitmap (binary) image of the entire index is usually small enough to fit in RAM. High-speed bit operations are used to make comparisons and search

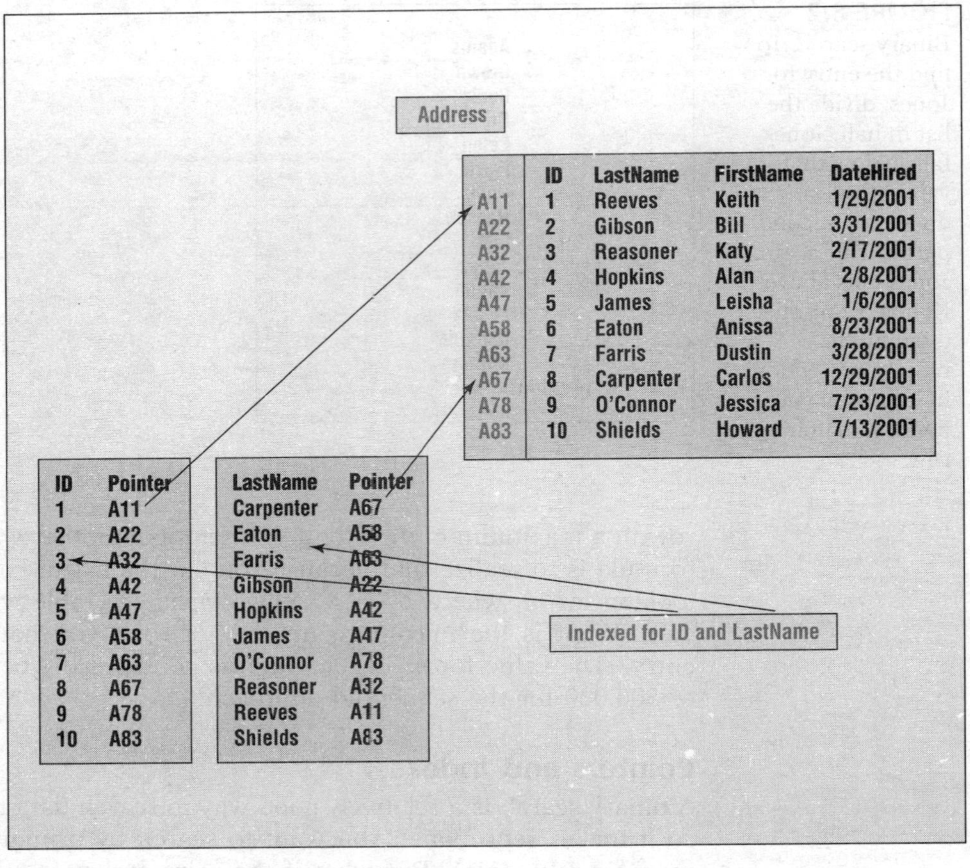

FIGURE 8.3
Pointers and indexes. Each piece of data is stored in a location with a specific address. An index consists of the column value to be searched along with the pointer to the rest of the row. Multiple indexes can be assigned to a table and quickly searched.

for key values. Hence, the bitmap indexes are extremely fast. Bitmap indexes are particularly useful for columns like secondary keys that contain large amounts of repeating data. They should not be used for a column that contains all unique values. For example, in a typical SaleItem(<u>SaleID</u>, <u>ItemID</u>, Quantity) table, you could consider using a bitmap index for the SaleID and ItemID columns. But you would not want to use a bitmap index for the SaleID column in the Sale table.

Some database systems also provide more sophisticated indexing methods. These methods examine the data within the indexed columns and store statistics on the structure of the data. For example, primary keys are unique within the main table. But a foreign key could appear several times in a table. For example, a CustomerID of 1173 occurs only once in the Customer table, but many times (once for each Sale) in the Sale table. If the DBMS knows which values occur most often in a table, it can use the statistics to search the data more efficiently. In particular, if it knows that one of your WHERE conditions has only a limited number of matches in a table, it can apply that condition first, thereby making it much easier and faster to join the result to other tables.

Problems with Indexes

Consider a table in which 10 indexes are defined. When a new row of data is added to the table, every index has to be modified. At a minimum, the database has to insert a new row into each of the 10 indexes. In most cases, it will also have to reorganize each index. This issue is the heart of the problem of deciding how to improve the performance of your application. By creating an index, you substantially improve the ability to search a data table. But for every index you create, the application will slow down every time you add new data or modify indexed columns. So your big decision is which columns to index.

The first step in the decision is to index only the columns that require random searches. The most important columns are the ones that are used to join tables in major queries. You could identify the queries that are commonly used in your application. Second, index the columns used in the JOIN condition. However, to be safe, you also need to identify the tables that experience rapid changes. Go to those tables and remove as many indexes as possible. The third step is to test your application with large amounts of sample data and heavy usage. Look for sections or forms that perform slowly. Then check to see whether you can speed up the access with an index. Test the index and the overall application to see whether it interferes with other components. Use indexes only if they provide a clear and significant improvement in performance in a critical area of the application. The fourth, and probably most important, step is to get a performance analyzer tool for your DBMS. A good analyzer can monitor usage, identify bottlenecks, and suggest which columns should be indexed.

Data Warehouses and Online Analytical Processing

Ultimately, the trade-offs with indexes can be insurmountable. To perform complex searches, you need many indexes on every table. But too many indexes slow down the transaction processing. Consider that a typical organization has data stored in several different databases and sometimes other files. Obviously, the transaction systems need priority—without them, the business cannot operate. But managers increasingly need complex analyses of data. The solution: Keep the transaction systems and create a new database for managers to perform online analytical processing.

Increasingly, managers want more than the traditional reports that are produced by OLTP systems. Managers want the ability to interactively examine the data. They do not always know what questions to ask or what they are looking for. They need the ability to quickly look at different views of the data. These types of queries can involve huge amounts of data and require JOINs across multiple tables. Fortunately, the access is almost always read-only—very little data is altered—and read-only queries can be several times faster than updateable queries. But the JOINs still take time to build with hundreds of tables and millions of rows of data. Additionally, tricks that can speed up the queries, such as indexing, will slow down the transaction processing.

Data Warehouse Goals

Many organizations have chosen to avoid these conflicts by creating a second copy of the database. A **data warehouse** holds a copy of the transaction data in a special database that is dedicated to answering managerial queries. Data may come from various sources, but all of it has been cleaned so that

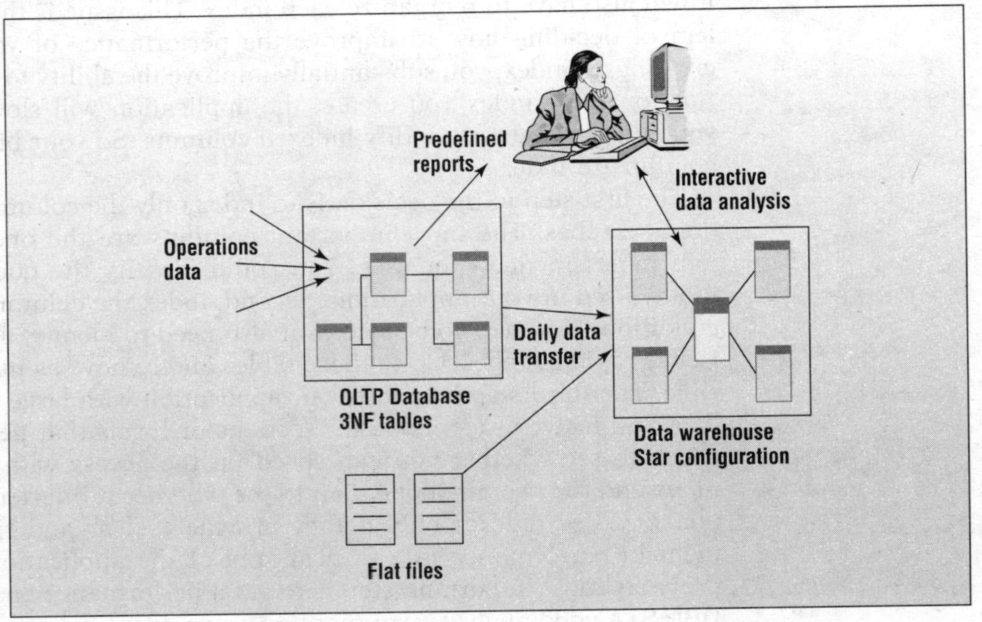

FIGURE 8.4
Data warehouse. Data from the OLTP system and other sources is cleaned and transferred into a data warehouse on a regular basis. The data warehouse is optimized for interactive data analysis.

it is consistent and meets referential integrity constraints. Multiple indexes are built on every table to improve the performance of JOINs. Special functions and query controls are included to rapidly create different views of the data. Generally, data is transferred from the transaction system once or twice a day and moved in bulk to the data warehouse. Additionally, data warehouses might be denormalized so that data is actually duplicated to improve retrieval performance.

The basic concepts of a data warehouse are shown in Figure 8.4. The transaction databases continually collect data and produce basic reports, such as inventory and sales reports. The data warehouse represents a separate collection of the data. Although it might use the same DBMS, it requires new tables. On a regular basis, data is extracted from the transaction databases and from other files. This data is checked to make sure it is consistent; for example, all of the key values must match for referential integrity. Then it is added to the data warehouse, which usually does not store data in normalized tables. Instead, it has special structures like the star configuration. In these cases, data is often duplicated. For example, the same city and state combination may show up in thousands of data records.

Online analytical processing is usually related to data warehouses, but technically, you can build OLAP systems on transaction databases without using the intermediate data warehouse. *OLAP* is a relatively new term so there are different interpretations of which features are included. A bigger challenge is that each vendor offers different technology and different implementations. In general terms, OLAP consists of a set of tools that makes it easier to analyze and compare data in the database.

Once the data warehouse is established, many tools are available to search it. Some people might use basic SQL queries and gradually refine their search. Others might use spreadsheets to extract and analyze the data. More sophisticated approaches use data mining techniques. **Data mining** consists of using automated tools to search for hidden patterns in the data.

Some tools include statistical methods (e.g., regression, discriminant analysis), pattern recognition (e.g., neural networks), and database segmentation (e.g., k-means, mixture modeling, and deviation analysis). These tools generally require substantial computing power and extremely high-speed data retrieval. Even with current high-speed systems, many of the techniques would need days or weeks to analyze some of the large datasets that exist. The point is that if users want to work on this type of analysis, the databases will have to be configured and tuned to their specific needs.

Data Warehouse Issues

Despite advances in database management systems and improvements in computer hardware, some queries take too long to run. Additionally, many companies have data stored in different databases with different names and formats, or even data stored in older files. The purpose of a data warehouse is to create a system that collects this data at regular intervals, cleans it up to make it consistent, and stores it in one location. A second primary goal of a data warehouse is to improve the performance of OLAP queries. In most cases, performance is improved by denormalizing the data. Joining tables is often the most time-consuming portion of a query, so new data structures are created that perform all of the JOINs ahead of time and store redundant data into fewer tables.

Three main challenges exist in creating a data warehouse: (1) Setting up a transfer system that collects and cleans the data, (2) Designing the storage structure to obtain the best query performance when handling millions or billions of rows of data, and (3) Creating data analysis tools to statistically analyze the data. Most companies choose to purchase data mining software for the third step. Few organizations have programmers with experience writing detailed statistical analysis procedures, and several companies sell prepackaged tools that can be configured to search data for patterns. The second issue—OLAP design—is discussed in the next section.

Cleaning and transferring data is often the most difficult part of establishing a data warehouse. Figure 8.5 shows the process known as **extraction, transformation, and transportation (ETT)**. You will quickly find that most companies have many different databases, with different table and column names, and different formats for the same type of data. For instance, one database might have a column Customers.LastName declared at 20 characters, and a second database uses Clients.LName set at 15 characters. The process of extracting data from these sources needs to be automated as much as possible; it is too hard and too expensive to try to clean data by hand. So you often have to write complex queries to merge data from different sources. In this small example, you would probably import one table (e.g., Customers), and then run a NOT IN query to get the list of names that are in the Clients table but not in the Customers table. These new names would then be added to the data warehouse. Some of the DBMS vendors have created import tools that will help you automate these data comparisons, but ultimately, most companies end up writing custom code to handle this complex process. A key element in the process is to extract the data from the OLTP systems without interfering with the ongoing operations. Specialized tools and queries utilizing parallel processing on multiple-processor machines are often used in this step, but the details depend on the DBMS, the hardware, and the database configuration.

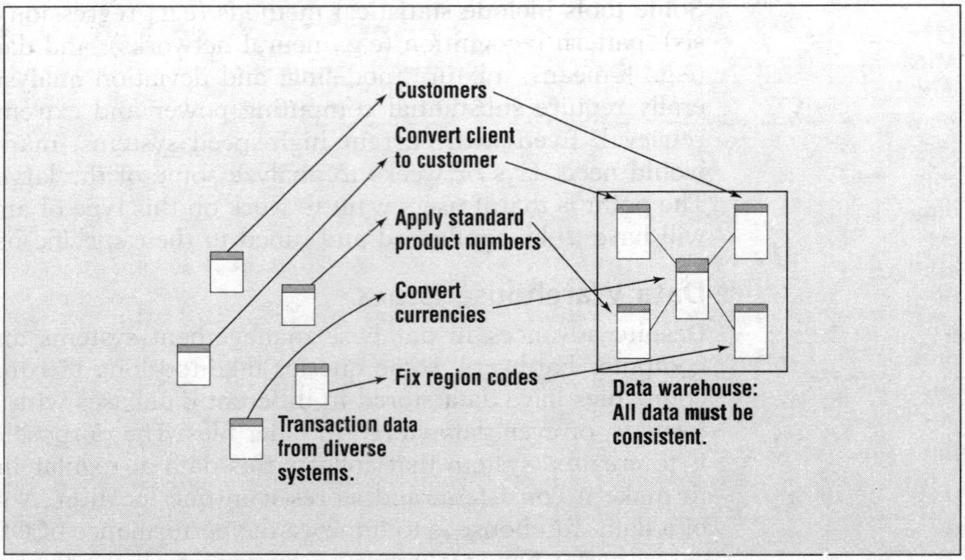

FIGURE 8.5 Extraction, transformation, and transportation (ETT). Transaction data usually has to be modified to make it completely consistent. This process must be automated so it can run unattended on a regular schedule.

One method that can sometimes be used to reduce the data volume is to extract and transfer only data that has been changed since the last transfer. However, this process requires that the OLTP system track the date and time of all changes. Many older systems do not record this information for all elements. For instance, a sales database has to record the date and time of a sale, but it probably does not record the date and time that a customer address was changed.

Transforming the data often involves replacing Null values, converting text to numbers, or retrieving a value from a joined table and updating a value in the base table. All of these operations can be handled by SQL statements, and you will have to create modules that can be executed on a regular basis to extract the data, clean the data, and insert it into the new database.

OLAP Concepts

A more specific description of OLAP is that most tools depict the data as multidimensional cubes. Managers use specific tools to examine various sections of the data. To illustrate the process, consider a simple example from the Pet Store database. Managers are interested in sales of merchandise. In particular, they want to look at sales by date, by the category of the item (cat, dog, etc.), and by the location of the customer. The attribute they want to measure is the value or amount of the items sold, which is the price times the quantity. Figure 8.6 shows how this small query could be pictured as a three-dimensional cube. The OLAP tools enable managers to examine any question that involves the dimensions of the cube. For instance, they can quickly examine totals by state, city, month, or category. They can look at subtotals for the different categories of products or details within individual states. The tools can provide detail items that can be pictured as a slice of the cube, or they can provide subtotals of any section.

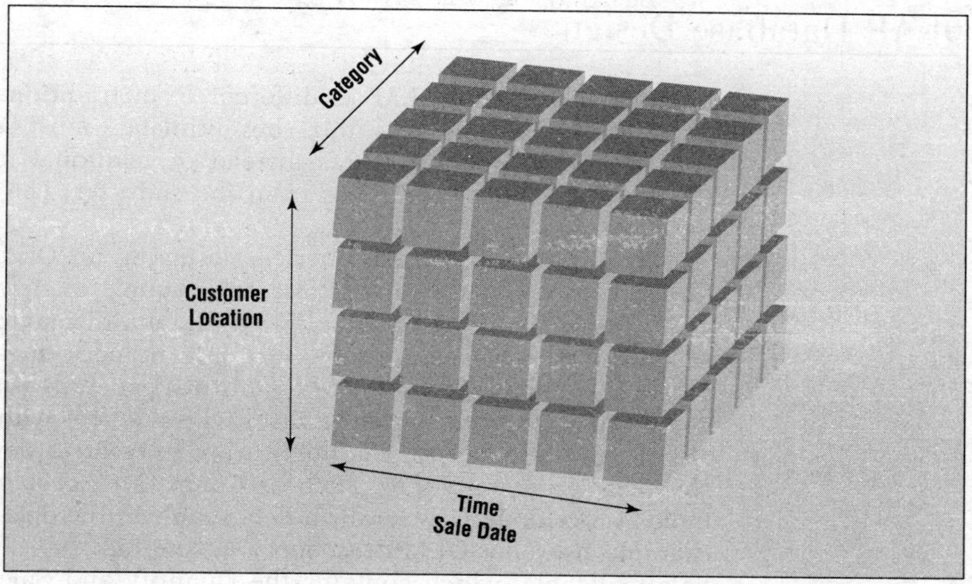

FIGURE 8.6
Multidimensional cube for Item Sales. Managers are interested in various combinations of the dimensions, for example, total item sales of dog items in the last quarter. OLAP tools rapidly provide answers to questions involving any perspective of this cube.

The most useful OLAP tools provide interactive capabilities to help the managers look at the data from any perspective. These tools generally start with summary totals, and then let the manager **drill down** to get more detail. In the example, a manager looking at totals for the year could drill down and get values for the quarter, then the month, and even a specific day. The opposite of drill down is to **roll up** the data into totals or averages. Instead of looking at detail sales for a given city, the manager might want to see the totals for the entire state. The terms are illustrated in Figure 8.7.

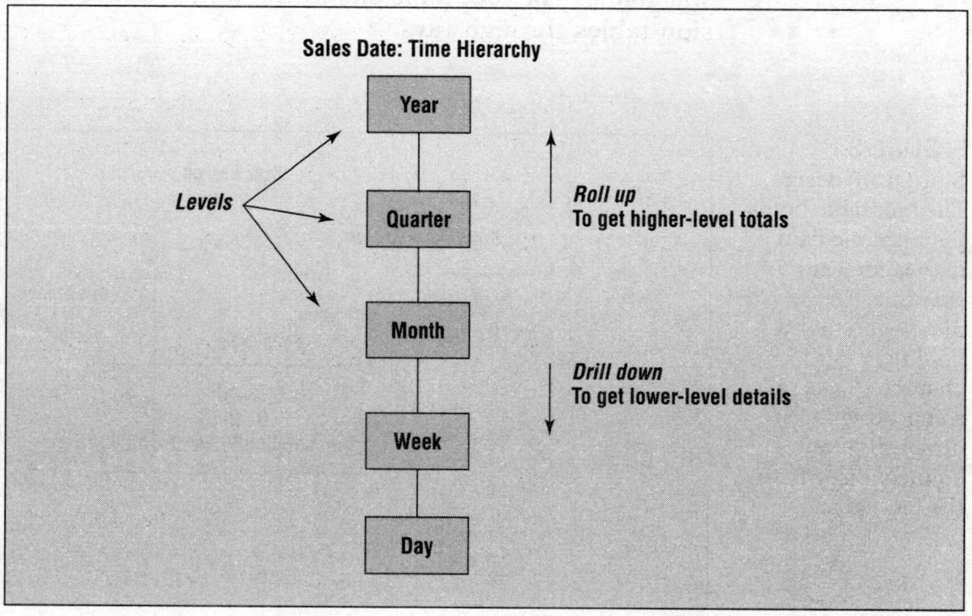

FIGURE 8.7
Drill down and Roll up. In a given dimension, drill down provides more detail. Roll up aggregates the values from subcategories.

OLAP Database Design

Database design for OLAP is different from traditional database design. Some of the concepts are similar, but ultimately, most OLAP tools store the data in these cube structures instead of relational tables. Additionally, OLAP design hides table joins from the end user. The manager sees only the cube.

If you understand basic queries, designing an OLAP cube is straightforward. However, you need to learn a couple of new terms and understand the basic idea of a cube. First, all data displayed in an OLAP cube is known as a measure. A **measure** is a numeric measurement of some attribute, such as sales value or quantity. It generally is selected to be some detail attribute from a table (a SELECT statement without a GROUP BY), although in some cases, you might want to create a new query to perform some basic computations, such as Count. Measures come from the fact table. A **fact table** is generally a detail table in the database. The Pet Store example uses the OLAPItem query as the fact table. It is based on the SaleItem table, which contains the Quantity and SalePrice of each item sold. The Amount column is a computed column that is calculated as Quantity * SalePrice. Generally, the fact table contains one or two pieces of data the managers want to examine, and then several columns that are foreign keys.

The second step is to choose the attributes that form the sides of the cube. Each attribute or side is called a **dimension.** The dimensions are attributes chosen from other tables. These dimension tables must be related to the fact table. Usually, they are joined to the foreign keys in the fact table. In theory, two OLAP designs exist: (1) All of the dimension tables are joined directly to the fact table—called a star design; or (2) At least one dimension table is joined through a second table before being joined to the fact table—known as a snowflake design. Figure 8.8 shows a simple **star design.** If you add enough dimension tables, you will see the reason for the star name. The fact table sits in the center and is connected to the dimension tables through rays.

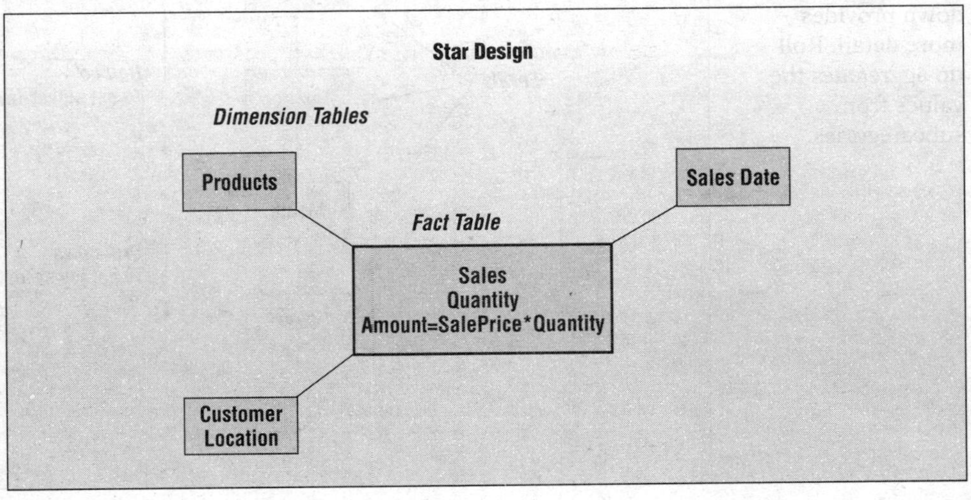

FIGURE 8.8
Star OLAP design. The fact table holds the numeric data managers want to examine. The dimension tables hold the characteristics. In a star design, all dimension tables connect directly to the fact table.

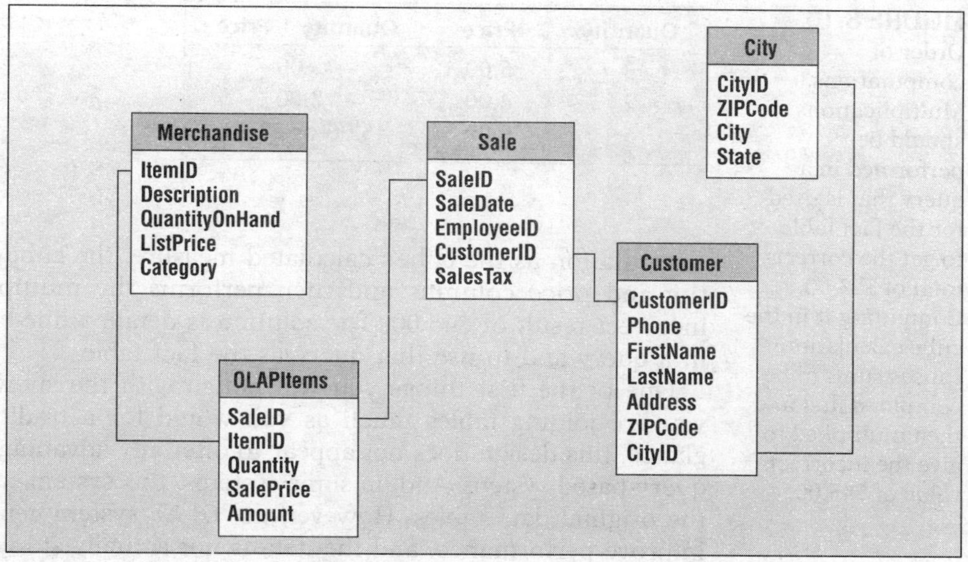

FIGURE 8.9
Snowflake design. It is less strict than the star design in that dimension tables can be joined to other dimension tables before being connected to the fact table.

The **snowflake design** has a more lenient definition in that the dimension tables may connect through other tables before being joined to the fact table. Figure 8.9 shows an example from the Pet Store database. If you place many tables in the diagram, you will see the reason for the name. The fact table sits at the center, like the star design, but dimension tables can extend outward through several levels. In a star design, all dimension tables connect directly to the fact table with no intermediaries.

The cube displayed in Figure 8.6 is created from the snowflake design shown here. PeetSaleDate, Location, and Category are the three main dimensions used. The Quantity and Amount are the measures taken from the fact table that will be used to produce the subtotals by each dimension. PetSaleDate is actually the hierarchy of dates shown in Figure 8.7, so managers can examine sales at several different levels. Likewise, Location can be defined as a geographical hierarchy encompassing country, state, and city.

Remember that the fact table is based on a query that computes the Amount value. What happens if you build the cube using the original SaleItem table? Then you could only use Quantity and SalePrice as measures. It would be tempting to create a calculated measure: Amount2 = Quantity * SalePrice. However, this approach can lead to incorrect results. It is critical that you understand the difference between these two approaches. The correct method is to build a query for any computation that needs to be done on a line-by-line basis (Price * Quantity is a common example). If you wait and build it in the OLAP design cube as a calculated measure, then the cube will (1) slice the data, (2) subtotal any measures separately (Price and Quantity), then (3) perform your calculations: Sum(Price) * Sum(Quantity). So your calculations will be performed on data that has already been totaled. Figure 8.10 shows the difference with a small example. When you use a query for the fact table to compute the multiplication, the columns are multiplied first and then summed, giving the correct total or $23.00. If you use the original table as the fact table and specify the

Quantity	Price	Quantity * Price
3	5.00	15.00
2	4.00	8.00
5	9.00	45.00 or 23.00

FIGURE 8.10
Order of computations. Multiplications should be performed in a query that is used for the fact table to get the correct total of $23.00. Computing it in the cube calculation causes sums to be computed first and then multiplied to give the incorrect value of $45.00.

computation as the cube's calculated measure, the cube first adds the quantity and price columns and then performs the multiplication, giving the incorrect result of $45.00. The solution is detailed line-by-line computations in a query and to use that query as the fact table.

One of the first things you will notice with the snowflake design is that you are joining tables much as you would for a traditional query. At first glance, this design does not appear to offer any advantages over a traditional query-based system. And, in some systems, this system can be analyzed using the original data tables. However, the OLAP system generally adds items to improve performance, and the data is not actually stored in separate tables. For example, data may be duplicated, such as repeating customer data for every order. Or internal pointers might be created to provide fast links from the fact table to the dimension data. Remember that the cube is designed to retrieve data, not to make changes, so it avoids the problems with INSERT and DELETE on unnormalized data. In some systems, you can create snapshots of queries to produce the same effect.

OLAP Data Analysis

Once the cube is created and processed, the data is available for analysis and browsing by the end users. As shown in Figure 8.11, most systems provide some type of cube browser. The browser makes it easy for managers to quickly obtain subtotals by any dimension, or filter to see only some elements within a dimension. In fact, it is this screen that you need to consider when designing the cube.

The manager can drill down the rows of the data grid by double-clicking the levels. Specific locations can be selected to compare subtotals. Similarly, selecting new values in the drop-down boxes provide a different slice of data from the cube. Even for large data sets, results are quickly displayed.

On the desktop, Microsoft provides a powerful cube browser that can run inside of Excel, or even deliver interactive Web pages. A **PivotTable** is an interactive interface to a multidimensional cube. PivotTables are created on the users' machines—most users will build PivotTables inside of Microsoft Excel. This tool has several options and provides a great deal of flexibility for the user. It can connect to OLAP cubes and databases built on a variety of systems.

Figure 8.12 shows the PivotTable report for the Pet Store example. By clicking on a row or column dimension, managers can see detail or subtotals. They can also select specific items to include in the subtotals. Managers even have the flexibility to drag the dimensions around—to move them from columns to rows—or to change the order of the summations. Additional options provide other statistics, such as averages. A powerful graphics option makes it easy to create charts using the Excel interface that is familiar to most business managers.

FIGURE 8.11
An OLAP cube browser. The location dimension is shown in the table of data; you can expand it or see subtotals by clicking on the grid. The other two dimensions (Category and SaleDate) are selected from the drop-down boxes at the top of the form. Here, the time dimension is expanded to show the selection of the second quarter. When values are changed, the new totals are displayed immediately.

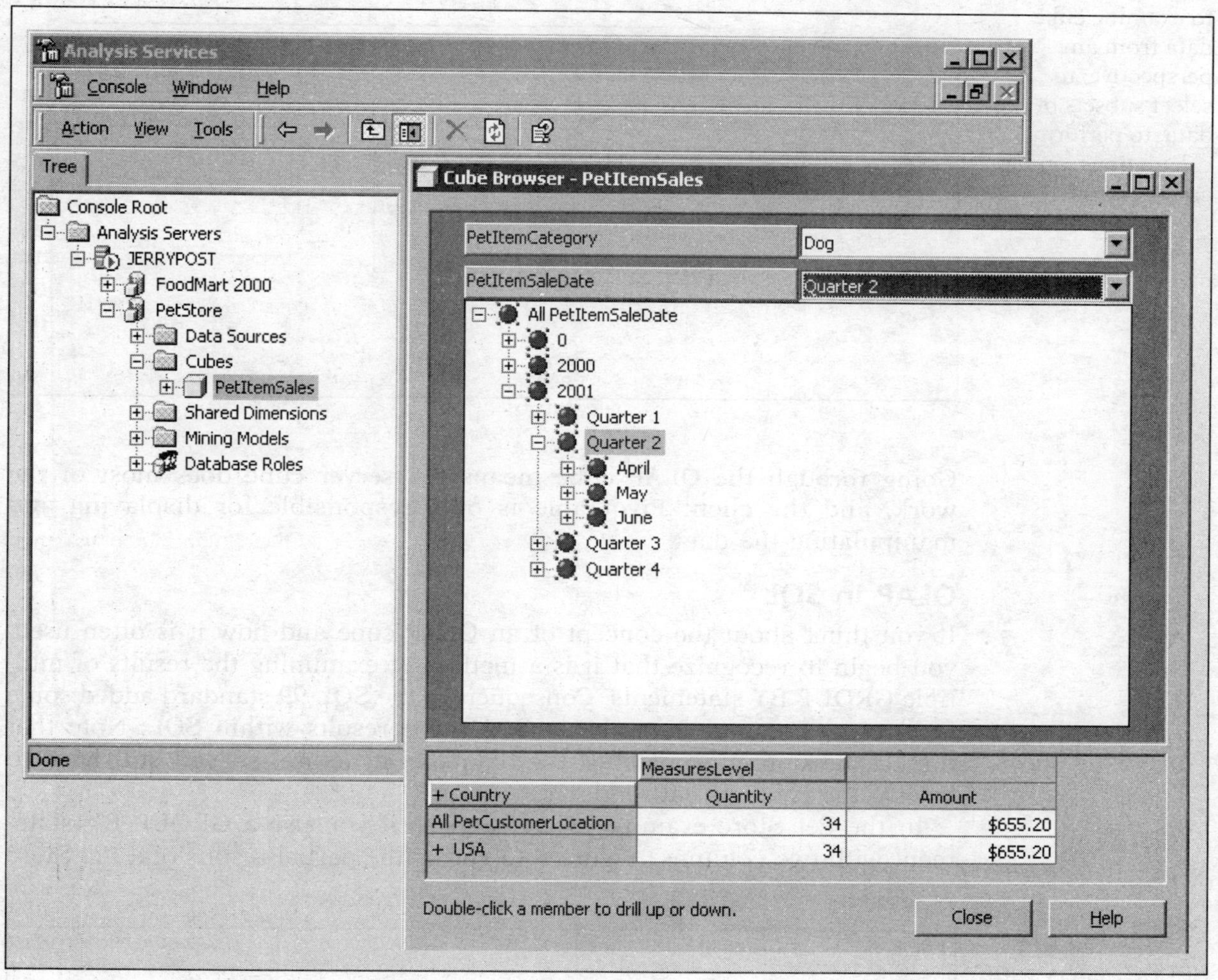

The PivotTable tool is powerful and can actually be used without an OLAP or data warehouse. However, when combined with an OLAP server, the PivotTable can run significantly faster. To create a PivotTable in Excel using the OLAP option, simply choose Data from the menu and then the PivotTable Report option. Once activated, the next step is to get the external data. Choose the OLAP Cubes tab; select a new data source. From here, the options are the same as a traditional PivotTable. Drag the dimensions to the row or column headings; then drag the fact table data (Amount) to the center of the table. From this point, several options can be used to customize the layout or create graphs. The important point is to select the OLAP Cube tab to retrieve the data from the cube instead of directly from the database. Pulling the data from the database means that the PivotTable does all of the work of extracting the data and performing computations.

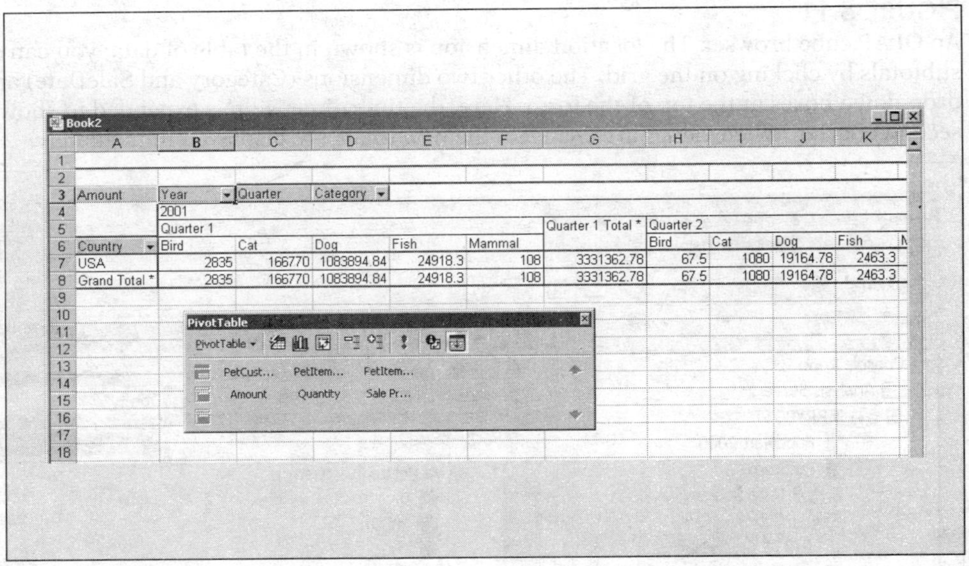

FIGURE 8.12 Microsoft PivotTable report. Pivot tools make it easy for managers to examine cube data from any perspective, to select subsets of the data, to perform calculations, and to create charts.

Going through the OLAP cube means the server cube does most of the work, and the client PivotTable is only responsible for displaying and manipulating the data.

OLAP in SQL

If you think about the concept of an OLAP cube and how it is often used, you begin to recognize that it is a method of examining the results of multiple GROUP BY statements. Consequently, the SQL 99 standard added some features to compute some basic OLAP-type results within SQL. Note that these extensions do not alter the database structure, so you still have to resolve the conflicts with indexes.

In the Pet Store example, what happens if you use a GROUP BY statement with two columns? Figure 8.13 shows the partial results of a Pet Store

FIGURE 8.13 SELECT query with two GROUP BY columns. You get subtotals for each animal category for each month. You do not see totals across an entire category (Birds for all months), and you do not get the overall total.

```
SELECT Category, Month(SaleDate) AS Month,
  Sum(Quantity * SalePrice) AS Amount
FROM Sale INNER JOIN (Merchandise
  INNER JOIN SaleItem
ON Merchandise.ItemID = SaleItem.ItemID)
ON Sale.SaleID = SaleItem.SaleID
GROUP BY Category, Month(SaleDate);
```

Category	Month	Amount
Bird	1	$135.00
Bird	2	$45.00
Bird	3	$202.50
Bird	6	$67.50
Bird	7	$90.00
Bird	9	$67.50
Cat	1	$396.00
Cat	2	$113.85
Cat	3	$443.70
Cat	4	$2.25

FIGURE 8.14
ROLLUP option. Adding the ROLLUP option to the GROUP BY statement generates the super-aggregate totals. In this case, the query provides totals for each Category element and the overall total. Notice that the corresponding Month is a null value.

```
SELECT Category, Month ..., Sum ...
FROM ...
GROUP BY ROLLUP (Category, Month ...)
```

Category	Month	Amount
Bird	1	135.00
Bird	2	45.00
...		
Bird	**(null)**	**607.50**
Cat	1	396.00
Cat	2	113.85
...		
Cat	**(null)**	**1,293.30**
...		
(null)	**(null)**	**8,451.79**

query that contains a GROUP BY computation with two columns (animal category and month sold). Notice that it provides a subtotal for each category element for each month. Assuming all animal types were sold in all months, you would see 12 values for birds, 12 for cats, 12 for dogs, and so on. What you do not get are **super-aggregate** totals, or totals for an entire category or across all rows. For instance, what is the total value of bird merchandise sold for the entire year?

ROLLUP

You could get these super-aggregate totals by using additional SELECT statements. However, SQL 99 added the ROLLUP option specifically to compute super-aggregate totals. Figure 8.14 shows the results for the Pet Store query. The total across all months is calculated for each element in the Category column. This total is displayed with a null value for the Month column. At the bottom, the overall total is displayed with two null values. Of course, the super-aggregate totals are not normally printed in bold, so they can be hard to spot. A bigger question is, What happens if there is a missing (null) value for some months? In the case of a missing date for a sale of bird items, the display would contain two similar lines with Bird as the category, a null/missing value for the Month, and some Amount. One value would be the total sales of bird products for months with missing dates. The second total would be the super-aggregate total across all months. But how do you know which is which? It is possible to scrutinize the numbers with totals and realize that the larger total should be the super-aggregate value. But with other functions, such as Average, there might not be any way to tell.

To help identify the super-aggregate lines, the SQL standard introduced the GROUPING function. As shown in Figure 8.15, the function usually returns a value of 0. When the row displayed is a super-aggregate computation, it displays a value of 1. In the example, the totals across months for each category produce a value of one for the GROUPING (Category) function. The overall total contains values of one in both indicator columns. This function could also be used in other computations or even in WHERE

FIGURE 8.15
GROUPING function. The GROUPING function returns a value of one when the row displayed is a super-aggregate for the selected column parameter.

```
SELECT Category, Month ..., Sum ...,
  GROUPING (Category) AS Gc,
  GROUPING (Month) AS Gm
FROM ...
GROUP BY ROLLUP (Category, Month ...)
```

Category	Month	Amount	Gc	Gm
Bird	1	135.00	0	0
Bird	2	45.00	0	0
. . .				
Bird	(null)	32.00	0	0
Bird	**(null)**	**607.50**	**1**	**0**
Cat	1	396.00	0	0
Cat	2	113.85	0	0
. . .				
Cat	**(null)**	**1,293.30**	**1**	**0**
. . .				
(null)	**(null)**	**8,451.79**	**1**	**1**

conditions. For instance, you might want to perform a computation with the super-aggregate totals.

CUBE

Looking at the results, it is clear that the ROLLUP option does not provide all of the information a manager might want. Notice that the super-aggregate totals only apply to the Category column in the examples. There are no corresponding totals for the Month column, which would represent sales of all categories for a given month. Of course, you could obtain those totals if you rewrite the query and reverse the order of the Category and Month columns in the GROUP BY clause.

The CUBE option provides the solution. The CUBE option is similar to ROLLUP, but it computes and displays the super-aggregates for all GROUP BY columns. In Figure 8.16, notice that the only change to the SQL was replacing the ROLLUP keyword with CUBE. The result still includes the super-aggregate totals across months for each category. These totals have a value of 1 for the Gc indicator column. But the query also produces the super-aggregate totals for each month across all categories of products. The values for the three months are displayed near the bottom of the results. Notice the null value under Category, and the Gm column value of 1 indicating that it is the super-aggregate total for the month.

Because of these additional totals, you will most likely use the CUBE option more often than ROLLUP. However, if you add several columns to the GROUP BY statement, you could get so many subtotals that you might prefer to use ROLLUP to simplify the display.

The SQL standard provides additional options, including the ability to create CUBEs or ROLLUPs based on the combined value from multiple columns. You can also use GROUPING SETS to hide the detail subtotals and only display the super-aggregate totals. As shown in Figure 8.17, the SQL is straightforward. The GROUPING SETS lets you specify the super-aggregate

FIGURE 8.16
CUBE option. The CUBE option computes super-aggregate values for all columns in the GROUP BY statement. The rows near the bottom with the Gm indicator value of 1 are the totals by month for all categories of products.

```
SELECT Category, Month, Sum, GROUPING (Category)
  AS Gc, GROUPING (Month) AS Gm
FROM ...
GROUP BY CUBE (Category, Month ...)
```

Category	Month	Amount	Gc	Gm
Bird	1	135.00	0	0
Bird	2	45.00	0	0
. . .				
Bird	(null)	32.00	0	0
Bird	**(null)**	**607.50**	**1**	**0**
Cat	1	396.00	0	0
Cat	2	113.85	0	0
. . .				
Cat	**(null)**	**1,293.30**	**1**	**0**
(null)	**1**	**1,358.8**	**0**	**1**
(null)	**2**	**1,508.94**	**0**	**1**
(null)	**3**	**2,362.68**	**0**	**1**
. . .				
(null)	**(null)**	**8,451.79**	**1**	**1**

totals for each column that you wish to see. In this case, three separate computations have been requested: (1) Category totals across months, (2) Month totals across categories, and (3) the grand total specified by the open parentheses. The result is that the query displays only the requested super-aggregate totals without the detailed subtotals.

Although the ROLLUP and CUBE options bring new features to SQL, the results can be difficult to read. In terms of OLAP value, you would not want to show the results to managers or expect them to be able to use these tools interactively. On the other hand, they could be useful for feeding data into

FIGURE 8.17
GROUPING SETS option. It is possible to hide the detail subtotals and display only the super-aggregate totals. Notice that this example calls for three totals: By Category, by Month, and overall with the empty parentheses.

```
SELECT Category, Month, Sum
FROM ...
GROUP BY GROUPING SETS
( ROLLUP (Category),
  ROLLUP (Month),
  ()
)
```

Category	Month	Amount
Bird	**(null)**	**607.50**
Cat	**(null)**	**1,293.30**
. . .		
(null)	**1**	**1,358.8**
(null)	**2**	**1,508.94**
(null)	**3**	**2,362.68**
. . .		
(null)	**(null)**	**8,451.79**

a procedure that you write which needs to perform more advanced computations or transfer the data to a spreadsheet.

SQL Analytic Functions

The SQL-99 standard added some mathematical functions that are useful for common OLAP analyses. For example, the statistical functions of standard deviation (STDDEV_POP and STDDEV_SAMP), variance (VAR_POP and VAR_SAMP), covariance (COVAR_POP and COVAR_SAMP), correlation (CORR), and linear regression (REGR_SLOPE, etc.) are now part of the standard. Because most database systems already had proprietary versions of these functions, the impact is not that great, but it will help if vendors adopt the standard names for the functions.

More interesting, the standard also defines several functions that produce ranking numbers automatically. Consider a manager who wishes to compare the sales by employees within the department (or you want to list the results of a sports tournament). Figure 8.18 shows the basic SELECT statement. Notice that the rank functions operate over a range of values, and each range must be sorted. Also notice the difference between the RANK and DENSE_RANK functions. In both cases, tie values are given the same rank. The difference lies in where to restart the numbering after a tie. The RANK function skips the values that would have been assigned (the third rank in the example). The DENSE_RANK function does not skip values and picks up with the next available rank. The standard also provides PERCENT_RANK and CUME_DIST functions that will compute the percentile and cumulative percentile ranking of each value. There is also a ROW_NUMBER function that returns the numbered row for each of the displayed rows in the query.

SQL OLAP Windows

The SQL-99 standard defines some useful extensions for OLAP that should make certain types of queries substantially easier in SQL. Although most databases do not yet implement this standard, companies will most likely add some of the features over time. Two elements are particularly useful: (1) window partitions and (2) computations against previous rows.

Partitions are similar to groups in computing totals, where you specify a column to partition or group the data. The difference is that when you use GROUP BY you retrieve only the summarized results for each group. When

FIGURE 8.18
RANK functions. The sort order for the rank function is specified separately. Ties are given the same rank. RANK skips values that would have been assigned to tie values. DENSE_RANK does not skip values.

```
SELECT Employee, SalesValue
RANK() OVER (ORDER BY SalesValue DESC) AS rank
DENSE_RANK() OVER (ORDER BY SalesValue DESC) AS dense
FROM Sales
ORDER BY SalesValue DESC, Employee;
```

Employee	SalesValue	Rank	Dense
Jones	18,000	1	1
Smith	16,000	2	2
Black	16,000	2	2
White	14,000	4	3

FIGURE 8.19

SQL-99 OLAP PARTITION versus GROUP BY. The window PARTITION statement enables you to display aggregate data (average) along with the detail rows. The GROUP BY statement only provides the summarized data. Also, note the use of the PRECEDING statement in the partition to calculate across previous rows of data.

```
SELECT Category, SaleMonth, MonthAmount,
 AVG(MonthAmount)
  OVER (PARTITION BY Category
  ORDER BY SaleMonth ASC ROWS 2 PRECEDING)
  AS MA
FROM qryOLAPSQL99
ORDER BY SaleMonth ASC;
```

Category	SaleMonth	MonthAmount	MA
Bird	200101	1,500.00	
Bird	200102	1,700.00	
Bird	200103	2,000.00	1,600.00
Bird	200104	2,500.00	1,850.00
. . .			
Cat	200101	4,000.00	
Cat	200102	5,000.00	
Cat	200103	6,000.00	4,500.00
Cat	200104	7,000.00	5,500.00
. . .			

```
SELECT Category, SaleMonth,
  AVG(MonthAmount) AS Average
FROM qryOLAPSQL99
ORDER BY SaleMonth ASC;
```

Category	SaleMonth	Average
Bird	200101	1,925.00
Cat	200101	5,500.00
. . .		

you use PARTITION, you retrieve the individual rows organized by the selected column. Figure 8.19 shows the difference.

The PARTITION statement also enables you to perform aggregations across a selected number of previous rows. This example asks for the moving average for the two rows of data that precede the current row. Although the DBMS is free to use any method to perform the calculations, think of the partitioning process as the following steps. First, the data is retrieved and sorted by Category and SaleMonth. Second, within each category, the system examines each row and computes the average of the two prior rows of data.

Note that it might take some time for vendors to implement all of the new features in SQL-99. Also, you should know that Oracle has used the PARTITION keyword in a different context for many years, so be careful about using this syntax. In Oracle, partitions represent different physical organizations of the underlying table.

The OVER statement enables you to specify a variety of ranges of rows. It is used to perform calculations relative to the current row, so you can compute differences and averages backward and forward. Figure 8.20 shows some commonly used options for the RANGE function. The entire query computes three values of totals. The first SUM command totals the values in the rows from the beginning of the query through the current row. The second SUM function does the same thing, but more explicitly states the beginning and ending rows. The third SUM function computes the total from the current row through the last row of the query. In the second and third examples, notice the use of the UNBOUNDED keyword to specify the start or end row. You could have replaced those with specific numbers if you

```
SELECT SaleDate, Value
SUM(Value) OVER (ORDER BY SaleDate) AS running_sum,
SUM(Value) OVER (ORDER BY SaleDate RANGE
  BETWEEN UNBOUNDED PRECEDING
  AND CURRENT ROW) AS running_sum2,
SUM (Value) OVER (ORDER BY SaleDate RANGE
  BETWEEN CURRENT ROW
  AND UNBOUNDED FOLLOWING) AS remaining_sum;
FROM ...
```

FIGURE 8.20
OVER and RANGE functions. The first SUM function computes the total from the beginning to through the current row. The second SUM function does the same thing more explicitly. The third SUM function totals the values from the current row through the remaining rows in the query.

wanted to compute only the totals for a specified number of preceding or following rows.

Most database systems also make it easy to use LAG and LEAD functions. These functions are designed to be used as inline functions that refer backward or forward to a specified number of rows. For example, the LAG function makes it easy to refer to a value on the previous row. Figure 8.21 shows the basic syntax and the result of a one-period lag and one-period lead. The power of the functions is that it is also easy to use the lag or lead variables in additional calculations. These functions are not part of the official SQL standard, so there are still some differences among the vendors. For example, you might not be able to specify the default value, which is useful for the first (or last) few rows that do not have defined values. But because most systems support the functions, and because they are so useful, they are worth studying.

Data Mining

The goal of data mining is to discover unknown relationships that can be used to make better decisions. Figure 8.22 shows that, compared to the other data retrieval technologies, data mining is a bottom-up approach. Highly specialized tools examine the database looking for correlations and other

```
LAG or LEAD: (Column, # rows, default)

SELECT SaleDate, Value,
  LAG (Value 1,0) OVER (ORDER BY SaleDate) AS prior_day
  LEAD (Value 1,0) OVER (ORDER BY SaleDate) AS next_day
FROM ...
ORDER BY SaleDate
```

SaleDate	Value	prior_day	next_day
1/1/2003	1,000	0	1,500
1/2/2003	1,500	1,000	2,000
1/3/2003	2,000	1,500	2,300
...			
1/31/2003	3,500	3,200	0

FIGURE 8.21
LAG and LEAD functions. As inline functions, they easily return a value from a prior or following line. You can specify how many lines to go backward or forward.

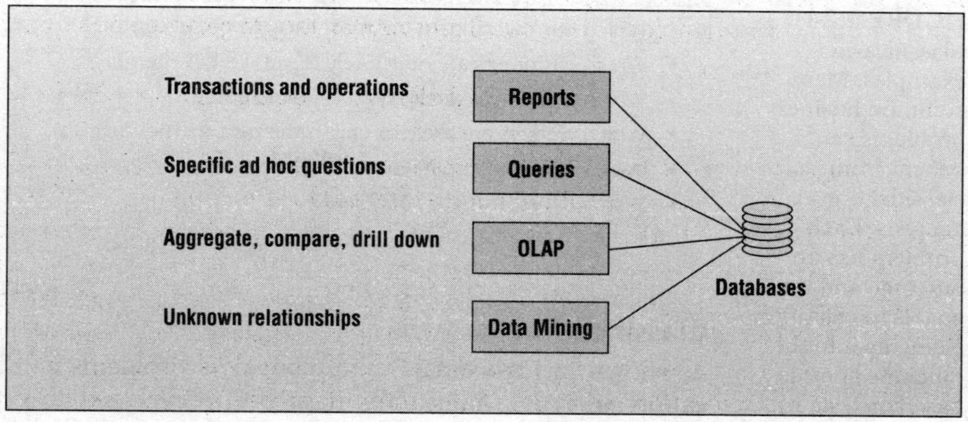

FIGURE 8.22
Data mining. With a goal of identifying unknown relationships. Data mining is a bottom-up approach. Highly specialized tools scan the data searching for information that might be useful.

useful tidbits of information. Some of these tools are relatively unsupervised and can spot patterns with little guidance. Others require more input and specification by model builders. Most of the technologies are exploratory, in the sense that you are searching for unknown relationships as opposed to trying to confirm a suspected one. Some of the routines are derived from statistical analysis; others are highly detailed and created for specialized tasks. This section presents an overview of some of the more popular technologies. Detailed statistical and programming issues are not covered here, but can be found in specialized textbooks.

Figure 8.23 lists some of the common data mining techniques. Occasionally, a DBMS vendor will include a few of the technologies with the base system. However, most vendors sell data mining as add-on products. Many other tools are available from specialized data mining companies. In either case, you generally require the services of a modeler to help build the proper models and interpret the results. Data classification and market basket analysis are two common methods of analyzing data in business because they are useful for many types of problems. Geographic systems are powerful solutions to specific questions. Website analysis through time-series evaluation of logs is increasingly popular. New technologies and new methodologies that can evaluate ever-larger datasets are being developed continually.

FIGURE 8.23
Data mining techniques. Classification and market basket analysis are popular technologies in business. New technologies and new methods of estimating relationships are still being developed.

- Classification/prediction/regression
- Association rules/market basket analysis
- Clustering
  - Data points
  - Hierarchies
- Neural networks
- Deviation detection
- Sequential analysis
  - Time series events
  - Website analysis
- Spatial/geographic analysis
- Textual analysis

FIGURE 8.24
Classification examples. Many common business problems can benefit from classification analysis. Each problem has an outcome and the goal is to classify elements into the outcome choices based on a set of attributes.

- Which borrowers/loans are most likely to be successful?
- Which customers are most likely to want a new item?
- Which companies are likely to file bankruptcy?
- Which workers are likely to quit in the next six months?
- Which startup companies are likely to succeed?
- Which tax returns are fraudulent?

Classification

As shown in Figure 8.24, many business problems can benefit from **classification analysis.** Many tools have been developed to estimate relationships that can predict an outcome. Statistical methods like regression are readily available. However, the two drawbacks to statistical methods are that they tend to assume linear relationships exist, and the estimates are based on averages—but often the most important hidden relationships are too small to be identified by averages. For example, you might be searching for new customers that can be encouraged to return and make more purchases. Since they are new, you might not have enough average data to create a statistically important effect.

Problems that can be evaluated by classification analysis have an outcome that is affected by a set of indicator attributes. The basic objective is to estimate the strength of the effect of each indicator variable and its influence on the outcome. For instance, a bank would have historical data on borrower attributes such as job stability, credit history, and income. The data mining system could estimate the effect of each of these variables on the ultimate outcome (paying off the loan or defaulting). These weights could be applied to future customer data to help determine whether to grant a loan, or to affect the interest rate to charge.

Figure 8.25 shows a tiny sample of data for the lending situation. Note that the data might be categorical (Yes/No) or continuous (e.g., Income). Some classification tools can work with either type of data; some require you to convert to categorical data. For example, the income data could be

FIGURE 8.25
Bank loan classification. The indicator attributes affect the outcome in some fashion. The data mining software estimates the strength of each attribute on a set of test data. The resulting model can be applied to future data to predict the potential success or failure of new loans.

Income	Married	Credit History	Job Stability	Success
50000	Yes	Good	Good	Yes
25000	Yes	Bad	Bad	No
75000	No	Good	Good	No

converted to bins, such as low: 0–30,000; medium: 30,000–70,000; high: 70,000–120,000, and wealthy: above 120,000. Of course, then you face the new data mining question of where to draw the lines to separate the categories. Some tools provide systems to help make this decision as well.

Common classification tools include various regression methods, Bayesian analysis, decision trees (particularly for hierarchical data), genetic algorithms, and neural networks. Of the group, neural networks typically require the least supervision, whereas advanced regression techniques rely on the skills of an experienced modeler. The key issue with any classification analysis is to determine how accurately the model can predict both existing and new cases.

Association Rules/Market Basket Analysis

Market basket analysis is the tool that is credited with driving the acceptance of data mining. Originally, the techniques were applied to analyzing consumer purchases at convenience stores, hence the term *market basket*. The more generic term of **association rules** indicates that the methodology can be used for other situations. The basic question these systems answer is, What items are customers likely to buy together? Or, in terms of rules, Does the existence of *A* imply the existence of *B*? In the classic example, a convenience store discovered that shoppers who purchase diapers often purchase beer at the same time—particularly on Thursday and Friday nights. The importance of this piece of information is that managers can use it to increase sales. For instance, you might consider placing the two items close to each other in the store to encourage even more customers to purchase both items. Likewise, manufacturers might use similar knowledge to cross-sell items by providing coupons or product descriptions in the packaging of the related items.

Market basket analysis requires that you have a set of transaction data that contains a list of all items purchased by one person. Today, this data is readily available from supermarkets and large chains that use bar-code scanners. Most companies sell this data to specialized firms that resell it to other companies. The analysis software then scans the data and compares each item against the others to see if any patterns exist. In the process, the software computes three numbers that you use to evaluate the strength of the potential relationship or rule. The definitions are easier to understand with pairs of items, but they also apply to multiple items. The **support** for a rule is measured by the percent of transactions that contain both items. Statistically, the probability is denoted as $P(A \cap B)$, and computed by counting the number of transactions with both items and dividing by the total number of transactions. Similar numbers can be computed for *A* and *B* alone, or the percentage of times each individual item has been purchased. Higher values of support indicate that both items are frequently purchased together—but the number does not tell us that one causes the other. The **confidence** of the rule (*A* implies *B*) is measured by the percentage of transactions with item *A* that also contain item *B*. Statistically, it is the probability that *B* is in the basket, given that *A* has already been chosen, denoted $P(B|A)$. By statistical definitions, $P(B|A) = P(A \cap B)/P(A)$, so it is relatively easy to compute. Again, higher values of confidence tend to indicate that purchases of item *A* lead to purchases of item *B*. The third statistic reported by most data mining tools

FIGURE 8.26
Evaluating a market basket association. Support is the percentage of both items being purchased in one transaction. Confidence is the probability of purchasing beer (B) given that diapers (D) are purchased. Lift is the contribution of the effect to sales and should be greater than 1.

Support:	$P(B \cap D) = .6 \quad P(D) = .7 \quad P(B) = .5$
Confidence:	$P(B\|D) = P(B \cap D)/P(D) = 0.857$
Lift:	$P(B\|D)/P(B) = 1.714$

is lift. **Lift** is the potential gain attributed to the rule, compared to purchases without the rule. If the value is greater than 1, the lift is positive. Conceptually, it indicates the gain in sales resulting from the association. Statistically, it can be computed as $P(A \cap B)/(P(A) * P(B))$ or as $P(B|A)/P(B)$.

Figure 8.26 shows how the numbers are computed for the diapers and beer example. The numbers are fictional but representative of the situation. Notice that the lift is substantially higher than 1 (1.714), indicating that the association strongly contributes to sales of beer. Data mining software computes all of these numbers for essentially all pairs of items. If there are many items, the process can take quite a while to run. Also, multiple items could be considered in the analysis: Does the purchase of sheets and pillowcases lead to the sale of more towels? However, combining too many dimensions leads to huge computational issues, so most analyses are done with a limited set of comparisons.

Working with market basket analysis, you will quickly encounter several problems. First, items with a small number of purchases can result in misleading values. If an item is purchased only once or twice, then almost anything else purchased with it will seem to be related. Consequently, you will have to examine the data and change groupings to ensure that most items are purchased with approximately the same frequency. Figure 8.27 shows a hypothetical situation at a hardware store that sells a lot of lumber but only a limited number of nails and screws. To prevent spurious rules, the answer is to combine the nails and screws into a broader hardware category, and split the lumber transactions into more detailed definitions. How do you know if problems exist? You can use additional queries to quickly count the number of sales of each item. The newer

FIGURE 8.27
Balanced frequencies. Items that are rarely purchased will lead to false rules. The solution is to define the items so that they balance. In this case, combine nails into a hardware category and split lumber into smaller categories.

Item	Freq.
1" nails	2%
2" nails	1%
3" nails	1%
4" nails	2%
Lumber	50%

Item	Freq.
Hardware	15%
Dim. lumber	20%
Plywood	15%
Finish lumber	15%

OLAP functions also make it easy to compute the percentages if the raw count numbers are hard to read.

The other problems that you can encounter with market basket analysis include the fact that some rules identified will be obvious to anyone in the industry. For example, a fast-food chain would undoubtedly see a relationship between burgers and fries. A tricky problem arises when the system returns rules that do not make sense or cannot be explained. For example, a hardware chain found that sales of toilet rings were closely tied to the opening of new stores. Even if this correlation is true, what do you do with it?

Cluster Analysis

Cluster analysis is used to identify groupings of data—data points that tend to be related to each other. It can be used to identify groups of people, for example, to categorize customers. If you know that customers fall within certain groupings, you can use the information about a few customers to help sell additional products to the others in the group. Most likely, customers in the same group will want similar products. For instance, a bookstore can use the purchases of some items to categorize a customer and then identify books that similar customers bought and suggest them to the other shoppers. Likewise, you could use cluster analysis to categorize the skills of employees that work in various departments and use that information when hiring new workers.

As shown in Figure 8.28, clusters are relatively easy to see in two dimensions. The objective of the software is to identify the data points that are close to each other (small intra-cluster distance), yet further away from other points (larger inter-cluster distance). Unfortunately, most datasets do not exhibit clustering as strongly as shown in this example. But cluster analysis is a useful data exploration technique because it can reveal patterns that you might not see with other tools. However, keep in mind that datasets with a large number of observations (rows) and many dimensions are extremely difficult to cluster. Even with relatively modern computers, it can take hours or days to evaluate large, complex problems. So start cautiously, and try to build clusters using smaller samples and a limited number of dimensions.

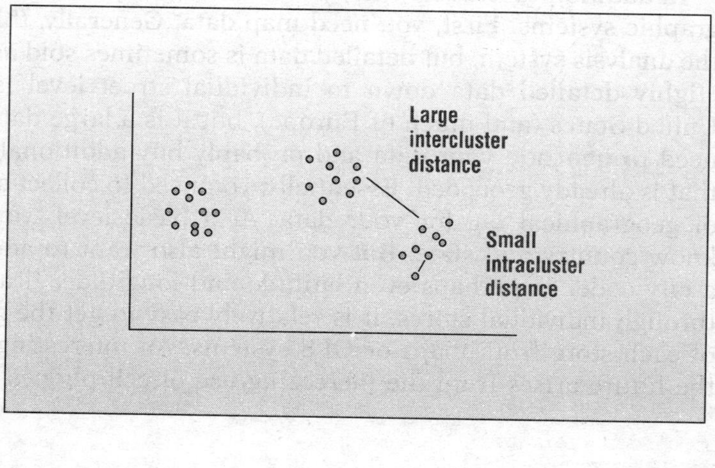

FIGURE 8.28
Cluster analysis. The goal is to find data points that are grouped close to each other and farther from other groups. Larger datasets with multiple dimensions are very difficult and time-consuming to evaluate.

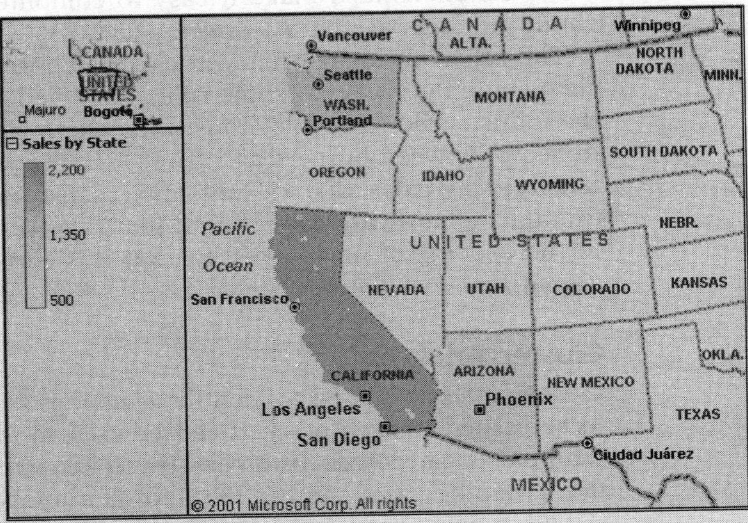

FIGURE 8.29 Geographic analysis. This basic map shows sales by state. As shown by the key, darker colors represent larger sales. Additional data, such as income, could be shown as overlays or compared in charts.

Geographic Analysis

Geographic information systems (GIS) display data in relation to their location. The systems are generally classified as visualization systems. They are useful for displaying geographical relationships and showing people how data is influenced by location. Few systems have true data mining capabilities for scanning the data to find patterns. Nonetheless, they are an important tool in analyzing data. Some relationships are much easier to understand if you see them on a map. Figure 8.29 shows a simple map of sales by western states. Additional data could be displayed with more colors, or charts could be placed on each state.

Larger DBMS vendors have begun incorporating spatial and GIS systems into their offerings. You can also purchase standalone systems from other vendors. Beyond drawing maps, a true GIS has several methods for displaying data on the map. Basic techniques include shading and overlays, often used to display sales by region. Overlays show multiple items on different levels, making it easier to see how several items relate to each other as well as to location. For instance, marketers might compare sales, income, and population by geographic region.

In addition to the software, you need two important components for geographic systems. First, you need map data. Generally, this data is sold with the analysis system, but detailed data is sometimes sold as an add-on option. Highly detailed data down to individual street level is available for the United States (and much of Europe), but it is a large database. Second, you need to **geocode** your data and probably buy additional demographic data that is already geocoded. Essentially, you need to collect and store some type of geographical tag for your data. At a basic level, you probably already know country and state. But you might also want to add a region code, or a city code, or perhaps even latitude and longitude. If all of your sales are through individual stores, it is relatively easy to get the geographic position of each store from maps or GPS systems. An interesting possible option in the future arises from the increasing use of cell phones. Because of federal emergency regulations (e-911), cell phones are required to have positioning systems. Eventually, it is conceivable that this information will be provided to businesses, so your transaction systems can record exact locations of salespeople, and possibly even of customers. Please keep in mind the serious privacy issues these technologies create, but as you build new databases, you should think about incorporating geocode information into the data capture tables. Once the data has been collected, the GIS makes it easy to display relationships.

Summary

Large databases are optimized for transactions processing—to handle day-to-day operations efficiently, data is stored in normalized tables. But most managers need to join several tables to retrieve and understand the data. Indexes speed joins and data retrieval, but slow down transactions. This dichotomy means that it is often better to create a separate data warehouse to use for data analysis. Data can be extracted and cleaned from transaction systems, and placed into star or snowflake designs enabling managers to focus on the dimensions that surround a particular fact.

OLAP cubes are a powerful tool to enable managers to quickly sift through data and examine subtotals from a variety of perspectives. Without writing intense SQL queries, managers can compare values across product categories, time, and even across multiple dimensions simultaneously. OLAP cube browsers also contain easy methods to filter the data to specific rows or cube sections.

Many statistical data mining tools have been developed to help managers analyze data. They often require training and specialized knowledge by the workers, but can be powerful tools to understand relationships among the data. Classification and clustering algorithms help break the data into groups. Comparing the various groups makes it possible to better understand customers and expand the market. Association or market basket rules are popular with stores that sell a large variety of items. Identifying items that are purchased together makes it possible to suggest products to other customers. It can also lead to insights in store layout and customer psychology. Geographic systems are useful for any problem involving location. Specialized tools and demographic data are available to see the geographic relationships that exist.

A Developer's View

Miranda saw that some business questions are difficult to answer, even with SQL. When managers are not exactly sure what they are looking for, you need to consider the OLAP and data mining approaches. Providing an OLAP cube is a good first step because it makes it easy for managers to see subtotals and slice the data to whatever level they want. More sophisticated statistical data mining tools are available, but generally require additional training and knowledgeable users. Just remember that performance often requires moving OLAP data into a separate data warehouse.

Key Terms

association rules, *321*
binary search, *300*
bitmap index, *301*
classification analysis, *320*
cluster analysis, *323*
confidence, *321*
data mining, *304*
data warehouse, *303*
dimension, *308*
drill down, *307*
extraction, transformation, and transportation (ETT), *305*
fact table, *308*
geocode, *324*
geographic information system (GIS), *324*
lift, *322*
market basket analysis, *321*
measure, *308*
online analytical processing (OLAP), *299*
online transaction processing (OLTP), *299*
PivotTable, *310*
pointer, *301*
roll up, *307*
snowflake design, *309*
star design, *308*
super-aggregate, *313*
support, *321*

Review Questions

1. Why are indexes so important in relational databases?
2. Given the power of a relational DBMS, why might a company still need a data warehouse?
3. What main problems are encountered in setting up a data warehouse?
4. How are OLAP queries different from traditional SQL queries?
5. What is an OLAP cube?
6. What are hierarchical dimensions and how do they relate to roll up and drill down operations?
7. What basic analytical functions are defined in SQL, particularly the newer standard?
8. What is the goal of data mining?
9. What are the main categories of data mining tools?

Exercises

1. Find at least two commercial OLAP tools and compare the features.
2. Find a commercial data mining tool and outline the steps needed to extract and transform data from a typical DBMS so it is usable by the system.
3. Find a commercial data mining tool and outline the steps needed to perform a market basket analysis.

Sally's Pet Store

Most of the following questions require an OLAP cube processor. You should have access to SQL, an OLAP browser within the DBMS, or a PivotTable. For the data mining tools, if you do not have access to specialized software, you can use Excel for simple analyses.

4. Create a cube to browse merchandise sales by time, state, employee, and item category.
5. Create a cube to browse animal sales by time, category, breed, gender, and registration.
6. Create a cube to browse both animal and merchandise sales by time, state, and category.
7. Create a cube to browse purchases of merchandise from suppliers based on time, employee, and location. As facts, include the value of the purchase, the shipping cost, and the delay between order and receipt.

8. What is the correlation between the age of an animal at the time of the sale and its price?
9. If you have access to market basket software, evaluate the sales tables to see if any associations exist.
10. As a simple time series analysis, extract the merchandise sales by week, plot the data, and estimate the trend line.
11. Are purchases of some categories of items significantly larger than others? For instance, does the company sell substantially more dog products?
12. Are there certain categories of customers who purchase more than others? This is a general clustering problem: If you do not have access to the specialized software, you can test attributes using regression.
13. Using weekly sales of merchandise, forecast sales for the next three weeks.
14. Is there a geographic pattern to sales? Do some states or regions have more sales?

Rolling Thunder Bicycles

15. Create an OLAP cube to evaluate sales (value and quantity) by model type, state, time, and sales employee.
16. Create a new size dimension to reduce the dimension of frame size down to three (small, medium, and large). Classify the bicycles into this dimension. If available, use clustering software; otherwise, use the mean and standard deviation. Remember that road bikes are measured in centimeters and mountain bikes in inches.
17. Add the reduced size dimension created in Exercise 16 to the OLAP cube created in Exercise 15.
18. Create an OLAP cube to evaluate production time by order date (time), model type, month, and employee who assembled the frame.
19. Create an OLAP cube to evaluate purchases of components by time, manufacturer, road or mountain bike, and component category.
20. What is the correlation between sales by city and its population? Evaluate both for quantity and value of the bicycles.
21. What is the correlation between the size of a bicycle (frame size) and its price?
22. Using monthly sales by model type, forecast sales for the next six months.
23. If you have market basket analysis software, evaluate the purchases of components. Do any patterns exist—outside of the defined groupo relationships?
24. Create an OLAP cube to evaluate sales (quantity) by paint type, letter style, and model type.
25. Ignoring capital costs but including salary, evaluate profit by month and forecast it for 6 months.

Website References

Site	Description
http://otn.oracle.com/products/warehouse/owb_calais_new_features/html/module4/04-0110.htm	Oracle 9i OLAP process.
http://www.microsoft.com/sql/evaluation/bi/default.asp	Microsoft SQL Server 2000 analysis tools.
http://www-3.ibm.com/software/data/db2/db2olap/features.html	IBM DB2 OLAP tools.
http://www.wintercorp.com/rwintercolumns/SQL_99snewolapfunctions.html	SQL 99 OLAP standards and example.
http://www.datawarehousing.org/	Data warehouse information.

Additional Reading

Apte, C., B. Liu, E. Pednault, and P. Smyth. "Business Applications of Data Mining." *Communications of the ACM* 45, no. 8 (August 2002), pp. 49–53. [Some examples of data mining, also part of a special issue on data mining.]

Golfarelli, M., and S. Rizzi. "A Methodological Framework for Data Warehouse Design." *Proceedings of the First ACM International Workshop on Data Warehousing and OLAP,* 1998, ACM Press, pp. 3–9. [Relatively formal definition of facts, dimensions, and hierarchies.]

Han, J., and M. Kamber. *Data Mining: Concepts and Techniques*. San Francisco: Morgan Kaufmann/Academic Press, 2001. [A general introduction to data mining techniques.]

Hastie, T., R. Tibshirani, and J. Friedman. *The Elements of Statistical Learning*. New York: Springer-Verlag, 2001. [A strong foundation book on the statistics and algorithms of data mining, including all of the math.]

Marakas, George M. *Modern Data Warehousing, Mining, and Visualization*. Upper Saddle River: Prentice Hall, 2003. [An introduction to core concepts in data mining that includes trial software.]

Peterson, T., J. Pinkelman, and B. Pfeiff. *Microsoft OLAP Unleashed*. Indianapolis: Sams/Macmillan, 1999. [Details on OLAP queries and data warehouses in SQL Server.]

Scott, J. "Warehousing over the Web." *Communications of the ACM* 41, no. 9 (September 1998), pp. 64–65. [Brief comments on Comcast using a Web interface for its data warehouse.]

Part 4

Database Administration

Large applications require careful support. Most organizations hire a database administrator to monitor application performance, assess security, and ensure database integrity. Chapter 9 highlights the tasks of the data administrator and the database administrator, with special emphasis on database security. Once again, SQL has a strong role in managing and protecting the database.

Information systems (IS) managers are increasingly concerned with issues of providing access to data regardless of location. Networks and the Internet provide multiple options for distributing data and providing answers throughout the organization. Chapter 10 explores some of the challenges and options of distributed databases, and providing access to databases through the Internet.

Chapter 9

Database Administration

Chapter Outline

What You Will Learn in This Chapter

- What administrative tasks need to be performed with a database application? 336
- What complications arise with database backups? 339
- How do you protect a database from physical disasters? 342
- What security threats should you be concerned about? 344
- How do you protect a database from various security threats? 348

A Developer's View

Miranda: Finally, everything seems to be running well.

Ariel: Does that mean you finally got paid?

Miranda: Yes. They gave me the check yesterday. They even liked my work so well, they offered me a job.

Ariel: That's great. Are you going to take it? What job is it?

Miranda: I think so. They want me to be a database administrator. They said they need me to keep the database running properly. They also hinted that they want me to help their existing programmers learn to build database applications.

Ariel: Wow! That means you'll get more money than the programmers.

Miranda: Probably. But I'll have to learn some new material. I'm really starting to worry about security. The accounting manager talked to me yesterday and gave me some idea of the problems that I can expect with the sales application.

Introduction

The power of a DBMS comes from its ability to share data. Data can be shared across many users, departments, and applications. Most organizations build more than one application and more than one database. Large organizations might use more than one DBMS. Most companies have several projects being developed or revised at the same time by different teams. Imagine what happens if you just turn developers loose to create databases, tables, and applications anyway they want to. It is highly unlikely the applications would work together. Just using a DBMS is not enough. An organization that wants to build integrated applications must have someone in charge of the data and the databases.

Data administration consists of the planning and coordination required to define data consistently throughout the company. Some person or group should have the responsibility for determining what data should be collected, how it should be stored, and promoting ways in which it can be used. This person or group is responsible for the integrity of the data.

Database administration consists of technical aspects of creating and running the database. The basic tasks are performance monitoring, backup and recovery, and assigning and controlling security. Database administrators are trained in the details of installing, configuring, and operating the DBMS.

Database security is a subset of computer security topics. However, because of the goal of sharing data, security is a crucial issue in database management. Also, some interesting twists in database security should be studied by all application developers and database managers. If database security is assigned properly, it has the ability to reduce many types of fraud. If database security is ignored or performed poorly, major assets of the company could be manipulated or stolen from any computer in the world. It pays to understand the security issues and to handle security properly.

Data Administrator

Data is an important asset to companies. Think about how long a modern company would survive if its computers were suddenly destroyed or all the data lost. Some organizations might survive as long as a few days or a week. Many, such as banks, would be out of business immediately.

A company should not have to lose any data before it recognizes the value of the information contained in the data. As indicated by Figure 9.1, companies have many databases for different purposes. Over time, organizations build many different databases and applications to support their operational, tactical, and strategic decisions. Each application is important by itself, but when the applications and databases can coordinate and exchange data, managers receive a complete picture of the entire organization.

Despite the power and flexibility of database systems, applications built at different times by different people do not automatically share data. The key to integrating data is to put someone in charge of the data resources of the company. In most companies the **data administrator (DA)** fills this position.

As summarized in Figure 9.2, the primary role of the DA is to provide centralized control over the data for the entire organization. The DA sets data definition standards to ensure that all applications use consistent formats and naming conventions. The DA coordinates applications and teams to ensure that data from individual projects can be integrated into a corporatewide information system. If disputes occur among developers or managers, the DA serves as the judge, making decisions to ensure compatibility across the organization. The DA also monitors the database industry and watches trends and technologies to advise the company on which database systems and tools to consider for long-term benefits.

The DA plays a crucial role as an advocate. Most managers and many developers are not aware of the power and capabilities of modern database systems. By understanding the managerial tasks and the database capabilities,

FIGURE 9.1
Data administration. With many projects and developers, a data administrator coordinates the projects so data can be integrated across applications.

FIGURE 9.2
Data administrator roles. The DA is responsible for maintaining the quality of the data and for integrating data across the organization. The DA also advocates the use of databases and is often in charge of security.

- Provide centralized control over the data
  - Data definition: format and naming convention
  - Data integration
  - DBMS selection
- Act as data and database advocate
  - Application ideas
  - Decision support
  - Strategic uses
- Coordinate data integrity, security, privacy, and control

the DA is in a position to suggest new applications and expanded uses of the existing data.

Ultimately, the DA is also responsible for the integrity of the data: Does the data contained in the DBMS represent a true picture of the firm? Does the firm have the proper systems and controls in place to ensure the accuracy and timeliness of the data?

The DA position is largely a management job. The DA tasks consist of organizing and controlling the design aspects of application development. Control is maintained by setting standards, monitoring ongoing development and changes, and providing assistance in database design as needed. The DA also spends time with business managers to evaluate current systems, monitor business trends, and identify future needs. The person hired for this position usually has several years of experience in designing databases and needs a detailed knowledge of the company. The DA also needs technical database skills to understand the various storage implications of the decisions. The DA must also be able to communicate easily with technical managers and business managers.

Database Administrator

A DBMS is a complex software package. Installing, running, and upgrading a DBMS are not trivial tasks. Even with personal computer–based systems, these tasks can require the services of a full-time person. Every database requires the services of a **database administrator (DBA)**. The DBA position is generally staffed by a specialist who is trained in the administration of a particular DBMS. In smaller companies, instead of hiring a specialist, one of the lead developers may be asked to perform DBA duties.

The DBA role is relatively technical. As highlighted in Figure 9.3, the DBA's responsibilities include installing and upgrading the DBMS. Additional tasks

FIGURE 9.3
Database administrator roles. The DBA tasks are fairly technical and require daily monitoring and changes to the DBMS.

- Install and upgrade DBMS
- Create user accounts and monitor security
- Manage backup and recovery of the database
- Monitor and tune the database performance
- Coordinate with DBMS vendor and plan for changes
- Maintain DBMS-specific information for developers

include creating user accounts and monitoring security. The DBA is also responsible for managing backups. Although the actual backup task may be performed by a system operator, the DBA is responsible for setting schedules and making sure the data backups are safe. The DBA also monitors the performance of the databases and plans upgrades and additional capacity. The DBA must stay in contact with the DBMS vendor to track system problems and to be notified of changes. As new utilities, tools, or information is provided, the DBA functions as a liaison to gather this knowledge and make it available to developers. The DBA has complete access to the data in the application. In many organizations the DBA is in charge of security for each database. Larger companies might appoint a special security officer to specify policies and procedures and to help with the monitoring. However, the DBA is generally in charge of carrying out the technical details of assigning security privileges for the database.

Data allocation and storage are an important part of the daily tasks of the DBA. Some large database systems require the DBA to preassign a space on the disk drive for each database. Many systems allocate physical space by creating datafiles and **tablespaces**, which are logical collections of space where data can be stored.

Separate space is usually allocated for the data tables, the indexes, and the transaction logs, and the DBA must estimate the size of each component. If the DBA allocates too little space, performance will suffer; on thc other hand, allocating too much space means that the company will waste money on unneeded disk drive capacity. Most systems provide tools to add space later, but it is best to get good estimates up front. The data volume estimates from Chapter 3 provide crucial information in determining the space requirements. For tables, the main concept is to determine the size of an average row (in bytes) and multiply by the expected number of rows in the table. Note that each DBMS stores data slightly differently, and some add bytes per row of storage. The documentation will provide details for each DBMS. A more accurate solution is to set up a temporary database, create a few rows of data in each table, and then use the actual average space to estimate future needs. Space required for the indexes and rollback log depend on the specific DBMS and the computer system. If you need highly accurate estimates, you will have to consult the documentation and support tools for your specific DBMS. Space for indexes and logs also depends on the number and length of transactions defined in the applications. For example, the transaction log in a database used for transaction processing will have to be substantially larger than the log in a database used primarily for decision support and data retrieval.

Database Structure

The DBA works on a daily basis with the structure of the database. Although each DBMS has slightly different characteristics, Figure 9.4 shows the overall structure of a database as defined by the SQL standard. Users are defined within the individual database instance and granted permissions by the DBA. The **schema** is a container that serves as a namespace so that duplicate table names can be avoided. Originally, it was defined so that each user would have a separate space to create tables. Two users could each create a table

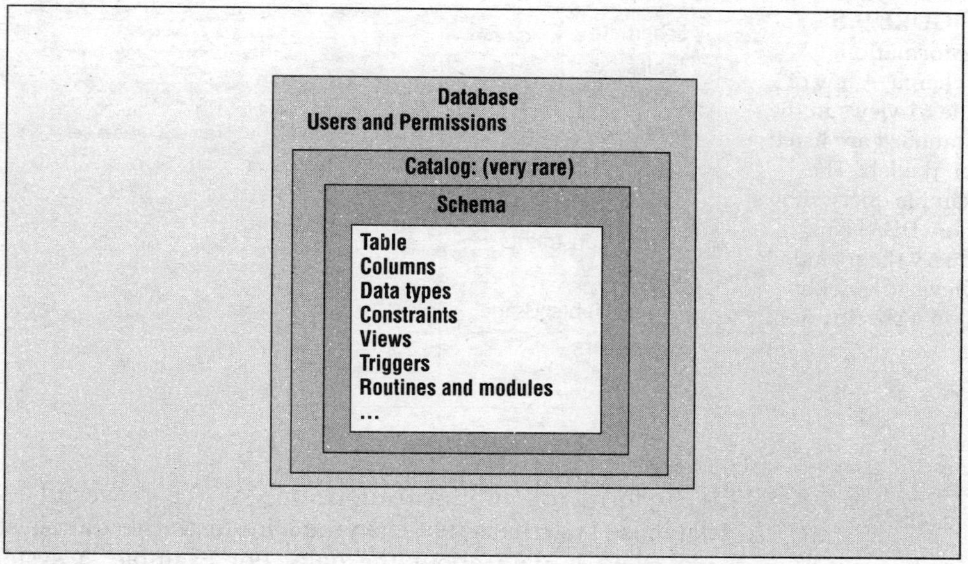

FIGURE 9.4
Database structure. The schema serves as a container for other elements to minimize potential naming conflicts.

named Employee without causing a problem. Today, schemas can be created for any purpose, not just for each user. The catalog was proposed in the SQL 99 standard, primarily to make it easier to find and access related schemas by placing them into one container. At this point, it is not likely that any DBMS supports the catalog element. However, the schema approach is relatively common. Users and applications are assigned to a default schema, and tables and views within that schema are directly accessible (depending on the security permissions, of course). But sometimes you need to access tables or views stored in a different schema. In these situations, you need to use the full name of the item. The full name includes the schema name (and eventually the catalog name). For example, if you want to access the Employee table in the Corporate schema, you would use SELECT * FROM Corporate.Employee to indicate the full name of the table. If you need to specify the catalog (e.g., Main), you would use Main.Corporate.Employee as the full name of the table. The standard database elements such as tables, views, and triggers reside within each schema. One of the tasks of the DBA (and the DA) is to identify when to create new schemas. Although there are no specific rules, keep in mind that the purpose of a schema is to isolate and compartmentalize applications.

Metadata

Each vendor provides tools to help DBAs accomplish common tasks. Most have a graphically oriented approach to make them easier to use. On the other hand, DBAs often choose to perform tasks using SQL by building specific procedures. The SQL commands provide detailed control over an operation and can be written to handle dozens or hundreds of operations at one time. For example, the graphical approach is easy to use for adding one user, but if you need to add 100 users, it is easier to write an SQL procedure that pulls the list of users from a file or a temporary table.

FIGURE 9.5
Information_schema. A few of the 61 views in the standard are listed on the left. The sample query shows how DBAs can query the metadata views to quickly find a specific item.

Schemata Tables Domains Views Table_Privileges Referential_Constraints Check_Constraints Triggers Trigger_Table_Usage Parameters Routines	SELECT Table_Name, Table_Type FROM Information_Schema.Tables WHERE table_name LIKE 'Emp%'

In terms of administration, one of the powerful aspects of relational database systems is that even the administrative data is stored in tables. This **metadata** is data about the data. For example, a system table contains a list of all the user tables. The SQL 99 standard describes the Information_Schema which consists of a set of views that provide documentation on the database. Technically, the Information_Schema views retrieve data from the Definition_Schema tables; however, DBMS vendors might choose not to implement the Definition_Schema. DBMS vendors have already developed proprietary system tables to hold the metadata. The drawback to this approach has been that there is no consistency across products, so DBAs have to learn different commands for each DBMS. As vendors implement the newer standards, DBAs should find it easier to work with products from multiple vendors.

Figure 9.5 shows some of the common elements of the Information_Schema. The SQL command illustrates how to obtain a partial list of the tables, based on the name. Commands of this type are useful when a database has hundreds of tables and views. Instead of scrolling through dozens of pages looking for a specific table, you can use the power of SQL to quickly find the exact table needed. In the example, note that you should always retrieve the Table_Type as well as the name. Tables can be base types (that actually hold the data), views, or derived tables.

Database Tasks by Development Stages

Whichever development methodology you follow (e.g., traditional systems development life cycle, rapid development, or prototyping), certain database tasks are required at each step. Most of the tasks are performed by the application developers. Some involve coordination with the DA. Many require communication with the DBA, both to get advice and to provide information to help the DBA set up the databases.

Database Planning

During the feasibility and planning stages, you will have to make an estimate of the data storage requirements. These initial estimates will be rough, but they will help determine the size and capacity of the hardware needed to support the application. For example, if you are building a simple database to track materials that will be used by five people, the database might require less than 100 megabytes of storage and run on a personal computer. If the initial size estimates start to exceed a few hundred megabytes of storage, a file server with high-speed disk drives might be more appropriate. As the database estimates approach gigabytes or terabytes, you should investigate special database hardware and parallel-processing systems.

The initial investigation should also provide some idea of the number of forms and reports that will be needed, as well as their complexity. These numbers will be used to estimate the time and cost required to develop the system. An experienced DBA can provide estimates of space requirements from similar projects. Company records on other projects can provide estimates of the average time to develop forms and reports.

Database Design

The basic goal of the design stage is to identify the user needs and design the appropriate data tables. Data normalization is the primary database-related activity in this stage. The final table definitions will also provide better estimates of the storage requirements.

Teamwork coordination and project management are important administrative tasks at this stage. As highlighted in Figure 9.6, teamwork is supported with data standards as defined by the DA. Projects can be split into pieces and assigned to each team member. The ability to integrate the pieces into a complete application is provided through standards and communication. Communication is enhanced through a shared data repository, networked tools, e-mail, and **computer-aided software engineering (CASE)** tools. Leading CASE tools include Oracle Designer/2000, Rational Rose, IEF, and IBM's Visual Age. These tools provide a centralized repository for all project work, including diagrams, data definitions, and programming code. As team members work on their portion of the project, they can see the rest of the project. In an OO project, they can use the objects created by other teams.

From the perspective of data design or normalization, the project is often split by assigning forms and reports to individual team members. Each person is then responsible for identifying the business assumptions and defining the normalized tables needed for the assigned forms. Periodically, the individuals combine their work and create a centralized list of the tables that

FIGURE 9.6
Managing database design. Database design requires teamwork and standards to ensure that individual components can be integrated into a complete application. CASE tools and networks improve communication through a centralized repository of design data.

- Teamwork
  - Data standards
  - Data repository
  - Reusable objects
  - CASE tools
  - Networks and communication
- Subdividing projects
  - Delivering in stages: versions
  - Normalization by user views
  - Assigning forms and reports

- Standards for application programming
  - User interface
  - Programming structure
  - Programming variables and objects
  - Test procedures
- Data access and ownership
- Loading databases
- Backup and recovery plans
- User and operating training

FIGURE 9.7
Implementation management. The user interface must be carefully chosen. Programming standards and test procedures help ensure compatibility of the components and provide quality control. Business managers should be assigned ownership of the data, so they can make final determinations of security conditions and quality. Backup and recovery plans have to be created and tested. Training programs have to be created for operators and users.

will be used in the database. This final list must follow the standards established by the DA.

Database Implementation

The primary database tasks required for implementation are listed in Figure 9.7. Development of the application and user interface are the major steps. Management and organizational tasks largely entail determining the overall look and feel of the application. Once the overall structure is determined, programming standards and testing procedures facilitate teamwork and ensure quality.

Another important management task is to assign ownership of the various databases. Owners should be from business management. Data owners are responsible for identifying primary security rules and for verifying the accuracy of the data. If the DBA has any questions about access rights or changes to the data, the DBA can obtain additional information and advice from the data owner.

Backup and recovery procedures have to be established and tested. If any component fails, the database logs should be able to fully restore the data. Backups are often handled in two forms: full backup at predefined checkpoints and incremental backups of changes that have occurred since the last full backup. Complete backups are easier to restore and provide safer recovery. However, they can be time-consuming and require large amounts of backup space. For small databases, full backups are not a problem. For large, continually changing transaction databases, it may only be possible to perform a full backup once a week or so.

Users and operators also have to be trained. No matter how carefully the user interface is designed, there should always be at least an introductory training session for users. Similarly, computer operators may have to be trained in the backup and recovery procedures.

Database Operation and Maintenance

Once the database is placed in operation, the DBA performs most of the management tasks. The primary tasks are to (1) monitor usage and security, (2) perform backups and recovery, and (3) support the user.

Monitoring performance and storage space is a critical factor in managing a database. Monitoring is used to fine-tune the application performance and to estimate growth and plan for future needs. Security access and changes are also monitored. Security logs can track changes to critical data.

They can also be specified to track usage (both read and write) by individual users if there is a suspected problem.

Monitoring user problems as well as performance provides useful feedback on the application. If users consistently have problems in certain areas, the design team should be encouraged to improve those forms. Similarly, if some users are running queries that take a long time to execute, the design team should be called in to create efficient versions of the queries. For example, do not expect a user to recognize or correct a correlated subquery. Instead, if the DBA sees users running complex queries that take too long to run, the team should add a new section to the application that stores and executes a more efficient query.

Similarly, if some people are heavily using certain sections of the database, it might be more efficient to provide them with replicated copies of the main sections. If the users do not need up-to-the-minute data, a smaller database can be set up on a server and updated nightly. The users end up with faster response times because they have a smaller database and less communication time. The rest of the database runs faster because there are fewer heavy users.

Database vendors provide some powerful tools to help analyze queries and database performance. With these tools, you can break apart the entire query process to see exactly which step is taking the most time. With this knowledge, developers can work on alternative solutions to avoid the bottlenecks. Other tools can monitor for deadlock and transaction problems, making it relatively easy to correct problems. **Tuning** a large database to improve performance is a complex issue and depends heavily on the capabilities and tools of the specific DBMS.

Backup and Recovery

Perhaps the most critical database management task is backup. No matter how well you plan, no matter how sophisticated your security system, something will go wrong. Database managers and developers have an obligation to plan for disasters. The most critical aspect of planning is to make sure that a current copy of the database is easily accessible. Any type of disaster—fire, flood, terrorist attack, power failure, computer virus, disk drive crash, or accidental deletion—requires backup data. Given the low cost of making and storing backup copies, there is no excuse for not having a current backup available at all times.

As shown in Figure 9.8, database backups provide some interesting challenges—particularly when the database must be available 24 hours a day, 7 days a week (abbreviated to **24-7**). The basic problem is that while the database is making a copy, changes could still be made to the data. That is, every copy of the database is immediately out of date—even while it is being made. A related issue is that the DBMS copy routines might have to wait to copy portions of the database that are currently in use (possibly creating a deadlock situation).

Fortunately, the larger database systems provide many tools to solve these problems. In most cases the DBMS takes a **snapshot** of the tables. The snapshot represents the status of a table at one instant in time. Then the database maintains a transaction log of every change made since the last snapshot.

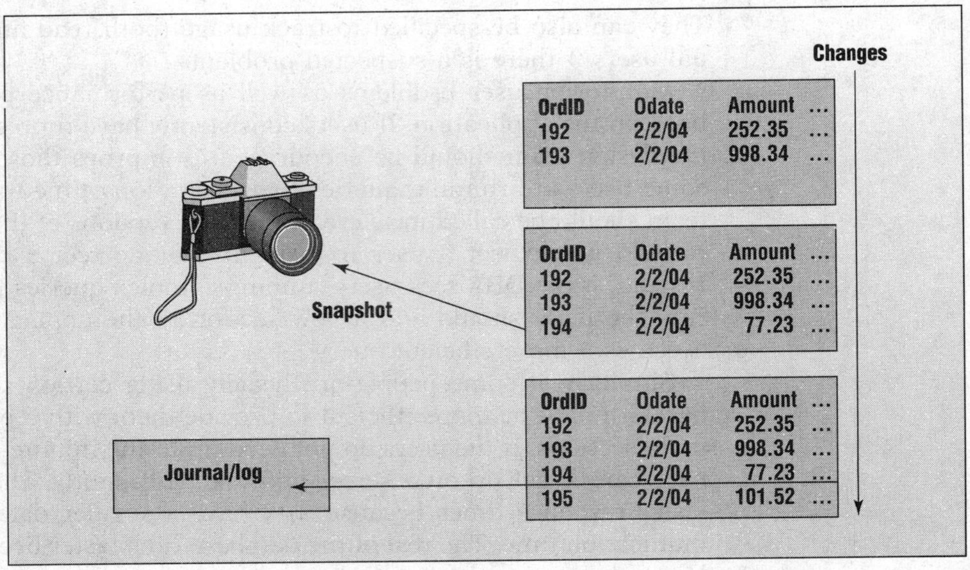

FIGURE 9.8 Backup of a changing database. Backup takes a snapshot at one point in time. New changes are stored in the journal or log. Recovery loads snapshot and adds or deletes changes in the journal.

The catch is that the DBA must decide how often to perform an incremental (partial) backup and how often a full backup (snapshot) is needed. A partial backup is faster to create and requires less storage space but takes longer to restore in the event of a disaster.

If there is a problem, the database has to be restored from the backup tapes. First the DBMS loads the most recent snapshot data. Then it examines the transactions. Completed transactions are rolled forward, and the changes are rewritten to the data tables. If the backup occurred in the middle of a transaction and the transaction was not completed, the DBMS will roll back or remove the initial changes and then restart the transaction. Remember that a transaction consists of a series of changes that must all succeed or fail together. The DBMS relies on the application's definition of a transaction as described in Chapter 7.

Backups have to be performed on a regular schedule. Occasionally, the schedule will have to be revised—particularly if the database records many changes. Remember that every change since the last backup is recorded in a journal or transaction log. The DBA has to watch the space on the transaction log. If it becomes too full, a backup has to be run earlier than scheduled. If these unexpected backups happen too often, the schedule should be changed.

Backup tapes must be stored offsite. Otherwise, a fire or other disaster might destroy all data stored in the building. Snapshot and journal logs should be copied and moved offsite at least once a day. Networks make it easier to transfer data if the company is large enough to support computer facilities at more than one location. Several companies provide disaster-safe vaults for storage of data tapes and disks. In extreme situations, it might pay to have duplicate computer facilities and to program the system to automatically mirror changes from the main database onto the secondary computer in a different location. Then when something goes wrong, the secondary computer can immediately pick up the operations. However, even in this situation, you should make physical backup copies.

Security and Privacy

Computer security is an issue with every company today, and any computer application faces security problems. A database collects a large amount of data in one location and makes it easy for people to retrieve and change data. In other words, a database is a critical resource that must be protected. Yet the same factors that make a database so useful also make it more difficult to secure. In particular, the purpose of a database is to share data. In a security context, you want to control who can share the data and what those users can do with it.

There are two basic categories of computer security: (1) physical security and (2) logical security. **Physical security** is concerned with physically protecting the computing resources and preparing for physical disasters that might damage equipment or data. **Logical security** consists of protecting the data and controlling access to the data.

Data Privacy

Privacy is related to security but with a slight twist. Companies and governmental agencies collect huge amounts of data on customers, suppliers, and employees. Privacy means controlling the distribution of this data and respecting the wishes of these external people. Figure 9.9 shows some of the demands placed on business data in terms of marketing, employee

FIGURE 9.9
Privacy. Many reasons exist to collect and analyze data. People might find some reasons invasive. Although few privacy laws exist, businesses and database administrators should consider the implications and trade-offs of using this data.

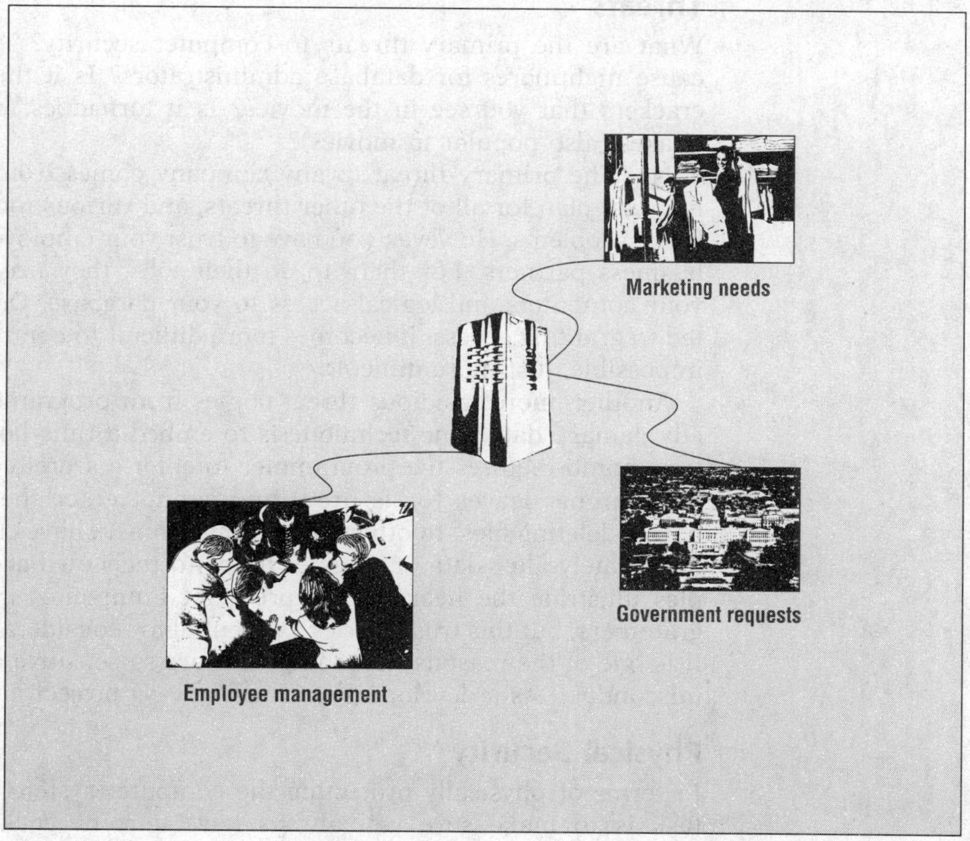

management, and governmental requests. The concepts of keeping data accurate and limiting who has access to it are the same for security and for privacy. The differences lie in the objectives and motivation. In terms of security, every company has a self-interest in keeping its data safe and protected. In terms of privacy—at least in the United States—there are few regulations or limitations on what a company can do with personal data. Whereas customers and employees may want a company to keep personal data private, companies may have a financial incentive to trade or sell the data to other companies.

In terms of data privacy, the most important question is, Who owns the data? In most cases the answer is the company or individual that collects the data. Some people, particularly in Europe, have suggested that the individuals should be considered to be the owners. Then companies would have to get permission—or pay for permission—to use or trade personal data. So far, technical limitations have prevented most of the suggested payment schemes from being implemented. However, companies must pay attention to changes in the laws regarding privacy.

Database workers have an ethical obligation in terms of data privacy. Many times, you will have access to personal data regarding customers and other employees. You have an obligation to maintain the privacy of that data: You cannot reveal the data to other people. In fact, you should avoid even reading the data. You should also not tolerate abuses by other workers within the organization. If you detect privacy (or security) violations by others, you should report the problems and issues to the appropriate supervisors.

Threats

What are the primary threats to computer security? What possible events cause nightmares for database administrators? Is it the outside hackers or crackers that you see in the movies? Is it tornadoes, hurricanes, or earthquakes (also popular in movies)?

No. The primary threat to any company comes from "insiders." Companies can plan for all of the other threats, and various tools exist to help minimize problems. However, you have to trust your employees, consultants, and business partners. For them to do their jobs, they need physical access to your computers and logical access to your database. Once you are committed to granting access, it becomes more difficult to control what they do. Not impossible, just more difficult.

Another, more insidious threat comes from programmers who intentionally damage data. One technique is to embed a time bomb in a program. A time bomb requires the programmer to enter a secret code every day. If the programmer leaves (or is fired) and cannot enter the code, the program begins deleting files. In other cases, programmers have created programs that deliberately alter data or transfer funds to their own accounts. These examples illustrate the heart of the problem. Companies must trust their programmers, but this trust carries a potential for considerable damage or fraud. It is one of the reasons that companies are so sensitive about MIS employee misconduct. As a developer, you must always project an image of trust.

Physical Security

In terms of physically protecting the computer system, the most important task is to make sure you always have current backups. This policy of maintaining backups also applies to hardware. In case of a fire or other physical disaster, you need to collect the data tapes and then find a computer to load and run them. Instead of waiting until a disaster happens, you really need to create a disaster plan.

A **disaster plan** is a complete list of the steps that the IS department will take if a disaster hits the information system. The plan details who is in charge, describes what steps everyone will take, lists contact numbers, and tells how you will get the systems up and running. One popular method of finding an alternative computer is to lease a hot site from a disaster planning company. A **hot site** consists of a computer facility that has power, terminals, communication systems, and a computer. You pay a monthly fee for the right to use the facility if a disaster occurs. If there is a disaster, you activate the disaster plan, collect the data tapes, load the system, load your backup tapes, and run the system from the hot site. A slightly cheaper alternative is to lease a cold site. A **cold site** or **shell site** is similar to a hot site, but it does not have the computer and telecommunications equipment. If a disaster occurs, you call your hardware vendor and beg for a new computer. Actually, vendors have been very cooperative. The catch is that it can still take several days to receive and install a new computer. Can your company survive for several days without a computer system? To replace smaller computers, some of the disaster recovery companies can deliver a truck to your site and run the system from your parking lot.

A more interesting problem arises with protecting personal computers. First, it is more challenging to back up data on many individual computers. If they are connected to a network, the data can be transferred to a central file server and copied from there. If there is a fire, at least the data can be recovered. Now, what about the computers? If you lose 5 or 10 computers, you can easily buy replacement units at your local computer store. But if you lose several hundred computers, it will be a little more difficult to replace them. One creative solution is to help employees purchase computers for their use at home. If there is a problem, they can work from home while you rebuild the central computer systems and replace the personal computers.

As summarized in Figure 9.10, prevention is another important step in providing physical security. Computer facilities should have fire detection and protection systems. Similarly, computer facilities should be located away from flood plains, earthquake faults, tidal areas, and other locations subject to known disasters. Physical access to computers, network equipment, and personal computers should be limited. Most companies have instituted

FIGURE 9.10
Physical security controls. Backup data is the most important step. Having a place to move to is a second step. Disaster plans and prevention help prevent problems and make recovery faster.

- Backup data
- Backup hardware
- Disaster planning and testing
- Prevention
  - Location
  - Fire monitoring and control
  - Control physical access

company badges with electronic locks. Access by visitors, delivery people, and temporary employees should be controlled.

Managerial Controls

Because the major threats to data security come from company insiders, traditional managerial controls play an important role in enhancing security. For example, one of the most important controls begins with the hiring process. Some firms perform background checks to verify the character and trustworthiness of the employees. Even simple verification of references will help to minimize problems. Similarly, firms have become more cautious when terminating employees—particularly MIS employees with wide access to databases. Even for routine layoffs, access rights and passwords are revoked immediately.

Sensitive jobs are segmented. For example, several employees are required to complete financial transactions. Transactions involving larger amounts of money are routed to higher level employees. Similarly, outside institutions like banks often call back to designated supervisors to verify large transactions. Transactions are often monitored and recorded in terms of the time, location, and person performing the operations.

In some cases, security can be enhanced through physical control over the hardware. Centralized computers are placed in locked and guarded rooms. Employees are often tracked through video monitors. Security badges are also used to track employee access to locations and computer hardware.

Consultants and business alliances also raise security concerns. Generally, you have less control over the selection of the consultant and any partnership employees. Although you have control in the selection of a consulting firm, you have little control over the specific employees assigned to your location. These risks can be controlled by limiting their access to the data and restricting their access to physical locations. In some situations, you may also want to pair an internal employee with each consultant.

Logical Security

The essence of logical security is that you want to allow each user to have some access to the data, but you want to control exactly what type of access the user will have. You also want to monitor access to the data to identify potential problems. Figure 9.11 notes the three basic problems that you want to avoid: unauthorized disclosure, unauthorized modification, and unauthorized withholding of information (or denial of service).

Some information needs to be protected so that only a select group of users can retrieve it. For example, the company's strategic marketing plans need to be protected so that no competitor can retrieve the data. To be safe, only a few top people in the company would have access to the plans.

Some information is safe to display to users, but you do not want the users to change it. For example, an employee should be able to check the human resource files to verify his or her salary, remaining vacation days, or merit

FIGURE 9.11
Logical security problems. Each situation can cause problems for the company, including financial loss, lost time, lost sales, or destruction of the company.

- Unauthorized disclosure
- Unauthorized modification
- Unauthorized withholding (denial of service)

evaluations. But it would be a mistake to allow the employee to change any of this data. No matter how honest your employees are, it would be a dangerous temptation to allow them to alter their salary, for example.

The third problem is subtle but just as dangerous. Consider what would happen if the chief financial officer needs to retrieve data to finalize a bank loan. However, the security system is set incorrectly and refuses to provide the data needed. If the data is not delivered to the bank by the end of the day, the company will default on several payments, receive negative publicity, lose 20 percent of its stock price, and risk going under. The point is that withholding data from authorized users can be just as dangerous as allowing access to the wrong people.

Assuming you have a sophisticated computer system and a DBMS that supports security controls, two steps are needed to prevent these problems. First, the computer system must be able to identify each user. Second, the owner of the data must assign the proper access rights to every piece of data. The DBA (or a security officer) is responsible for assigning and managing user accounts to uniquely identify users. The application designer and data owners are jointly responsible for identifying the necessary security controls and access rights for each user.

User Identification

One of the major difficulties of logical computer security is identifying the user. Humans recognize other people with sophisticated pattern-recognition techniques applied to appearance, voice, handwriting, and so on. Yet even people can be fooled. Computers are weak at pattern recognition, so other techniques are required.

The most common method of identifying users is by accounts and passwords. Each person has a unique account name and chooses a password. In theory, the password is known only to the individual user and the computer system. When the user enters the correct name and matching password, the computer accepts the identity of the person.

The problem is that computers are better than people at remembering passwords. Consequently, people make poor choices for passwords. Some of the basic rules for creating passwords are outlined in Figure 9.12. The best passwords are long, contain nonalphabetic characters, have no relationship to the user, and are changed often. Fine, but a user today can easily have 10, 20, or more different accounts and passwords. Almost no one can remember every account and the convoluted passwords required for security. So there is a natural inclination either to write the passwords in a convenient location (where they can be found by others) or choose simple passwords (which can be guessed).

Passwords are the easiest system to implement at this time. Some work is being done at storing passwords in a central security server (e.g., Kerberos),

FIGURE 9.12
Password suggestions. Pick passwords that are not in a dictionary and are hard to guess. The catch is, Can you remember a convoluted password?

- Do not use "real" words.
- Do not use personal (or pet) names.
- Include nonalphabetic characters.
- Use at least six characters.
- Change it often.

where a user logs into the main server and all other software verifies users with that server. Another approach is to use password generator cards. Each user carries a small card that generates a new password every minute. At login, the computer generates a password that is synchronized to the card. Once the password is used, it is invalidated, so if an interloper observes a password, it has no value. The system still requires users to memorize a short password just in case a thief steals the password card. Of course, if a user loses the card, that user cannot get access to the computers. Encrypted software variations can be loaded onto laptop computers, which then provide access to the corporate network.

Other alternatives are being developed to get away from the need to memorize passwords. Biometric systems that measure physical characteristics already exist and are becoming less expensive. For example, fingerprint, handprint, iris pattern, voice recognition, and thermal imaging systems now work relatively well. The advantage to biometric approaches is that the user does not have to memorize anything or carry around devices that could be lost or stolen. The main drawback is cost, since the validating equipment has to be installed anywhere that employees might need access to a computer. A secondary problem is that although the devices are good at preventing unauthorized access, many of them still have relatively high failure rates and refuse access to authorized users.

After individual users are identified, most systems enable you to assign the individuals to groups. Groups make it easier to assign permissions to users. For example, by putting 100 employees into a clerical group, you can grant permissions to the group, which is much faster than assigning the same permissions 100 times.

Access Controls

After users are identified, they can be assigned specific permissions to any resource. From a database perspective, two levels of access must be set. First, the user must be granted access to the overall database, using operating system commands. Second, the user must be granted individual permissions, using the database security commands.

Remember that the DBMS is just another piece of software that runs in the environment of the computer. It stores data in files that are controlled and monitored by the operating system. Before anyone can get access to the data controlled by the DBMS, the computer must give that person permission to access the entire database directory and its files. This situation also requires users to be identified twice: once by the operating system and once by the DBMS. On some systems (e.g., Windows 2000), the DBMS might accept the user identification directly from the operating system. On operating systems that have no security provisions (such as personal computer–based Windows), the DBMS is responsible for providing all security. Even with advanced database systems, you might need to create user accounts within the DBMS for some applications. For example, Web-based applications avoid using the operating system log in, and it is often easier to assign users and passwords within the database itself.

Operating system permissions consist of permissions at the directory level (read, view, write, create, and delete). Similar permissions apply to individual files (read, write, edit, and delete). On larger systems the DBMS logs in as a separate user. The DBA grants this DBMS user full directory and file

FIGURE 9.13
DBMS privileges. These privileges apply to the entire table or query. The first three (read, update, and insert) are commonly used. The design privileges are usually granted only to developers.

- Read data
- Update data
- Insert data
- Delete data
- Open/run
- Read design
- Modify design
- Administer

permissions to his or her own files. If you are running a personal computer–based system over a network, you will have to use the network operating system to give users access to your files. For example, users should be given read access to the directory where you store the file. They should also be given read and write permissions on the specific file and on the lock file. Avoid giving them delete permission to any files, however. A disgruntled user with delete permission could delete your entire database—even if he or she cannot change individual items. Of course, you have a backup, but the delay in finding the problem and restoring the database can be annoying to users.

When the operating system user has access to the overall files, you can use the DBMS security system to control access to individual tables. In most cases the DBA will have to create user accounts within the DBMS to identify each user. In some situations this technique means that users will have to log in twice: once for the operating system and once for the database. All of the database systems have a DBA security tool to make it easy to add or delete users and to change passwords.

The privileges listed in Figure 9.13 apply to the entire table or query. The most common privileges you will grant are read, update, and insert. Delete permission means that a user can delete an entire row; it should be granted to only a few people in specific circumstances. Privileges that are more powerful can be granted to enable users to read and modify the design of the tables, forms, and reports. These privileges should be reserved for trusted users. Users will rarely need to modify the design of the underlying tables. These privileges are granted to developers.

With most database systems the basic security permissions can be set with two SQL commands: **GRANT** and **REVOKE**. Figure 9.14 shows the standard syntax of the GRANT command. The REVOKE command is similar. SQL 92 provides some additional control over security by allowing you to specify columns in the GRANT and REVOKE commands, so you can grant access to just one or two columns within a table. However, the privilege applies to every row in the table or query.

FIGURE 9.14
SQL security commands. Most systems also provide a visual tool to assign and revoke access rights.

```
GRANT privileges
ON objects
TO users

REVOKE privileges
ON objects
FROM users
```

Most of the database systems provide a visual security tool to help assign access rights. The SQL commands are useful for batch operations when you need to assign permissions to a large number of tables or for several users at the same time. The visual tools are easier to use for single operations. They also make it easy to see exactly which permissions have currently been assigned to individuals.

The GRANT command offers an additional option that is sometimes useful. As the owner of a database element, you have the ability to pass on some of your powers when you grant access. If you add the phrase **WITH GRANT OPTION**, then whoever just received the privileges you specified can also pass those on to someone else. For example, you could grant SELECT (read) privilege on a table WITH GRANT OPTION to the head of the marketing department. That person could then give read access to the other employees in the marketing department.

Database Roles

Imagine the administrative hassles you would face if you have to assign security permissions for hundreds or thousands of employees. Each time an employee is hired or leaves, someone would have to assign or remove rights to possibly hundreds of tables and views. The task would be time-consuming and highly error-prone. Even if you build SQL procedures to help, it would require almost constant maintenance. A far more effective solution is to define database roles. A **role** is often associated with a group of users and consists of a set of permissions that are assigned together. As shown in Figure 9.15, you create a role and assign the desired permissions to the role instead of to the individual users. Then you assign the role to the specific users. When a new employee is hired, adding the role to that user provides all of the necessary permissions. The SQL 99 standard supports the ability to assign roles to other roles. For instance, you could define smaller sets of tasks as roles (sell item, add customer, update inventory) and then assign those tasks to broader roles (sales clerk, inventory clerk, and so on).

Queries as Controls

With many systems, the basic security commands are powerful but somewhat limited in their usefulness. Many systems only grant and revoke privileges to an entire table or query. The true power of a database security system lies in the ability to assign access to individual queries. Consider the example in Figure 9.16. You have an Employee table that lists each worker's name, phone number, and salary. You want to use the table as a phone book so employees can look up phone numbers for other workers. The problem is that you do not want employees to see the salary values. The solution is to create a query that contains just the name and phone number. Remember that a query does not duplicate the data—it simply retrieves the data from the other tables. Now, assign the SELECT privilege on the Phonebook query to all employees and revoke all employee privileges to the original Employee table. If you want, you can also choose specific rows from the Employee table. For example, you might not want to display the phone numbers of the senior executives.

Chapters 4 and 5 showed you the power of queries. This power can be used to create virtually any level of security that you need. Virtually all user

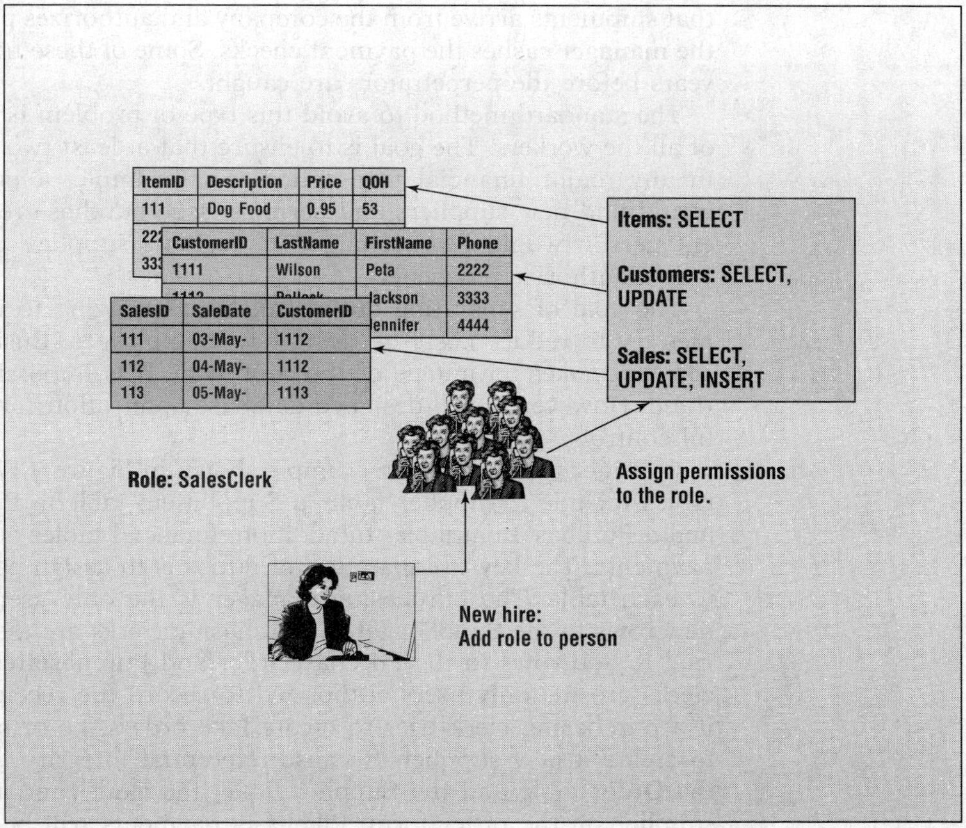

FIGURE 9.15
Database roles. Create a role and assign permissions to the role. When an employee is added or released, you simply assign or remove the desired roles to instantly provide the appropriate permissions.

access to the database will be through queries. Avoid granting any access directly to a table. Then it will be easier to alter the security conditions as the business needs change.

The basic process is to confer with the users and to determine exactly which type of access each user needs to the data. In particular, determine which users need to add or change data. Then create the users and assign the appropriate security conditions to the queries. Be certain to test the application for each user group. If security is a critical issue, you should consider assigning a couple of programmers to "attack" the database from the perspective of different users to see whether they can delete or change important files.

Division of Duties

For years, security experts have worried about theft and fraud by people who work for the company. Consider a classic situation that seems to arise every year. A purchasing manager sets up a fake supplier. The manager then pretends

FIGURE 9.16
Security using queries. You wish to let all employees look up worker phone numbers. But employees should not be able to see salaries. Define a query that contains only the data needed, and then give employees access to the query—not to the original table.

```
Employee(ID, Name, Phone, Salary)

        Query: Phonebook
        SELECT Name, Phone
        FROM Employee
```

that shipments arrive from the company and authorizes payments. Of course, the manager cashes the payment checks. Some of these frauds run for several years before the perpetrators are caught.

The standard method to avoid this type of problem is to divide the duties of all the workers. The goal is to ensure that at least two people are involved in any major financial transaction. For example, a purchasing manager would find new suppliers and perhaps issue purchase requisitions. A different person would be in charge of receiving supplies, and a third person would authorize payments.

The goal of separating duties can be challenging to implement. Companies try to reduce costs by using fewer employees. Business picks up, and someone takes advantage of the confusion. It is impossible to eliminate all fraud. However, a well-designed database application can provide some useful controls.

Consider the purchasing example shown in Figure 9.17 in which the basic tables include a Supplier table, a SupplyItem table, a PurchaseOrder table, and a PurchaseItem table. In addition, financial tables authorize and record payments. The key to separation of duties is to assign permissions correctly to each table. The purchasing manager is the only user authorized to add new rows to the Supplier table. Purchasing clerks are the only users authorized to add rows to the PurchaseOrder and PurchaseItem tables. Receiving clerks are the only users authorized to record the receipt of supplies. Now if a purchasing clerk tries to create fake orders, he or she will not be able to create a new supplier. Because referential integrity is enforced between the Order table and the Supplier table, the clerk cannot even enter a false supplier on the order form. Likewise, payments will be sent only to legitimate companies, and a purchasing manager will not be able to fake a receipt of a shipment. The power of the database security system is that it will always enforce the assigned responsibilities.

Software Updates

Modern software is large and complex. Software vendors and other researchers often find security problems after the software has been released. Typically, the company has a process to evaluate security threats, create patches to fix the problems, and notify users to update their systems. The difficulty is that announcing the security flaw to users also means that potential hackers are alerted to the problem. As long as all users patch their systems immediately, these announcements would be effective. But as a database administrator, the issue is not that simple. Even if you receive the notice, you still need to test the patch and ensure that it does not cause problems with your applications. Several major attacks have been launched against companies by attackers using known security holes that were not patched.

Consequently, a major task of database administrators is to monitor security releases for the DBMS and operating system software. These patches need to be installed on test machines and moved to the production systems as soon as possible. In the meantime, the network administrators can block specific ports and prevent outsiders from accessing features on the database. The DBAs and the network administrators also have to carefully monitor the network and the servers to see if rogue processes have been started.

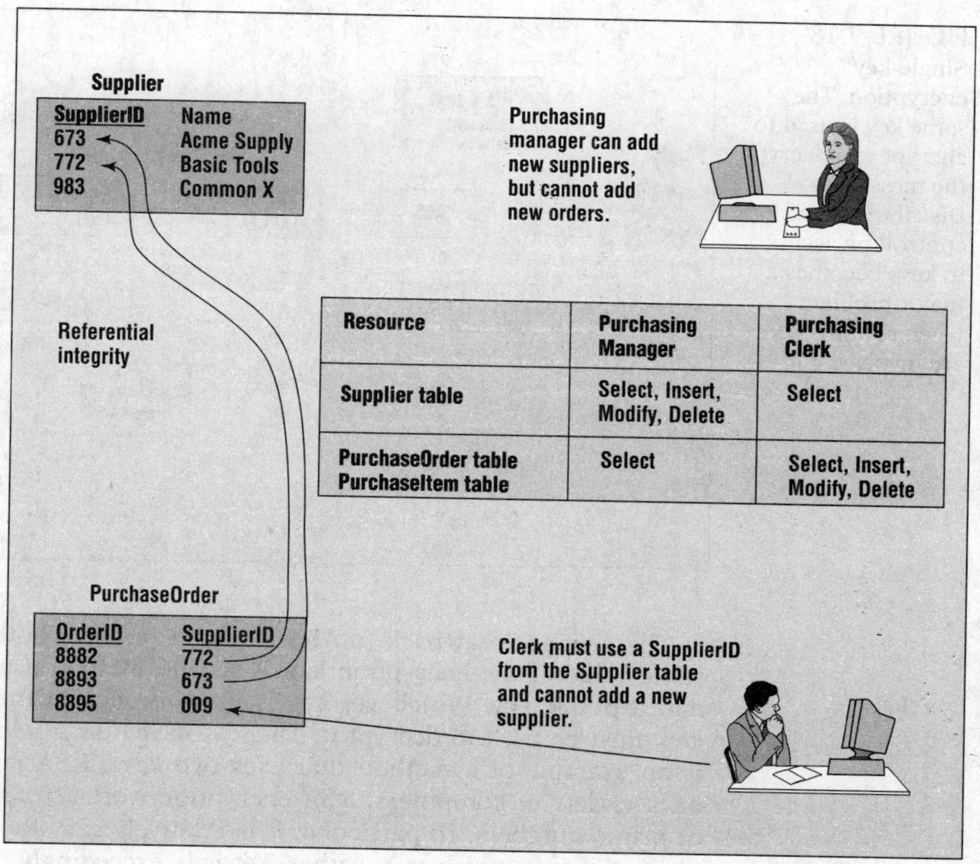

FIGURE 9.17
Separation of duties. The clerk cannot create a fake supplier. Referential integrity forces the clerk to enter a SupplierID from the Supplier table, and the clerk cannot add a new row to the Supplier table.

Encryption

Encryption is a method of modifying the original information according to some code so that it can be read only if the user knows the decryption key. Encryption can be used to transmit information from one computer to another. Information stored on a computer also can be encrypted. Without the encryption key, the files are gibberish. Encryption is critical for personal computer–based systems that do not provide user identification and access controls. Encryption is also important when transmitting data across networks—particularly the Internet.

Two basic types of encryption are commonly used today. Most methods use a single key to both encrypt and decrypt a message. For example, the **advanced encryption system (AES)** method uses a single key. Although AES is a U.S. standard, versions of it are available throughout the world because it is based on Rijndael created by two Belgian cryptographers. The AES algorithm is fast and supports key lengths of 128, 192, and 256 bits—protecting it from a **brute force attack** that tries all possible key values. Note that adding one bit to the key length provides twice as many keys; for example, moving from 56 to 128 bits adds 2 to the 72nd power more possibilities to test, making it virtually impossible to attack with brute force—using today's computers. Figure 9.18 shows a basic use of the AES encryption method.

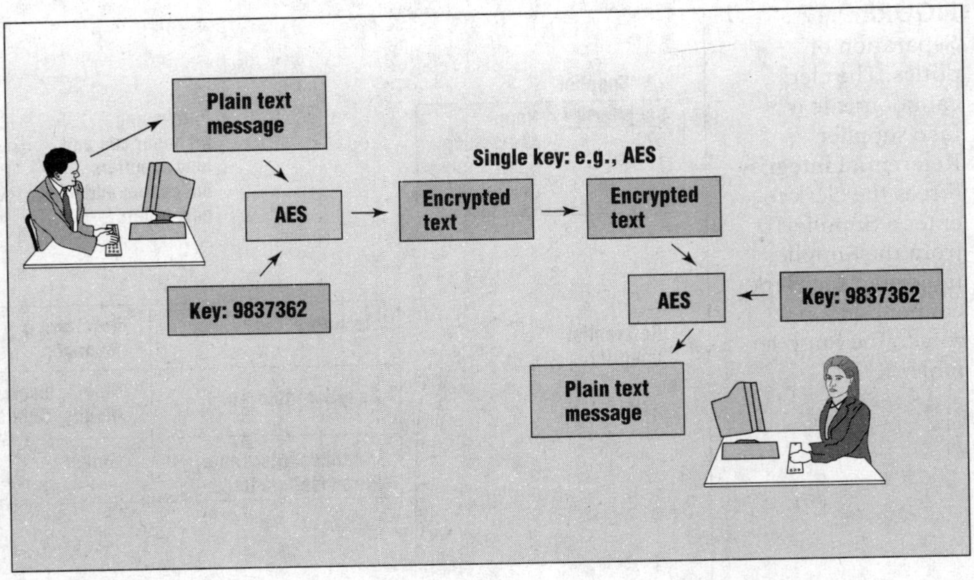

FIGURE 9.18
Single-key encryption. The same key is used to encrypt and decrypt the message. Distributing and controlling access to keys becomes a major problem when several users are involved.

The primary drawback to AES is that it requires both parties to have the same value of the encryption key. A second method uses both a **private key** and a **public key**. Whichever key is used to encrypt the message, the other key must be used to decrypt it. The **Rivest-Shamir-Adelman (RSA) algorithm** is an example of a method that uses two keys. RSA protection is available on a variety of computers. RSA encryption works because of the properties of prime numbers. In particular, it is relatively easy for computers to multiply two prime numbers together. Yet it is exceedingly difficult to factor the resulting large number back into its two component parts. The security of the RSA approach relies on using huge numbers (128 digits or more), which would take many years to factor with current technology.

Methods that use two keys have some interesting uses. The trick is that everyone knows your public key, but only you know the private key. Consider a situation in which Bob wants to send a database transaction to Alice across the Internet. Bob looks up Alice's public key in a directory. Once the message is encrypted with Alice's public key, only her private key can decrypt it: No one else can read or change the transaction message. However, someone might be able to destroy the message before Alice receives it.

There is a second use of dual-key systems called **authentication**. Let's say that Bob wants to send a message to Alice. To make sure that only she can read it, he encrypts it with her public key. However, Bob is worried that someone has been sending false messages to Alice using his name, and he wants to make sure that Alice knows the message came from him. If Bob also encrypts the message with his private key, it can be decrypted only with Bob's public key. When Alice receives the message, she applies her private key and Bob's public key. If the message is readable, then it must have been sent by Bob. This situation is displayed in Figure 9.19.

Modern encryption schemes are powerful tools. They can be used to automatically ensure safe storage and transmission of data—even in open networks like the Internet. Keep in mind that all encryption schemes are subject to a brute force attack. As computers get faster, older encryption schemes become risky.

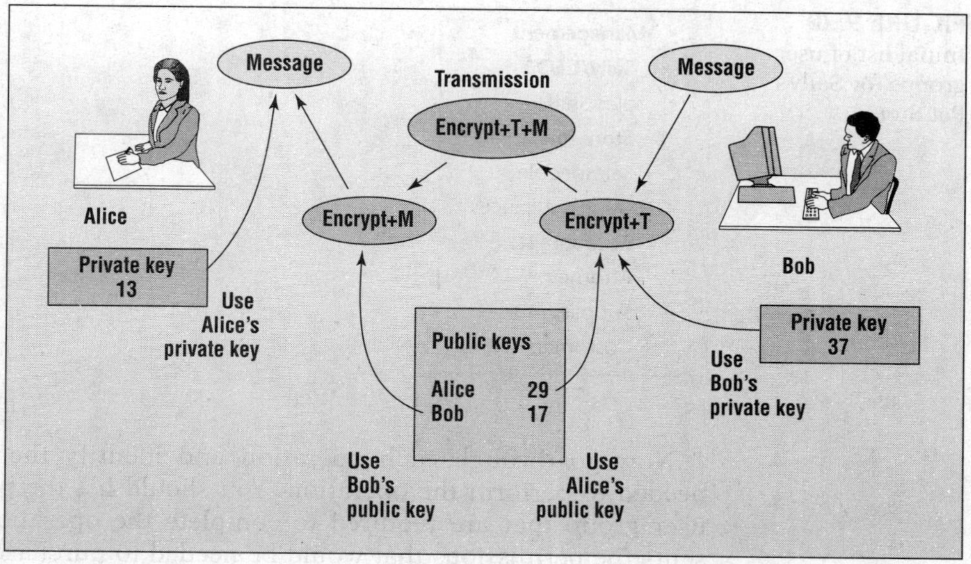

FIGURE 9.19
Dual-key encryption. Bob sends a message to Alice. By encrypting it first with his private key, Bob authenticates the message. By encrypting it next with Alice's public key, only Alice can read the message.

Dual-key encryption systems are useful in all aspects of information communication. They do have one complication: The directory that lists public keys must be accurate. Think about what would happen to authentication if someone impersonated Bob and invented a private and public key for him. This interloper would then be accepted as Bob for any transaction. Hence, the public keys must be maintained by an organization that is trusted. Additionally, this organization must be careful to verify the identity of anyone (individual or corporation) who applies for a key. Several companies have begun to offer these services as a **certificate authority**. One of the leading commercial firms is Verisign.

For internal use, it is relatively easy to set up a company server that functions as a certificate authority. With this approach, you can generate internal security certificates that will protect transmissions among employees and internal database applications. This approach is significantly less expensive than purchasing annual certificates for every employee. Of course, your certificates will probably not be accepted by anyone outside the company, so you will still need to obtain commercial certificates for applications that deal with external firms and people.

Sally's Pet Store

The first step in assigning security permissions for Sally's Pet Store is to identify the various groups of users. The initial list is shown in Figure 9.20. As the company grows, there will eventually be additional categories of users. Note that these are groups and that several people might be assigned to each category.

The second step is to identify the operations that various users will perform. Separate forms will be designed to support each of these activities. Figure 9.21 contains a partial list of the major activities.

The user and group accounts need to be created within the operating system and within the DBMS. After the tables, queries, and forms are created, the DBA should make sure that only the DBA should be able to read or modify data.

FIGURE 9.20
Initial list of user groups for Sally's Pet Store.

- Management
  - Sally/CEO
- Sales Staff
  - Store manager
  - Salespeople
- Business Alliances
  - Accountant
  - Attorney
  - Suppliers
  - Customers

Now go through each operation and identify the queries and tables needed to perform the operation. You should list the permissions for each user group that are required to complete the operation. Figure 9.22 presents the permissions that would be needed to purchase items from suppliers. Notice that only the store managers (and the owner) can order new merchandise. (Add permission on the MerchandiseOrder and OrderItem tables.) Also note that only the owner can add new suppliers. Remember that a referential integrity constraint is in place that forces the MerchandiseOrder table to use only Suppliers already listed in the Supplier table. Therefore, a store manager will not be able to invent a fictitious supplier. Also note that you would like to permit store managers to add items to the OrderItem table, but they should not be able to alter the order once it has been completed. The DBMS might not support this restriction, and you probably have to give the managers Write permission as well. If available, the distinction would be useful. Otherwise, a manager is charge of receiving products could steal some of the items and change the original order quantity. If Sally has enough managers, this problem can be minimized by

FIGURE 9.21
Primary operations at Sally's Pet Store. All of these transactions will have forms or reports built into the database.

- Products
  - Sales
  - Purchases
  - Receive products
- Animals
  - Sales
  - Purchases
  - Animal health care
- Employees
  - Hiring/release
  - Hours
  - Paychecks
- Accounts
  - Payments
  - Receipts
  - Management reports

FIGURE 9.22
Permissions for purchases. Notice that only the owner can add new suppliers, and only top-level managers can create new orders.

	Purchase Query				PurchaseItem Query	
Purchase	Merchandise Order	Supplier	Employee	City	Order Item	Merchandise
Sally/CEO	W/A	W/A	R: ID, Name	R	W/A	W/A
Store manager	W/A	R*	R: ID, Name	R	A	R
Salespeople	R	R*	R: ID, Name	R	R	R
Accountant	R	R*	R: ID, Name	R	R	R
Attorney	———	———	———	———	———	———
Suppliers	R	R*	———	R	R	R
Customers	———	———	———	———	———	———

*Basic supplier data: ID, Name, Address, Phone, ZIPCode, CityID.
R = Read; W = Write; A = Add.

dividing the duties and having one manager place orders and another manager record the shipments.

Also note that Sally wants to record the identity of the employee who placed the order. For this purpose, you need only read permission on the EmployeeID and Name columns. This privilege can be set by creating a separate EmployeeName query that only retrieves a minimal number of columns from the Employee table. Then you can use this query for purchases instead of the original Employee table.

Summary

Several steps are involved in managing a database. The DA performs management tasks related to design and planning. Key priorities are establishing standards to facilitate sharing data and integrating applications. The DA also works with users and business managers to identify new applications. In contrast, the DBA is responsible for installing and maintaining the DBMS software, defining databases, ensuring data is backed up, monitoring performance, and assisting developers.

Each stage of application development involves different aspects of database management. Planning entails estimating the size and approximate development costs. Project management skills and teamwork are used in the design stage to split the project and assign it to individual workers. Implementation requires establishing and enforcing development standards, testing procedures, training, and operating plans. Once the application is operational, the DBA monitors performance in terms of space and processing time. Physical storage parameters and other attributes are modified to improve the application's performance.

Backup and recovery are key administrative tasks that must be performed on a regular basis. Backup is more challenging on systems that are running continuously. The DBMS takes a snapshot and saves the data at one point in time. All changes are saved to a journal, which is also backed up on a regular basis. If the system has to be recovered, the DBMS loads the snapshot and then integrates the logged changes.

Security is an important issue in database management. Physical security consists of problems that involve the actual equipment, such as natural disasters or physical theft of hardware. Data backup and disaster planning are the keys to providing physical security. Logical security consists of protecting data from unauthorized disclosure, unauthorized modification, and unauthorized withholding. The first step to providing logical security is to create a system that enables the computer to identify the user. Then application designers and users must determine the access rights that should be assigned to each user. Access rights should be assigned to enforce separation of duties.

Encryption is a tool that is often needed to protect databases. Encryption is particularly useful when the operating system cannot protect the database files. Encryption is also used when data must be transmitted across networks—particularly open networks like the Internet.

A Developer's View

Miranda will quickly see that the tasks of a DBA are different from those of a developer, yet the developer must work closely with the DBA. As a developer, you need to understand the importance of data standards. You also need to work with the DBA in planning, implementing, and maintaining the database application. Before implementing the application, you need to establish the database security rights and controls. For your class project, identify all users and determine their access rights. Use queries to give them access only to the data that they need. Test your work. Also, run any performance monitors or analysis tools.

Key Terms

24-7, *339*
advanced encryption system (AES), *351*
authentication, *352*
brute force attack, *351*
certificate authority, *353*
cold site, *343*
computer-aided software engineering (CASE), *337*
data administration, *331*
data administrator (DA), *332*
database administration, *331*
database administrator (DBA), *333*
disaster plan, *343*
encryption, *351*
GRANT, *347*
hot site, *343*
logical security, *341*
metadata, *336*
physical security, *341*
private key, *352*
public key, *352*
REVOKE, *347*
Rivest-Shamir-Adelman (RSA) encryption, *352*
role, *348*
schema, *334*
shell site, *343*
snapshot, *339*
tablespace, *334*
tuning, *339*
WITH GRANT OPTION, *348*

Review Questions

1. What is the role and purpose of a data administrator?
2. What tasks are performed by a database administrator?
3. What tools are available to monitor database performance?
4. What aspects of a database should be monitored to avoid performance problems?
5. How does the DA facilitate teamwork in developing database applications?
6. What are the primary security threats to a business?
7. How is a hot site used to protect the business applications?
8. What are the three problems faced by logical security systems?
9. What basic methods are available to identify users in a security system?
10. What are the basic database privileges that can be assigned to users?

11. How do queries provide detailed access controls?
12. How does a good DBMS application provide for division of duties?
13. Why is encryption an important step in securing databases?
14. How does a dual-key encryption system provide for security and authentication at the same time?

Exercises

1. Extend the example in Figure 9.16. Add Title to the Employee table. Now create two phone books. One is accessible to all employees and lets them see phone numbers for anyone without the word *Executive* in his or her title. The second book is for executives and lists phone numbers of all employees.
2. A DBMS is halfway through recording a transaction with several related updates, when someone trips over the computer's power cord. Describe the steps the DBMS uses to protect and restore the database.
3. Briefly describe how you would protect a computer system from the following problems.
   a. An employee who was just fired steals the entire customer table and sells it to a competitor.
   b. The candles on the CEO's birthday cake ignite his PDA, which he drops in the trash can. The ensuing fire burns down the data center.
   c. A disk drive fails.
   d. A car flies off the road and wipes out a major power line; it takes 6 hours to restore power to your facility.
   e. The CFO loses his cell phone/PDA and someone uses the stored passwords to steal money from his benefits accounts.
   f. An investigator has accused your company of violating the Health Insurance Portability and Accountability Act of 1996 (HIPPA) privacy law.
   g. An executive's administrative assistant inflated supplier payments and moved the excess money to her bank account.
   h. A programmer you hired is now living in Brazil on the $2.5 million his software stole by transferring data to his personal accounts.
   i. Investigators are charging the CEO and CFO under the Sarbanes-Oxley Act for falsifying financial reports.
   j. An automated attack just wiped out your database server using a known problem with the DBMS software.
4. Explain why 24-7 access to a transaction database makes it more difficult to provide backup and security.
5. What are the current U.S. laws on data privacy? What are the current European rules concerning customer privacy? What steps should a database administrator take to ensure privacy of data?
6. You are setting up security for an e-commerce site. The application uses the following tables:

```
Customer(CustomerID, Name, Address,...)
Items(ItemID, Description, ListPrice, QOH)
Sale(SaleID, CustomerID, SaleDate, IPAddress,
CCNumber,...)
SaleItem(SaleID, ItemID, SalePrice, Quantity)
```

Define the access rights to each table for the following users: managers, shipping clerks, and customers who use the website. Define any queries you need to add security conditions.

7. You are setting up a small billing database for a physician's office with the following tables:

```
Client(ClientID, Name, Address, DOB, Gender,...)
Staff(StaffID, Name, Specialty,...)
Visit(VisitID, ClientID, DateTime, Charge, InsuranceCompany,
InsuranceID)
TreatmentCode(TreatmentCode, Description, Cost)
Treatment(VisitID, TreatmentCode, Comments, Charge)
Insurance(CompanyID, Contact, Phone, EDIAddress)
```

Define the access rights to each table for the following users: physicians, accountants, clerks (reservations), clients (if you create a website), insurance company. Define any queries you need to add additional security conditions.

8. Employees and other insiders present the greatest security problems to companies. Outline basic policies and procedures that should be implemented to protect the computer systems. (*Hint:* Research employee hiring procedures.)

Sally's Pet Store

9. Devise a security plan for Sally's Pet Store. Identify the various classes of users and determine the level of access required by each group. Create any queries necessary to provide the desired security.
10. If it does not already exist, create a sales query that uses data from the Customer, Sales, SaleItems, Employee, and City tables to produce a report of all sales sorted by state. Use a query analyzer to evaluate the query and identify methods to improve its performance.
11. Create a backup and recovery plan that will be used at Sally's Pet Store. Identify the techniques used, who will be in charge, and the frequency of the backups. Explain how the process will change as the store and the database grow larger.
12. What physical security controls will be needed to protect the database and hardware?

Rolling Thunder Bicycles

13. Devise a security plan for Rolling Thunder Bicycles. Identify the various classes of users and determine the level of access required by each group. Create any queries necessary to provide the desired security.
14. Devise a backup and recovery plan for Rolling Thunder Bicycles. Be sure to specify what data should be backed up and how often. Outline a basic disaster plan for the company. Where are security problems likely in the existing application? How should duties be separated to improve security?
15. Use the performance analyzer tools available for your DBMS to evaluate the tables, queries, forms, and reports. Provide an explanation of the top five recommendations.
16. Analyze the BikeOrderReportQuery and identify and changes that could be made to improve the performance of the query.
17. The managers want to switch to a wireless network, and they would even like to allow managers to connect to the database and check on progress using remote PDAs and cell phones. Write a security plan to protect the database using these systems.
18. The company is planning to set up a website to enable customers to enter and track their orders using the Internet. Explain the additional security procedures that will be needed.

Website References

Site	Description
http://www.dama.org	Data management organization.
http://www.aitp.org	Association for Information Technology Professionals organization.
http://www.acm.org/sigsac	Association for Computing Machinery: Special Interest Group on Security, Audit, and Control.
http://www.cert.org	Internet organization tracking security topics.
http://www.benchmarkresources.com	A related site that explores issues in benchmarking and performance.
http://www.databasejournal.com	Database security and other database management topics.

Additional Reading

Bertino, E., B. Catania, E. Ferrari, and P. Perlasca. "A Logical Framework for Reasoning about Access Control Models." *ACM Transactions on Information and System Security (TISSEC)* 6, no. 1 (February 2003), pp. 71–127. [A detailed discussion of various security access complications.]

Brown, L., M. Mohun, J. Deep, and E. Kear. *The Complete Oracle DBA Training Course.* Upper Saddle River, NJ: Prentice Hall, 1999. [Introduction to DBA tasks in Oracle.]

Castano, S., ed. *Database Security.* Reading, MA: Addison Wasley, 1994. [Collection of articles from the Association of Computing Machinery.]

Fayyad, U. "Diving into Databases." *Database Programming & Design,* March 1998, pp. 24–31. [Good summary of OLAP, data warehouses, and future uses of databases.]

Loney, K. *Oracle DBA Handbook.* Berkeley: Osborne, 1997. [One of many Osborne books on Oracle.]

Oracle 7 Server Administrator's Guide. Oracle, 1996. [Available on CD-ROM with the Oracle DBMS. Appendix A describes the technique used to estimate space required for tables, indexes, and rollback logs.]

Stuns, D., B. Thomas, and G. Hobbs. *OCP: Oracle8i DBA Architecture & Administration and Backup & Recovery Study Guide.* Alameda, CA: Sybex, 2000. [You need to read many books to become an Oracle DBA or to pass the certification tests.]

Theriault, M. L., R. Carmichael, and J. Judson. *Oracle DBA 101.* Berkeley: Osborne/McGraw-Hill, 1999. [Good introduction to DBA tasks in Oracle.]

______, and W. Heney. *Oracle Security.* Cambridge, MA: O'Reilly & Associates, 1998. [Setting policies and plans for securing Oracle databases.]

Chapter 10

Distributed Databases and the Internet

Chapter Outline

What You Will Learn in This Chapter

- Why do companies need distributed databases? 362
- What problems are created or exacerbated with distributed databases? 367
- What are the strengths and weaknesses of a client/server application? 373
- How does a three-tier client/server application provide flexibility in an application? 375
- How do you use databases on Web servers to build interactive Internet applications? 380
- What problems arise with forms in distributed client/server applications? 385

A Developer's View

Ariel: How is the new job going, Miranda?

Miranda: Great! The other developers are really fun to work with.

Ariel: So you're not bored with the job yet?

Miranda: No. I don't think that will ever happen—everything keeps changing. Now they want me to set up a website for the sales application. They want a site where customers can check on their order status and maybe even enter new orders.

Ariel: That sounds hard. I know a little about HTML, but I don't have any idea of how you access a database over the Web.

Miranda: Well, there are some nice tools out there now. With SQL and a little programming, it should not be too hard.

Ariel: That sounds like a great opportunity. If you learn how to build websites that access databases, you can write your ticket to a job anywhere.

Introduction

Today even small businesses have more than one computer. At a minimum they have several personal computers. More realistically, most organizations today take advantage of networks of computers by installing portions of their database and applications on more than one computer. As companies open offices in new locations, they need to share data across a larger distance. Increasingly, companies are finding it useful and necessary to share data with people around the world. Manufacturing companies need to connect to suppliers, distributors, and customers. Service companies need to share data among employees or partners. All of these situations are examples of distributed databases. Many applications can take advantage of the network capabilities of the Internet and the presentation standards of the World Wide Web.

Building applications that function over networks and managing distributed databases can be complicated tasks. The goal is to provide location transparency to the users. Users should never have to know where data is stored. This feature requires a good DBMS, a solid network, and considerable database, network, and security management skills. However, a well-designed distributed database application also makes it easier for a company to expand its operations.

The Internet and the World Wide Web are increasingly used to share data. One of the fundamental strengths of the Internet is the set of standards that define how users connect to servers and how data will be displayed. By developing applications to run on a website, you ensure the widest possible compatibility and accessibility to your system. Building applications that use a database on the Web is similar to building any database; you just have to learn to use a few more tools and standards.

Sally's Pet Store

Now that the database is operating in Sally's store and the store is making money, she wants to expand. She is talking about adding a second store. She is also pushing for creation of a website, so that customers can order products, check on new animals, and get some help in caring for their pets. As a first step you have decided to talk to Sally about making your job a full-time position. She needs someone to manage the computers on a regular basis, modify the programs, and train other workers.

Sally's request to expand the database to a second store raises many questions. Does she need "instant" access to the sales data from both stores all the time? Do the stores need to share data with each other? For example, if a product is out of stock at one store, does Sally want the system to automatically check the other store? Will the stores operate somewhat independently—so that sales and financial data are maintained separately for each store—or will the data always be merged into one entity? How up-to-date does data need to be? Is it acceptable to have inventory data from yesterday, or does it need to be up-to-the-minute?

The answers to these questions determine some crucial design aspects. In particular, the primary design question to answer is whether one central database should handle all sales or separate, distributed databases should handle each store. The answer depends on how the stores are managed, the type of data needed, the network capabilities and costs, and the capabilities of the DBMS.

In many ways, initially the cheapest solution is to keep the second store completely independent. Then there is no need to share data except for some basic financial information at the end of each accounting period. A second advantage of this approach is that it is easy to expand since each new store is independent. Similarly, if something goes wrong with the computer system at one store, it will not affect the other stores.

However, at some point Sally will probably want a tighter integration of the data. For example, the ability to check inventory at other local stores can be a useful feature to customers, which means that the application will need to retrieve data from several databases, located in different stores. These distributed databases must be networked through a telecommunications channel. There are many ways to physically link computers, and you should take a telecommunications course to understand the various options. Once the computers are physically linked, you need to deal with some additional issues in terms of creating and managing the distributed databases.

The Internet has rapidly become a leading method to contact customers and share information. Connecting a database to a website is a powerful method of providing up-to-date information and enabling customers to find exactly the information they need. To understand how to link a database to a website, it is helpful to first understand the details of distributed databases.

Distributed Databases

A **distributed database** system consists of multiple independent databases that operate on two or more computers that are connected and share data over a network. The databases are usually in different physical locations. Each database is controlled by an independent DBMS, which is responsible for maintaining the integrity of its own databases. In extreme situations, the databases might be installed on different hardware, use different operating systems, and could even use DBMS software from different vendors. That last contingency is the hardest one to handle. Most current distributed

FIGURE 10.1
Distributed database. Each office has its own hardware and databases. For international projects, workers in different offices can easily share data. The workers do not need to know that the data is stored in different locations.

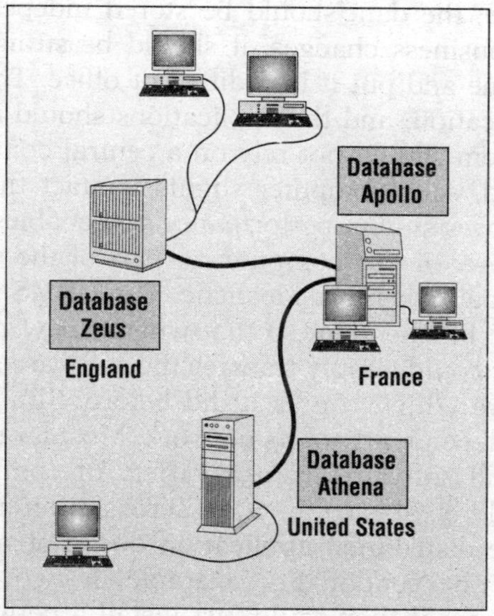

databases function better if all of the environments are running DBMS software from the same vendor.

In the example shown in Figure 10.1, a company could have offices in three different nations. Each office would have its own computer and database. Much of the data would stay within the individual offices. For example, workers in the United States would rarely need to see the daily schedules of workers in France. On the other hand, workers in France and England could be working on a large international project. The network and distributed database enable them to share data and treat the project as if all the information were in one place.

Distributed databases can be organized in several configurations. The most popular method today involves a client/server approach. In a **client/server** system, the server computer is more powerful and provides data for many clients. The client computers are usually personal computers with a graphical user interface. The role of the client is to provide the interface to the user, collect and display data, and return the data to the appropriate server.

Goals and Rules

It is difficult to create a DBMS that can adequately handle distributed databases. (The major issues will be addressed in later sections.) In fact, early systems faced various problems. Consequently, a few writers have created a set of goals or rules that constitute the useful features of a distributed DBMS. C. J. Date, who worked with E. F. Codd to define the relational database approach, lists several rules that he feels are important. This section summarizes Date's rules.

In anyone's definition of a distributed database, the most important rule is that the user should not know or care that the database is distributed. For example, the user should be able to create and run a simple query just as if the database were on one computer. Behind the scenes the DBMS might connect to three different computers, collect data, and format the results. But the user does not know about these steps.

As part of this rule, the data should be stored independently of location. For example, if the business changes, it should be straightforward to move data from one machine and put it in a different office. This move should not crash the entire application, and the applications should run with a few simple changes. The system should not rely on a central computer to coordinate all the others. Instead, each computer should contact the others as needed. This separation improves system performance and enables the other offices to continue operations even if one computer or part of the network goes down.

Some additional goals are more idealistic. The DBMS should be hardware and operating system independent so that when a newer, faster computer is needed, the company could simply transfer the software and data to the new machine and have everything run as it did before. Similarly, it is beneficial if the system runs independently of its network. Most large networks are built from components and software from a variety of companies. A good distributed DBMS should be able to function across different networks. Finally, it is preferable if the distributed application does not rely on using DBMS software from only one vendor. For example, if two companies were to merge, it would be great if they could just install a network connection and have all the applications continue to function—even if the companies have different networks, different hardware, and database software from different vendors. This idealistic scenario does not yet exist. However, some systems, such as Oracle, provide many components of these goals.

These features are desirable because they would make it easier for a company to expand or alter its databases and applications without discarding the existing work. By providing for a mix of hardware, software, and network components, these objectives also enable an organization to choose the individual components that best support its needs.

Advantages and Applications

The main strength of the distributed database approach is that it matches the way organizations function. Business operations are often distributed across different locations. For example, work and data are segmented by departments. Workers within each department share most data and communications with other workers within that department. Yet some data needs to be shared with the rest of the company as well. Similarly, larger companies often have offices in different geographical regions. Again, much of the data collected within a region is used within that region; however, some of the data needs to be shared by workers in different regions.

Three basic configurations exist for sharing data: (1) one central computer that collects and processes all data, (2) independent computer systems in each office that do not share data with the others, and (3) a distributed database system.

The second option is a possibility—as long as the offices rarely need to share data. It is still a common approach in many situations. Data that needs to be shared is transmitted via paper reports, fax or telephone calls, or possibly e-mail messages. Of course, these are ineffective methods for sharing data.

Some early computer systems used the first option. However, routing all transactions to a central computer has several drawbacks. In particular, transferring the data to one location is expensive, and if the one computer is unavailable, everyone suffers.

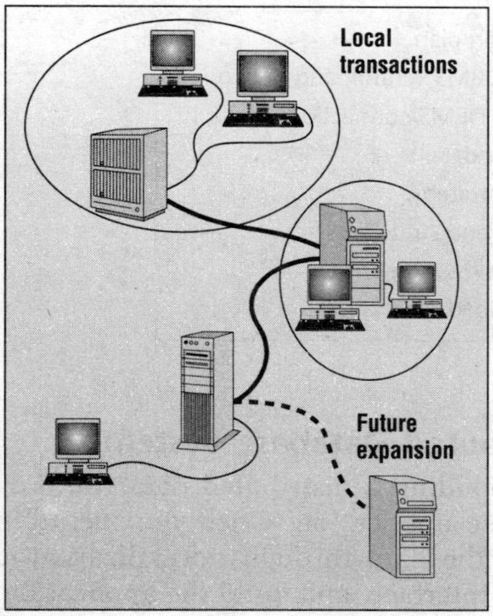

FIGURE 10.2
Distributed database strengths. Most data is collected and stored locally. Only data that needs to be shared is transmitted across the network. The system is flexible because it can be expanded in sections as the organization grows.

Figure 10.2 illustrates several advantages of the distributed database approach. First, distributed systems provide a significant performance advantage through better alignment with the needs of the organization. Most updates and queries are performed locally. Each office retains local control and responsibility for the data. Yet the system enables anyone with the proper authority to retrieve and integrate data from any portion of the company as it is needed.

A second advantage to distributed databases is that, compared to centralized systems, they are easier to expand. Think about what happens if the company is using one large, centralized computer. If the company expands into a new region, requiring more processing capacity, the entire computer might have to be replaced. With a distributed database approach, expanding into a new area would be supported by adding another computer with a database to support the new operations. All existing hardware and applications remain the same. By using smaller computer systems, it is easier and cheaper to match the changing needs of the organization.

Because the distributed database approach can be tailored to match the layout of any company, it has many applications. Two common categories are transaction processing and decision support applications. In a transaction processing system, each region would be responsible for collecting the detailed transaction data that it uses on a daily basis. For instance, a manufacturing plant would have a database to collect and store data on purchases, human relations, and production. Most of this data would be used by the individual plant to manage its operations. Yet as part of the corporate network, summary data could be collected from each plant and sent to headquarters for analysis. As another example, consider a consulting firm with offices in several countries. The workers can store their notes and comments in a local database. If a client in one country needs specialized assistance or encounters a unique problem, the local partners can use the database to search for similar problems and solutions at other offices around the world. The distributed database enables workers within the company to share their knowledge and experiences.

- Design administration plan.
- Choose hardware, DBMS vendor, and network.
- Set up network and DBMS connections.
- Choose locations for data.
- Choose replication strategy.
- Create backup plan and strategy.
- Create local views and synonyms.
- Perform stress test: loads and failures.

FIGURE 10.3 Additional steps to creating a distributed database. After the individual systems and network are installed, you must choose where to store the data. Data can also be replicated and stored in more than one location. Local views and synonyms are used to provide transparency and security. Be sure to stress test the applications under heavy loads and to ensure that they handle failures in the network and in remote computers.

Creating a Distributed Database System

The basic steps to building a distributed database are similar to those for creating any database application. Once you identify the user needs, the developers organize the data through normalization, create queries using SQL, define the user interface, and build the application. However, as shown in Figure 10.3, a distributed database requires some additional steps. In particular, a network must connect the computers from all the locations. Even if the network already exists, it might have to be modified or extended to support the chosen hardware and DBMS software.

Another crucial step is to determine where to store the data. The next section examines some of the issues you will encounter with processing queries on a distributed database. For now, remember that the goal is to store the data as close as possible to the location where it will be used the most. It is also possible to replicate heavily used data so that it can be stored on more than one computer. Of course, then you need to choose and implement a strategy to make sure that each copy is kept up-to-date.

Backup and recovery plans are even more critical with a distributed database. Remember that several computers will be operating in different locations. Each system will probably have a different DBA. Yet the entire database must be protected from failures, so every system must have consistent backup and security plans. Developing these plans will probably require negotiation among the administrators—particularly when the systems cross national boundaries and multiple time zones. For example, it would be virtually impossible to back up data everywhere at the same time.

Once the individual systems are installed and operational, each location must create local views, synonyms, and stored procedures that will connect the databases, grant access to the appropriate users, and connect the applications running on each system. Each individual link must be tested, and the final applications must be tested both for connections and for stress under heavy loads. It should also be tested for proper behavior when a network link is broken or a remote computer fails.

Operating and managing a distributed database system is considerably more difficult than handling a single database. Identifying the cause of problems is much more difficult. Basic tasks like backup and recovery require coordination of all DBAs. Some tools exist to make these jobs easier, but they can be improved.

Do you remember the rule that a distributed database should be transparent to the user? That same rule does not yet apply to DBAs or to application developers. Coordination among administrators and developers is crucial to making applications more accessible to users.

FIGURE 10.4
Network transfer rates. Transfers from disk drives are faster than LAN transfers, which are faster than WAN transfers. High-speed WAN transfers are much more expensive than other transfer methods.

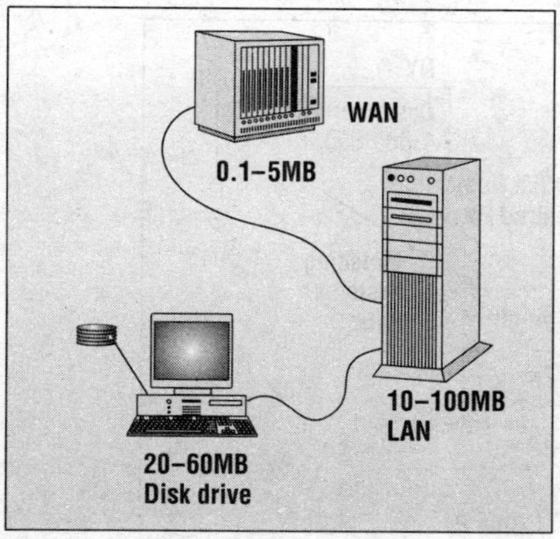

Distributed Query Processing

The challenge with distributed databases comes down to physics and economics. As illustrated in Figure 10.4, data that is stored on a local disk drive can be transferred to the CPU at transfer rates of 20 to 60 megabytes per second (or higher). Data that is stored on a server attached to a **local area network (LAN)** can be transferred at rates from 1 to 10 megabytes per second (10 to 100 megabits per second). That is, the average speed of a LAN can be 10 times slower than a direct disk transfer. Using public transmission lines to connect across a **wide area network (WAN)** provides transfer rates from 0.01 to about 5 megabytes per second. To get that 5 megabytes per second (on a T3 line), your company would probably have to pay at least $10,000 a month. As technology changes these numbers are continually improving, but the comparative relationships tend to hold true. That is, transfer to a local disk drive is faster than it is to transfer across a LAN, which is faster than to transfer across a WAN. However, note that advances in local speeds have facilitated the use of a storage area network (SAN), which uses gigabit network speeds to separate the drives from the processors. Although a SAN offers several benefits to running servers, it does not solve the distributed database problem because the distance is still limited.

The goal of distributed processing is to minimize the transfer of data on slower networks and to reduce the costs of network transfers. Part of this goal can be accomplished through design—developers must carefully choose where data should be located. Data should be stored as close as possible to where it will be used the most. However, trade-offs always arise when data is used in several locations.

Another issue in transferring data arises in terms of query processing. If a query needs to retrieve data from several different computers, the time to transfer the data and process the query depends heavily on how much data must be transferred and the speed of the transmission lines. Consequently, the result depends on how the DBMS joins the data from the multiple tables. In some cases, the difference can be extreme. One method could produce a result in a few seconds. A different approach to the same query might take several days to process! Ideally, the DBMS should evaluate the query, the databases used, and the transmission times to determine the most efficient way to answer the query.

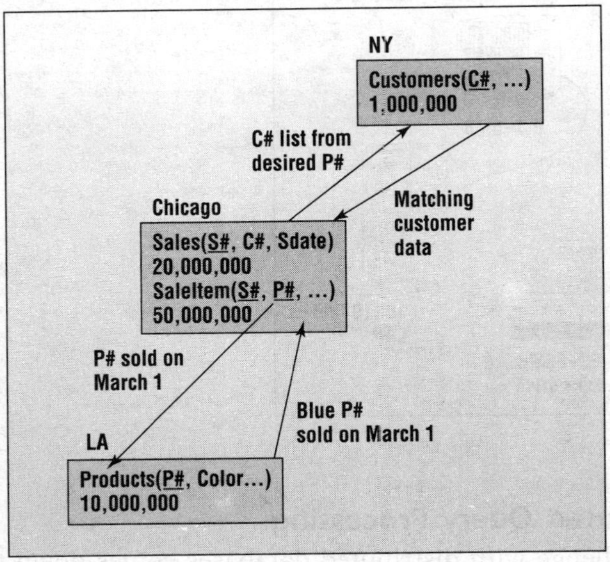

FIGURE 10.5 Distributed database query example. List customers who bought blue products on March 1. A bad idea is to transfer all data to Chicago. The goal is to restrict each set and transfer the least amount of data.

Figure 10.5 illustrates the basic problem. Consider tables on three different databases: (1) a Customer table in New York with 1 million rows, (2) a Production table in Los Angeles with 10 million rows, and (3) a Sales table in Chicago with 20 million rows. A manager in Chicago wants to run the following query: List customers who bought blue products on March 1.

This query could be processed in several ways. Consider a bad idea. Transfer all of the rows to Chicago; then join the tables and select the rows that match the query. This method results in 11 million rows of data being transferred to Chicago. Even with a relatively fast WAN, anything less than 30 minutes for this query would be amazingly fast.

A better idea would be to tell the database in Los Angeles to find all of the blue products and send the resulting rows to Chicago. Assuming only some of the products are blue, this method could significantly cut the number of rows that need to be transmitted. The performance gain will depend on what percentage of rows consists of blue products.

An even better idea is to get the list of items sold on March 1 from the Chicago table, which requires no transmission cost. Send this list to Los Angeles and have that database determine which of the products are blue. Send the matching CustomerID to the New York database, which returns the corresponding Customer data.

Notice that to optimize the query, the DBMS needs to know a little about the data in each table. For example, if there are many blue products in the Los Angeles database and not very many sales on March 1, then the database should send the Sales data from Chicago to Los Angeles. On the other hand, if there are few blue products, it will be more efficient to send the product data from Los Angeles to Chicago. In some cases, the network also needs to know the transfer speed of the network links. A good DBMS contains a query optimizer that checks the database contents and network transfer speeds to choose the best method to answer the query. You still might have to optimize some queries yourself. The basic rule is to transfer the least amount of data possible.

Data Replication

Sometimes there is no good way to optimize a query. When large data sets are needed in several different places, it can be more efficient to **replicate** the tables and store copies in each location. The problem is that the databases involved have to know about each of the copies. If a user updates data in one location, the changes have to be replicated to all the other copies. The DBMS uses a **replication manager** to determine which changes should be sent and to handle the updates at each location. Replications can be sent automatically at certain times of the day or triggered manually when someone feels it is necessary to synchronize the data.

Developers and database administrators can tune the performance by specifying how the database should be replicated. You can control how often the changes are distributed and whether they are sent in pieces or as a bulk transfer of the entire table. The biggest difficulty is that sometimes a network link might be unavailable or a server might be down. Then the DBMS has to coordinate the databases to make sure they get the current version of the table and do not lose any changes.

Figure 10.6 illustrates the basic concepts of replication. Marketing offices in each location have copies of Customer and Sales data from Britain and Spain. Almost all updates are based on data in the local country. Managers probably do not need up-to-the-minute data from the other countries, so the tables can be replicated as batch updates during the night. The data will be available to managers in all locations without the managers worrying about transfer time, and the company can minimize international transmission costs by performing transfers at off-peak times.

Transaction processing databases generally record many changes—sometimes hundreds of changes per minute. These applications require fast response times at the point of the transaction. It is generally best to run these systems as distributed databases to improve the performance within the local region.

On the other hand, managers from different locations often need to analyze the transaction data. If you give them direct access to the distributed

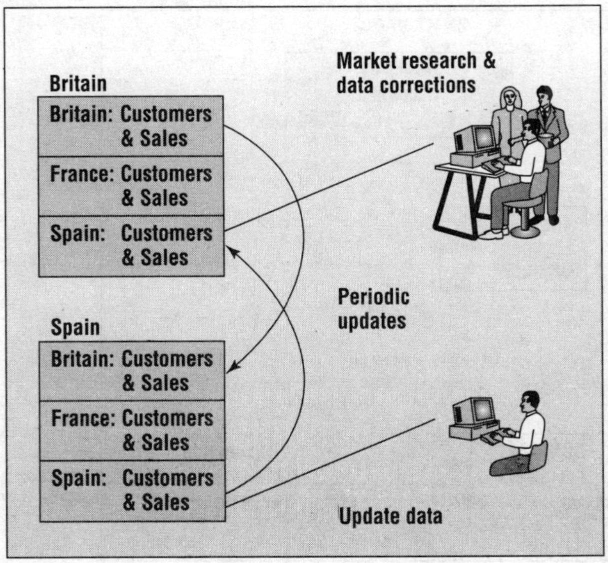

FIGURE 10.6
Replicated databases. If managers do not need immediate data from other nations, the tables can be replicated and updates can be transferred at night when costs are lower.

transaction databases, the analysis queries might slow the performance of the transaction system. A currently popular solution is to replicate the transaction data into a data warehouse. Routines extract data from the transaction processing system and store it in the data warehouse. Managers run applications and build queries to retrieve the data from the warehouse and analyze it to make tactical and strategic decisions. Because the managers rarely make changes to the underlying data, the data warehouse is a good candidate for replication. The underlying transaction processing system retains its speed, and the raw data is not shared. Managers have shared access to the warehouse data.

Automatic key generation is a difficult challenge with replicated databases. What happens if two people in different locations create a new customer? If the key generator is not synchronized, then it is highly likely that both locations will generate the same key, and when the data is updated from the two locations, a collision will occur that must be resolved by hand. Two common methods can be used in distributed databases to generate keys safely: (1) randomly generated keys, and (2) location-specific keys. Randomly generated keys work if the generator chooses from a sufficiently large number of possible keys. Then there is only a small probability that two keys would ever be generated the same at the same time. To be safe, the generator immediately checks to see if the key just created already exists. The second approach can use either sequential keys or random keys, but it relies on each location being allocated a certain range of values. For instance, one region might be given the range from 1 to 1 million, the next from 1 million to 2 million, and so on. With location-specific generators, you must be careful to isolate the key generation data tables. For example, your key tables would contain the location identifier and the starting or current value of the key.

Concurrency, Locks, and Transactions

Concurrency and deadlock become complex problems in a distributed database. Remember that concurrency problems arise when two people try to alter the same data at the same time. The situation is prevented by locking a row that is about to be changed. As shown in Figure 10.7, the problem with a

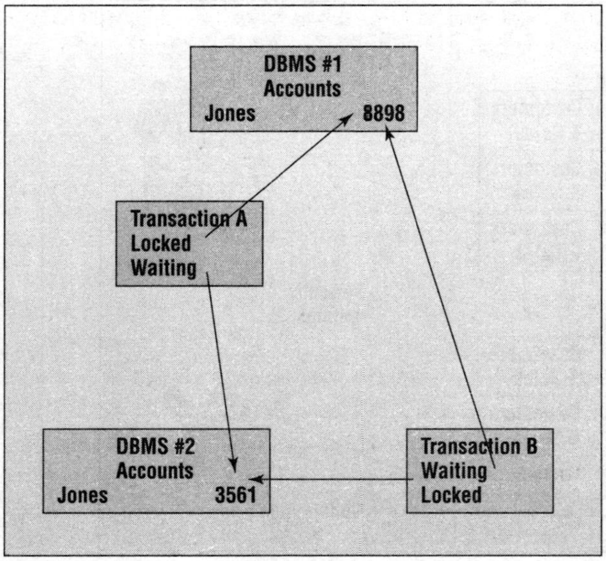

FIGURE 10.7
Concurrency and deadlock are more complicated in a distributed database. The deadlock can arise across many different databases, making it hard to identify and resolve.

distributed database is that the application could create a deadlock that involves different databases on separate computers. One user could hold a lock on a table on one computer and be waiting for a resource on a different computer. Now imagine what happens when there are five databases in five locations. It can be difficult to identify the deadlock problem. When the locks are on one computer, the DBMS can use a lock graph to catch deadlock problems as they arise. With distributed databases, the DBMS has to monitor the delay while waiting for a resource. If the delay is too long, the system assumes a deadlock has arisen and rolls back the transaction. Of course, the delay might simply be due to a slow network link, so the method is not foolproof. Worse, the time spent waiting is wasted. In a busy system, the DBMS could spend more time waiting than it does processing transactions.

Handling transactions across several databases is also a more complex problem. When changes have to be written to several computers, you still have to be certain that all changes succeed or fail together. To date, the most common mechanism for verifying transactions utilizes a **two-phase commit** process. Figure 10.8 illustrates the process. The database that initiates the transaction becomes a coordinator. In the first phase it sends the updates to the other databases and asks them to prepare the transaction. Each database must then send a reply about its status. Each database must agree to perform the entire transaction or to roll back changes if needed. The database must agree to make the changes even if a failure occurs. In other words, it writes the changes to a transaction log. Once the log is successfully created, the remote database agrees that it can handle the update. If a database encounters a problem and cannot perform the transaction (perhaps it cannot lock a table), it sends a failure message and the coordinator tells all the databases to roll back their changes. A good DBMS handles the two-phase commit automatically. As a developer, you write standard SQL statements, and the DBMS handles the communication to ensure the transaction is completed successfully. With weaker systems you will have to embed the two-phase commit commands within your program code. If you know that you are building an application that will use many distributed updates, it is

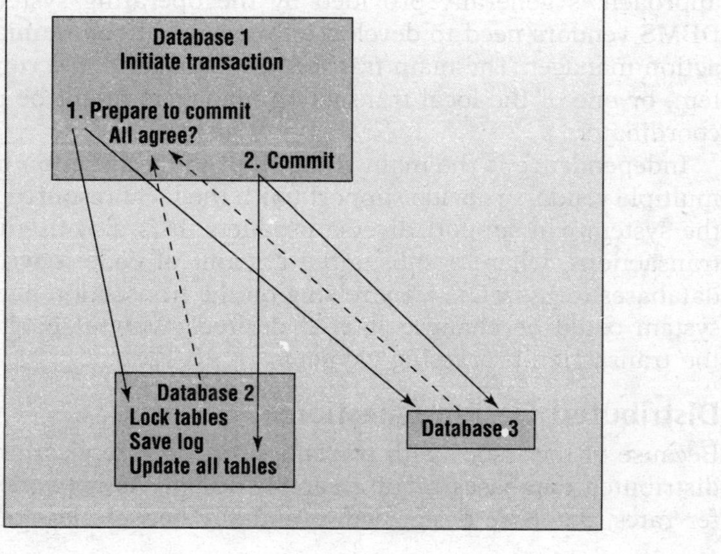

FIGURE 10.8
Two-phase commit. Each database must agree to save all changes—even if the system crashes. When all systems are prepared, they are asked to commit the changes.

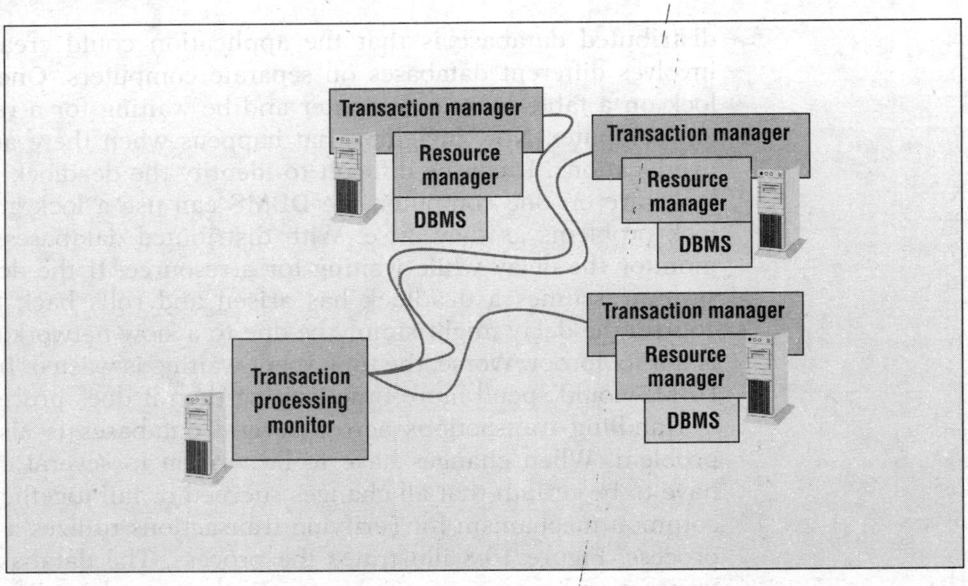

FIGURE 10.9 Distributed transaction processing monitor. This software handles the transaction decisions and coordinates across the participating systems by communicating with the local transaction managers.

generally better to budget for a better DBMS that can handle the two-phase-commit process automatically.

Notice that the two-phase commit system relies on pessimistic locking. Because of transmission delays, it could significantly slow down all of the systems involved in the transaction—as it waits for each machine to lock records. Although optimistic locking might help with some aspects of the transaction, it does not help when a system or communication link fails.

Independent Transaction Managers

The problem of distributed systems—particularly when database systems are from diverse vendors—is difficult to solve efficiently. One common approach, shown in Figure 10.9, is to use an independent transaction processing monitor or distributed transaction coordinator. This system is a separate piece of software that coordinates all transactions and makes the decision to commit or abort based on interactions with the local transaction managers. This approach is generally provided by the operating system vendor, and the DBMS vendors need to develop interfaces that communicate with the transaction manager. The main transaction manager could run on a separate system, or one of the local transaction managers might be promoted to be the coordinator.

Independence is the main strength of the transaction manager. As long as multiple vendors provide support (with the local resource manager software), the system can support diverse products. It is also useful for program-level transactions, where a substantial amount of code is written outside of the databases (e.g., in C++). By relying on the transaction manager, the database system could be changed later if desired—without having to rewrite all of the transaction-processing elements.

Distributed Design Questions

Because of the issues with transmission costs, replication, and concurrency, distributed databases require careful design. As networks gain better transfer rates, database design will eventually become less of a problem. In the

FIGURE 10.10
Design questions. Use these questions to determine whether you should replicate the database or provide concurrent access to data across the network. Transaction operations are generally run with concurrent access. Decision support systems often use replicated databases. However, the exact choice depends on the use of the data and the needs of the users.

Question	Concurrent	Replication
What level of data consistency is needed?	High	Low–medium
How expensive is storage?	Medium–high	Low
What are the shared access requirements?	Global	Local
How often are the tables updated?	Often	Seldom
Required speed of updates (transactions)?	Fast	Slow
How important are predictable transaction times?	High	Low
DBMS support for concurrency and locking?	Good–excellent	Poor
Can shared access be avoided?	No	Yes

meantime you need to analyze your applications to determine how they should be distributed. Figure 10.10 lists some of the questions you need to ask when designing a distributed database. The main point is to determine what portions of the databases should be replicated. If users at all locations require absolute consistency in the database, then replication is probably a bad idea. On the other hand, you might have a weak DBMS that poorly handles locking and concurrency. In this situation it is better to replicate the data rather than risk destroying the data through incomplete transaction updates.

Client/Server Databases

The client/server approach is currently the most popular system of distributing data (and computers) on networks. With this system, powerful machines with multiuser operating systems function as servers. Smaller computers—usually personal computers—operate as clients. The servers hold software and data that will be shared by the users. Individual client computers hold data that is used by the individual using that machine.

The client/server approach was driven largely by the limited capabilities of personal computer operating systems. Early operating systems could not support multiple users and provided no security controls. Hence, powerful operating systems were installed on servers that handled all the tasks that required sharing data and hardware. The client/server approach is also somewhat easier to manage and control than monitoring hundreds of PCs. Any hardware, software, or data that needs to be shared is stored in a centralized location and controlled by an MIS staff. With the client/server approach, all data that will be shared is first transferred to a server.

As indicated by Figure 10.11, a client/server database operates the same way. The actual database resides on a server computer. Individual components can be run from client machines, but they store and retrieve data on the servers. The client component is usually a front-end application that interacts with the user. For example, a common approach is to store the data tables on a server but run the forms on personal computers. The forms handle user events with a graphical interface, but all data is transferred to the server.

You need to understand a few important concepts to design and manage client/server databases. Like any distributed database, where you store the

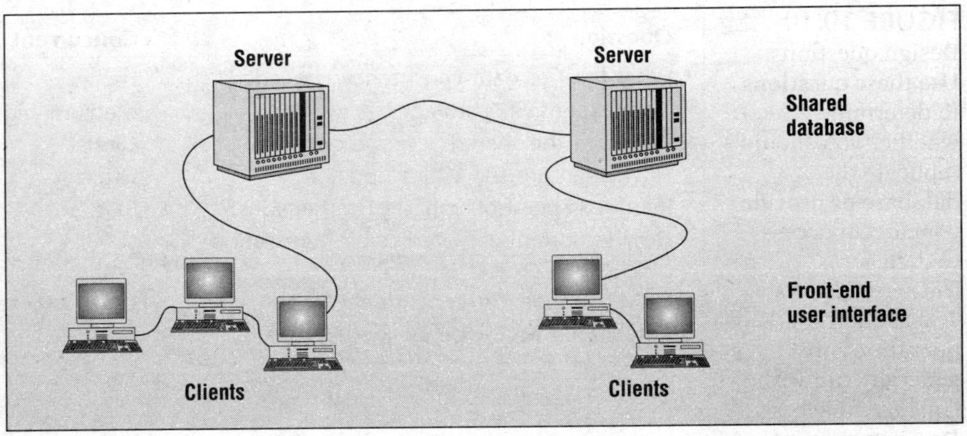

FIGURE 10.11 Client/server system. The client computers run front-end, user interface applications. These applications retrieve and store data in shared databases that are run on the server computers. The network enables clients to access data on any server where they have appropriate permissions.

data and how you access it can make a substantial difference in performance. This section also demonstrates some of the tools available to build a client/server database application.

Client/Server versus File Server

To understand the features and power of a client/server database, it is first useful to examine a database application that is not a true client/server database. Initial local area networks were based on file servers. A file server is a centralized computer that can share files with personal computers. However, it does not contain a database. The file server stores files, but to the personal computers it appears as a giant, passive disk drive. The sole purpose of the server is to provide secure shared access to files. The client personal computers do all of the application processing.

Figure 10.12 illustrates the basic problem. The database file is stored on the file server but the DBMS itself runs on the client. Security permissions are set so that each user has read and write permission on the file. When the application is run, the forms and your code are downloaded to the client

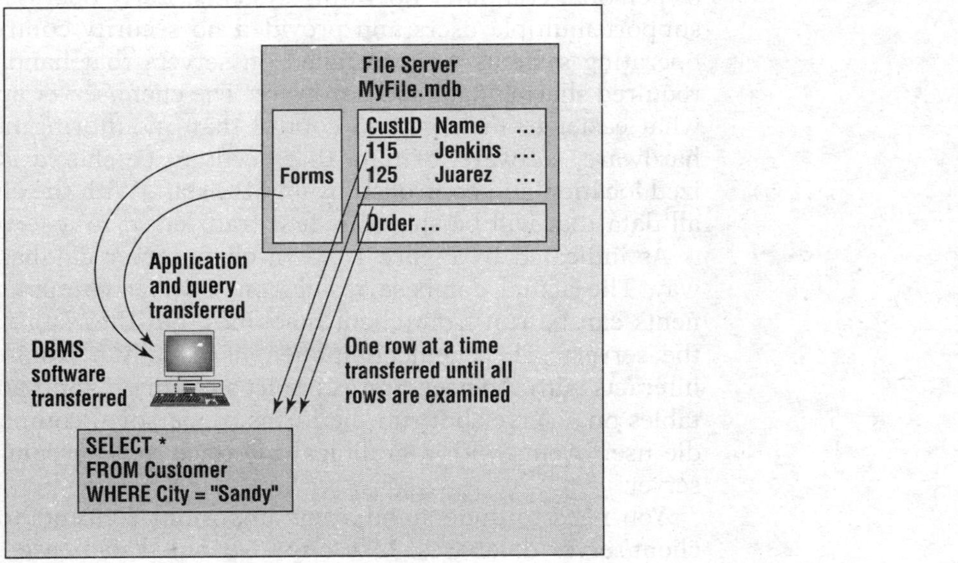

FIGURE 10.12 File server problems. The file server acts as a large, passive disk drive. The personal computer does all the database processing, so it must retrieve and examine every row of data. For large tables, this process is slow and wastes network bandwidth.

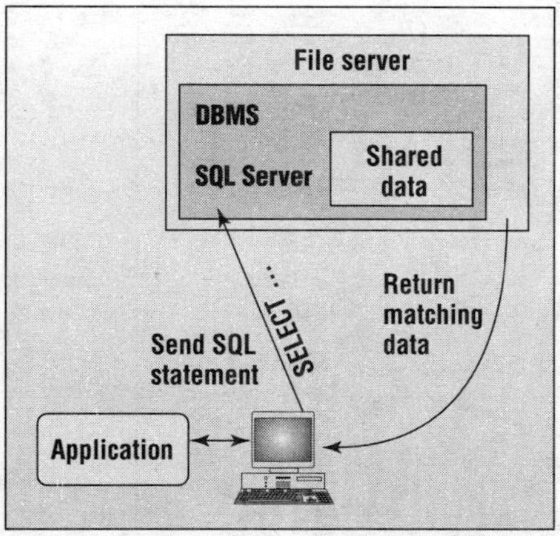

FIGURE 10.13
Database server. The client computer sends a SQL statement that is processed on the server. Only the result is returned to the client, reducing network traffic.

computer. The problem arises when your application runs a query. The processing of the query is done on the client computer. That means that the personal computer has to retrieve every row of data from the server, examine it, and decide whether to use it in the computation or display. If the database is small, if the network connection is fast, and if users often want to see the entire table, then this process does not matter. But if the table is large and users need to see only a small portion, then it is a waste of time and network bandwidth to transfer the entire table to the client computer.

The problem is that the file server approach relies on transferring huge amounts of data when the application needs only some of the data. The client/server database approach was designed to solve this problem. With a client/server database, the binary code for the database actually runs on the server. As shown in Figure 10.13, the server database receives SQL statements, processes them, and returns only the results of the query. Notice the reduction in network transfers. The initial SQL statement is small, and only the data needed by the application is transferred over the network. This result is particularly important for decision support systems. The server database might contain millions of rows of data. The manager is analyzing the data and may want summary statistics, such as an average. The server database optimizes the query, computes the result, and transfers a few simple numbers back to the client. Without the server database, millions of rows of data would be transferred across the network. Remember that even fast LAN transfer rates are substantially slower than disk drive transfers.

Of course, the drawback to the server database approach is that the server spends more time processing data. Consequently, the server computer has to be configured so that it can efficiently run processes for many users at the same time. Fortunately, processor speeds have historically increased much more rapidly than disk drive and network transfer speeds. The other drawback is that this approach requires the purchase of a powerful DBMS that runs on the server. However, you rarely have a choice. Only small applications used by a few users can be run without a database server.

Three-Tier Client/Server Model

The **three-tier client/server** model has been suggested as an approach that has some advantages over the two-tier model. The three-tier approach adds a layer between the clients and the servers. The three-tier approach is particularly

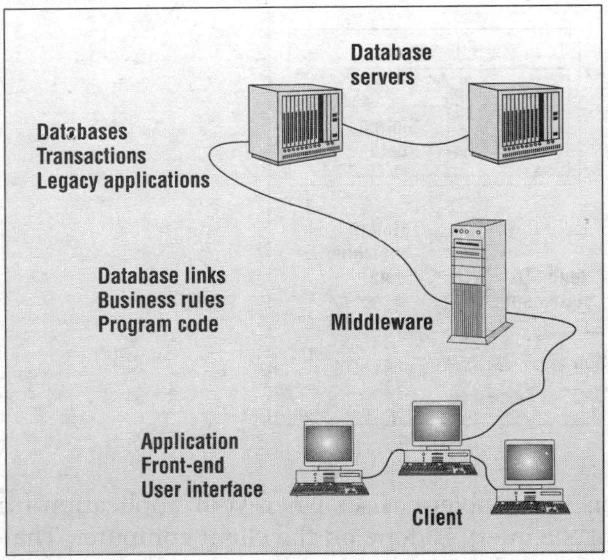

FIGURE 10.14
Three-tier client/server model. The middle layer separates the business rules and program code from the databases and applications. Independence makes it easier to alter each component without interfering with the other elements.

useful for systems having several database servers with many different applications. The method is useful when some of the servers are running legacy applications.

As shown in Figure 10.14, one role of the middle layer is to create links to the databases. If necessary, the middle layer translates SQL requests and retrieves data from legacy COBOL applications. By placing the access links in one location, the server databases can be moved or altered without affecting the client front-end applications. Developers simply change the location pointers, or alter the middleware routines. Some people refer to this approach as *n*-tier because you can have any number of middle-level computers—each specializing in a particular aspect of the business rules.

Another important role of the middle layer is to host the business rules. For example, creating identification numbers for customers and products should follow a standard process. The routine that generates these numbers should be stored in one location, and all the applications that need it will call that function. Similarly, common application functions can be written once and stored on the middle-layer servers.

This middleware system is well suited to an object-oriented development approach. Common objects that are used for multiple business applications can be written once and stored on the middle servers. Any application can use those objects as needed. As the business rules change or as systems are updated, developers can alter or improve the base objects without interfering with the operations of the applications on the client side. The three-tier approach separates the business rules and program code from the databases and from the applications. The independence makes the system more flexible and easier to expand. Some recent programming tools, such as the enterprise edition of VB, facilitate development of the middle layer. You can create a middle-tier object using Visual Basic. It can retrieve data from any server, or it can simply perform calculations. You create the component as a dynamic link library (DLL) that runs without any forms. You install it on the middle-tier computer, and then you build the client application. With the enterprise edition of VB, your application can open and use a component on any connected computer—as long as you set permissions correctly. You configure distributed COM (DCOM) to establish access rights.

The Back End: Server Databases

Server databases are available from many companies, and the various products have specific strengths and weaknesses. Some must run on certain brands of computer; others will run on several machines. Fortunately, most of the leading DBMS vendors support some version of SQL. Hence, defining the database and building queries will follow the steps you already know. Of course, the database vendors also add new features that you will have to learn.

Server database systems tend to be considerably more complex and require more administrative tasks than personal computer–based systems. The server environment also provides more options, which makes administration and development more complicated. Server computers use more sophisticated operating systems to support multiple users. The DBA must work closely with the system administrator to set up the software, define user accounts, and monitor performance.

Server databases also user the trigger procedures to define and enforce business rules. One of the more difficult design questions you must address is whether to store these rules on the back-end database as database triggers and procedures, or move them to a middle-level server using lower-level languages such as C++ or Visual Basic. Sometimes you are constrained by the tools and time available. But when possible, you should consider the various alternatives in terms of cost, performance, and expandability.

Placing procedures in the back-end database ensures that all rules are enforced by the DBMS, regardless of how the data is accessed. But, this approach ties you in to a particular DBMS vendor. Because most systems contain proprietary elements, it is difficult to switch to a different DBMS in the future. Placing rules in a middle tier also makes it easier to physically move the database. Generally, the systems are built with reference links to the databases. To move the database, you simply change the reference pointers.

One rule of thumb is to write user-interface code for the client computers and to write data manipulation and control programs to run on the server. Middle-layer programs are used to encode business rules and provide data translation and database independence. The primary objective is to minimize the transfer of data across the network. However, if some computers are substantially slower than others, you will have to accept more data transfers in order to execute the code on faster machines.

The Front End: Windows Clients

Windows-based computers are commonly used as client machines, so Microsoft has created several technologies to provide database connections from the PCs to back-end databases. Various tools and many vendors support the technologies, so they are relatively standardized. The tools have evolved over time as hardware and networks have improved and applications became more complex. Visual Basic is often used as a front-end tool to create the forms and reports. The application is compiled and distributed to user machines, which connect through the Microsoft data components to a back-end server. The PC has a network connection and a database connection that enables it to find the central database on the server. The VB application code simply selects the appropriate database connection. From that point,

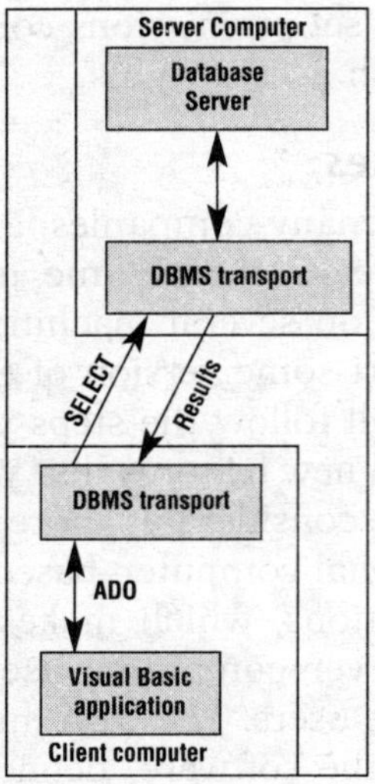

FIGURE 10.15
Active Data Objects connections. In a distributed environment, ADO handles the connection between your application and the underlying data transport layer. The fastest method is to use the DBMS vendor's data transport, but open database connectivity can be used if no other mechanisms are available.

your application no longer cares where the data is located—it simply passes SQL requests to the server.

Open database connectivity (ODBC) is an early Microsoft technology to connect Windows clients to servers. Some systems still utilize the technology, but it is relatively slow. The newer technology is **Active Data Objects (ADO)**, and it is faster because it uses fewer layers and also provides more functionality. The most recent version is ADO .NET that has additional functions for Microsoft's .NET environment.

ADO runs on top of the vendor's networking system; hence it provides more direct access to the data. ADO can also utilize ODBC to handle files and other systems that do not provide their own data transport. Figure 10.15 shows the use of ADO in a distributed environment. You need to install the database vendor's data transport layer. Then your application selects the appropriate ADO driver, which connects to the underlying database transport services. ADO passes your SQL statements to the transport service and handles the basic data translation tasks (e.g., recognizing date, integer, and currency data) for returning data. It also handles the data cursors consistently. Hence, your application written with the ADO tools can access a variety of databases.

Maintaining Database Independence in the Client

One of the trickiest aspects of distributed databases is the issue of maintaining database independence. When you first build an application, it is often created to run with a single, specified database on the back end. Consequently, it is tempting to simply build the application assuming that the same database will always be there, and use the tools and shortcuts available for that particular system. But what happens later when someone wants to change the back-end database? In extreme cases, the entire application will have to be rewritten. As a developer pressed for time, you might ask why it matters. If someone wants to change the database at a later date, then should they be willing to pay the costs at that time? Yet, with only a little extra effort up front, the application can support most common database systems on the back end, making it easy to change later.

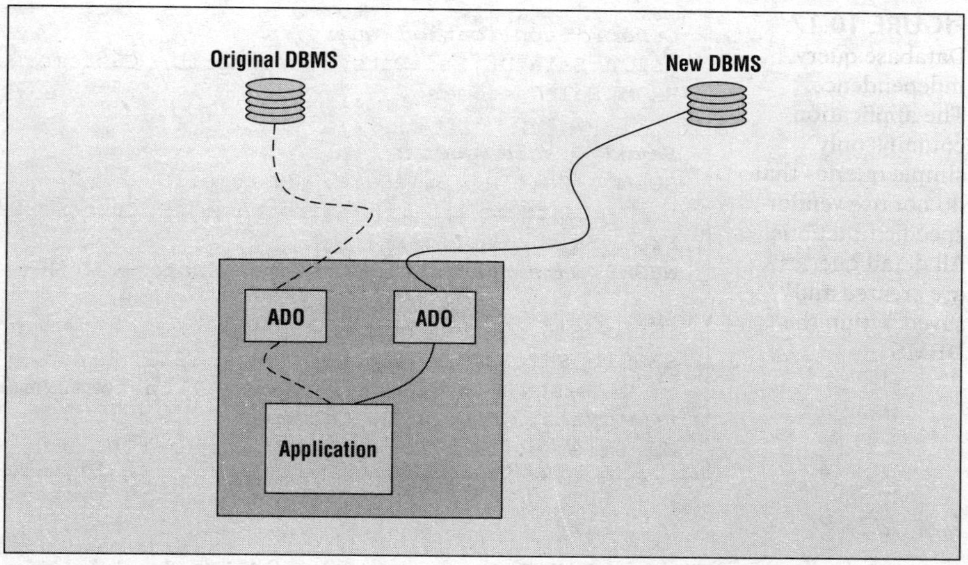

FIGURE 10.16
Database independence. ADO is a useful buffer between the application and the DBMS. Changing the connection makes it relatively easy to switch the back-end DBMS.

The database connection is one issue in building a generic application. Using adopted standards such as ADO or ODBC make it easier to change databases. Figure 10.16 shows that by changing the connection, your application can connect to a different DBMS. Of course, it is never quite that simple, but the ADO buffer is an important element. In many cases, you can specify the ADO connection string dynamically, making it easy for the application to connect to a different DBMS without rewriting the code. If you are careful, you can build the application so that it can switch DBMS connections at any time. You can build the system using one DBMS and run the production system against a different one.

It is important that you understand that the connection is only one element in making an application DBMS independent. In most situations, the actual SQL commands are a much bigger issue. DBMS vendors tend to provide different levels of support for the SQL standard. They also add proprietary options and commands that are enticing. In particular, vendors offer many variations within the SELECT command. For example, string and date operations are notoriously nonstandardized across vendors. And, if you are using an older version of Oracle or SQL Server, you will not be able to use the INNER JOIN syntax. Because of these differences, a key step in making an application DBMS independent is to move all queries to the DBMS and save them as views. Then your application only contains simple SELECT (or INSERT/UPDATE/DELETE) queries that pull data from the saved view. These simple queries should use only basic standard SQL elements. All of the vendor-specific functions are coded into the query that is saved in the DBMS. To transfer to a new DBMS, you just recreate the queries on the new DBMS using that vendor's specific tools and syntax. This technique is particularly important for applications that might begin small and grow. At a small size, you might be able to use a small, inexpensive DBMS; but as the number of users grows and demand on the system increases, you will have to scale up to a larger DBMS. If the application queries were carefully built to remain independent, it will be relatively easy to transfer to a new DBMS.

FIGURE 10.17
Database query independence. The application contains only simple queries that do not use vendor-specific functions. All detail queries are created and saved within the DBMS.

```
Generic application query:
SELECT SaleID, SaleDate, CustomerID, CustomerName
FROM SaleCustomer

Saved Oracle query:
SELECT SaleID, SaleDate, CustomerID,
      LastName ||',' || FirstName AS CustomerName
From Sale, Customer
WHERE Sale.CustomerID=Customer.CustomerID

Saved SQL Server query:
SELECT SaleID, SaleDate, CustomerID,
      LastName + ',' + FirstName AS CustomerName
FROM Sale INNER JOIN Customer
ON Sale.CustomerID = Customer.CustomerID
```

Figure 10.17 shows an example of using simple queries to maintain DBMS vendor independence.

Trigger functions are a more complex issue. Some systems do not support triggers at all, and those that do generally provide different functionality. At this point in time, the only method to guarantee compatibility across vendors is to avoid database triggers. Instead, write the same functionality into middleware code that also relies on generic queries.

Electronic Commerce Databases

In many ways, electronic commerce (e-commerce) is similar to traditional database applications. The differences come from some additional data and usability issues. When users enter data over the Web, the Internet transmits important information to the server that you should keep. For example, you can keep the IP address of the customer, any source page or advertisement that directed the customer to your site, as well as payment information and confirmation data.

The essence of the Web is to let users make choices and enter their own data into your forms. Consequently, these forms have to be easy to use. In this situation, standardization is an important aspect of ease of use. Over time, websites have developed standard formats for handling basic tasks. Your application needs to follow these basic formats so users can follow familiar tasks.

Today, e-commerce websites generally contain a database of products with prices, descriptions, and images. Your application must display item descriptions, and it must provide a search engine to help customers find specific products. You also need a shopping cart that contains a list of items temporarily selected by the users. The shopping cart is often developed as a basic table that holds the list of items for each person. Your application also needs a checkout page that enables the user to make final changes to the items in the shopping cart, collects payment and shipping information, and then records the order. Additionally, you need to let users return later and check on the status of their orders.

On top of all of these user interface items, websites also need several administrative pages. Someone in the company needs the ability to update descriptions, images, and prices. Other workers need to check on orders, enter data on shipping dates, and solve basic order problems. The marketing department wants the ability to monitor sales, evaluate the effects of advertising campaigns, and examine customer attributes. All of these administrative tasks require additional forms. Rather than write a new Web application from scratch, many firms have chosen to buy standard merchant software systems that incorporate all of the desired features. But for many other firms, it is still necessary to write custom database applications.

Because of the rapid growth of the Internet, tools are still being developed. The back-end database concepts are similar to the concepts discussed in the previous chapters. However, the front-end forms and reports are developed as Web pages that require connections to the database. Several technologies are being developed to make it easier to create these pages. For example, Microsoft has Active Server Pages (ASP) in the .NET family; IBM has WebSphere products; Oracle sells OracleWeb tools; and Sun is marketing its Java and Java Database Connectivity (JDBC). It is impossible to cover all of these technologies in one book, let alone one chapter. So this chapter discusses the general concepts and some specific problems that arise with Web-based distributed database applications.

The Web as a Client/Server System

The **World Wide Web** was designed as a client/server system. The objective was to enable people (physicists and researchers) to share information with their colleagues. The fundamental problem was that everyone used different hardware and software—both for clients and for servers—and the solution was to define a set of standards. These evolving standards are the heart of the Web. They define how computers can connect, how data can be transferred, and how data can be found. Additional standards define how data should be stored and how it can be displayed. The clients run **browser** software that receives and displays data files. The servers run Web server software that answers requests, finds the appropriate files, and sends the required data. Both the clients and the browsers are becoming more sophisticated, but the essence of the method is presented in Figure 10.18.

HTML-Limited Clients

Today the Web server can be tied to a database. The database can hold traditional data, or it can hold complex graphics and other objects that can be retrieved with browsers. To build applications in this environment, you must understand and follow the rules to display data on the browsers.

The basic rule of browsers is that they only know how to display certain types of data, such as text and graphics. Each type of data must be created in a predefined format. For the most part, you are not allowed to create new formats or new types of data. The browser capabilities are continuously being expanded to handle new types of data, such as sound and video. However, your application and the database must follow the standards for the new data types. Also, there are differences in the ways the various browsers display information. If you want a wide audience for your data, you have to be careful to avoid the incompatibilities.

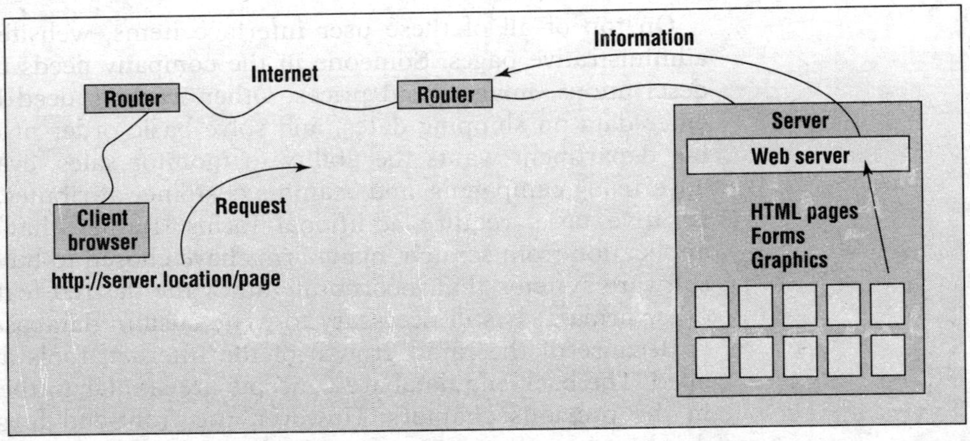

FIGURE 10.18 Web servers and client browsers. Browsers are standardized display platforms. Servers are accessible from any browser.

Hypertext markup language (HTML) is the foundation of the display system for browsers. It is a simplified page description language. For maximum compatibility, all information sent to browsers should be sent as an HTML page. Several sources for learning HTML are available on the Internet, and many tutorial books are available to help you learn the language. For the basics, you control the page layout and text attributes with tags. A *tag* is just a short term enclosed in brackets, such as <B>. HTML uses pairs of tags; for example, to boldface a word, you surround it with a start tag and an end tag, like <B>my text</B>. A simple example of HTML is shown in Figure 10.19 with the output in Figure 10.20.

Database applications often use two special sets of tags: one set to create tables and another to create forms. Tables display output from the database, whereas forms collect data for the database and get parameters from the users to build queries. You should learn more about these basic tags if you want to build database applications on the Web. Fortunately, several

FIGURE 10.19 Typical HTML page. The tags set the page layout and control text formatting. Database applications often use tags to create tables to display results. Forms tags are used to collect data to interact with the server.

```
<HTML>
<HEAD>
<TITLE>My main page</TITLE></HEAD>
<BODY BACKGROUND="graphics/back0.jpg">
<P>My text goes in paragraphs.</P>
<P>Additional tags set <B>boldface</B> and
<I>Italic</I>
<P>Tables are more complicated and use a set of tags for
rows and columns.</P>
<TABLE BORDER=1>
<TR><TD>First cell</TD><TD>Second cell</TD></TR>
<TR><TD>Next row</TD><TD>Second column</TD>></TR>
</TABLE>
<P>There are form tags to create input forms for
collecting data.
But you need CGI program code to convert and use the
input data</P>
</BODY>
</HTML>
```

FIGURE 10.20
HTML page display.

My text goes in paragraphs.
Additional tags set **boldface** and *Italic.*
Tables are more complicated and use a set of tags for rows and columns.

First cell	Second cell
Next row	Second column

There are form tags to create input forms for collecting data. But you need CGI program code to convert and use the input data.

tools exist to help automate the creation of HTML pages, so you do not have to memorize the HTML syntax. Most word processors today can store documents such as input forms in HTML format.

Graphics are a little more restrictive. You need to store images in one of three formats: GIF, JPEG, or PNG. Modern graphics software can perform the conversion. Because of the limitations in displaying graphics and data, you should consult with a graphics designer when developing applications for the Web.

Hypertext links are an important feature of the Web. Each page contains references or links to other pages. The basic format of a link uses the **anchor tag** (<A>). For example: <A HREF='newfile.html'>Text to display </A>. Typical static pages have fixed links so that each person sees exactly the same page and the same links. A database enables developers to create more interactive pages and links. The links (and the text) can be stored in a database table. Based on the actions of the user, the application can retrieve the desired data from a table and build a page with links for any situation. A common example is an order form. The user can select a category and the application will retrieve a list of items in that category. In addition to displaying the list, each item will be linked to a description page and a picture. Users who want more information can click on the links. The key is that the category and link information are stored in a database, which makes the list easier to search and easier for product managers to change. Your application simply needs to retrieve the data and format it with the <A> tag.

Browser capabilities and standards continue to improve rapidly. Browsers now support an object model that you can use to create applications. Much like a database form, the browser records user events and enables you to attach code to these events. This client-side code can record user choices, manipulate the display, and interact with your server. Similarly, server-side code can retrieve data from databases, track user connections, and maintain transaction integrity. When coupled with a server-side DBMS, the Web can be used to create client/server applications. The main advantage to using the Web is that users can access your applications from anywhere in the world, using a variety of client computers.

Web Server Database Fundamentals

There is no standard mechanism for connecting databases to the Web server. Consequently, the method you use depends on the specific software (Web

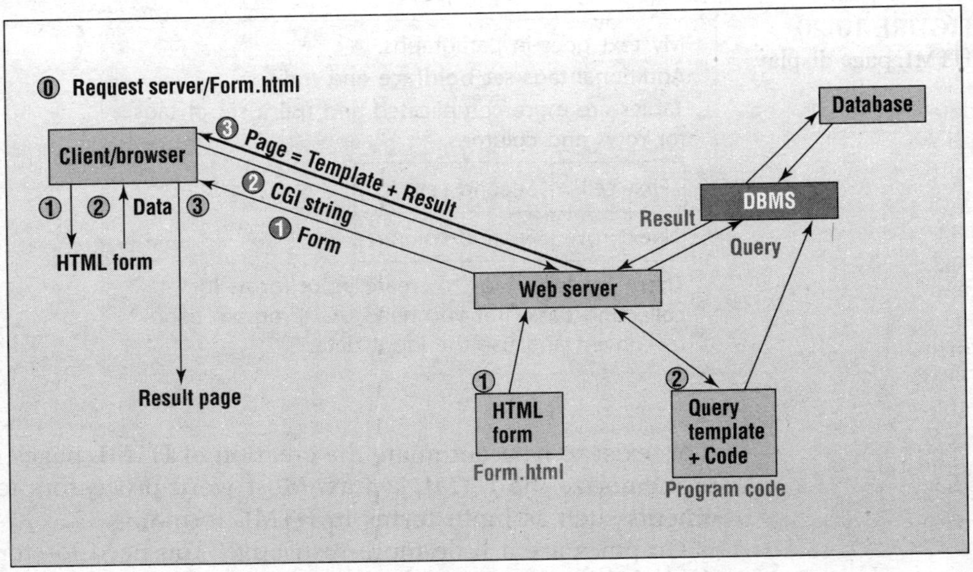

FIGURE 10.21
Web server database fundamentals. The developer builds the initial form, the query, and a template to display the results. The Web server merges the input data with the query and passes it to the DBMS (SQL Server). The query results are merged into the template and sent to the user as a new page.

server and DBMS) that you install. Most of the methods follow a similar structure but vary in the details. Several tools exist to help you build forms in a graphical designer, supported by a programming language to process the data. These tools then generate the raw HTML files that are sent to the client browsers. One issue to watch for when selecting tools is that some of them require users to download special add-in software for the browsers. Most users are wary of downloading nonstandard components. When you are dealing with users outside of the main company, it is best to stick with tools that use only standard browser features.

Figure 10.21 shows the basic process of connecting a DBMS to a Web server. The numbers indicate the three basic steps that take place. Remember that there are two perspectives of these actions: the client and the server side. (0) You first have to create a form, which is requested by the client. (1) Then the user receives the form and enters data. The data might comprise constraint values for a condition in a query. For example, a user might select an animal category and color. (2) This data is returned to the Web server in the form of a **common gateway interface (CGI)** string. CGI specifies the format of data that is transmitted between computers. The data also tells the Web server which file to open and transfer the data to. (3) A new page is constructed and returned to the user.

Client Perspective

On the client browser the user will see a simple sequence like the forms shown in Figure 10.22. Once someone chooses a Search option, the AnimalSearch form is displayed on his or her browser. The user chooses a category and enters a color. When the Search button is clicked, the choices are sent to a new page on the server. This page retrieves the data and formats a new page. The data is generally stored in a table, similar to the one shown in Figure 10.22. The user never needs to know anything about the DBMS: Users see only forms and new pages. Each new page should provide additional choices and links to other pages.

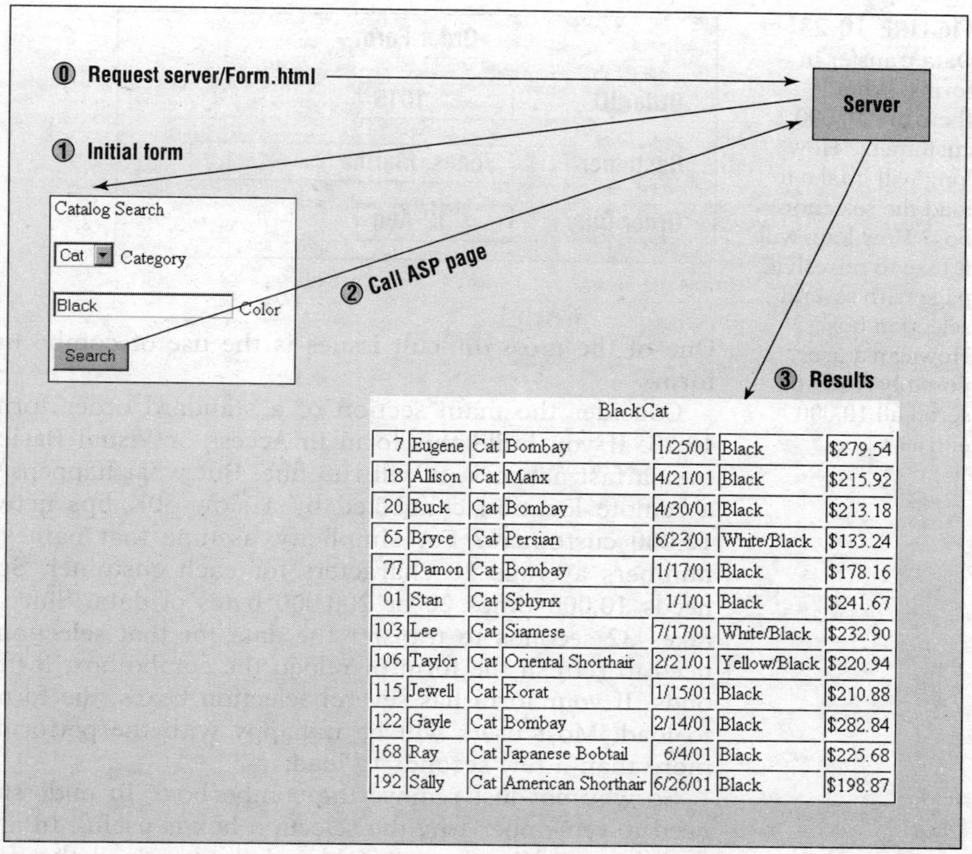

FIGURE 10.22
Client perspective. The client enters data into a form. Clicking the Search button sends the data to a server page. The server page retrieves the matching data from the DBMS and formats a new HTML page. This table is returned to the user, along with additional choices.

Server Perspective

Vendors are busy creating and refining tools to create Web-based forms that can interact easily with the database. The details vary enormously depending on which tool you use. However, the basic process remains similar. The server takes the values from the client form, validates them for rules you specify, and writes SQL queries to insert them or update existing rows in the database. You should review all of the issues discussed in Chapter 6 for building forms and reports. The main difference with the Web is that today's tools generally require more programming and individualized attention. On the other hand, Web-based applications create some potentially difficult problems that must be addressed. Data transmission, concurrency, and server loads are significant issues that arise in Web-based applications. In fact, some of the most important differences in vendor tools can be found in how these problems are solved.

Data Transmission Issues in Applications

At first glance, it seems straightforward to build a client/server application. You simply move the database to a central server and use the network connections to handle the data transfer. However, client/server applications can present some challenging issues for data transfer and usability of forms.

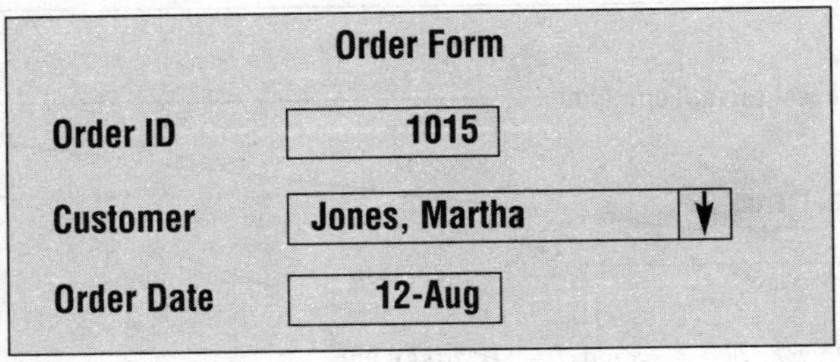

FIGURE 10.23
Data transfer in forms. What if there are 10,000 customers? How long will it take to load the selection box? How long will it take to refresh a page with several selection boxes? How can a user possibly read and scroll all 10,000 entries?

One of the most difficult issues is the use of combo or select boxes on a form.

Consider the main section of a standard order form shown in Figure 10.23. If you build this form in Access or Visual Basic and run it locally over a fast network, it will run fine. But what happens if the form runs at a remote location connected by a slow 50K bps network and there are 10,000 customers? For simplicity, assume that names and identification numbers average 20 characters for each customer. So the selection box needs 10,000 times 20 or 200,000 bytes of data. Since a byte is 8 bits, it takes 32 seconds to transfer the data for that selection box. Anytime you need to refresh the form or reload the combo box, it takes another 32 seconds. If your form has several selection boxes, the form takes even longer to load. Most users will be unhappy with the performance if forms take more than a few seconds to load.

So why not just remove the combo box? To understand the issues, you need to remember why the selection box is useful. In a relational database, data is stored in separate tables that are joined through key data. In this case, the Order table contains the CustomerID. Theoretically, to place an order you simply need the customer's ID. (Eventually you will also need individual identification numbers for products as well.) You cannot expect your customers or clerks to memorize ID numbers, so the order form uses the combo box to list customers alphabetically and return the matching ID number for the selected customer. If you remove the combo box, you need to rethink the usability and find another method for customers and clerks to enter data.

Even without the data transfer issue a selection box might not be the best solution when it has thousands of entries. Some boxes try to automatically find a matching entry as a user enters the first few characters of a name or product, but this method still requires the user to know the first few characters. Hence, a potentially better solution is to create a more detailed search mechanism. Instead of a selection box containing all customers, the user could enter the first few characters of a customer's last name, click a button, and receive a small list of matching names.

Order items present similar problems. Two common solutions exist: (1) For in-store sales, attach the product ID numbers to the individual items (e.g., bar codes); or (2) for Web sales, let the customer search for items and keep a collection of the selected ID numbers in a shopping cart.

For situations where you still want to use selection boxes, you need to be more creative with programming. For example, Oracle recommends that you do not use selection boxes for lists with more than 30 items. Instead, Oracle suggests the use of a standard text box, along with a **list of values (LOV)**.

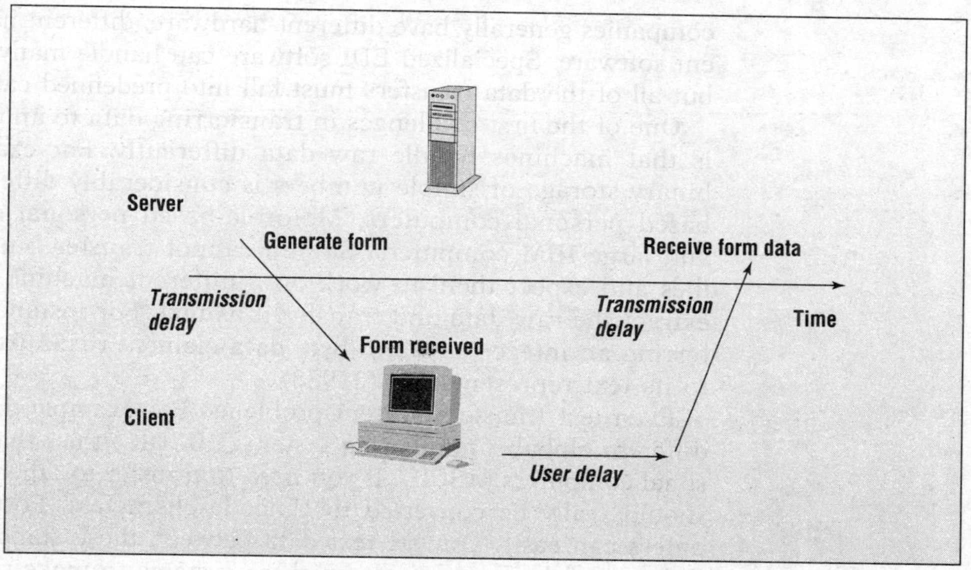

FIGURE 10.24
Latency. Transmission delays and user delays can create long latency for Web forms. Avoid pessimistic locking and carefully test for changes in the underlying database.

A list of values can be defined as a query. When the user enters the text box, the item can be selected from the list of values. How is this approach different from a selection box? The main difference lies beneath the surface. The LOV retrieves data in chunks instead of trying to transfer the entire set at one time. To the user, the list appears continuous, but by transferring only the currently displayed section of the list, the LOV reduces transmission time. It also transfers data while the user is reading, so the time is less noticeable. This approach can be used, even if your tool or vendor does not support it directly. In Web forms, simply create a second form that holds the list of items on multiple pages with a search function. When users find the specific item, you can write a function to transfer the selected item to the main form.

For similar data transmission reasons, concurrency is also a problem with Web forms. In engineering terms, **latency** is a time delay in a system. In the context of forms, latency is the time between generating the form and receiving a response from the user. With a long latency, there is a greater opportunity for someone else to modify the same data elements, so concurrency is a greater problem. As shown in Figure 10.24, latency is typically longer on Web forms because of slow transmission lines and because users may be casual browsers who wander off and do other tasks before submitting the form. Consequently, Web-based applications should avoid pessimistic locking so that the data is available to more people at the same time. Consequently, your application has to test and handle optimistic concurrency issues when the data has been changed by another process.

XML: Transferring Data to Diverse Systems

Partly due to the rise of the Internet, organizations increasingly want to transfer data to computers that are managed by other companies. For example, a retailer might want to send orders to suppliers using **electronic data interchange (EDI)**. The challenge with these transfers is that the two companies generally have different hardware, different networks, and different software. Specialized EDI software can handle many of these problems, but all of the data transfers must fall into predefined categories.

One of the first challenges in transferring data to an unknown computer is that machines handle raw data differently. For example, the internal binary storage of simple numbers is considerably different between Intel-based personal computers, Motorola-based personal computers (Apple), and large IBM computers. So you cannot transfer binary (e.g., database) files and expect them to work on a different machine. Instead, you must extract the raw data and transfer it as text. For instance, instead of transferring an integer as a two-byte data element (0x55 0xE4), you convert it to its text representation (21988).

Even text transfers present problems. For example, IBM machines use a different alphabet/numbering system (EBCDIC) than that used by most personal computers (ASCII). If you need to transfer to other languages, the data should really be converted to Unicode characters. Fortunately, most computers can easily convert text data between these standards. You just have to be careful when you set up these systems to make sure everyone knows the format of the text data.

However, even transferring data as text does not solve all of the problems. Simple text data files do not contain metadata: information about the content of the file. For instance, if you received a table of numbers, how would you know the purpose of each column? A column heading would help, but it might not contain enough information; and more complex data transfers would be even harder to understand. Consider the common order shown in Figure 10.25. It contains a separate order line with multiple elements for each item ordered.

The **extensible markup language (XML)** was created to resolve these problems. In some ways, XML is similar to HTML—they are both derived from a more complex language known as the standard generalized markup language (SGML). However, HTML is designed for displaying data, and XML is designed for transferring data. XML uses tags to indicate the purpose of the data. The power of XML is that you can create any tags you desire.

When transferring data to others, it is also important to specify the layout of the file and provide the metadata to describe each element expected in the data file. The XML schema definition (XSD) file is designed to show the overall layout of an XML file. Figure 10.26 shows a partial xsd file for the basic order problem. This version was automatically generated by the Microsoft .NET xsd.exe tool. You could get by with a simpler definition. The main thing to note is that the definition file shows the layout of the data and provides the metadata to describe each field element.

FIGURE 10.25
Hierarchical data file. Notice the structure of the file: Basic order date followed by repeating elements of order items, where each order item consists of ItemID, Description, Quantity, and Cost.

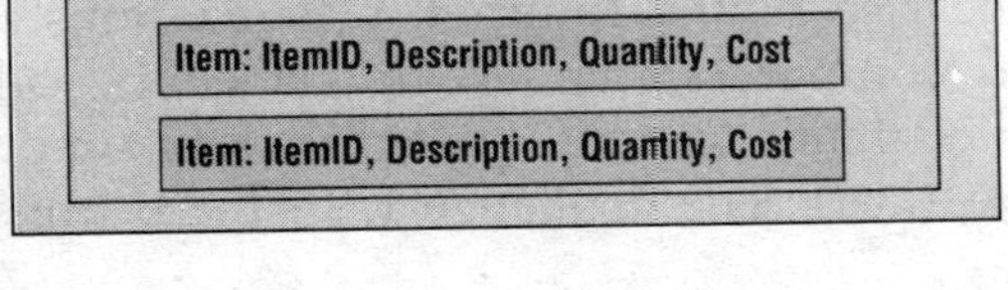

FIGURE 10.26
Partial XSD file. The schema definition describes the layout of the XML data file and the types of data that will be transferred. Note the hierarchical layout and the individual field definitions.

```
<?xml version="1.0" encoding="utf-8"?>
<xs:schema id="OrderList" xmlns="" xmlns:xs="http://www.w3.org/2001/XMLSchema"
xmlns:msdata="urn:schemas-microsoft.com:xml-msdata">
 <xs:element name="OrderList" msdata:IsDataSet="true">
  <xs:complexType>
   <xs:choice maxOccurs="unbounded">
    <xs:element name="Order">
     <xs:complexType>
      <xs:sequence>
       <xs:element name="OrderID" type="xs:string" minOccurs="0"/>
       <xs:element name="OrderDate" type="xs:date" minOccurs="0"/>
       <xs:element name="ShippingCost" type="xs:string" minOccurs="0"/>
       <xs:element name="Comment" type="xs:string" minOccurs="0"/>
       <xs:element name="Items" minOccurs="0" maxOccurs="unbounded">
        <xs:complexType>
         <xs:sequence>
          <xs:element name="ItemID" nillable="true" minOccurs="0"
          maxOccurs="unbounded">
           <xs:complexType>
            <xs:simpleContent msdata:ColumnName="ItemID_Text"
            msdata:Ordinal="0">
             <xs:extension base="xs:string">
             </xs:extension>
            </xs:simpleContent>
           </xs:complexType>
          </xs:element>
          <xs:element name="Description" nillable="true" minOccurs="0"
          maxOccurs="unbounded">
           <xs:complexType>
            <xs:simpleContent msdata:ColumnName="Description_Text"
            msdata:Ordinal="0">
             <xs:extension base="xs:string">
             </xs:extension>
            </xs:simpleContent>
           </xs:complexType>
          </xs:element>
```

An XML file with sample data from the Pet Store Merchandise Order is shown in Figure 10.27. The OrderList is the root tag for the document, indicating that the file can contain more than one order, but only a portion of the file is displayed here. Each order contains several elements to describe the order (OrderDate, ShippingCost, and Comment). Each order can contain a list of several items being ordered. Each item has its own list of identifiers (ItemID, Description, Quantity, and Cost). The data for these items is included in the file and surrounded by the appropriate opening and closing tags.

You can use Microsoft's Internet Explorer browser to examine the contents of an XML file. As shown in Figure 10.28, the browser provides a simple hierarchical view of the data. Clicking on the +/− marks to the left of the

FIGURE 10.27
Sample XML file. The XML file contains the actual data. Each element is surrounded by an opening tag and a closing tag.

```
<?xml version="1.0"?>
<!DOCTYPE OrderList SYSTEM "orderlist.dtd">
<OrderList>
<Order>
<OrderID>1</OrderID>
<OrderDate>3/6/2004</OrderDate>
<ShippingCost>$33.54</ShippingCost>
<Comment>Need immediately.</Comment>
<Items>
<ItemID>30</ItemID>
<Description>Flea Collar-Dog-Medium</Description>
<Quantity>208</Quantity>
<Cost>$4.42</Cost>
<ItemID>27</ItemID>
<Description>Aquarium Filter &amp; Pump</Description>
<Quantity>8</Quantity>
<Cost>$24.65</Cost>
</Items>
</Order>
</OrderList>
```

display will expand or contract the hierarchical list. The basic browser provides only a simple view of the raw data. You would never use it to actually present the data to users. Instead, you can build an XSL style sheet to specify the layout and format of each element. However, the simple view is an easy way to check the data for XML files that are being sent to other companies.

FIGURE 10.28
XML file in Internet Explorer browser. The browser provides a hierarchical view of the raw data in an XML file. You can also build XSL style sheets to improve the display.

```
 <?xml version="1.0"?>
 <!DOCTYPE OrderList (View Source for full doctype...)>
- <OrderList>
  - <Order>
      <OrderID>1</OrderID>
      <OrderDate>3/6/2004</OrderDate>
      <ShippingCost>$33.54</ShippingCost>
      <Comment>Need immediately.</Comment>
    - <Items>
        <ItemID>30</ItemID>
        <Description>Flea Collar-Dog-Medium</Description>
        <Quantity>208</Quantity>
        <Cost>$4.42</Cost>
        <ItemID>27</ItemID>
        <Description>Aquarium Filter & Pump</Description>
        <Quantity>8</Quantity>
        <Cost>$24.65</Cost>
      </Items>
    </Order>
  +<Order>
  +<Order>
 </OrderList>
```

The strength of XML is that it is relatively easy to build a parser to extract the data and use it in other applications. In fact, several companies provide general-purpose XML parsers. Your application code can activate the parser and tell it to extract the various portions of the data automatically. The other powerful aspect of XML is that an enormous number of vendors are supporting it. It is also a major addition to the next version of the SQL standard (200x). Consequently, many tools and applications already support conversion from internal data formats to XML and back. For a growing number of tasks, you do not need to understand XML at all. You can simply tell one application to generate the XML and the XSD files, transfer them to the other system, and have it read the data correctly. All of the conversions are automated, driven by the XSD file.

Java and JDBC

Java is a language developed by Sun Microsystems, used largely with web-based operating systems. One of the goals is to provide a software platform that can be used with any common hardware. As part of this environment, **JDBC** was introduced to handle the interaction between Java and commercial databases. As a side note, JDBC is a trademarked name that is not technically an acronym, but people often refer to it as Java database connectivity. JDBC is an important component of the **Java 2 enterprise edition (J2EE)**, which is a server-based platform technology for building data-driven websites.

As shown by the small excerpt in Figure 10.29, the structure of JDBC is similar to other database languages such as ADO: Your code must first establish a connection to the database. Next you create a statement that contains an SQL query. Then you write a cursor-based loop that tracks through the query (ResultSet) row by row. Basic JDBC commands will transfer data from the query into Java variables.

FIGURE 10.29
Structure of JDBC code. The overall structure and features are similar to those in the Microsoft ADO approach.

```
Connection con = DriverManager.getConnection(
                    "jdbc.myDriver:myDBName",
                    "myLogin",
                    "myPassword");
Statement smt = con.CreateStatement();
ResultSet rst = smt.executeQuery(
                "SELECT AnimalID, Name, Category, Breed
                FROM Animal");

while (rst.next()){
        int iAnimal = rst.getInt("AnimalID");
        String sName = rst.getString("Name");
        String sCategory = rst.getString("Category");
        String sBreed = rst.getString("Breed");

  \\ Now do something with these four variables
}
```

Of course, you need to do considerably more setup and programming to get this example to work. For instance, you have to install all of Java, JDBC, and the JDBC driver that connects to the database you wish to use. The purpose of this example is to show you that the structure of the code is the same as the structure of the code used throughout the other chapters in this book. The syntax and commands you use are different, but the logic is the same.

Summary

As organizations grow, distributed databases become useful. Distributed databases enable the company to expand individual departments without directly affecting everyone else. Distributed databases also give individual departments increased control and responsibility for their data.

However, distributed databases, with independent database engines running in different locations, increase the complexity of developing and managing applications. One of the primary goals is to make the location of the data transparent to the user. To accomplish this goal, developers and DBAs need to carefully define the databases, networks, and applications.

Some of the major complications generated by distributed databases are query optimization; data replication questions; and support for transactions, concurrency controls, and deadlock resolution. These issues become even more complex when multiple databases are involved. Network transfers of data are substantially slower than transfers from local disk drives. Transfers over wide area networks can be slow and costly. These factors imply that developers must carefully design the applications and the data distribution strategy. The applications also have to be tested and monitored for performance and cost.

One of the major strategies in designing and controlling distributed databases is to replicate data. Instead of maintaining one source, it is often more efficient to replicate data that is heavily used in multiple locations. Of course, replication requires additional disk space, along with periodic updates and transfers of the data changes to each copy. Replication saves time by providing local access to data. It reduces costs by reducing the need for a full-time high-speed connection. Instead, bulk data is transferred at regular intervals—preferably at off-peak communication rates.

Client/server networks and client/server databases are a common means to design applications and distribute databases. Clients usually run applications on personal computers, and most of their power is devoted to the user interface. The data is maintained on a limited number of database servers, which are more efficient than simple file-server transfers. With a server database, the client sends an SQL query, and the server processes the request and returns only the desired data. With a file server, the client computer performs all the processing and must retrieve and examine all the data.

Larger, object-oriented applications are being built using a three-tier client/server architecture. The additional layer is in the middle and consists of business rules and program code (business objects) that execute on servers. The middle layer is also responsible for pulling data from the database servers and reformatting it for use by the client applications. Separating the three layers makes it easier to modify each component without interfering with the other elements.

The World Wide Web is becoming a popular mechanism to create client/server applications. The clients have limited capabilities, but standards make it easier for everyone to get access to the applications and data. Capabilities of all Web tools are increasing rapidly, making it easier for developers to extend the reach of their applications. Tools and applications are also supporting XML to make it easier to transfer data across companies, machines, and applications.

A Developer's View

Like Miranda, most developers understand the importance of the Web. The client standards make it easier to distribute data and connect with users around the world. Additionally, as applications expand, it becomes necessary to create distributed databases to improve performance and to support different regions. Distributed databases can significantly complicate application development. First, be sure the application runs on one computer. Then get the best software you can afford. As much as possible, let the server databases perform the data manipulation and computation tasks. Use the client computers to display the results. Learn as much as you can about the Internet: It changes constantly, but will become increasingly important in your applications. For your class project, you should identify where the company might expand and where you would position distributed computers to support it. Explain how the database design would change in a distributed environment.

Key Terms

Active Data Objects (ADO), *378*
anchor tag, *383*
browser, *381*
client/server, *363*
common gateway interface (CGI), *384*
distributed database, *362*
electronic data interchange (EDI), *387*
extensible markup language (XML), *388*
hypertext link, *383*
java, *391*
Java 2 enterprise edition (J2EE), *391*
JDBC, *391*
latency, *387*
list of values (LOV), *386*
local area network (LAN), *367*
open database connectivity (ODBC), *378*
replicate, *369*
replication manager, *369*
three-tier client/server, *375*
two-phase commit, *371*
wide area network (WAN), *367*
World Wide Web, *381*

Review Questions

1. What are the strengths and weaknesses of distributed databases?
2. Which features are needed to make the distributed database transparent to the user?
3. Why might a query on a distributed database take a long time to run?
4. When would you want to replicate data in a distributed database?
5. Why is concurrency a bigger problem with distributed databases than with stand-alone databases?
6. How does the two-phase commit process work?
7. Why is a client/server database more efficient than a database on a simple file server?
8. Which tools help connect databases from different vendors?

9. What are the advantages of the three-tier client/server approach?
10. What are the capabilities of an Internet Web client?
11. What is XML and why is it useful in transferring data?

Exercises

1. Research software that can be used to build three-tier client/server applications. Describe the capabilities of the software. Explain how components are assigned to each tier. For example, consider VB enterprise edition of J2EE.
2. You have the following distributed databases:

Location	Link Speed	Tables	Sizes
Boston	53kbps	Part(PartID, Description, Size, ListPrice) Order(OrderID, OrderDate, DateShipped, DateReceived) OrderPart(OrderID, PartID, Quantity, SalePrice)	1,500 rows 300,000 rows 3,000,000 rows
Seattle	1.544mbps	Part(PartID, Description, Size, ListPrice) Order(OrderID, OrderDate, DateShipped, DateReceived) OrderPart(OrderID, PartID, Quantity, SalePrice)	1,000 rows 200,000 rows 2,000,000 rows
Miami	128kbps	Item(BarCode, Description, ListPrice) Sales(SaleID, SaleDate, SalesTax, RegisterID) SaleItem(TransactionID, SaleID, BarCode)	70,000 rows 1,000,000 rows 40,000,000 rows
Denver (HQ)	local	Assembly(EmployeeID, BarCodeID, PartID, DateTime) Shipment(ShipID, CustomerID, ShipDate) ShipItem(ShipID, BarCode, Quantity)	1,000,000 rows 50,000 rows 10,000 rows

You are working for a firm that has suppliers in Boston and Seattle, and a major customer in Miami. The suppliers have systems that enable you to send XML queries and retrieve data on when parts were shipped. Likewise, the customer provides access to the main sales database so you can check on item sales. Your CEO noted that one product apparently assembled over the past 10 days has been returned several times to the customer, and she wants you to find out which employees and suppliers contributed to that particular product. Based on the communication speeds and table sizes, design the best performing query to answer this question. Could the database and query performance be improved by changing the distributed design?

3. A company has two satellite offices about 100 miles apart in the same state. Main data processing is handled at a data center about 1,000 miles away. Both offices are connected to the main site with a T1 (1.544mbps) line. A manager wants you to develop a database to be used by employees at both offices. The database will track customer interactions. Each local employee (about 10 at each location) will track his or her clients (about 50 active clients per employee at any point in time), and the data will be reviewed by the manager once a month. What is the best distributed design for this database?
4. You are hired as a consultant to a firm with plants in several different states. At best, the plants are connected by a T1 line at 1.544mbps, a few are running ISDN connections at 128kbps. The application maintains detailed data about each plant's operations, as well as prices, rules, and procedures created at the headquarters. The application performs complex processing for each plant and generates large amounts of data that is used by both the plants and specialists at headquarters. The company wants the application to run on an Oracle database,

with processing handled by Visual Basic. Set up the basic structure of the database. Which parts should be distributed? Which parts centralized?

5. For distributed systems, what are the advantages and disadvantages of using a central website with all of the data in one primary location and all client access through Web browsers?

Sally's Pet Store

6. Sally is planning to add a second store. Write a plan that describes how the data will be shared. How will you control and monitor the new system? Which tools will you add?
7. Sally wants to connect to some of the breeders so that she can get up-to-date information on their animals—including health and genealogy records. Explain how you would set up a system to enable this sharing of data.
8. Define a three-tier system for the Pet Store. In particular, what business rules and applications would you store on the middle tier?
9. Create a website so Sally can let potential customers search for a particular animal.
10. Expand the database and create a website for Sally's best customers. When customers purchase more than $1,000 in a year, they will receive an e-mailed newsletter, and be directed to a special website where they can check their recent purchases and order new items.

Rolling Thunder Bicycles

11. Rolling Thunder is planning to expand to a second location across the country. How should the database be distributed? Where should each table be stored? Which tables should be replicated, and how should the data changes be reconciled?
12. Rolling Thunder is planning to expand by sending sales representatives around the country to various bike shops. They will have laptops to configure and take new orders. But most bike shops will not have Internet connections, so the system will have to work offline. Describe how this system will work. What security provisions will be needed?
13. If you have a three-tier client/server system, describe which components you would store in each location (client, server, middleware). Justify your choices and examine your options.
14. Build a Web form that enables customers to check on the progress of their bicycle orders.
15. Separate the purchasing-related tables from the database and move them to a new database on a second server. Modify or recreate the purchasing and manufacturing forms so that they continue to work from the original computer.

Website References

Site	Description
http://www.w3.org/	Web standards body.
http://www.stardeveloper.com/	General information on databases, particularly Microsoft (ASP) and Java.
http://msdn.microsoft.com	Search for Microsoft's .NET framework and documentation.
http://www.xml.org	Standards organization for XML.
http://www.xml.com	O'Reilly website on XML.
http://www.w3.org/TR/xquery	A query language for XML.
http://java.sun.com/products/jdbc	Java and JDBC documentation and references.

Additional Reading

Burns R., D. Long, and R. Rees. "Consistency and Locking for Distributing Updates to Web Servers Using a File System." *ACM SIGMETRICS Performance Evaluation Review* 28, no. 2 (September 2000), pp. 15–21. [Performance issues in replicated databases.]

Date, C. J. *An Introduction to Database Systems,* 8th ed. Reading, MA: Addison-Wesley, 2003. [In-depth discussion of distributed databases.]

Fortier, P. J. *Database Systems Handbook.* Burr Ridge, IL: McGraw-Hill, 1996. [Technical discussion on building applications using multiple database systems.]

Holzner, S. *Inside XML.* Indianapolis: New Riders/MTP, 2000. [One of several books describing XML.]

Simon, E. *Distributed Information Systems: From Client/Server to Distributed Multimedia.* Burr Ridge, IL: McGraw-Hill, 1996. [General but technical discussion on building distributed systems.]

White, S., M. Fisher, R. Cattell, G. Hamilton, and M. Hapner. *JDBC API Tutorial and Reference,* 2nd ed. Boston: Addison-Wesley, 1999. [Details of Java database access connectivity.]

Glossary

24-7 Operation of an application or database 24 hours a day, 7 days a week. Because the database can never be shut down, performing maintenance is a challenge.

abstract data types In SQL 1999, the ability to define more complex data domains that support inheritance for storing objects.

accessibility A design goal to make the application usable by as many users as possible, including those with physical challenges. One solution is to support multiple input and output methods.

ACID transactions The acronym for transactions that specifies the four required elements of a safe transaction: atomicity, consistency, isolation, and durability.

active data objects (ADO) Microsoft's component (COM) approach to connect program code and Web server scripts to a database. Provides SQL statement and row-level access to virtually any database.

active server pages (ASP) Microsoft's Web pages that enable you to run script programs on the server. Useful for providing access to a server database for Internet users.

Advanced Encryption System (AES) A single-key encryption system to replace DES, based on a Belgian encryption system: Rijndael. It supports key lengths of 128, 192, and 256 bits, making it considerably more secure than DES.

aesthetics An application design goal, where layout, colors, and artwork are used to improve the appearance of the application—not detract from it. By its nature, the value of any design is subjective.

aggregation The generic name for several SQL functions that operate across the selected rows. Common examples include SUM, COUNT, and AVERAGE.

aggregation association A relationship where individual items become elements in a new class. For example, an Order contains Items. In UML, the association is indicated with a small open diamond on the association end. *Also see* composition.

alias A temporary name for a table or a column. Often used when you need to refer to the same table more than once, as in a self-join.

ALL A SQL SELECT clause often used with subqueries. Used in a WHERE clause to match all of the items in a list. For example, Price > All (. . .) means that the row matches only if Price is greater than the largest value in the list.

ALTER TABLE A SQL data definition command that changes the structure of a table. To improve performance, some systems limit the changes to adding new columns. In these situations, to make major changes, you have to create a new table and copy the old data.

anchor tag The HTML tag that signifies a link. Denoted with <A>.

ANY A SQL SELECT clause often used with subqueries. Used in a WHERE clause to match at least one of the items in a list. For example, Price > ANY (. . .) means that the row matches as long as Price is greater than at least one item in the list.

application A complete system that performs a specific collection of tasks. It typically consists of integrated forms and reports and generally contains menus and a Help system.

Application Design Guide A standard set of design principles that should be followed when building applications. The standard makes it easier for users to operate new applications, since techniques they learn in one system will work in another.

application generator A DBMS tool that assists the developer in creating a complete application package. Common tools include menu and toolbar generators and an integrated context-sensitive Help system.

association Connections between classes or entities. Generally, they represent business rules. For example, an order can be placed by one customer. It is important to identify whether the association is one-to-one, one-to-many, or many-to-many.

association role In UML, the point where an association attaches to a class. It can be named, and generally shows multiplicity, aggregation, or composition.

association rules A data mining technique that examines a set of transactions to see which items are commonly purchased together.

atomicity The transaction element that specifies that all changes in a transaction must succeed or fail together.

attribute A feature or characteristic of an entity. An attribute will become a column in a data table. Employee attributes might include name, address, date hired, and phone.

authentication Providing a verification system to determine who actually wrote a message. Common systems use a dual-key encryption system.

autonumber A type of data domain where the DBMS automatically assigns a unique identification number for each new row of data. Useful for generating primary keys.

B^+-tree An indexed data storage method that is efficient for a wide range of data access tasks. Tree searches provide a consistent level of performance that is not affected by the size of the database.

base table A table that contains data about a single basic entity. It generally contains no foreign keys, so data can be entered into this table without reference to other tables. For example, Customer would be a base table; Order would not.

BETWEEN A SQL comparison operator that determines whether an item falls between two values. Often useful for dates.

binary large object (BLOB) A data domain for undefined, large chunks of data. A BLOB (or simple object) type can hold any type of data, but the programmer is often responsible for displaying, manipulating, and searching the data.

binary search A search technique for sorted data. Start at the middle of the data. If the search value is greater than the middle value, split the following data in half. Keep reducing by half until the value is found.

bitmap index A compact, high-speed indexing method where the key values and conditions are compressed to a small size that can be stored and searched rapidly.

Boolean algebra Creating and manipulating logic queries connected with AND, OR, and NOT conditions.

bound control A control on a form that is tied to a column in the database. When data is entered or changed, the changes are automatically saved to the data table.

Boyce-Codd normal form (BCNF) All dependencies must be explicitly shown through keys. There cannot be a hidden dependency between nonkey and key columns.

browser A software package on a client personal computer used to access and display Web pages from the Internet.

brute force attack An attempt to break a security system by trying every possible combination of passwords or encryption keys.

call-level interface (CLI) A set of libraries that enable programmers to work in a language outside the DBMS (e.g., C++) and utilize the features of the DBMS. The DBMS provides the communication libraries and handles much of the data exchange itself.

cascading delete When tables are linked by data, if you delete a row in a higher level table, matching rows in other tables are deleted automatically. For example, if you delete Customer 1173, all orders placed by that customer are also deleted.

cascading triggers Multiple events that arise when a change that fires a trigger on one table causes a change in a second table, that triggers a change in a third table, and so on.

CASE A SQL operator supported by some systems. It examines multiple conditions (cases) and takes the appropriate action when it finds a match.

certificate authority A company that ensures the validity of public keys and the applicant's identity for dual-key encryption systems.

check box A square button that signifies a choice. By the design guide, users can select multiple options with check boxes, as opposed to option buttons that signify mutually exclusive choices.

clarity The goal of making an application easier to use through elegant design and organization that matches user tasks so that the purpose and use of the application is clear to the user.

class A descriptor for a set of objects with similar structure, behavior, and relationships. That is, a class is the model description of the business entity. A business model might have an Employee class, where one specific employee is an object in that class.

class diagram A graph of classes connected through relationships. It is designed to show the static structure of the model. Similar to the entity-relationship diagram.

class hierarchy A graph that highlights the inheritance relationships between classes.

classification analysis A data mining technique that classifies groups of objects, such as customers. It determines which factors are important classifier variables.

client/server A technique for organizing systems where a few computers hold most of the data, which is retrieved by individuals using personal computer clients.

cluster analysis A data mining technique that groups elements of a dataset, often based on how close the items are to each other.

cold site A facility that can be leased from a disaster backup specialist. A cold site contains power and telecommunication lines, but no computer. In the event of a disaster, a company calls the computer vendor and begs for the first available machine to be sent to the cold site.

collaboration diagram A UML diagram to display interactions among objects. It does not show time as a separate dimension. It is used to model processes.

combo box A combination of a list box and a text box that is used to enter new data or to select from a list of items. A combo box saves space compared to a list box since the list is displayed only when selected by the user. Known as a select box on Web forms.

command button A button on a form that is designed to be clicked. The designer writes the code that is activated when the button is clicked.

common gateway interface (CGI) With Web servers, CGI is a predefined system for transferring data across the Internet. Current scripting languages hide the details, so you can simply retrieve data as it is needed.

composite key A primary key that consists of more than one column. Indicates a many-to-many relationship between the columns.

composition association A relationship in which an object is composed of a collection of other objects. For example, a bicycle is built from components. In UML, it is indicated with a small filled diamond on the association end.

computer-aided software engineering (CASE) Computer programs that are designed to support the analysis and development of computer systems. They make it easier to create, store, and share diagrams and data definitions. Some versions can analyze existing code and generate new code.

concatenate A programming operation that appends one string on the end of a second string. For example, LastName & "," & FirstName could yield "Smith, John".

concatenated key *See* composite key.

concurrent access Performing two (or more) operations on the same data at the same time. The DBMS must sequence the operations so that some of the changes are not lost.

confidence In data mining with association rules, a measure of the strength of a rule measured by the percentage of transactions with item A that also contain item B. The probability that B is in the basket given that A is already there.

consistency, application The goal of making an application easier to use by using the same features, colors, and commands throughout. Modern applications also strive for consistency with a common design guide.

consistency, transaction The transaction requirement that specifies all data must remain internally consistent when changes are committed and can be validated by application checks.

constraint In SQL, a constraint is a rule that is enforced on the data. For example, there can be primary-key and foreign-key constraints that limit the data that can be entered into the declared columns. Other business rules can form constraints, such as Price > 0.

context-sensitive help Help messages that are tailored to the specific task the user is performing.

context-sensitive menu A menu that changes depending on the object selected by the user.

control break A report consisting of grouped data uses control breaks to separate the groups. The break is defined on the key variable that identifies each member of the group.

controls The generic term for an item placed on a form. Typical controls consist of text boxes, combo boxes, and labels.

correlated subquery A subquery that must be reevaluated for each row of the main query. Can be extremely slow. Can often be avoided by creating a temporary table and using that in the subquery instead.

CREATE DOMAIN A SQL data definition command to create a new data domain that is composed of existing domain types.

CREATE SCHEMA A SQL data definition command to create a new logical grouping of tables. With some systems it is equivalent to creating a new database. This command is not available in Oracle or SQL Server.

CREATE TABLE A SQL data definition command to create a new table. The command is often generated with a program.

CREATE VIEW A SQL command to create a new view or saved query.

Cross JOIN Arises when you do not specify a JOIN condition for two tables. It matches every row in the first table with every row in the second table. Also known as the Cartesian product. It should be avoided.

crosstab A special SQL query (not offered by all systems) that creates a tabular output based on two groups of data. Access uses a TRANSFORM command to create a cross tabulation.

cursor (1) The current location pointer in a graphical environment. (2) A row pointer that tracks through a table, making one row of data active at a time.

cylinder Disk drives are partitioned into cylinders (or sectors) that represent a portion of a track.

data administration Planning and coordination required to define data consistently throughout the company.

data administrator (DA) The person in charge of the data resources of a company. The DA is responsible for data integrity, consistency, and integration.

data definition language (DDL) A set of commands that are used to define data, such as CREATE TABLE. Graphical interfaces are often easier to use, but the data definition commands are useful for creating new tables with a program.

data device Storage space allocated to hold database tables, indexes, and rollback data. *See* tablespace.

data dictionary Holds the definitions of all of the data tables and describes the type of data that is being stored.

data independence Separates the data from the programs, which often enables the data definition to be changed without altering the program.

data integrity Keeping accurate data, which means few errors and means that the data reflects the true state of the business. A DBMS enables you to specify constraints or rules that help maintain integrity, such as prices must always be greater than 0.

data manipulation language (DML) A set of commands used to alter the data. *See* INSERT, DELETE, and UPDATE.

data mining Searching databases for unknown patterns and information. Tools include statistical analysis, pattern-matching techniques, and data segmentation analysis, classification analysis, association rules, and cluster analysis.

data normalization The process of creating a well-behaved set of tables to efficiently store data, minimize redundancy, and ensure data integrity. *See* first, second, and third normal form.

data replication In a distributed system, placing duplicate copies of data on several servers to reduce overall transmission time and costs.

data type A type of data that can be held by a column. Each DBMS has predefined system domains (integer, float, string, etc.). Some systems support user-defined domains that are named combinations of other data types.

data volume The estimated size of the database. Computed for each table by multiplying the estimated number of rows times the average data length of each row.

data warehouse A specialized database that is optimized for management queries. Data is extracted from online transaction processing systems. The data is cleaned and optimized for searching and analysis. Generally supported by parallel processing and RAID storage.

database A collection of data stored in a standardized format, designed to be shared by multiple users. A collection of tables for a particular business situation.

database administration The technical aspects of creating and running the database. The basic tasks are performance monitoring, backup and recovery, and assigning and controlling security.

database administrator (DBA) A specialist who is trained in the administration of a particular DBMS. DBAs are trained in the details of installing, configuring, and operating the DBMS.

database cursor A variable created within a programming language that defines a SELECT statement and points to one row of data at a time. Data on that row can be retrieved or edited using the programming language.

database engine The heart of the DBMS. It is responsible for storing, retrieving, and updating the data.

database management system (DBMS) Software that defines a database, stores the data, supports a query language, produces reports, and creates data entry screens.

datasheet A gridlike form that displays rows and columns of data. Generally used as a subform, a datasheet displays data in the least amount of space possible.

deadlock A situation that exists when two (or more) processes each have a lock on a piece of data that the other one needs.

default values Values that are displayed and entered automatically. Used to save time at data entry.

DELETE A SQL data manipulation command that deletes rows of data. It is always used with a WHERE clause to specify which rows should be deleted.

deletion anomaly Problems that arise when you delete data from a table that is not in third normal form. For example, if all customer data is stored with each order, when you delete an order, you could lose all associated customer data.

DeMorgan's law An algebraic law that states: To negate a condition that contains an AND or an OR connector, you negate each of the two clauses and switch the connector. An AND becomes an OR and vice versa.

dependence An issue in data normalization. An attribute A depends on another attribute B if the values of A change in response to changes in B. For example, a customer's name depends on the CustomerID (each employee has a specific name). On the other hand, a customer's name does not depend on the OrderID. Customers do not change their names each time they place an order.

derived class A class that is created as an extension of another class. The programmer need only define the new attributes and methods. All others are inherited from the higher level classes. *See* inheritance.

DESC The modifier in the SQL SELECT . . . ORDER BY statement that specifies a descending sort (e.g., Z . . . A). ASC can be used for ascending, but it is the default, so it is not necessary.

dimension An attribute in an OLAP cube that is used to group and search the data.

direct access A data storage method where the physical location is computed from the logical key value. Data can be stored and retrieved with no searches.

direct manipulation of objects A graphical interface method that is designed to mimic real-world actions. For example, you can copy files by dragging an icon from one location to another.

disaster plan A contingency plan that is created and followed if a disaster strikes the computer system. Plans include off-site storage of backups, notifying personnel, and establishing operations at a safe site.

DISTINCT An SQL keyword used in the SELECT statement to remove duplicate rows from the output.

distributed database Multiple independent databases that operate on two or more computers that are connected and share data over a network. The databases are usually in different physical locations. Each database is controlled by an independent DBMS.

dockable toolbar A toolbar that users can drag to any location on the application window. It is generally customized with options and buttons to perform specific tasks.

domain-key normal form (DKNF) The ultimate goal in designing a database. Each table represents one topic, and all of the business rules are expressed in terms of domain constraints and key relationships. That is, all of the business rules are explicitly described by the table rules.

drag-and-drop A graphical interface technique where actions are defined by holding down a mouse key, dragging an icon, and dropping the icon on a new object.

drill down The act of moving from a display of summary data to more detail. Commonly used in examining data in a data warehouse or OLAP application. *See* Roll up.

drive head The mechanism that reads and writes data onto a disk. Modern drives have several drive heads.

DROP TABLE A SQL data definition command that completely removes a table from the database—including the definition. Use it sparingly.

dual-key encryption An encryption technique that uses two different keys: one private and one public. The public key is published so anyone can retrieve it. To send an encrypted message to someone, you use the person's public key. At that point, only the person's private key will decrypt the message. Encrypting a message first with your private key can also be used to verify that you wrote the message.

durability The transaction element that specifies that when a transaction is committed, all changes are permanently saved even if there is a hardware or system failure.

edit The Microsoft DAO command to alter data on the current row.

electronic data interchange (EDI) Exchanging data over networks with external agents such as suppliers, customers, and banks.

encapsulation In object-oriented programming, the technique of defining attributes and methods within a common class. For example, all features and capabilities of an Employee class would be located together. Other code objects can use the properties and methods but only by referencing the Employee object.

encryption Encoding data with a key value so the data becomes unreadable. Two general types of encryption are used today: single key (e.g., DES) and dual key (e.g., RSA).

entity An item in the real world that we wish to identify and track.

entity-relationship diagram (ERD) A graph that shows the associations (relationships) between business entities. Under UML, the class diagram displays similar relationships.

equi-join A SQL equality JOIN condition. Rows from two tables are joined if the columns match exactly. Equi-join is the most common JOIN condition. Rows that have no match in the other table are not displayed.

EXCEPT A SQL operator that examines rows from two SELECT statements. It returns all rows from one statement except those that would be returned by the second statement. Sometimes implemented as a SUBTRACT command. *See* UNION.

exists A SQL keyword used to determine if subqueries return any rows of data.

expert system (ES) A system with a knowledge base consisting of data and rules that enables a novice to make decisions as effectively as an expert.

extensible markup language (XML) A tag-based notation system that is used to assign names and structure to data. It was mainly designed for transferring data among diverse systems.

extraction, transformation, and transportation (ETT) The three steps in populating a data warehouse from existing files or databases. Extraction means selecting the data you want. Transformation is generally the most difficult step and requires making the data consistent. Transportation implies that the data has to be physically moved over a network to the data warehouse.

fact table The table or query holding the facts to be presented in an OLAP cube.

feasibility study A quick examination of the problems, goals, and expected costs of a proposed system. The objective is to determine whether the problem can reasonably be solved with a computer system.

feedback A design feature where the application provides information to the user as tasks are accomplished or errors arise. Feedback can be provided in many forms (e.g., messages, visual cues, or audible reminders).

FETCH The command used in SQL cursor programming to retrieve the next row of data into memory.

first normal form (1NF) A table is in 1NF when there are no repeating groups within it. Each cell can contain only one value. For example, how many items can be placed in one Order table? The items repeat, so they must be split into a separate table.

fixed-width storage Storing each row of data in a fixed number of bytes per column.

fixed-with-overflow storage Storing a portion of the row data in a limited number of bytes, and moving extra data to an overflow location.

focus In a window environment, a form or control has focus when it is the one that will receive keystrokes. It is usually highlighted.

For Each . . . Next In VBA, an iteration command to automatically identify objects in a group and apply some operation to that collection. Particularly useful when dealing with cells in a spreadsheet.

foreign key A column in one table that is a primary key in a second table. It does not need to be a key in the first table. For example, in an Order table, CustomerID is a foreign key because it is a primary key in the Customer table.

forms generator A DBMS tool that enables you to set up input forms on the screen.

fourth normal form (4NF) There cannot be hidden dependencies between key columns. A multivalued dependency exists when a key determines two separate but independent attributes. Split the table to make the two dependencies explicit.

FROM The SQL SELECT clause that signifies the tables from which the query will retrieve data. Used in conjunction with the JOIN or INNER JOIN statement.

FULL JOIN A JOIN that matches all rows from both tables if they match, plus all rows from the left table that do not match, and all rows from the right table that do not match. Rarely used and rarely available. *See* LEFT JOIN and RIGHT JOIN.

function A procedure designed to perform a specific computation. The difference between a function and a subroutine is that a function returns a specific value (not including the parameters).

generalization association A relationship among classes that begins with a generic class. More detailed classes are derived from it and inherit the properties and methods of the higher level classes.

geocode Assigning location coordinates of latitude and longitude to a dataset.

geographic information system (GIS) Designed to identify and display relationships among business data and locations. A good example of the use of objects in a database environment.

GRANT The SQL command to give someone access to specific tables or queries.

graphics interchange file (GIF) One standard method of storing graphical images. Commonly used for images shared on the Internet.

group break A report that splits data into groups. The split-point is called a break. Also known as a control break.

GROUP BY A SQL SELECT clause that computes an aggregate value for each item in a group. For example, SELECT Department, SUM(Salary) FROM Employee GROUP BY Department;

computes and lists the total employee salaries for each department.

HAVING A SQL clause used with the GROUP BY statement. It restricts the output to only those groups that meet the specified condition.

heads-down data entry Touch typists concentrate on entering data without looking at the screen. Forms for this task should minimize keystrokes and use audio cues.

Help system A method for displaying, sequencing, and searching Help documentation. Developers need to write the Help files in a specific format and then use a Help compiler to generate the final Help file.

hidden dependency A dependency specified by business rules that is not shown in the table structure. It generally indicates that the table needs to be normalized further and is an issue with Boyce-Codd or fourth normal form.

hierarchical database An older DBMS type that organizes data in hierarchies that can be rapidly searched from top to bottom, e.g., Customer—Order—OrderItem.

horizontal partition Splitting a table into groups based on the rows of data. Rows that are seldom used can be moved to slower, cheaper storage devices.

hot site A facility that can be leased from a disaster backup specialist. A hot site contains all the power, telecommunication facilities, and computers necessary to run a company. In the event of a disaster, a company collects its backup data, notifies workers, and moves operations to the hot site.

human factors design An attempt to design computer systems that best accommodate human users.

hypertext link Hypertext (e.g., Web) documents consist of text and graphics with links that retrieve new pages. Clicking on a link is the primary means of navigation and obtaining more information.

hypertext markup language (HTML) A display standard that is used to create documents to be shared on the Internet. Several generators will create HTML documents from standard word processor files.

icon A small graphical representation of some idea or object. Typically used in a graphical user interface to execute commands and manipulate underlying objects.

IN A SQL WHERE clause operator typically used with subqueries. It returns a match if the selected item matches one of the items in the list. For example, WHERE ItemID IN (115, 235, 536) returns a match for any of the items specified. Typically, another SELECT statement is inserted in the parentheses.

index A sorted list of key values from the original table along with a pointer to the rest of the data in each row. Used to speed up searches and data retrieval.

indexed sequential access method (ISAM) A data storage method that relies on an index to search and retrieve data faster than a pure sequential search.

inequality join A SQL JOIN where the comparison is made with an inequality (greater than or less than) instead of an equality operator. Useful for placing data into categories based on ranges of data.

inheritance In object-oriented design, the ability to define new classes that are derived from higher level classes. New classes inherit all prior properties and methods, so the programmer only needs to define new properties and methods.

INNER JOIN A SQL equality JOIN condition. Rows from two tables are joined if the columns match exactly. The most common JOIN condition. Rows that have no match in the other table are not displayed.

InputBox A predefined simplistic Window form that might be used to get one piece of data from the user. But it is better to avoid it and create your own form.

INSERT Two SQL commands that insert data into a table. One version inserts a single row at a time. The other variation copies selected data from one query and appends it as new rows in a different table.

insertion anomaly Problems that arise when you try to insert data into a table that is not in third normal form. For example, if you find yourself repeatedly entering the same data (e.g., a customer's address), the table probably needs to be redefined.

Internet A collection of computers loosely connected to exchange information worldwide. Owners of the computers make files and information available to other users.

INTERSECT A set operation on rows of data from two SELECT statements. Only rows that are in both statements will be retrieved. *See* UNION.

Intranet A network internal to a company that uses Internet technologies to share data.

isolation The transaction requirement that says the system must give each transaction the perception that it is running in isolation with no concurrent access issues.

isolation level Used to assign locking properties in transactions. At a minimum, it is used to specify optimistic or pessimistic locks. Some systems support intermediate levels.

iteration Causing a section of code to be executed repeatedly, such as the need for a loop to track through each row of data. Typical commands include Do . . . Loop, and For . . . Next.

Java A programming language developed by Sun Microsystems that is supposed to be able to run unchanged on diverse computers. Originally designed as a control language for embedded systems, Java is targeted for Internet applications. The source of many bad puns in naming software products.

Java 2 enterprises edition (J2EE) A back-end server-based system for building complex applications. It is based on Java but consists of an entire environment.

JDBC A set of methods to connect Java code to databases. Similar in purpose to ADO, but works only in Java. Sometimes referred to as Java Database Connectivity.

JOIN When data is retrieved from more than one table, the tables must be joined by some column or columns of data. *See* INNER JOIN and LEFT JOIN.

latency Time delay in a system. In a Web-based system, the delay created by slow links. Long download times create higher latency which leads to more server conflicts.

LEFT JOIN An OUTER JOIN that includes all of the rows from the "left" table, even if there are no matching rows in the "right" table. The missing values are indicated by Nulls. *See* RIGHT JOIN and INNER JOIN. Left and right are defined by the order the tables are listed; left is first.

lifetime The length of time that a programming variable stays available. For example, variables created within subroutines are created when the routine is executed and then destroyed when it exits. Global variables stay alive for all routines within the module.

lift The potential gain attributed to an association rule compared to purchases without the rule.

LIKE The SQL pattern-matching operator used to compare string values. The standard uses percent (%) to match any number of characters, and underscore (_) to match a single character. Some systems (e.g., Access) use an asterisk (*) and a question mark (?) instead.

list box A control on a form that displays a list of choices. The list is always displayed and takes up a fixed amount of space on the screen.

list of values (LOV) An important technique for selecting data on Oracle forms. Used instead of combo/select boxes, the Oracle form maintains a small, buffered list of data that can be selected for a text box. Particularly useful in distributed databases because only portions of the list are sent to the user.

local area network (LAN) A collection of personal computers within a small geographic area. All components of the network are owned or controlled by one company.

local variable A variable defined within a subroutine. It can be accessed only within that subroutine and not from other procedures.

logic Logic statements that define a program's purpose and structure. Can be written in pseudocode independently of the program's syntax. Logic structures include loops, conditions, subroutines, and input/output commands.

logical security Determining which users should have access to which data. It deals with preventing three data problems: (1) unauthorized disclosure, (2) unauthorized modification, and (3) unauthorized withholding.

loop Each loop must have a beginning, an end condition, and some way to increment a variable. *See* iteration.

market basket analysis *See* association rules.

master-detail A common one-to-many relationship often found on business forms, where the main form (e.g., Order) displays data for the master component, and a subform (e.g., Order Items) displays detail data. Sometimes called a parent-child relationship.

measure The numeric data displayed in an OLAP cube.

menu A set of application commands grouped together—usually on a toolbar. It provides an easy reference for commonly used commands and highlights the structure of the application.

metadata Data about data, or the description of the data tables and columns. Usually held in the data dictionary.

method A function or operation that a class can perform. For example, a Customer class would generally have an AddNew method that is called whenever a new customer object is added to the database.

metadata Data about data, typically stored in a data dictionary. For example, table definitions and column domains are metadata.

modal form A form that takes priority on the screen and forces the user to deal with it before continuing. It should be avoided because it interrupts the user.

module (or package) A collection of subroutines, generally related to a common purpose.

MsgBox A predefined method in Windows for displaying a brief message on the screen and presenting a few limited choices to the user. Because it is modal and interrupts the user, it should be used sparingly.

multiplicity The UML term for signifying the quantities involved in an association. It is displayed on an association line with a minimum value, an ellipses (. . .), and a maximum value or asterisk (*) for many. For example, a customer can place from zero to many orders, so the multiplicity is (0 . . . *).

***N*-ary association** An association among three or more classes. It is drawn as a diamond on a UML class diagram. The term comes from extending English terms: un*ary* means one, bin*ary* means two, tern*ary* means four; so *N*-ary means many.

naming conventions Program teams should name their variables and controls according to a consistent format. One common approach is to use a three-letter prefix to identify the type of variable, followed by a descriptive name.

nested conditions Conditional statements that are placed inside other conditional statements. For example, If (x > 0) Then . . . If (y < 4) Then . . . Some nested conditions can be replaced with a Case statement.

nested query *See* subquery.

network database An older DBMS type that expanded the hierarchical database by supporting multiple connections between entities. A network database is characterized by the requirement that all connections had to be supported by an index.

normalization *See* data normalization.

NOT The SQL negation operator. Used in the WHERE clause to reverse the truth value of a statement. *See* DeMorgan's law.

NotInList An event corresponding to a combo box in Access. It is triggered when a user enters a value that does not yet exist in the selected list. Often used to add new data to a table, such as new customers.

NULL A missing (or currently unassigned) value.

object An instance or particular example of a class. For example, in an Employee class, one individual employee would be an object. In a relational environment, a class is stored as a table, while an individual row in the table contains data for one object.

object browser A tool provided within Microsoft software that displays properties and methods for available objects.

object-oriented (OO) database management system (OODBMS) A database system that holds objects, including properties and methods. It supports links between objects, including inheritance.

object-oriented programming A programming methodology where code is encapsulated within the definition of various objects (or classes). Systems are built from (hopefully) reusable objects. You control the system by manipulating object properties and calling object methods.

online analytical processing (OLAP) The use of a database for data analysis. The focus is on retrieval of the data. The primary goals are to provide acceptable response times, maintain security, and make it easy for users to find the data they need.

online transaction processing (OLTP) The use of a database for transaction processing. It consists of many insert and update operations and supports hundreds of concurrent accesses. High-speed storage of data, reliability, and data integrity are primary goals. Examples include airline reservations, online banking, and retail sales.

open database connectivity (ODBC) A standard created by Microsoft to enable software to access a variety of databases. Each DBMS vendor provides an ODBC driver. Application code can generally be written once. To change the DBMS, you simply install and set up the proper ODBC driver.

optimistic lock A transaction lock that does not block other processes. If the data is changed between read and write steps, the system generates an error that must be handled by code.

option button A round button that is used to indicate a choice. By the design guide, option buttons signify mutually exclusive choices, as opposed to check boxes.

ORDER BY The clause in the SQL SELECT statement that lists the columns to sort the output. The modifiers ASC and DESC are used to specify ascending and descending sort orders.

OUTER JOIN A generic term that represents a *left join* or a *right join*. It returns rows from a table, even if there is no matching row in the other table.

pack A maintenance operation that must be periodically performed on a database to remove fragments of deleted data.

package A UML mechanism to group logical elements together. It is useful for isolating sections of a design. Packages can provide an overview of the entire system without having to see all the details.

page footer A report element that appears at the bottom of every page. Often used for page numbers.

page header A report element that appears at the top of every page. Often used for column headings and subtitles.

parameter A variable that is passed to a subroutine or function and used in its computations.

pass-by-reference A subroutine parameter that can be altered within the subroutine. If it is altered, the new value is returned to the calling program. That is, the subroutine can alter variables in other parts of the code. Usually a dangerous approach. *See* pass-by-value.

pass-by-value A subroutine parameter that cannot be altered within the subroutine. Only its value is passed. If the subroutine changes the value, the original value in the calling program is not changed.

pass-through query SQL queries that are ignored by Access on the front end. They enable you to write complex SQL queries that are specific to the server database.

persistent objects In object-oriented programming, the ability to store objects (in a file or database) so that they can be retrieved at a later data.

persistent stored modules (PSM) In SQL-99 a proposed method for storing methods associated with objects. The module code would be stored and retrieved automatically by the DBMS.

pessimistic lock A complete isolation level that blocks other processes from reading a locked piece of data until the transaction is complete. Program code will receive an error message if the data element is locked.

physical security The branch of security that involves physically protecting the equipment and people. It includes disaster planning, physical access to equipment, and risk analysis and prevention.

pivot table Microsoft's tool for enabling managers to examine OLAP data dynamically—typically inside of an Excel spreadsheet. The data is extracted from the database or OLAP cube, and managers can click buttons to examine summaries or details.

pointer A logical or physical address of a piece of data.

polymorphism In a class hierarchy each new class inherits methods from the prior classes. Through polymorphism you can override those definitions and assign a new method (with the same name) to the new class.

primary key A column or set of columns that identify a particular row in a table.

private key In a dual-key encryption system, the key that is never revealed to anyone else. A message encrypted with a public key can be decrypted only with the matching private key.

procedural language A traditional programming language that is based on following procedures and is typically executed one statement at a time. Compared to SQL, which operates on sets of data with one command.

procedure A subroutine or function that is designed to perform one specific task. It is generally wise to keep procedures small.

property An attribute or feature of an entity that we wish to track. The term is often applied in an object-oriented context. *See* attribute.

prototype An initial outline of an application that is built quickly to demonstrate and test various features of the application. Often used to help users visualize and improve forms and reports.

public key In a dual-key encryption system, the key that is given to the public. A message encrypted with a public key can only be decrypted with the matching private key.

query by example (QBE) A fill-in-the-form approach to designing queries. You select tables and columns from a list and fill in blanks for conditions and sorting. It is relatively easy to use, requires minimal typing skills, generally comes with a Help system, and is useful for beginners.

rapid application development (RAD) A systems design methodology that attempts to reduce development time through efficiency and overlapping stages.

referential integrity A data integrity constraint where data can be entered into a foreign key column only if the data value already exists in the base table. For example, clerks should not be able to enter an Order for CustomerID 1173 if CustomerID 1173 is not in the Customer table.

reflexive association A relationship from one class back to itself. Most commonly seen in business in an Employee class, where some employees are managers over other employees.

reflexive join A situation that exists when a table is joined to itself through a second column. For example, the table Employee(EmployeeID, . . . , ManagerID) could have a join from ManagerID to EmployeeID.

relational database The most popular type of DBMS. All data is stored in tables (sometimes called relations). Tables are logically connected by the data they hold (e.g., through the key values). Relational databases should be designed through data normalization.

relationship An association between two or more entities. *See* association.

repeating groups Groups of data that repeat, such as items being ordered by a customer, multiple phone numbers for a client, and tasks assigned to a worker.

replicate Make a deliberate copy of a database so it can be distributed to a new location and the contents later synchronized with the master copy.

replication manager In a distributed database that relies on replication, the manager is an automated system that transfers changes to the various copies of the database. It has to handle conflicts if two people changed the same data before it was replicated.

report footer A report element that appears at the end of the report. Often used for summary statistics or graphs.

report header A report element that appears only at the start of the report. Often used for title pages and overviews.

report writer A DBMS tool that enables you to set up reports on the screen to specify how items will be displayed or calculated. Most of these tasks are performed by dragging data onto the screen.

resume A VBA error-handling operator that tells the processor to return to a new location and continue evaluating the code. Resume by itself returns to the line that caused the error. Resume Next returns to the line immediately following the error. Resume <label> sends the processor to a new location.

REVOKE The SQL command used to remove permissions that were granted to certain users.

RIGHT JOIN An OUTER JOIN that includes all the rows from the "right" table, even if there are no matching rows in the "left" table. The missing values are indicated by NULLS. See RIGHT JOIN and INNER JOIN. Left and right are defined by the order the tables are listed; left is first.

Rivest-Shamir-Adelman (RSA) encryption A dual-key encryption system that was patented in the United States by three mathematicians. *See* dual-key encryption.

role Security group where permissions are assigned by the task or role that is performed instead of to individual people. Roles make it easier to change employee permissions.

roll back A database system transaction feature. If an error occurs in a sequence of changes, the preceding changes can be rolled back to restore the database to a safe state with correct data.

roll forward If an error occurs in processing transactions, the database can be restarted and loaded from a known checkpoint. Then partially completed transactions can be rolled forward to record the interrupted changes.

roll up The act of aggregating detail data into a display of category summaries. Commonly used in examining data in a data warehouse or OLAP application. *See* drill down.

row-by-row calculations The way that SQL performs in-line calculations. For example, the statement SELECT price * Quantity AS Extended goes through each row and multiplies the row's value for Price times the matching value of Quantity.

schema A collection of tables that are grouped together for a common purpose.

scope Refers to where a variable is accessible. Variables defined within a subroutine can typically be accessed only by code within that subroutine. Variables defined within a module are globally accessible by any code within that module.

scroll bars A common graphical interface feature used to move material horizontally or vertically.

second normal form (2NF) A table is in 2NF if every nonkey column depends on the entire key (not just part of it). This issue arises only if there is a concatenated key (with multiple columns).

SELECT The primary data retrieval command for SQL. The main components are SELECT . . . FROM . . . INNER JOIN . . . WHERE.

self-join A table joined to itself. *See* reflexive join.

serialization A transaction requirement that specifies that each transaction is treated completely separately and run as if there were no other transactions.

shell site *See* cold site.

single-row form An input form that displays data from one row of a table at a time. The most common input form, since the designer has full control over the layout of the form.

snapshot In a constantly changing database, you can take a snapshot that provides a copy of the data at one point in time.

snowflake design A database design used for OLAP. A fact table is connected to dimension tables. The dimension tables can be joined to other dimension tables. It is less restrictive than the star design.

SQL A standardized database language, used for data retrieval (queries), data definition, and data manipulation.

SQL 1999 (SQL3) Approved in 1999, SQL 1999 was largely designed to add object-oriented features to the SQL language.

SQL 200x An almost completed new version of SQL. Its primary contribution is a formal definition of integrating XML and multimedia into relational databases.

star design A database design used for OLAP. A fact table is connected to dimension tables that provide categories for analysis. More restrictive than the snowflake design, all dimension tables are directly connected to the fact table.

style sheet A special file that describes the desired layout, fonts, and styles for a set of Web pages. It is a powerful method to establish and change styles on many Web pages through making minor changes to one file.

subform form A form that is displayed inside another (main) form. The data in the subform is generally linked to the row currently being displayed on the main form.

subquery Using a second query to retrieve additional data within the main query. For example, to retrieve all sales where price was greater than the average, the WHERE clause could use a subquery to compute the average price.

subroutine A separate section of code designed to perform one specific purpose. A subroutine can use parameters to exchange data with the calling routine.

subtable In SQL 1999 a subtable inherits all of the columns from a base table. It provides inheritance similar to that of the abstract data types; however, all data is stored in separate columns.

super-aggregate In a query, totals of totals. An important concept in OLAP queries provided by the ROLLUP option.

support A data mining measure in association rules, measured by the percent of transactions that contain both items.

switchboard form A form that is used to direct users to different parts of the application. Often used as the first form to appear. Options on the form should match the tasks of the users.

synonym A short name for the full database path. Advantages of the short name are that it is easy to remember and the user never needs to know where the data is located. In addition, if everyone uses the synonym, database administrators can easily move the server databases to different locations just by altering the synonym's properties.

syntax The specific format of commands that can be created in a program. Programs consist of logical steps, but each command must be given in the proper syntax for the compiler to understand it. Compilers generally check for syntax and prompt you with messages.

tab order The sequence of controls followed on a form when the user presses the tab or return keys.

table A collection of data for one class or entity. It consists of columns for each attribute and a row of data for each specific entity or object.

tablespace In Oracle, a tablespace is disk space that is allocated to hold tables, indexes, and other system data. You must first know the approximate size of the database.

tabular form An input form that displays data in columns and rows. It is used when there are few columns of data or when the user needs to see multiple rows at the same time.

third normal form (3NF) A table is in third normal form (3NF) if each nonkey column depends on the whole key and nothing but the key.

three-tier client/server A client/server system with a middle layer to hold code that defines business rules and consolidates access to various transaction servers.

toggle button A three-dimensional variation of the check box. It is used to signify a choice of options.

toolbar A small object in applications that can hold buttons and text menus. Users can execute commands with one or two mouse clicks. Used to hold frequently used commands, and commands that are used across the entire application, such as printing.

tooltip A short message that is displayed when the user moves the mouse cursor over an item on the screen. Extremely useful for identifying the purpose of icons.

TOP A SQL SELECT clause provided by Access that restricts the displayed output to a specified number of rows. You can set the number of rows directly or use a percentage of the total number.

transaction In a database application a transaction is a set of changes that must all be made together. Transactions must be identified to the DBMS and then committed or rolled back (if there is an error). For example, a transfer of money from one bank account to another requires two changes to the database—both must succeed or fail together.

transaction processing Collecting data for the purpose of recording transactions. Common examples include sales, human resource management, and financial accounting.

trigger An event that causes a procedure to be executed. For example, clicking a button can be a trigger, as can a change in a data value.

tuning Setting indexes, rewriting queries, and setting storage and other parameters to improve the database application performance.

two-phase commit A mechanism for handling concurrency and deadlock problems in a distributed database. In the first phase the coordinating DBMS sends updates to the other databases and asks them to prepare the transaction. Once they have agreed, the coordinator sends a message to commit the changes.

unicode A standard method of storing and displaying a variety of character sets. Almost all current world character sets have been defined, as well as several ancient languages. It uses 2 bytes to represent each character, enabling it to handle over 65,000 characters or ideograms.

Unified Modeling Language (UML) A standardized modeling language for designing and documenting computer and business systems.

UNION An SQL clause to combine rows from two SELECT statements. Both queries must have the same number of columns with the same domains. Most systems also support INTERSECT and EXCEPT (or SUBTRACT) operators.

UPDATE An SQL data manipulation command that changes the values in specified columns. A WHERE clause specifies which rows will be affected.

User Interface The look and feel of the application as it is seen by the user. Graphical interfaces are commonly employed in which users can manipulate icons and data on the screen to perform their tasks.

validation tables Simple tables of one or two columns that contain standardized data for entry into other tables. For example, a list of departments would be stored in a validation table. To enter a department name into an Employee table, the user would be given a choice of the rows in the validation table.

VARCHAR A common method for storing character data. It stands for variable characters. Each column of data uses the exact amount of bytes needed to store the specific data.

variable A location in memory used to hold temporary values. Variables have a scope and a lifetime depending on where they are created and how they are defined. They also have a specific data type, although the Variant data type in VBA can hold any common type of data.

vertical partition Splitting a table into groups based on the columns of data. Large columns or columns that are seldom used (e.g., pictures) can be moved to slower, cheaper storage devices.

view A saved query. You can build new queries that retrieve data from the view. A view is saved as an SQL statement—not as the actual data.

Visual Basic (VB) A stand-alone programming language sold by Microsoft and used to develop applications for the Windows environment. The professional version supports database connections. The program can be compiled into a stand-alone executable file.

Visual Basic for Applications (VBA) The programming language that underlies almost all of Microsoft's tools, including Access.

volume table of contents (VTOC) A design tool that can be used to outline the overall structure of an application. It generally shows a sequence of interrelated menus.

WHERE The SQL clause that restricts the rows that will be used in the query. It can also refer to data in subqueries.

wide area network (WAN) A network that is spread across a larger geographic area. Parts of the network are outside the control of a single firm. Long-distance connections often use public carriers.

With . . . End With In VBA, a shortcut for examining or altering several properties for a single object. Once the object is specified in the With statement, you simply refer to the properties inside the "loop."

WITH GRANT OPTION A security permission option that transfers the ability to assign permissions to the specified role or user.

World Wide Web (WWW) A first attempt to set up an international database of information. Web browsers display graphical pages of information. Hypertext connections enable you to get related information by clicking highlighted words or icons. A standard method for displaying text and images on client computers.

Index

D

E

U

V